THE UNEXPLAINED

MYSTERIES OF MIND, SPACE AND TIME

This edition reprinted 1993
Published in this edition 1992 by Blitz Editions
an imprint of Bookmart Ltd
Registered Number 2372865
Trading as Bookmart Limited
Desford Road, Enderby, Leicester LE9 5AD

Printed in Hungary

ISBN 1 85605 123 4

THE UNEXPLAINED

MYSTERIES OF MIND, SPACE AND TIME

BLITZ EDITIONS

OURS IS A UNIVERSE FULL OF MYSTERIES...
...from the deepest recesses of the subconscious mind to the infinity of outer space.

POLTERGEISTS, UNLIKE GHOSTS, 'HAUNT' BY CAUSING COMMOTIONS, MAKING NOISES, THROWING THINGS AROUND AND CREATING CHAOS. ARE THEY MALEVOLENT SPIRITS, OR MERELY PROJECTIONS, PERHAPS, OF THE UNCONSCIOUS MIND?

SPIRITS ON THE RAMPAGE

Mysterious bangs, loud crashes, objectionable smells and furniture that moves about on its own; sudden cold spells, inexplicable voices, objects that appear and disappear, and the uncontrolled levitation of victims – these are all symptoms of poltergeist activity. (The word poltergeist is derived from two German words – a folklore term, *polter,* meaning 'noisy' and the word for spirit, *geist*). The development of psychical research and parapsychology during the last 100 years has also introduced into the language a more cumbersome phrase sometimes used to describe the same phenomena – recurrent spontaneous psychokinesis (or RSPK).

EVIL FORCES?

Such disturbances have been recorded since at least the 12th century. At one time, they were believed to be caused by mysterious, evil forces. Writing in the 13th century, a Welshman, for instance, noted that a 'spirit' was heard to converse with a group of men in a most alarming fashion. But it was not until 300 years later, in 1599, that one of the first authentic examinations of this type of incident was undertaken by Martin del Rio. He described 18 kinds of demon, including one that seemed to specialise in causing disturbances:

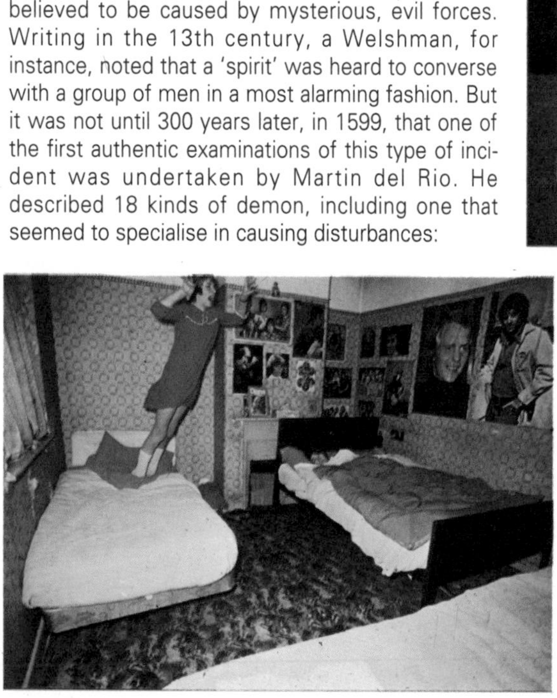

In May 1985, teacher Ken Webster experienced violent poltergeist activity at his cottage in the village of Dodleston, near Chester. Much of the disturbance centred on the kitchen, left, *where furniture was upended and small items thrown about.*

PERSPECTIVES

THE PHANTOM FACE

Poltergeists, it seems, sometimes haunt commercial premises as well as invading the home. In 1973, Manfred Cassirer – member of the council of Britain's Society for Psychical Research – was called in to investigate an odd series of events that had occurred at a garden centre occupying two rough sheds in Bromley, Kent. Planks of wood often mysteriously vanished, only to reappear out of the blue. A clock was seen to jump off a desk, apparently of its own accord. Then, to crown it all, garden fertilizer started falling from the ceiling, even though not stored at a height. On one occasion, it even formed the shape of a face, modelled in two distinct types of fertilizer (grey and white), on a counter. Stranger still, the skull-like shape remained static when looked at, but would disintegrate somewhat whenever Cassirer looked away. Finally, after Cassirer had investigated on two occasions, it disappeared just as mysteriously as it had arrived.

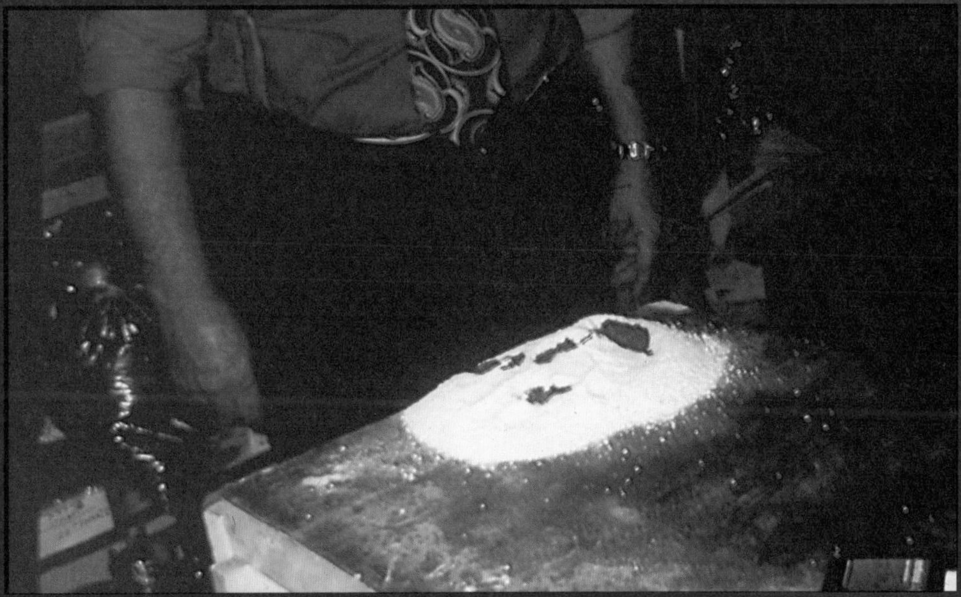

As shown in the sequence of photographs below, *12 year-old Janet seemed to be the focus of the dramatic and long-lasting Enfield poltergeist, and was often dragged out of bed by an invisible force. Even when she took to sleeping on the floor, she was still forcibly moved; and researcher Maurice Grosse,* far right, *always found it very difficult to hold her down.*

> 'The 16th type are spectres which in certain times and places or homes are wont to occasion various commotions and annoyances. I shall pass over examples since the thing is exceedingly well known... Some disturb slumbers with clattering of pots and hurling of stones and others pull away a mattress and turn one out of bed.'

Although there are some people today who maintain that poltergeist activity can be attributed to 'elementals', it is more generally accepted by authorities on the subject that 'hauntings' of this kind have a natural and not a supernatural origin. Yet we still do not understand the nature of the strange forces that seem to cause them.

AN INEXPLICABLE HAUNTING

The most spectacular case ever recorded lasted from August 1977 to September 1978. During this time, a woman and her four children, who were living in a council house in Enfield, on the northern outskirts of London, experienced practically every type of poltergeist phenomenon ever identified. No fewer than 1,500 separate incidents were recorded in all, and this astonishing barrage of disturbances

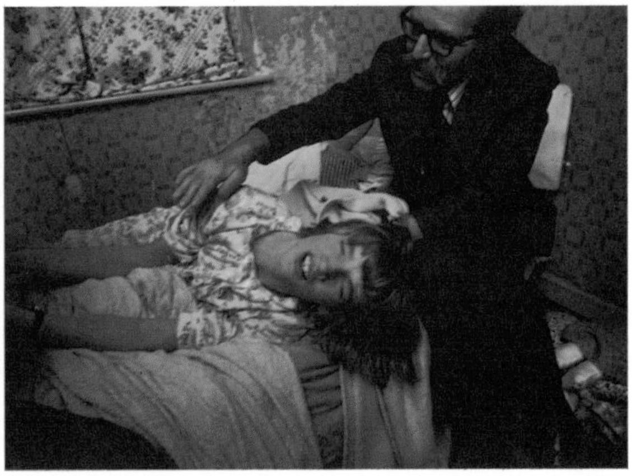

thoroughly mystified all those involved in the investigations, including social workers, a speech therapist, photographers, psychologists, priests and two poltergeist researchers.

As is usual in such cases, the 'haunting' started in a comparatively quiet fashion. A 'sort of shuffling sound' seemed to come from the floor of a bedroom, rather like the noise made by someone shambling across the room in slippers, according to the mother of the family. Then the knocking started, and this continued for nearly 11 months.

Mysterious Voice

A voice – deep, gruff and often crude – was tape-recorded on many occasions. Several attempts were made to identify it. The voice itself claimed to belong to a 72 year-old man from a nearby road. But a listener to a local radio phone-in programme had heard a recording of the voice and identified it as that of her uncle, Bill Haylock, whom she described as a 'gypsy type'. Every attempt at proving the validity of such claims failed, however – a fairly common experience in cases of this kind.

There were many other inexplicable incidents, too. On one occasion, a toy brick suddenly appeared, flew across the room and hit a photographer on the head. Paper and pieces of cloth caught fire spontaneously, and a box of matches that was lying in a drawer burst into flames which then extinguished themselves without igniting anything else in the drawer. A message, patched together from lengths of sticky tape, was also found on the lavatory door. Cutlery, a metal teapot lid and a brass pipe were all seen to bend and twist of their own accord. Three pieces of stone, found scattered about the house, were later discovered to be fragments of a single stone that had been split.

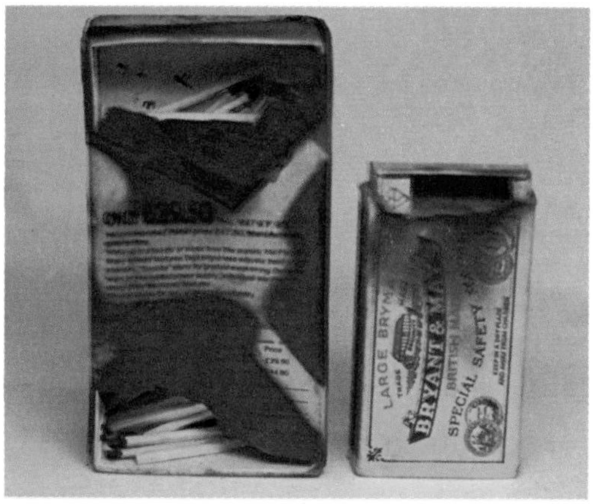

The phantom drummer of Tidworth – a poltergeist whose activity was recorded in 1666 – is depicted* above. *He produced a strange scratching or drumming noise in a bedroom that was occupied by two young girls.

Maurice Grosse,* far left, *has studied many household objects that were burnt or broken by the Enfield poltergeist.

The boxes of matches,* left, *were first set alight and then mysteriously extinguished by a London poltergeist.

The strength of the force at work in the house can be gauged from more impressive incidents. Part of a gas fire was wrenched away from the fireplace, and its grille was thrown across the sitting-room, for instance. Large pieces of furniture, among them a chest-of-drawers, a heavy sofa and a double bed, were also tossed around the house.

Janet, the 12 year-old daughter of the house, seems to have been the epicentre or focus of all this activity, and it was from her that the mysterious deep voice seemed to emanate. She even experienced levitation (witnesses on two occasions said that she seemed to be suspended in mid-air). She and her sister, Rose, were also thrown out of bed so often that in the end they decided to sleep on the floor; but that did not put an end to the poltergeist's activities, for Janet was often found fast asleep on top of a radio in her bedroom.

Although the family was very frightened at first, as time wore on the children and their mother became mystified rather than alarmed. Indeed, their reaction was typical of the attitude adopted by many of those who experience RSPK, as poltergeists generally cause no physical injury. As one investigator has pointed out: 'RSPK is really a series of nuisance incidents, rather like the actions of a frustrated adolescent or a child-like personality'. Interestingly, this is not entirely true of American cases, however; and experts, such as W G Roll, have noted that many victims of poltergeist activity in the United States do suffer minor physical injury.

The Enfield case was certainly remarkable for the extent and duration of the phenomena that the family experienced. But many of its features have

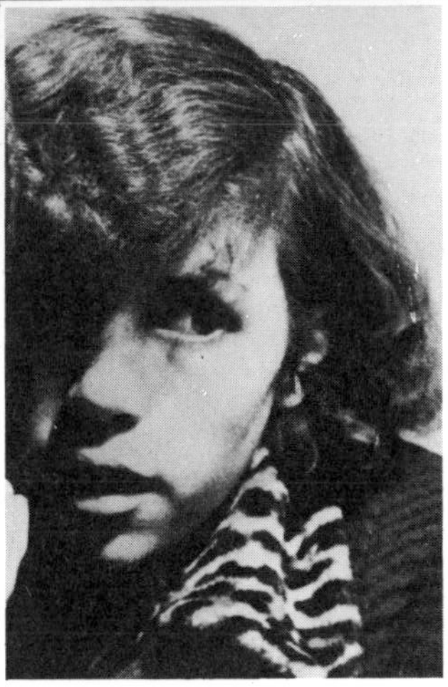

been observed by countless other people in other places and in other ages.

Mysterious knockings and rappings, for example, are often the first indication of the presence of a poltergeist (although some people notice first that objects are moved from their usual place). An early classic case, which became known as that of the Drummer of Tidworth, was recorded in 1666 by the Reverend Joseph Glanvill, who lived in a house on the site of the present Zouch Manor in Wiltshire. Two girls were occupying a bedroom from which a 'strange drumming sound' seemed to emerge. The noise was traced to a point 'behind the bolster'; but sceptics argued that the girls themselves were the cause. Eventually, they were cleared of suspicion. Their hands were always outside the bedclothes and, as for the noise, the Reverend Glanvill reported that he could find 'no trick, contrivance or common cause' to explain it.

Spirit Rappings

In America, in 1848, the celebrated Fox case appeared to confirm that such raps were indeed an early indication of incipient poltergeist activity; and it was this case that actually later prompted the founding of the Spiritualist movement. Hysterical and highly imaginative witnesses assumed that spirits were trying to communicate through another two girls who were apparently (but unconsciously) responsible for the sounds that were heard.

In 1960, a similar case was investigated in Alloa in Scotland, where a girl of 11 heard a curious 'thunking' noise, rather like a ball bouncing (or a drumming sound?), that seemed to come from the head of her bed. An unusual aspect of what later developed into an extremely fascinating case was that the girl herself was so calm about the experience that investigators were able to record the incidents in a rational and detailed manner. Like the Reverend Glanvill, 300 years earlier, the Reverend Lund – one of the investigators involved in the case – found that the violent vibrations were indeed coming from the head of the bed, and he, too, ruled out the possibility of fraud.

In a case in Battersea, south London, in the 1950s, however, the poltergeist announced its arrival by placing an unidentified key on the bed of a 14 year-old girl, Shirley Hitching. This incident remained as puzzling as Shirley's ability to produce raps, several paces from her body, as a form of coded answer to questions that were put to her.

To prevent hysteria and mental stress, she and her parents, like many other victims, invented a personality for the poltergeist, whom they called Donald. They decided that he was the spirit of a 14 year-old illegitimate son of Charles II of France. Donald was irrepressible. He decorated the walls and ceiling of Shirley's bedroom with graffiti and pictures of film stars, and he wrote letters (or so it was claimed) to a number of dignitaries.

Obscenities

Alien voices are a common feature of RSPK, and various theories have been advanced to explain this phenomenon. The most plausible is that put forward by a 19th-century French doctor, Gilles de la Tourette, who identified certain symptoms of severe stress, classifying them as forms of *copropraxia* (delight in the inappropriate use of obscene language) and *echolalia* (meaningless repetition of speech patterns). He further observed that some of his patients made 'obscene gestures and explosive utterances', and many of the noises and barking sounds that he described seem to have been identical to those produced by 12 year-old Janet of Enfield who, like the Frenchman's patients, was under great stress at the time (caused by, among other things, her parents' separation).

We still have to learn a very great deal about the sources of such 'commotions and annoyances', typical of poltergeist activity. But one thing is certain – the phenomenon is far too common to be ignored or explained away as the product of fevered minds. On the other hand, such experiences should probably not be taken too seriously either. Perhaps just the right blend of scepticism and acceptance was displayed by an insurance company in 1942, when it paid out £400 against an £800 claim for damage that seemed to have been caused by a poltergeist.

Harry Hanks,* top, *a psychic, is seen giving his views on the Battersea poltergeist to an interviewer following a seance.

Shirley Hitching,* above, *was the 14 year-old focus for the Battersea 'haunting'.

Blocks of heavy paving stones, depicted* right, *were hurled with great violence at a coachman's house in Paris in 1846. The missiles continued to smash the house even when it was guarded by police and soldiers. Then, after several weeks, the poltergeist abruptly ceased its activities.

INSIDE A BLACK HOLE

BLACK HOLES CAN TURN EVERYTHING WE KNOW ABOUT REALITY ON ITS HEAD. INFINITELY DENSE, THEY WARP SPACE AND TIME, AND THEY MAY EVEN CONNECT DIRECTLY WITH OTHER UNIVERSES

For years, scientists the world over have argued whether black holes are in fact a dead-end to nowhere or perhaps secret passages through space and time. The debate is a fascinating one, particularly as it seems to indicate that much of science fiction could perhaps, after all, be science fact.

But what exactly is a black hole? Quite literally, it is a gap in the fabric of space, torn from our Universe by a star collapsing in on itself. It is a region into which matter has fallen and from which nothing, not even light, can escape. Within the black hole, there is no up or down, no left or right; and time and space have changed roles.

Just as on Earth we cannot help but travel forward in time, so any space traveller unfortunate enough to fall into a black hole would be sucked into the centre by an infinite density and crushed out of existence. Around the black hole itself, there is, too, another gaping hole, a few miles across, where space does not even exist. Here, the pull of gravity is stronger than anywhere else in the Universe, and nothing can ever escape from it.

What is more, even if we could fly into a black hole, we could never inform the rest of the Universe what lies within, since signals could never be relayed through this exceptional gravity.

However, the mathematics of gravity, based on Einstein's theory of relativity, can tell us much about the nature of these odd phenomena. Both the theory of black holes and the evidence for their existence are products of 20th-century science. But, surprisingly, the first predictions of black holes was made in 1798 by the French astronomer Pierre Laplace. In his *Exposition du Systeme du Monde,* Laplace proposed the startling and seemingly contradictory theory that the most luminous stars might in fact be invisible.

INVISIBLE STARS

Laplace derived this theory from Newton's law of gravitation. If a star has the same density as the Earth, Laplace argued, it would be so massive that its surface gravity would prevent light from escaping. Since such heavy stars should produce a lot of light, Laplace therefore concluded that the most brilliant of the stars must be invisible.

The modern view, however, is that stars as heavy as those described by Laplace cannot exist in reality. Indeed astronomers now think that black holes are formed not by the massive explosion predicted by Laplace but by a cataclysmic implosion – matter being dragged inwards and compressing to an incredible density.

The main source of contemporary theories about black holes was in fact Albert Einstein. In his *General Theory of Relativity*, published in 1916, Einstein replaced Newton's 'force' of gravity with an entirely new concept of time and space 'warps'. Subsequent measurement and experimentation

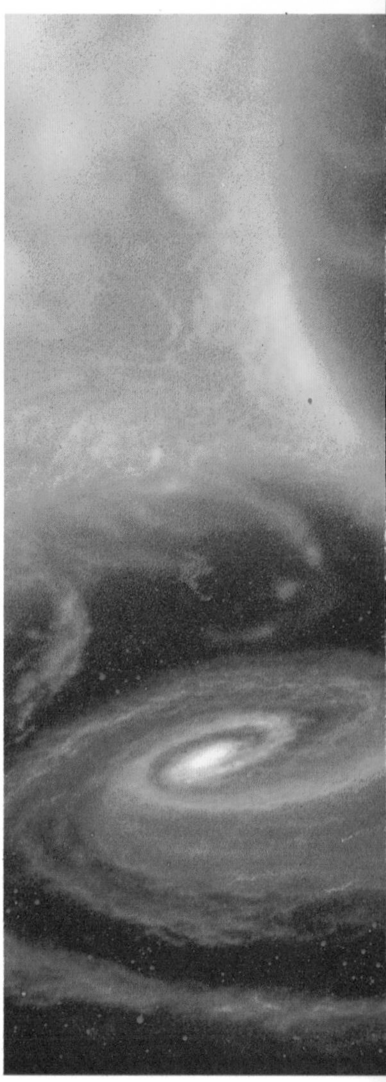

Clusters – such as Hercules X-1, left *– are tightly packed collections of individual stars. The heaviest will end their existence by swallowing themselves up into black holes.*

The artist's impression, below, *shows a binary star system. This comprises a normal star and a black hole. Gas is pulled from the atmosphere of the normal star by the immense gravitational field of its companion, and fleetingly emits X-rays.*

In 5,000 million years, the Sun will become a red giant like the one shown, right. *100 times its present size, it will engulf both Venus and Mercury, and burn up life on Earth.*

Sirius B, below right, *is a white dwarf, some nine light years from Earth. Our Sun, too, will end its long life as a white dwarf.*

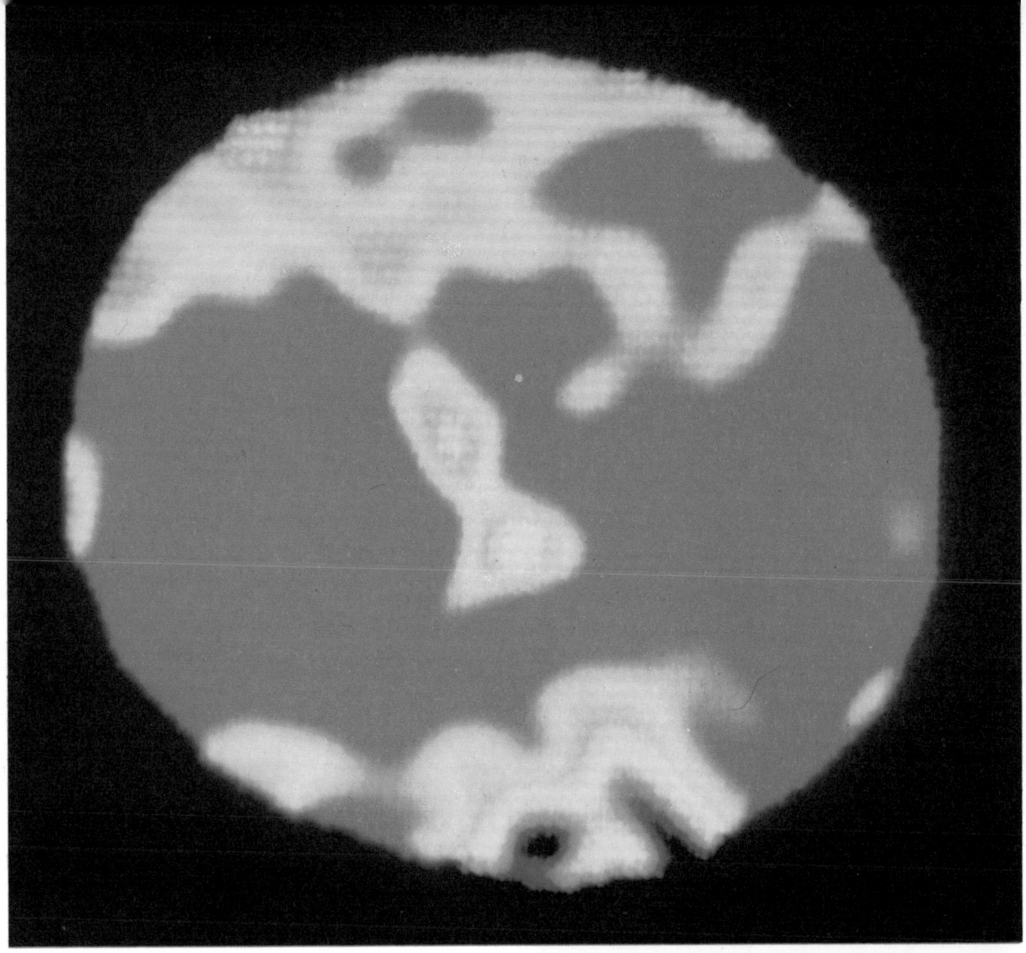

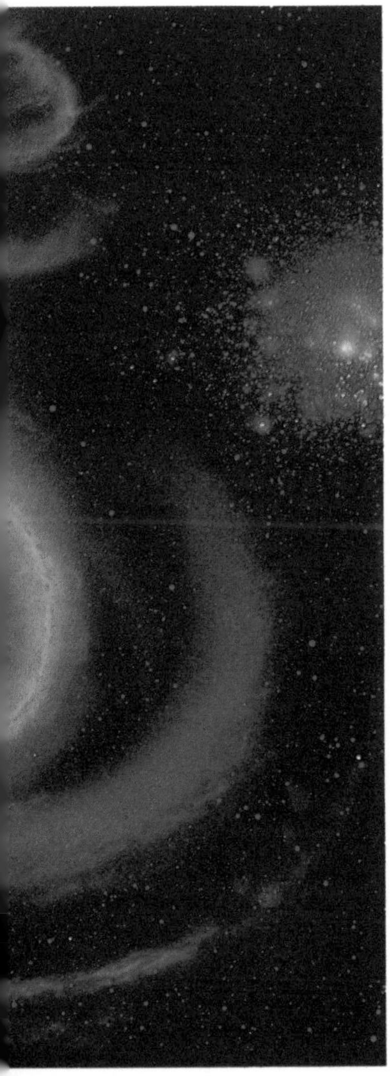

"WITHIN THE BLACK HOLE, THERE IS NO UP OR DOWN, NO LEFT OR RIGHT; AND TIME AND SPACE HAVE CHANGED ROLES."

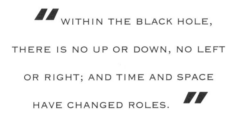

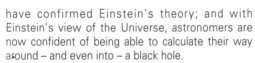

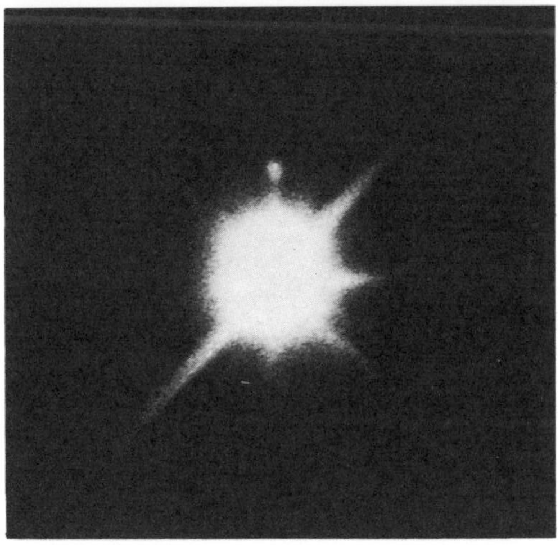

have confirmed Einstein's theory; and with Einstein's view of the Universe, astronomers are now confident of being able to calculate their way around – and even into – a black hole.

Using Einstein's equations, the German astronomer Karl Schwarzschild produced a general description of black holes only months after publication of the general theory. At the time, however, no one could conceive of such strong gravitation as predicted by Schwarzschild, so his calculations lay in obscurity, collecting dust. But by 1939, American physicists J Robert Oppenheimer ('father of the atom bomb') and H Snyder had calculated that black holes could form at the heart of a massive implosion of a star.

INTO TURMOIL

Yet black holes were still not taken seriously by the astronomical establishment. How could you possibly detect an entirely black, extremely small object, millions of miles away? It seemed that no advances in black hole theory were possible. Then, in the 1960s and 1970s, thanks to advances made in radio astronomy, strange objects were seen on the fringe of the Universe that suddenly put astronomy into turmoil and led to the resurrection of interest in black hole theory.

Astronomers had spotted objects that emitted huge amounts of radiation, but no light. Although black holes cannot themselves emit radiation, they could perhaps capture streamers of gas which wrap around a black hole in a rotating disc before being sucked into the hole. Caught in the intense gravitation near the hole, the gas may then become hot and turbulent, and its energy may shine out as radiation. Astronomers now think that some celestial X-ray sources consist of a black hole pulling gas off a companion star. Quasars (quasi-stellar objects) were even thought to be huge black holes capturing gas in the centre of a whole galaxy of stars. Schwarzschild had assumed that, if black holes do exist, they would not rotate. But all real stars rotate; and as a dying star collapses into a black hole, it should, in theory, spin round even faster. So what was the explanation?

One of the most important contributions to black hole theory in recent years has been the work of New Zealand mathematician Roy Kerr. Calculations based on Einstein's theory convinced Kerr of the existence of 'rotating black holes'. However, although the collapsed star's matter ends up as a central point, the space around it is still distorted, curved by its original rotation. Kerr therefore theorised that there is a region surrounding the hole where matter is dragged around by virtue of the hole's actual rotation.

This work on rotating black holes was further elaborated by Oxford mathematician, Roger Penrose. Although some have thought that the collapsed star can sometimes be visible, Penrose suggested that such a 'naked singularity' is always 'decently clothed' by a surrounding black hole that keeps its light from reaching the Universe beyond.

Evaporating Holes

Other important work on black hole theory has been carried out by Stephen Hawking of Cambridge University, described as the man who has contributed more to our understanding of gravity than anyone since Einstein himself. Hawking revealed his amazing results in 1974: his research had shown that black holes are very slowly evaporating away.

In practice, Hawking's evaporation mechanism is far too slow to affect black holes formed from collapsed stars. But it is very important for smaller holes. If black holes, the size and density of small hills, had formed when the Universe began some 15,000 million years ago, they should have evaporated so fast that, by now, they would be exploding in a burst of energy. Astronomers have looked for such explosions but failed to detect them. This, however, is not a refutation of Hawking's theory: rather, it may just indicate that there were few such holes created in the early Universe.

But with evidence for star-mass black holes, astronomers are on firmer ground. Indeed, the general consensus is that the heaviest stars in the Universe must end their lives by swallowing themselves up in black holes.

Birth of a Star

To understand how this happens, we must begin with the birth of a star. Stars are formed in huge clouds of diffuse gas which come together under their own gravitational inpull. Near the centre, turbulent gas becomes so dense that it breaks up into individual fragments, each of which becomes a new-born star. The result is a cluster of stars, all of

New-born stars of Orion Nebula light the surrounding gas cloud,* above. *Eventually, the nebula will break up to form individual stars.

The X-ray photograph,* below, *shows some of the most distant parts of the Universe. The bright object, lower right, is quasar 2C278 – the size of the Earth but with the brilliance of 100,000 million suns.

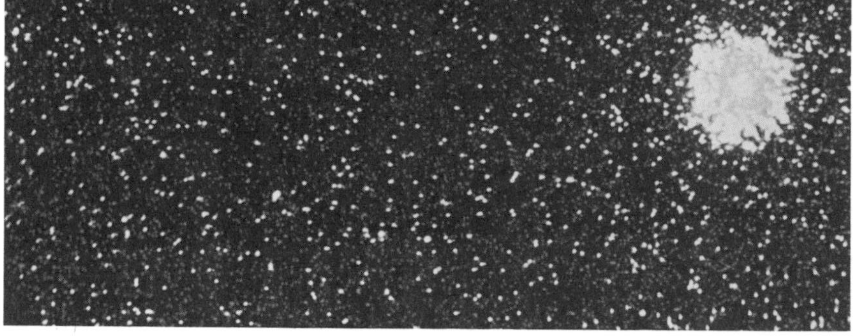

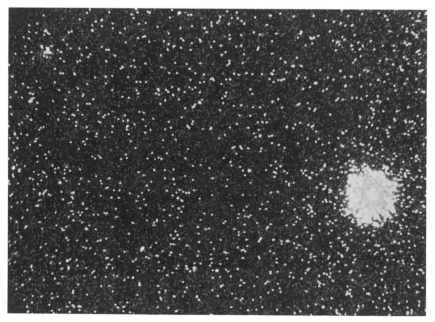

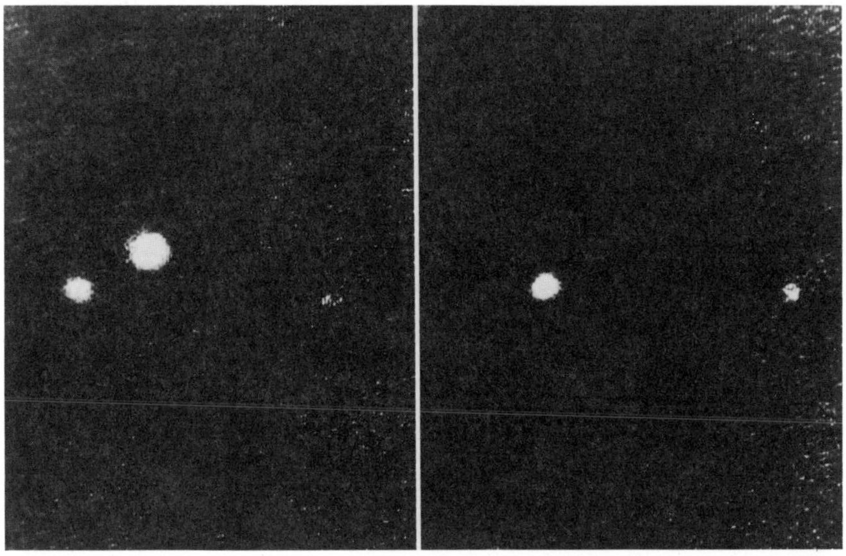

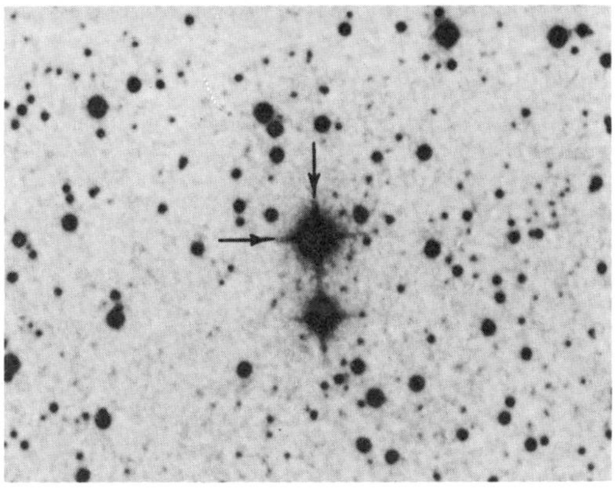

Pulsars are stars that spin rapidly in space, emitting radio waves that are received on Earth as a pulse every few seconds. In the picture, above, of the Crab pulsar, the pulse is 'on', while in the picture next to it, the pulse is 'off'.

Some 6,000 light years from Earth, the recently-discovered X-ray star Cygnus X-1, right, is thought to provide the best evidence for the existence of black holes. The arrowed star shows HDE 226868, a companion star with three times the density of our Sun.

"MATTER IN OUR UNIVERSE CAN INDEED COLLAPSE PAST THE POINT OF NO RETURN, AND TEAR OUT OF THE STRUCTURE OF SPACE A BLACK HOLE."

different masses, ranging from one that is a ten-thousandth of the Sun's mass to one that is 100 times heavier than our star.

At first, the new-born stars light up the surrounding gas cloud or nebula, as we see in the Orion Nebula today. Eventually, however, the gas cloud is blown away, and the cluster breaks up into individual stars. Our Sun, a typical star, was born in this way, around 4,600 million years ago.

During a star's lifetime, its core is a raging nuclear furnace where hydrogen is continually turning into helium – as in a hydrogen bomb; and the nuclear energy released keeps the star shining. Eventually, though, the hydrogen at the centre will be replaced by helium 'ash'. Now the star must change. Its core shrinks, while its outer layers swell up enormously – to around a hundred times the star's previous size. When our Sun's central reactor becomes choked with helium, it will expand to become a red giant, engulfing Mercury and Venus in the process.

White Dwarfs

A star exists as a red giant at the most for a few hundred million years. Eventually, it ejects its distended outer gas as a beautiful 'planetary' nebula (so-called because it resembles a planet's disc in a small telescope), while its core settles down as a small, dense star, or a white dwarf. White dwarfs are very small – about the size of the Earth and one hundredth the Sun's present size – and are made of a 'gas' some million times denser than water.

Heavier stars live for a shorter time, since they consume their central hydrogen much more quickly. They have a more chequered career as red giants, too. The core of a heavy star can convert helium into other elements – carbon, silicon and iron, in particular. But they, too, must die, blowing themselves apart in a vast supernova explosion, during which they outshine 1000 million suns.

While the outer layers explode outwards, the central core of the supernova collapses inwards on itself. The subatomic particles (electrons and protons) within it then amalgamate to make up neutrons. Because neutrons are much smaller than atoms, the resulting neutron star is tiny, smaller even than a white dwarf. It is only 15 miles (25 kilometres) across, and so dense that a drop of matter from it would weigh over a million tonnes.

Many neutron stars spin rapidly, and send out beams of radio waves. When these sweep across the Earth, a radio telescope can detect the star appearing to 'flash' or 'pulse', just as a lighthouse seems to flash as the beam of light from its rotating lantern sweeps across our eyes. Radio astronomers at Cambridge discovered these flashing neutron stars in 1967 and labelled them 'pulsars'.

Invisible Companion Stars

Studying X-rays from space, astronomers have also found neutron stars in orbit around normal stars. Here, the compact neutron star pulls gas off its companion. As gas spirals down through the neutron star's gravitational field, it heats up by friction until it is hot enough to beam out X-rays, not light.

Satellites have revealed many of these unequal double acts, and astronomers studying the ordinary star's light in each case have found that it is indeed in mutual orbit about a star that cannot be seen. Theory suggests that neither a white dwarf nor a neutron star can be heavier than three suns; yet some stars associated with X-ray sources seem to have invisible companions heavier than this limit.

The best-known is Cyg X-1, an X-ray star in the constellation Cygnus. Uhuru, the X-ray detecting satellite, discovered that the radiation comes from the spiralling disc of gas which surrounds the unseen companion of a giant star (catalogued as HDE 226868). But the motion of the giant star, revealed by its light, shows that its companion is at least six times heavier than the Sun. Too heavy to be a neutron star (or a white dwarf), the invisible star in the Cyg X-1 system must therefore be a black hole. Millions of years ago, it must have been an ordinary but very heavy star which lived its life in a rush, exploded as a supernova, and left its invisible corpse still in orbit about its companion HDE 226868. Streams of gas from the latter fall towards the black hole, and fleetingly emit X-rays before disappearing into the hole.

Half-a-dozen other X-ray sources have similar characteristics to Cyg X-1, and probably also harbour black holes. Indirect though the evidence is, most astronomers now accept that these sources clearly indicate that black holes are not just a theorist's dream. Matter in our Universe can indeed collapse past the point of no return, and tear out of the structure of space a black hole – a hole that may lead out of our Universe and into another, perhaps even more mysterious.

TESTING TELEPATHY

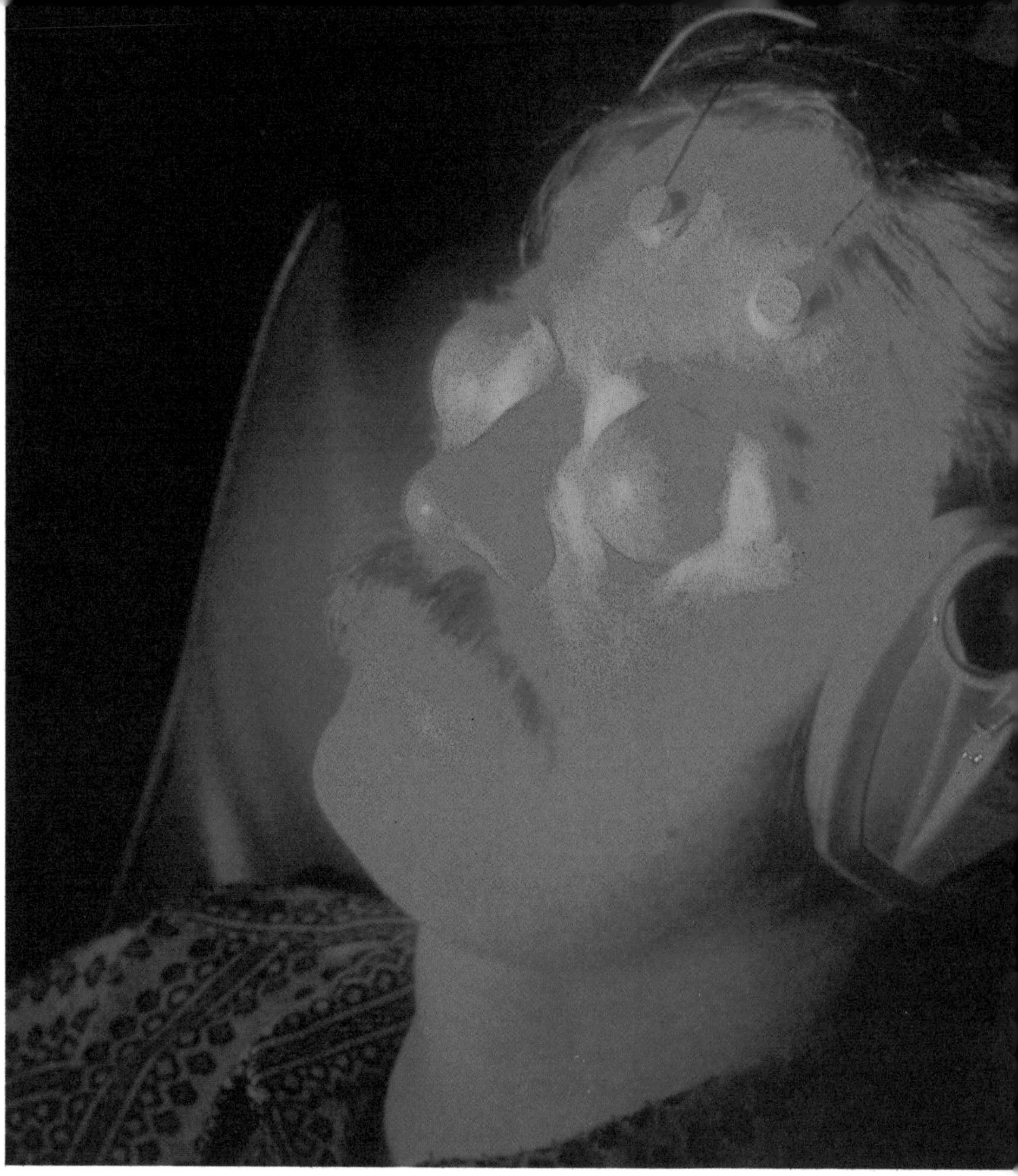

SOME OF US, IT SEEMS, ARE ABLE TO READ THE THOUGHTS OF OTHERS. SCIENCE, HOWEVER, STILL CANNOT EXPLAIN THIS MYSTERIOUS 'TUNING IN'

Early one morning in 1980, a very frightened old lady walked feebly into a Barcelona police station. Senora Isabel Casas, an 81 year-old widow, had been so scared by a terrible dream that, despite her age and infirmity, she had managed to walk to the local police station to raise the alarm. Almost incoherent with fear, she told the officer on duty that she had seen the familiar face of her friend and neighbour, Rafael Perez, 'twisted in terror', and had heard a voice saying: 'they are going to kill us'.

The Spanish police were inclined to dismiss Senora Casas' experience as a mere nightmare. But they became curious when they learned that she had not seen Perez, the only other resident in the block of flats where she lived, for 10 days. Normally, the 56 year-old chef called by every day, but he had written her a note saying he was going away for several weeks. It was odd, the police thought, that this note had not been delivered until three days after she had last seen her neighbour. Why had Perez not called to see her personally?

They decided to investigate, and eventually found Perez tied up in a shed on the roof of the block of flats. He told them that two men had broken into his apartment, made him sign 28 cheques so that they could draw his £15,000 life savings, a little at a time, and forced him to write the letter to Senora Casas so that her suspicions would not be aroused. Then they tied him up, saying they would be back, once they had all the money, to kill him and his neighbour.

Astonishingly, the old woman seems to have picked up the thoughts of her friend as he waited in terror for his captors to return. His life had been saved by her vivid telepathic dream. The police then ambushed and arrested the men when they returned to the scene of their crime.

This ability of one person to 'look into' the mind of another was one of the first subjects studied by early psychical researchers a century or so ago.

THE CASE OF CANON WARBURTON

Typical of the spontaneous cases of telepathy investigated by these early researchers was the experience of an English clergyman in 1883. Canon Warburton was seated in an armchair in his brother's flat when he began to doze. Suddenly, he woke with a start, and exclaimed 'By Jove! He's down!' The canon had just had a vivid dream in which he had seen his brother come out of a drawing room on to a brightly illuminated landing, catch his foot on the edge of the top stair and fall headlong, only just managing to save himself from serious injury by

Psychic powers – and telepathy in particular – are known to become heightened during dream states. This, it has been found, can be echoed in a laboratory setting through Ganzfeld (German for 'whole field') experiments. The subject, shown above, relaxes in a darkened room with a dim red light, halved ping-pong balls covering his eyes, and headphones providing white noise. The aim is then to focus on any images that enter the mind while, elsewhere, a 'sender' concentrates hard and tries to communicate.

using his hands and elbows. The house in the dream was not one that he recognised. All the canon knew, having just arrived in London from Oxford, was that his brother had left him a note explaining that he had gone to a dance in the West End and would be back about 1 a.m.

Recovering from the experience, Canon Warburton then dozed off again, until his brother eventually came in and woke him. 'I have just had as narrow an escape of breaking my neck as I ever had in my life!' he exclaimed. 'Coming out of the ballroom, I caught my foot, and tumbled full length down the stairs.'

This uncanny dream experience is just one of many hundreds of equally impressive cases collected by the Society for Psychical Research in both Britain and America.

CONTROLLED EXPERIMENTS

The word 'telepathy' was originally coined in 1882 by a leading Cambridge scholar and investigator, F.W.H Myers; and the first major study of such experiences – the *Census of Hallucinations,* published in 1890 – examined replies to 20,000 questionnaires. But science needed to examine telepathy under more controlled conditions.

Sir William Barrett, pioneer of scientific research into telepathy and professor of physics at the Royal College of Science, Dublin, conducted a large number of experiments in this area, and finally became satisfied that telepathy was real.

When he first submitted his paper – *Some Phenomena associated with Abnormal Conditions of the Mind* – to the British Association for the Advancement of Science, however, it was refused by the biological committee. But it was eventually accepted by the anthropological sub-section on the casting vote of its chairman, Dr Alfred Russell Wallace, who was also a keen investigator of psychical phenomena.

By the early part of this century, many groups of researchers were involved in imaginative telepathy tests. In the 1920s, for example, René Warcollier conducted group telepathy experiments between France and the United States, many of which produced very impressive results. But not all early research is acceptable by today's strict scientific standards. The famous physicist Oliver Lodge, for example had carried out tests with two girls who claimed to be able to read each other's minds. He found their demonstrations convincing, and described them in his book *The Survival of Man,* published in 1909. But since the girls were allowed to hold hands while 'sending' telepathic images of playing cards, the possibility that they were using a code cannot be eliminated. This suspicion is reinforced by Lodge's statistics, which show that, when the girls were not touching, results dropped to almost chance level.

TELEPATHIC PICTURES

During the 1930s, the work of writer Upton Sinclair caught public imagination quite strongly. His wife had considerable psychic abilities and was able to 'receive' by telepathy pictures that were drawn by her husband or other senders. Sometimes their

PERSPECTIVES

IN THE MIND'S EYE

The most impressive scorer in a series of telepathy experiments carried out at Cambridge University by Dr Carl Sargent was Hugh Ashton, who worked with computers by day and played in a punk rock group at night. During one session in 1979, for example, he produced the following taped comments, which are a sample only of the total transcript:

'Buildings in corner. Picture is longer than high. Postcard...concrete, urban, town. Perhaps in Cambridge. Keep thinking of firemen and fire station... Officialdom. Uniforms...Firemen definitely seen. Black and white... People but not face...

'I think one face at bottom in foreground...Policemen's helmet or hat. Facing...smiling...All wearing same uniform...

"Wet, rainy day...White silvery badge on helmet of him looking towards us...Shot looking down...'

The actual target picture, reproduced here, was of firemen taking part in a fire-drill practice in Cambridge. Any comment on the accuracy of Ashton's description would be superfluous, but especially striking have to be the one face turned towards us (all the rest are facing away), the silvery badge on the helmet, and the firemen, who are all wearing the same uniform.

experiments were carried out in adjoining rooms; at other times, over long distances. The results were published in Sinclair's book *Mental Radio,* and reveal that, in 290 experiments, Mrs Sinclair scored 23 per cent successes, 53 per cent partial successes and 24 per cent failures.

The similarity between the original drawings and Mrs Sinclair's 'copies' were often striking, ruling out coincidence but making statistical analysis of the results difficult. In fact, partial successes were often as impressive as direct hits because they provided fascinating insight into how Mrs Sinclair perceived the images. On one occasion, Upton Sinclair drew a volcano with billowing black smoke. His wife drew a very good likeness, but was unable to say what it was, and suggested a beetle. Had this been a telepathy test which required a verbal response, her description of a beetle would have been judged a miss. But her actual drawing showed that she had in fact picked up the image with extraordinary accuracy.

Sinclair, a committed socialist, was well aware that most intelligent people still regarded the phenomenon of telepathy with scepticism. Indeed, some of his socialist friends felt that his interest in ESP conflicted with their rationalist outlook on the world. One of them even attacked him in a newspaper article headed 'Sinclair goes spooky'.

It was to give the subject respectability in the eyes of science that the American Dr J B Rhine began to research in the laboratory, using new methods and easily identifiable targets to ensure there was no doubt whether a subject was scoring a hit or a miss. The results were impressive and satisfied Rhine, as well as many other scientists, that mind-to-mind communication was real.

SCEPTICS

But there were still sceptics, one of whom was the psychologist Bernard Riess. Once, when Dr Rhine was invited to lecture on ESP at Barnard College, Riess questioned him so fiercely that Rhine protested he was, in effect, accusing him of lying. Instead of going on to defend his experiments, however, Rhine suggested to Riess that he should carry out his own tests, using any controls he believed necessary. Riess' students urged him to accept the challenge, and they found a young woman with supposed psychic abilities who agreed to act as a subject. For several months, Riess conducted his own card-guessing experiments with her. Seventy-four runs of 25 cards were made (1,850 trials), and they averaged a phenomenal 18 hits out of 25.

Riess, once a denigrator of ESP research, was then called upon to defend his own experiments in 1938, when the American Psychological Association organised an ESP symposium.

'There can be no criticism of the method used. I had the deck of cards on my desk, shuffled them, and at the stated time turned them over one by one, making a record of each card. I kept the records locked up in my desk and sometimes it was a week before I totalled up the scores and found the number of high scores she was making... The only error that may have crept in is a possibility of deception, and the only person who could have done the deceiving was myself since the subject at no time knew how well she was doing nor had any idea of which cards were being turned over by myself...' he told the meeting.

*In*Focus

ESP IN DREAMS

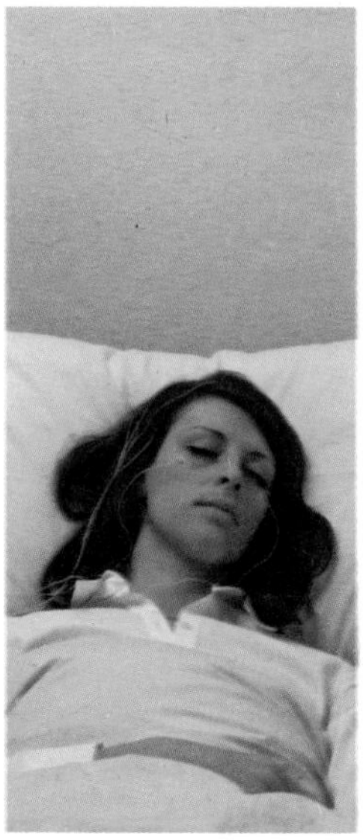

Recent research suggests that telepathy may occur much more often than is generally thought.

In a series of experiments carried out at the Dream Laboratory in Brooklyn, New York, an experimenter studied a picture postcard and transmitted the image telepathically while the subject was asleep in another room. An electro-encephalograph monitored the sleeper's brain patterns; and when a change in the patterns indicated the subject was dreaming, he or she was woken up and asked to describe the dream.

A high degree of similarity between the transmitted images and the dreams of the sleeper was noted, although the target pictures were never received whole but interwoven with the dream the subject was having at the time.

ESP-IONAGE!

Rhine's work continued to be a subject of public debate for many years; but with more and more investigators carrying out their own research programmes into various ESP subjects, telepathy was soon overshadowed by such phenomena as clairvoyance and precognition, which brought startling experimental results. Then, in the late 1950s, telepathy was suddenly back in the news with the publication in the French press of reports that successful telepathy tests had been carried out between a submerged American submarine, *USS Nautilus,* and an agent on shore. The possible military implications of such methods of communica-

tion, if they could actually be proved reliable, were obvious.

Despite the United States Navy's denial of the Nautilus story, however, the Soviets took it seriously, with the result that the work of Russian psychical investigators, which had been classed as top secret for 30 years, was at last made public. Among these investigators was Dr Leonid Vasiliev, who claimed that Soviet parapsychologists had received encouragement for their research from high up in the party organisation. Indeed, it is thought that Stalin himself may have been interested in the use of telepathy for military purposes.

TELEPATHIC ORDERS

Dr Vasiliev had been using hypnotised subjects to investigate 'mental radio'; and when a book about this work was published in 1962, he revealed that he and other researchers had been able to make certain individuals carry out instructions by telepathic order. He even claimed to be able to hypnotise by telepathy. In one extraordinary case, a woman whose body was paralysed down the left side was the subject of experiments. Her condition was psychosomatic, however, and without physical cause. Vasiliev discovered that he had only to give mental

The nuclear submarine USS Nautilus, shown **top**, *was rumoured to have been carrying out telepathy experiments between an agent on shore and a sender aboard the submerged craft during the late 1950s.*
Karl Nikolaiev and Dr Yuri Kamensky, **above left** *and second from* **right**, *took part in a number of experiments involving the sending of Morse messages telepathically.*

Dr Leonid Vasiliev, the Soviet psychical researcher who used hypnosis to enhance telepathy experiments, is shown **left**.

commands and she would be able to move her left hand, arm or foot as requested, even without the use of hypnotism.

Demonstrating this form of mental communication before a group of observers as an extra precaution, he blindfolded the subject and did not speak a word. Instead, each instruction was written down and witnessed by the group before either Vasiliev or his co-worker, hypnotist Dr Finne, began concentration. The woman obeyed with remarkable accuracy, and was even able to say whether it was Vasiliev or Finne giving the instruction.

More recently, Russian researchers have carried out even more startling demonstrations of telepathy using a biophysicist, Yuri Kamensky, and an actor and journalist, Karl Nikolaiev. Kamensky was in Novosibirsk in Siberia; Nikolaiev, in Moscow – and a committee of scientists supervised the session. The results provided overwhelming evidence for mental communication.

In one test, Nikolaiev correctly described six objects that had been given to Kamensky, and was also able to identify 12 out of 20 ESP test cards. What is particularly impressive about these Russian tests, however, is that the scientists succeeded in producing independent instrumental confirmation that something paranormal was going on.

They wired Nikolaiev to an electro-encephalograph (EEG) machine which monitors brain waves. As soon as Kamensky began to transmit images, they found that his brain waves altered. Using this knowledge, they then devised a technique for sending messages in Morse code. Instead of asking Kamensky to think of an object, they asked him to imagine he was fighting Nikolaiev. As the scientists in Moscow watched the recording of Nikolaiev's brain waves on the EEG, they found there was a distinct change in the pattern whenever Kamensky imagined he was fighting him. Kamensky was able to transmit Morse 'dots' and 'dashes' by imagining 'fighting bouts' of various lengths: a 45-second bout produced a burst of activity that was interpreted as a dash, while a 15-second bout was read as a dot. In this way, the scientists in Moscow found they were able to identify the Russian word *mig* – meaning 'instant' – which Kamensky had transmitted in Morse code from as far as 2,000 miles (3,200 kilometres) away in Siberia.

Interestingly, a similar technique using different methods followed the accidental discovery by a Czechoslovakian researcher, Dr Stepan Figar, that intense thought about a person produced an increase in that individual's blood volume – a change that could be accurately measured by a device called a plethysmograph.

MENTAL RADIO

Douglas Dean, a British-born electrochemist and professor of computing, and a leading psychical researcher, saw the potential of this discovery for telepathy tests. His research revealed that, when a telepathic sender concentrates on the name of someone with whom a subject – wired to a plethysmograph – has an emotional tie, a change in the subject's blood volume is often recorded. Together with two engineers from the Newark College of Engineering in New Jersey, Dean went on to design a system using a plethysmograph for sending messages in Morse code.

Its mode of operation is an intriguing one. If the sender concentrates on the name of a person who is emotionally significant to the subject, the plethysmograph produces a measurable response which is interpreted as a Morse dot. If no response is registered during a specified time, however, this is noted as a Morse dash. Using this technique, Dean managed to send a telepathic Morse message over a distance of 1,200 miles (2,000 kilometres) between New York and Florida.

But despite these discoveries and the outstanding individual results that some experiments have produced, not all researchers are so successful when they attempt to duplicate telepathy tests. 'Mental radio' remains an elusive phenomenon, although it is one that has occurred often enough – spontaneously and in the laboratory.

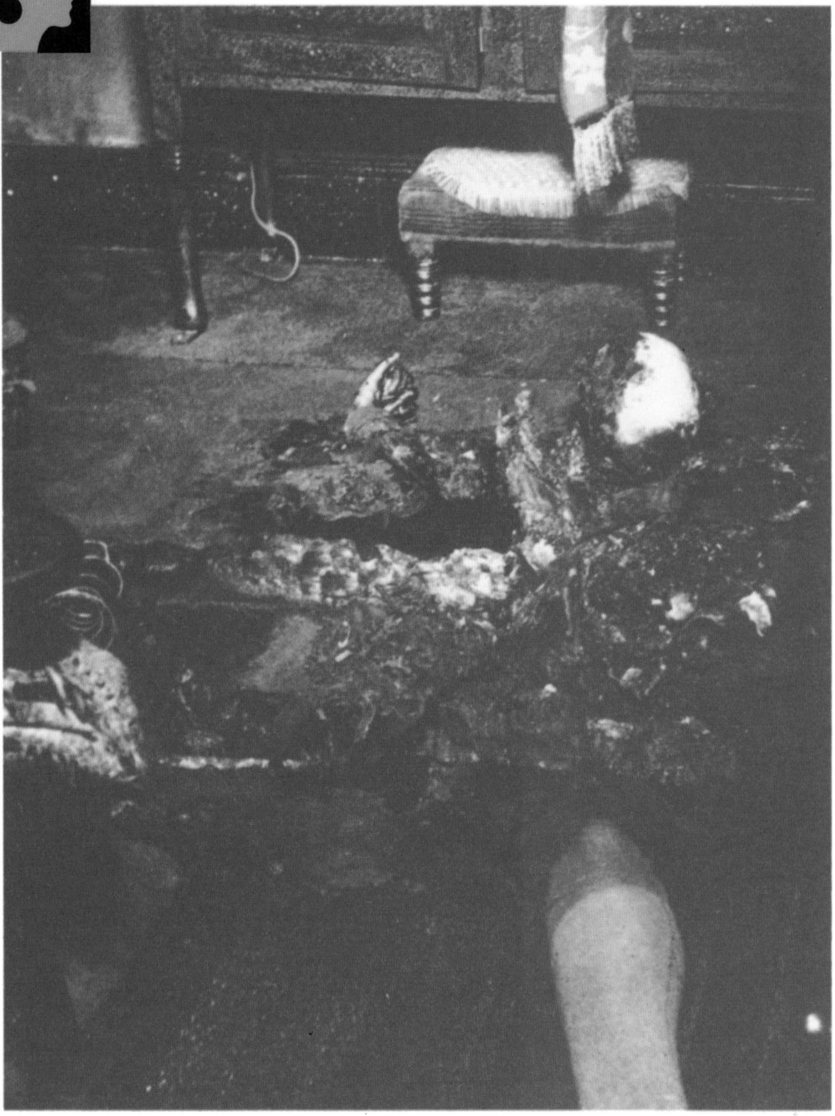

FIRE OF UNKNOWN ORIGIN

OF ALL THE STRANGE AND INEXPLICABLE FATES THAT MAY BEFALL SOMEONE, PERHAPS THE MOST BIZARRE IS SPONTANEOUS HUMAN COMBUSTION. IT IS A FATAL PHENOMENON THAT OCCURS WITHOUT WARNING AND WITHOUT APPARENT CAUSE

People have long believed that, in certain circumstances, the human body can burst into flames of its own accord – flames, furthermore, of such ferocity that within minutes the victim is reduced to a heap of carbonised ashes. This idea – some would call it a superstition – has been around for centuries, smouldering in a belief in divine retribution. 'By the blast of God they perish,' says the author of Job, 'and by the breath of his nostrils are they consumed.'

Such Gothic horrors were hugely popular in the 18th and 19th centuries, and their literary use is still extensively discussed in the pages of the magazine, *The Dickensian*, stimulated by author Charles Dickens' own fascination with the subject. Dickens had examined the case for spontaneous human combustion (SHC) thoroughly, and knew most of the early authorities and collections of cases. Indeed, he probably based his description of Krook's death in *Bleak House* (1852-3) upon the real-life case of Countess Bandi.

The death of 62 year-old Countess Cornelia Bandi, near Verona, is certainly one of the first more reliable reports of SHC. According to one statement, dated 4 April 1731, the Countess had been put to bed after supper, and fell asleep after several hours' conversation with her maid. In the morning, the maid returned to wake her and found a grisly scene. As the *Gentleman's Magazine* reported in vivid detail shortly afterwards: 'The floor of the chamber was thick smear'd with gluish moisture, not easily got off... and from the lower part of the window trickl'd down a greasy, loathsome yellowish liquor with an unusual stink.'

In a typical case of spontaneous human combustion – shown above – fire has reduced most of the body to ashes, leaving only parts of the lower legs, the left hand and portions of the skull. Enormously high temperatures must have been involved; yet for some mysterious reason, the fire has been contained, causing little further damage to surroundings.

Heaps of Ashes

Specks of soot hung in the air, covering all the surfaces and the smell had also penetrated adjoining rooms. The bed was undamaged, and the sheets, turned back, indicating that the Countess had got out of bed.

'Four feet (1.3 metres) from the bed was a heap of ashes, two legs untouch'd, stockings on, between which lay the head, the brains, half of the back-part of the skull and the whole chin burn'd to ashes, among which were found three fingers blacken'd. All the rest was ashes which had this quality, that they left in the hand a greasy and stinking moisture.'

> "...FLAMES, FURTHERMORE, OF SUCH FEROCITY THAT WITHIN MINUTES THE VICTIM IS REDUCED TO A HEAP OF CARBONISED ASHES."

Due primarily to the efforts of Charles Fort, pioneer collector of accounts of strange phenomena, and the people and journals who continue his work, a fair number of reports of SHC right up to the present have been accumulated from newspaper and medical journal sources. Very few of the accounts actually refer to SHC as such, however, simply because, officially, it does not exist as a phenomenon. Coroners and their advisers therefore have the unenviable task of dealing with evidence that seems to contradict both accepted physical laws and medical opinion. Inevitably, suppositions are made about knocked-over heaters, flying sparks, careless smoking and, in the case of child victims, playing with matches. Faced with the alternative – a terrifying mystery – it is not really surprising that these causes of death by fire are more readily accepted.

There are occasional exceptions, though, and these are, of course, far more useful to those who wish to solve the enigma. In *Lloyds Weekly News* for 5 February 1905, for instance, it was reported that a woman asleep by a fireplace woke to find herself in flames and later died. The honest coroner said he could not understand the data with which he was presented. Apparently, the woman had gone to sleep facing the fire, so any cinder that shot out of the grate would presumably have ignited the front of her clothes. Yet it was her back that bore severe burns.

CASEBOOK

THE CASE OF MARY REESER

On the evening of 1 July 1951, Richard Reeser made his usual nightly visit to his 67 year-old widowed mother, Mary, below, and found her already changed for bed, sitting in an easy-chair and reading by the light of a standard electric lamp at her one-room apartment in St Petersburg, Florida. It was to be the last time he saw her alive. Her only remains were found to be a velvet-slippered foot when, the very next morning, the landlady and a workman opened the red-hot door knob and entered her heat-filled room. No ordinary fire, investigators have confirmed, could possibly have burnt her to ashes in this terrible way. Workmen – seen above – cleared away the remains of the easy-chair in which Mary Reeser burned to death. Damage to the rest of the apartment was minimal, however: the floor beneath the chair was scorched and there was soot on the ceiling, but no damage was done to a pile of papers nearby.

FEAR OF THE TRUTH

At worst, a story may be rejected out of fear or disbelief, as in the case of the elderly spinster, Wilhelmina Dewar, who combusted near midnight on 22 March 1908, in the Northumberland town of Whitley Bay. Wilhelmina was found by her sister Margaret who, although in a state of shock, managed to summon her neighbours. Inside the house, they found the severely charred body of Wilhelmina in an upstairs bed. Yet the bedclothes were unscorched and there was no sign of fire anywhere else in the house.

When Margaret told this story at the inquest, the coroner thought her evidence preposterous and asked her to think again. But she repeatedly said she was telling the truth and did not change her story – even after a policeman had testified that Margaret was so drunk that she could not have known what she was saying. As Fort pointed out, however, the policeman was not called upon to state how he distinguished between signs of excitement and terror, and intoxication. The coroner finally adjourned the inquest to give Margaret more time to think; and when it was re-convened a few days later, it was obvious that a great deal of pressure had been placed upon poor Margaret.

Both sisters were retired school teachers and, until then, had lived respectably. Now the coroner was calling her a liar, the papers labelled her a drunk, and friends and neighbours had turned away, leaving her to face a hostile court. It was hardly surprising, therefore, that Margaret gave in and said she had been inaccurate. This time, she said she had found her sister burned, but alive, in the lower part of the house. She then went on to say that she had helped her upstairs to bed, where Wilhelmina died, so she said.

PROPER TESTIMONY

Superficially more plausible, this story was accepted, and the proceedings promptly closed. The court was not interested in how Wilhelmina had been transformed into the cindered corpse with charred abdomen and legs; nor how, if she had continued to smoulder after being helped into the bed, there was no other sign of fire. 'But the coroner was satisfied', Fort wrote sarcastically. 'The proper testimony had been recorded.'

Yet, ironically enough, it is actually medico-legal interest that has kept alive the notion of SHC, with pathologists endorsing the phenomenon and then rejecting it. There is, of course, also the possibility that a murderer might simulate a case of SHC to hide a crime. One of the earliest test cases along these lines occurred in Rheims, France, in 1725, when an inn-keeper, Jean Millet, was accused of having an affair with a pretty servant girl and killing his wife. The wife, who was often drunk, was found one morning, about a foot (30 centimetres) away from the hearth.

'A part of the head only, with a portion of the lower extremities, and a few of the vertebrae, had escaped combustion. A foot-and-a-half (45 centimetres) of the flooring under the body had been consumed, but a kneading-trough and a powdering tub very near the body sustained no injury.' A young assistant doctor, named Le Cat, was staying at the inn and managed to convince the court that this was no ordinary death by fire but a 'visitation of God' upon the drunken woman, and an obvious result of soaking one's innards with spirits. Millet was vindicated, and Le Cat went on to qualify with distinction, and to publish a treatise on SHC.

Eyewitnesses Sought

Spontaneous human combustion subsequently received what has perhaps been its severest criticism from a great pioneering chemist, Baron Justus von Liebig, who wrote a spirited refutation on the grounds that no one had actually seen it happen. As a scientist, he regarded historical evidence as an unsupported record of the belief in SHC rather than an actual proof of it. He also lamented the lack of expert witnesses, and dismissed most accounts because, in his opinion, they 'proceed from ignorant persons, unpractised in observation, and bear in themselves the stamp of untrustworthiness'.

Despite Liebig's assertion, however, there is plenty of evidence from both medical and police sources. Many of these bear witness to the ferocity of SHC, as in the case investigated by Merille, a surgeon in Caen, recorded in Trotter's *Essay on Drunkenness,* 1804. Merille was asked, on 3 June 1782, by the king's officers to report on the death of Mademoiselle Thaurs, a lady of over 60 who had been observed, that day, to have drunk three bottles of wine and one of brandy. Merille wrote:

'The body lay with the crown of the head resting against one of the hand-irons... 18 inches (45 centimetres) from the fire, the remainder of the body was placed obliquely before the chimney, the whole being nothing but a mass of ashes. Even the most solid bones had lost their form and consistence. The right foot was found entire and scorched at its upper junction; the left was more burnt. The day was cold but there was nothing in the grate except two or three bits of wood about an inch (2.5 centimetres) in diameter, burnt in the middle.'

Dr Wilton Krogman, who has experimented with sophisticated crematorium equipment, has commented: 'Only at 3000° F (1500° C) plus have I seen bone fuse or melt so that it ran and became volatile.' Such a heat would certainly char everything within a considerable radius and set the house ablaze, yet the meticulous Merille writes:

'None of the furniture in the apartment was damaged. The chair on which she was sitting was found at the distance of a foot (30 centimetres) from her, and absolutely untouched... the consumption of the body had taken place in less than 7 hours, though according to appearance, nothing around the body was burnt but the clothes.'

Elementary Chemistry

An officially rejected theory, current until the end of the 18th century, held that a substance known as Phlogiston was the principle or element of heat inherent in all matter. When latent, it was said to be imperceptible; but when operative, it was believed to produce all the effects of combustion.

As any student of elementary chemistry will be aware, bring metallic sodium into contact with ordinary tap water, and the sodium will explode into violent flames. Expose phosphorous to the air, and it, too, will burst into flame. It is not impossible,

"Some human beings may have within them a fatal inherent response to the force that lies behind the SHC phenomenon."

The great chemist, Baron Justus von Liebig – shown left – rejected accounts of spontaneous human combustion because of the lack of expert witnesses. His attempts to make flesh burn with the same intensity as SHC were, without exception, a dismal failure.

How did the body below burn so thoroughly without setting fire to the rest of the room? The death of this anonymous victim of what seems to be SHC remains an intriguing mystery.

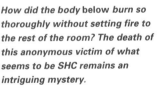

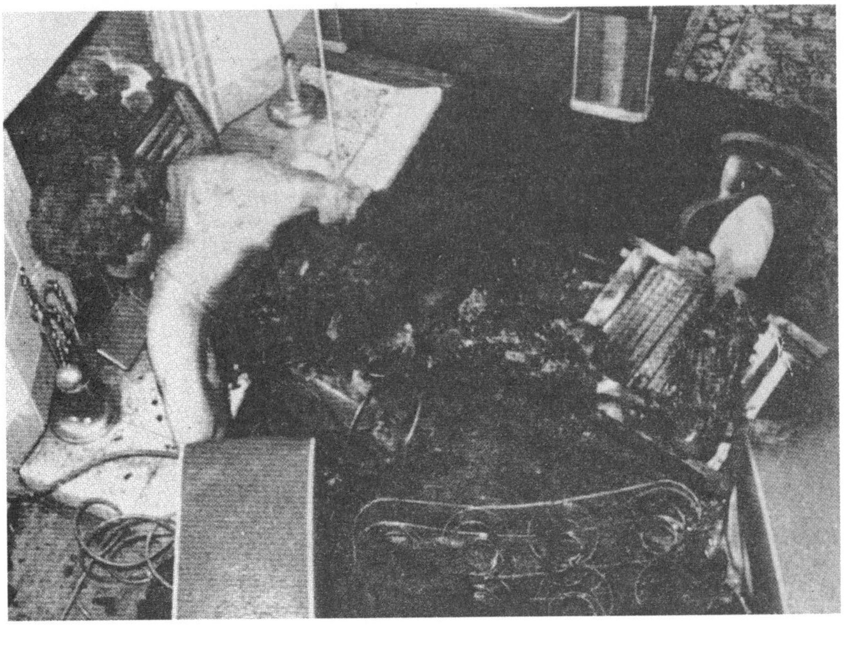

CASEBOOK

THE BURNING OF DR BENTLEY

Dr J. Irving Bentley, a retired physician, lived on the ground floor of an apartment building in Coudersport, northern Pennsylvania. On the rather cold morning of 5 December 1966, Don Gosnell entered the building's basement to read the meter for the North Penn Gas Company. In the basement, a light-blue smoke of unusual odour hung in the air. Scattering an unfamiliar heap in the corner with his boot, Gosnell found it was ashes. There had been no answer to his greeting on the way in, so he decided to look in on the old man. There was more strange smoke in the bedroom but no sign of Bentley. Gosnell peered into the bathroom and was confronted with a sight he would never forget. A large hole had burned through the floor, exposing the joists and pipework below. On the edge of the hole, he saw '... a brown leg from the knee down, like that of a mannequin. I didn't look further!' The coroner's verdict of asphyxiation was thought unsatisfactory by many.

therefore, that some human beings may have within them a fatal inherent response to the force that lies behind the SHC.

No one has yet been able to offer an explanation for all the various forms of SHC that have been reported. But the phenomenon is as prevalent today as it ever was. The *Washington Post* of 29 May 1990, for instance, reported the following rather curious death by fire: 'Los Angeles – Sheets covering a patient caught fire during surgery at UCLA Medical Center, filling the operating room with smoke so thick that staff members could not extinguish the flames. The patient, 26 year-old Angela Hernandez, died. "The sheets just caught fire", Fire Department Chief Pat Marek said. "It's bizarre."

UP LIKE A ROCKET

Even stranger is the case of Horace Trew Nicholas of Hampton Hill, Middlesex. The London *Daily Telegraph* of 28 December 1938 (a year in which no fewer than 17 SHC-type fires were reported in the British press alone) gave details of his extraordinary death by fire.

Nicholas was walking along Windmill Road, when there was a loud bang. Suddenly, he went up like a rocket and landed against the chimney of an adjacent house, his clothes ablaze, his hair burnt off, and his rubber boots melted on his feet.

The medical authorities, eager to find a cause other than SHC, claimed that a gas leak was responsible. When gas workers opened up the main, however, there was no leak to be found. The authorities then suggested that an explosion of sewer gas had caused Nicholas' death; but, again, no such gas could be detected. Finally, the coroner closed the case with the rather more traditional verdict of 'accidental death'.

RELUCTANT ADMISSIONS

Today, researchers into SHC readily quash the idea that the phenomenon does not exist, and a growing number of cases has also been authenticated by doctors and pathologists. Indeed, this number would most probably be far higher, some say, if fear of ridicule for belief in the phenomenon could be completely removed.

American physician Dr B.H Hartwell was sufficiently confident, however, about what he once personally witnessed to report it to the Massachusetts Medico-Legal Society. He had been driving through Ayer in Massachusetts when he was stopped and called into a wood. There he saw a most horrible sight: in a clearing, a woman was crouching in flames at the shoulders, both sides of the abdomen, and both legs. Neither he nor the other witnesses to this horrific event could think of an obvious rational cause for the fire.

This doctor's experience was not unique; and support for the suspicion that many a physician would be able to tell of similar mysterious deaths by fire has come from a number of forthright members of the medical profession. Some have even admitted to coming across the phenomenon several times in the course of their career; and a certain Dr David Price has stated that he met with it approximately once every four years. SHC may indeed be a far more common occurrence than we have previously been led to believe.

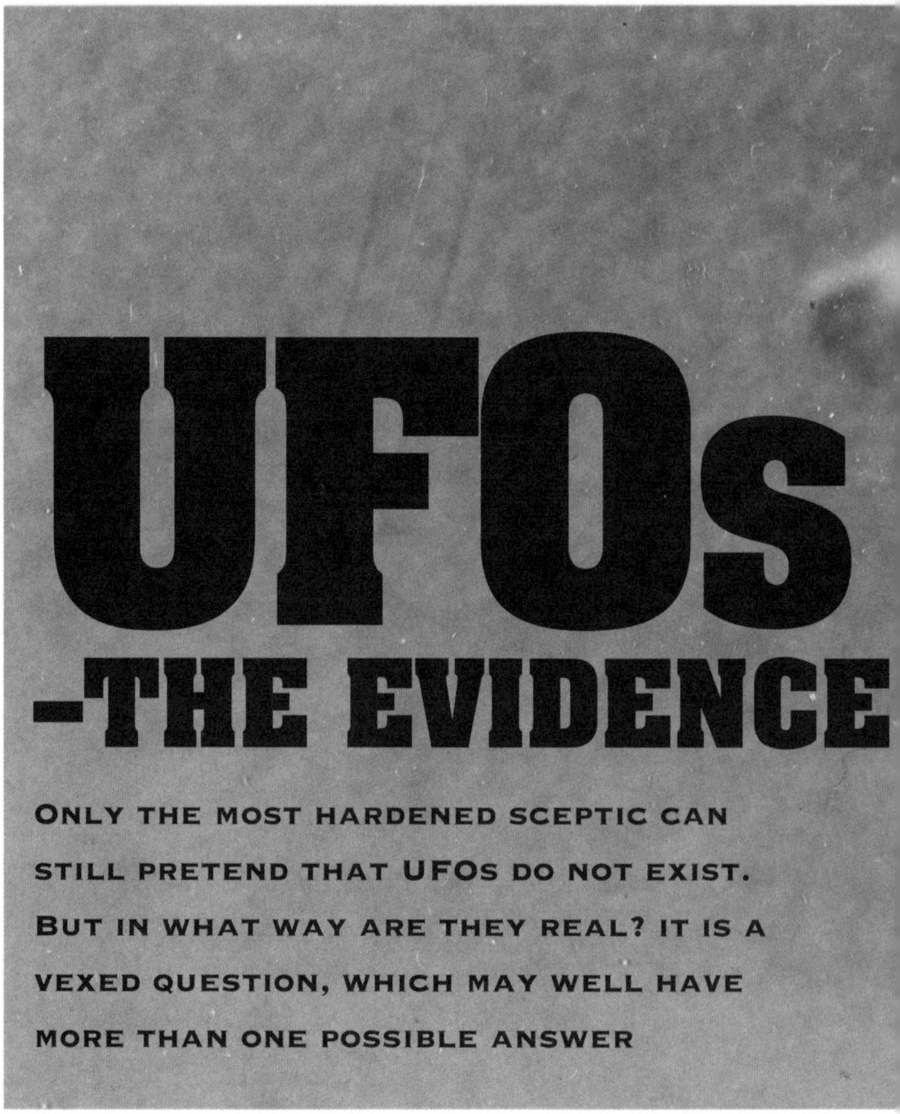

UFOs –THE EVIDENCE

ONLY THE MOST HARDENED SCEPTIC CAN STILL PRETEND THAT UFOs DO NOT EXIST. BUT IN WHAT WAY ARE THEY REAL? IT IS A VEXED QUESTION, WHICH MAY WELL HAVE MORE THAN ONE POSSIBLE ANSWER

'They flew like a saucer would if you skipped it across the water.' This is how, on 24 June 1947, American airman Kenneth Arnold, an experienced pilot, described some unusual flying craft he had seen over the mountains of America's west coast. Newspapermen applied his phrase to the craft themselves, and the misleading label 'flying saucer' has followed the UFO ever since, like a tin can tied to a cat's tail.

This fanciful name has, perhaps not unexpectedly, deepened the reluctance of professional scientists to take the UFO seriously. Indeed, only a few have taken the trouble to investigate this bizarre phenomenon, which surely qualifies as the strangest of our time. But even that phrase 'of our time' is a subject of controversy: many people claim that the UFO has in fact been with mankind throughout history. Yet the evidence they offer is meagre and their case far from proven. There seems little doubt that our earliest ancestors were considerably more advanced than has generally been supposed, but that is a long way from the theory that our planet has been regularly visited by extraterrestrial voyagers throughout the ages.

Whether or not UFOs existed in the past, there is no doubt that UFO sightings have proliferated in astonishing numbers over the past 40 years. This fact seems to be in some way linked with Man's first steps towards exploring space, and the connection is undoubtedly an important clue in trying to explain the nature of the UFO.

Estimates of the total number of UFO sightings vary so widely as to be meaningless: but more helpful figures are provided by the catalogues of reported sightings prepared by individual investigative organisations. Recently, for instance, a French team catalogued more than 600 encounter cases in France alone, each vouched for by responsible investigators; but how many more were not reported or investigated?

TANGIBLE EVIDENCE

In spite of this, many people do wonder whether UFOs are 'real' in the sense that, say, spacecraft or satellites are real. The surest proof would be actually to get hold of one, and there are persistent rumours that certain governments – notably that of the United States – have indeed captured a UFO, now kept in total secrecy. This is, however, more a matter of conjecture than anything else, despite the sworn affidavits of alleged witnesses. Indeed, the whole question of possible governmental involvement is a further fascinating aspect of the great UFO controversy.

Yet despite the absence of an actual UFO that we could touch and examine, a tremendous amount of evidence has been presented in the form of both still photographs and movies. The majority are likely to be fakes. Those with good credentials, meanwhile, are often so blurred or distant that they add a further dimension to the problem. Why, if UFOs exist, in an age when so many people travel about with a camera to hand, have we not obtained more and better photographic evidence?

We do have strong evidence, nevertheless, from certain effects that seem to have been caused by UFOs on surrounding objects, especially machinery. In November 1967, for example, a truck and a car approaching each other on a Hampshire road in the early hours of the morning simultaneously suffered engine failure when a large egg-shaped object crossed the road between them. The police, and subsequently the Ministry of Defence, investigated the incident, but no official explanation was ever issued. Such a case may leave investigators puzzled, but it makes one thing very likely: if they are indeed capable of causing physical effects, UFOs must surely by physically real.

ENEMY ACTION

What is more, as concrete physical objects, UFOs must originate from somewhere. Originally, back in the 1940s, when the very first UFOs of the current spate were seen, it was assumed they were from somewhere on Earth. The Americans even suspected they were a Russian secret device, perhaps developed using the expertise of German scientists captured during World War II.

But as more reports came in, it became clear that no nation on Earth could be responsible. Nor was there sufficient evidence to support other ingenious theories – that they came from the Himalayas, long a favoured source for hidden wisdom, or Antarctica where, of course, unexplored tracts of land and climatic anomalies provide fertile ground for speculation.

Instead, ufologists began to look beyond the Earth, encouraged by the fact that our own space

The first full study of UFOs,* above, *was published in 1952. Kenneth Arnold, one of its authors, began his collection of accounts of sightings soon after he himself saw several disc-shaped objects in the sky during June 1947.

UFOs have been reported by most astronauts. The object shown* right, *in a shot taken from Skylab III in 1973, rotated for several minutes before disappearing.

> "I am convinced that UFOs exist because I have seen one... It was big, it was very bright, it changed colours, and it was about the size of the moon. We watched it for ten minutes, but none of us could figure out what it was."
>
> **Former US President Jimmy Carter, 1976**

exploration programme was beginning. We were just starting to take an active interest in the possible existence of worlds beyond, and it seemed reasonable that other civilisations might have a similar interest in us.

Today, it is widely recognised that the UFO poses a problem not only for the astronomer and the engineer but also for behavioural scientists. Psychologists, for instance, confirm that an individual's response to a sighting is generally conditioned by his or her psychological make-up. The sociologist, meanwhile, places such responses in a rather wider context, relating them to cultural patterns. The anthropologist often detects parallels with myths and traditional beliefs, while the parapsychologist has been known to report that sightings are frequently accompanied by psychic manifestations, such as precognition or poltergeist activity.

Looking much like a spinning top, the unidentified object,* above, *was photographed hovering above Joshua Tree, California, in 1965.

Sceptics claim that the objects shown in the photograph,* right, *taken at Taormina, Sicily, are nothing more than lentil-shaped clouds, or perhaps the result of lens flare. Others, however, remain utterly convinced that they are UFOs.

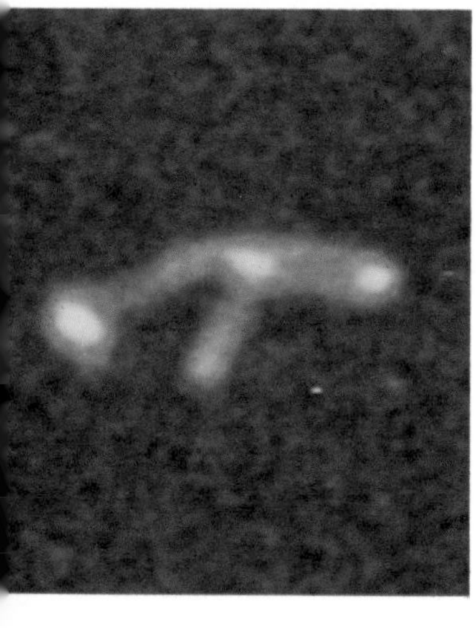

Messages from Outer Space?

This is particularly true of 'encounter' cases, in which the observer claims to have had actual meetings with UFO occupants. The entities are usually described as extraterrestrial aliens, often ambassadors from an intergalactic power, their purpose being to examine the human form, to warn us of our misuse of resources and to bring reassuring messages from some cosmic brotherhood. With only one or two such cases on file, these reports could certainly be dismissed as fantasy. But there are hundreds of such cases on record.

Each and every incident, however, remains a mystery. Did it actually occur or is it simply a fabrication – deliberate, unconscious, or perhaps induced by some external force? Hypotheses range from brainwashing by extraterrestrial invaders to deliberate invention by the CIA.

A great number of people would probably agree that UFOs exist on both a physical and psychological level. But even though they may be real enough, the likelihood is that they are not what they seem. This is the paradox that lies at the heart of all UFO mysteries, such as the dramatic account of a recent sighting that follows.

CASEBOOK

A DRAMATIC UFO SIGHTING WAS MADE BY THE KNOWLES FAMILY AS THEY DROVE FROM PERTH TO MELBOURNE. THEIRS WAS A TERRIFYING EXPERIENCE

The Knowles family are seen above, with their two dogs, shortly after their dramatic 'close encounter'.

January 1988 was an exciting time in Australia. The country was preparing to mark its bi-centennial, and the eyes of the world were closely focused on all the celebrations underway in this southern continent. But according to certain sources, other-worldly eyes may also have been watching the jubilations.

The Knowles family had left their home in Perth on 19 January, following a sudden decision to take the coastal desert highway to Melbourne, where they wanted to surprise relatives.

Head of the party was Faye Knowles, who had brought along her sons, Sean, Patrick and Wayne, aged between 18 and 24, and their two dogs. They had been on the road several hours when things first started to go wrong.

JUMPING LIGHTS

It was just after 4 a.m. on Wednesday 20 January, some way to the west of the small town of Mundrabilla when Sean Knowles reported what at first he assumed to be headlights some distance in front. But all at once these lights began to jump about and then vanished, before reappearing and heading straight at them.

A frightening game of cat and mouse followed. Sean accelerated in an attempt at escaping the now glowing mass. But the object kept appearing and disappearing, both in front and behind them. One moment they could see it; the next, it disappeared.

Absolute panic set in when the Knowles became convinced that a UFO was now overhead. They could not see it, but Faye put her hand out of an open window and placed it on the roof. There, she felt something soft and rubbery, and later found her hand covered in a sort of smooth 'soot'.

Much else was happening simultaneously. Everyone noticed that their voices were suffering an odd slurred effect. A greyish-black 'mist' with a bad smell had also entered the car, and a humming noise surrounded the road. The family's two dogs, meanwhile, were becoming highly irritable.

The most frightening event of all, however, occurred when the vehicle began to shake violently from side to side, as if it was being sucked up. Then it was seemingly dumped back with a thud, at which point a tyre blew.

Sean pulled the car off the road, and the family leapt out to hide in scrubland. The light was seen again in the distance; and only after it disappeared for the final time did the family dare hurriedly to fit the spare tyre and drive on as fast as they could.

Graham Henley was driving a truck 10 kilometres ahead of the Knowles when he, too, saw what he described as a 'twinkling light' in his rear mirror.

Henley attested to several things. Firstly, he had noted that the Knowles family were obviously terrified, and that even the dogs were cowering. There was also very evident damage to the car. There were dents in the roof and traces of grey ash inside the vehicle, which also had an unusual smell.

After the Knowles family had continued on their way, Henley went back to the spot where the vehicle had skidded off the road. It was now daylight, and he soon found the evidence – tyre marks, an indentation caused by a jack, and footprints. But the jack itself, as well as clothes and suitcases which the Knowles family said had tumbled out of the boot, had all strangely disappeared.

It was about 1 p.m. when the police at Ceduna, South Australia, were approached by Sean and Patrick Knowles. According to them, the light had been 'extremely bright... white with a yellow core.'

The Ceduna force decided to contact the South Australia branch of UFO Research Australia (UFORA). Eventually, a combined effort by several leading investigators procured data from all the witnesses, and a sample of dust from the vehicle was examined, just as it had been by the police.

> " THE MOST FRIGHTENING EVENT OF ALL, HOWEVER, OCCURRED WHEN THE VEHICLE BEGAN TO SHAKE VIOLENTLY FROM SIDE TO SIDE, AS IF IT WAS BEING SUCKED UP. "

A REGULAR HAUNT?

Many UFO researchers became convinced that the Knowles family had indeed been in close proximity to some sort of alien craft, and all sorts of links with other cases were sought.

Research into the incident yielded further evidence of strange happenings that night. Several drivers reported sudden freak weather during what was otherwise a clear, calm and dry night. The occupants of one car spoke of suddenly driving into a wall of buffeting winds of near hurricane force that rocked their vehicle from side to side.

Debunkers have tried to suggest that the sighting might have been a mirage caused by the desert heat (but, of course, it occurred at night when it is very much cooler). Those, however, who have invested considerable time and effort into investigating this case have all reached a fairly unanimous conclusion: namely that the witnesses were sincere and truthful, and had been confronted by something which they genuinely could not explain.

WHO ARE THE HUMANOIDS?

MANY PEOPLE CLAIM TO HAVE MET THE OCCUPANTS OF UFOS; BUT ACCOUNTS OF HUMANOIDS' BEHAVIOUR AND APPEARANCE SEEM STRANGELY INCONSISTENT

The sighting of nine unusual flying craft in Washington State, USA, by American airman Kenneth Arnold in June 1947, marked the advent of modern publicity for the 'flying saucer' or UFO phenomenon. The frequently reported ultra-high speeds and breath-taking manoeuvrability of the objects inevitably led to speculation by observers, newsmen and the public alike that what was being witnessed were intrusions into our airspace by extra-terrestrial visitors – beings from outer space. And, as the behaviour of these objects seemed to indicate superior technology and its fluent control, the big question was: control by whom, or by what?

The question was not quickly resolved, however; for although the phenomenon was so persistent that the US Air Force set up an investigatory unit (Project Blue Book), officialdom did not appear to want to know the answer. By 1952, many accounts of sightings and even landings had been filed with the Project; but in his book *The Report on UFOs,* Blue Book's commanding officer, Captain Edward Ruppelt, stated he had been plagued by reports of landings and that his team had conscientiously ignored them.

There are, however, always those whose sense of wonder overcomes official intransigence. Groups of doggedly inquisitive civilian researchers drifted together and, to the limits of their slender resources, they gathered and recorded information from all around the world. Among them were people like Aimé Michel and Jacques Vallée from France (Vallée subsequently lived and worked in the USA); Coral and Jim Lorenzen and their Aerial Phenomena Research Organisation (APRO) in Arizona; Len Stringfield in Ohio; Major Donald Keyhoe's National Investigations Committee on Aerial Phenomena (NICAP) in Washington DC (who, like Ruppelt, were at first none too happy about the many landing reports) and, in Britain, the supporters of the *Flying Saucer Review.*

A purported humanoid,* above, *stands to the left of an alleged grounded UFO in the Bernina Mountains, Italy, on 31 July 1952.

The controversial picture,* above right, *shows a dead crew member from a crashed UFO found near Mexico City in the 1950s. The creature was apparently taken to Germany for examination – never to be heard of again.

ALIEN PHENOMENON

From the impressive body of evidence collected by these veterans, and others, it is quite obvious now that the occupants of UFOs constitute a phenomenon in their own right. Indeed, the shapes, sizes, appearance and behaviour of these 'pilots', as reported by their alleged observers, are often quite extraordinary. Out of the thousands of reported sightings, no coherent picture emerges of their nature and intentions, however, and their actions seldom seem to be related to any kind of organised surveillance of our planet. Sometimes, sightings of these aliens are even reported without the apparent presence of a UFO.

From 1947 to 1952, while the reality of UFOs and their occupants was often the subject of heated debate, allegedly man-like creatures had already been observed either close to, or actually in, UFOs in widely different parts of the world.

Brazilian Landing

At Bauru, in the state of Sao Paulo, Brazil, on 23 July 1947, for instance, – less than a month after Kenneth Arnold's aerial encounter near Mount Rainier – a survey worker named José Higgins, and several of his fellow workers, saw a large metallic disc come to earth and settle down on curved legs.

Higgins stood his ground while his colleagues fled, and he soon found himself face to face with three 7-foot (2.1 metres) tall beings, all wearing transparent overalls with metal boxes on their backs. One entity pointed a tube at him and moved as though to apprehend him. But Higgins dodged the creature and observed that it was shy of following him into the sunlight.

The creatures had large bald heads, big round eyes, no eyebrows or beards and long legs. They leapt and gambolled, picking up and tossing huge boulders about. They also made holes in the ground, perhaps trying to indicate what could have been the positions of planets around the sun, and pointing particularly to the seventh hole from the centre. (Could that seventh 'planet' signify Uranus?) The creatures then re-entered their craft, which took off with a whistling noise. Higgins' subsequent account appeared in two Brazilian newspapers.

Three weeks later, far away in north-eastern Italy, a Professor Johannis was on a mountain walk on 14 August 1947, near Villa Santina, Carni, in the province of Friuli, when he suddenly saw a red metallic disc in a rocky cleft and emerged from trees to look at it. He then noticed that two dwarf-like creatures were following him, moving with tiny strides, hands perfectly motionless at their sides, and heads still. As they came nearer, Johannis' strength failed him: he seemed paralysed.

The little beings – less than 3 feet (1 metre) tall – wore translucent blue coveralls, with red collars and belts. The witness could detect no hair, but he described their facial skin colour as 'earthy green'. He also noted straight noses, slits for mouths that opened and closed like fishes' mouths, and large, round, protruding eyes.

Johannis says he shouted to them on an impulse and waved his alpine pick, whereupon one dwarf raised a hand to his belt, the centre of which apparently emitted a puff of smoke. The pick flew out of Johannis' hand, and he fell flat on his back. One entity then retrieved the pick, and the pair retreated to the disc, which soon shot up, hovered briefly over the panic-stricken professor, and then suddenly seemed to shrink and vanish.

Captain Edward J. Ruppelt,* top, *was the commanding officer of the highly-criticised Project Blue Book; Aimé Michel,* centre, *a famous French UFO investigator; and Major Donald E. Keyhoe, the head of the National Investigations Committee on Aerial Phenomena (NICAP), based in Washington DC, USA.

***Artist's impressions of the humanoids reported by José Higgins in Brazil and Professor Johannis in Italy in 1947 are shown* left *and* top right.**

Crash Landing

On 19 August 1949, in Death Valley, California, two prospectors saw the apparent crash-landing of a disc. Two small beings emerged and were chased by the prospectors until the aliens were lost among sand dunes. But when the two men returned to their site, the disc-shaped object had gone.

Argentine rancher Wilfredo Arévalo saw one 'aluminium' disc land while another hovered over it on 18 March 1950. The object that landed was surrounded by a greenish-blue vapour, and in its centre was a transparent cabin in which Arévalo saw 'four tall, well-shaped men dressed in Cellophane-like clothing'. They shone a beam of light at the rancher, the disc glowed a brighter blue, flames shot from the base, and it rose from the ground. The two objects then disappeared swiftly towards the Chilean border.

Such reports seemed to promise interesting material for future investigation, but did not appear to indicate a serious threat of alien ('take me to your leader') invasion. There was, too, an official reluctance even to consider landing reports, which were

A 'Venusian scout ship', photographed by George Adamski on 13 December 1952 at Palomar Gardens, California, USA, is shown **right**, *while his picture of an 'interplanetary carrier' and six 'scouts' is featured* **below.**

George Adamski is seen, **bottom**, *with the 6-inch (15-centimetre) telescope through which he took these controversial UFO photographs.*

" A PERSON THEN APPEARED AND APPROACHED HIM...THERE WAS AN AURA OF FRIENDLINESS ABOUT HIM, AND ADAMSKI SAID THAT THEY WERE ABLE TO COMMUNICATE TELEPATHICALLY ABOUT MANY THINGS, THE VISITOR SPECIFICALLY INDICATING THAT HE CAME FROM VENUS. "

said to be flooding in, due possibly to a fear of being swamped with crazy stories of 'little green men', which might well have become ready targets for ridicule in the media. (Serious researchers eventually coined the term 'humanoids'.)

Back in 1953, however, something happened that shocked most serious-minded investigators, for it was in that year that a certain George Adamski broke in on the UFO scene with a book co-authored with Desmond Leslie – *Flying Saucers Have Landed.* In this controversial title, Adamski claimed to have conversed with a being from a flying saucer and to have taken photographs of the craft. The book rapidly became a bestseller and was a boon to those early serious researchers – although they would never admit it – in that it brought to thousands of casual readers an interest in ufology.

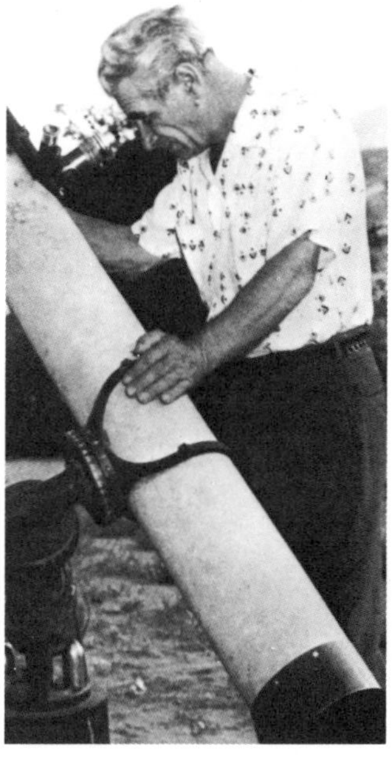

George Adamski (1891-1965) was an amateur astronomer who operated Newtonian reflector telescopes from his home at Palomar Gardens, California. He developed an obsessive interest in flying saucer reports, frequently claimed to have seen the objects and to have photographed them telescopically – as on 5 March 1951, when he captured on film a giant cigar-shaped object surrounded by emerging scout craft, and on 1 May 1952, when he took a picture of another giant cigar-shaped 'mother ship'. Then, on 20 November 1952, with a small party of friends, Adamski was driven out to a place just off the road to Parker, in Arizona. The purpose of the trip was to look for, and then possibly to photograph, UFOs.

Venusian Visitor

A 6-inch (15-centimetre) portable telescope was set up at a convenient place and Adamski settled down to wait, while his companions retreated to watch from a distance. Before long, he said, he was rewarded with the sight of an object landing among the hills before him, and he photographed it at long range before it disappeared.

A 'person' then appeared and approached him. The stranger was about 5 feet 6 inches (1.7 metres) tall, wore ski-suit type clothing and had long hair down to his shoulders. There was an aura of friendliness about him, and Adamski said that they were able to communicate telepathically about many things, the visitor specifically indicating that he came from Venus.

The stranger's 'scout craft' then turned up and, refusing Adamski's request for a ride, the 'Venusian' departed, taking one of Adamski's film plate-holders with him. The ufonaut left footprints in the sand, and a member of the party produced plaster of Paris to make casts of the imprints.

On 13 December 1952, the Venusian returned to Earth, bringing back the plate-holder; and it was then, so Adamski claims, that he took close-up pictures of the craft.

In his second book, *Inside the Space Ships,* Adamski stated that he finally made that trip – round the Moon – and that a space companion had pointed out the rivers on the unseen far side.

All of this seems to indicate that Adamski was not telling the truth, or perhaps that he had been deliberately misled by entities that had a vested interest in spreading a little confusion on Earth. Then again, perhaps the story Adamski told was real enough to him.

UFO PHOTO FILE

The photograph, *left,* is one of the few shots of a nocturnal UFO to show more than an indeterminate blur of light. It was taken by a 14-year-old paper-boy in Tulsa, Oklahoma, USA, on 2 August 1965. The object was observed by many witnesses, who stated that the tricoloured lights changed slowly to a uniform blue-green. The Condon Committee, set up at the University of Colorado, confirmed that the photograph represented a large object seen against the sky, and that the dark stripes between the bright patches were neither space nor sky, but part of the UFO itself. With characteristic caution, the US Air Force concluded that the photograph represented either a genuine UFO or a Christmas tree light! The UFO organisation Ground Saucer Watch, on the other hand, considers it strong UFO evidence.

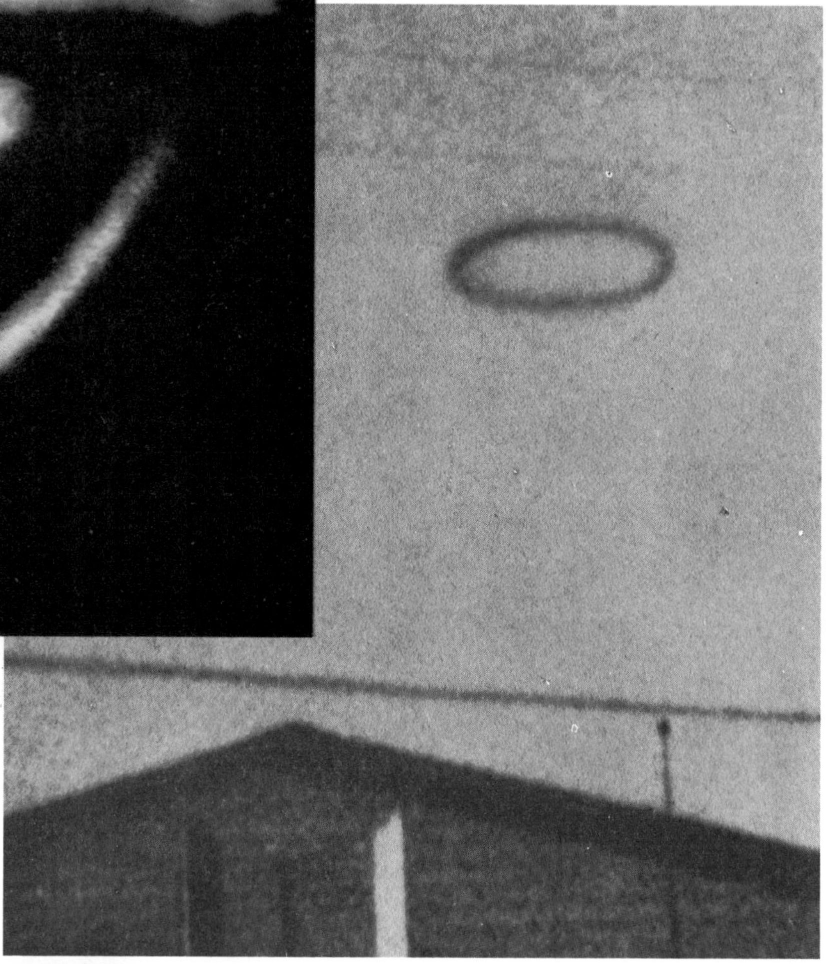

At about 9.00 a.m. one day in September 1957, the strange, ring-shaped object, *right,* was seen in the sky over Fort Belvoir, Virginia, USA. It 'seemed solid', very black with no reflection and was about 60 feet (18 metres) in diameter. The ring gradually became engulfed in black smoke and finally disappeared. The Condon Committee later identified the sighting, however, as having been 'an atomic bomb simulation demonstration of the type commonly carried out at Fort Belvoir at this period'.

The still, *left,* is from a film taken by Ralph Mayher in Miami, Florida, USA on 29 July 1952. Using computer techniques to analyse the photograph, the American UFO organisation Ground Saucer Watch has established that it is probably genuine and that it shows an object 30-40 feet (9-12 metres) long. Mayher reported that its speed appeared to be less than that of a falling meteorite as it shot away over the ocean.

Puzzled by his sighting, Mayher turned his film over to the US Air Force for investigation. It was never returned. Many people see the incident as part of a deliberate campaign on the part of the US authorities to suppress evidence of UFOs. Luckily, Mayher had foreseen the possibility of his film getting 'lost': so before handing it over, he carefully snipped off the first few frames. This is one of them.

The photograph of an alleged flying saucer over Venezuela, *above,* is in fact a hoax by an engineer in Caracas. He placed a photograph of a button on an enlargement of an aerial shot, which was then rephotographed; and the 'saucer's' shadow was 'burned' in at the printing stage.

The photograph, *right,* confirmed as probably genuine by Ground Saucer Watch, was taken early in the afternoon of 8 May 1966 by James Pfeiffer, an airline executive on holiday in Ipameri, Brazil. The object was seen by a couple of dozen witnesses. GSW's computer analysis of the photograph shows that the object was approximately 450 yards (400 metres) from the camera at an altitude of about 160-230 feet (50-70 metres). The witnesses heard a 'high-, then a low-pitched whining sound' as the object crossed the river. It brushed against trees as it disappeared from view; and broken branches were found in the area later. The entire sighting lasted about 90 seconds.

THE SINKING OF THE TITANIC, THE ASSASSINATIONS OF THE KENNEDY BROTHERS, AND THE ABERFAN DISASTER – ALL HAVE BEEN THE SUBJECT OF REMARKABLE SUCCESSES ON THE PART OF THOSE WITH THE EXTRAORDINARY GIFT OF PRECOGNITION

THE WARNING VOICE

At 5 o'clock one morning in 1979, a knock at her apartment door woke Helen Tillotson from a very deep sleep. Suddenly, she heard her mother calling out: 'Helen, are you there? Let me in!' Helen hurried to the door to find out what was wrong. Her mother, Mrs Marjorie Tillotson, who lived in a Philadelphia apartment block just across the street, demanded to know why Helen had been knocking on her door a few minutes earlier.

Helen, 26, assured her mother that she had gone to bed at 11 o'clock the previous night and had not woken at all until she heard her mother knocking at the door. 'But I saw you. I spoke to you,' said Mrs Tillotson. She said Helen had told her to follow her home immediately without asking questions.

Suddenly, there was a loud noise from outside. Both women rushed to the window: across the street, a gas leak in Mrs Tillotson's block had caused an explosion, and her apartment was gutted. 'If she had been asleep there at the time,' said a fire chief, 'I doubt whether she would have got out alive.'

Had Helen been sleep-walking? Or did her mother have a psychic vision? Whatever the explanation, either mother or daughter had apparently sensed the danger of an explosion, and saved Mrs Tillotson's life. Such incidents are known as premonitions; and although they are rare, enough cases have been documented to suggest that some people are able to catch a glimpse of the future.

PREMONITION OF DEATH

Early in 1979, Spanish hotel executive Jaime Castell had a dream in which a voice told him he would never see his unborn child, which was due in three months. Convinced that he would die, Castell took out a £50,000 insurance policy – payable only on his death, with no benefits if he lived. Weeks later, as he drove from work at a steady 50 mph (80 km/h), another car travelling in the opposite direction at over 100 mph (160 km/h) went out of control, hit a safety barrier, somersaulted and landed on top of Castell's car. Both drivers were killed instantly.

After paying the £50,000 to Castell's widow, a spokesman for the insurance company said that a death occurring so soon after such a specific policy had been taken out would normally have to be investigated thoroughly. 'But this incredible accident rules out any suspicion. A fraction of a second either way and he would have escaped.'

Sometimes a number of people will even have forebodings of the same event. Many of them have no direct connection with the tragedy they foresee; but some, like Eryl Mai Jones, become its victims. On 20 October 1966, this nine-year-old Welsh girl told her mother she had dreamt that, when she had gone to school, it was not there. 'Something black had come down all over it,' she said. Next day she went to school in Aberfan – and half a million tons of coal waste slithered down onto the mining village, killing Eryl and 139 others, most of them children.

After the disaster, many people claimed to have had premonitions about it. They were investigated

The terrible events of 21 October 1966, when a large part of the Welsh mining village of Aberfan, above, was obliterated by coal waste, were foreseen by many people. Among them was nine-year-old Eryl Mai Jones (inset), who became one of the victims.

The Titanic, the 'safest ocean liner ever built,' sank on her maiden voyage in 1912. Journalist W.T. Stead, shown far right, one of the many who drowned, had published a strangely prophetic story a few years earlier about a similar tragedy.

by a London psychiatrist, Dr John Barker, who narrowed them down to 60 he felt were genuine. So impressed was he by this evidence for premonitions of the tragedy that he helped set up the British Premonitions Bureau, to record and monitor such occurrences. It was hoped the Bureau could be used to give early warning of similar disasters and enable lives to be saved.

When Dr Barker analysed the Aberfan premonitions, he noticed that there had been a gradual build-up during the week before the Welsh tip buried the school, reaching a peak on the night before the tragedy. Two Californian premonitions bureaux – one at Monterey, south of San Francisco, the other at Berkeley – have since sifted through predictions from members of the public in the hope of detecting a similar pattern.

Sceptics often point out that information about premonitions is published only after the event, and that the vast majority of such predictions are discarded when they are found to be wrong. This may be true in many cases, but there are exceptions.

PROPHET ARRESTED

A Scottish newspaper, the *Dundee Courier & Advertiser,* carried a story on 6 December 1978, headlined 'Prophet didn't have a ticket'. It told of the appearance of Edward Pearson, 43, at Perth Sheriff Court, charged with travelling on the train from Inverness to Perth on 4 December without paying the proper fare.

Pearson – described as 'an unemployed Welsh prophet' – was said to have been on his way to see the Minister of the Environment to warn him about an earthquake that would hit Glasgow in the near future. The *Courier*'s readers doubtless found it very amusing. But they were not so amused by the earthquake that shook them in their beds three weeks later, causing damage to buildings in Glasgow and other parts of Scotland. Earthquakes in Britain are rare; and prophets who predict them are even rarer.

But the most remarkable prophecy ever made must surely be the story of the *Titanic,* the great ocean liner which sank on her maiden voyage in 1912 with terrible loss of life. In 1898, a novel by a struggling writer, Morgan Robertson, had predicted the disaster with uncanny accuracy.

Robertson's story told of a 70,000-tonne vessel, the safest ocean liner in the world, which hit an iceberg in the Atlantic on her maiden voyage. She sank and most of her 2,500 passengers were lost because, incredibly, the liner had only 24 lifeboats – less than half the number needed to save all the passengers and crew on board.

FICTION BECOMES FACT

On 14 April 1912, the real-life tragedy occurred as the 66,000-tonne *Titanic* was making her maiden voyage across the Atlantic. She, too, hit an iceberg; she, too, sank. And, like the liner in the novel, she did not have enough lifeboats on board – only 20, in fact – and there was terrible loss of life. Of the 2,224 people on board the luxury liner, 1,513 perished in the icy waters. Robertson even came remarkably close to getting the vessel's name right – he had called it the *SS Titan.*

Curiously, another work of fiction about a similar tragedy had appeared in a London newspaper some years earlier. The editor was a distinguished journalist, W.T. Stead, who added a prophetic note to the end of the story: 'This is exactly what might take place, and what will take place, if liners are sent to sea short of boats.' By a particularly ironic twist of fate, Stead was one of the passengers on the *Titanic* who died for that very reason.

Such cases are rare, however, and for every prediction that is fulfilled there are perhaps a thousand that are not. In 1979, the Mind Science Foundation of San Antonio, Texas, USA, came up with a novel experiment to test how accurately people could predict an event. The American Skylab space station had begun to fall out of orbit and, although it was known for certain that it

Nostradamus, above, *the 16th-century seer, is credited with having prophesied many major world events, among them the recent Gulf War,* above left. *But many say the predictions are only given credibility with hindsight.*

would eventually fall to Earth, scientists did not know when this would occur nor where it would land. The foundation therefore invited people known to have psychic powers – and anyone else who wanted to participate – to predict the date of Skylab's fall and the spot on Earth where its remains would land. It called the exercise 'Project Chicken Little', and over 200 people responded to the appeal. Their predictions were analysed and published before Skylab fell. Virtually all were wrong: very few even came close to the date of Skylab's return (11 June), and even fewer guessed that it would land in Australia.

Bombs and Assassinations

While such experiments to prove that the future can be predicted have not been very successful, some individuals nevertheless seem to excel at prophecy. Nostradamus, for example, the 16th-century seer, made many prophecies that have apparently come true. Not everyone agrees with their interpretation, however. Take this one for example:

'Near the harbour and in two cities will be two scourges, the like of which have never been seen. Hunger, plague within, people thrown out by the sword will cry for help from the great immortal God.'

But what does it predict? Nostradamus' followers say it is a prediction of the atom bomb attacks on Nagasaki and Hiroshima in 1945. But no one could have used his prophecy to foretell these events. In other words, it is hindsight that gives credibility to writing such as this.

Jeane Dixon, a modern seer, successfully predicted the assassinations of President John F. Kennedy, his brother, Robert Kennedy, and civil rights leader Martin Luther King. Intriguingly, her premonition of the American President's murder came 11 years before the event and before he had even been elected President.

A devout woman, she had gone to St Matthew's Cathedral in Washington one morning in 1952 to pray, and was standing before a statue of the Virgin Mary when she had a vision of the White House. The numerals 1 – 9 – 6 – 0 appeared above it against a dark cloud. A young, blue-eyed man stood

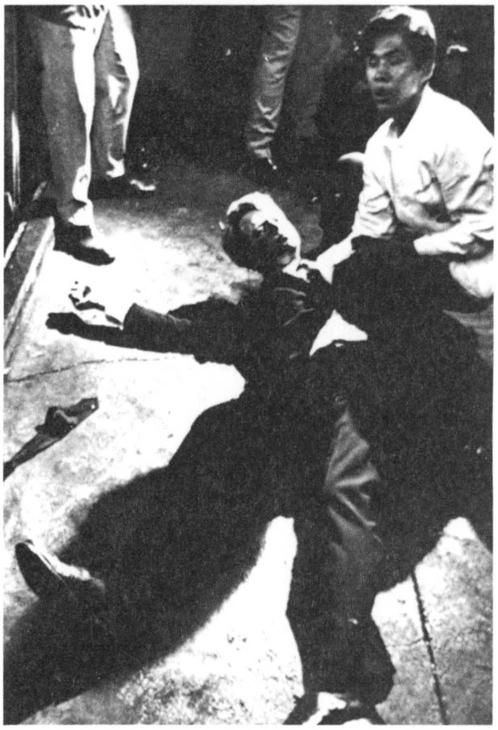

at the door. A voice then told her that a Democrat, who would be inaugurated as President in 1960, would be assassinated while in office.

She predicted Kennedy's brother's death in 1968 – in an even more startling way – while addressing a convention at the Ambassador Hotel, Los Angeles. She invited questions from the floor and someone asked if Robert Kennedy would ever be president. Suddenly, Jeane Dixon saw a black curtain fall between her and the audience, and she told the questioner: 'No, he will not. He will never be President of the United States, because of a tragedy right here in this hotel.' A week later Robert Kennedy was gunned down in that very hotel.

But Jeane Dixon is not always right. In fact, even the best seers claim only a 70 per cent success rate, and sceptics argue that it appears so high only because their predictions are vague.

Jeane Dixon, below, *is a modern American seer who predicted the assassinations of both President John F. Kennedy and his brother, Robert,* left, *as well as civil rights leader, Martin Luther King.*

"THERE REMAIN ON RECORD SOME EXTRAORDINARY STORIES OF PREMONITIONS THAT ARE DIFFICULT TO EXPLAIN ACCORDING TO THE LAWS OF CONVENTIONAL SCIENCE – UNLESS THERE IS SOMETHING WRONG WITH OUR CONCEPT OF SPACE AND TIME."

Sceptics, of course, will argue that it is impossible to look into the future, many of them feeling that, until the existence of precognition is proved in the laboratory, it cannot be taken seriously. But, although it may not be easy to look ahead at will, there remain on record some extraordinary stories of premonitions that are difficult to explain according to the laws of conventional science – unless there is something wrong with our concept of space and time.

A first-class example of this is the experience of Mark Twain. Before he became a famous writer – and while he was still known by the name of Samuel Clemens – he worked as an apprentice pilot on a steamboat, the *Pennsylvania*, which plied the Mississippi river. His younger brother, Henry, worked as a clerk on the same boat. Samuel went to visit his sister in St Louis; and, while he was there, had a vivid dream, featuring a metal coffin resting on two chairs. In it was his brother and, resting on his chest, a bouquet of white flowers with a crimson one in the middle.

A few days later, back on the boat, Samuel had an argument with the chief pilot of the *Pennsylvania* and was transferred to another boat, the *Lacey*. His brother, however, stayed aboard the *Pennsylvania*, which was travelling up the river two days ahead of the *Lacey*. When Samuel reached Greenville, Mississippi, he was told that the *Pennsylvania* had blown up just outside Memphis with the loss of 150 lives. His brother Henry, however, was still alive, though badly scalded, and Samuel spent six days and nights with him until he died. Exhausted, he fell into a deep sleep. When he awoke, he found his brother's body had been removed from the room, so he went to find it.

It was just as he had seen it in the dream. Henry was in a metal coffin, which rested on two chairs. But one detail was missing – the flowers. Then, as Samuel watched, an elderly woman entered the room carrying a bouquet of white flowers with a single red rose in the centre. She placed them on Henry's body and left. Mark Twain's glimpse of the future had been fulfilled in practically every detail.

The Mind Science Foundation of Texas carried out an experiment in 1979 to detect whether people could foretell where Skylab would fall to Earth. Very few, however, accurately predicted Australia.

CASEBOOK

A NIGHTMARE COMES TRUE

On the evening of Friday, 26 May 1979, the world was shocked to learn that an American Airlines DC-10 airliner had crashed – a mass of flames and twisted wreckage – on take-off from Chicago's O'Hare International Airport. The lives of 273 people were lost in the worst disaster in the history of flying ever to occur in the United States.

In Cincinnati, Ohio, 23-year-old office manager David Booth sat slumped in horrified disbelief in front of his television. For 10 consecutive nights before the disaster, he had slept through the same terrible nightmare. First, he had heard the sound of engines failing and then looked on helplessly as a huge American Airlines aeroplane swerved sharply, rolled over and crashed to the ground in a mass of red and orange flames. Not only did he see the crash and hear the explosion in his dreams, he also felt the heat of the flames. Each time he awoke in terror and was obsessed all day by the memory of the hideous occurrence. He was sure it was a premonition.

'There was never any doubt to me that something was going to happen,' he said. 'It wasn't like a dream. It was like I was standing there watching the whole thing – like watching television.'

After several nights, he could no longer keep his terrible premonition to himself; and, on Tuesday, 22 May 1979, he telephoned the Federal Aviation Authority at the Greater Cincinnati Airport. Then he called American Airlines and a psychiatrist at the University of Cincinnati. They listened sympathetically, but that failed to make Booth feel any better. Three days later, almost out of his mind with worry, he heard the news of the DC-10 crash.

The Federal Aviation Authority had taken David Booth's call seriously enough to attempt, in vain, to match up the details of his nightmare with some known airport or aeroplane somewhere in the country. When they heard the news of the crash, of course, the details tallied all too well. 'It was uncanny,' said Jack Barker, public affairs officer for the southern region of the FAA. 'There were differences, but there were many similarities. The greatest similarity was his calling [naming] the airline and the aeroplane ... and that [the plane] came in inverted.' Booth had mentioned a 'three-engine aircraft' resembling a DC-10, and the crash site he described was similar in many aspects to the airport at Chicago.

David Booth stopped having nightmares once the disaster had happened, but he continued to feel disturbed by the whole affair. 'How can you make sense of something like that?' he asked. 'There's no explanation for it. No meaning. No conclusion. It just doesn't make sense.'

THE POWER TO OVERCOME THE FORCE OF GRAVITY IS SAID SOMETIMES TO OCCUR SPONTANEOUSLY, AMAZING LEVITATOR AND ONLOOKERS ALIKE. HOW REAL IS THE PHENOMENON?

DEFYING THE LAW OF GRAVITY

Three notable members of London society witnessed, on 16 December 1868, an incident so extraordinary that it is still a focus of controversy. Viscount Adare, the Master of Lindsay and Captain Wynne saw the famous medium Daniel Home rise into the air and float out of one window in a large house in fashionable London and then float in at another – over 80 feet (24 metres) from the ground, it is claimed. D.D. Home became known primarily for his levitations, of himself and of objects – on one occasion, a grand piano – but he was not alone in having this apparently 'impossible' ability to defy the law of gravity.

St Joseph of Copertino (1603-1663) flew into the air every time he was emotionally aroused. Being of an excitable nature, he often made levitations, and they were well witnessed. A simple peasant – some say he was actually feeble-minded – this boy, from Apulia in Italy, spent his youth trying to achieve religious ecstasy by such means as self-flagellation, starvation and wearing hair-shirts. He became a Franciscan at the age of 22, and then his religious fervour 'took off', quite literally.

D.D. Home,* above, *ascribed his levitations to the work of spirits, and is seen,* above right, *floating into the air with no visible means of support.

SAINTLY GIDDINESS

Joseph soon became something of an embarrassment to his superiors. During Mass one Sunday, he rose into the air and flew onto the altar in the midst of the candles, becoming badly burned as a result.

For 35 years, Joseph was excluded from all public services because of his disconcerting habits, but still tales of his levitations spread. While walking with a Benedictine monk in the monastery gardens, for instance, he suddenly flew up into an olive tree. Unfortunately he was unable to fly back down, so his fellow-monks had to fetch a ladder.

A surgeon, at least two cardinals and one Pope (Urban VIII), among many others, witnessed Joseph's extraordinary spells of weightlessness – which he called 'my giddinesses' – and the Church concluded the levitations must be the work of God.

Another levitator was St Teresa of Avila, who died in 1582. This remarkable mystic experienced the same feelings as many people do during common 'flying dreams'.

'It seemed to me, when I tried to make some resistance, as if a great force beneath my

St Joseph of Copertino, depicted* below, *owed his canonisation to an ability to levitate.

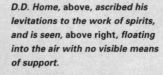

feet lifted me up ... I confess that it threw me into great fear, very great indeed at first; for in seeing one's body thus lifted up from the earth, though the spirit draws it upwards after itself (and that with great sweetness, if unresisted), the senses are not lost; at least I was so much myself as able to see that I was being lifted up. After the rapture was over, I have to say my body seemed frequently to be buoyant, as if all weight had departed from it, so much so that now and then I scarce knew my feet touched the ground', she said.

Indeed, so insistent were St Teresa's levitations that she begged the sisters to hold her down when she felt an 'attack' coming on, but often there was no time for such measures – she simply rose off the floor until the weightlessness passed.

Most levitators are believers in one particular system, be it Christianity, Hindu mysticism, ancient Egyptian mysteries or Spiritualism; and it was to this last category that D.D. Home belonged.

Born in Scotland and brought up in America, Home was a puny, artistic child. At the age of 13, he had a vision of a friend, Edwin, and announced to his aunt's family that this must mean that Edwin had been dead for three days. Amazingly, it was proved to be true. Home's career as a medium had begun; but it was not until he was 19 that he would actually defy the law of gravity.

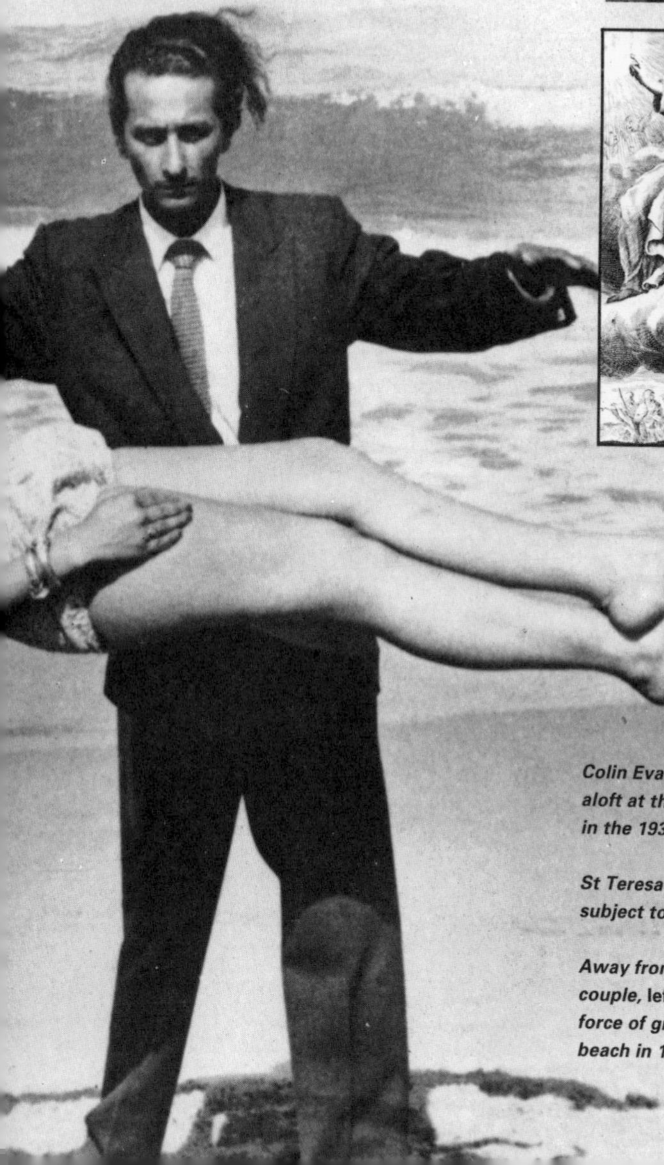

Colin Evans, top, seems to drift aloft at the Conway Hall, London, in the 1930s.

St Teresa of Avila, above, was also subject to 'attacks of levitation.

Away from all artificial aids, the couple, left, appears to defeat the force of gravity on a South African beach in 1962.

Ward Cheney, a prosperous silk-manufacturer, held a seance at his home in Connecticut in August 1852, and D.D. Home was there to provide the usual 'spiritualist' manifestations – table-turning, rappings, floating trumpets and mysterious lights.

Home was quite capable of keeping the guests entertained in this fashion; but something happened, completely unannounced, that made his name overnight. He suddenly floated up into the air until his head was touching the ceiling.

Up to the Ceiling

Among the guests was a sceptical reporter, F.L. Burr, editor of the *Hartford Times*. He wrote of this bizarre and unexpected incident:

> 'Suddenly, without any expectation on the part of the company, Home was taken up into the air. I had hold of his hand at the time and I felt his feet – they were lifted a foot (30 centimetres) from the floor. He palpitated from head to foot with the contending emotions of joy and fear which choked his utterances. Again and again he was taken from the floor, and the third time he was carried to the ceiling of the apartment, with which his hands and feet came into gentle contact.'

Home's career advanced rapidly and he was lionised in seance parlour and royal court alike. Indeed, wherever he went there were bizarre phenomena – winds howled in still rooms, apports of fresh flowers fell from the ceiling, doors opened and shut, fireballs zigzagged around the room – and Home levitated.

The famous occasion, when he floated out of one window and in through another, is still the subject of heated debate, particularly since the incident was documented by respectable witnesses. One of

them, the Master of Lindsay (later the Earl of Crawford) wrote:

> 'I was sitting with Mr Home and Lord Adare and a cousin of his [Captain Wynne]. During the sitting, Mr Home went into a trance and in that state was carried out of the window in the room next to where we were, and was brought in at our window. The distance between the windows was about seven feet six inches [2.3 metres], and there was not the slightest foothold between them, nor was there more than a 12-inch [30 centimetres] projection to each window, which served as a ledge to put flowers on. We heard the window in the next room lift up, and almost immediately after we saw Home floating in the air outside our window. The moon was shining full into the room; my back was to the light, and I saw the shadow on the wall of the windowsill, and Home's feet about six inches [15 centimetres] above it. He remained in this position for a few seconds, then raised the window and glided into the room feet foremost and sat down.'

SUBTLE SCEPTICISM

Sceptics such as Frank Podmore or, more recently, John Sladek, have tried to disprove this levitation, although neither of them was among the witnesses. Sladek attempted to discredit the three who were present by comparing the details of their stories – such as how high the balconies were from the street or, indeed, whether there were actually any balconies at all.

Podmore, on the other hand, was more subtle in his scepticism. He mentions the fact that a few days before the levitation, and in front of the same witnesses, Home had opened the window and stood on the ledge outside. He had pointedly drawn their attention to himself standing on the narrow ledge some considerable distance from the ground. As Podmore remarked drily: 'The medium had thus, as it were, furnished a rough sketch of the picture which he aimed at producing.'

In a classic stage levitation,* top, *the girl, Marva Ganzel, is first hypnotised into a cataleptic trance while balanced on two swords. When one is taken away, she somehow remains suspended in mid-air.
Frank Podmore,* above, *suggested that D.D. Home's most famous levitation was merely an hallucination.

On another occasion, Home suddenly announced 'I'm rising, I'm rising', before proceeding to levitate in front of several witnesses. Again, Podmore implied that Home's levitations were nothing more than hallucinations produced by his hypnotic suggestion, rather in the same manner that the Indian rope trick is said to be a mass hallucination, the secret being in the magician's patter.

But even in the face of extreme hostility, Home remained a successful levitator for over 40 years. Among his witnesses were Emperor Napoleon III, John Ruskin and many hundreds more, not all of whom were as inconsistent in their testimonies as Adare, Wynne and Lindsay. Moreover, during that long span of time and mostly in broad daylight, Home was never proven to be a fraud. And despite Podmore's accusations, Home never went out of his way to build up an atmosphere heavy with suggestibility. In fact, he was one of the few mediums actively to eschew 'atmosphere'. He preferred a normal or bright light to darkness and encouraged sitters to chat in a relaxed fashion rather than 'hold hands and concentrate'.

Although, in his mature years, Home could levitate at will, he apparently also levitated without being aware of it. On one occasion, for example, when his host drew his attention to the fact that he was hovering above the cushions of his armchair, Home seemed most surprised.

Stage illusionists frequently pride themselves on their *pièce de résistance* – putting their assistant into a 'trance', balancing her on the points of two swords, and then removing the swords so that she hangs in the air without apparent support. Sometimes she is 'hypnotised' and seen to rise further into the air, again without visible means of support. One of two things must be happening: either she does not rise into the air at all (that is, we all suffer some sort of mass hallucination), or she rises

Accounts of levitation and other manifestations of the seance room obviously did not impress* Punch *which, in 1863, published the lampoon,* right, *showing that some surprises, at least, could be administered by all too explicable means.

Ridicule has long been poured on the notion that people can free themselves from the force of gravity. The cartoon, **left,** *entitled 'The Day's Folly' was published by Sergent in 1783. But Alexandra David-Neel,* **below,** *came back from 14 years in Tibet with no doubt that adepts could indeed achieve weightlessness.*

aided by machinery that is hidden and therefore invisible to us.

Home was also able to make tables levitate, complete with any objects that happened to be on them; and when he raised a grand piano into the air, he also levitated the astounded Countess Orsini, who was playing it at the time. But his amazing talents did not stop there. Home could also elongate his physical form, and was able to hold hot coals without flinching.

Of course, Home and other spiritualists would also attribute their feats of apportation or levitation to 'machinery invisible to us' – but in their case, the machinery would be the agency of spirits. Indeed, to the end of his life, Home maintained that he could only fly because he was lifted up by the spirits, who thus demonstrated their existence. He described a typical levitation as follows:

'I feel no hands supporting me and, since the first time, I have never felt fear; though, should I have fallen from the ceiling of some rooms in which I have been raised, I could not have escaped serious injury. I am generally lifted up perpendicular!'

And yet we do not refer in a spiritualistic way to the 'unseen power' that keeps us on the floor. Every schoolboy knows about Newton and his discovery of the law of gravity. But psychical research points to the relative ease with which certain sensitives can turn this law on its head.

MYSTICAL TRAINING

In her book *Mystère et Magique en Tibet* (1931), Madame Alexandra David-Neel, the French explorer who spent 14 years in and around Tibet, told how she came upon a naked man, weighed down with heavy chains. The man's companion explained to her that his mystical training had made his body so light that, unless he wore iron chains, he would float away.

It seems that gravity does not necessarily always have the hold on us we have been taught it has. Sir William Crookes, the renowned scientist and psychical researcher, had this to say about D.D. Home's levitations:

> 'The phenomena I am prepared to attest are so extraordinary, and so directly oppose the most firmly-rooted articles of scientific belief – amongst others, the ubiquity and invariable action of the force of gravitation – that, even now, on recalling the details of what I have witnessed, there is an antagonism in my mind between reason, which pronounces it to be scientifically impossible, and the consciousness that my senses, both of touch and sight, are not lying witnesses.'

In some special cases – such as saints or particularly gifted mediums – levitation may well exist. But there is a growing body of thought that puts forward the idea that anyone can do it, providing he or she has been through the right sort of training. Students of transcendental meditation even claim to do it all the time.

"I FEEL NO HANDS SUPPORTING ME AND, SINCE THE FIRST TIME, I HAVE NEVER FELT FEAR; THOUGH, SHOULD I HAVE FALLEN FROM THE CEILING OF SOME ROOMS IN WHICH I HAVE BEEN RAISED, I COULD NOT HAVE ESCAPED SERIOUS INJURY. I AM GENERALLY LIFTED UP PERPENDICULAR!"

D.D. HOME

MASTERY OF FIRE

PEOPLE WHO ARE PROOF AGAINST FIRE CAN BE FOUND ALL OVER THE WORLD – ON EVERY CONTINENT AND IN EVERY KIND OF SOCIETY. WHERE DOES THE TRADITION OF 'FIRE MASTERY' HAVE ITS ROOTS? AND WHAT DOES IT MEAN TO THOSE WHO PRACTISE ITS UNLIKELY RITUALS?

George Sandwith was fascinated, like many a Westerner before him, by the fire-walking ceremonies he saw while working as a British government surveyor on the island of Suva in the Fijian group. Local adherents of one of the many Hindu sects made a practice of walking over red-hot embers, laid down in special trenches 30-40 feet (9-12 metres) long, to celebrate the feasts of local deities.

After his retirement in the 1950s, Sandwith wrote a book, *The Miracle Hunters*, in which he gave details of what he had witnessed. He also recorded the reaction of a fellow European, a banker, who was watching the phenomenon for the first time:

> 'Very grudgingly he admitted the fire-walking was genuine, for he had thrown something on the pit and it caught fire at once, but he was strongly of the opinion that the Government ought to stop it! When asked why, he became annoyed, replying that it does not conform with modern scientific discoveries. When I suggested that something of value might be learned from the firewalkers, he was so furious that he turned on his heel and left me.'

While the banker's 'rationalist' attitude may be understandable, it is one that has been adopted by scientists in the face of such 'fire phenomena' for well over a century. More interestingly, it is paralleled by the attitudes of the leaders of those religions – Hinduism, Buddhism and Shintoism, for instance – whose followers practise 'fire-handling'. To them, such activities occupy a peripheral place at best, in relation to orthodox religion and are not in any way encouraged since they do not fit in with, and may even be contrary to, established thought.

Jatoo Bhai*, above, *a 'fakir' from Calcutta, dances in the midst of a blazing fire, and will emerge unscathed. During the ritual of preparation for the firewalk,* below, *Jatoo Bhai goes into an attitude of prayer.

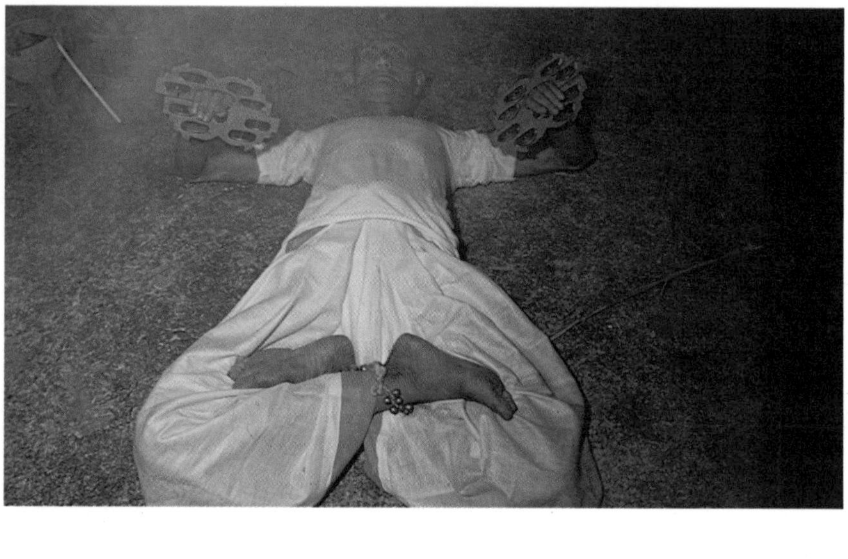

Occasionally, an example of 'fire power' turns up in a primitive society that has no tradition of such esoteric skills, and here again the practitioner is often viewed with disapproval. The late Frank Clements, a journalist and rancher from what was then Southern Rhodesia, and who served as Mayor of Salisbury during the 1950s, gave an account of one such isolated instance that he encountered among the Shona tribe. He and a veterinary surgeon had been inoculating Shona cattle and were invited for a meal. Afterwards, squatting by the fire, Clements lit a cigarette with a Zippo lighter. As he recalled afterwards:

> 'It was an old one and was slightly overfuelled, and the resulting flame was, I suppose, rather spectacular to those of the tribe who were not familiar with cigarette lighters – mostly the younger children. But there was a tribal elder present who had taken rather a dislike to my companion and me. As if showing what *he* could do, he plucked a burning brand from the fire and, holding it up to his grey-bearded face, licked the flame slowly, letting it flicker around his cheeks and nostrils. Then he quenched the flame quite deliberately between his palms, gave a snort of contempt in our direction, and tossed the stick away. He seemed to suffer no injury and his beard was not even singed.'

Jatoo Bhai works himself into a state of religious ecstasy,* below, *as part of the 'fireproofing' process. He then handles fire, before the dance in the flames.

Interestingly, the Shona are an agricultural people whose traditions lack any element of fire mastery – unlike, for instance, the Katanga, the BaYeke, the Mosengere and other tribes of the Congo area who are metal-working people and practise complex fire rituals and initiation rites. The Shona 'fire-eater' also appears to have been unique among his people: an individual who either had learned his skill from a wandering expert or was one of those apparently born with the gift.

Anthropologically, it is possible to trace the activities of most fire ritual societies back to a probable central source – the Iron Age shamanists of central Asia. These Tartars, Mongols and Yakuts thought of fire as one of the greatest of nature's mysteries, to be feared and revered. 'The first smith, the first shaman, and the first potter were blood brothers,' says an ancient Yakut proverb, referring to their importance in the community; but beyond doubt the smith was held in the highest esteem. He was 'master of fire' and he proved it by swallowing burning coals, walking on hot embers, and holding red-hot iron in his hands. Significantly, the greatest Tartar hero of all, Ghengis Khan, was said to have begun life as a blacksmith, and to have flown his leather apron as a battle pennant at the peak of his lance when riding to war. As a corollary to fire mastery, the smith could also endure intense cold by cultivating inner, or 'spiritual', heat, so that by overcoming both extremes of temperature he was, in the eyes of his community, super-human and on the level of a spirit or demi-god.

MASTERS OF THE FURNACE

Over the course of centuries, the knowledge and practice of fire-handling filtered out from Asia during prehistoric migrations, until about 500 BC, by when it had spread to China and Japan, Tibet and the Indian sub-continent. In Bulgaria and Greece, meanwhile, the ancient Cabiri peoples were described as 'masters of the furnace' and 'mighty in fire', for their secret knowledge eventually found its way all around the eastern Mediterranean and then down into the continent of Africa.

Fire mastery was subsequently easily absorbed into the practices of Hinduism on the Indian subcontinent. The aim of devout Hindus is to achieve the 'Brahman', or essential self, and they attempt this by following one or more of the 10 or so 'yoga' paths of self discovery. Hatha yoga, perhaps the most familiar form to Westerners, is the way to both physical control and mastery of the occult. The initiate works his way through seven stages of hatha yoga until he reaches the eighth stage, *samadhi,* which cannot be taught but is recognised by the practitioner achieving it. *Samadhi* brings with it preternatural abilities, or *siddhis;* and the men who achieve these are called *sadhus* – erroneously known to Europeans as *fakirs,* a word that properly denotes an Islamic holy man.

The majority of *sadhus* seem content to remain in one place and quietly meditate. It is the more eccentric 'fakir' types who capture the popular imagination. Some of these are genuinely sincere, setting themselves dramatic but apparently pointless tasks in their search for holiness. They may set out, for instance, to bathe in as many sacred rivers

"THE IDEA IS THAT THE SADHU TAKES ON ALL THE PAIN TO HIMSELF AND THEN NEGATES IT BY WILLPOWER ... THERE SEEMS TO BE NO RATIONAL EXPLANATION."

and water holes as possible, or sit motionless in a thorn bush for years until the spiky growth completely enfolds them, or permanently clench their fists so that their fingernails grow into the palms of their hands. Some, on the other hand, set out on what amounts to a deliberate circus career, and it is from among these that most of the fire masters of India are drawn. To devout and sophisticated Hindus, however, such 'showmen' are anathema, and yet the genuineness of their powers is never doubted – a contradiction that has caused a good deal of Western scepticism. It is almost as if a medieval saint were to have levitated, exhibited stigmata, and performed miracles of healing in the market place for cash.

Fire-trench walking seems to be among the most popular of the fakirs' feats. On the feast day of a local deity – there are dozens of Hindu sects and numerous gods – a fakir will arrive at a village and order the trench to be prepared and filled with hot stones. He will then lead the 'faithful' across. There are many accounts of Europeans having joined in the walks and, remarkably, few instances of serious injury. 'The idea is,' explained one commentator, 'that the *sadhu* takes on all the pain to himself and then negates it by willpower. The stones are genuinely hot, the bodies of the walkers untreated by any artificial preparation. There seems to be no rational explanation... '

Jatoo Bhai dances in the flames at the climax of his ritual,* above. *After the dance, the fakir displays his unburnt feet,* right, *and, equally remarkable, his unscorched clothing.

Firewalking Feats

Significantly, it is among the Hindu sects that the firewalkers of Polynesia, Malaya and Tahiti flourish. But the Buddhists of China, Tibet and Japan go in for almost exactly the same practices; while in Hong Kong, firewalking feats are a highly popular tourist attraction. Shintoism, the ancient nature and ancestor worship of the Japanese, also has its firewalking devotees.

E.G. Stephenson, a professor of English literature, attended a Shinto ceremony in Tokyo during which a 90-foot (27-metre) blazing trench was prepared. Professor Stephenson bravely asked if he might try. The officiating priest took him to a temple

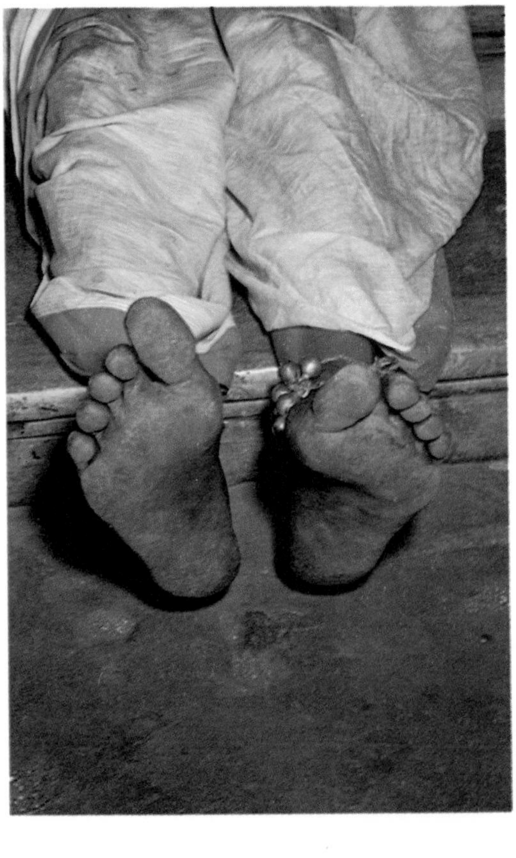

At the Buddhist firewalking festival 'hi watari', which is held every year at the foot of Mt Takao in Japan, the ceremony is dedicated to prayers for peace and to the health of the onlookers, who rub their ailing parts with wooden boards before throwing these on to the fire.

nearby and sprinkled salt over his head, after which the professor 'strolled over the trench in quite a leisurely way', feeling only a 'faint tingling' in the soles of his feet.

There is also a strong element of showmanship about many of the voodoo rituals of the West Indies, in which fire mastery in various forms plays an important part. In Trinidad, for example, fire eaters and firewalkers abound; but it is in Haiti, where voodoo still forms the basis of most political, social and religious activity, that fire masters are most spectacular.

Dr William Sargant, author and psychiatrist, made Haitian voodoo a subject of close study for several years, coming to the conclusion that most of the phenomena take place after the participants have worked themselves into a state of deep trance. Interestingly, such voodoo practices can be traced back by way of the African Congo, Arab traders, Asia Minor and Persia to the Mongol and Tartar shamans.

INNER AND OUTER FIRE

Many West Indian slaves were exported from the Congo, among them great numbers of Yoruba. The principal god of the Yoruba tribe was Ogun, a celestial smith who taught his people to handle fire and work with metal. The Yoruba secret society, Ogboni, still has Ogun as its patron, and practises fire-handling and eating. In Haiti, meanwhile, Ogun has become Ogun Badagris, the 'bloody warrior' who demands that his followers cultivate immunity to both 'inner' and 'outer' fire.

They fulfil these requirements quite literally, firstly by dancing on live coals, and secondly by drinking prodigious quantities of fiery white rum into which ground cayenne pepper has been liberally poured. At one all-woman ceremony, Dr Sargant saw the participants not only consume this apparently lethal mixture without collapsing, but rub it into their open eyes without damaging their sight in any way. Haitian voodoo is a complex mixture of African and European influences, and Dr Sargant was interested to note that some of the women dancers wore modern welders' and metal-workers' goggles, which they removed only to anoint their eyes with the rum and pepper.

The North American Indians, meanwhile, are a Mongol race in origin, their prehistoric ancestors nursed in the same Asiatic cradle as the Tartars, and carrying shamanism and its accompanying fire mastery with them from Siberia to Alaska and, from there, down the American continent. Literally every Indian tribe has at least the remnants of fire worship as part of its culture. The Canadian Hurons, for example, have retained the old skills more or less intact, as have the Apaches of the South-West and several of the Plains Indians, such as the Sioux and Cheyenne. Some tribes – the Blackfoot and Pueblo, for instance – less dramatically smear themselves with ashes, which they regard as the 'seeds of fire'.

PURIFICATION BY FIRE

Perhaps the most intriguing fire purification ceremony among North American Indians, however, is that practised by the Navajo, which combines elements of shamanism with those of the Finnish sauna. The village people prepare themselves for annual purification by building a roaring fire in the *hogan* or ritual hut. The tribe then strips naked and, led by the shaman, enters and circles the fire, while the shaman makes offerings of incense to the four quarters. A ritual dance follows, during which the women shuffle around the edge of the fire, while the men leap over and run through it. When this is over, the men and women segregate themselves, and the shaman heats long stakes of wood until they are charred and glowing. These are applied first to his own legs and then to the legs of his patients. Anyone suffering burns is considered to be in need of extra prayers. Each person then drinks a bowl of salt water, and vomits into a bowl of sand. Again, anyone who does not vomit is considered to be impure and must undergo the ritual again. Finally, the doorway of the *hogan* is sealed, and both shaman and followers sit around the fire until the flames die down and the ashes cool. These are later mixed with the vomit, taken outside and left to dry and be blown away on the wind. The purification is over for another year.

A Navajo fire dance, as depicted by the painter William Leigh, is shown below.

VOICES FROM THE DEAD

Has the modern tape recorder provided evidence of survival after death? Thousands of voices – purporting to be those of the dead – have been recorded without rational explanation for their origin. What are we to make of them?

Thomas Alva Edison was one of the greatest practical scientists of the 19th century. His achievements included the perfection of the 'duplex' telegraph, the invention of the phonograph and the introduction into the United States of the first electric light. In 1882, his generating station brought electric street lighting to New York for the first time; and 12 years later, his moving picture show, which he called his 'kinetoscope parlour', was opened in the city.

Despite such solid successes, however, an interview he gave to the *Scientific American* in 1920 caused concern among his contemporaries, some of whom must have thought that the 73-year-old inventor had lapsed into senility. What he proposed, in the issue of 30 October, was no less than an instrument for communicating with the dead.

> 'If our personality survives, then it is strictly logical and scientific to assume that it retains memory, intellect and other faculties and knowledge that we acquire on this earth. Therefore, if personality exists after what we call death, it is reasonable to conclude that those who leave this earth would like to communicate with those they have left here...
> I am inclined to believe that our personality hereafter will be able to affect matter. If this reasoning be correct, then, if we can evolve an instrument so delicate as to be affected, or moved, or manipulated... by our personality as it survives in the next life, such an instrument, when made available, ought to record something.'

Edison worked on the development of such an instrument, but was unsuccessful in his attempts to record voices from the dead. However, in the opinion of many modern scientific researchers, his views were apparently vindicated in 1959.

Ghosts in the Machine

At that time, a celebrated Swedish painter, musician and film producer named Friedrich Jürgenson took his battery-operated tape recorder out into a remote part of the countryside near his villa in order to record birdsong. Playing the tapes back later, Jürgenson found not only bird sounds but faint human voices, speaking in Swedish and Norwegian and discussing nocturnal birdsong. Despite the 'coincidence' of subject matter, Jürgenson first thought that he had picked up a stray radio transmission. On repeating the experiment, however, he heard further voices, this time addressing him personally and claiming to be dead relatives, as well as friends of his.

Over the next few years, working from his home at Mölnbo, near Stockholm, Jürgenson amassed the evidence that he was to present in his book *Voices from the Universe* in 1964. This proved sufficiently convincing to attract the attention of the eminent German psychologist Professor Hans Bender, director of the Government-funded parapsychological research unit at the University of Freiburg, who in turn set up a team of distinguished scientists to repeat the experiments and analyse the results.

Thomas Alva Edison (1847-1931), above, invented the phonograph and the electric light bulb. In 1920 he also worked on a device that would, he believed, make possible a form of telepathic contact with the dead.

"THE IMPLICATIONS OF THESE VOICES FROM NOWHERE ARE ENORMOUS. DR BANDER IS EVEN REPORTED TO CONSIDER THEM OF MORE IMPORTANCE TO HUMANITY THAN NUCLEAR PHYSICS."

PERSPECTIVES

RECORDING THE VOICES YOURSELF

An ordinary cassette tape recorder can be used to record 'electronic voices'; but, generally speaking, the better the equipment, the more satisfactory the results. Machines with volume, tone and level controls make the task of deciphering the voices on playback much easier, and a good set of headphones is essential.

Experts agree that the hours between sunset and sunrise are the best time for experiments. Most researchers prefer to work in a quiet room, although a portable tape recorder in a quiet place in the countryside can yield good results, as Jürgenson proved. The date and time should be spoken into the microphone before each session, followed by an invitation to the voices to speak. Each recording session should be no longer than approximately two minutes, as intense concentration is needed in listening to the playback of the voices.

Three basic recording methods are most likely to be of use. With the first, the tape recorder is simply switched to 'record'; then questions are asked aloud and details of them noted on paper.

With a second method, preliminary announcements are made through a microphone which is then unplugged and a radio attached to the recorder instead. The radio is tuned between frequencies, to a band of 'white noise', and the recording level is set mid-way between maximum and minimum.

A third method involves the use of a diode receiver, a small crystal set that is plugged into the microphone socket of a tape recorder.

Klaus Schreiber, retired German fire equipment inspector, right, *claims to have gone one step beyond the recording of voices, and to have captured on television the image of his deceased daughter, Karin,* above.

Under differing conditions and circumstances, a factory-clean tape, run through an ordinary tape-recording head in an otherwise silent environment, they found, will contain human voices speaking recognisable words when played back. The origin of these voices is apparently inexplicable in the light of present day science, and the voices themselves are objective in that they yield prints in the same way as normal voices, registering as visible oscillograph impulses on videotape recordings. The implications of these 'voices from nowhere' are enormous. Dr Bender himself is even reported to consider them of more importance to humanity than nuclear physics.

Other scientists, too, were to become fascinated by Jürgenson's odd discovery. Dr Konstantin Raudive, former professor of psychology at the Universities of Uppsala and Riga, was living in Bad Krozingen, Germany, when he heard of the Jürgenson-Bender experiments in 1965. A former student of Carl Jung, Dr Raudive had been forced to flee from his native Latvia when it was invaded and annexed by the Soviet Union in 1945. Thereafter, he became well-known as a writer on experimental psychology.

Dr Raudive also began recording tests on the mysterious voices with conspicuous success; and between 1965 and his death in 1974, in partnership with physicist Dr Alex Schneider of St Gallen, Switzerland, and Theodor Rudolph, a specialist in high-frequency electronic engineering, he made over 100,000 tapes under stringent laboratory conditions. An exhaustive analysis of his work was published in Germany in the late 1960s, under the title *The Inaudible Made Audible.* This caught the attention of British publisher Colin Smythe, who subsequently brought out an English language edition, entitled *Breakthrough.*

Peter Bander, who wrote the preface to the book, later gave an account of how he first heard a strange voice on tape. This nicely illustrates what happens as a rule, and also points out the objective nature of the phenomenon. Colin Smythe had bought a new tape and had followed Dr Raudive's instructions on how to 'contact' the voices. A certain rhythm resembling a human voice had been recorded, but it was unintelligible to Smythe. Peter Bander played the relevant portion of tape over two or three times, and suddenly became aware of what the voice was saying. It was a woman's, and it said: *'Mach die Tur mal auf'* – German for *'Open the door'*. Bander immediately recognised the voice as that of his dead mother – he had been in the habit of conducting his correspondence with her by tape recordings for several years before she died. What is more, the comment was apt: his colleagues often chided him for shutting his office door.

Dr Konstantin Raudive is seen,* right, *with the 'goniometer', an instrument that was designed for him by Theodor Rudolph of Telefunken to record 'spirit' voices.

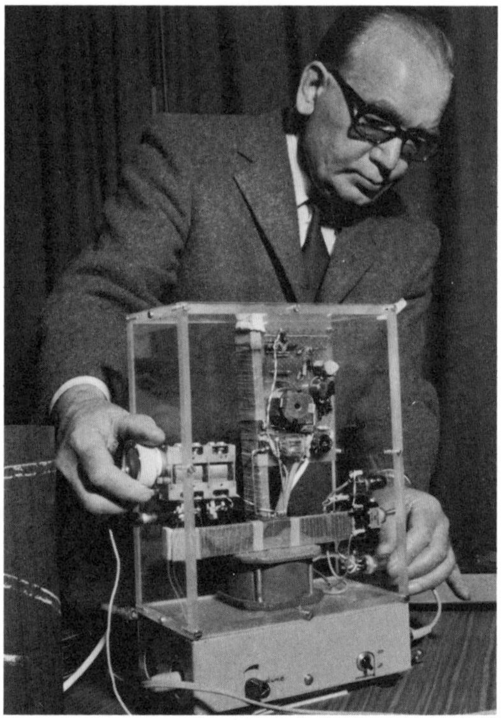

The Right Reverend Monsignor Stephen O'Connor, Vicar General and Principal Roman Catholic Chaplain to the Royal Navy at the time, listens to a voice recorded by Dr Raudive,* below. *The voice seemed to be that of a young naval officer who had committed suicide two years earlier.

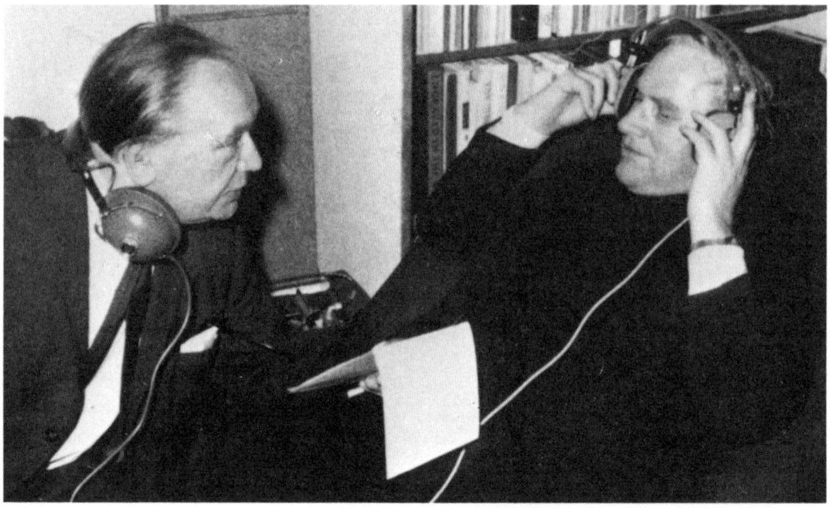

Pope Paul VI,* right, *decorated Friedrich Jürgenson with the Commander's Cross of the Order of St Gregory the Great in 1969. The Catholic Church has never expressed an official opinion on the nature of his mysterious voices, but Jürgenson has said that he found 'a sympathetic ear' in the Vatican.

Startled by the voice, Bander asked two people who did not speak German to listen and write down what they heard phonetically. Their versions matched what he had heard exactly. Dr Bander was now convinced of the authenticity of the voices.

Since the publication of *Breakthrough* in 1971, serious research has begun in all parts of the world, and the interest of two very different bodies reflects the spiritual and temporal aspects of the voices. Even the Vatican has shown a great deal of 'off the record' awareness of the phenomena, and a number of distinguished Catholic priest-scientists have conducted experiments of their own. Pre-eminent among these researchers was the late Professor Gebhard Frei, an internationally recognised expert in the fields of depth psychology, parapsychology and anthropology. Dr Frei was the cousin of the late Pope Paul VI who, in 1969, decorated Friedrich Jürgenson with the Commander's Cross of the Order of St Gregory the Great, ostensibly for documentary film work about the Vatican. But, as Jürgenson told Peter Bander in August 1971, he had found 'a sympathetic ear for the voice phenomenon in the Vatican'.

The interest of the National Aeronautics and Space Administration (NASA) also came to light in the late 1960s when two American engineers from Cape Kennedy visited Dr Raudive at Bad Krozingen. The visitors examined Dr Raudive's experiments minutely and asked many 'unusually pertinent questions', as well as making helpful comments. They refused, unfortunately, to give the scientist any indication of what relevance the voice phenomena might have to America's space programme.

But as Dr Raudive reasoned, if he could achieve clear and regular results on his relatively simple equipment, how much more likely was it that the sophisticated recorders carried in spacecraft would pick up the voices? From whatever source they spring, Jürgenson's voices represent the start of a whole new field in the study of the paranormal.

HYPNOSIS IS A HIGHLY POPULAR FORM OF STAGE ENTERTAINMENT. NO ONE IS QUITE SURE HOW THE TRANCE-STATE COMES ABOUT; BUT THE TECHNIQUE CAN ALSO BE HELPFUL AS A FORM OF MEDICAL TREATMENT IN CRIME DETECTION AND IN EXPLORING POSSIBLE EVIDENCE FOR PAST LIVES

THE POWER OF SUGGESTION

Most people still think of hypnotists as slightly shady characters, practising a highly dubious craft. We see in our mind's eye the evil Svengali, the character in George du Maurier's novel who lived off the unfortunate Trilby, by putting the 'fluence on her so that she became an internationally acclaimed concert artist, though her ordinary voice was truly terrible. Today's stage hypnotist, however, is no longer the seedy villain of such a story – merely an entertainer.

Performances tend to follow a standard formula. Volunteers are called for; and one by one, the hypnotist addresses soothing words to them, like a mother putting her child to sleep. Those who respond remain on stage: the rest are sent back into the audience. Then, in groups or individually, those still on stage are told that they are very hot or very cold, very thirsty or very drunk; and they behave and feel just as they are told to do, even if they make themselves look ridiculous.

The Riddle Of Hypnosis

There is not, as yet, any clear explanation of the nature of hypnotism. It is generally defined as a trance – that is, an altered state of consciousness, the extent of the alteration depending on the individual. In any group, some volunteers will remember everything that has been done while they are on stage, but others may recall nothing. Nevertheless, they all will have come under the hypnotist's influence.

What this means is that each of them has shed some of his or her controls, or thrown off certain inhibitions that training and habit normally impose. If somebody said to any of them, in ordinary conversation, 'You are a watchdog and you hear a burglar', it would raise only a laugh. On stage, however, the hypnotised subject gets down on hands and knees, and barks. The hypnotist is he-who-must-be-obeyed; and commands from other people are ignored, unless the hypnotist has given instructions that they should be obeyed, too.

Even more impressively, the accomplished hypnotist can give commands that will be obeyed after subjects have come out of their trances and returned to their seats in the audience. If he gives them a 'post-hypnotic suggestion' that they should stand up and shout 'hip-hip-hooray' whenever the orchestra plays a certain tune, for instance, they will do so, without knowing why.

Hypnosis appears to switch off some part of our minds that ordinarily monitors our behaviour, instructing us what to do in any given set of circumstances without thought on our part. We hand this control system over to the hypnotist, much as an airline pilot may hand over the controls of his aircraft to somebody on the ground, who then guides it in by radar with the help of an automatic pilot.

Hypnosis has been exploited by tribal witch doctors and by priests in the temples of ancient Greece. But we owe the form in which it is practised today to Franz Mesmer and his disciples. Two hundred years ago, they realised that subjects in the trance state could be made to obey every command. But more importantly, in the course of their experiments, they made two discoveries of great potential significance.

Who, it is often asked, make the best hypnotic subjects? And can someone be hypnotised against his or her will? The hypnotist is, in fact, merely a guide; and his or her subject can only be 'put under' if the willingness is there. Often a trigger will be used – a snap of the fingers, perhaps, or simply a word or phrase – to induce the trance-state at a later stage. But, again, this will only work when the subject has every intention of cooperating.

Some stage hypnotists can give their profession a bad name. In one French hypnotist's show,* below*, a girl from the audience, apparently under hypnosis, stripped off. But it was the same girl every night! Hypnotist Martin Taylor,* below*, also gives stage performances. However, no compromising situations are introduced. In any event, it is highly unlikely that a volunteer would do anything outside his or her moral code. The hypnotised subject,* inset*, is merely obeying instructions to put on yet another tie.

For a start, they found that if they told a subject, 'You will feel no pain,' he could be struck, pricked and even burned without giving out so much as a yelp – and this was before the invention of anaesthetic drugs. Mesmerists further proceeded to demonstrate that pain-free surgical operations could be performed under hypnosis.

The medical profession refused to accept the evidence, however; and when distinguished surgeons were invited to watch the amputation of a leg under hypnosis, they insisted the man was only pretending to feel no pain. Hypnosis, they argued, was occult in its principles: it could not work.

The second discovery was that some hypnotised subjects suddenly found themselves enjoying talents they did not know they had in their ordinary lives. One might draw well under hypnosis; another, sing melodiously. A few even appeared to become clairvoyant, describing events or places that they could not have seen. This, too, was dismissed as occultism. And to this day, hypnotism has never quite rid itself of its reputation of lying beyond the boundaries of orthodox science.

> "If a hypnotised subject is told he is going to be touched with a red-hot skewer, not only will he cry out in pain even if the skewer is stone cold, its touch will often actually raise a blister."

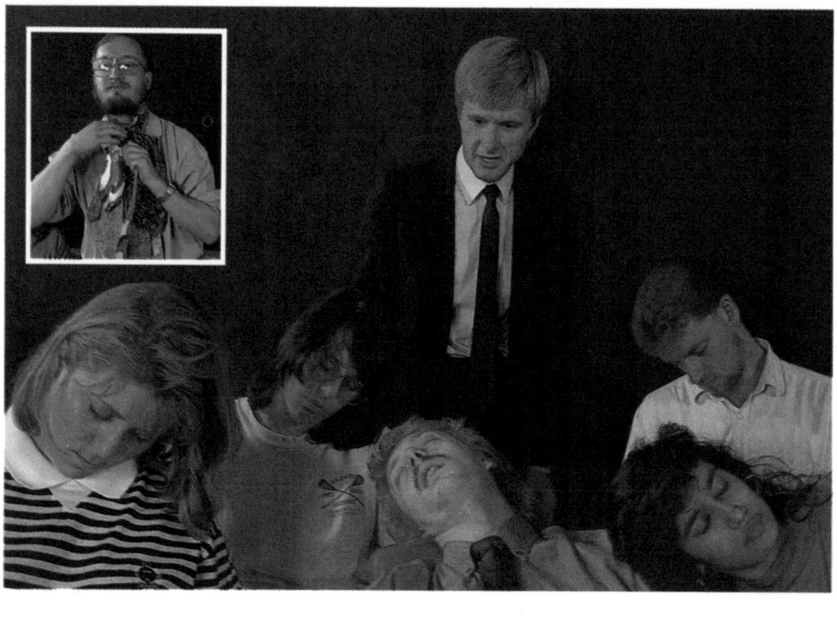

Yet we know now that the Mesmerists' claims were largely justified. Endless demonstrations have shown that a subject under hypnosis can put his finger into a candle flame and, if told he will feel no pain, will feel no pain. Even more remarkable, if told he will have no blister, no blister appears.

Certain researchers have taken this even further. If a hypnotised subject is told he is going to be touched with a red-hot skewer, not only will he cry out in pain even if the skewer is stone cold, its touch will actually raise a blister.

Scepticism about the possibility that some subjects become clairvoyant under hypnosis has also been shaken by recent research into hypnotic regression. It has long been known that hypnotised subjects can be escorted back in time to earlier occasions in their lives. Asked to recall what they were doing on, say, New Year's Day 10 or 20 years ago, they will describe in detail episodes they have long since consciously forgotten. Where it has been possible to check such accounts, they have been found to be accurate. In the United States, the police have even exploited this faculty by asking witnesses of crimes and accidents to allow themselves to be hypnotised in order to find out whether they can recall, say, the number of a stolen car.

Hypnotic Regression

Hypnotic regression has also been carried further. A hundred years ago, researchers in Europe found that some hypnotised subjects appeared ro be able to recall events from past centuries. Recently, this line of investigation has been taken up again, and the results are described in detail in works like Jeremy Iverson's *More Lives Than One*, an account of Arnall Bloxham's investigations, and Joe Keeton's *Encounters With The Past*.

It remains to be established whether such hypnotised subjects are regressing to their own past lives, or tuning into what might be described as a 'videotape from the collective unconscious', but it seems clear they are genuine. The material, even if not accurate in details, is certainly being picked up from sources other than books and conversations.

Hypnosis, then, involves a trance or altered state of consciousness, (some people prefer to describe it as a state of altered awareness of consciousness), in which certain faculties and abilities can be liberated. Clearly, the potential benefits, for anybody prepared

PERSPECTIVES

SELF-HYPNOSIS

Today, self-hypnosis is practised as a therapy by thousands of people worldwide. It has been used successfully as a technique for, among other things, reducing stress and tension, losing weight, giving up smoking, revitalising both mental and bodily energies, overcoming phobias and generally becoming more self-assertive.

One of the most popular forms involves the use of self-help cassettes. These usually start by relaxing the listener – often with soothing, light music or with sounds recorded from nature, such as the rustling of wind through leaves or the breaking of waves on the seashore.

Once relaxed, the subject is in a more fit state to take on-board suggestions and instructions that are long-lasting, if not permanent. Such instructions may be related either directly or subliminally.

to master the art of auto-hypnosis, can be considerable. Why, then, is more use not made of it?

Fear is partly responsible – the lingering suspicion that hypnosis is in the occult category and not scientifically resepctable, or the more reasonable fear that to undergo it is to put oneself into the hands of a Svengali.

WILLING SUBJECTS

Yet the fact that a stage hypnotists can so easily manipulate volunteers is somewhat misleading. The volunteers know it is a game. They choose to play it, presumably out of curiousity in most cases, and would not volunteer if they thought they might be made to do something dangerous, criminal, or even immoral, by their standards.

A celebrated occasion demonstrated this a century ago. A girl taking part in an experiment in Paris, who had been told to kill one of the students, appeared to try to do so and had to be restrained. Yet when asked to take off her clothes, she blushed, came out of the trance and ran from the room.

Presumably, she must have sensed in some way that she would be prevented from doing anything dangerous or criminal, and so agreed to join in. But actually to have undressed would almost certainly have compromised her own moral code to a marked degree – something unacceptable.

The implications of hypnosis for medicine are striking too; yet, until very recently, they have been largely ignored. It is only in the last 20 years or so that the results of research into hypnosis have been confirmed and amplified with the help of investigation involving biofeedback. These have shown how individuals can actually learn to control many bodily functions – heartbeat, blood pressure and gastric secretions, for instance – by auto-suggestion or self-hypnosis.

Hypnosis, or auto-suggestion, can also accomplish much more. Individuals, like the American Jack Schwartz, have even demonstrated how they are able to control bleeding, staunching blood flow as if turning off a tap. Similarly, it has been shown that much the simplest way to remove warts and other skin blemishes is by suggestion under hypnosis. It can also help in curing allergies and in getting a subject to stop smoking (though good hypnotherapists emphasize that they can only help those who want to help themselves).

PAIN CONTROL

The distinguished Australian psychiatrist, Ainslie Meares, and Americans Carl and Stephanie Simonton, have shown how hypnosis and auto-hypnosis can be used to help terminal cancer patients in particular, not merely by enabling them to control pain, but also by giving them a welcome distraction from their worries. In some cases, this has prolonged survival; and in others, X-rays have revealed actual regression of tumours. No false hopes of miracle cures are raised, as has so often happened with other forms of cancer treatment. Rather, patients are told that it is how they react to their own voyages of discovery in altered states of consciousness that counts.

Self-hypnosis has two major advantages. It can be taught, so that patients can learn to control, for instance, their own headaches and sometimes even prevent them. And it costs nothing – except, of course, for the practitioner's initial time in passing on the technique.

Post-hypnotic suggestion can also help in other spheres, such as golf. It will, for instance, send a golfer out onto the course in an utterly relaxed frame of mind – which, in golf, is said to be half the battle. Outside the medical field, too, it seems the possibilities for hypnosis are only just beginning to be appreciated.

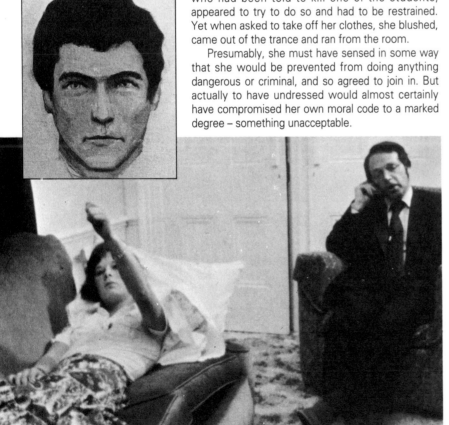

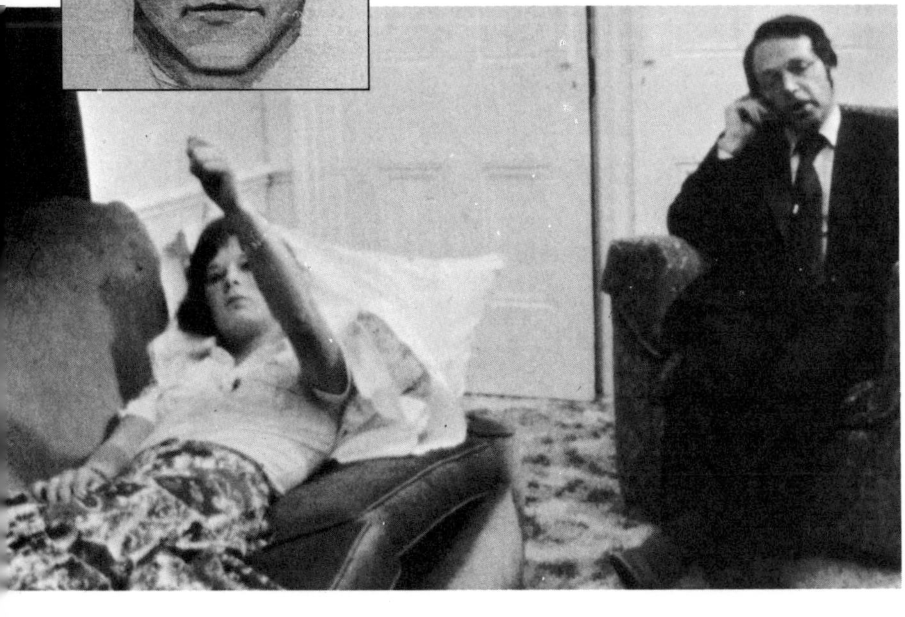

Dr Malcolm Rawson, chief neurologist at Hull Royal Infirmary, questions 13 year-old Gail Rogers,** below, **after putting her into a hypnotic trance. The aim was to try to cast light on the mysterious disappearance of Genette Tate, also aged 13, who had vanished while delivering evening papers on Friday 18 August 1978, in her home town of Aylesbeare in Devon. The painting,** inset, **was produced by an artist from descriptions given by Gail and her mother, Mrs Matilda Rogers, under hypnosis. For a time, police were hopeful it might give them a lead. The case, however, remains unsolved.

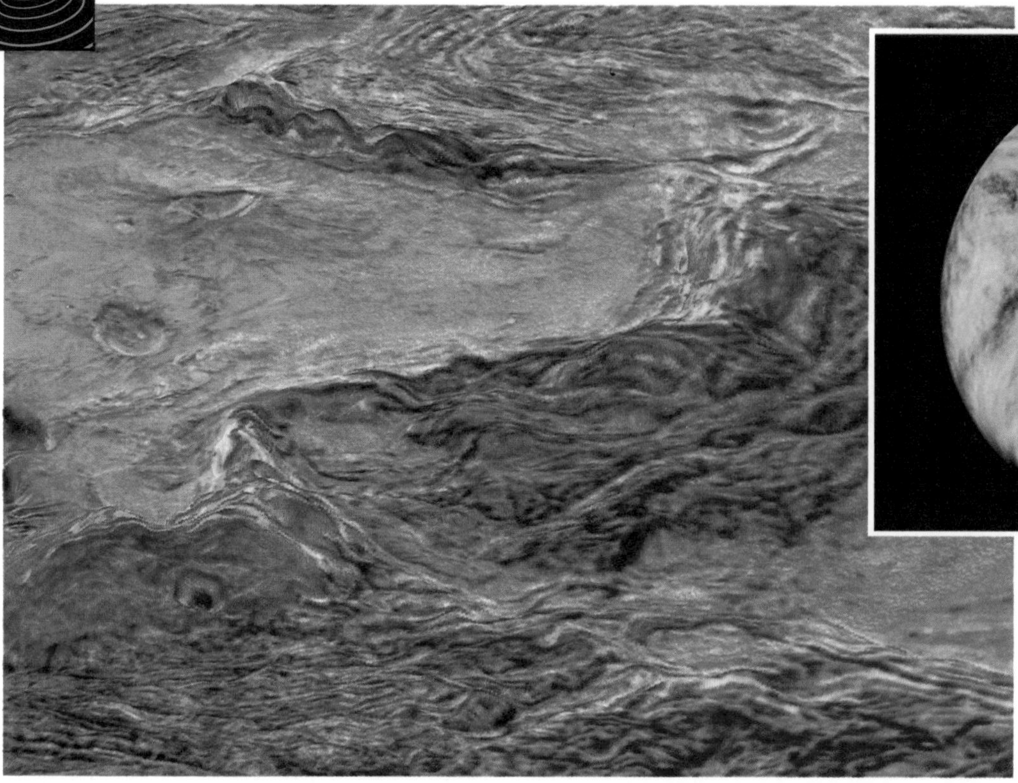

The planet Venus, above, *is some 26 million miles (48 million kilometres) from Earth. With a surface temperature reaching 900°F (480°C), it is virtually impossible that anything could live on Venus, shown* left *in an artist's impression.*

SPINNING THROUGH SPACE

REPORTS OF UFOS DESCRIBE DISC-SHAPED, HIGHLY MANOEUVRABLE, IMMENSELY FAST-FLYING MACHINES, CAPABLE OF FEATS THAT DEFY ALL KNOWN PHYSICAL LAWS. WHAT KIND OF CIVILISATIONS MIGHT HAVE PRODUCED THEM?

The term UFO – unidentified flying object – officially means simply something that has not been, or cannot be, accounted for by any of the known laws of physics. But the seemingly rational behaviour reported in many UFO sightings, as well as the accounts of meetings with humanoids, have led to frequent speculation that UFOs are, in fact, spacecraft bringing creatures from outer space to Earth.

If this is so, the spaceships must be able to cover immense distances. Indeed, people who claim to have had contact with extra-terrestrials often say they have spoken with Venusians. Yet Venus is highly unlikely to be inhabited. So any intelligent life forms must be coming from still further away; and, even assuming that lifespans of creatures from other planets may be much longer than our own, it is clear that UFOs must be able to travel very fast indeed if they are not to take hundreds of years to travel between inhabited planets.

Reports of the movement of UFOs are also remarkably consistent. Most people describe them as hovering and then taking off at very high speed, often executing manoeuvres that would be impossible in conventional aircraft. Even allowing for exaggeration, the consistency of reports suggests that UFOs must be using a very powerful force indeed to produce such dramatic accelerations.

None of the rocket fuels we use at present can produce either the speed or acceleration observed in UFOs, because they store only a small amount of energy for a given mass. Right from the beginning, space travel has been faced with the problem of enabling rockets to carry enough fuel for a journey – they must lift the fuel, which can be very heavy if the journey is long, as well as themselves and their occupants. The solution has been the multi-stage rocket: initial acceleration is given by a rocket that is jettisoned when its fuel is used up and a second rocket takes over.

Although our rockets eventually reach quite high speeds, they are nowhere near fast enough to reach planets outside our solar system within a

Apollo 8 blasts off for the Moon, below. *To reach planets beyond our solar system, however, would require a spacecraft powered by a vastly more efficient fuel.*

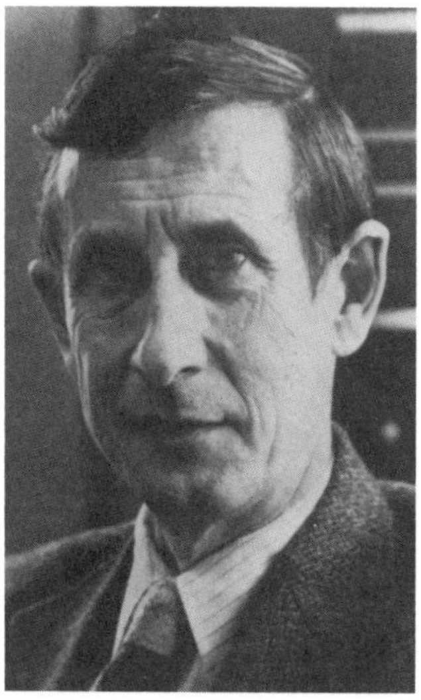

Professor Freeman Dyson, above, is the American physicist who designed a nuclear-powered spacecraft as long ago as 1958.

human lifetime. If we assume UFOs are subject to the same laws of physics as we are, in order to operate on and near the Earth with the rapid accelerations and manoeuvres at high speeds that are often reported, they must be using a different source of energy from conventional chemical fuels. Indeed, their fuel must be highly compact, with a high energy yield for a small mass, for which the obvious source is nuclear.

As long ago as 1958 – just after the Russians launched the first man-made satellites into space – a brilliant theoretical physicist called Freeman Dyson embarked on a plan for a nuclear-powered spaceship. He had previously worked on the development of the atom bomb and had a comprehensive understanding of nuclear power. Assembling a group of scientists at La Jolla, in southern California, to work with him, he now embarked upon 'Project Orion' – a serious attempt to build a spacecraft powered by nuclear explosions.

PROJECT ORION

Freeman Dyson's ultimate aim was to build a spacecraft the size of a small city that would take a group of people to a distant comet on the edge of the solar system, where they would settle. This may have been a pipe-dream, but the design was real enough.

The spacecraft was to be powered by hydrogen bombs. Essentially, his idea was to carry a number of hydrogen bombs aboard the spacecraft: these would be moved, one by one, to a position underneath the craft where they would be exploded. The base of the spacecraft would absorb the shock, and the craft would be driven along. Obviously, the

> "UFOS MUST BE ABLE TO TRAVEL VERY FAST INDEED IF THEY ARE NOT TO TAKE HUNDREDS OF YEARS TO TRAVEL BETWEEN INHABITED PLANETS"

bomb system would have to be designed so that the craft was propelled and not simply blown apart; but – in principle, at least – this was staightforward. However, Dyson was never able to test his ideas: he was prevented by public concern about pollution of the atmosphere by radioactive fallout.

UFOs are often reported as disappearing rapidly – going off 'like a television set' and reappearing just as quickly. This aspect of the phenomenon has puzzled scientists for a long time and has led to suggestions that UFOs use some kind of 'anti-optic device' to prevent them being seen. There are, however, some simpler explanations that could account for the majority of reports. UFOs 'disappearing' in the darkness of night could do so by simply switching off their lights; and daytime discs could appear to vanish by turning themselves sideways on to the observer. (It would be difficult to pick out the thin edge of a disc against the sky.) These explanations do not, of course, account for radar-visual sightings that suddenly vanish. But if a UFO disappeared behind a patch of disturbed air, a mirage-like effect could easily screen it both from sight and from radar detectors.

There are, however, cases on file for which none of these explanations is credible. Indeed, it seems that the phenomena involved can only be explained as products of a technology much further advanced than our own.

PERSPECTIVES

WHY SAUCERS?

By far the majority of UFO reports describe the objects seen as disc or cigar-shaped; and it could even be that most UFOs reported as cigar-shaped are in fact discs. Whether or not this is actually the case, the number of reports of saucer-shaped UFOs is overwhelming. There has also been a great deal of speculation as to why this should be so, some people suggesting that the mystical significance of the circle may have something to do with it. But there could be a simpler explanation.

On long inter-stellar voyages, a spacecraft will pass through vast regions of empty space - far from the regions of gravitational attraction of any major objects - where there is no wind resistance, no 'up' or 'down', no east or west, nothing. The most logical shape for a vessel travelling in these circumstances is circular, for a circle is symmetrical about an infinite number of axes. The fact that most UFOs are disc-shaped rather than spherical can be explained as a design feature that allows spacecraft to operate at high speeds once they have entered the atmosphere of planets. By flying with their edges into the wind, they can - in theory, at least - cut down the effect of air resistance almost to zero.

UFO PHOTO FILE

The photograph, **above,** was taken by a coastguard, R. Alpert, at 9.35 a.m. on 16 July 1952 from the control tower at Salem Air Base in Massachusetts, USA. The objects were reported to be moving at great speed; but they appear much brighter in the photograph than they actually were because the aperture of the camera was set for the brightness of the surrounding landscape. Consequently, the UFOs themselves are over-exposed.

But is the photography genuine? The images are unlikely to have been caused by lens flares, as these almost always appear in straight lines. But it is reported that the picture was taken through a laboratory window; and sceptics have suggested that the objects could actually be reflections of lights inside the laboratory. Photographic experts, however, point out that reflected lights are rarely as opaque as these.

The picture, **right,** was taken by London photographer Anwar Hussein in the Spanish Pyrenees in July 1978. After finishing filming one day, he found he had left one of his lenses at the top of a mountain. The next morning, at about 9 o'clock, he returned to look for it. He found the lens and took some pictures, his camera set on motor-drive. At the time, he noticed nothing unusual except the brightness of the light and the uncanny quietness. Back in London, he sent the film to be developed, and later received a worried telephone call from the lab, who pointed out the 'object ' on the film and thought it must be a fault that had appeared during developing. On examination, however, the emulsion was found to be undamaged. This is typical of many of the best UFO pictures, which are often of objects that go unnoticed at the time of filming but which show up later on the negatives.

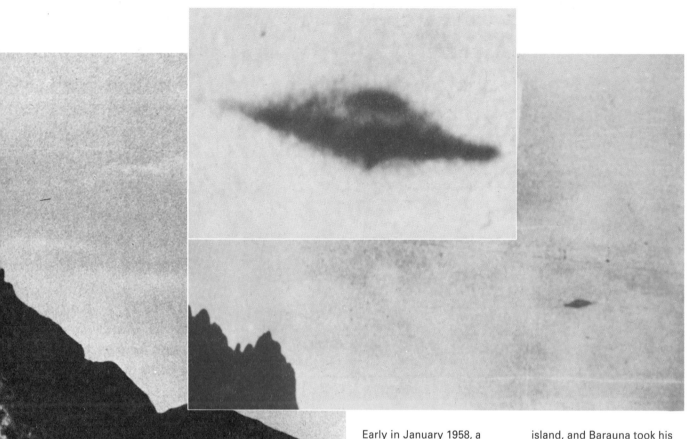

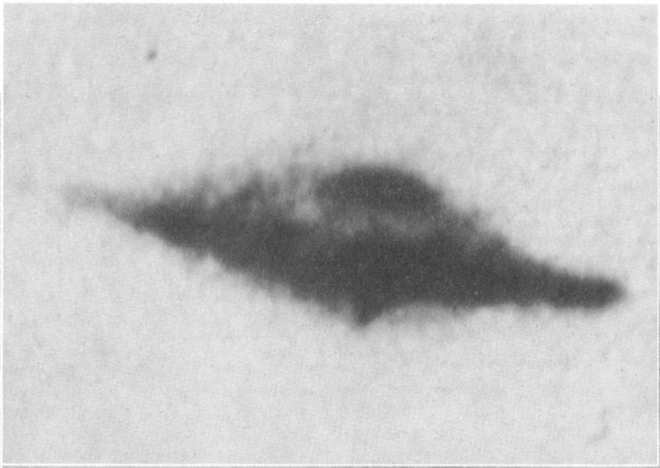

Early in January 1958, a survey ship of the Brazilian Navy, the Almirante Saldanha, set off from Rio de Janeiro, bound for the rocky island of Trindade, where the Navy had an oceanographic station. Among those on board was Almiro Barauna, a specialist in underwater photography.

Just before the ship was due to set sail on the return journey at 12.15 p.m. on 16 January 1958, a retired Air Force officer, Captain Viegas, who was on deck with other officers and technicians, called to Barauna that there was a bright object in the sky. Barauna located it and watched the moving object until it was silhouetted against some cloud. Then he shot the two photographs, **above.** The UFO disappeared behind the main peak of the island for a few seconds. When it reappeared, it was flying in the opposite direction. Barauna took a third photograph, then a fourth and fifth, but these last two were wasted shots because the photographer was jostled by the other people aboard the ship, who were by now extremely excited about what they were witnessing. The UFO appeared briefly to halt its passage away from the island, and Barauna took his last picture of the object as it moved swiftly away.

The photographer said the object was silent, dark grey in colour, and apparently surrounded by a greenish vapour or mist.

Barauna developed his film on board ship in the presence of the skipper, Commander Bacellar. (As there was no photographic paper on board, prints were made once the ship had returned to Rio.) Barauna said that, in the urgency and excitement of the sighting, he had not thought to check the settings of his camera and the pictures were consequently over-exposed.

Back in Rio de Janeiro, the Brazilian Navy examined the negatives. They found them to be genuine, and any possibility of a hoax was eliminated. Based on Barauna's account, the naval authorities then set up a mock re-run of the incident, and were able to compute the speed of the object as about 550-600 mph (900-1000 km/h). The diameter of the Saturn-shaped UFO was estimated at around 40 yards (37 metres). At least 100 people had seen the UFO, and the photographs seem to be unimpeachable.

WHEN FISH POUR

FOR CENTURIES, THERE HAVE BEEN INCIDENTS OF FISH FALLING FROM THE SKY. THIS STRANGE, WORLD-WIDE PHENOMENON IS ONE OF THE LEAST EXPLICABLE QUIRKS OF NATURE

Despite the fact that the phenomenon of fish falling from the sky has been the subject of discussion and eyewitness reports for centuries, no 'natural' explanation-has yet been found. The illustration of falling fish, right, comes from a book by Claus Magnus, Historia de gentibus septentrionalibus *(1555), in which the author discusses falls of fish, frogs and other animals.*

One of the most reliably recorded incidents in Britain involved a timber yard worker, John Lewis, of Mountain Ash, Glamorganshire. On 9 February 1859, he was hit by falling fish, as illustrated, far right, in Charles Tomlinson's Raincloud and Snowstorm *(1864).*

On 28 May 1984, builder Edward Rodmell and his son were astonished to find that fish had rained on the house they were renovating in the London Borough of Newham. Dabs were lying in the yard; and there were also fish on the red-tiled roof and in the gutter. Then, on 7 June, a man living nearby found some 30 fish in his garden. Extraordinary as such events may seem, they have occurred on many occasions

On 16 February 1861, for instance, a violent earthquake shook the island of Singapore. For the following six days, rain fell in torrents. Then, later that year, after a last furious downpour, it stopped. François de Castelnau, a French naturalist staying on the island, reported what happened next to the Academy of Sciences in Paris.

'At 10 a.m. the sun lifted, and from my window I saw a large number of Malays and Chinese filling baskets with fishes which they picked up in the pools of water which covered the ground. On being

asked where the fishes came from, they answered that they had fallen from the sky. Three days afterwards, when the pools had dried up, we found many dead fishes.'

Although de Castelnau did not see the rain of fish himself, he was convinced that they had fallen from the sky. Dr A.D. Bajkov, an American marine scientist, was luckier. On 23 October 1947, he was having breakfast with his wife in a café in Marksville, Louisiana, USA, when shortly after a sudden shower of rain, he noticed fish lying in the streets: 'sunfish, goggle-eyed minnows and black bass up to 9 inches [23 centimetres] long'. More fish were found on rooftops, cold and dead, but nevertheless still fit to eat.

On their own, such accounts are not much to go on. Much of the evidence for fish falling from the sky is circumstantial – fish being found, usually after heavy rain, in places and on surfaces where no fish were before. But there are eyewitness accounts.

One of the best attested cases occurred in Britain at Mountain Ash, Glamorganshire, Wales, in 1859. In a paper published in the *Fortean Times* of autumn 1979, Robert Schadwald established, on the evidence of eyewitness accounts published at the time, that it had happened on 9 February 1859. It was not blowing very hard, but uncommon wet... They came down in the rain... '

A similar experience happened 86 years later to Ron Spencer of Lancashire, while serving with the RAF at Kamilla, India, near the Burmese border. Speaking on BBC Radio 4 in April 1975, after another listener had described his experience of a fish fall, Spencer said that he had loved going out into the monsoon rains to wash himself. On one occasion he was standing naked in the middle of this ritual when:

'Things started to hit me, and looking round, I could see myriads of small wriggling shapes on the ground and thousands being swept off the roofs, along channels and into the paddy fields. They were small sardine-sized fish. Needless to say, very shortly after the heavy storm, none were left. Scavengers had gobbled them up.'

FREQUENT FALLS

Records are widely scattered and there is not a full study available that has collected all known cases. But it seems that only falls of frogs and toads are more abundant than fish. For example, Dr E.W. Grudger, of the US Museum of Natural History, collected accounts, and found only 78 reports that

DOWN LIKE RAIN

John Lewis, working in a timber yard at Mountain Ash, was startled at 11 a.m. when he was suddenly struck by small objects falling out of the sky. One of the objects fell down the back of his neck.

'On putting my hand down my neck, I was surprised to find they were small fish. By this time, I saw that the whole ground was covered with them. I took off my hat, the brim of which was full of them. They were jumping all about... The shed [pointing to a large workshop] was covered with them... My mates and I might have gathered bucketsful of them, scraping with our hands. There were two showers...

spanned 2,350 years. Seventeen of these had occurred in the USA; 13 in India; 11 in Germany; 9 in Scotland; 7 in Australia; and 5 in England and Canada. But Gilbert Whitley, working from the records in the Australian Museum, lists over 50 fish falls in Australasia alone between 1879 and 1971.

One of the earliest references to a fish fall is to be found in the ancient Greek text, the *Deipnosophistai,* compiled at the end of the second century AD by Athenaeus. These fragments, drawn from the records of nearly 800 writers, contain the report:

'I know also that it rained fishes. At all events Phoenias, in the second book of his *Eresian Magistrates,* says that in the Chersonesus it once rained fishes uninterruptedly for three days, and Phylarchus in his fourth book says that the people had often seen it raining fish.'

The earliest known case in England happened in Kent in 1666, and was reported in the *Philosophical Transactions* of 1698.

But despite the wealth of authenticated and reliable reports that fish falls have occurred, no one has yet produced a convincing account of why they happen. One of the most plausible explanations is that they are caused by tornadoes, waterspouts or whirlwinds that lift water containing fish high up into a cloud mass and carry them inland.

Other explanations include the suggestion that the phenomenon is caused by fish 'migrating over land'; that fish-eating birds regurgitate or drop their food; that fish are left behind by ponds and streams overflowing; and that fish hibernating in mud are brought to life again by rain. But these do not account for the variety of eyewitness reports, the assortment of species found in the same place, the

*"*ON PUTTING MY HAND DOWN MY NECK, I WAS SURPRISED TO FIND...SMALL FISH...THE WHOLE GROUND WAS FULL OF THEM. THEY WERE JUMPING ALL ABOUT.*"*

One popular theory as to how fish could be transported overland and then 'dropped' from the sky is that water containing quantities of fish is gathered up by tornadoes, such as the one,* above, *photographed in Nebraska.

variety of terrain where fish have been found, and the sheer number of fish involved in some cases. And even though there are well-documented cases of whirlwinds and waterspouts transporting fish, this explanation is inadequate to cover all cases.

ORDERLY PATTERNS

But whirlwinds, tornadoes and waterspouts are very messy, and tend to pick up anything in their way, scattering it in every direction. This conflicts dramatically with the great majority of cases of fish falls. In the Mountain Ash case, for example, the fall was restricted to an area 80 yards by 12 yards (73 metres by 11 metres); and in the Kent case of 1666, it was claimed that the fish were dumped in one particular field and not in any of the surrounding ones. Most falls, in fact, seem to follow this localised pattern. What is perhaps the most extreme example of this orderly fall of fish took place south of Calcutta on 20 September 1839. An eyewitness said: 'The most strange thing which ever struck me was that the fish did not fall helter-skelter... but in a straight line not more than one cubit [an ancient measurement deriving from the length of the forearm] in breadth'.

Whirlwinds, of course, move continuously; and there is considerable evidence that fish falls have lasted much longer than the time possible for them to have been caused in this way. The torrent of many hundreds of sand eels on Hendon, a suburb of Sunderland, north-east England, on 24 August 1918, for example, is a case in point. A. Meek, a marine biologist, reported seeing a fall that lasted a full 10 minutes and that was confined to one small area.

Even if whirlwinds do retrace their path, some fish falls have occurred in such a rapid succession that they could not possibly have been caused by a single whirlwind. John Lewis of Mountain Ash, for example, witnessed 'two showers, with an interval of ten minutes [between them] and each shower lasted about two minutes or thereabouts'.

ALIVE AND THRASHING

The length of time during which fish have been transported through the air seems, according to the evidence, to vary considerably. In many accounts, the fish are alive and thrashing when found on the ground: in other cases, they have been found dead, but fresh and edible. It is difficult to believe that fish could be hurled against the ground and not be killed, but evidence suggests that even those found dead were not killed by their fall.

More puzzling still are the falls of dead fish. On two occasions in India, at Futtepoor in 1833 and at Allahabad in 1836, the fish that fell from the sky were not only dead, but dried. In the former case, the number of fish that fell was estimated to be between 3,000 and 4,000, all of one species. It is difficult to imagine how a whirlwind could keep so many fish in the air long enough for them to have dried out. But, despite widespread publicity in the Indian press at the time, no one came forward to report that a whirlwind had snatched up a valuable heap of dried fish! Perhaps even more extraordinary is the case from Essen, Germany. In 1896, a Crucian carp, encased in ice, fell out of the sky during a storm. Here, the fish must have been kept aloft by vertical currents, long enough to let it become the nucleus of an egg-sized hailstone.

In falls of other animals and insects, there is a tendency for only one species to descend at any one time. But the evidence available concerning fish falls shows that they can be equally divided between falls of a single species and mixed falls. Up to six different species have even been identified in a single fall, for instance, lending support to the idea that the phenomenon is caused by a waterspout, scooping randomly from seas and lakes.

Falls of single species present many problems. The Mountain Ash fall in Glamorganshire, for example, was found to contain mostly sticklebacks, with just a few minnows. Sticklebacks live in freshwater streams and do not congregate in shoals. So how was it possible for a whirlwind to have scooped out such a vast quantity of sticklebacks from a single

source and deposit them all in one place? Similar questions apply to other cases of fish falls involving just one species. Another curious feature is the absence of any accompanying debris.

Objects caught up in the currents of a whirlwind might be expected to be hurled out at different times and distances according to their mass, size or shape. Contrary to this expectation, however, fish falls often involve many different sizes of fish. At Feridpoor, India, for example, two species of fish fell in 1830, one larger and heavier than the other. Similarly, fish ranging in length from 6-12 inches (15-39 centimetres) fell in several gardens in Harlow, Essex, on 12 August 1968, according to the next day's newspapers.

Teleportation

Charles Fort, who spent a lifetime collecting accounts of strange phenomena, suggested that fish falls are the result of what he called 'teleportation', a force that can transport objects from place to place without traversing the intervening distance. Such a force, Fort claimed, was once more active than it is now, and survives today as an erratic and feeble semblance of its former self. Through this agency, fish are snatched away from a place of abundance to a point in the sky, from which they fall. Sometimes this point is not very high off the ground, which would account for the fact that the fish are often found alive. At other times, the point is very close to the ground, accounting for the many observations of fish that seem to have appeared on the ground during a rainstorm.

Fort further suggested that fish falls might be the result of a new pond 'vibrating with its need for fish'. There is the case of Major Cox, for example, a well-known writer in England after the First World War. In an article published in the *Daily Mail* on 6 October 1921, Cox reported that the pond at his Sussex home had been drained and scraped of mud. The pond was then left dry for five months before refilling with water in November 1920. The following May, Cox was astonished to find it teeming with tench.

In 1941, the *American Journal of Science* published a story of a farm in Cambridge, Maryland, USA, where work on a new system of drains was halted because of rain. When work resumed, the ditch was found to be full of rainwater, as might be expected; but here were also hundreds of perch, of two different species, measuring between 4 and 7 inches (10-18 centimetres).

In neither case, however, had there been time for spawning. Overflows and migrating fish were also ruled out because of the distance of both sites from any surrounding water. Fort ruled out, too, the possibility that the fish fell from the sky since they were found only in the new water. If they had fallen from the sky, one would expect there to be at least a few dead fish lying around on surrounding ground; but there were none.

Most fish falls occur during heavy rains, so the whirlwind theory seems to be partially acceptable. A look at the range of reported cases, however, shows that a number of falls have occurred in cloudless skies and quite independently of any accompanying strong wind. At present, the only rational explanation in terms of known causes seems to be the whirlwind theory. But this, as we have seen, cannot account for every single case. Some other unknown force must surely be at work.

The drawing,* left, *from Claus Magnus'* Historia de gentibus septentrionalibus *(1555) shows fish falling from the sky onto a town.

The woodcut,* below, *showing a man struggling through a torrential shower of rain and fish, was based on an 18th century incident in Transylvania.

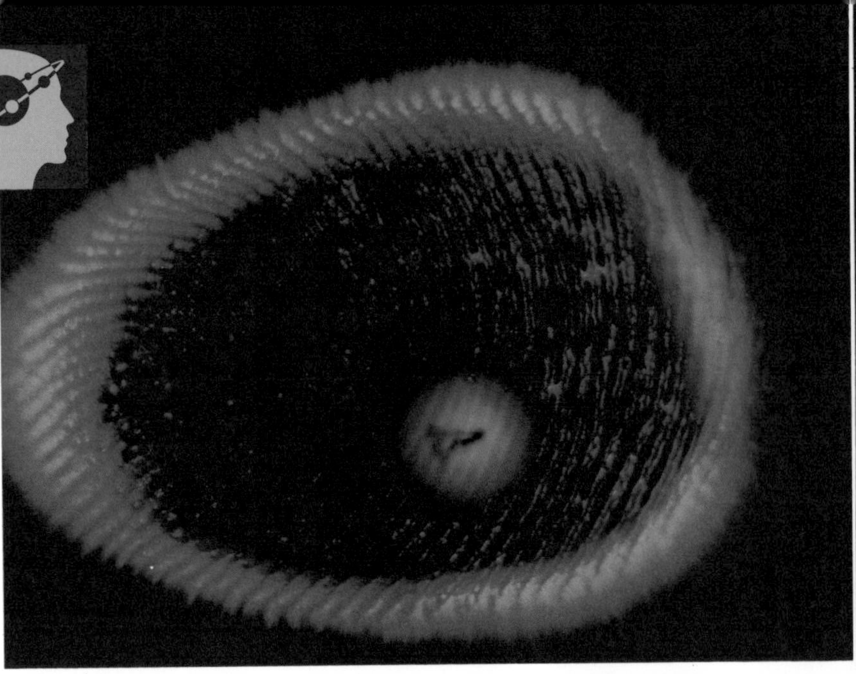

IMAGES OF THE UNSEEN

MYSTICS AND CLAIRVOYANTS HAVE LONG CLAIMED THAT THERE IS A NORMALLY INVISIBLE HALO OF LIGHT SURROUNDING THE HUMAN BODY. THEN, IN 1970, NEWS WAS RECEIVED THAT RUSSIAN SCIENTISTS HAD ACTUALLY PHOTOGRAPHED THIS 'AURA'

In 1939, a Russian engineer, Semyon Kirlian, was repairing an electro-therapy machine in a research laboratory in the Ukrainian town of Krasnodar when he accidentally allowed his hand to move to close to a 'live' electrode. The shock he received was accompanied by a brilliant flash of light given off by a large spark of electricity. Curiosity aroused, Kirlian wondered what would happen if he placed a sheet of light-sensitive material in the path of the spark. Placing his hand behind a piece of light-sensitised paper, Kirlian found, on developing the film, strange streamer-like emanations surrounding the image of his fingertips. On closer inspection, he then noticed that each emanation had a different radiation pattern.

Fascinated by his discovery, Kirlian set up a laboratory in his tiny two-roomed flat and spent all his spare time investigating this phenomenon. His subsequent research into high-voltage photography over the next 40 years led to intense scientific speculation and debate of the claim that the strange emanations captured on film were proof of the existence of the so-called 'astral body'.

For centuries, the psychically-gifted have spoken of a brilliant circle of light surrounding the physical body of all living organisms. This 'halo', they believed, was the spiritual 'double' of our physical selves, but independent of it and surviving the death of the body.

It is still not at all clear, however, in spite of extensive research, what it is exactly that causes the brilliant glow surrounding the hands, feet, plant leaves and other objects that have been photographed using the Kirlian technique.

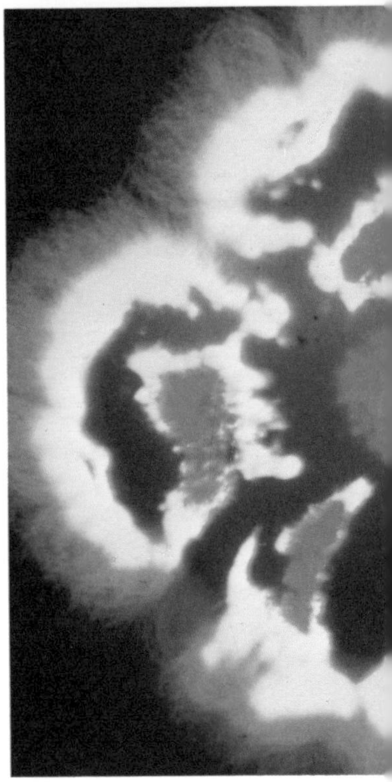

A fingertip photographed by the Kirlian method,* top left, *shows a surrounding radiation pattern. But the vivid colour may not be significant, since this tends to vary according to the type of film used.

Semyon and Valentina Kirlian,* left, *spent over 40 years developing a technique to capture on film the strange streamer-like emanations that, in varying degrees of strength, surround all objects.

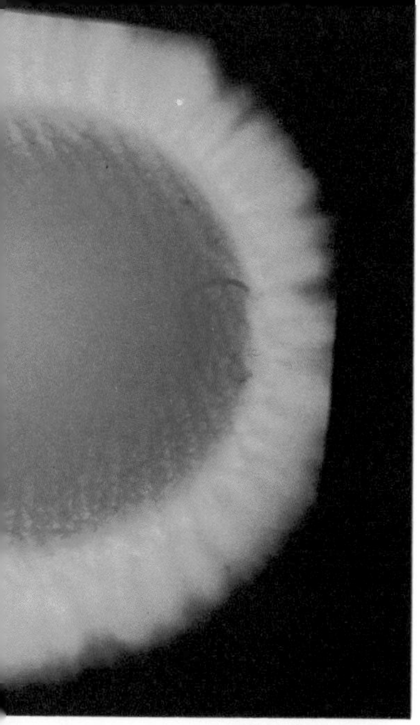

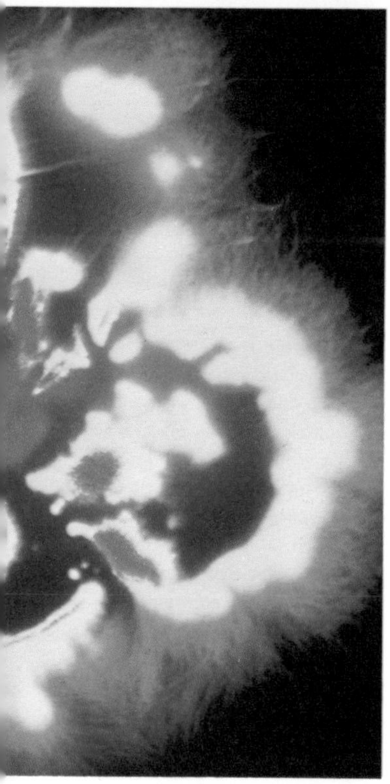

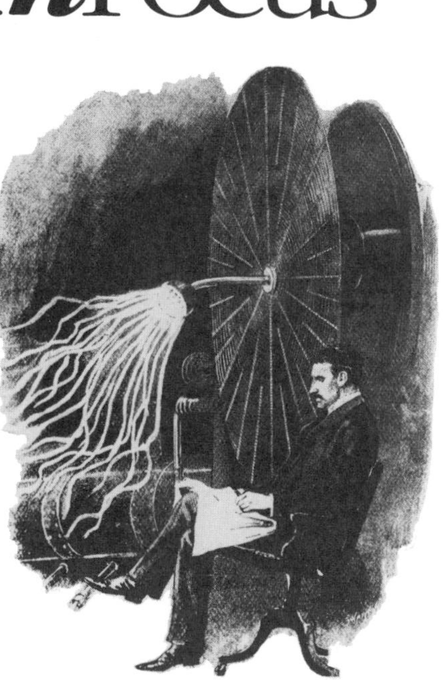

AMAZING INVENTOR

Born in Smiljan, Yugoslavia, in 1856, Nikola Tesla was to become a driving force in the invention of electrical equipment, as well as being something of a prophet. Unable to interest European engineers in a new alternating current motor he had conceived, Tesla left for the United States in 1884 and joined Thomas Edison in the designing of dynamos. But the two men soon fell out, and Tesla went on to set up his own laboratory where, in 1891, he unveiled his famous coil, still widely used today. It is an electrical device for producing an intermittent source of high voltage and consists of an induction coil with a central cylindrical core of soft iron onto which are wound two insulated coils. The inner (primary) coil has a few turns of copper wire, while a surrounding, secondary coil comprises a large number of turns of thin copper wire. An interrupter is used for making and breaking the current in the primary coil automatically. This magnetises the iron core and produces a large magnetic field through the induction coil. For experimentation with the high voltage output of power from his coil, Tesla produced a gas-filled, phosphore-coated tubular light - a forerunner of today's fluorescent light.

A further measure of Tesla's inventiveness can be seen in his tele-automatic boat of 1898 which was guided by remote control. Then, in 1900, he made what many have claimed to be his finest discovery – terrestrial stationary waves. He proved with this discovery that the Earth could be used as a conductor and would be as responsive as a tuning fork to electrical vibrations of a certain pitch. He also managed to light 200 electric lamps without wires from a distance of 25 miles (40 kilometres) and created man-made lightning, producing flashes of some 135 feet (42 metres).

Tesla was also convinced at one time that he was receiving signals from another planet at his Colorado laboratory. But his claims met with derision on the part of the scientific press.

His later ideas became even more speculative. He asserted, for instance, that he was able to split the world in half, like an apple, and that he had invented a 'death ray' that could destroy aircraft 250 miles (400 kilometres) away. Such theories also met with incredulity. Yet, in 1917, he accurately forecast the coming of radar, and achieved similar results to Semyon Kirlian with high-voltage photography.

Particularly brilliant Kirlian 'auras', such as that shown top, are said to indicate ESP powers, sometimes latent, in the subject of the photograph.

As the picture of an oleander leaf, above, shows, plants also respond to the Kirlian method. This fact has been taken by some as proof that all life is essentially spiritual.

In any event, the effects that Kirlian thought he had discovered were not entirely new. In the 1890s, Nikola Tesla, a Serbian scientist working in the US, had used high-voltage photography, with much the same results as those achieved by Kirlian. In the early 1930s, too, an English researcher, George de la Warr, had discovered the existence of weak 'electromagnetic force fields' surrounding areas of the human body and at a distance from it. These fields extended in a lattice-like formation and contained voltage peaks as high as 70 millivolts. Their vividness was also seen to fluctuate according to the physical and emotional state of the subject.

But the major advances in the field of high-voltage photography were undoubtedly made by Kirlian himself, even though some of his most interesting contributions came about quite by chance. On one occasion, Kirlian was preparing his equipment for a demonstration he was giving to a distinguished visitor. To his dismay, on the day the visitor was to arrive, the machine failed to produce the normal clear pictures. Kirlian took his machine apart, checked for faults and made further tests, but with the same negative results. In frustration, he asked his wife, Valentina, to be the subject. To their mutual surprise, a perfect image was produced. A few hours later, however, Kirlian discovered what he believed to be the cause of his failure to produce a clear image. He had developed a particularly virulent form of influenza, and to Kirlian it seemed reasonable to suppose that it was his illness that had caused the weak image. The photograph, Kirlian claimed, had in some way given warning of the influenza.

A further possible use of the Kirlian method was revealed when the chairman of a major scientific research institution arrived. He brought with him two apparently identical leaves for the Kirlians to photograph. The two samples had been taken from the same species of plant, and had been torn off at

PERSPECTIVES

CONTROLLING THE KIRLIAN AURA

From the age of 11, Matthew Manning, *below left,* has been aware of possessing a wide range of psychic powers that he can, with practice, turn on at will. In 1974, a group of 21 scientists met to investigate these powers. Was Manning being used by supernatural forces outside himself, or could his 'gift' be explained in terms of science? The evidence remains inconclusive. But Kirlian photographs taken of Manning's finger-tips produced startling results. The picture, *left,* shows his 'normal' aura; but the picture, below, taken when he had 'switched the power on', shows a remarkably more intense corona.

The Kirlian photograph of a rose petal,* top right, *shows a characteristic aura. But when a portion of the petal is cut away,* below right, *the Kirlian photograph still shows, quite clearly, the section that has been removed. This is known as the 'phantom leaf effect'. Russian investigators say that it proves that 'bioplasma' surrounds all living things.

The 50p coin,* below, *has a characteristic outer 'glow' using Kirlian's methods. If, as some claim, this glow is really the 'aura', then it would imply that even inanimate matter has some form of spiritual existence. Intriguingly, when the same coin is photographed after two psychic healers have placed their hands 4 inches (10 centimetres) above it for five minutes, the outer 'glow' is noticeably brighter.

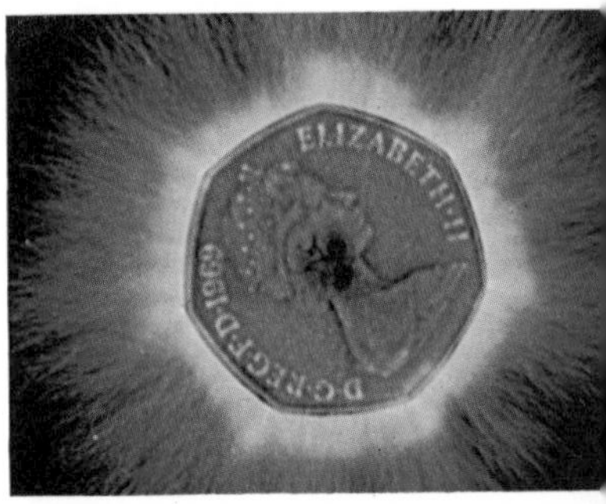

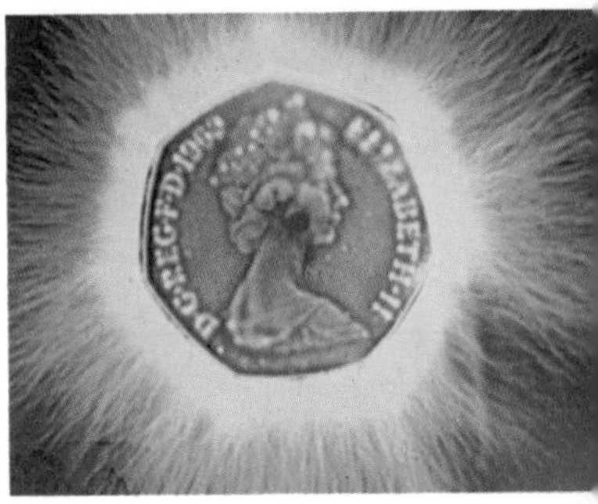

the same time. From one leaf, the husband and wife team obtained the characteristic flare patterns surrounding the leaf. But from the other leaf, no clear patterns were obtained. The Kirlians adjusted their machine in every possible way, but with the same inconsistent results. Next morning, they related to their visitor their failure to produce the same results. To their surprise, he was delighted. The leaf with the weak pattern, he told them, had been taken from a plant that had contracted a serious disease. The other leaf, with the clear pattern, had been taken from a perfectly healthy plant. The experiment seemed to confirm Kirlian's hypothesis: his machine was able to give warning of disease. The high voltage photograph had actually detected illness and disease *in advance* of any physical symptoms appearing on the surface.

Further experiments seemed to produce equally startling results. If a section of a leaf was cut off and photographed, for example, an image of the whole outline appeared on the photograph. This phenomenon, known as the 'phantom leaf' effect, seemed to confirm the claims of certain clairvoyants that they could see clearly the 'phantom limb' on people who had undergone amputations, but who continued to feel pain from the severed arm or leg.

ASTRAL BODY

Though the Kirlians themselves did not describe the results of their investigations as evidence for the existence of an 'astral body', many were only too eager to do so. What other explanation was there, they asked, for the startling pictures Kirlian was able to take? But, in one sense, even the clairvoyants were disappointed with the results of Kirlian photography, since the richly colourful images achieved by Kirlian lacked the subtlety of the 'aura' seen by clairvoyants.

While working at St Thomas' Hospital in London at the turn of the century, Dr Walter Kilner had found that, if he observed his patients through a glass screen coated with a blue dye, he could see a 'faint cloud' surrounding them. This seemed to vary according to the physical and mental state of the patient. The dye, Kilner later came to believe, acted as a stimulant to his own innate ability to perceive

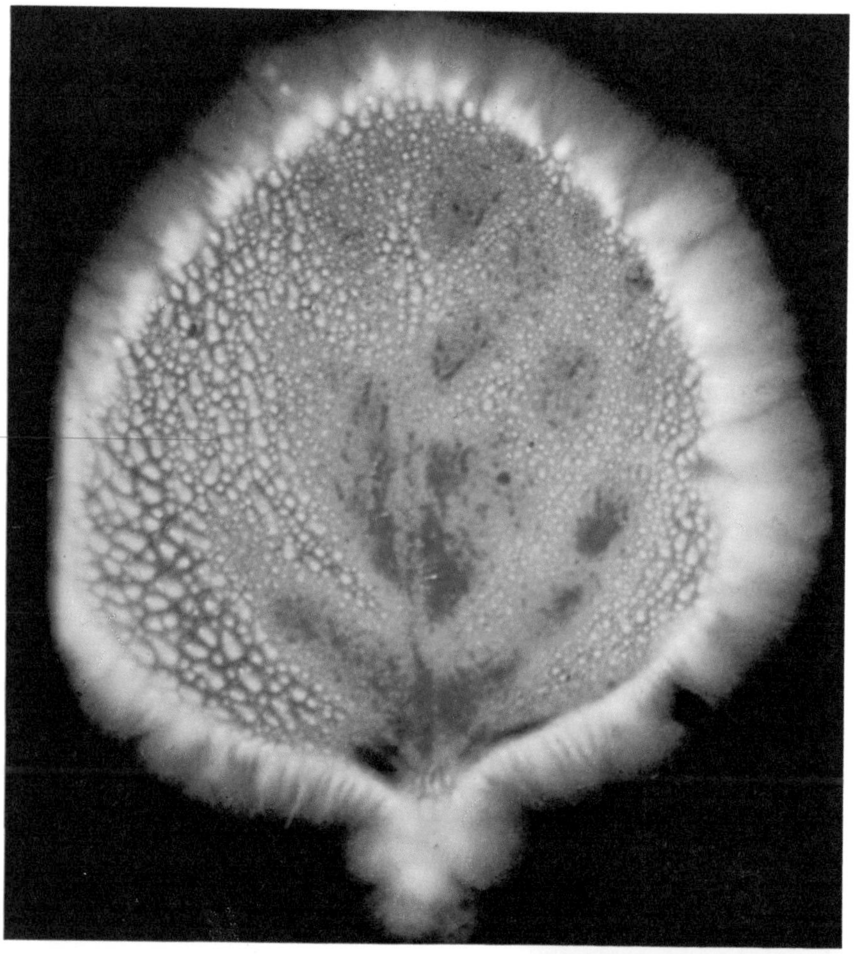

describes 'biological plasma' in terms that closely resemble those used by clairvoyants to describe the nature of the 'astral body'. 'All living things,' writes Dr Inyushin, 'plants, animals and humans, not only have a physical body made of atoms and molecules, but also a counterpart body of energy.'

Critical Viewpoints

Much evidence already exists, claim the enthusiasts, to support Inyushin's theory. And there is also evidence that the nature and extent of these fields of energy, surrounding every living organism, correspond to the image on the Kirlian print. Not so, reply the critics: Kirlian photography cannot be considered of scientific interest, since it is not repeatable under stringent laboratory conditions – a necessary requirement of all scientific phenomena. Sceptics also argue that experiments have produced different results every time, not due to underlying physical or psychological causes, as Kirlian claimed, but to factors such as sweat secretion and the primitive nature of the equipment used in Kirlian photography.

The debates continues. No one knows for certain the nature of those images first photographed by the Kirlians. Some, while rejecting spiritual aspects, accept that, whatever the emanations mean, they can be used to achieve insight into the physical and psychological condition of the subject. Others, including some practising scientists, claim far more. But all are agreed that Kirlian succeeded in opening up a hitherto invisible world, once known only to the clairvoyants and mystics – the exceptional few – for everyone to see.

> "THERE IS EVIDENCE TO SUGGEST THAT THE NATURE AND EXTENT OF THE FIELDS OF ENERGY SURROUNDING EVERY LIVING ORGANISM CORRESPOND TO THE IMAGE OF THE KIRLIAN PRINT."

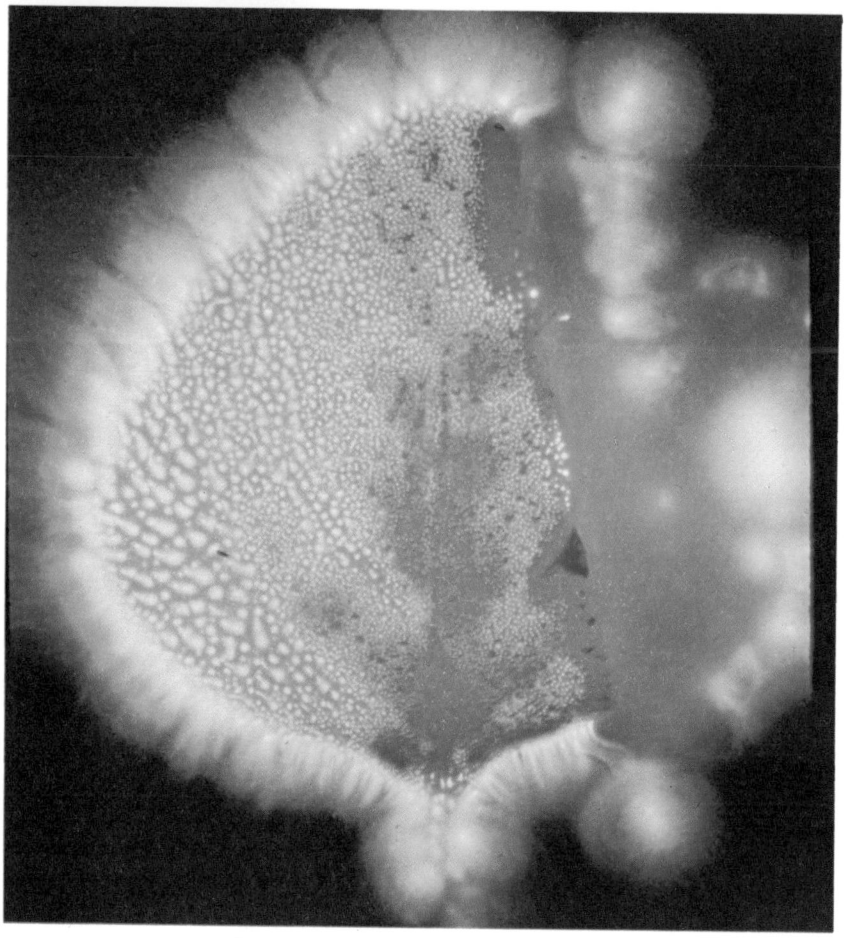

the 'glow' without any artificial aid. But the ability of those who, like Kilner, are able to see this 'aura' clearly is of little help to scientists who cannot see the phenomenon for themselves. Because it is such a personal quality, it is difficult – if not impossible – to measure, control and analyse it in the laboratory.

Research in the West into the possible nature of Kirlian photography is still in its infancy, and no definite conclusions have been reached. Research in Russia, meanwhile, has been of much longer duration and has contributed many interesting theories as to the possible cause of the Kirlian effect. Working at the University of Alma Atta, for instance, Dr Victor Inyushin has spent several years investigating Kirlian photography. As a result of these studies, he has come to the conclusion that the 'aura' effect showing up in Kirlian photography is evidence of what he calls 'biological plasma' and not the result of any electrical state of the organism. Dr Inyushin

THE CROP CIRCLE CONTROVERSY

APPEARING OUT OF THE BLUE EACH YEAR, CROP CIRCLES ARE AS BAFFLING AS EVER. COULD THEY BE UNEARTHLY? OR ARE THEY NOTHING MORE THAN ELABORATE HOAXES?

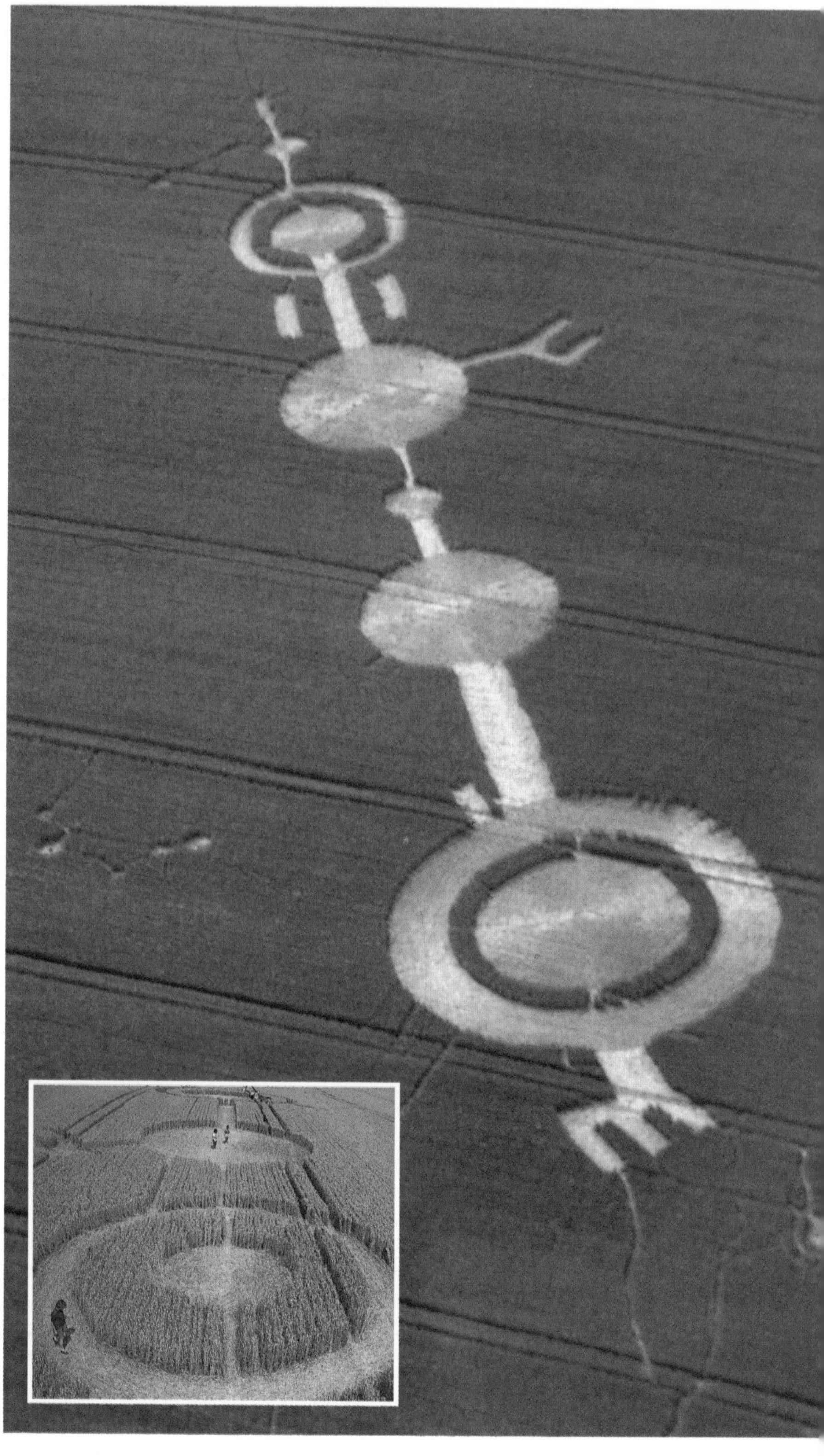

The most popular current enigma; an intellectual challenge strong enough to baffle the entire planet; a continually changing phenomenon: all these phrases, and many more, have been used to describe the bizarre – even beautiful – circular designs that over recent years have regularly appeared in British cereal fields – and elsewhere, too – during the high summer months.

They come in swirls: they come in rings: they come as singles, doubles, triples, and even complex formations like dials, and have manifested in ever-increasing profusion since August 1980 when research began at White Horse Hill, near Westbury in Wiltshire.

We have not seen the likes of it for a long time in the world of unexplained phenomena: and, certainly, the nature of these mysterious formations still eludes us. Are they always created by intrepid hoaxers? Is there a natural solution, possibly triggered by changes in our atmosphere or even the controversial greenhouse effect? Or, could it be, as some researchers insist, that we are the subject of alien visitations? Is someone, somewhere, trying to tell us something?

POWERFUL VIBRATIONS

Probably the most remarkable formation to date appeared right on cue on Friday, 13 July 1990. It arrived just after a scientific conference in Oxford had gathered physicists and meteorologists from three continents to dismiss corn circles as a novel weather phenomenon, and the day before a UFO conference in Sheffield met in order to support the same conclusion.

The scene of this timely wonder was Alton Barnes in the Vale of Pewsey, Wiltshire. This is an area where circles appear, like a rash of extra-terrestrial pimples each May, June, July and August. It is an evocative place, scattered with ancient sites, such as the stone circle at Avebury and the imposing mound of Silbury Hill. The esoteric community loves this region: if you are psychically in tune, they say, then you sense its powerful vibrations.

Numerous researchers regularly investigate crop circles, such as the one shown right, *for authenticity, using a variety of instruments. The origin of these recurrent formations remains, nevertheless, uncertain.*

The Alton Barnes formation attracted tremendous global interest because it had a series of six interlocking rings, circles, straight lines and arms with spokes emanating from them – by far the most elaborate grouping ever seen, and almost impossible not to accept as intelligently designed, and also perhaps highly symbolic in content. Researchers soon found that this kind of mark bears a curious resemblance to ancient picture writing from the Sumerian culture – to such an extent that, within just a few days, the formations became known as 'pictograms' rather than crop marks.

Most crop marks are single circles. Rings, ringed circles, triplets, and more complex formations, like that found at Alton Barnes and shown left, *with a detail* inset, *are more rare. However, during 1990, many increasingly bizarre crop pictograms were found.*

The farmers who owned the land were insistent that a hoax was impossible because the pattern was so complex that it would have taken a very long time to fabricate. Noted circle researcher Colin Andrews agreed that it was far too elaborate, adding that it seemed to have been created by some sort of intelligent life force as an attempt to communicate with us.

Crop circles have been appearing since 1678 when they were found in a Hertfordshire field and blamed on the Devil. He is seen below *mowing an oval formation.*

The Westbury Mystery

Officially, the crop circle mystery was born in a field in August 1980. There was sporadic local interest and an immediate suggestion that its very regular edges (it seemed a giant cookie-cutter might have descended from the sky) indicated an intelligence, rather than a natural phenomenon. What is more, it seemed that the most likely candidate for that intelligence was located in outer space – especially as UFO phenomena had apparently centred on nearby Warminster some 20 years earlier.

Circles from Outer Space?

Tourists from all over the world started skywatching from local hills to look out for 'the thing', as the UFO was quaintly nicknamed. Crop circles had become a centre of attention.

More circles then appeared in 1981 and 1982 at other sites in the counties of Hampshire and Wiltshire; and subsequently local media regenerated the story every year, eagerly awaiting the first circle of summer with as much enthusiasm as nature-watchers traditionally anticipate the first cuckoo of spring.

By 1983, the phenomenon was still little more than a local enigma, but it was debated in various UFO societies, and some fascinating research was conducted by the research group PROBE, the British UFO Research Association (BUFORA) and Dr Terence Meaden, a physicist specialising in unusual vortex mechanisms within the atmosphere and who operated TORRO (the Tornado and Storm Research Organisation). The general conclusion was that a natural phenomenon was to blame, and researchers did a fine job of defusing the 'alien myth' that some UFO spotters, sometimes displaying more imagination than common sense, tended automatically to read into such matters.

However, this was not the end of the mystery, merely the beginning. The main proponent of an 'alien intelligence' interpretation of the phenomenon was *Flying Saucer Review* consultant Pat Delgado, later to be joined by colleague Colin Andrews. Their approach – that crop circles were some sort of warning from another intelligence – was the most popular with the media, and Delgado was successful in interesting the national press in the first 'quintuplets' (a formation of five circles, with a large one at the centre and four smaller satellites). This latest development ensured escalation of the subject to a nationwide level.

A 'Cosmic Joker?'

The first proven hoax occurred in July 1983, when one national newspaper paid a farmer 'compensation' for a quintuplet to be 'created' on his land, right alongside an identical and allegedly 'real' pattern that had achieved great publicity in a rival daily. The hoax would probably have gone unrecognised but for some diligent investigation by serious UFOlogists, blamed in *New Scientist* magazine for actually fanning the flames of mystery.

Over the next few summers, there was occasional interest in the subject, especially when another new type of formation (a ring) appeared in 1986. Rings differ from circles in that only a narrow band of crop is laid down, whereas circles contain a whole area of flattened cereal. Ringed circles also began to appear; but simple circles still predominated in the British countryside.

It was from a mixture of gradually escalating activity, and claim and counter-claim between 'rival' researchers, that the first signs of the possibility of a 'cosmic joker' – some sort of force from beyond that could be playing tricks on us – began to appear. Various strange things suddenly had been discovered in the centre of some circles.

Columnist Jean Rook visited a circle and found a single lone poppy staring up at her from the corn. In July 1989, this was reproduced at Mansfield and hailed as the first circle in Nottinghamshire. However, after careful investigation, the circle was found to be a hoax, a diagnosis supported by full confession on the part of the hoaxers. But the presence of another lone poppy at the centre of a circle was seemingly a 'coincidence' – or was it?

A white 'goo' then turned up inside another formation, and speculation resulted about litter-bugging aliens who had visited our planet. Analysis, however, revealed the most likely source to be Earth-based confectionery that had 'gone off', then interacting in some strange way with the soil. Much jovial commentary about Martians dumping a 'Mars bar' as a cosmic signal resulted.

Many circles, like the formation below, are surrounded by tractor lines which to some, suggests more often than not the possibility of a hoax.

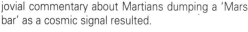

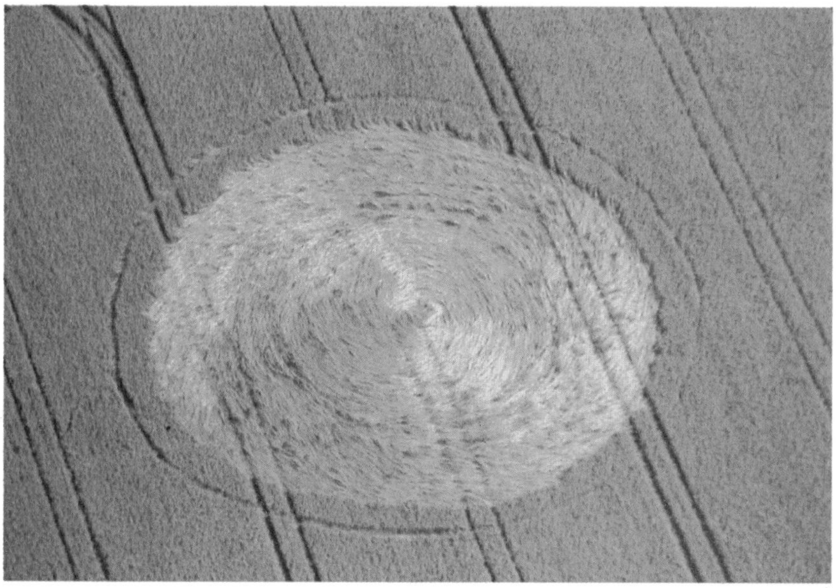

The Name Game

Name games were another feature of the increasingly perplexing phenomenon. Circles (a quintuplet formation) also appeared for the first time in Sussex. Remarkably, the pattern was astride Cradle Hill, which bears the same name as the famous UFO-watching location at Warminster in Wiltshire, where circles now appear today.

Researchers have also looked for some sort of logic in the placement of circles. Some of the earliest, at Warminster and Westbury in Wiltshire, and Wantage in Oxfordshire, were at places with names starting with the letter 'W', forming the so-called 'Wessex Triangle', but this lost meaning when circles began to dot the map all over the UK.

> "If a joke-playing intelligence does indeed lie behind some of the circles, the question remains as to whether it comes from a cosmic source or from rather closer to home."

The remarkable formation, left, appeared during July 1991 in a field at Barbary Castle near Swindon, Wiltshire. Locals refer to it as 'the bicycle' because of obvious similarities.

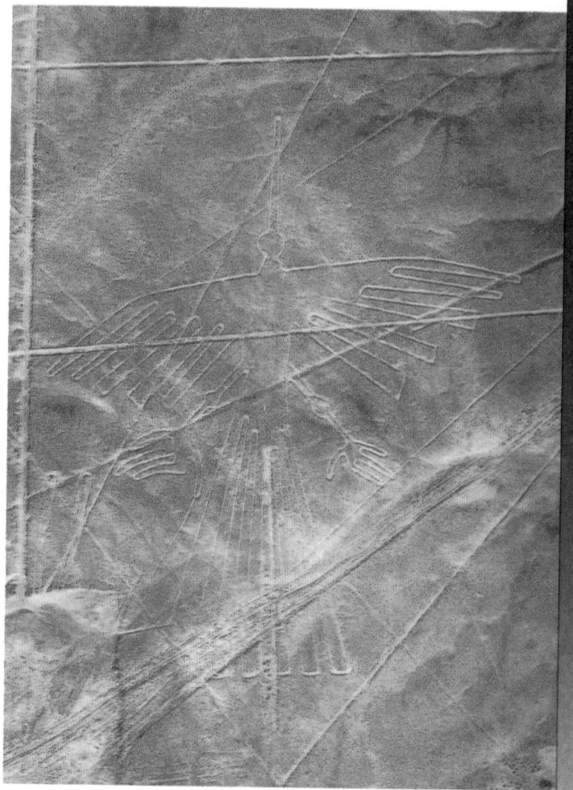

Almost as mysterious as crop formations are ancient Nazca lines, such as these on a hillside in Peru, right. Some bear a remarkable similarity to modern crop pictograms.

Particularly intriguing was the message 'We are not alone', which was found cut into crop at one site. Thought by many to be an obvious hoax, the perpetrators have never been identified, however. Other circle researchers, meanwhile, have chosen to cover up this particular story because they believe it could well damage the credibility of all their investigations to date.

Many have also had fun trying to align the circle locations with ancient monuments, stone circles, ley lines, and the like; but such theories are now generally disputed.

Mounting Operations

In 1989, Operation Whitecrow was mounted, and watch was kept for several days on a field where circles were expected to appear. Hundreds took part, with cameras permanently trained on the suspect zone. Nothing was spotted; but as the operation shut down, new circles appeared in a field right behind the observers' backs.

Then, in the early summer of 1990, a group of meteorologists led a weekend expedition with sophisticated equipment. No circles were seen to form, although several did appear in a nearby field, out of line of sight as they sat and waited.

Operation Blackbird followed. A sequel to Operation Whitecrow, this had backing from the BBC and Nippon TV in Japan. It involved expensive cameras with thermal imaging equipment, necessary because most circles are known to form during pre-dawn hours.

CASEBOOK

KILLER FORCES

On 18 February 1977, at 4 a.m., a Uruguayan rancher, together with his family and several farmhands, suffered a nasty shock while herding cattle. The generator that provided the farm with light suddenly cut out as a rotating shape with a central bulge and glowing bright orange descended on to the farmland. Cows ran away and dogs barked in panic; but Topo, the family guard dog, large and police-trained, rushed immediately towards the 'thing' as it rocked from side to side, giving out terrific blasts of strong wind that tore off branches from adjacent trees.

When almost on top of the terrifying 'object', Topo froze in his tracks and began to howl in pain. Streaks of white 'lightning' emerged from the beneath the shape and were earthed when they made contact with the ground. The farmer, who had been chasing his dog, felt a wave of heat strike him from some distance, and his skin tingled in response to an electrical charge. He stood paralysed, his muscles convulsing.

As the glow shot upwards and vanished, the generator immediately began to work again. However, all the wiring to the lights had been burnt right through by a power surge.

When their fear had been somewhat allayed, the farmworkers approached the spot and discovered that the ground beneath where the Saturn-like mass had hovered was a classic swirled crop circle, some 36 feet (11 metres) in diameter.

The farmer had a severe skin rash that lasted several days, felt unwell, but thankfully recovered; not so the dog. Topo was found dead at the very spot where he had confronted the unbelievably powerful force. An autopsy by the local vet revealed that the animal had been 'cooked' from within by a powerful electro-magnetic force that had generated intense energy.

Fortunately, most other cases of a close encounter with the cause of a crop circle are far less traumatic; but the force that is generating these marks is clearly powerful and, at times, perhaps even a killer.

Yet again, however, the observers fell victim to a joker. Cameras at the Nippon site detected orange lights shortly after 4 a.m. on 25 July (only hours after major national press coverage for the mission, and three days after one tabloid newspaper had offered £10,000 to the first person who could solve the mystery). As the sun rose, there was a brand new formation of circles in the field. Were 10 years of research about to be rewarded?

The dramatic news immediately spread around the world, and there was talk of a major scientific breakthrough. Journalists then flocked to the scene, only to find the complex formation crudely trampled into the corn and very obviously a hoax. At the centre of each circle, they also found two strange objects – a ouija board and a wooden cross – researchers had been foiled again.

This ouija board, right, was found at the centre of a circle in July 1990, left behind by a hoaxer.

PERSPECTIVES

ALL IN A NIGHT'S WORK

On 9 September 1991, *Today* newspaper led with an article on its front page entitled: 'The men who conned the world'. The paper claimed that the crop circle debate was over. Two British artists, Doug Bower and David Chorley, both in their 60s, demonstrated how they first designed a circle at home and then, using 4 ft (1.2 m) wooden plinths, a ball of string and a baseball cap with a piece of wire threaded through its visor, executed their designs in the middle of the night at a preselected site. They offered to create a circle for the paper which would fool the experts.

Having shown their design to the *Today* reporter, the two men set off at 1.30 am. First, they tied string to each end of a plinth to form a pair of reins. Chorley then placed his foot on one end of the plinth while Bower worked it round; this gave them the basic circle. From then on, each man took turns at holding the reins and walking round with his foot on the plinth – always with the plinth half way up the corn. In this way, the corn was flattened, but never trampled. The men kept walking around until they were satisfied the circle was big enough.

Then, wearing the baseball hat with the wire fed into its visor, Bower lined up a point on the horizon and started to walk in a straight line backward and forward until he had formed what was to become the corridor between two circles. When this was completed, another circle was created at the other end using the same technique. When the men had finished, they left the way they had come in – along a tramline made by the farmer's tractor.

The following day, the newspaper called in Pat Delgado, best-selling author and crop circle expert, who examined and then 'authenticated' the circles describing them as '... the greatest of modern mysteries'.

Bower and Chorley went on to describe how they had first learned about crop circles in Australia. They had become drinking partners in England, had found the idea amusing – and decided to try them out here. The publicity the circles received only increased their desire to make them more and more intricate. Despite the men's claims, however, most scientists are not convinced that all circles are the work of hoaxers. The debate continues.

Doug Bower and Dave Chorley planning a crop circle.

Plasma Vortex Theory

One of the most derided, but least understood, explanations for crop circles is that they are the product of some sort of atmospheric force, usually dismissed as a 'whirlwind' or 'tornado'. Dr Terence Meaden, of the Tornado and Storm Research Organisation (TORRO), has been involved in circle studies far longer than anybody else, and has developed an extensive and complex set of ideas that have won growing support. Indeed, in a survey of 50 meteorologists conducted in 1990 by Paul Fuller, almost all were willing to accept the theory, or believed it worthy of further research.

Essentially, Dr Meaden suggests that spinning columns of air above the surface during certain weather conditions and at key geographical sites (gentle hill slopes being prime examples) produce an electrical field by ionizing the surrounding air. This can, in some circumstances, drop to Earth like a curtain of electric rain. It is very short-lived but interacts with the resistive properties of cereal fields to leave geometric marks. The 'curtain' (or plasma vortex to give it its technical name) is confined to a well-defined shape by surface tension, just as floating soap bubbles retain their precise and seemingly 'artificial' design in the same way. Critics of Dr Meaden's theory, however, suggest that it fails to take into account the highly complex pattern of some circles.

A Psychological Approach

Carl Jung, the Swiss psychologist who developed a theory of archetypal images that are buried deep inside us, would probably have loved to tangle with the crop circle mystery, just as he theorised about the true nature of UFOs. Indeed, perhaps the full solution will not require a cereal specialist, UFO enthusiast or even a meteorologist after all. Instead, it may take a psychologist to unravel the innermost secrets of crop circles.

GREAT BALLS OF FIRE!

Taken by Roy Jennings at 2 a.m. one day in August 1961 in Castleford, Yorkshire, the photograph above is alleged to show ball lightning. The woman who owns the house in the background of the photograph remembers hearing a loud explosion at the time. The photographer used a long exposure to record the 'wake' of the lightning on film. Critics, however, have claimed that a similar result could have been obtained by pointing the camera towards a street light and swinging it – but there were no street lights.

FOR CENTURIES, SCIENTISTS REFUSED TO BELIEVE THAT BALL LIGHTNING EVEN EXISTED. THE PHENOMENON IS NOW ACKNOWLEDGED, BUT ITS CAUSES STILL REMAIN VERY MUCH A MYSTERY. WHAT LIES BEHIND THESE REMARKABLY POWERFUL GLOWING SPHERES?

Flying towards Elko, Nevada, USA on a routine mission to refuel B47 bombers in flight on 16 June 1960, a USAF KG97 tanker aircraft suddenly ran into a layer of cloud at 18,000 feet (5,500 metres).

The pilot was concentrating on the instrument panel, when he was surprised to see a yellow-white ball of light, 18 inches (45 centimetres) in diameter, emerge silently through the windshield. It passed at a fast running pace between his seat and the co-pilot's, and travelled down the cabin passageway, past the navigator and engineer.

The pilot had been struck by lightning twice on previous flights and knew that an explosion was imminent. His immediate reaction, as an experienced airman, was to concentrate on flying rather than to turn round and watch the ball drift to the back of the aircraft.

After a few seconds of shocked silence, the four men in the flight compartment heard over the intercom the excited voice of the boom operator, who was sitting in the rear of the aircraft. A ball of fire had come rolling through the cargo compartment, and then danced out over the right wing, and rolled off harmlessly into the night.

This remarkable report concerns ball lightning – one of the many natural phenomena for which science has no explanation. In fact, the properties of ball lightning are so hard to explain that, for years, scientists doubted its very existence. Their principle was that what cannot be explained cannot exist.

This attitude, unfortunately, is by no means rare among scientists. The fall of meteors to Earth was for many years considered a superstition of ignorant peasants, for instance. Indeed, despite many well-documented observations of these fiery bodies, sceptics were at one point so sure of their case that rare meteorite specimens were removed from museum collections and destroyed on the grounds that stories of meteorites falling from the sky were mere superstition.

Luminous Globes

The ball lightning controversy has divided the scientific community since the early 19th century, when comprehensive reports were first prepared on the subject. Then, in 1890, a large number of luminous globes resembling ball lightning appeared in a tornado and were the subject of a meeting of the French Academy of Sciences. The glowing spheres entered houses through the chimneys, and bored circular holes in the windows as they departed.

A member of the Academy stood up at the end of the account and commented that the extraordinary properties supposedly attributed to ball lightning should be taken with a liberal pinch of salt, since the observers must have been suffering from hallucinations. In the heated discussion that followed, it was agreed that the observations made by uneducated peasants were valueless. At this point, the former Emperor of Brazil, a foreign member of the Academy, silenced the meeting by remarking that he himself had actually seen ball lightning!

Even today, many such reports still have a certain medieval aura of witchcraft and magic about them, which scarcely serves to endear the subject to sceptics. Yet over the centuries, literally hundreds of sightings have been made, so that the evidence for ball lightning now seems to be irrefutable.

Fire From The Sky

One observation reported in great detail was made by a Russian chemist, M.T. Dmitriev, in 1967. He was camping on the banks of the River Onega in western Russia when there was an intense flash of lightning. A ball of fire appeared, hovering over the water. It took the form of an oval mass of light with a yellow-white core, surrounded by layers of dark violet and blue.

Apparently unaffected by the wind, it hovered across the water at a height of about one foot (30 centimetres). Dmitriev heard it crackling and hissing as it flew across his head and on to the river bank, where it hung motionless for about 30 seconds.

It left a trail of acrid, bluish smoke as it passed into a group of trees. Then it bounced like a billiard ball from tree to tree, emitting burst after burst of sparks. After a minute, it disappeared from view.

From this and many similar reports, it is possible to sketch out the properties 'typical' of ball lightning. Firstly, it usually occurs at the same time as cloud-to-ground lightning. The balls are generally spherical or pear-shaped with somewhat fuzzy edges, and they range from half-an-inch to a yard (1-100 centimetres) across. They shine as brightly as a domestic electric lamp; they vary in colour, but are often red, orange or yellow; and they last for anything from just a second to over a minute.

The disappearance of a lightning ball may be silent or accompanied by an explosion. Probably the best known report of a lightning ball causing material damage was reported in 1936 by a correspondent to the *Daily Mail*. He wrote that, during a thunderstorm, he saw a large 'red hot' ball, later described as the 'size of an orange', come down from the sky. It struck the house, cut the telephone wire, burnt the window frame and then buried itself in a tub of water underneath the window. The water boiled for some minutes; but when cool enough to search, nothing could be found.

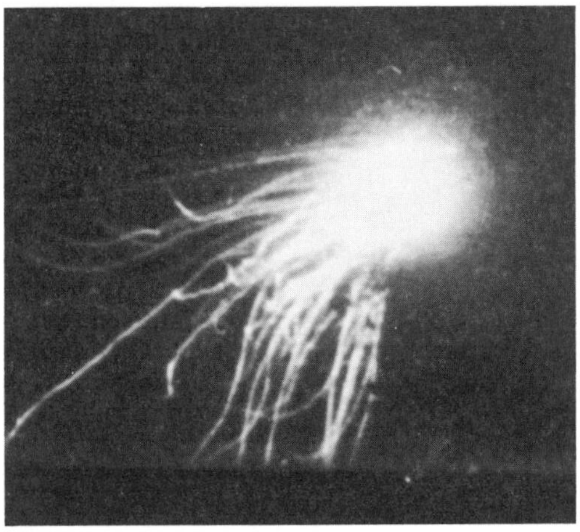

Like ball lightning, meteorites,* top, *were long believed by scientists to be creations of the imagination.

The photograph,* above, *was taken in 1933 by an insurance expert on storm damage who made a practice of photographing lightning. The intensely luminous ball appeared during a thunderstorm and, observed by several people, floated gently towards the ground. The ball had a diameter estimated at just over one foot (30 centimetres) and disappeared after about 10 seconds.

The 'firework ball lightning',* above left, *appeared during a thunderstorm in 1951. It fell straight downwards and flew apart like a firework a few yards above the ground.

Surprisingly, perhaps, ball lightning may not be that rare. In one survey, for instance, 4,000 NASA employees were asked whether they had seen ball lightning, and their answers indicated that it might occur more commonly than had been thought. As the report states:

'A comparison of the frequency of observation of ordinary lightning impact points [with appearances of ball lightning] reveals that ball lightning is not a particularly rare phenomenon. Contrary to widely accepted ideas, the occurrence of ball lightning may be nearly as frequent as that of ordinary cloud-to-ground strokes.'

All In The Imagination

The Canadian scientist Edward Argyll, however, claims that ball lightning is merely an optical illusion. When lightning strikes the ground, he says, it creates such a bright flash that an observer will see a persistent after-image that can easily be mistaken for ball lightning.

By embracing this theory, Dr Argyll finally makes sense of the extraordinary properties of ball lightning that are the despair of theoreticians who attempt identification of a plausible physical mechanism for it.

'Passage through physical surfaces, such as metal screens, is possible for after-images and is reported for lightning balls. After-images last for 2-10 seconds, and most lightning balls are reported to have a duration in the same range,' he explains, linking the two phenomena.

Unlike lightning balls, after-images generate no sound. But this is no problem for the sceptical scientist. The typical observer finds it easy to imagine 'suitable accompanying sounds'. But what does Dr Argyll make of cases where the lightning ball leaves behind actual physical signs of its presence? He simply rejects the evidence that contradicts his theory. 'If ball lightning is an optical illusion, it would not be unreasonable to categorise these reports as unreliable,' he says.

Yet there can be little doubt that, however imperfect the observations and in spite of the outlandish behaviour of ball lightning, it does occur. No one will deny the existence of after-images, and most of us have experienced them. But how could

Ball lightning,* left, *was seen near St Petersburg, Russia, on 30 July 1888. The spheres moved down the ravine and promptly vanished without a sound.

they possibly explain fireballs that appear to more than one observer, on the same occasion, and that have precisely the same form and travel along the same path?

Inflammable Gas

One early theory suggested that the balls were burning puffs of inflammable gas, released by the impact of lightning on the ground. But if this were so, how could a puff of gas rise to the height of an aeroplane? And could it pass through solid walls, as so many lightning balls reportedly do?

According to one report, a red lightning ball about two feet (60 centimetres) in diameter dug a trench a full 100 yards (91 metres) long and over three feet (one metre) deep in soft soil near a stream, and then literally tore away another 75 feet (23 metres) of the stream bed. To dig this trench, the ball would have had to have an enormous amount of power, and to account for this, it has been suggested that some sort of atomic reaction would have to be involved.

However, ball lightning has been observed by some people at close quarters and does not appear to involve any nuclear effects. A characteristic incident was reported by a housewife after a violent thunderstorm in Staffordshire, England, on 8 August 1975. She was in the kitchen when a flaming sphere of light suddenly appeared over the cooker. It came towards her, making a strange rattling sound and moving too quickly for her to be able to dodge out of the way.

'The ball seemed to hit me below the belt and I automatically brushed it away. Where I had touched it, there was a redness and swelling on my hand. It seemed as if the gold wedding ring was burning into my finger.' The ball exploded with a bang and scorched a small hole in her skirt, but she was otherwise unharmed.

An even more bizarre suggestion is that ball lightning may be due to minute particles of meteoric anti-matter that fall to Earth from the upper atmosphere. It is suggested that thunderstorms act as giant vacuum cleaners that suck up anti-matter dust particles. As the anti-matter then comes into contact with normal matter, it is gradually annihilated, releasing the energy that produces the glowing ball.

Peasants,* below, *were terrified by the ball lightning that appeared at Salagnac, France, in 1845.

A further artist's impression,* bottom, *shows the glowing sphere said, by some, to be an after-image, rather than ball lightning as such.

Yet another theory is that ball lightning is generated by currents flowing from thunder clouds to the ground. By postulating an external energy source for the ball, this theory elegantly accounts for the long life of lightning balls; but unfortunately it does not explain how a ball could enter the metallic skin of an aircraft, in the way that it did with the USAF tanker aircraft, and as witnessed by the crew.

Ball lightning is as much a puzzle today as when it was first reported some 1,500 years ago. In the sixth century, St Gregory of Tours is said to have watched in absolute horror as a fireball of blinding brightness appeared in the air above a procession of religious and civil dignitaries during a ceremony marking the dedication of a chapel. The sight was so terrifying that everyone in the procession immediately threw themselves to the ground. Since there was no reasonable explanation for the ball, he concluded that it was a miracle.

CLUES FROM

THE UNCANNY ABILITY THAT WE CALL CLAIRVOYANCE TAKES MANY FORMS, FROM A VAGUE AWARENESS OF A DISTANT EVENT TO A VIVID REVELATION. THOUGH NOT ALWAYS RELIABLE, CLAIRVOYANCE HAS SOMETIMES PROVIDED STARTLING AND UNEXPECTED CLUES IN CASES OF CRIME

In October 1978, the Los Angeles police called in a local psychic, known simply as Joan, **left,** *to help locate a missing small boy. Convinced that he had been murdered, she provided a description of his killer, on which a police artist based his sketch,* **below left.** *In spite of certain obvious differences, the missing boy's father immediately identified it as a family acquaintance, and 'Butch' Memro,* **bottom,** *was convicted.*

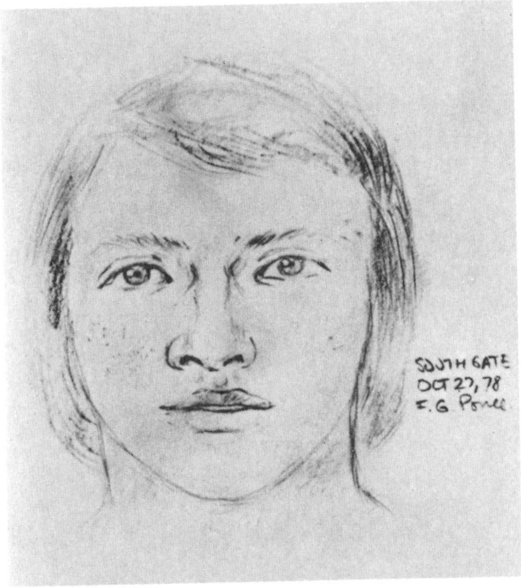

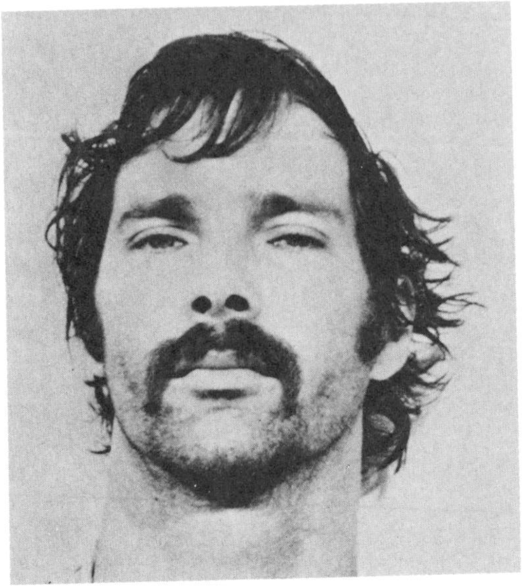

One day in late October 1978, seven-year-old Carl Carter disappeared from his Los Angeles home. The police were baffled: they did not know whether he had been kidnapped, or had simply wandered off and got lost.

It was then that a retired police officer suggested that a local psychic – known only by the name of Joan – might be able to help. Within hours of her involvement, the case had changed from a lost-child investigation to one of triple murder.

The psychic told the police that the boy was dead, and she even described the man she thought was responsible for his murder. Joan tried drawing his portrait, and a police artist was called in to make a more accurate sketch of the suspect, based on her description. When the drawing was shown to Carl's parents, his father said at once: 'That looks like Butch.'

Within the hour, Harold Ray 'Butch' Memro was arrested; and by the end of the day, he had confessed to strangling Carl, and to murdering two other boys two years earlier.

Psychic Sleuths

Psychics often volunteer their services to the police, and there are countless stories of people whose extra-sensory powers have given glimpses of crimes. But all too often the accuracy of their statements cannot be verified until after the criminals have been caught by conventional means. In other words, ESP seldom leads the police directly to a culprit, as appears to have happened in the Memro case.

It has to be remembered that for every impressive case reported in the press, there are probably a hundred or more where volunteered 'psychic' help only leads the police on a wild goose chase. Following the mysterious disappearance of schoolgirl Genette Tate in August 1978, for example, the Devon police received calls from over 200 mediums and others interested in psychic detection who

CLAIRVOYANCE

*In*Focus THE DELPHI METHOD

Named after the ancient oracle at the Greek Temple of Apollo, the Delphi method of researching predictions was developed by two American mathematicians at the Rand Corporation, shortly after World War II.

The procedure involves asking several experts in particular fields to make predictions. These experts are then shown forecasts made by others, as a result of which their own predictions are refined.

Results – particularly in the business field – have been extraordinarily accurate. According to one theory, this is because the method utilises both parts of the brain. At first, when predictions are made, the right intuitive side of the brain is at work. Later revised predictions, after sight of colleagues' forecasts, however, call for logical analysis, as provided by the left side.

In many respects, of course, the Delphi method does not rely on clairvoyance alone. It does, nevertheless, require an all-important element of intuition initially. Indeed, professional psychics – such as Missouri-born Beverly Jaegers – are now sometimes being called in by various large companies to advise on stocks and commodities. According to Jaegers, when the name of a stock is placed in an envelope which feels 'hot' to her when she holds it, the investment is a sure one. Psychic Uri Geller, meanwhile, has used his sixth sense to find oil and minerals for large corporations who have employed him as a dowser.

believed their paranormal powers could produce useful clues.

The definition of clairvoyance is 'extra-sensory knowledge about material objects or events which is not obtained from another person's mind' – in other words, not simple telepathy. It can take many different forms, ranging from a vague awareness of a distant event to a vision in which scenes unfold vividly before the eyes of the clairvoyant. For ordinary people, clairvoyance is most likely to occur in stressful situations or when people or places connected with them are in danger. A well authenticated instance concerns the 18th-century Swedish scientist and seer, Emanuel Swedenborg, who was investigated by the distinguished German philosopher, Immanuel Kant. On one occasion, Swedenborg arrived in Gothenburg from England at around 4 p.m. on a Saturday. Soon he became restless and left his friends to go for a walk.

On his return, he described a vision he had experienced of a fire which, he said, had broken out just three doors away from his home, 300 miles (480 kilometres) away. A fierce blaze was raging, he said, and he continued to be disturbed until 8 p.m. when he announced that the fire had been extinguished. News of this clairvoyant vision spread rapidly through the city and Swedenborg was asked to give a first-hand account to the Governor of Gothenburg. It was not until a royal messenger arrived in Gothenburg on the following Monday that the events of Swedenborg's vision were confirmed.

Pioneer of ESP research, Dr J. Rhine, and his colleagues at Duke University, USA, decided in the 1930s to investigate clairvoyance. They had earlier conducted successful telepathy tests in which one person concentrated on a symbol while someone else, in another room, tried to read his mind. A pack of Zener cards, featuring a number of symbols, was

Dutch clairvoyant Gerard Croiset, seen below, has frequently assisted the police in cases concerning missing persons, including that of Pat McAdam, whose photograph he is holding.

used. The investigators at Duke University decided to see what would happen if, instead of looking at the cards, the agent simply shuffled them and then removed them one at a time from the pack, face down. The subject of the experiment had to use clairvoyance, instead of telepathy, to guess their running order. (The agent could then note down the order of the cards by going through the pack after the experiment.)

In one series of experiments in which J. Pratt was the experimenter and Hubert Pearce the subject, Pearce scored 558 correct responses out of a total of 1850 guesses. If chance alone had been at work, he should have scored only 370 correct answers. On this basis, the odds against Pearce's score were calculated as being as unlikely as 22,000 million to one.

Not everyone is impressed with laboratory results, however; and one criticism that has been levelled at the Pearce-Pratt experiments is that Pearce was unsupervised while making his guesses. Professor C.E.M. Hansel, a non-believer in ESP, has argued that, under the circumstances, the

results cannot be taken seriously. It was possible, after all, for Pearce to have sneaked out of the building after the experiment and to have peered through the window of Dr Pratt's room in order to see the cards he was turning over. He could have noted them down or memorised them, and then dashed back to his room to compile a running order with enough mistakes to make it look genuine. But another psychical researcher, Professor Ian Stevenson, has subsequently investigated the theory and has asserted that it would have been physically impossible for Pearce to have cheated in this way, since the cards would not have been visible through the window.

Even where the methodology of clairvoyant research is beyond criticism, however, the statistical nature of the results often leaves many people unimpressed. For them, individual cases of spectacular clairvoyance are far more impressive than repeated card-guessing tests that produce staggering, above-average results.

The clairvoyance of Polish engineer Stephan Ossowiecki attracted the attention of top psychical researchers in the early 1900s. Holding a sealed envelope or a folded piece of paper, he could often describe in detail its contents or even give the name of the signatory.

During an international conference on psychical research held in Warsaw in 1923, Ossowiecki's powers were actually put to the test. An English investigator, Dr Eric Dingwall, sketched a flag with a bottle etched in its upper left-hand corner. He then wrote the date, 22 August 1923, beneath his drawing and sealed it in a package comprising three envelopes, one within the next. Dingwall sent the package from England to Baron Albert von

Important research was carried out at Duke University, USA,* top, *during the 1930s. The experiments used Zener cards as targets. The agent, Dr Pratt,* above left, *sat in either room A or room B, and withdrew cards one at a time, face down, while the subject, Hubert Pearce,* above right, *sat in room C and tried to name the cards as they were drawn. He was spectacularly successful, the odds against his results being 22,000 million to one.

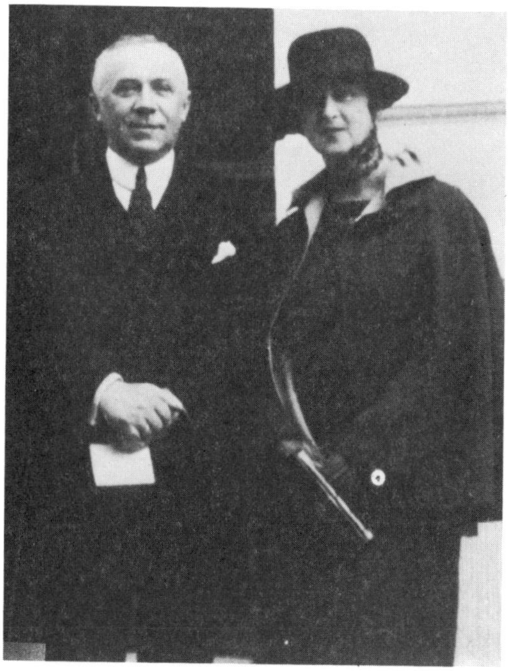

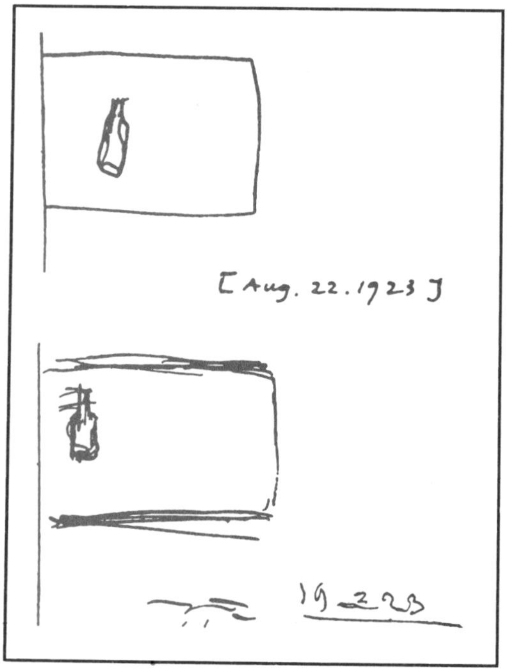

Polish engineer Stephan Ossowiecki, pictured* far left, *with his wife, had extraordinary clairvoyant powers. In one experiment, an English investigator sketched a flag with a bottle on it, wrote the date beneath it, and sent the drawing in a sealed package to a noted Polish psychic researcher, Baron von Schrenck-Notzing,* below, *in Warsaw. The Baron handed the sealed envelope to Ossowiecki and asked him for his impressions. Ossowiecki immediately realised that the Baron had not written the message. Then he suddenly grabbed a pen and agitatedly began to draw what he 'saw' inside the envelope. The drawing,* left, *was startlingly similar to the original, shown* above *it.

"For ordinary people clairvoyance is most likely to occur in stressful situations or when people or places connected with them are in danger."

Schrenck-Notzing in Warsaw. Baron von Schrenck-Notzing was a well-known pathologist of the day, and also a noted psychic investigator. Neither the Baron, nor the two other researchers involved in the experiment knew what was inside the envelope. They simply gave it to Ossowiecki without explanation and asked for his impressions.

The Polish clairvoyant told them at once that the Baron had not written the message: and that there were several envelopes, something greenish – cardboard – and a little bottle. Then he grabbed a pen and, in an agitated manner, drew an almost identical replica of the target. He also wrote '1923' and said something was written before it, but he was unable to say what this was. The test left Dingwall and the other researchers in no doubt that Ossowiecki had paranormal powers.

Second Sight

The ability to pick up impressions from objects was investigated as early as 1949 by J. Rhodes Buchanan, a physician in Ohio, USA. He found that some people he tested were able, for example, to identify medicines hidden in sealed envelopes or to give accurate descriptions of the writers of letters. He then went on to coin the word *psychometry* – which means, in Greek, 'measure of the soul' – to describe this ability.

One of the most detailed studies of clairvoyance and psychometry was carried out by a German physician, Dr Gustav Pagenstecher, who practised medicine in Mexico for 40 years. One day, a certain Maria Reyes Zierold consulted Dr Pagenstecher, complaining of insomnia. He decided to treat her by hypnosis. While in trance, she told him she could see his daughter listening at the door. To his great surprise, when he opened the door, the child was there, just as the patient had claimed. With her permission, he then set about investigating Maria Zierold's paranormal vision and soon discovered that, if an object was put in her hand while she was in trance, astonishingly, she was able to give a vivid description of events connected with it.

Once, for example, she was handed a piece of string. Immediately, she began describing a battlefield on a cold, foggy day, with groups of men and continuous rifle fire. 'Quite of a sudden,' she said, 'I see coming through the air and moving with great rapidity a big ball of fire...which drops just in the middle of the 15 men, tearing them to pieces.' The string, it transpired, had originally been attached to a German soldier's dog tag. The psychic had reported with startling accuracy a scene that the man described as 'the first great impression I received of the war'.

In an attempt to discover whether some element of telepathy was involved, or whether Maria Zierold was a genuine clairvoyant, the American Society for Psychical Research sent its research officer, Walter Prince, to conduct tests. One experiment he carried out involved two identical pieces of silk ribbon, enclosed in identical boxes. He mixed them up so that even he did not know which was which. Holding one box, Señora Zierold described a Mexican church and dancing Indians. The other gave her impressions of a French ribbon factory. She was absolutely right: one piece had come direct from the manufacturers, the other from a church altar.

With many outstanding cases of clairvoyance on record, it is not surprising to find possessors of these abilities being consulted in particularly baffling crime cases. The one consolation for criminals is that only a few outstanding clairvoyants are as spectacularly successful or as reliable as Ossowiecki or Zierold.

Lightning,* left, *strikes the surface of the sea. According to one theory, primitive life forms may first have come about after lightning had fused together elements of the Earth's atmosphere to create the potential for life. The fern-like crystals,* above, *are of the amino acid tryptophan, one of the basic building blocks of life.

THE MIRACLE OF LIFE

ESTABLISHED SCIENCE HOLDS THAT LIFE CAME ABOUT BY ACCIDENT AND CAN BE EXPLAINED ENTIRELY BY THE LAWS OF PHYSICS AND BIOLOGY. BUT THERE IS ANOTHER, MORE EXCITING POSSIBILITY. COULD LIFE BE A FORCE INDEPENDENT OF MATTER, WHICH SOMEHOW CONTROLS MECHANICAL PROCESSES FOR A PURPOSE OF ITS OWN?

According to the theories of modern astronomy, our Universe began about 10 billion years ago with a tremendous explosion. After a billion or so years, great clouds of steamy gas formed into galaxies, and eventually the whirls and eddies in this spinning gas contracted into stars. Until this point, there had been nothing in the Universe but the two 'simplest' gases – hydrogen and helium. But as the stars contracted, the pressure became great enough to crush together these simple atoms to form carbon – the basic building block of life.

But life cannot exist without various heavy elements, such as iron, phosphorus and sulphur, and these were also locked up in the cores of gigantic stars. Billions more years had to pass, until the original stars grew old, gave off most of their energy in the form of radiation, then collapsing and

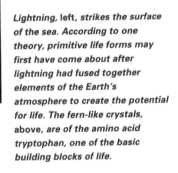

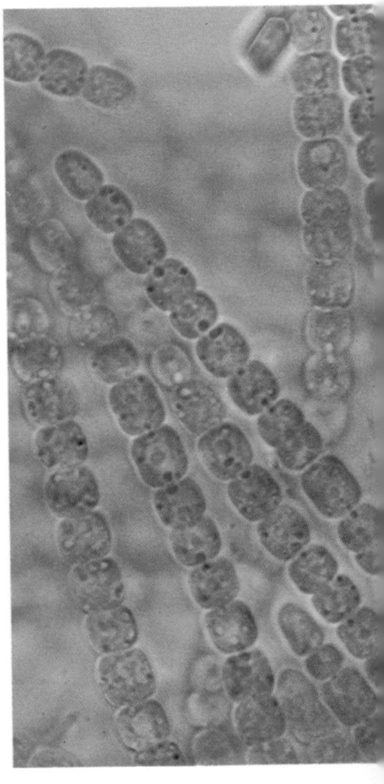

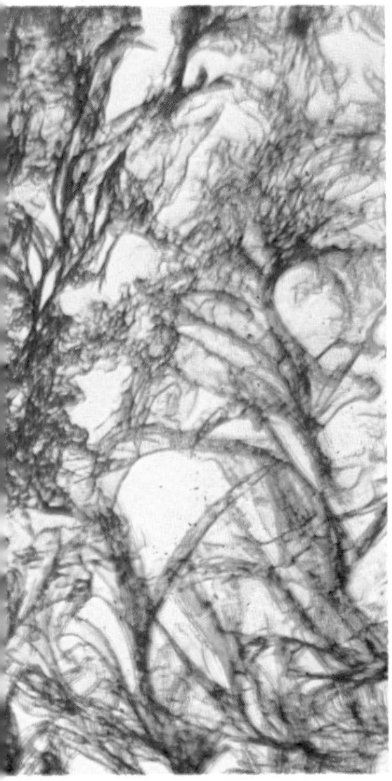

The 'mechanical' argument for evolution runs into difficulties when faced with primitive organisms like the amoeba, **right,** magnified 500 times and the blue-green alga, **below,** magnified 180 times. No one knows how the simple cell of the alga could evolve into the complex nuclear cell of the amoeba.

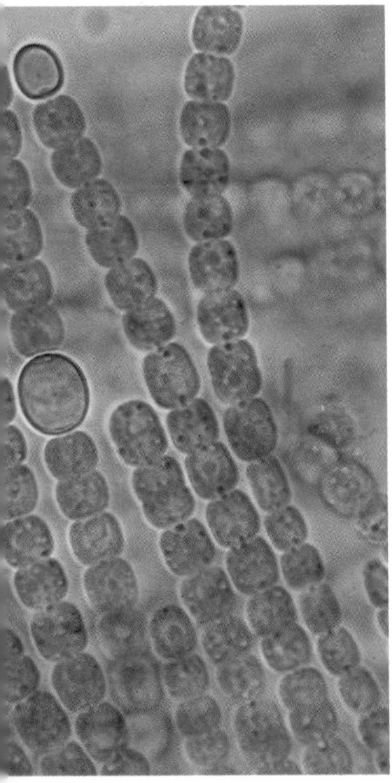

exploding, before the essential elements finally began to float free.

The usual account is that the various elements – carbon, nitrogen, phosphorus, oxygen, hydrogen, iron – somehow came together in the great witches' cauldron of our cooling planet, were fused by lightning, and formed complex molecules called amino acids, the basic constituents of all living organisms. But in 1963, astronomers discovered molecules of combined oxygen and hydrogen out in deep space: science calls them 'hydroxy groups'. A few years later, radio astronomers also discovered water, ammonia, formaldehyde and methyl alcohol in space. No one is quite sure how these atoms came to be formed, but they could have come into existence in outer space and been brought to Earth by comets, as astronomer Fred Hoyle argued.

And now we come to the more difficult and controversial part of the story. How did this dead matter actually turn into life? The standard account is that the organic molecules found their way into the oceans and, over millions of years, accidental collisions formed every conceivable shape and size of molecule. Finally, a molecule was formed that had the amazing power to reproduce itself.

But there are problems with this explanation. Life begins with 'protein chains', each made up of many amino acids, with 20 possibilities for each link in the chain. In his book *Human Destiny,* the French biophysicist Lecomte de Noüy pointed out that, even if a new combination were tried every millionth of a second, it would still take longer than the lifetime of our Earth to form a chain associated with life – the odds against this being a one followed by 95 zeros.

In 1953, the American scientist Stanley Miller conducted an experiment in which electrical discharges – artificial lightning – were passed through a mixture of water, ammonia, methane and hydrogen, substances believed to have formed the primitive atmosphere of the Earth. At the end of a day, the mixture turned pink; and at the end of a week, Dr Miller found that two of the simplest amino acids had been formed. Latest findings also suggest that the early atmosphere of the Earth was in fact made up of carbon dioxide and water vapour. But, when Dr Miller's experiments were repeated using carbon dioxide and water, similar results were obtained – again, simple amino acids were formed.

Alternative Theory Of Life

It seems that in the Earth's primitive atmosphere, lightning and chance could together have produced the building blocks of life. But this still leaves unanswered Lecomte de Noüy's objection that it would take thousands of billions of years for these acids to form a protein chain. Still, scientists can take comfort from the notion that there seem to be 'natural laws' that favour the formation of living cells.

An alternative theory about life has been in existence for more than two centuries. It was conceived one day in 1762, when an Italian professor of anatomy named Luigi Galvani was studying amputated frogs' legs on a bench in his laboratory. (Legend has it that they were waiting to be made into soup!) On a nearby bench, someone was turning the handle of an electrical machine. Galvani happened to touch one of the frogs' legs with a metal scalpel; and, to his surprise, it 'kicked'. What had happened, it seemed, was that the electric sparks caused a 'wave' of electricity which was picked up by the scalpel. This, in turn, transmitted it to a nerve, which behaved just as if the frog's brain had ordered the leg to move. The implication was that the brain gives its orders by electrical telegraph. In fact, Galvani's observation led to the discovery that human beings are, in one sense, electrical machines; every time we think, the brain discharges electric currents.

Blueprints

Late last century, a young German biologist, Hans Driesch, tried an experiment with the fertilised egg of a sea urchin. He waited until it divided, and then killed off one half with a hot needle. To his surprise, the surviving half did not turn into 'half' a sea urchin; it developed into a perfect but smaller embryo of a whole sea urchin. Clearly, each half of the egg contained a 'blueprint' of the whole.

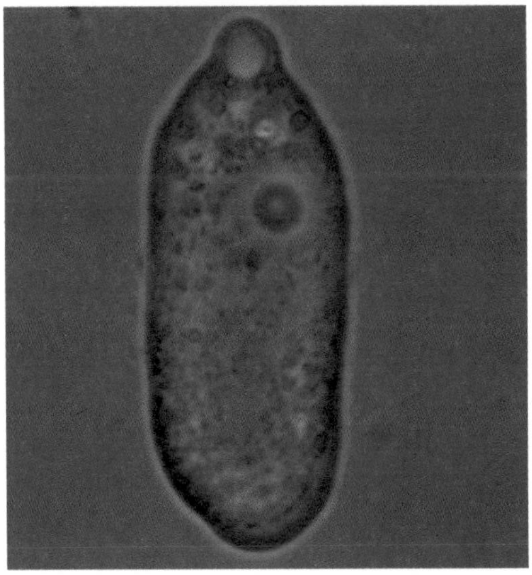

He also tried pressing two eggs together; they fused and then developed into a larger than normal embryo.

Driesch argued, sensibly, that organisms can only be understood as living wholes, not as machines made up of bits and pieces. That, today, sounds unexceptionable. What upset Driesch's contemporaries was that he went on to suggest that if organisms had a purpose, then the 'purpose' must be quite separate from their 'mechanical' parts – the biological bits and pieces, so to speak. In other words, the life in a living creature is something quite separate from its chemistry. Driesch's scientific contemporaries were indignant. They growled 'vitalist' or 'mystic', and ignored him.

Still, not all scientists were obsessed by the idea of explaining nature in purely mechanistic terms. Across the Atlantic, another professor of anatomy, Harold Saxton Burr of Yale University, was deeply interested in Driesch's ideas – particularly in the notion that cells contain a 'blueprint'. The first thing he wanted to examine was the electrical forces that seem to set the whole thing in motion. The problem, of course, is that these currents are so tiny that they are very difficult to measure. Burr was not discouraged, however: together with a colleague,

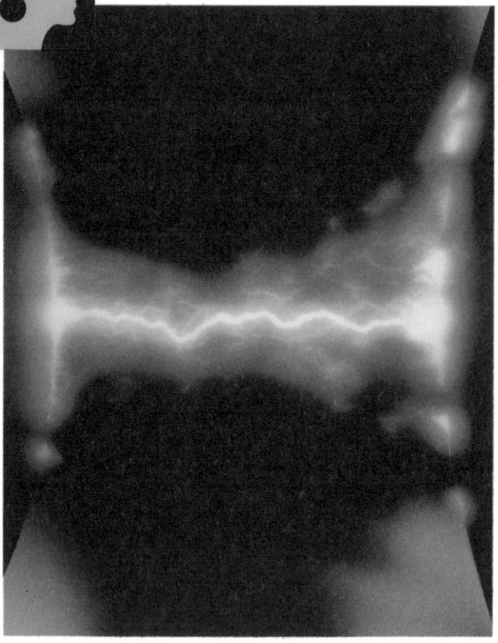

F.S.C Northrop, he developed methods of attaching a voltmeter to trees – and other living organisms – and kept a continuous record of their voltages.

The trees showed a regular seasonal variation in voltage, which also varied with sunspot activity and phases of the Moon. When the voltmeter was attached to a rabbit's ovary, it showed a sudden jump in voltage as the follicle ruptured, releasing the egg. It was discovered that this technique could be used to help women who were having difficulty becoming pregnant. When the voltmeter was attached to mental patients, it also showed quite clearly who were the most 'disturbed'. It could record, too, the ups and downs in physical illness, and even detect cancer at an early stage.

Fields Of Life

Burr's experiments confirmed him in his conclusion that all living organisms are influenced by their electric fields. He called them L-fields (life-fields) for short. If a salamander embryo is placed in an alkaline solution, its individual cells 'disaggregate', or separate; but if these are then placed back in a slightly acid solution, they come together again and re-form into an embryo. Burr compared this to what happens when a magnet is held underneath iron filings on a sheet of paper – they form into a pattern. And he concluded that the 'blueprint' of life is contained in the L-field, which causes the cells to come together into a certain shape. A frog's egg shows various lines of electrical force; and when it develops into a tadpole, these lines turn out to be its nervous system. The electric field seems to be a kind of jelly-mould into which the living matter is poured.

In the late 1930s, a Russian professor, Semyon Kirlian, made a discovery that seems to support Burr's theory. When living matter – anything from a human hand to a leaf – was photographed, it showed sparks flowing from the stem. It certainly looked very much as if Professor Kirlian had succeeded in photographing the L-field – although sceptical scientists continue to insist that this is just a freak effect due to irregularities in the high-voltage current. Perhaps the most exciting of Kirlian's experiments involved a torn leaf; the photograph appeared to show the missing portion of the leaf in dim outline. Unlike Burr's experiments, those of Kirlian are still a matter of violent disagreement among scientists; but many respected experimenters are now convinced that Kirlian indeed discovered how to photograph the 'fields of life', that shows up as an aura.

Of course, all this does not prove Driesch's theories. It only proves his assertion that life seems to aim at 'wholeness'. And the controversial word here is 'aim'. Scientists do not like works implying purpose: they prefer to believe that life 'aims' at wholeness in the same sense that a snowflake 'aims' at getting to the ground. But new discoveries are continually upsetting their old mechanistic models.

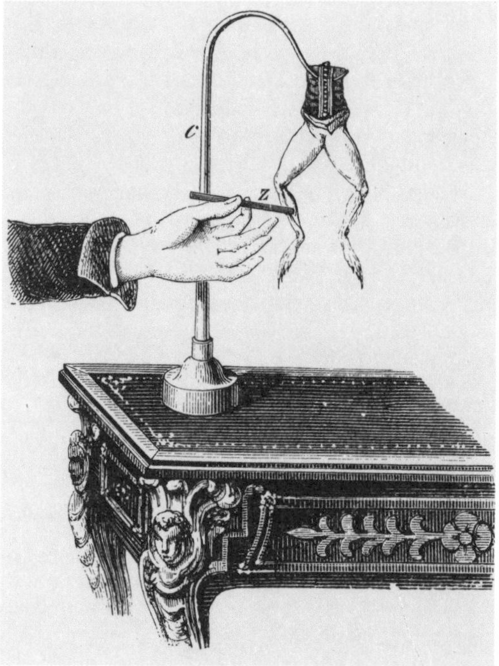

Electrical discharge – as created, above left, in the laboratory between two metal objects – is believed by some to have contributed towards the building blocks of life in the form of lightning. Experiments on frogs' legs, left, conducted by 18th-century scientist Luigi Galvani, further showed that the brain gives its orders by electrical impulses.

Semyon Kirlian, above, the Russian scientist, discovered how to photograph the electrical or life-fields surrounding all objects, as the Kirlian photograph of a human outer ear, below, shows.

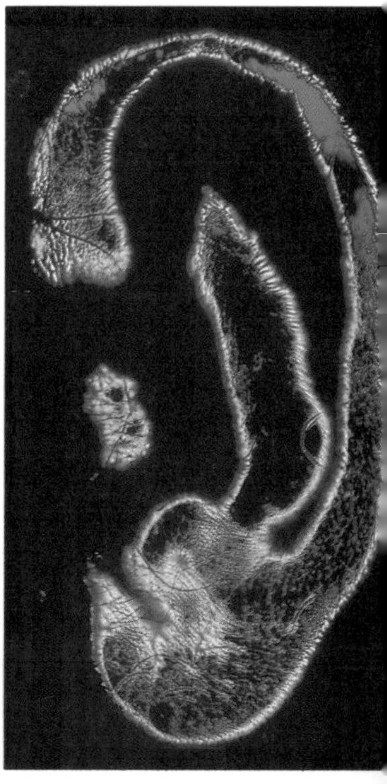

An odd kind of 'freedom' was demonstrated, for example, in experiments conducted at the University of Wisconsin in the mid-1970s by Daniel Perlman and Robert Stickgold. They grew bacteria in a solution containing an antibiotic that would normally destroy it. The bacteria used has a gene that can produce an enzyme to destroy the antibiotic, so it can, in fact, survive. But according to the mechanistic view, it should do this by 'switching on' its defence system, then switching it off when the danger has passed. In fact, the bacteria reacted by making vast numbers of copies of the protective gene – as if the bacteria had decided to choose a more reliable defence policy.

Professor C.H. Waddington made a suggestion that comes very close to Burr's 'vital blueprint' – that life may be a matter of rhythms and vibrations, like the patterns that develop on a glass plate strewn with sand if your stroke it with a violin bow. He even suggests that life may develop like a musical composition – as an ordered series of vibrations. (Cancer is a disease of disorganisation.)

At the moment, all these exciting ideas are very much in the melting pot: the slag has not settled to the bottom and the scum has not floated to the top. Yet the suggestion that is beginning to emerge is

> **"** IF LIFE AND MATTER SOMEHOW EXIST SEPARATELY, THIS MEANS IN EFFECT THAT LIFE – OR MIND – COULD OVERRULE THE LAWS OF NATURE. THERE IS A NAME FOR THIS BELIEF: IT IS MAGIC. **"**

clear enough. Perhaps life, after all, is not just a 'product' of matter, as heat is a product of fire; perhaps it is an organising principle beyond matter. In other words, once chance and the laws of nature had formed the basic building blocks – the amino acids – life intervened to organise them into more complex forms.

This view is known as vitalism, and most respectable biologists would shudder and turn away at the very idea. Bernard Shaw, however, expressed this view well when he said that life permeates the Universe, and is striving to gain a foothold in matter. The philosopher T.E. Hulme even believed that the process of evolution can be described as the insertion of more and more freedom into matter – so that amoebas could be regarded as a small 'leak' of freedom, while man is a larger leak.

Astonishing Consequences

Here we come to the heart of the matter. Science does not recognise the word 'freedom'. Science deals with mechanical procedures. If you say that you have done something of your own free will, the scientist can produce a thousand reasons to prove that you had to do it, as a river has to flow downhill. If you reply that you can decide whether to contradict him or not, or whether to go off and do something more rewarding, he will tell you that your freedom of thought is also an illusion. If you decline to accept this, then you are opting for the view that life – or freedom – somehow stands above matter and mechanism.

If this heretical notion is true, the consequences for science are astonishing. If life is a mere product of matter – as heat is of burning – then life is a slave of matter. But if it somehow exists separately, then it is potentially the master. This means, in effect, that life (or mind) could overrule the laws of nature. And there is a name for this belief: it is *magic*.

This is the question with which science will one day have to come to terms: whether the Universe is basically 'magical'. Some scientists are willing to concede that it probably is. For example, cybernetician David Foster has made a study of the 'programming' of DNA, which carries the genetic coding of human beings, and has concluded that Darwinian biology is probably mistaken. Cybernetics is the study of systems of control – like a thermostat, which switches off the heat when the room gets above a certain temperature. One of the basic laws of cybernetics says that a man who devises such a system must always be more intelligent than the system itself; in other words, a programmer must always be more intelligent than the system he programmes, no matter how high the 'artificial intelligence' of that system.

Now, a gene is, in fact, a programme; and it is Foster's contention that the complexity of our genetic programming indicates higher energies and higher intelligences than anything we can find on Earth. This suggests very definitely that Man is not the highest intelligence in the Universe. There must, says Foster, be higher intelligences 'out there'. Indeed, perhaps the universe itself is one vast intelligence.

When we move into these realms, we come alarmingly close to certain questions that are ignored by the majority of scientists – questions, for example, about the 'paranormal', about UFOs, about other dimensions of space and time. At the beginning of his book *Lifetide,* the zoologist Lyall Watson claims that he watched a small girl stroke a tennis ball, and – incredibly – saw the ball turn itself inside out, without breaking its surface. This may seem impossible. But in a universe with even one extra dimension of reality, it could be as commonplace as turning a glove inside out. And if life is not a product of matter, but somehow exists 'beyond' it, our Universe does have that magical level, and cannot be described in purely physical terms.

***The computer graphic image,* below, *shows the double helix of DNA, which carries the genetic code of living beings. One theory concerning the origin of life holds that the complexity of our genetic programming must indicate higher intelligences than anything on Earth. Astrophysicist Fred Hoyle, however, put forward the theory that atoms may first have come into existence in outer space and then been brought to Earth by comets, such as the one* inset.**

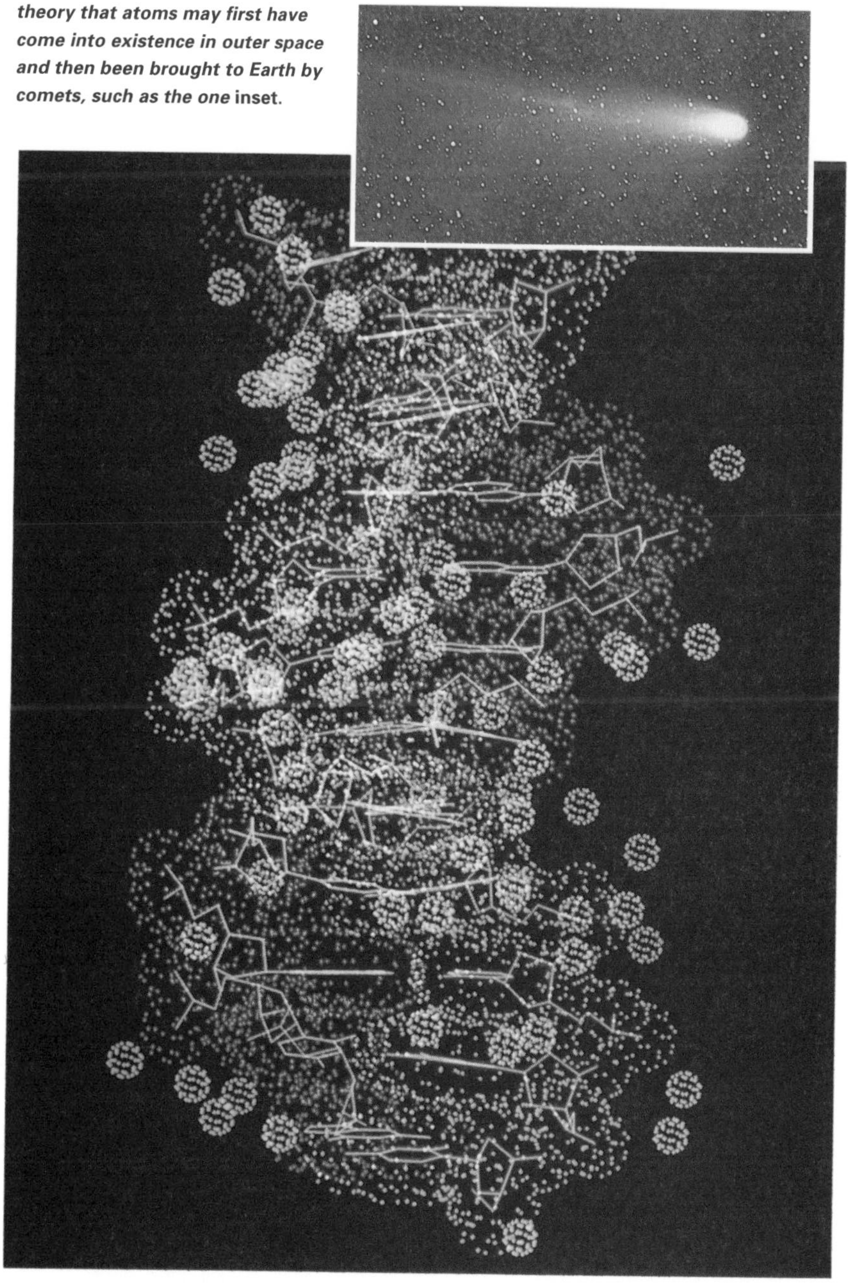

SILENTLY, OUT OF THE NIGHT SKY

SCIENTISTS GENERALLY CONSIDER UFOS THAT GIVE RESPONSES ON RADAR SCOPES THE MOST RELIABLE FOR THEIR PURPOSES. THE SIGHTING DESCRIBED BELOW TOOK PLACE AT CASELLE AIRPORT IN TURIN, ITALY, AND IS ONE OF THE MOST WELL DOCUMENTED RADAR-VISUAL SIGHTINGS ON RECORD

In all, it lasted for five months in the winter of 1973 to 1974. It was heralded by a first impressive sighting at Turin in November 1973 – an event of profound significance for the science of ufology that attracted the attention of Jean-Claude Bourret, a top reporter from the French radio station *France-Inter*, who broadcast a series of programmes about UFOs, culminating in a startling and important interview with the then Minister of Defence, Robert Galley.

On 30 November 1973, Riccardo Marano was preparing to land his Piper Navajo at Caselle Airport when he was advised by control that there was an unidentified object at a height of about 4,000 feet (1,200 metres) above the runway, close to where he was due to land. Control had the object on its radar screens and gave Marano permission to approach it to see what it was. As he neared his target, control reported that it was heading for the Susa Valley. Accordingly, Marano changed course to follow it, when suddenly control announced that the target had disappeared from its radar.

At that moment, Marano received a message from another aircraft; the UFO was behind him at about 12,000 feet (3,600 metres). Marano's Navajo was then flying at about 10,000 feet (3,000 metres). He began to turn, and saw in front of him what appeared to be a bright, white luminous sphere, which was emitting light of all colours of the spectrum. The light pulsated from bright to dim, but never went out completely. As he approached the UFO, Marano reported that it was 'flying in a most irregular fashion, making fantastic lateral deviations and sudden vast jumps to and fro'. Taking advantage of a moment when the object was below him, Marano put his plane into a dive, accelerating to a speed of over 250 mph (400 km/h), but he could not catch up with the UFO. When he abandoned the chase, it was heading south-eastwards. He estimated its speed at about 550 mph (900 km/h).

The artist's impressions, **below and opposite,** *show the luminous spheres witnessed at Caselle Airport, Turin in 1973 from the aircraft,* **above right.**

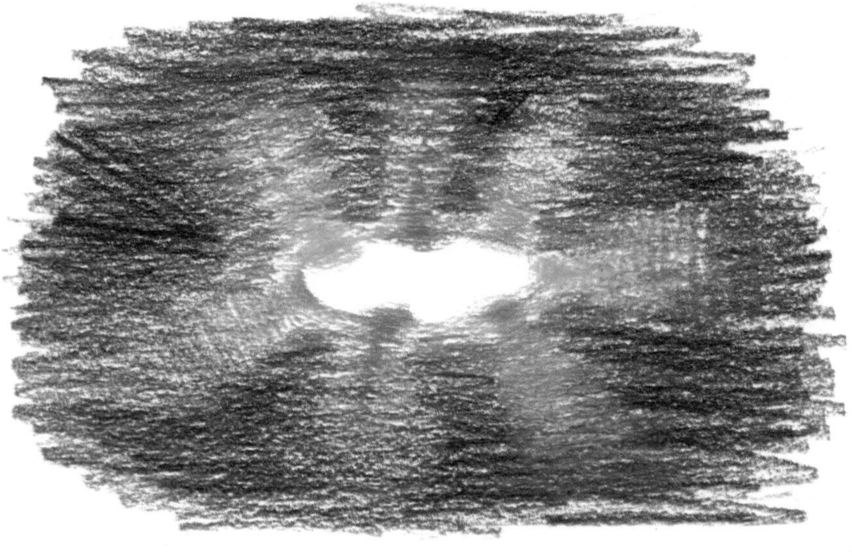

SIGHTING CONFIRMED

Two other pilots confirmed the presence of the object. They were Comandante Tranquillo, who had just taken off in his Alitalia DC-9, and Comandante Mezzalani, who was bringing in his Alitalia DC-9 from Paris. Comandante Tranquillo advised control that he dared not approach the 'shining object giving out flashes' and thereupon adjusted his course.

Comandante Mezzalani observed the object as he was touching down. He said it was large and bright, yet somehow dimmer than a star or an artificial satellite.

There was another very reliable witness, too – none other than the commander of the neighbouring Caselle military airfield, Colonello Rustichelli, who stated that he had observed the UFO on his radar screen. It was, he said, something solid, which lit up like an aircraft on his radar screen, giving the

"COMANDANTE TRANQUILLO ADVISED CONTROL THAT HE DARED NOT APPROACH THE SHINING OBJECT GIVING OUT FLASHES AND THEREUPON ADJUSTED HIS COURSE."

same sort of return as a DC-9. He said that it had looked like a star; but when he got it on his radar, it stayed firm. Soon afterwards, it had headed off westwards.

A curious event, which may be connected with the UFO sightings described above, had taken place earlier on the same evening. At 5.00 p.m., Franco Contin, an amateur photographer, saw an extremely bright object in the sky. At first he thought it was a star; but when he saw it begin to move about, he realised it must be something else. A slightly misshapen luminous globe, it was white at first and then suddenly turned deep orange. Contin fetched his camera and took a total of eight photographs. These show an enormous object, oval in shape and brightly luminous.

Radio Coverage

The Turin sighting was remarkable not only because it was followed by a world-wide wave of UFO reports, but also because it attracted the attention of two very important people. The first of these was Jean-Claude Bourret, chief reporter of the radio station *France-Inter,* who was so impressed by the report of the sighting that he made a series of 39 radio programmes entirely devoted to UFO research, which were broadcast between January 1973 and March 1974.

Robert Galley, then French Minister of Defence, is seen* below *in his historic interview with reporter Jean-Claude Bourret of the French radio station* France-Inter *on 21 February 1974. Galley admitted that the French government had been secretly studying UFOs for 20 years.

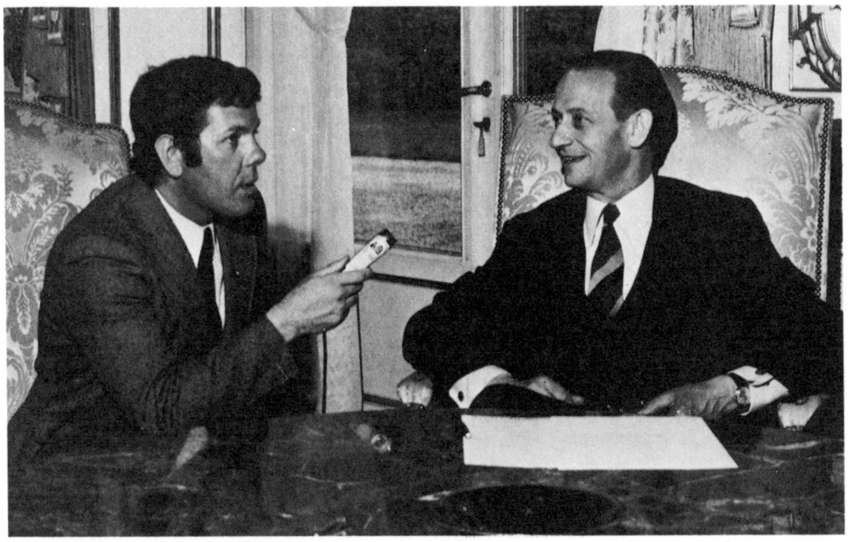

The other person whose interest was aroused by the Turin incident was Robert Galley, Minister of Defence for France, who granted an exclusive interview to Bourret, broadcast to the nation on 21 February 1974.

Secret Section

This interview was of immense importance for the science of ufology. In it, the serving Minister of Defence admitted not only that UFOs exist, but also that in 1954 his government had set up a secret section devoted to their study. Galley spoke of the massive nature of the UFO phenomena, of the many detailed eyewitness reports he had read, and of the volume of reports received from the Air Force in the early days of the project. Since 1970, UFO research in France has been in the hands of the *Centre Nationale d'Etudes Spatiales* (The National Centre for Space Studies), which evaluates reports of UFO sightings from both the Air Force and the Gendarmerie. Unfortunately, however, the French UFO group has no contact with international military groups.

This startling interview was immediately given wide coverage in the French papers, including *France-Soir, Le Parisien Libéré, L'Aurore* and *Le Figaro,* as well as all the big provincial papers. It was soon reported in German, Spanish, Swiss, Italian, Brazilian and American newspapers, too, but not in the British press, nor on radio or television. In his English translation of Jean-Claude Bourret's book *The Crack in the Universe,* Gordon Creighton describes his unsuccessful attempts to convince the BBC that the interview was important enough to warrant a mention on one of its radio science programmes. He even suggests that the scant and biased reporting of the UFO phenomena by the British media may be the result of an official debunking attitude on the part of the authorities. Their methods are certainly different from those used in the USA.

Indeed, Creighton says: 'Quieter and more subtle techniques of ridicule and denigration plus, no doubt, the occasional discreet telephone call to the newspaper that has offended by printing a serious looking UFO report, have yielded far better results than the CIA's methods.'

This scepticism on the part of the authorities no doubt accounts for the fact that very little serious scientific research is carried out into UFOs in Britain. Amateur UFO societies can do little more than monitor sightings. Suppression of information can only be harmful to research, and it is disturbing to think there may be many UFO sightings we simply never hear about.

UFO PHOTO FILE

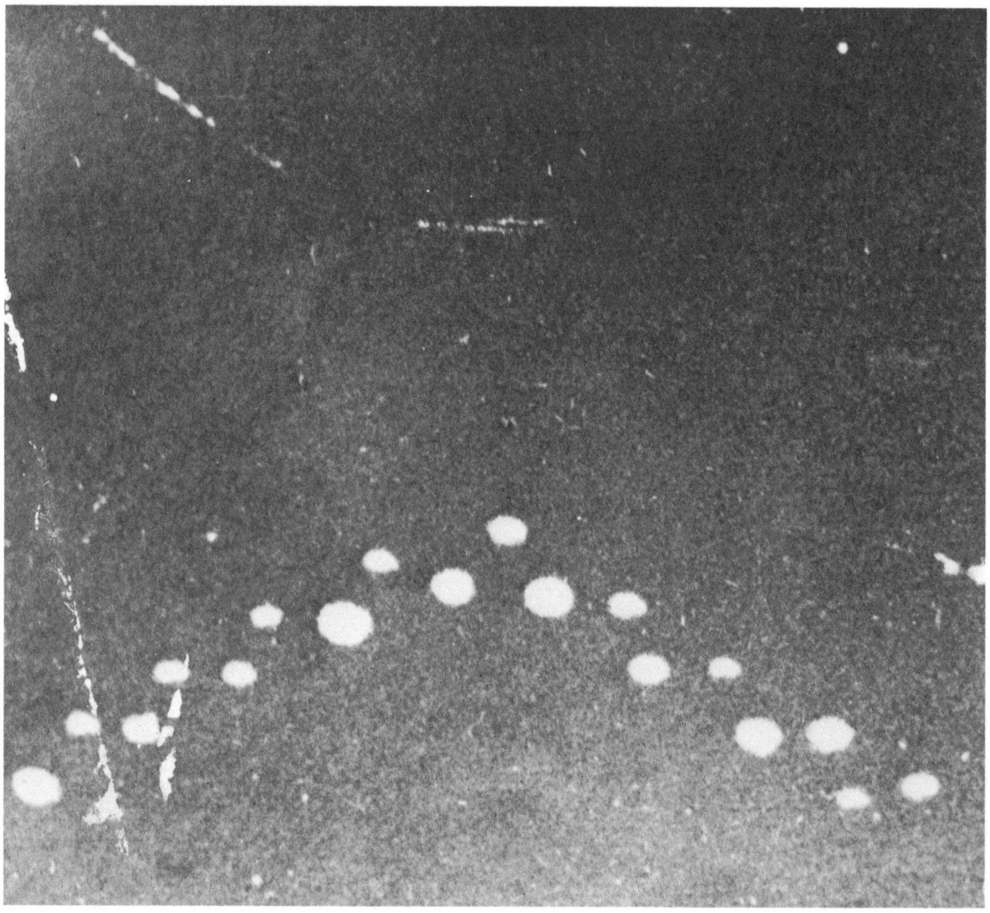

The impressive photograph, **above,** was taken during the Gemini XII space mission on 12 November 1966. Analysis has shown that the UFO on the right of the picture is a distant object; but the NASA Photo Evaluation Lab claimed this was actually rubbish discarded from the Gemini XII spacecraft itself.

At about 9.10 p.m. on 25 August 1951, a group of five professors and a post-graduate student were relaxing outside the house of Professor W.I. Robinson in Lubbock, Texas. Suddenly they saw a formation of bright lights flying rapidly across the sky. The professors estimated their speed at around 1,800 miles per hour (2,900 km/h) at a height of about one mile (1.5 kilometres). Sceptics, however, claim that the lights were nothing more than reflections from the bellies of flying ducks; but if so, they would have been flying at more than 125 miles per hour (200 km/h) – surely a world record for ducks!

The UFO **below** was observed by three witnesses near Saas Fee, Switzerland, on 26 July 1975. It seemed to be metallic and was difficult to make out against the mountain fog. It was also reported to be humming softly.

The photograph has been rigorously analysed by the American UFO organisation Ground Saucer Watch of Phoenix, Arizona. The techniques they use can reveal a number of details not immediately apparent from a photograph, including the time, to within an hour, at which the shot was taken, the apparent size of the UFO, its distance from the camera, and any supporting threads or structures that may indicate a hoax.

The black-and-white picture, **right,** shows a computer digital image enhancement of the original. It passed the test.

The photograph, **below,** also passed GSW's computer test. It was taken by Deputy Sheriff Strauch while on a hunting trip in Gibbon, Minnesota, USA on 21 October 1965. It shows a typical UFO – a bright, blurred, disc-shaped light – and illustrates the difficulty of taking accurate colour pictures of UFOs in poor light conditions. The strange colour of the sky makes it possible to deduce that the original object was probably a shade of red, another feature that links it with other UFO sightings.

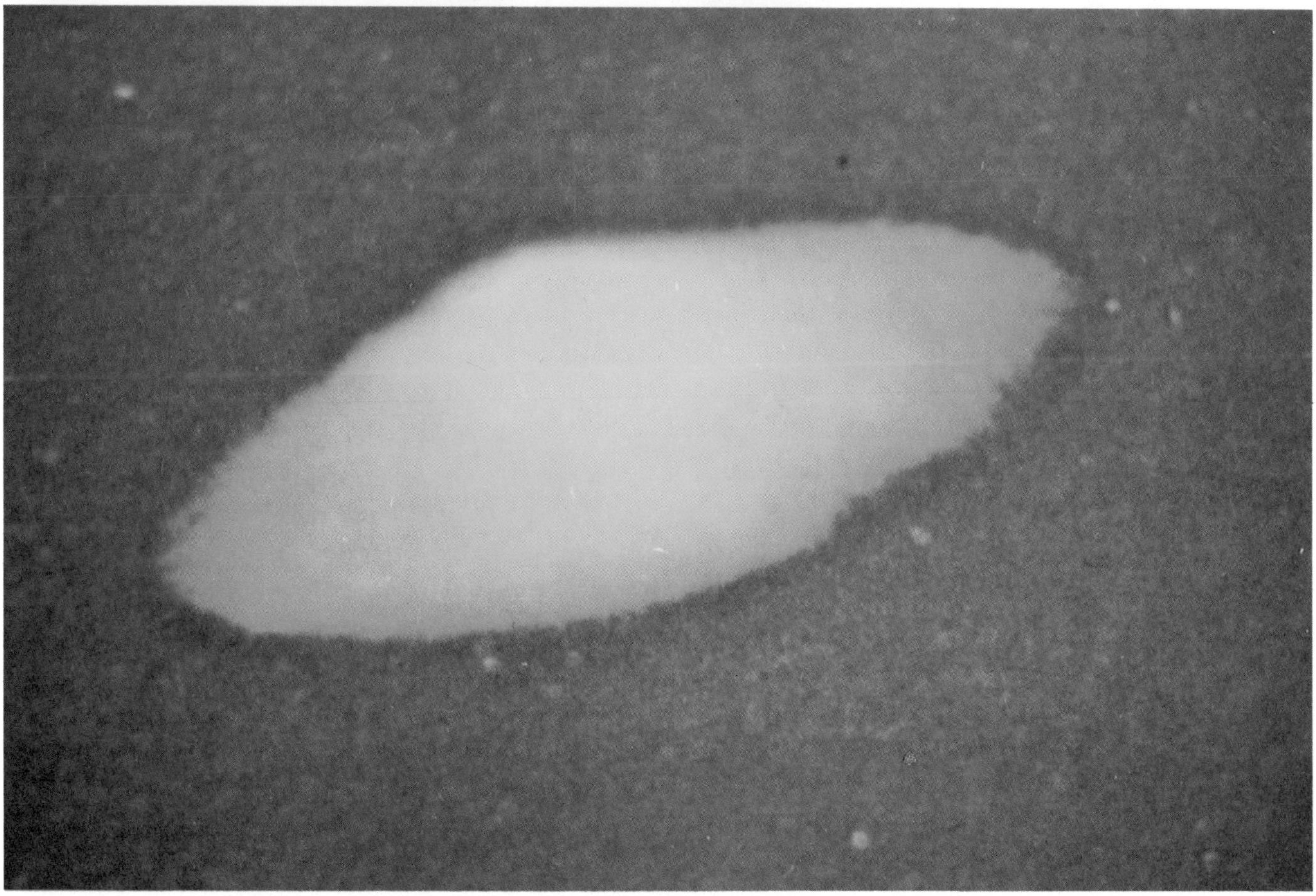

PICTURES FROM BEYOND THE GRAVE

DOES ARTISTIC GENIUS DIE WITH THE ARTIST – OR COULD IT POSSIBLY SURVIVE, TO FIND EXPRESSION THROUGH THE HANDS OF LIVING PSYCHICS?

Pablo Picasso, who died in April 1973, produced several drawings in both pen-and-ink and colour, three months afterwards – through British psychic Matthew Manning. While concentrating, Manning found his hand being controlled with an assertive force, apparently by the spirit of the great master. He had specifically asked Picasso to produce a drawing for him.

Psychic art presents many of the same questions to the psychical researcher that are posed by the prize-winning psychic literature of Patience Worth or Beethoven's 1980 symphony. Is the painting, poetry or music, believed by many to be evidence of the artist's survival beyond the grave, merely an exhibition of the medium's own repressed creativity, finally finding expression? Or is it really as simple as the psychics would have us

The style of the work* above left *is unmistakably Aubrey Beardsley's, but the pen-and-ink drawing was actually produced through the hands of English psychic Matthew Manning.

The posthumous Picasso,* above, *was also painted by Matthew Manning, who remarked on the 'energy and impatience' of the artist. Picasso is one of the few artists who 'chose' to use colour when working through Manning.

A Manning-Monet is shown,* above right. *The style certainly seems to be consistent with that of the great French impressionist.

The drawing,* right, *of a hanged man, is by Leonardo da Vinci. Manning once found himself drawing something very similar but suddenly felt physically ill and wanted to stop the drawing.

believe – that the world's great musicians, writers and artists are 'proving' their continued existence by carrying on their arts through selected 'sensitives'?

Some examples of psychic art are highly impressive, both in their own right and, more significantly, as examples of the styles of the great painters. Some collections of psychic art are also impressive in their diversity of style and sheer quantity.

It was Matthew Manning's enormous collection of sketches and paintings, seemingly produced psychically by him as a teenager in the early 1970s, that utterly convinced his publisher that he was a very special young man, particularly as Manning claims to have no ability at all to draw.

Contact With The Dead

Manning's intelligent, articulate and objective approach to all the strange phenomena in his life makes fascinating reading. In his first book, *The Link,* he discusses his method of 'contacting' dead artists. He simply sat quietly with a pad and pen in hand and concentrated on the artist. As he himself put it: 'I empty my mind as completely as possible and in that state I think of the person I am trying to contact – sending all my energy out to this person who then writes or draws through my hand'. Almost immediately, the pen would begin to move, usually starting in the centre of the page and finally filling it with what seemed like a well-planned work of art. Almost always, the result was recognisably in the style of the artist on whom he had been concentrating: sometimes it was even signed. Occasionally, however, although bearing a strong resemblance to the style of the artist he had wanted to 'reach', the pictures were not signed. In these instances, it seemed to Manning that some other discarnate artist, perhaps even a pupil of the greater one, had intervened.

The communicators also showed very distinct personalities. 'No other communicator tires me out

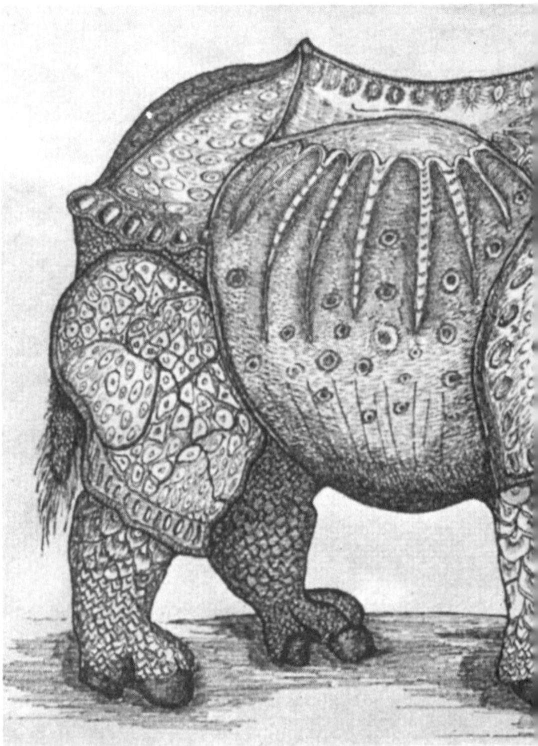

mistakes made and covered over. It took between one and two hours to produce a finished work, whereas most living artists would perhaps take days to produce a painting of similar size and complexity – and then not necessarily of the same high quality. More time would also have been spent in planning and sketching.

But one psychic artist has produced 'new' old masters at the rate of 21 in 75 minutes. In March 1978, the Brazilian Luiz Gasparetto appeared on BBC's *Nationwide* and was seen by millions to go into a trance and produce 21 pictures – sometimes

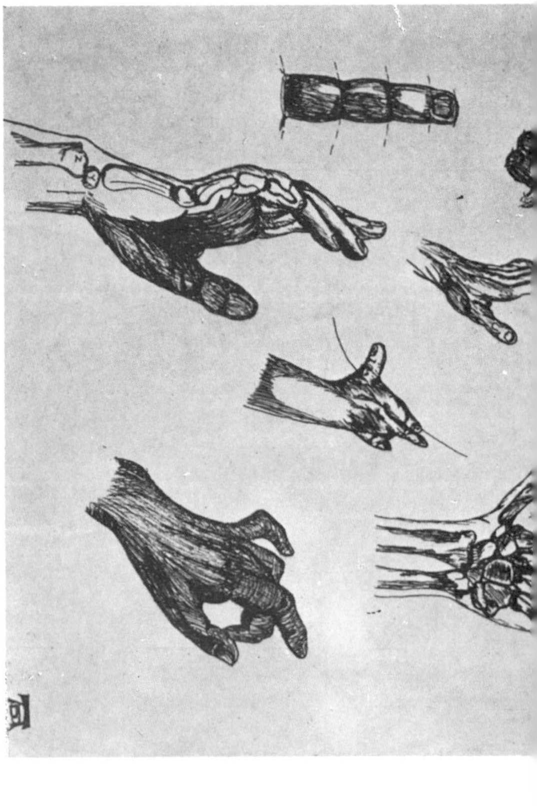

as much as Picasso does,' Manning has said. 'After only a few minutes, the time it takes him to do one drawing, I feel worn out and cannot continue for at least 24 hours...'

Pablo Picasso was also one of the few communicators who was not confused about using colour: indeed, he directed Matthew Mannings's hand to pick out certain felt-tipped pens from a box of mixed colours. (Most of Manning's other discarnate artists used pen-and-ink.)

Diversity of Style

Among the signed works in his collection are drawings recognisably in the styles of Arthur Rackham, Paul Klee, Leonardo da Vinci, Albrecht Dürer, Aubrey Beardsley, Beatrix Potter, Pablo Picasso, Keble Martin and the Elizabethan miniaturist, Isaac Oliver.

Sometimes a finished picture would be very similar to a famous work by a particular artist, but usually these similarities had to be pointed out to him. A virtual reproduction of Beardsley's famous *Salome*, for example, took place under his very eyes as he concentrated on Beardsley.

The 'new' work usually came at an incredible speed. There was no preliminary sketching, nor – except in the case of Aubrey Beardsley – were any

Four centuries after his death, Isaac Oliver – the Elizabethan miniaturist – executed and signed such detailed – and typical – work as the picture* above, *via Matthew Manning.

Albrecht Dürer (1471-1528), inventor of engraving and true son of the Renaissance, was another of Matthew Manning's alleged communicators. The rhinoceros,* above right, *and the study of human hands,* right *– 'transmitted through' Matthew Manning – are characteristic of Dürer's minute observation and the scope of his interests.

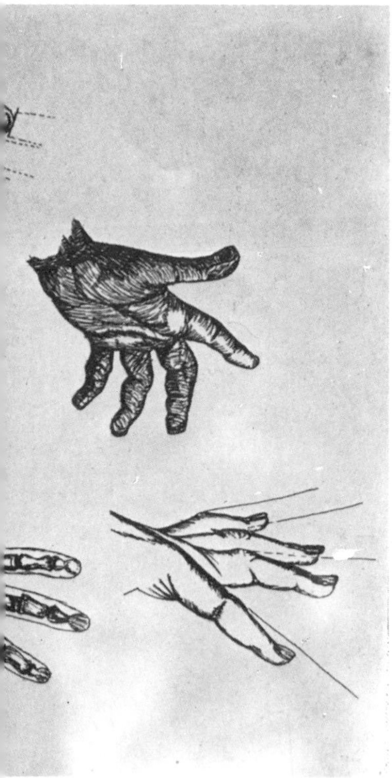

The crayon drawing by Brazilian trance artist Luiz Antonio Gasparetto, right, is in the style of Henri de Toulouse-Lautrec (1864-1901). Whereas most of Gasparetto's paintings take only a few minutes to complete, this one took several hours. The drawing was made in 1978 while the medium was living in London, studying English.

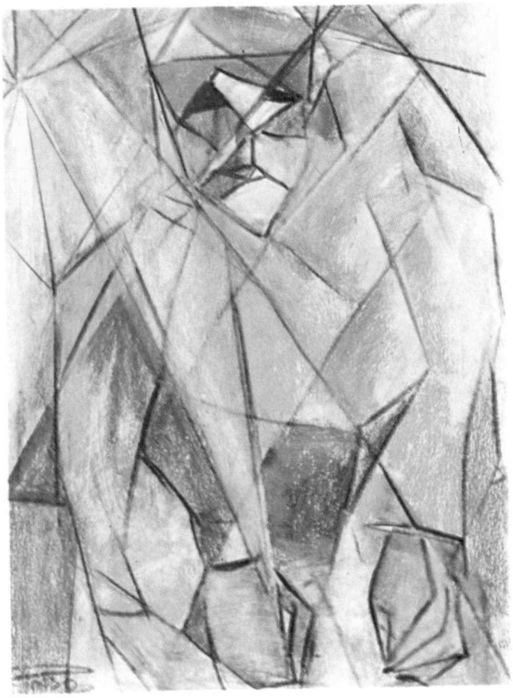

Sometimes painted with both hands simultaneously, sometimes with his toes, and almost always within a few minutes, Luiz Gasparetto's trance-paintings bear striking resemblances to the works of famous, dead artists. Often the 'spirit' paintings are signed, such as the typical Van Gogh, right *– signed 'Vincent' – and the slightly unusual Picasso,* far right. *Others do not need a full signature: the style is sufficient. Who else could have painted the closely-observed portrait,* below, *but Toulouse-Lautrec, or Gasparetto?*

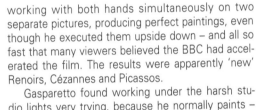

working with both hands simultaneously on two separate pictures, producing perfect paintings, even though he executed them upside down – and all so fast that many viewers believed the BBC had accelerated the film. The results were apparently 'new' Renoirs, Cézannes and Picassos.

Gasparetto found working under the harsh studio lights very trying, because he normally paints – in a trance – in the dark or, at most, in a very weak light. A psychologist by profession, he views what he produces with some objectivity. But, although familiar with others who write or paint by psychic means, he says: 'I've never seen anyone else who can draw with both hands in the dark – in 30 different styles.' In a state of normal consciousness, he even says that, like Manning, he cannot paint at all.

This Brazilian says he sees, senses and talks to all the great artists who 'come through'. Interestingly, particularly in view of Matthew Manning's experience, Gasparetto has revealed: 'Picasso sometimes used to be violent. If anyone whispered, he would throw the paper away.'

Gasparetto travels extensively with journalist and fellow spiritist Elsie Dubugras, giving demonstrations of psychic painting. After each session, the paintings are then auctioned and the proceeds go to charity.

Although Gasparetto is still producing vast numbers of psychic paintings, Matthew Manning has done little automatic art or writing since adolescence. At first, he did it because he found it quelled the poltergeist activity that seemed always to surround him; but now it appears that the power, whatever it is, has been harnessed for the healing with which he has become involved.

Researchers and sceptics alike have come up with theories of repressed creativity, or even a secondary personality, to account for the strange phenomenon of psychic art. Perhaps we will never know how, or why, it happens; but out of all the vast array of paranormal phenomena, this threatens no one – and often produces works of great beauty.

WHAT IS IT LIKE SUDDENLY TO FIND YOURSELF IN THE PECULIAR POSITION OF EXISTING OUTSIDE YOUR OWN BODY, LOOKING DOWN AT THE WORLD FROM SOME DETACHED, EXTERNAL POINT?

THE DISEMBODIED SELF

'For a split second, I saw my own face, as if reflected in a mirror. It was a grey spirit face, screwed up in terror. I tried to turn my head away, but some force held it there, wanting me to see this room and what was in it.'

This is how Shirley Wood describes a near death experience on 17 May 1987. But the circumstances in which out-of-body experiences occur vary considerably. Stress particularly seems a significant factor, and many people have reported experiencing the sensation of leaving their bodies when undergoing an operation, after an accident or when seriously ill, for instance. But there are also numerous cases of people who were asleep or going about everyday tasks, such as shopping or gardening, when the experience occurred.

From accounts given by those who have had an out-of-body experience (OOBE), the general sensation is at first indistinguishable from the ordinary physical state, except for a feeling of buoyancy and positive well-being. But some subjects have mentioned that their 'phantom' or 'astral' body seemed to remain attached to their physical form by a thin cord, enabling them to return to their normal state.

Astral Projection

The term 'astral' is used to describe a second body within the physical one. It is an exact copy of the flesh and blood version, but is made of finer material and has a luminous appearance. It is apparently capable of separating itself from the physical body and travelling about, passing through solid objects. The astral body exists in what is called the astral plane, which includes the everyday world, but extending beyond it. It is also said to survive death.

References to the astral body abound in ancient literature. Ancient Indian writings, for instance, tell of eight *siddhis* (supernatural powers) that can be acquired through meditation. The sixth *siddhi* is 'flying in the sky', presumably indicating astral projection; and a religious belief common to some cultures is that the shaman (a kind of priest-doctor) is able to leave his body at will and escort the soul of the dead to the land of tribal ancestors.

In this image – one of a series – photographer Duane Michals illustrates a typical out-of-body experience, in which the spirit is freed from the physical world.

> "Every human being has already had an experience like that of travellers who return from the land of death; the sensation of flight and the emergence from darkness into light... It is called birth."

CASEBOOK

THE NEAR-DEATH EXPERIENCE

Many people have experienced an OOBE for the first time through being involved in a serious accident. In 1964, David Taylor and a friend were spending the last few weeks of their tour of East Africa in northern Tanzania, when they had a serious collision with a lorry. David nearly died as a result of his injuries.

'We had been driving through the game park and had just turned on to the main road to Moshi. It was dusk, and I was sitting half-asleep in the passenger seat.

'I was suddenly woken by my friend who was delighted to see the first vehicle we had come across in six hours, driving down towards us. Either my friend or the other driver must have been half-asleep, too, for within seconds the two vehicles drove smack into each other.

'As the two vehicles collided, I suddenly found that I was watching the scene from several yards up in the air, as if I were suspended above the road. I saw our own Land-Rover colliding with a large lorry, and I watched as I was thrown from the Land-Rover. My friend then climbed out unhurt and came back to examine my body. I also saw the lorry drive off. I remember thinking that I looked a terrible mess lying there on the road and could well be dead.

The next thing I knew was coming to in Moshi Hospital. I had been unconscious for two days with serious injuries. I told my friend what I had seen and he confirmed that it was indeed a lorry that had run into us and that it had driven on. I had only been saved because another car had come down the road afterwards and taken me to the hospital.

'The whole experience, even after all these years, has left me completely unafraid of death.'

It appears from drawings that the ancient Egyptians believed that the astral plane was entered by 10 gates and seven doors. Indeed, they thought of the soul or astral body as a bird, independent of gravity, that would hover close to an individual's physical form following death. (A puny soul, however, was symbolised as a mouse!)

Widespread Beliefs

The modern idea that it is wrong to awaken a sleepwalker may even be traced back to the primitive belief that to do so would prevent the soul, or astral body, from returning. Even more frightening is the belief, still common in Haiti, that the soul can be stolen by evil beings and its owner subsequently enslaved. (The zombies of Haiti are deemed to be bodies without souls.)

In 1978, Dean Shiels, Associate Professor at the University of Wisconsin, USA, published the results of his cross-culture study of beliefs in OOBEs. He had collected data from nearly 70 non-Western cultures and found that a belief in OOBE occurred in about 95 per cent of them. Despite the need for further research, Professor Shiels was sufficiently confident in the results of his survey to remark that 'the near-universality of OOBE beliefs and the consistency of the beliefs is striking'.

The notion of the astral body has a continuous history in the West, too. One of the few men whose ability to travel astrally was acknowledged by the Roman Catholic Church was St Anthony of Padua (1195-1231). St Anthony was a Portuguese Franciscan friar who won a great reputation as a preacher in southern France and Italy. He is the patron saint of the poor, and is often called upon by those who have mislaid items accidently or been robbed for the return of their lost property.

It is said of St Anthony that, one day in 1126, when he was preaching in a church in Limoges, he suddenly remembered that he was supposed to be

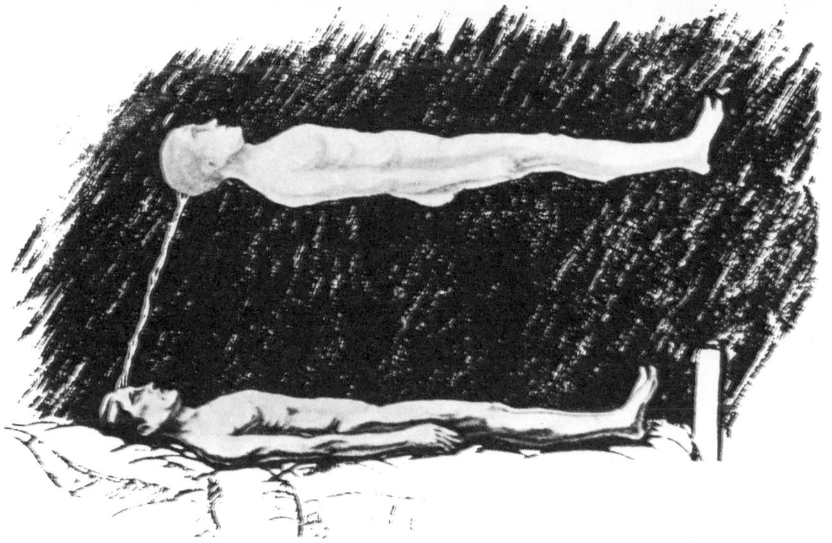

reading a lesson at another church on the other side of town. St Anthony stopped his sermon, pulled his hood over his head and knelt silently for several minutes. During that time, monks in the other church saw the saint suddenly appear in their midst, read the lesson, and then just as suddenly disappear again. St Anthony then returned to his kneeling body and, without explanation to his congregation, continued his sermon.

During recent centuries, many notable writers have described their own experiences of spontaneous projection or those of colleagues, among them Walter de la Mare, T.E. Lawrence, Jack London and Guy de Maupassant. Ernest Hemingway experienced the sensation of quitting his body when he was hit by shrapnel during the First World War. He later described it in rather shocking fashion as:

'... my soul or something coming right out of my body, like you'd pull a silk handkerchief out of a pocket by one corner. It flew around and then came back and went in again, and I wasn't dead anymore.'

The ancient Egyptians thought of the astral body, or* ba*, as a bird with a human face, as shown,* top. *At death, the bird would leave the physical body, and then hover close to it.

The astral body, lying above the physical body at the start of an OOBE, is shown,* above. *The 'cord' that connects the two bodies has been mentioned by some subjects as the means by which they can return to a normal state of consciousness.

***The great mystic poet and painter William Blake portrays the reunion of the soul and the physical body in the illustration,* left, *of Robert Blair's poem,* The Grave.**

The phenomenon of OOBE raises considerable problems for philosophers and psychologists. Many sceptics maintain that any suggestion of an OOBE should be dismissed as an hallucination or delusion. But people who have had such experiences are adamant that they have, indeed, taken place. Even when unconscious at the time of the experience, some people have later described in considerable detail what was going on around them; and those present have been able to confirm their accounts. Subjects who experience this phenomenon are also fully aware at the time that they are in an out-of-the-body state.

DISPELLED FEARS

Many subjects who have had an OOBE while on the operating table or after a serious accident say that the experience has profoundly changed their view of life and dispelled any fears about dying. An interesting theory on this type of projection, or near-death experience (NDE), has been put forward by Carl Sagan, director of the Laboratory for Planetary Studies in New York. He describes the phenomenon of NDE in terms that relate it to an experience shared by all but generally forgotten:

'Every human being has already had an experience like that of travellers who return from the land of death; the sensation of flight and the emergence from darkness into light; an experience in which the heroic figure may be dimly perceived, bathed in radiance and glory. There is only one common experience that matches this description. It is called birth.'

Could it be that, in times of mortal danger or acute emotional stress, we are able to retrieve these memories of birth, and once again, leave the darkness – the suffering body – and rise towards freedom and light?

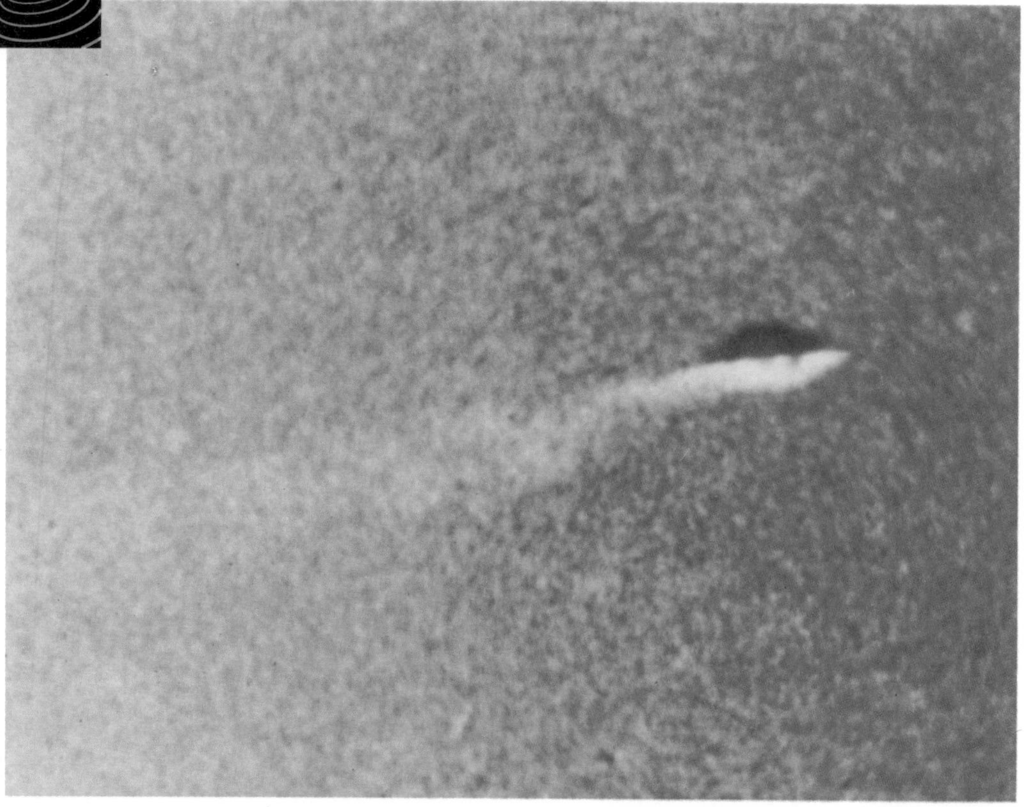

The daylight disc, left, *has an unusual feature – an apparent trail of smoke streaming behind it.*

The phenomenon, below, *is known as an 'airglow' – luminescence of the sky at night. Odd enough to be taken for a UFO, it is actually caused by atoms in the upper atmosphere, releasing energy absorbed from solar radiation.*

MAKING A UFO REPORT

IF YOU SEE AN UNIDENTIFIED FLYING OBJECT, WHAT SHOULD YOU DO, AND WHOM SHOULD YOU TELL ABOUT YOUR SIGHTING?

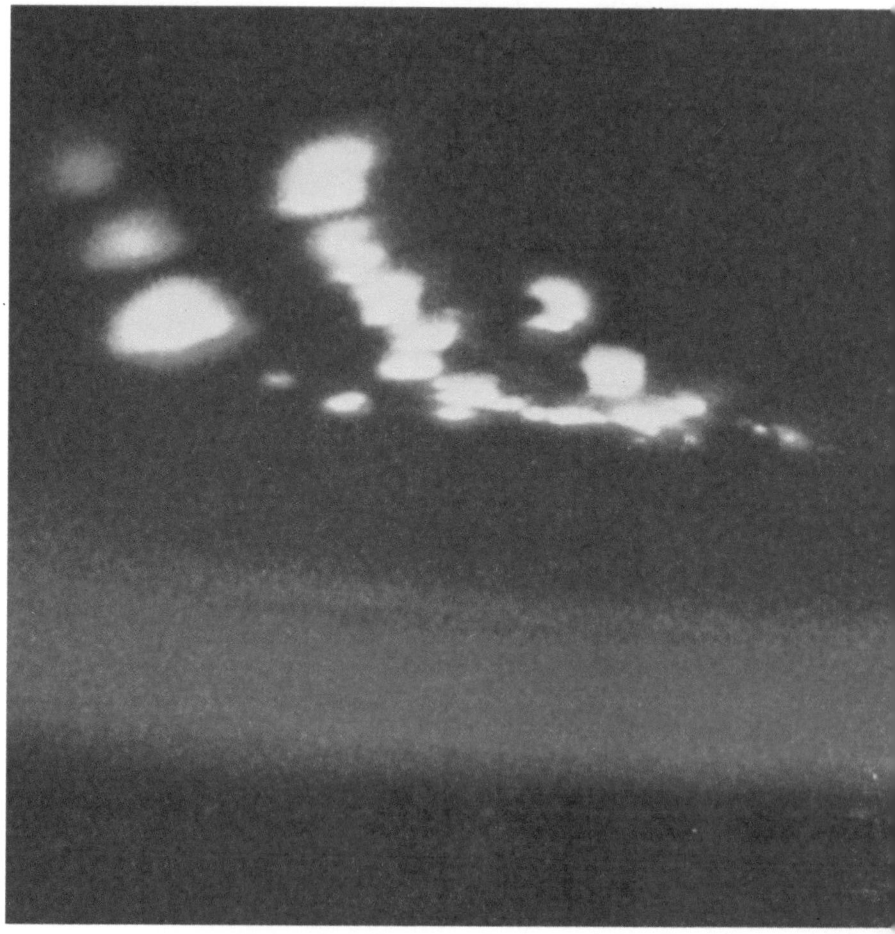

In July 1978 a middle-aged couple in Manchester saw a brilliant red cog-wheel float across the sky. They thought they had seen a UFO. Not knowing anything about the subject, they wrote to Patrick Moore, the astronomer, whose programmes they had watched on television. Perhaps they did not express themselves fully and Patrick Moore did not question them in depth. In any event, he advised them that what they had seen was probably a meteor, albeit a spectacular one. The couple thought no more of the matter until, six months later, they happened to watch a programme in which a well-known UFO investigator appeared.

They contacted her and related their story. Whatever it was they had seen, it was now clear that it was not a meteor. The object had been too large, and had been seen in daylight for several minutes. (Meteorites usually remain visible for only a few seconds.) What they had experienced, according to the UFO investigator, was an impressive close encounter of the first kind: and it was only by chance that their valuable eyewitness report was not lost forever.

Fobbed Off

Two years earlier, just a few miles from this sighting, Detective Sergeant Norman Collinson of the Manchester police force was returning from duty in the early hours of the morning when he saw a strange white disc in the sky. Naturally, he reported his sighting to what he believed to be the 'proper authorities' and waited for a reply, if not an explanation. He was told by his superiors, to whom he had reported the incident, that his account would be passed on to the Ministry of Defence. But, despite several attempts to get an answer, Collinson heard no more. Frustrated by this, he contacted his local university, but received only non-committal replies to his questioning. When he asked for the address of the local UFO group, for example, he was told, 'Oh... you don't want to bother with them'.

But with persistence, Collinson did contact such a group. As it turned out, not only was his case a valuable addition to the evidence for the UFOs, but Collinson became a keen UFO investigator himself.

Both these cases illustrate the importance of what can happen after someone has sighted a true UFO. But, as both these cases also show, it is not always easy to find out who is the right person to contact. So if you have seen something strange in the sky, what should you do?

Many UFO reports describe craft that are much more complex than a simple, featureless 'flying saucer'. The drawing, right, shows a number of details that crop up in sighting after sighting – but how much detail would you remember if this UFO flashed by at high speed? Try drawing it from memory in 24 hours' time and check how much you have recalled accurately. It is a technique requiring practice.

Other Witnesses

If you believe that what you have seen might be a true UFO, first of all it is important to try to find corroborative witnesses. It is not, however, advisable to knock on people's front doors – some may not take too kindly to your intrusion. This does not mean that you should not try to call the attention of those close by. Their presence may add weight to your sighting, or they may be able to provide some other explanation of the phenomenon you have seen. It could, after all, simply be an identified flying object (or IFO).

Another important step is to make notes about the environment and the area in which the sighting is made. Factors such as the barking of dogs or the sudden silence of birds may be significant. Of course, if you have a camera within reach, use it! It is surprising how many people who are perfectly equipped to take photographs are so overwhelmed by what they have seen that they fail to do so. If it is dark, and there is a controlled shutter speed on your camera, set it for a reasonably long exposure – probably about one second. This offers a much better chance of recording what may be a relatively dim phenomenon, even if it appears to the eye to be reasonably bright.

If you are in a car, switch on the ignition and, if you have one, the radio. There are enough stories to support the belief that some UFO phenomena can cause interference with electrical systems; and such evidence can be extremely important to your eventual report.

Floaters

As you watch the 'thing' in the sky, try a couple of quick experiments. Move your head from side to side and watch what happens to the UFO. This will help to eliminate one claim commonly made by disbelievers – that pieces of dead matter in the eye's optical system, known as floaters, are often taken to be UFOs. If a floater is the cause, the 'UFO' will move as your eyes move.

Secondly, try willing the UFO in a particular direction! This may sound ridiculous, but there is a

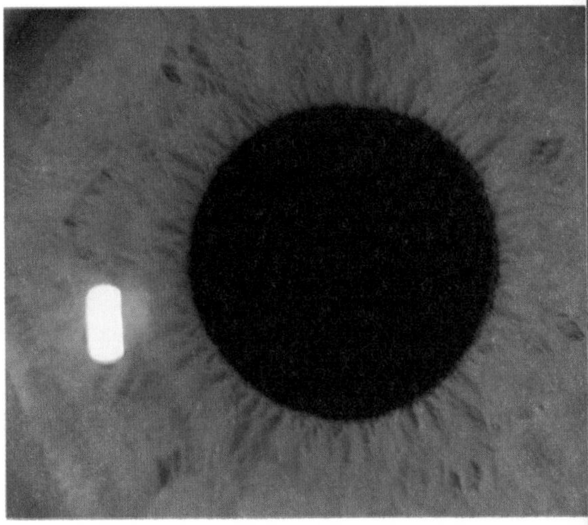

According to one theory, 'floaters' – pieces of dead matter in the eye, right – are sometimes mistaken for UFOs.

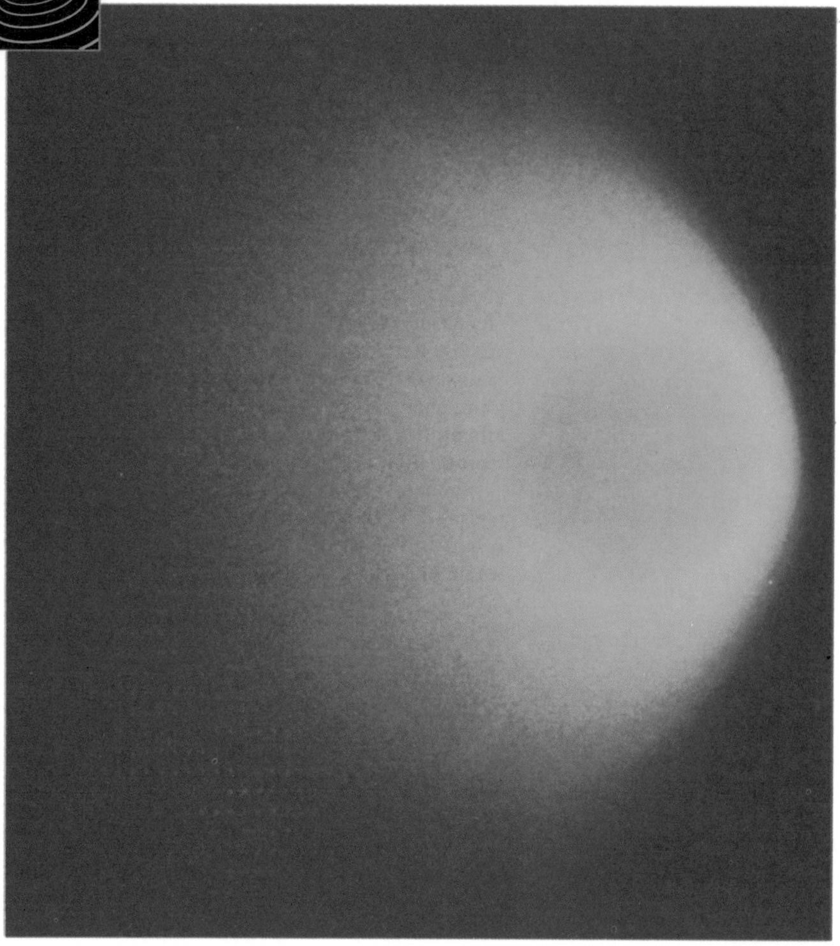

The weird light, **above,** *is a barium cloud, launched into the upper atmosphere as part of an investigation of the Earth's electrical and magnetic fields conducted by NASA. While bodies like NASA tend to deny the existence of UFOs, they can in fact help identify unusual but explicable phenomena that appear in the skies.*

school of thought that says UFOs are related to psychic phenomena. If this is so, then it should be possible for a witness to exert some degree of control over them. Interesting evidence may conceivably emerge from this exercise.

Eye for Detail

UFO encounters rarely last for long, and there is unlikely to be the opportunity to telephone anyone while the object is still in view. Time is better spent taking in as much detail as possible. This is a skill that improves with practice. Look at the picture of the 'UFO' on page 85 for about a minute. Then, tomorrow, try drawing it from memory in as much detail as possible, without cheating by looking at the original. Try the same experiment with various other UFO illustrations, varying the length of time from as little as an hour to as long as a week between examining the picture and redrawing it. The importance of being able to recall in detail what you have seen is paramount, and requires practice.

After the UFO has disappeared, do not discuss details of what you have seen with anyone else who might be around. Simply exchange telephone numbers and addresses, just as you would if you were involved in a road accident. Agree with other witnesses on who is to report the sighting and to whom. Finally, advise all the witnesses that, at the first possible opportunity, they should draw the object you have all seen, and write out a statement describing the sighting. Each witness should do this independently, and not talk about it to anyone else until they have done so. It is surprising how easy it is to be unwittingly influenced by what others say.

> "What they had experienced, according to the UFO investigator, was an impressive close encounter of the first kind."

To whom should you report your UFO sighting? There are several possibilities, and you should think carefully before acting. The most obvious choice is the police. They will probably regard it as their duty to check your story; but in most countries, with the exception of France and the USA, where certain official procedures exist, there will be little they can actually do.

Corroboration

In some cases, the police may refer the matter to the Defence Ministry. But, as often as not, the sighting will get no further than your local police station. Unfortunately, this is inevitable. The police have many tasks to perform and experience has taught them that most UFO reports are not really very important. Consequently, they tend to be given a low priority. But the police should certainly be contacted if you think that the object you have seen has landed. Their presence at the scene of the landing would provide very valuable corroboration. Otherwise, it is probably advisable not to waste their time.

Another agency you may think of notifying is the local airfield, either civil or military. As with the police, there is generally little they can do, or are prepared to do, unless it seems to them that your report justifies calling in a defence establishment. Airport staff may be able to tell you if any aircraft were in the area at the time of your sighting, but it is not advisable to ask them if they have read anything unusual on their radar. A denial might mean that they genuinely had not, or it could be that they had, but for some reason were not willing to tell you. The matter, for example, might already have been passed on to the Defence Ministry, who would want to make their own investigations.

As far as newspapers, radio and television are concerned, try to resist the temptation to approach them. The media will probably be interested only if they think they can use your story, and that may depend on whether it is quiet or busy in the newsroom, rather than on the credibility or intrinsic interest of your sighting.

Scientific Appraisal

The most sensible step to take if you have seen what you believe to be a UFO is to contact a UFO investigator as soon as possible. They are trained to help you and to record accurately the necessary information for scientific appraisal.

There are many kinds of UFO investigator and UFO investigation group. Some are motivated by an almost religious belief in UFOs and will be biased. Others may border on the eccentric, attracting cranks and frauds. Most, however, are serious-minded and will be concerned with establishing the authenticity of your sighting. A list of reputable UFO organisations and their addresses is given at the end of this article. If your country is not included in

*In*Focus

TEST YOUR POWERS OF OBSERVATION

When witnessing any strange or dramatic event, such as spotting a UFO, it is very important to be able to recall exactly what you saw. But try this experiment: look at the picture on the left for about 10 seconds. Now stop reading this article, while you try to remember what was in the picture. Draw it from memory. You will probably find that your attempt is far from being a perfect reproduction of the original.

You might think this experiment has little relevance to UFO spotting. Surely a UFO would present such an unusual sight that it would make an indelible impression on the memory? Experience with witnesses of accidents or crimes, which are not everyday observations for most people, does not bear this out. What we see is not always the same as what we are able to recall having seen.

After looking at the picture, men will probably be more likely to have recall of the attractive young woman walking along the street. Women, on the other hand, are more likely to remember details of her clothing.

Our memories of what we have seen tend to be conditioned by what interests us personally. And what we remember also depends to some extent on past experiences – what we are used to seeing. People unfamiliar with the type of lamp post in this street will probably have noticed one in the picture, but may not remember certain other details. Similarly, there will be some who fail to spot the UFO on first glancing at the picture, or even after staring at it for a while. How much did *you* take in?

the list, it does not necessarily mean that there is no serious UFO society there. Write to the British address. All the groups listed are associated with the international UFO magazine *Flying Saucer Review,* which is distributed in over 60 countries. Your letter will be forwarded to a local agency.

Each report is treated confidentially and almost all UFO groups use a standard report form. You will probably be asked to fill in one of these forms. You might also be asked if it is possible for a UFO investigator to come and see you at a time and place of your choosing.

Naturally, if you happen to come face to face with what you may think is a UFO, it is not always easy to remember exactly what to do. The oddness of the occasion may well lead you to panic. Yet it is always worth trying to remain calm and remembering the procedures outlined in this article. The more well-authenticated, well-documented, cases there are, the more will eventually be discovered about these elusive intruders.

UFO ORGANISATIONS

IF YOU ARE CONVINCED YOU HAVE SEEN A UFO, YOU MAY LIKE TO SEND YOUR OUTLINE REPORT TO ONE OF THE FOLLOWING BODIES. DETAILED FORMS ARE AVAILABLE FOR RECORDING EVERY ASPECT OF SUCH SIGHTINGS.

UK
British UFO Research Association
16 Southway
Burgess Hill
Sussex RH15 9ST

Flying Saucer Review
PO Box 162
High Wycombe
Bucks HP13 5DZ

GERMANY
Journal für UFO-Forschung
Postfach 2361
D-5880 Lüdenscheid 1
Germany

NORTH AMERICA
MUFON
103 Oldtowne Road
Seguin
Texas 78155
USA

AUSTRALASIA
ACUFOS
Box 728
Lane Cove
NSW 2066
Australia

CASEBOOK

FLYING SAUCERS ON FILM

ONE OF THE MOST IMPRESSIVE UFO SIGHTINGS OF ALL TIME TOOK PLACE WHEN A NEW ZEALAND TELEVISION CREW MADE TWO FLIGHTS IN ORDER TO SEARCH FOR UFOS, AND ACTUALLY SUCCEEDED IN MAKING A FILM OF THEM

Late in the evening of 30 December 1978, an Argosy freight plane set off from Wellington, New Zealand. Its skipper was Captain Bill Startup, who had 23 years' flying experience behind him, and the co-pilot was Bob Guard. On board were an Australian TV crew from Channel 0-10 Network; reporter, Quentin Fogarty; and cameraman, David Crockett and his wife, sound recordist Ngaire Crockett. Their purpose was to film UFOs, for there had been reports of 'unknowns' during the preceding weeks in the region of Cook Strait, which separates New Zealand's North and South Islands. They were spectacularly successful in the quest, so successful in fact that, after the story had appeared in hundreds of newspapers and clips from the films had been shown repeatedly on television around the world – the BBC, for instance, gave it pride of place on the main evening news – critics and droves of debunkers lined up to try to explain what the television crew had seen, in terms ranging from the sublimely astronomical to the ridiculously absurd.

The Argosy had crossed Cook Strait and was flying over the Pacific Ocean off the north-east coast of South Island when the excitement began. The television crew was down by the loading bay, filming 'intros' with Quentin Fogarty, when Captain Startup called over the intercom for them to hurry to the flight deck: the pilots had seen some strange objects in the sky. According to Crockett, they had already checked with Wellington air traffic control for radar confirmation of their visual sighting.

Fogarty stated that, when he reached the flight deck, he saw a row of five bright lights. Large and brilliant, although a long way off, they were seen to pulsate, growing from pinpoint size to that of a large balloon full of glowing light. The sequence was then repeated, the objects appearing above the street lights of the town of Kaikoura, but between the aircraft and the ground.

The spinning, luminous sphere above, was filmed by a New Zealand television crew on the night of 30 December 1978. The crew made two flights, looking for UFOs, on the same night and saw them both times.

UNKNOWN TARGET

Crockett, who was wearing headphones, received a call from Wellington control, warning the pilots that an unknown target was following the Argosy. Captain Startup put his plane into a turn to look for the unidentified object but the passengers and crew saw nothing. Control, however, was insistent: 'Sierra Alpha Eagle... you have a target in formation with you... target has increased in size.' This time, lights were seen outside the plane; but because of interference from the navigation lights of the plane, Crockett was unable to film. So First Officer Bob Guard switched off the navigation lights, and everyone saw a big, bright light. The plane was now back on automatic pilot, so Guard gave up his seat for Crockett, who obtained a clear shot of the object with his hand-held camera. Crockett has since

PERSPECTIVES

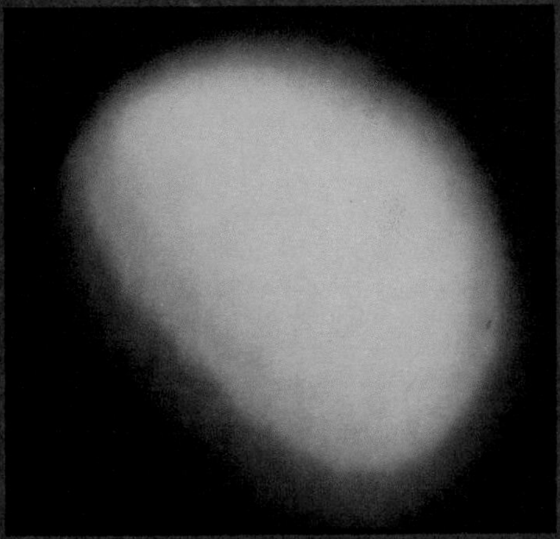

ROGUE PLANETS?

For a time it was thought that the New Zealand films might provide solid scientific evidence for the existence of UFOs, since they seemed to offer instrumental evidence both on film and on radar. Whatever they were, the objects were not hallucinations. Scientists were quick to react by putting forward a whole range of alternative explanations for what the objects in the films might be. Some of their theories were wildly implausible: one even claimed that the television crew had seen 'reflections from moonlight via cabbage leaves'.

A more reasonable explanation was that the films showed a planet – but which one was it? One newspaper claimed it was Venus, *left;* another said it was Jupiter, *below.* But even the quickest glance at the planets themselves show these explanations to be unlikely. The *Daily Telegraph,* surprisingly, printed a remarkably strong condemnation of the Venus theory: 'The scientist who suggested that all they [the television crew] were seeing was Venus on a particularly bright night can... be safely consigned to Bedlam' was the British paper's conviction.

Two stills from the New Zealand television crew's film, right, *show the presence of strange objects, as confirmed by Wellington air traffic control, who saw their traces on their radarscopes.*

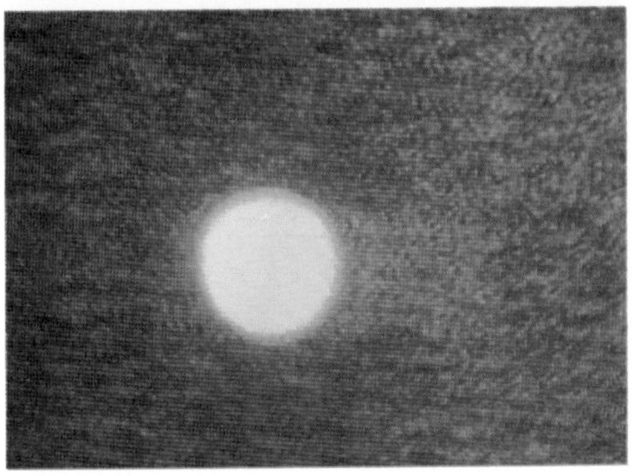

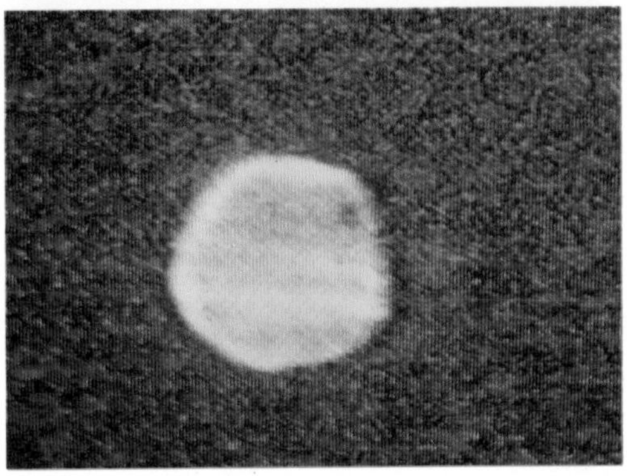

Captain Bill Startup, below, *was pilot of the aircraft from which the UFO film was taken.*

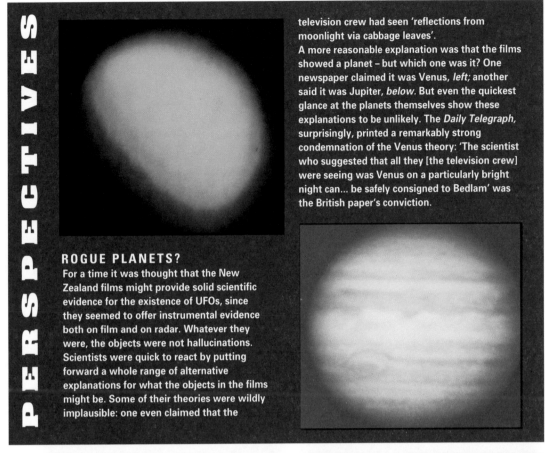

explained that this changing of seats with the camera running was responsible for the violent shake seen at that point in the movie film they made.

After this, Startup decided to put the plane into another 360-degree turn to see if they could spot the objects again, but they had now lost sight of the UFOs, although Wellington control said their echo was still on the radarscope.

Although there was no room for a camera tripod to be mounted on the flight deck, the unidentified object stayed steady enough for Crockett to be able to keep it dead centre in his camera viewfinder for more than 30 seconds.

As the plane approached Christchurch, the fuel gauge went into a spin, but the captain said that this occasionally happened and was not necessarily due to interference by the UFO. At this point, they were out of touch with Wellington control. Christchurch control, however, had the object on its radarscope but later, when Captain Startup and American investigating scientist Dr Bruce Maccabee asked to see the radar tapes, the Christchurch supervisor replied that they had been 'wiped' clean as part of routine procedure.

The Argosy landed at Christchurch and journalist Dennis Grant joined the team in place of Dave Crockett's wife, Ngaire. They left on the return flight at about 2.15 a.m. on 31 December 1978.

PULSATING LIGHTS

Early in this flight, the observers saw two more strange objects. Through the camera lens, Crockett saw what he described as a sphere with lateral lines around it. This object focused itself as Crockett watched through his camera, without adjusting the lens. He said the sphere was spinning. Significantly, one of the objects swayed on the Argosy's weather radar continuously for some four minutes. Later, they all saw two pulsating lights, one of which suddenly fell in a blurred streak for about 1,000 feet (300 metres) before pulling up short in a series of jerky movements.

Were the objects true 'flying saucers'? Many alternative explanations have been put forward. The film perhaps depicted a 'top secret American military remote-control drone vehicle', plasma or ball lightning, a hoax, meteorites, 'helicopters operating illegally at night', mutton birds, lights on Japanese squid boats, or 'reflections from moonlight via cabbage leaves' (at Kaikoura); while Patrick Moore hedged his bets with a guess of 'a reflection, a balloon or even an unscheduled aircraft'.

PLANETARY SIGHTINGS

One newspaper claimed the film showed the planet Venus, out-of-focus because it was filmed with a hand-held camera. Another offered Jupiter as a candidate, stating that an amateur astronomer had enhanced the light values of the film by putting it through a line-scan analyser, thereby identifying four small points of light, possibly Jupiter's four largest moons.

But because the television crew were so vague about the possibility of the lights relative to the aircraft as they were filming them, it was impossible to make a positive identification.

One of the most exciting aspects of the incident however, is that it appears to offer independent instrumental evidence of the sighting both on film and radar. But even here there are problems. Although both ground radar and the Argosy's own radar picked up unidentified traces, the number of UFOs the television crew claimed to have seen – about eight – conflicts with the 11 reported by ground radar. And the crew actually filmed only one object. The radar controller at Wellington, Ken Bigham, was dismissive about the whole affair.

'I managed to plot three of the echoes for 20 minutes or so before they faded completely. They definitely moved, varying between 50 and 100 knots (92.5 km/h and 185 km/h). I certainly couldn't identify them as anything. It's pretty inconclusive. They were purely the sort of radar echoes that constantly pop up. It is not unusual to get strange echoes appearing on what we call primary radar. They usually amount to nothing at all.'

Nevertheless, the Royal New Zealand Air Force was concerned enough about the incident to put a Skyhawk jet fighter on full alert to intercept any other UFOs that might appear in the area. By the end of January, however, the fuss had died down and the New Zealand Defence Ministry then stated that the unidentified objects were 'atmospheric phenomena'.

So what is the truth of the New Zealand affair? The film appears to be genuine; and computer enhancement has not proved it to be a fake. However, it seems almost too good to be true that a television crew that had set out with the deliberate intention of filming 'flying saucers' should come up with such spectacular results. Yet it has to be assumed that the objects were real enough to those who beheld them, and were not mere hallucinations. The case remains on file, accompanied by a fascinating question mark.

> "A TOP SECRET AMERICAN MILITARY REMOTE-CONTROL DRONE VEHICLE, PLASMA OR BALL LIGHTNING, A HOAX, METEORITES, HELICOPTERS OPERATING ILLEGALLY AT NIGHT, REFLECTIONS FROM MOONLIGHT VIA CABBAGE LEAVES ... OR UFOs?"

A unique frame from New Zealand, below, seems to show the UFO performing an extraordinary feat of acrobatics – looping the loop in 1/24 of a second. An alternative explanation is that the hand-held camera was jogged.

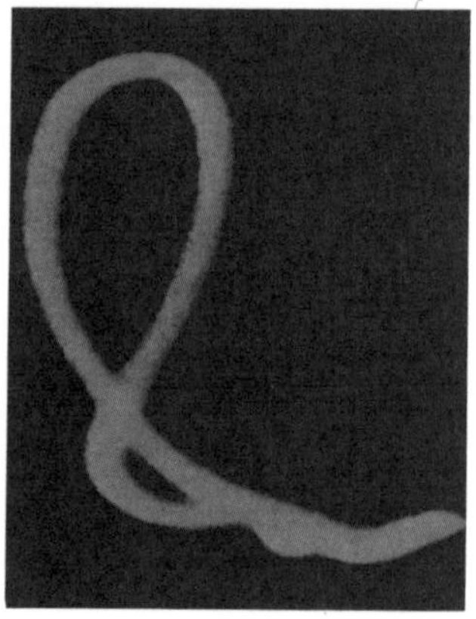

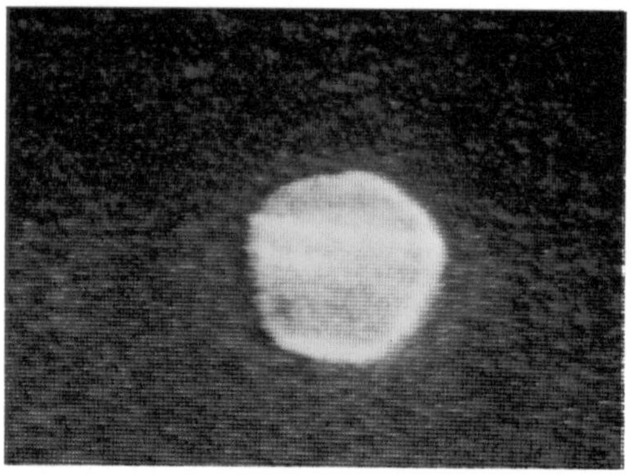

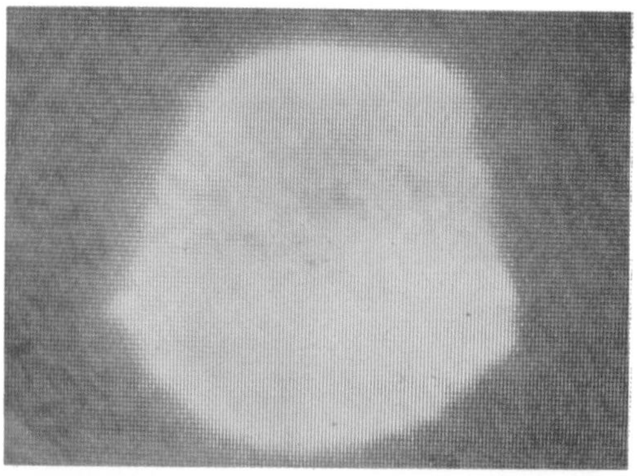

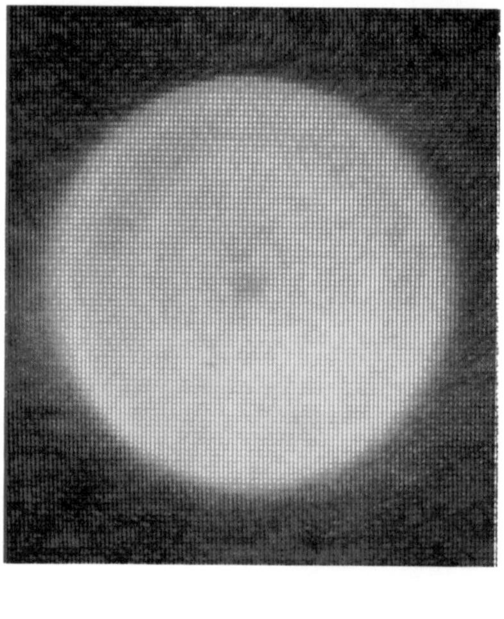

With the navigation lights of the aircraft switched off, the television crew was able to obtain film of one of the objects, seen left in a series of three images, pulsating to the size of 'a large balloon'.

RAISING THE DEAD, HEALING THE SICK, PRODUCING RELIGIOUS MEDALS AND EVEN FOOD OUT OF THIN AIR – THESE ARE JUST SOME OF THE MIRACLES OF SAI BABA

A small, chubby figure in a bright red robe and with a halo of crinkly black hair stood before a typically huge crowd eagerly awaiting him. He turned an empty hand palm down and began moving it in circles. When he turned it over, it contained a gold necklace. The spectators were delighted. Satya Sai Baba had performed another miracle. The necklace is one of more than 10,000 objects he is said to have materialised in this way, including diamonds, gold rings, beads, books, and even food.

The miracles of Satya Sai Baba are so incredible that they automatically invite disbelief. Yet witnesses who have come forward to testify to his astonishing powers often have impeccable credentials, and include government officials, scientists, religious leaders and other respected people.

His followers run into tens of thousands around the world, though the majority are in his native India, which now has some 3,000 Sai centres to promote his teachings, as well as Sai universities. Many of his devotees even regard him as an *avatar* – a god incarnate. Colin Wilson has described him as a 'contemporary Hindu saint'. And some who have written about him find many parallels between his miracles and those of Christ.

MAN OF MANY MIRACLES

Significantly, Sai Baba's robes have no pockets and only narrow wrists: so there seems to be nowhere he could hide the 'apports' he produces.

The powers Sai Baba possesses have always been special. When he was young, right, his father even sought to have him exorcised.

When he was born on 23 November 1926, Satyanarayana Raju was a normal robust child, though he soon caused consternation by refusing to eat meat and bringing beggars home so that his mother could feed them. At school, he was fun-loving and popular. He would arrive early in order to conduct worship with other children, most of whom were attracted by his ability to dip his hand into an empty bag and bring out sweets, or everyday objects they had lost.

Despite these early signs that he was special, the Raju family had hopes that he would be well educated and go on to become a government officer. Instead, a strange incident occurred when he was 13 which proved to be a major turning point in his life.

While working with friends, he suddenly leapt in the air with a loud shriek, holding a toe of his right foot. Everyone thought he had been stung by a scorpion, but next day he showed no sign of pain or sickness... until the evening, when he suddenly fell unconscious to the ground.

When he recovered consciousness next day, he seemed to be another person, bursting into song, reciting poetry and quoting long passages in Sanskrit that were far beyond his knowledge.

His worried parents consulted various doctors who prescribed different remedies; and when these failed to cure Satya, they arranged for the 'demon' in him to be exorcised. The young boy took it all in his stride, showing no sign of suffering despite the ghastly treatment that was administered to him by the exorcist.

Then, one morning, while his father was at work at his store, Satya called the rest of the family together. He waved his hand in front of them and produced candy and flowers. When the neighbours heard what had happened, they crowded in, and Satya obliged his audience by producing candy and flowers for them, too.

News of these 'conjuring tricks' reached his father who was so incensed that he found a stout stick and went to the house to chastise his wayward son. 'This is too much! It must stop!' he shouted when he confronted Satya. 'What are you? Tell me – a ghost, a god, or a madcap?'

Satya replied simply: 'I am Sai Baba.' Then, addressing everyone present, he continued: 'I have come to ward off your troubles; keep your houses clean and pure'.

The reply was hardly helpful. The Raju family did not know of anyone named Sai Baba, but others in the village had heard of such a person – a Hindu holy man who had performed many miracles, including healing the sick with ash from a fire which he had kept burning constantly at a mosque in Shirdi. He had died in 1918, but he told his followers that he would be born again. That promise, it seems, was fulfilled with the birth of Satya, eight years later, though many were sceptical of his claim. Eventually someone challenged Satya to prove that he really was who he claimed to be. 'Bring me those jasmine flowers,' he ordered. Then he threw them on the floor. To everyone's amazement, they landed in such a way that they spelt 'Sai Baba'.

"I GIVE YOU WHAT YOU WANT IN ORDER THAT YOU MAY WANT WHAT I HAVE COME TO GIVE, AND THAT IS TO AVERT A NUCLEAR HOLOCAUST."

The Hindu holy man, Sai Baba of Shirdi, who died in 1918, is shown **left.** ***Satyanarayana Raju, born in 1926, 'became' Sai Baba after suffering the physical trauma of a scorpion sting when he was 13. On a visit to Shirdi, he recognised the first Sai Baba's friends, although he had never met them in his present life.***

Photographic Evidence

In time, Satya came face to face with devotees of Sai Baba of Shirdi and he invariably recognised them. On one occasion, he took a photograph from someone, looked at it, and named the person it pictured – though it was a man Satya had never met. Having named the man and said he was the visitor's uncle – 'your father's elder brother, and my old devotee at Shirdi'.

For many people, however, it does not matter whether Satya Sai Baba is a reincarnation or not. The miracles he performs leave them in no doubt that he is a very special person. A recurring miracle is the materialisation of holy ash *(vibhuti)*, sometimes scooped from the air and sprinkled into the hands of visitors, but at other times made to pour out of an empty, upturned urn into which his hand has been placed. This ash has a variety of uses. He tells many of his followers to eat it, and it is reputed to have cured many ailments.

But it is the materialisation of solid objects which stretches belief to its limit. Sceptics argue that any competent stage conjuror can make objects appear as if from nowhere; but Sai Baba's talents – if we accept the numerous testimonies that have been made – are in a very different league. Often he invites people to name what they would like. Then he plucks it out of the air, or the 'Sai stores' as he jokingly call the invisible dimension from which it suddenly appears.

A holy medallion created by Sai Baba is shown **above.** ***On one side is the image of Sai Baba of Shirdi; on the other, the AUM symbol, signifying the word of creation. Baba says: 'To hear that sound one has to approach, as near as possible, the core of one's being... the Truth is AUM'.***

Sai Baba explains that he materialises objects by *sankalpa,* a strange form of creative will power. Psychotherapist Phyllis Kristal, in her book *Sai Baba: The Ultimate Experience,* describes how Sai Baba materialised a 32-inch (81-cm) necklace made of gold and precious stones as a gift for her. She also witnessed countless other examples of his power to pick objects from 'out of thin air'.

Howard Murphet, author of *Sai Baba, Man of Miracles,* tells of an occasion when Sai Baba asked him the year of his birth and then said he would get for him an American coin minted in that year.

'He began to circle his down-turned hand in the air in front of us, making perhaps half-a-dozen small circles, saying the while "It's coming now... coming... here it is!" Then he closed his hand and held it before me, smiling as if enjoying my eager expectancy. When the coin dropped form his hand to mine, I noticed first that it was heavy and golden. On closer examination, I found, to my delight, that it was a genuine milled American ten-dollar coin, with the year of my birth stamped beneath a profile head of the Statue of Liberty.'

***Sai Baba is believed to be an* avatar, *god incarnate, three forms of which are shown* above.**

MATERIALISED OBJECTS

Among the many reports which Murphet collected for his book is one by Mrs Nagamani Pourniya, widow of a Government District Transport Officer, who told him of a visit she and a small group of followers paid to the sands of the Chitravati river with Sai Baba. Instead of plunging his hands into the sands to produce materialised objects – which is a method he frequently uses – the miracle man simply scraped away sand to reveal statuettes, which then slowly rose out of the sand 'as if driven up by some power beneath'.

This may be hard to believe; but Jesus Christ worked many similar miracles. Indeed, Christians who accept the raising of Lazarus without question should not find it difficult to believe the story of V. Radhakrishna, a 60-year-old Indian factory-owner who visited Sai Baba's Puttaparti headquarters in 1953 in the hope of finding relief from the severe gastric ulcers that were making his life a misery.

He was given a room and spent all his time in bed, waiting for a visit from Sai Baba. When that came, the holy man made no attempt to cure him. He just laughed when Radhakrishna said he would rather die than go on suffering, and left the room without making any promises.

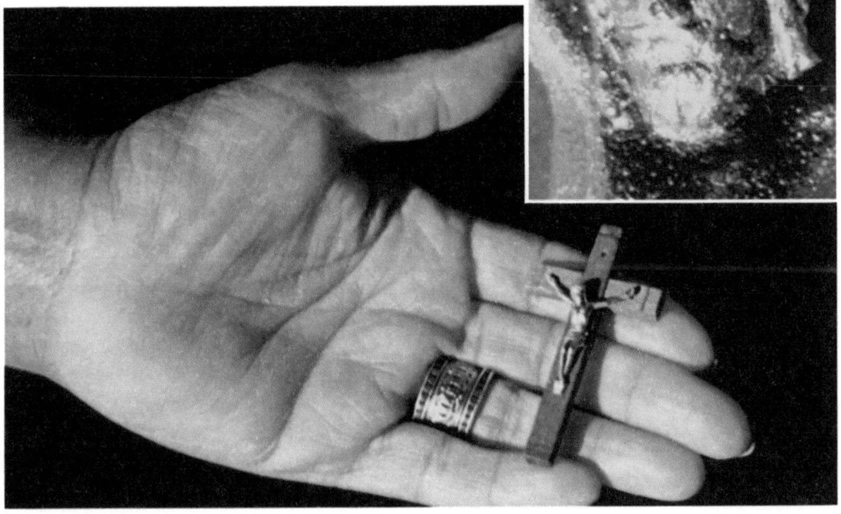

Sai Baba often materialises crucifixes for his Christian friends. The detail, shown* above, *depicts Jesus at the point of death. Sai Baba reveres Christ as a Master who came to unite all men through peace, sacrificing himself in order to atone for their violence and aggression.

Eventually, the man's condition got worse and he went into a coma. When Sai Baba learned of this, he said to the man's wife: 'Don't worry. Everything will be all right'. But when there was no improvement next day, the sick man's son-in-law sent for a male nurse who said the patient was now near death and that there was no hope of saving him. An hour later, Radhakrishna became very cold and his family heard what they took to be the 'death rattle' in his throat. Slowly, he turned blue and stiff.

When told what had happened, Sai Baba laughed: and when he visited the room to see the man for himself, he left without saying a word.

By the morning of the third day, the body was even more corpse-like: it was dark, cold and beginning to smell of decomposition. Some people advised the family to have it removed; but when Mrs Radhakrishna told Sai Baba this, he replied: 'Do not listen to them, and have no fear; I am here'.

Eventually, Sai Baba went to the room again and found the family distraught. He asked them to leave and remained with the body for a few minutes. Then he opened the door and called them in. To their great relief and astonishment, they found the 'dead' man conscious and smiling. Next day, he was strong enough to walk, and the gastric ulcers were found to be completely cured, never to return.

But such miracles are said to be the least important part of his work. Indeed, he refers to his psychic phenomena as 'small items'. His real mission is to attract attention to his spiritual teachings – to lead Man away from violence and hatred towards compassion and higher consciousness, and to unite many religions. He explains it this way: 'I give you what you want in order that you may want what I have come to give'. And that, he says, is to avert a nuclear holocaust.

But his incarnations as Sai Baba of Shirdi and Satya Sai Baba will not be enough to achieve that aim. He has already said he will be born again, as Prema Sai, in the 21st century, in order to complete

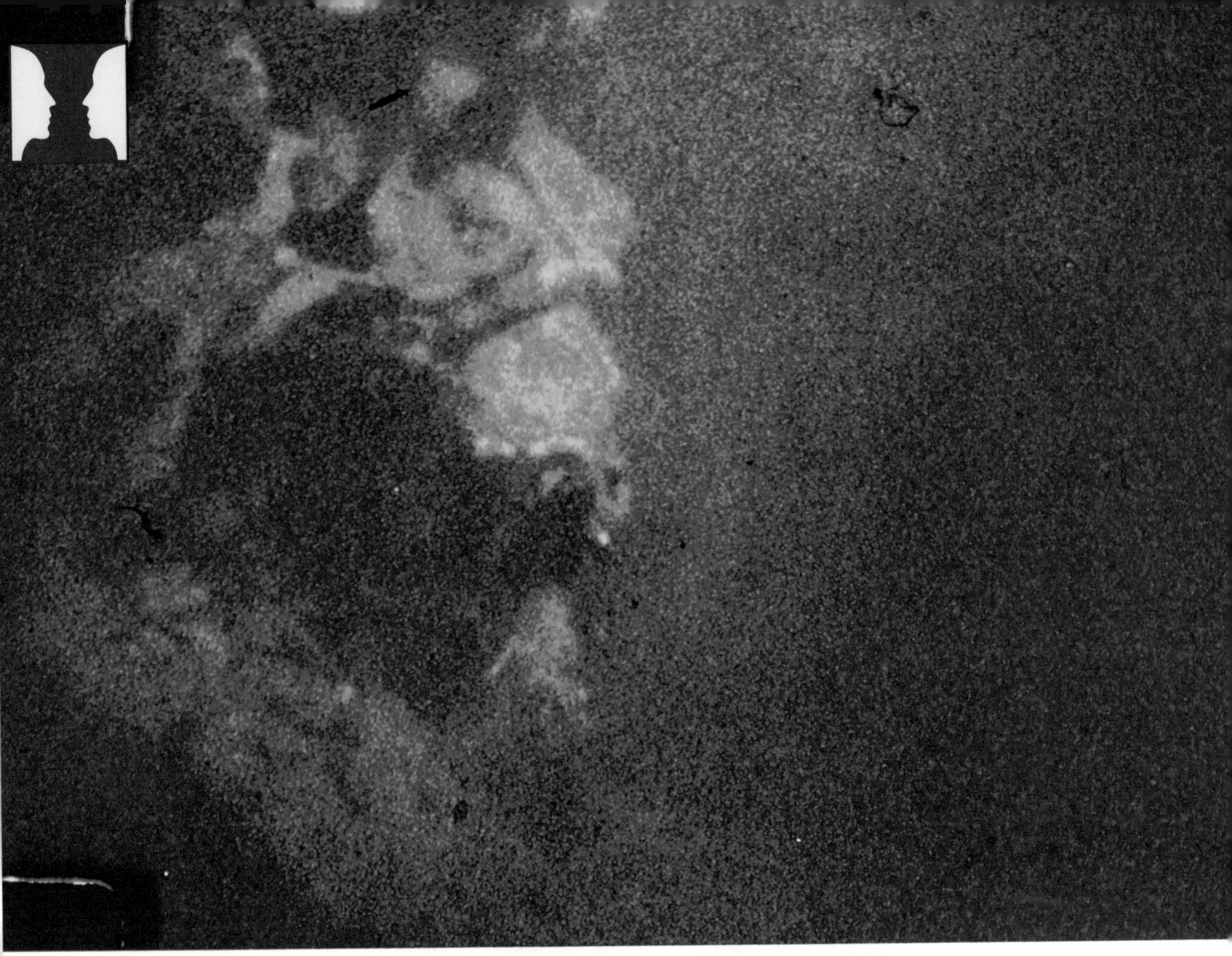

SOUNDING OUT THE SIGHTINGS

FOR DECADES NOW, PEOPLE HAVE BEEN TRYING TO CAPTURE THE LOCH NESS MONSTER ON FILM. ARCHIVES ARE FULL OF ALLEGED PHOTOGRAPHIC EVIDENCE OF THE EXISTENCE OF THE MONSTER – BUT HOW MUCH OF IT IS DEFINITELY GENUINE?

The explosion of interest over recent years in what may or may not lurk in the dark depths of Loch Ness was sparked off by a sighting on 14 April 1933 when, as the *Inverness Courier* reported: 'The creature disported itself for fully a minute, its body resembling that of a whale'. Since then, the volume of evidence has grown steadily – there were 50 other sightings in that year alone – and has been sustained by many more sightings, photographs, films and other evidence as attempts have been made to investigate the 'monster'.

In addition to the better view afforded by tree-felling on the north side of the loch, press interest soon led to many sightings being documented. Once Loch Ness was known to contain a mystery, people were obviously on the lookout for any signs of the unusual and, by the same token, such interest probably induced strong expectations.

But the major difficulty in evaluating eyewitness accounts and evidence is, of course, one of subjectivity. An honest man may easily be mistaken or fooled; a dishonest one may nevertheless give a

Is this the head of the Loch Ness monster,* above*? The photograph was taken, using an underwater camera, by Dr Robert Rines of the Academy of Applied Science, Massachusetts Institute of Technology, USA on 20 June 1975. Although the peaty waters of the bottom of the loch make it difficult to identify exactly what the photograph represents, it has been argued that its symmetry shows it to be animate. On the other hand, many experts hold that the photograph shows merely the bottom of the loch.

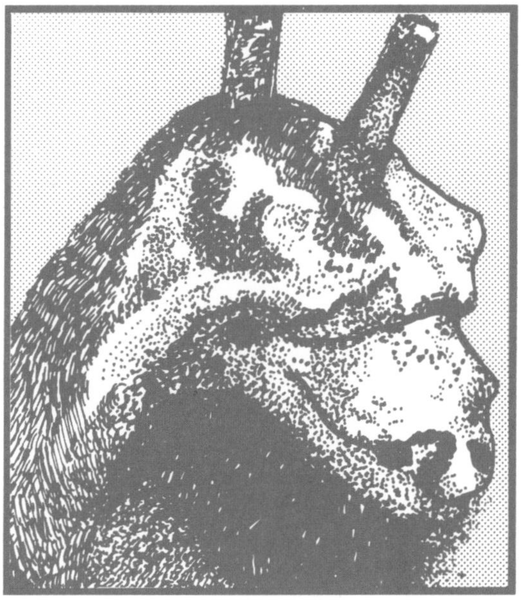

The artist's impression,* left, *of the object in Dr Robert Rines's photography,* far left, *shows the horns that may be used by the monster as snorkel tubes to enable it to breathe without surfacing.

good impression; and an educated one may be imaginative. The fact is that, without very specific experience, it is extremely difficult to judge time, size, distance or speed with any accuracy, especially over water. By pressing a witness to commit himself to just such details, moreover, the investigator may inadvertently contrive to make an honest man appear a liar or a fool. So it is almost impossible to construct a particularly accurate picture of what has been seen by using this kind of material.

OPTICAL ILLUSIONS

The loch itself also presents problems because it plays tricks on the eyes. It is a large mass of water, sometimes completely calm in a way that the sea, for example, rarely is; and its high shorelines cast deep shadows and reflections. In these conditions, you can get a visual impression totally out of proportion to an actual cause, such as small animals, water birds, boat wakes or the wind. The wakes from a boat passing through the loch, for example, can be reflected from the shore to form a standing wave in the centre of the loch even after the particular boat has passed out of sight.

Despite these problems, thousands of eyewitness sightings are now on record thanks to the press, individual authors and investigative organisations such as the Loch Ness Investigation Bureau. Descriptions are remarkably consistent, and point to a long-necked, hump-backed creature that sometimes moves at speed, both with neck raised and lowered, at other times simply appearing for a while and submerging quietly.

ISOLATED SPECIMEN

The first chronicler of the Loch Ness sightings was Lieutenant-Commander Rupert Gould who, in his book *The Loch Ness Monster* (1934), described 42 sightings from 1923 to 1933. He felt that the creature was an isolated specimen that had become trapped in the loch. His account was followed up by Constance White, wife of the manager of the Caledonian Canal. Her book, *More than a Legend*, published in 1957, contained references to over 60 sightings, and established that the phenomenon had not ceased after 1934, as some had believed, and that sometimes more than one animal was seen at a time, suggesting a resident population. More recent authors include Tim Dinsdale, Ted Holliday, Peter Costello and Nick Witchell, all of whom have added examples of eyewitness evidence, many drawn from the extensive files of the Loch Ness Investigation Bureau.

NEGATIVE FAKES?

Besides eyewitness evidence, there are photographic records of surfacings, too. But although a photographic image may appear irrefutable, and may be seen to present measurable evidence that can be independently assessed, the limitations of the camera lens in fact make any such assessment very difficult. Photographs taken with ordinary equipment give far less information than the naked eye; and sadly, the photographic print process is very easy to manipulate in order to produce fakes. Loch Ness is fair game for hoaxers of all kinds.

From a series of underwater photographs taken by Dr Robert Rines, an artist was able to build up the picture,* below, *showing what the Loch Ness monster might look like. The long neck, small head and flippers are mentioned in a number of reports of sightings.

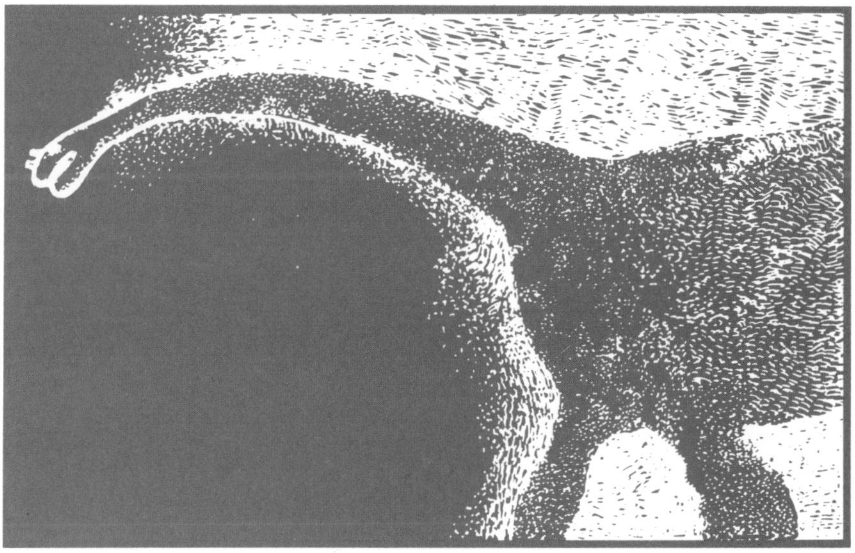

The usual view of an object on the loch is that of a dark image on a light background. This renders the making of a 'negative' fake simplicity itself, since all that is needed is to draw a silhouette on the negative or print and re-photograph the result, thereby producing an 'original' negative. One of the easiest and most frequently used ways of faking pictures is to photograph ordinary objects out of context. These range from the simple ruse of a pair of motor tyres, with a stone thrown in the water to cause disturbance, to quite sophisticated Loch Ness 'Muppets'. These photographs can, of course, be produced anywhere; and background is generally absent since this tends to provide scale and make the object appear smaller and less significant. But where identifiable Loch Ness backgrounds are used, it is common to find existing features that have been slightly adapted, such as rocks in a line, logs or even a fence post adorned with a sock!

From time to time, however, photographs are produced that stimulate real interest. These may be divided into two main types – 'bad' ones that could well be genuine, and 'good' ones that are probably not. Ciné films are far harder to fake than still pictures; so, although their subject matter may still be open to debate, they often provide more valuable evidence. Two film sequences, in particular, are exceptional.

The first was shot on 23 April 1960 by Tim Dinsdale from the mouth of the River Foyers, which flows into Loch Ness from the south, about a third of the way up from Fort Augustus. It shows a hump moving slowly away from him, and then quickly across his field of vision while submerging. The film was submitted to the Joint Air Reconnaissance Intelligence Centre (JARIC) by David James of the Loch Ness Investigation Bureau. In very broad terms, the analysts concluded the object was 'probably animate'. It was nearly 5 ½ feet (1.7 metres) wide, moved through the water at a speed of about 10 mph (16 km/h), and appeared to submerge.

> "Descriptions are remarkably consistent and point to a long-necked, humped-backed creature that sometimes moves at speed, both with neck raised and lowered..."

The second film, shot by Richard Raynor during the Loch Ness Expedition of 1967 on the morning of 13 June, is exceptional for its technical quality. The film, taken from opposite Dores at the north end of the loch, shows a wake, at the head of which a solid object appears from time to time. The object submerges as a boat enters the field of vision. Raynor is quite ready to entertain the possibility that the animal was an otter (the object was definitely animate); and this is really the only possible candidate, apart from an unknown animal. However JARIC – especially likely to be accurate in view of the photographic quality – estimates a possible length of 7 feet (2 metres) for the part of the 'creature' that breaks the surface of the water. (An otter of this proportion would be, to say the least, remarkable.)

Although these examples do suggest that a large animal is involved, they also demonstrate the limitations of this kind of evidence in terms of identification. Aquatic creatures cannot be studied on the basis of what proportions of their bodies are, by chance, exposed above water.

The still, above, from Tim Dinsdale's famous film of 23 April 1960 is very probably genuine; but, like most genuine photographs of the Loch Ness monster, it shows very little detail.

Underwater Pictures

It was not until 1970 that underwater photography was used as an investigative method. Its potential is enormous, since it should allow a complete profile view of the target to be obtained. In practice, however, the peaty water and limitations of normal underwater equipment reduce the range and coverage drastically. This makes interpretation of underwater pictures very difficult. The most interesting are two computer-enhanced pictures of a fin-like object taken in 1972 by Dr Robert Rines of the Academy of Applied Science, Boston, Massachusetts, USA, with a time-lapse camera fitted with a strobe flash. Whatever the biological discussions of this evidence, if the object is a fin, it does not resemble that of any creature known to inhabit the loch.

Perfectly natural objects can sometimes be utterly misleading. The wake shown in the photograph, below, experts agree, shows nothing more than a standing wave left by one of the heavy trawlers that regularly ply the Caledonian Canal, of which Loch Ness forms a part.

Subsequent pictures taken by Rines show six images, other than the underside of the boat, from which the camera was slung; and it has been suggested that two of these are animate. Other upward shots showing the surface of the loch have brought suggestions of a 'major disturbance' and agitation of the camera. However, the time lapse between these 'events' is 70 seconds; and one sequence of these surface shots would actually imply that the camera was more or less at rest for at least two minutes rather than swinging. It has also been argued that one object, the 'head', has sufficient symmetry to suggest a living creature, with horns used for breathing without creating ripples, although this is obviously a matter of individual interpretation.

Unfortunately, this argument can be countered by the fact that two-thirds of the images photographed in the same 24-hour period under the same conditions could by no stretch of the imagination be animate. Either the camera had touched the bottom through miscalculation of the depth or it had, in fact, come into contact with inanimate objects in midwater.

Led by Dr Robert Rines,* left, *an expedition team,* above, *succeeded in taking the first ever underwater pictures of what was alleged to be the Loch Ness monster in 1972-73. A number of sophisticated techniques were employed to obtain the picture, including the use of sonar to trigger one of the cameras when large objects approached. A second expedition, mounted in 1975, also produced spectacular results, although some still think them controversial.

The photograph,* below, *is an enlarged detail of a general view of Loch Ness taken in 1982 by Jennifer Bruce of Vancouver. She had noticed nothing unusual at the time.

Sound Evidence

But, without doubt, the most important class of evidence is that of the echo sounder and sonar. Developed during the Second World War as a submarine detection device, sonar relies on the reflection of transmitted sound waves by underwater targets. It is the only really effective instrument for 'seeing' underwater, particularly where the water is not clear, and by 1960 had been refined to a stage where it was used commercially in fishing – and in the Loch Ness investigations.

By far the most logical and relevant system of enquiry, sonar has also proved the most successful; and most reasonably equipped teams have secured positive contacts with it. The 'hard evidence' that the system has provided is to some extent measurable. The problem, however, is that it requires some considerable degree of expertise to assess the results, and this expertise is not generally found among zoologists.

At best, a sonar record is a trace on a paper chart or a blip on a cathode ray tube. Fish shoals, temperature changes and rising gases are all possible causes of sonar contacts. On the positive side, however, with sonar it is possible to follow the movements of a target under water and to judge from this whether or not it is animate. It is even possible to gain some hints as to its identity.

So far, teams from Oxford and Cambridge, Birmingham University, Vickers Oceanics, the Loch Ness Investigation Bureau, Klein Associates and the Academy of Applied Sciences, and the Partech Company have all produced results that they consider indicate the presence of an animate contact larger than a salmon, and displaying movement and diving rates different from those expected of fish. For the most part, the teams involved have been experienced and, in some cases, expert; and their evidence is not open to dispute, only to further investigation.

HAVE OUR LIVES BEEN SHAPED NOT ONLY BY EXPERIENCES AND IMPRESSIONS GAINED SINCE BIRTH, BUT ALSO BY THOSE FROM SOME OTHER, PREVIOUS EXISTENCE? ONE REMARKABLE CASE CERTAINLY SEEMS TO POINT TO THIS

A CASE FOR REINCARNATION?

In 1956 and 1957, Emile Franckel conducted a series of live experiments for a Los Angeles television programme called *Adventures in Hypnotism*. Franckel's aim was to bring to the public's attention the possibility that individuals under hypnosis can relive previous lives. His attitude was sceptical: he believed that recollections of previous lives arose from promptings from the hypnotist or deep subconscious memory. Some of the experiences he was able to draw from his subjects, however, seemed unaccountable by this explanation. Since the hypnotist did not know his subjects, he could scarcely have induced their responses except by a series of coincidences too remarkable to be mere chance.

Yet Franckel was right to have remained sceptical. For although some of the results seemed almost miraculous, hypnosis is a mental state that many people may experience, given the right circumstances. This does not mean, however, that hypnosis is fully understood by the medical profession even today.

What appears to happen under hypnosis is that the layers of experience we have all acquired during our lives – experiences that have pushed our memory of previous existences deep into the subconscious – come to the surface. When the hypnotist suggests, for example, to a 30-year-old subject that 'It is now 1981. You are now 20 – you are waking up on your 20th birthday, tell me where you are, what is happening', the subject's life and development of the past 10 years are as if they had never been.

FANTASY PERSONALITY

But what of past lives? In many subjects there seems to be a 'shadow' – a fantasy personality that is only revealed in dreams or under hypnosis. And the suggestion is that it is this 'fantasy personality' that is revealed in regression hypnosis, not a recollection of a previous life as such.

How, then, are we to distinguish between what may be mere fantasy and a true account of a previous life? As early as 1906, the Society for Psychical Research reported the case of an unnamed clergyman's daughter who, under hypnosis, recounted her life during the reign of Richard II. In that life, she was no great lady herself – despite the claim by cynics that subjects in regression imagine themselves

The account given by Virginia Tighe,* right, *of her 'previous life' as 'Bridey Murphy' led Morey Bernstein,* shown with her, *to become a firm believer in reincarnation.

It was in 18th-century Cork,* below, *that Virginia Tighe claimed she had previously been born as Bridey Murphy in 1798.

to be famous people – but an acquaintance of Maud, Countess of Salisbury, her friend Blanche Poynings, née Mowbray and Richard's mother, otherwise known as the 'Fair Maid of Kent'.

In this case, almost every historical fact stated under hypnosis was found to be true, as were details of the dress and food described by the girl. Moreover, she had no recollection of ever having read about either the period or the people.

From the Subconscious?

Some early psychical researchers into hypnotic phenomena would wake their subjects and place their hands on a planchette board, usually screened from the subjects' view. They would then proceed to interrogate them. The planchette – it is claimed – wrote down true answers to the questions from knowledge in the subjects' subconscious minds. Under these conditions, one girl revealed that she had just read an historical romance from which every person and fact came up in her regression, except for some minor details, though she had devised a new setting for them.

If all cases were as straightforward as this, there would be no need for further investigation, and believers in reincarnation would have to look elsewhere for evidence. How complicated the majority of cases are, however, is shown by the story of Bridey Murphy. This is no more remarkable than a hundred other cases of hypnotic regression, but was brought to the public's attention by heated debate in a number of American newspapers, as well as a film shown widely throughout the English-speaking world.

In a number of sessions taking place between November 1952 and October 1953, Morey Bernstein, an amateur American hypnotist, regressed Virginia Tighe to a life in early 19th-century Ireland. Mrs Tighe, 29 years-old at the time, a native of Maddison, Wisconsin, and resident in Chicago from the age of three until her marriage,

"What appears to happen under hypnosis is that the layers of experience we have acquired during our lives – experiences that have pushed our memory of previous existences deep into the subconscious – come to the surface."

had never visited Ireland, nor had she ever had much to do with Irish people. (She strongly denied allegations to the contrary and there is evidence to support her denials.) Under hypnosis, she began to speak with an Irish accent, and said she was Bridget (Bridey) Murphy, daughter of Duncan and Kathleen Murphy, Protestants living at the Meadows, Cork. Her brother Duncan, born in 1796, married Aimée, daughter of Mrs Strayne, who was mistress of a day school attended by Bridey when she was 15.

In about 1818, she had married a Catholic, Brian MacCarthy, whose relatives she named, and they travelled by carriage to Belfast through places she

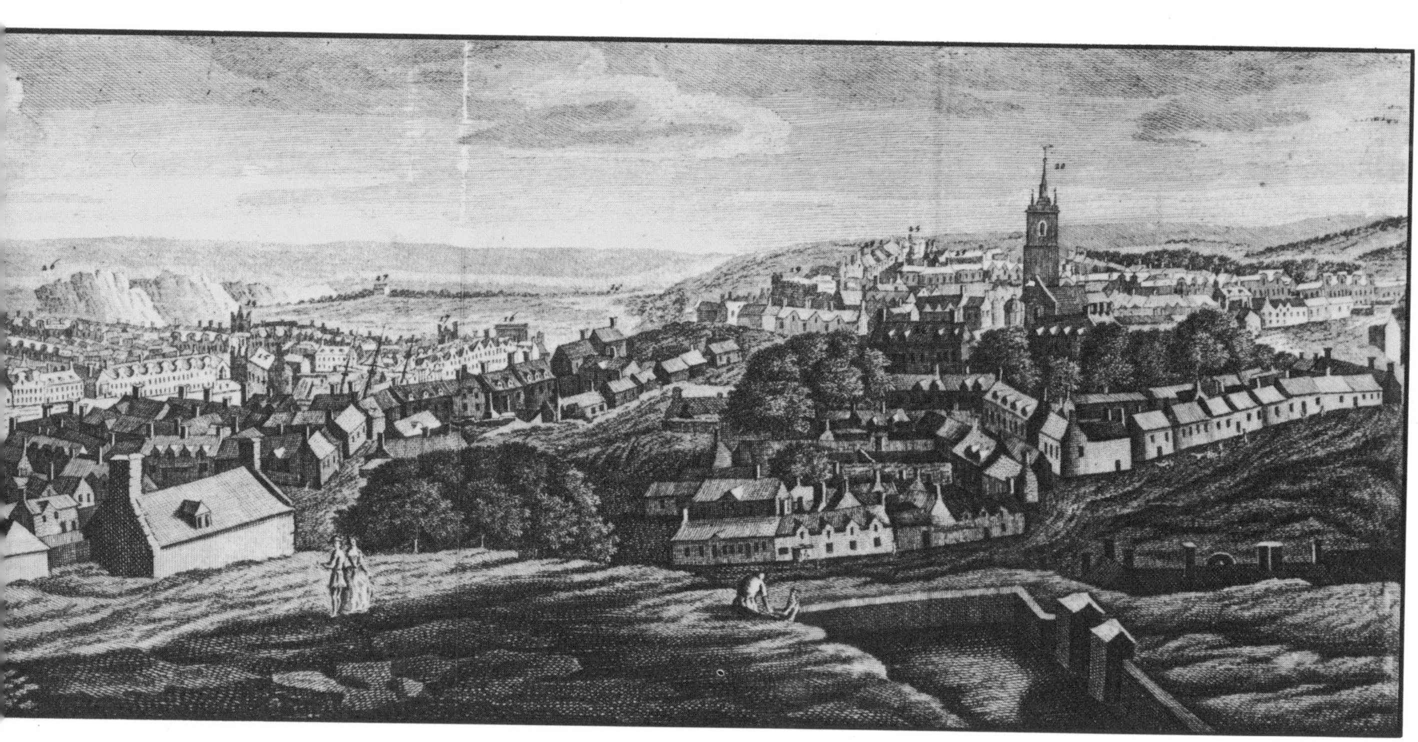

Today, what one does when kissing the Blarney Stone, right, *is to lie on the back, hold on to two bars attached to the wall, lower the head and kiss the underside of the Stone. The earlier method, used at the time of 'Bridey Murphy' and shown,* far right, *would not have been known by Virginia Tighe, unless she had done a great deal of research.*

To counter the claim that he had in some way rigged his experiments, Morey Bernstein, below, *hypnotised Mrs Tighe in the presence of two witnesses.*

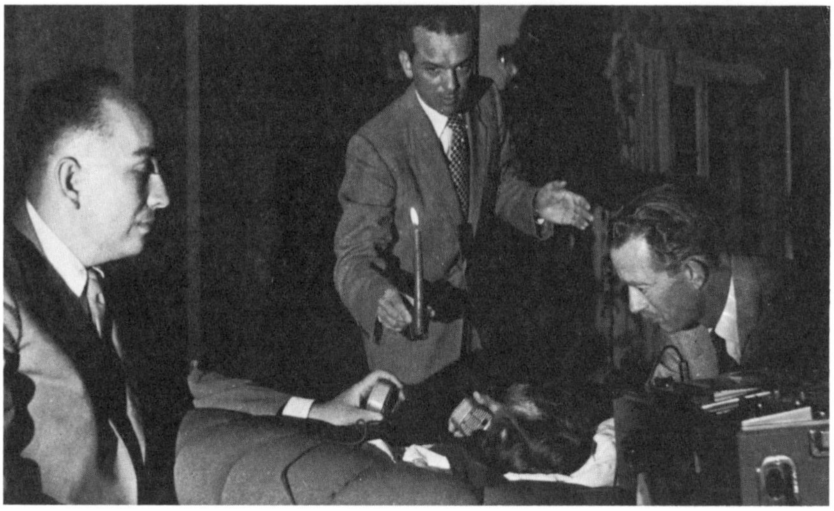

also named, but the existence of which has never been found on any map.

The couple apparently worshipped at Father John Gorman's St Theresa's Church. They shopped at stores that Bridey named, using coins correctly described for the period. In addition, Bridey produced a number of Irish words when asked, using some as they were used then, though their meaning had changed since. ('Slip', for example, referred to a child's pinafore, and not petticoat – the more common modern word.) Bridey Murphy had read some Irish mythology, knew some Irish songs and was a good dancer of Irish jigs. Indeed, at the end of one sitting, Mrs Tighe, aroused from her trance, yet not fully conscious, danced 'The Morning Jig', ending her performance with a stylised yawn. Her description of another dance was also confirmed in detail by a lady whose parents had danced it. A further telling detail was that she described the correct procedure, as used in Bridey's day, for kissing the Blarney Stone, reputed to confer eloquence on those who manage to do so.

Bridey's story was investigated by the American magazine *Empire*, and William Barker was commissioned to spend three weeks in Ireland checking the facts 'Bridey' had given. His visit resulted in a 19,000-word report. Barker's account is typical of regression cases. Some facts were confirmed, some unconfirmed, others proved incorrect. Mysteriously, memories of insignificant detail proved true, while Bridey displayed total ignorance of more important events.

Confirmation of facts proved impossible in many instances, however. There was no way, for example, of confirming dates of birth, marriages and deaths, as no records were kept in Cork until 1864; and if the Murphy family kept records in a family bible, a customary procedure, its whereabouts are not known. No information could be discovered concerning St Theresa's Church nor Father Gorman in Belfast, but the two shops mentioned by Bridey had both existed. Bridey had also said that uillean pipes were played at her funeral, and these were found to have been customarily used because of their soft tone.

So the neutral enquirer is left puzzled. Where had Mrs Tighe learnt about uillean pipes, kissing the Blarney Stone and the names of the shops in Belfast, the existence of which was only confirmed after painstaking research? Why should her subconscious have created a vivid picture of life in Ireland at the beginning of the 19th century? And from where did she – along with many other regressed subjects with no pretence of acting ability – draw the talent to dramatise so effectively a life in another age, in another country?

Furthermore, if reincarnation is a fact, why should trivialities be remembered, while great emotional experiences that you would expect to have contributed to your development in this life be forgotten or go unmentioned?

MEMORIES OF A DISTANT STAR?

THE DOGON PEOPLE OF WEST AFRICA HAVE A DETAILED KNOWLEDGE OF THE UNIVERSE THAT IS ASTONISHINGLY ACCURATE. WAS IT, AS THEY CLAIM, PASSED ON BY ANCIENT ASTRONAUTS?

Like many African tribes, the Dogon people of the Republic of Mali have a shadowed past. They settled on the Bandiagara Plateau, where they now live, some time between the 13th and 16th centuries. For most of the year, their homeland – 300 miles (500 km) south of Timbuktu – is a desolate, arid, rocky terrain of cliffs and gorges, dotted with small villages built from mud and straw.

Although most anthropologists would class them as 'primitive', the two million people who make up the Dogon and surrounding tribes would not agree with this epithet. Nor do they deserve it, except in the sense that their way of life has changed little over the centuries. Indifferent though they are to Western technology, their philosophy and religion is both rich and complex. Outsiders who have lived with them, and learned to accept the simplicity of their lives, speak of them as a happy, fulfilled people whose attitude to the essential values of life dates back millennia.

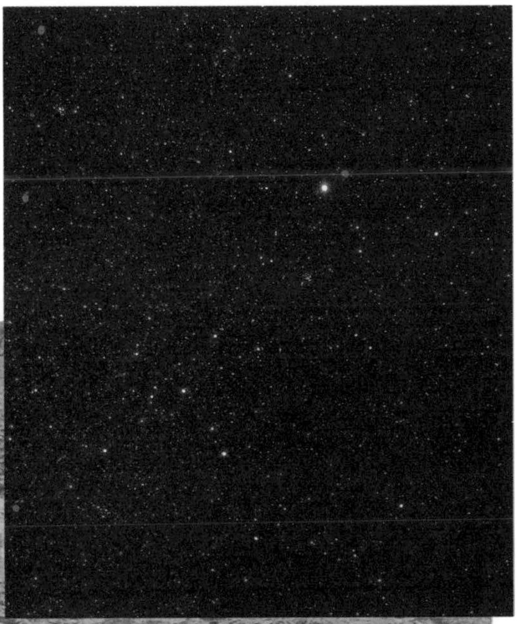

Sirius lies in the constellation Canis Major, right, *near the foot of Orion. It can be readily identified as it sits in a line with the three bright stars of Orion's belt.*

A Dogon settlement at the foot of the Bandiagara cliffs is shown below. *They are a primitive people, yet have a very profound belief that they were originally taught and 'civilised' by beings from the star system Sirius.*

Visitors From Sirius

The Dogon do, however, make one astounding claim: that they were originally taught and 'civilised' by creatures from outer space – specifically, from the star system Sirius, 8.7 light years away. And they back up this claim with what seems to be extraordinarily detailed knowledge of astronomy for such a 'primitive' and isolated tribe. Notably, they know that Sirius, the brightest star in the sky, has a companion star, invisible to the naked eye, which is small, dense, and extremely heavy. This is perfectly accurate. But its existence was not even suspected by Western astronomers until the middle of the 19th century; and it was not described in detail until the 1920s, nor photographed (so dim is this star, known as Sirius B) until 1970.

This curious astronomical fact forms the central tenet of Dogon mythology. It is enshrined in their most secret rituals, portrayed in sand drawings, built into their sacred architecture, and can be seen in carvings and patterns woven into their blankets – designs almost certainly dating back hundreds, if not thousands of years.

Interplanetary Connection

All in all, this has been held as the most persuasive evidence yet that Earth had, in its fairly recent past, an interplanetary connection – a close encounter of the educational kind, one might say. The extent of Dogon knowledge has also been subjected to scrutiny, in order to establish whether all that they say is true, or whether their information may have come from an Earthbound source – a passing missionary, say.

So, how did we in the West come to know of the Dogon beliefs? There is just one basic source, fortunately very thorough. In 1931, two of France's most respected anthropologists, Marcel Griaule and Germaine Dieterlen, decided to make the Dogon the subject of extended study. For the next 21 years, they lived almost constantly with the tribe; and, in 1946, Griaule was invited by the Dogon priests to share their innermost sacred secrets. He attended their rituals and their ceremonies, and learned – so far as it was possible for any Westerner to do – the enormously complex symbolism that stems from their central belief in amphibious creatures, which they called Nommo, and that came from outer pace to civilise the world. (Griaule himself came to be revered by the Dogon as much as their priests, to such an extent that at his funeral in Mali in 1956, a quarter of a million tribesmen gathered to pay him homage.)

The findings of the two anthropologists were first published in 1950, in a cautious and scholarly paper entitled *'A Sudanese Sirius System'* in the *Journal de la Société des Africainistes.* After Griaule's death, Germaine Dieterlen remained in Paris, where she was appointed Secretary General of the Société des Africainistes at the Musée de l'Homme. She wrote up their joint studies in a massive volume entitled *Le Renard Pële,* the first of a planned series, published in 1965, by the French National Institute of Ethnology.

Elliptical Orbit

The two works make it overwhelmingly clear that the Dogon belief system is indeed based on a surprisingly accurate knowledge of astronomy, mingled with a form of astrology. Lying at the heart of it is Sirius, and the various stars and planets that they believe orbit around this star. They also say that its main companion star, which they call *po tolo,* is

Sirius,* above left, *is the brightest star in the sky. But its white dwarf companion, Sirius B, is so dim that it was not even photographed until 1970. Yet the Dogon have always made sand drawings portraying Sirius, accompanied by another star.

Marcel Griaule and Germaine Dieterlen,* above, *are two French anthropologists who lived with the Dogon tribe for over 20 years. We owe much of our knowledge of Dogon mythology to their careful study.

The cave paintings,* right, *depict many of the myths of the Dogon.

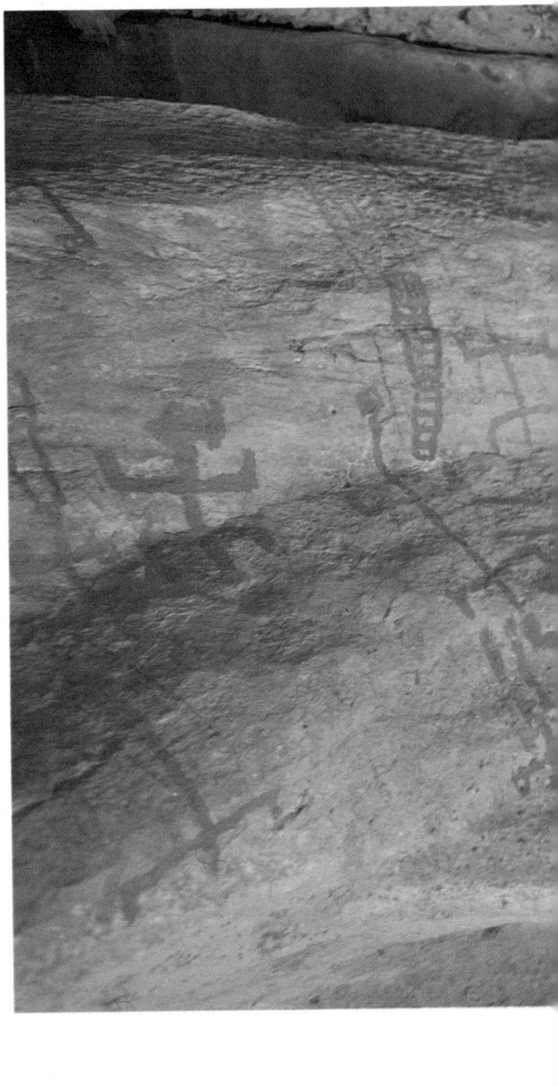

***The Dogon belief system is clearly based on a knowledge of astronomy, and worship takes place at highly decorated shrines, such as the one,* right.**

The designs on the mask worn by a Dogon dancer,* far right, *is said to represent the descent of a Nommo 'ark'.

Carved wooden figures, like the Dogon ancestor,* below, *are essential to the tribe's rituals.

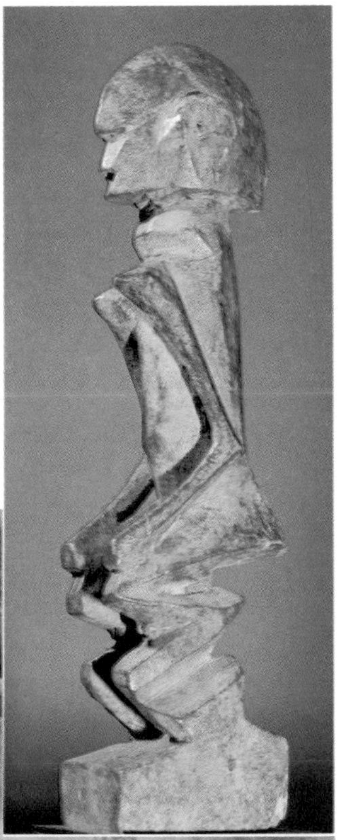

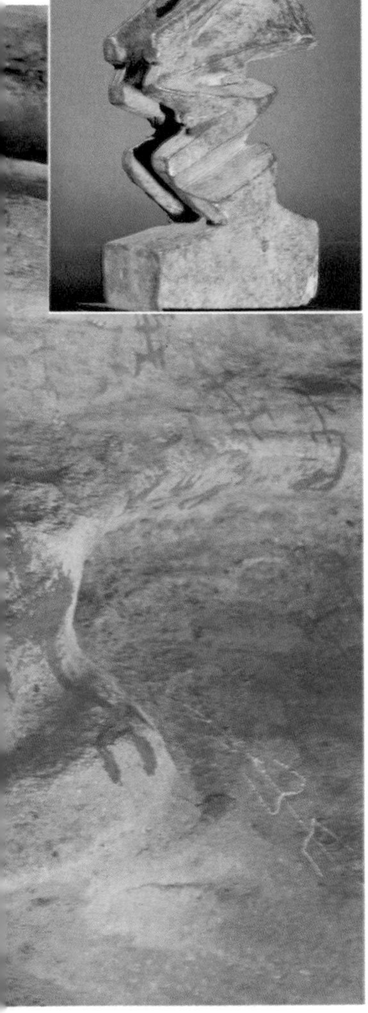

"THE DOGON BELIEVE PROFOUNDLY THAT AMPHIBIOUS CREATURES FROM A PLANET WITHIN THE SIRIUS SYSTEM LANDED ON EARTH IN DISTANT TIMES AND PASSED ON THE INFORMATION TO INITIATES, WHO IN TURN HANDED IT DOWN OVER THE CENTURIES. THEY CALL THE CREATURES *NOMMO,* AND WORSHIP THEM AS THE MONITORS OF THE UNIVERSE, THE FATHERS OF MANKIND, GUARDIANS OF SPIRITUAL PRINCIPLES, DISPENSERS OF RAIN AND MASTERS OF THE WATER."

made of matter heavier than anything on Earth, and moves in a 50-year elliptical orbit.

All these things are true. But Western astronomers only deduced that something curious was happening around Sirius about 150 years ago. They had noted certain irregularities in its motion, and they could explain this only by postulating the existence of another star close to it, which was disturbing Sirius' movements through the force of gravity. In 1862, the American astronomer Alvan Graham Clark actually spotted the star when testing a new telescope, and called it Sirius B.

However, it was to take another half-century from the first observation of Sirius' peculiarities for a mathematical and physical explanation to be found for such a small object exerting such massive force. Sir Arthur Eddington, in the 1920s, formulated the theory of certain stars being 'white dwarfs' – stars near the end of their life that have collapsed in on themselves and become superdense.

A BAFFLING PROBLEM

The description fitted the Dogon version precisely. But how could they have learned about it in the three years between Eddington's announcement of the theory in a popular book in 1928, and the arrival of Griaule and Dieterlen in 1931? The two anthropologists were baffled. 'The problem of knowing how, with no instruments at their disposal, men could know of the movements and certain characteristics of virtually invisible stars has not been settled', they wrote.

At this point, another researcher entered the scene – Robert Temple, an American scholar of Sanskrit and Oriental Studies living in Europe – who became deeply fascinated by two questions raised.

Firstly, was the evidence of the Dogon understanding of astronomy to be believed? And secondly, if the answer to the first question was positive, how could they conceivably have come by this knowledge?

Ancient Wisdom

A careful reading of the source material, and discussions with Germaine Dieterlen in Paris, convinced him after a time that the Dogon were indeed the possessors of an ancient wisdom that concerned not just Sirius B, but the solar system in general. They said the Moon was 'dry and dead like dry dead blood'. Their drawing of the planet Saturn had a ring round it. (Two other exceptional cases of primitive tribes privy to this information are known.) They knew that planets revolved round the sun, and recorded the movements of Venus in their sacred architecture. They knew of the four 'major moons' of Jupiter, first seen by Galileo. (There are now known to be at least 14.) They knew correctly that the Earth spins on its axis. And they believed there was an infinite number of stars, and that there was a spiral force involved in the Milky Way, to which Earth was connected.

Much of this came down in Dogon myth and symbolism. Objects on Earth were said to represent what went on in the skies, but the concept of 'twinning' made many of the calculations obscure, so that it could not be said that the evidence was totally unambiguous. But with Sirius B, in particular, the central facts seemed unarguable. Indeed, the Dogon deliberately chose the smallest yet most significant object they could find – a grain of their essential food crop – to symbolise Sirius B. (*Po tolo* means, literally, a star made of *fonio* seed.) They also stretched their imaginations to describe how massively heavy its mineral content was: 'All earthly beings combined cannot lift it.'

The doors,* right, *to the Dogon granaries,* below, *are decorated with painted figures, depicting the tribe's heavenly ancestors.

Temple found their sand drawings particularly compelling. The egg-shaped ellipse might perhaps be explained away as representing the 'egg of life', or some such symbolic meaning. But the Dogon were insistent that it meant an orbit – a fact discovered by the great astronomer Johannes Kepler in the 16th century, and certainly not known to untutored African tribes. They also put the position of Sirius exactly where it ought to be, rather than where someone might naturally guess – that is, at a focal point near the edge of the ellipse, rather than in the centre.

The Nommo

So how did the Dogon come to have this unearthly knowledge? So far as the Dogon priests are concerned, there is no ambiguity whatsoever in the answer to this question. They believe profoundly that amphibious creatures from a planet within the Sirius system landed on Earth in distant times and passed on the information to initiates, who in turn handed it down over the centuries. They call the creatures Nommo, and worship them as 'the monitors of the universe, the fathers of mankind, guardians of its spiritual principles, dispensers of rain and masters of the water'.

Temple found that the Dogon also drew sand diagrams to portray the spinning, whirling descent

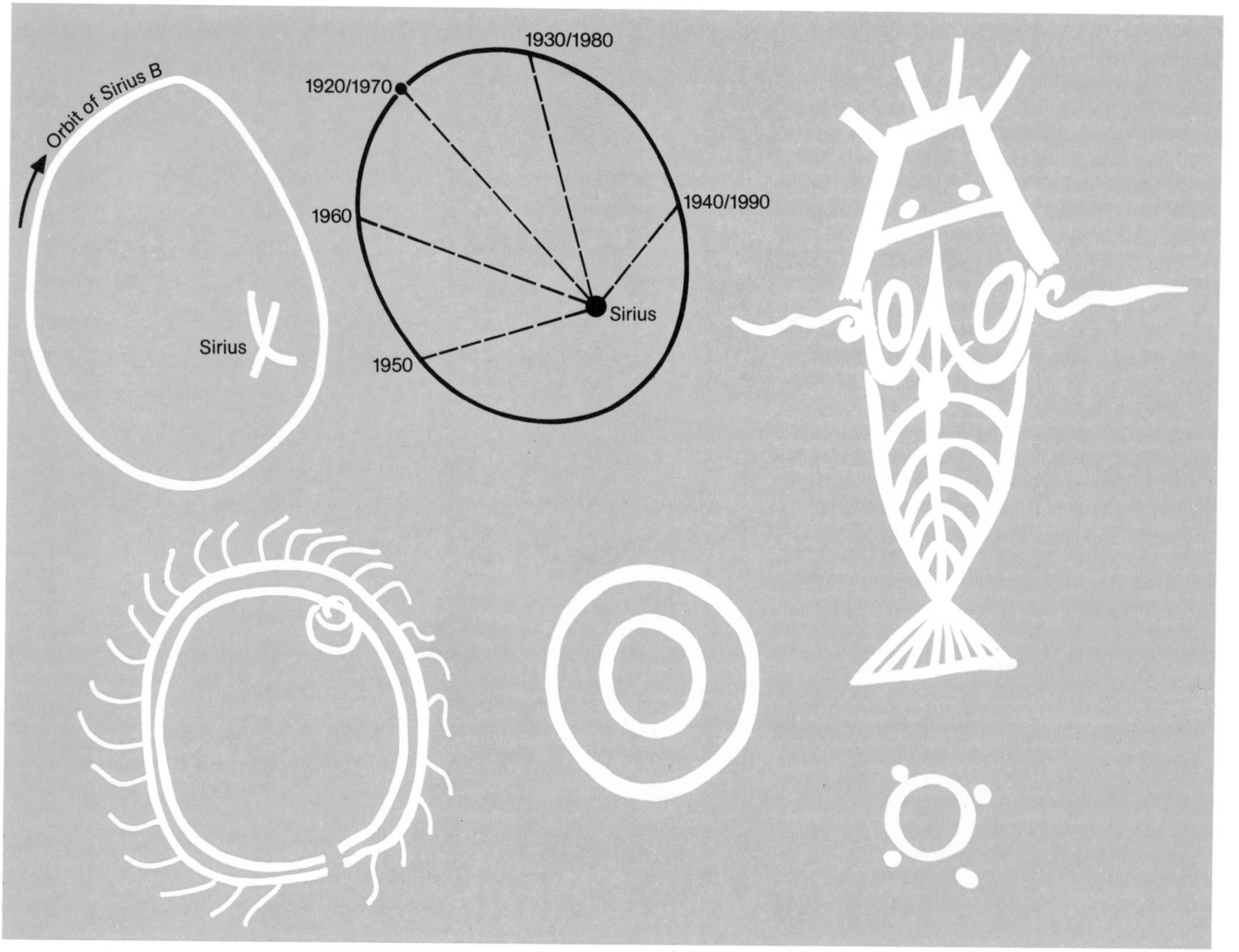

***The Dogan drawing,* top right, *is of one of the Nommo amphibious creatures, said to have given the Dogon information about the solar system when it came down in its 'ark' or spaceship, depicted* above. *The Dogon's knowledge of astronomy is also illustrated in their drawings. A portrayal of the orbit of Sirius B around Sirius,* top left, *is, for example, remarkably similar to a modern astronomical diagram,* top centre. *They also show Saturn with its ring,* above centre, *and depict the four 'major moons' of Jupiter, discovered by Galileo,* above right.**

of a Nommo 'ark', which he took to mean some sort of spaceship. As he put it:

'The descriptions of the landing of the ark are extremely precise. The ark is said to have landed on the Earth to the north-east of the Dogon country, which is where the Dogon claim to have come from originally.

'The Dogon describe the sound of the landing of the ark. They say the 'word' of Nommo was cast down by him in the four directions as he descended, and it sounded like the echoing of the four large stone blocks being struck with stones by the children, according to special rhythms, in a very small cave near Lake Debo. Presumably a thunderous vibrating sound is what the Dogon are trying to convey. One can imagine standing in the cave and holding one's ears at the noise. The descent of the ark must have sounded like a jet runway at close range.'

Other descriptions that the Dogon priests used to refer to the landing of the 'ark' tell how it came down on dry land and 'displaced a pile of dust raised by the whirlwind it caused. The violence of the impact roughened the ground... it skidded'.

Conclusive Proof

Robert Temple's conclusions, first published in 1976 in his book *The Sirius Mystery,* are at once highly provocative and extensively researched. As such, his findings have been used as ammunition both by those who believe in extra-terrestrial visitations in Earth's formative past, and by those (including the majority of scientists and historians) who believe the idea is bunkum.

Erich von Däniken, for instance, whose best-selling books on the subject have now been shown to be based, in the main, on distorted evidence, has welcomed the Dogon beliefs, calling them 'conclusive proof... of ancient astronauts'. Against him range a number of science writers – among them Carl Sagan and Ian Ridpath – who believe the case is by no means proved, and that Temple has read too much into Dogon mythology.

Robert Temple himself, years after first becoming interested in the subject, found nothing to retract from in the answer he gave to his publisher, who expressed his central doubt about the manuscript thus: 'Mr Temple, do you believe it? Do you believe it yourself?'

Temple answered: 'Yes, I do. I have become convinced by my own research. In the beginning I was just investigating. I was sceptical. I was looking for hoaxes, thinking it couldn't be true. But then I began to discover more and more pieces which fit. And the answer is: Yes, I believe it.'

The crucial question is whether the Dogon's knowledge could have been obtained in any more ordinary, mundane way.

THE POWER BEHIND THE HUNCH

COULD THE 'HUNCHES' ON WHICH MANY EXECUTIVES SEEM TO RELY BE EXTRA-SENSORY IN THEIR ORIGIN?

At the New York Stock Exchange,** above, **in the Wall Street district,** right, **many of the men who successfully play the Market admit that they are often guided by precognition and other forms of extra-sensory perception.

After a two-year development programme costing $2 million, the Electric Hydracon Company in Altoona, Pennsylvania, USA, discovered a serious flaw in its new extruded metal installation, which moulds metal by pushing it through dies. Only when the work was completed did the company realise that, if the machinery were run continuously, the regular dies and tooling used would last only a week.

'Financial disaster would be our reward,' said Richard Haupt, who was then executive vice-president. He consulted five major companies to see what could be done and they all gave the same advice. If Electric Hydracon wanted its new plant to last longer, it had to use harder materials for the container, dies and tooling. But Haupt had a nagging doubt: somehow he was sure that it would be better to use softer materials.

'Our president directed me to abide by the decision of the major steel mills,' Haupt recalled.

Dr Douglas Dean,* above left, *together with Dr John Mihalasky, carried out extensive research into the role of ESP in business life. Among the many top executives whose lives and achievements he examined were Conrad Hilton,* top left, *international hotel magnate; William C. Durant,* top right, *founder of General Motors; Charles Kemmons Wilson,* above, *chairman of Holiday Inns; and Charles Chester Carlson,* below, *inventor of the Xerox photocopying technique.

'Nevertheless, I followed my own intuition and spent two-and-a-half times more money for the softer material. The result was an outstanding success with the softer tooling. It lasts six times as long as harder steels. The entire industry has now followed this procedure.'

Richard Haupt, like many other top executives, recognises that there are times when an element of extra-sensory perception emerges in his decision-making, urging him to follow a course of action that often flies in the face of logic or expert advice. This talent, dubbed 'executive ESP', has been the subject of several studies.

Psychic Acumen

Most businessmen would deny that they were psychic, and it is admittedly difficult to know where subconscious assessment for normal sensory clues ends, and extra-sensory perception begins. Executives who recognise that there is a difference between the two use many different words to describe it: sixth sense, business acumen, gut feeling, hunch or intuition.

Psychical researcher Dr Douglas Dean says that executive ESP is an essential ingredient in business life where decisions have to be made about future events, often without enough information to justify them. 'Businessmen use it every week, every month, every year, continually. And the best ones go on doing it very happily without worrying about it. They pile up tremendous profits year after year because they really are stupendous at this ability.'

This statement is based on the research he carried out with the PSI Communications Project at Newark College of Engineering, New Jersey. An English electrochemist with a keen interest in the paranormal, Dean worked on the project with a professor of industrial engineering who was originally sceptical – Dr John Mihalasky.

Among those who gave financial support to the project was the late Chester Carlson, inventor of the Xerox photocopying technique, who – through personal experience – had no doubts at all about the existence of ESP and other psychic phenomena, and often used his special abilities to advantage.

During the course of the PSI Communications Project, the researchers interviewed many top executives and looked at the lives of others. William C. Durant, the founder of General Motors, was typical. One of his colleagues, Alfred P. Sloan, a former president of the giant automobile company, said Durant, 'would proceed on a course of action guided solely, as far as I could tell, by some intuitive flash of brilliance. He never felt obliged to make an engineering hunt for the facts.'

Choosing the right sites for his hotels was the responsibility of Charles Kemmons Wilson, founder and chairman of Holiday Inns Inc. He described the task as like 'going on an Easter egg hunt and sometimes you find the golden egg'. There were times when he would insist on weeks of study by his company before he would make a decision on a site. But there were other times when he would give an emphatic 'no' for no other reason than 'I don't like the smell of it'.

Another hotel man who believed in following his hunches was Conrad Hilton. In the 1940s, Hilton advised Duncan Harris, president of a large real

estate firm, to buy Waldorf-Astoria bonds. Hilton himself had snapped up a considerable number at 4½ cents, much to the surprise of other businessmen. The Depression had made the bonds tumble in price and wartime was adding to the difficulties of maintaining hotels.

Harris was sceptical about his friend's advice and he invited Hilton to listen in on an extension when he telephoned his broker about the bonds. 'Some wild man from the West has forced them up to 8 cents,' said the broker with amusement. 'We're unloading by the bushel. This is the first time in years that anyone holding hotel paper has believed in Santa Claus.'

The cynicism did not dismay Hilton, who remarked later: 'Harris bought, and so, sweating and swearing, did a small faithful group who backed Connie's hunches. Later, hotel securities boomed and the wild man who bought at 4½ cents was considered an astute fellow when he sold at 85 cents. Santa Claus had planted $22,500 and reaped almost $500,000. I've been accused more than once of playing hunches... I further believe most people have them, whether they follow them or not.'

Another of Hilton's hunches paid off when, during the war, he made a bid for the Stevens Corporation. He had wanted the Stevens Hotel, Chicago, but it had been taken over by the Air Force. He decided, when the Stevens Corporation came on the market, that its assets might prove profitable and, in time, if ever the government released the Chicago hotel, it would be his. But the Corporation's trustees called for sealed bids. The business empire would go to the highest bidder. In such a situation, interested parties run the risk of losing a bid by a narrow margin, or unnecessarily outbidding their rivals by many thousands.

There are other ways, too, it seems – apart from relying on hunches – of tapping into financial success. Alison Harper, above, operates as an astrologer, and uses her predictions to help British businessmen make the right commercial decisions. One office systems company even has her on a retainer, contacting her regularly for advice.

'No businessman likes sealed bids,' Hilton remarked. 'My first bid, hastily made, was $165,000. Then somehow it didn't feel right to me. Another figure kept coming, $180,000. It satisfied me. It seemed fair. It felt right. I changed my bid to the larger figure on that hunch. When the sealed bids were opened , the closest to mine was $179,800. So I got the Stevens Corporation by a narrow margin of $200. Eventually the assets returned me $2 million.'

Intuitive Bidding

A similar situation arose in 1969 when the Alaskan oil lands were sold off. The international oil companies also had to make sealed bids, and one particular area of six square miles (16 square kilometres) was of interest to many of them, including the Amarada-Hess-Getty Oil Combine. It had already made a bid but, suddenly, on the weekend before the land was awarded, Leon Hess decided to increase the amount he was prepared to pay to $72.3 million. If he had not done so, he would have lost. When the bids were announced, his combine's offer was just $200,000 above its nearest competitor. Why did Leon Hess decide to boost his offer? 'I suddenly had a hunch,' he explained.

Playing the Stock Market successfully may also depend at times on a willingness to follow hunches. Jesse Livermore, a Wall Street multi-millionaire with intuitive talents was so confident of his ESP powers that he even interrupted a holiday in order to obey a hunch to 'sell short on Union Pacific'. It was a strange decision to make because the railway's stock looked as solid as a rock, but he obeyed the impulse. A few days later, the San Francisco earthquake wrecked miles of the railway company's track and its stock fell drastically. The hunch netted Livermore over a quarter of a million dollars.

So what is a hunch? The top executives who rely on it do not seen to know. Benjamin Fairless, former Chairman of the Board of US Steel, has said: 'You don't know how you do it; you just do it.'

The 1906 San Francisco earthquake destroyed miles of track belonging to the Union Pacific railway, right, and the company's stock fell drastically as a result. But one stockholder, Jesse Livermore, saved himself over a quarter of a million dollars: only a few days before, he had obeyed an impulse to 'sell short on Union Pacific'.

The oil pipeline,* below, *is sited on the Alaskan oil lands that were sold off in 1969. Several companies had showed an interest in one small area. Sealed bids were invited and the Amarada-Hess-Getty Oil Combine made the highest offer – but only because, at the last moment and acting on a hunch, Leon Hess increased the amount he was prepared to pay.

It would seem that executive ESP is often a deciding factor in an individual's business career, enabling those who possess the gift to rise to the top and help their companies to prosper. But would it be possible to spot such people in advance? Surprisingly, the answer which the PSI Communications Project came up with is 'Yes'. Dean and Mihalasky, as well as interviewing top businessmen and actually testing them for ESP, also examined their outlook in a search for clues that would differentiate between those who had produced high scores in the tests and those who, as it turned out, scored below average.

They were greatly influenced by the work of a leading American psychical researcher, Dr Gertrude Schmeidler, professor of psychology at the City College of New York. Dr Schmeidler had been investigating precognition for some considerable time and had compared the results of the participants in her experiments with their responses to a specially devised, so-called Time Metaphor Test. Individuals were asked if they thought of time as a dashing waterfall, a motionless sea, or in the form of an old man.

Those whose images of time were fast-moving were classed as 'dynamics', whereas those who regarded it as a motionless sea were said to be 'naturalistics'. For the few for whom time conjured up an image of an old man, the term 'humanistic' was used – they were the neutrals. When Dr Schmeidler analysed her results she discovered that the dynamics scored high in precognition tests, where they knew they would subsequently be told the outcome.

Time and again in these tests, the two Newark researchers found dynamics out-scoring naturalistics (whom they called oceanics) in the ESP tests,

> " My first bid, hastily made, was $165,000. Then somehow it didn't feel right to me. Another figure kept coming, $180,000. It satisfied me... It felt right... So I got the Stevens Corporation by a narrow margin of $200. Eventually the assets returned me $2 million. "
>
> **Conrad Hilton**

which usually involved attempting to guess a number they set participants, that a computer would generate randomly.

Dynamic Scores

On one occasion, 40 top-flight executives were subjected to a test. Once again, the dynamics, as a group, outscored their oceanic colleagues. This time, Mihalasky also compared the results with the financial success of each individual's company. As he commented:

'Some of the presidents were company owners. I asked if they were also the chief decision makers. If the answer was no, I discarded them. Others were chief decision makers but didn't have the title of president, and I threw them out too.' In this way he reduced the number to a dozen, all of whom were presidents who had held office for at least five years.

'Of these,' Mihalasky reports, 'every man who improved his company's profits by 100 per cent or more scored above the ten mark (average) on the precognition test.' He then combined the statistics with those attained at a similar survey of top executives, giving him 25 chief executives of small, medium and large companies. Twelve of these ran companies which had performed outstandingly, at least doubling profits in five years. When he checked their scores in the ESP test, he found that 11 of the 12 scored above average, and the twelfth man scored exactly at chance. Not one of them showed a negative ESP score.

An examination of the other 13 chief executives, who had not doubled their profits in five years, showed that five who had scored above chance had improved profits by between 51 and 100 per cent. One man scored at chance level, and of the seven who scored below chance only two had improved profits by more than 50 per cent.

Though not a large enough study to claim proof of the theory, these results do suggest very strongly that there is a correlation between profit-making and ESP abilities.

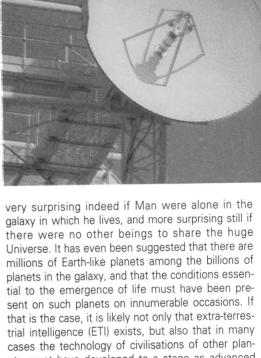

IS ANYBODY OUT THERE?

EVEN IF SOMEONE IS INDEED LISTENING, WILL OUR MESSAGES NECESSARILY BE UNDERSTOOD?

Mankind's first radio message to the stars was transmitted at 5 p.m. on 16 November 1974 by the world's largest radio telescope, a disc 1,000 feet (300 metres) in diameter, situated in Puerto Rico. The message was a three-minute signal sent out across the vastness of space towards a group of stars 24,000 light years away. It is believed to be the strongest signal yet radiated by mankind; and in the words of the Arecibo staff, it was intended to be 'a concrete demonstration that terrestrial radio astronomy had now reached a level of advance entirely adequate for interstellar radio communication over immense distances'.

The Arecibo transmission was a statement of faith by the scientific community. It bore witness to the confidence of scientists that intelligent extra-terrestrial beings exist and are 'out there' listening. In fact, many people would argue that it would be very surprising indeed if Man were alone in the galaxy in which he lives, and more surprising still if there were no other beings to share the huge Universe. It has even been suggested that there are millions of Earth-like planets among the billions of planets in the galaxy, and that the conditions essential to the emergence of life must have been present on such planets on innumerable occasions. If that is the case, it is likely not only that extra-terrestrial intelligence (ETI) exists, but also that in many cases the technology of civilisations of other planets must have developed to a stage as advanced as, or even much more advanced than our own.

From the Arecibo observatory in Puerto Rico,* above, *astronomers sent out Earth's first radio message to a group of stars, 24,000 light years away. Microwave receiving dishes, such as the one,* inset above, *meanwhile, have for years been leaking signals into space.

The impulse to attempt to make contact with beings on other planets is clearly very strong in Man. In the mid-19th century – a hundred years before sophisticated technology made such ambitions at all realistic – many people took it more or less for granted that there were civilisations on other planets that could be reached with the aid of science, and various methods of communicating with these civilisations were proposed.

The French inventor Charles Cros (1842-88), for example, suggested the construction of a vast mirror that could be used to reflect sunlight from Earth to Mars. It could be tilted, he thought, to flash out a form of code. (The idea was ingenious, but it raised an insurmountable problem: there was, of course, no guarantee that a Martian civilisation would recognise or be able to respond to such a code.)

SPECTACULAR MESSAGES

Nevertheless, interest in establishing communication with extra-terrestrial beings soon grew to fever pitch. In Paris, in 1900, for example, a prize of 100,000 francs was offered to the first person who would manage to make contact with ETI. The competition excluded communication with Mars, however – that was thought to be far too easy a feat to be worth the money!

These enthusiastic early experiments proved fruitless, however. It is doubtful whether the crude techniques that were suggested could have served the purpose of initiating contact with extra-terrestrial civilisations, and it has since been established that there is no ETI on the Moon, on Venus or on Mars. Yet the search for intelligent life on other planets continues; and, ironically enough, in the 20th century, we have transmitted spectacular messages to the stars with no special effort.

Since the 1940s, powerful microwave beams from radar and TV transmitters have been leaking out into space. This radio noise is already washing over the stars nearest to Earth like a tide of electromagnetic flotsam; and although its intensity is minute, a sufficiently sensitive receiver could pick up the signal as far as 40 light years away.

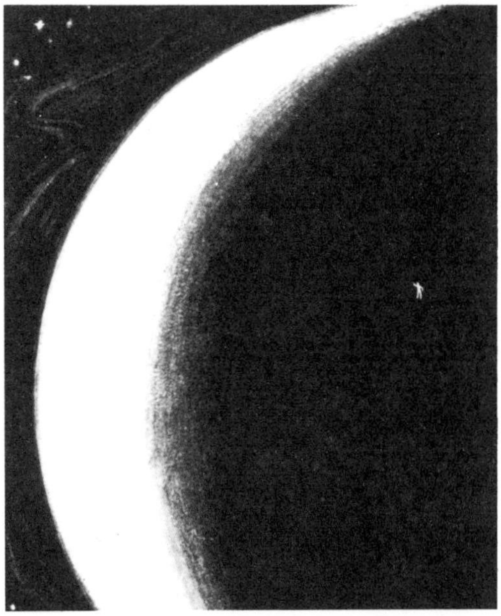

The tiny human outline in the picture,* right*, is an artist's impression of what an illuminated figure would look like from Mars. The shape – which was to be formed by illuminating 'several square miles' of snow with electric lamps – was proposed in 1893 as a means of communicating with other planets.

Another late-Victorian proposal – a cross of powerful electric lights to be strung across Lake Michigan – is demonstrated* below*. The lights would flash on for 10 minutes and off for another 10 – an artificial phasing that, it was hoped, would attract interstellar attention.

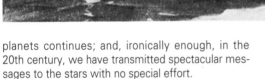

Hydroxyl and hydrogen, which together make water,* right*, could be widespread emitters of microwaves in space. Indeed, the wave band from 17-21 centimetres is sometimes called the 'waterhole'. The name is also apt because of the hope that different extra-terrestrial civilisations may send and receive messages in this band, just as different species come to drink at waterholes on Earth.

MEANINGFUL SIGNALS

So what would an extra-terrestrial astronomer make of this swelling tide of radio noise? If he had sustained his observations over a long period of time, he would have made an interesting discovery: today, Earth is emitting radiation at the frequency of radio waves that is a million times more intense than it was a few decades ago. And if he used his radio telescope to measure the radio power emerging from this small planet at metre wavelengths, he would make an even more astounding discovery: Earth is emitting almost as much radiation as the Sun at a time of low sunspot activity. In fact, in the radio spectrum, our planet is as bright as a star!

Extra-terrestrial scientists would perhaps attempt to formulate a 'natural' explanation for the phenomenon; but any such attempt would eventually prove unsatisfactory. They would be forced to acknowledge that the radio emission could not be explained by the action of natural forces: it could only be produced by artificial means. However, scientists on other planets might not regard such weak signals as incontrovertible proof of the existence of a civilisation somewhere near our Sun. Even if they concluded that a civilisation did exist, they would probably find it impossible to make sense of the complicated mix of signals.

One solution to this dilemma is for us to indicate our presence unambiguously by transmitting a constant and deliberate message via a powerful radio beam, aimed at the stars. Existing radio telescopes provide us with the technological means to do this.

Meanwhile, if we are trying to contact civilisations that may exist on other planets, it is conceivable that such civilisations may be attempting to communicate with Earth – perhaps some are even transmitting messages right now. Our radio telescopes would probably be sensitive enough to pick up their signals, but for two problems: we know neither where their transmissions might come from, nor the wavelength into which we should tune.

Imagine a transistor radio that is unable to pick up a radio station unless its aerial is pointed directly at the transmitter. The search for a particular station would involve not only exhaustive research to identify the direction of the transmitter, but also tuning through all the wavebands to find the right channel. Radio astronomers face just this problem, except that they are obliged to search through a vastly greater frequency band. There is the added disadvantage, too, that they may need to listen for several minutes on each wavelength in order to detect any faint signal against the background noise.

Tuning In

Radio telescopes can be tuned to receive a specific wavelength; but if a message were being transmitted on another wavelength, it would be missed. Clearly, it would be impracticable to construct radio telescopes tuned to every possible wavelength in the hope of picking up signals from other planets. Is there, then, some way in which the task could be simplified? Might it be possible to determine which wavelengths might be chosen for the transmission of messages from other planets?

During the Second World War, the Dutch astronomer Hendrick Christoffel van den Hulst calculated that hydrogen atoms might sometimes change from one energy state to another and, in so doing, might emit a photon (a quantity of electromagnetic radiation energy) with a frequency corresponding to a radio wavelength of 21 centimetres. Individual hydrogen atoms, he postulated, would undergo this transition very rarely. However, because hydrogen is the predominant element in the Universe, he predicted that the microwave 'notes' emitted by vast quantities of hydrogen atoms should build up to a level detectable by super-sensitive equipment. Then, in 1951, the American physicist Edward Mills Purcell made some observations that confirmed Van den Hulst's prediction.

Dr Frank Drake,* above, *started Project Ozma, which represented the first intensive search for messages from outer space. His team listened for 150 hours for an intelligible signal, but heard nothing that could be construed as a message.

The radio telescope at the National Observatory in Green Bank, West Virginia,* below, *was used in Project Ozma.

Since hydrogen is the most abundant substance in the Universe, it is reasonable to assume that any civilisation with an advanced technology would discover this property of hydrogen atoms and would conclude, as radio astronomers on Earth have done, that the 21 centimetre wavelength is one on which signals could be transmitted and received anywhere in the Universe, given sophisticated technology.

The idea of listening for interstellar communications transmitted on the 21-centimetre wavelength was first suggested in 1959 by physicists Giuseppe Cocconi and Philip Morrison, and has been widely adopted by subsequent signal searchers.

The Waterhole

Another suggestion along the same lines is to make use of hydroxyl, the two-atom combination of hydrogen and oxygen that, next to hydrogen itself, is the most widespread emitter of microwaves in space. Its microwave emission has a wavelength of 17 centimetres. Since hydrogen and hydroxyl together make water, the wave band from 17 to 21 centimetres is sometimes call the 'waterhole'. This region of the radio spectrum happens to have the least interference from background radiation and thus makes an ideal, naturally defined search band for interstellar communication. Its name is particularly apt, because the hope is that different civilisations will send and receive messages in this band in the same way as different species of animals come to drink at waterholes on Earth.

In 1960, the first serious attempt was made to listen to the 21 centimetre wavelength in the hope of detecting messages from the stars. This was Frank Drakes's Project Ozma. The listening began at 4 a.m. on 8 April 1960 with no publicity, as the astronomers feared ridicule. For 150 hours, they listened for signs of an intelligible signal, but they found absolutely nothing.

At Green Bank Observatory, in 1976, Benjamin Zuckerman and Patrick Palmer completed a four-year survey of the 659 stars most likely to harbour life between six and 76 light years away from the Sun. Although their equipment was far more sensitive than that used in Ozma, they too drew a blank.

Such lack of results may, of course, indicate that we are on the wrong trail. Up to this point, we have considered only interstellar radio contact among civilisations at, or just beyond, our own state of technical advance. Yet the bulk of technical civilisations may be immensely more advanced than ours. So perhaps we should consider how these technologies might communicate with us.

The Soviet astronomer Kardashev has suggested that civilisations might exist at three levels. A *Level I* civilisation might be regarded as Earth-like, able to exploit only a portion of the energy resources available to it; a *Level II* civilisation might tap the entire energy of its star, thus harnessing energies 100 trillion times those of *Level I* civilisations; and a *Level III* civilisation might tap entire galaxies, thus disposing of energies 100 billion times greater than those of *Level II* civilisations. If

> **"** ARE WE LISTENING IN THE RIGHT WAY? OR ARE WE DEAF TO A SIGNAL THAT WE ARE ACTUALLY RECEIVING LOUD AND CLEAR? **"**

Kardashev's theory is sound, a *Level II* civilisation should easily be detectable throughout its galaxy, and a *Level III* civilisation throughout the Universe. Thus we might be tempted to dismiss the possibility of the existence of such civilisations on the grounds that we can detect no signs of them anywhere. But are we listening in the right way? Or are we deaf to a signal that we are actually receiving loud and clear?

In 1965, Soviet radio astronomer Scholomitski studied the radio source CTA 102 and announced that it was varying significantly in intensity, with an apparent period of 100 days, and transmitting at a wavelength near 18 centimetres that had previously been proposed for interstellar communication. It was speculated that the oscillation might serve as a beacon calling attention to CTA 102, and that on a much shorter timescale than 100 days the individual words of an interstellar communication channel might be deciphered. In the Soviet press, some astronomers openly speculated that CTA 102 bore all the signs of an artificial source.

CTA 102 was later identified as a quasar – a natural source. But even so, might it not be under the control of a *Level II* or *Level III* civilisation? And might not the same be true of pulsars, stars that also send out regular pulses of radiation?

The artist's impressions on this page show the proposed NASA scheme, Project Cyclops, designed to achieve optimum efficiency in detecting radio signals from other intelligences.

The densely-packed array of radio telescopes,* below, *shows how they would look on the Moon's surface.* Below right, *they are shown as they would appear in the pilot scheme, based on Earth. The lunar Cyclops project is, however, at present very much a scientist's dream.

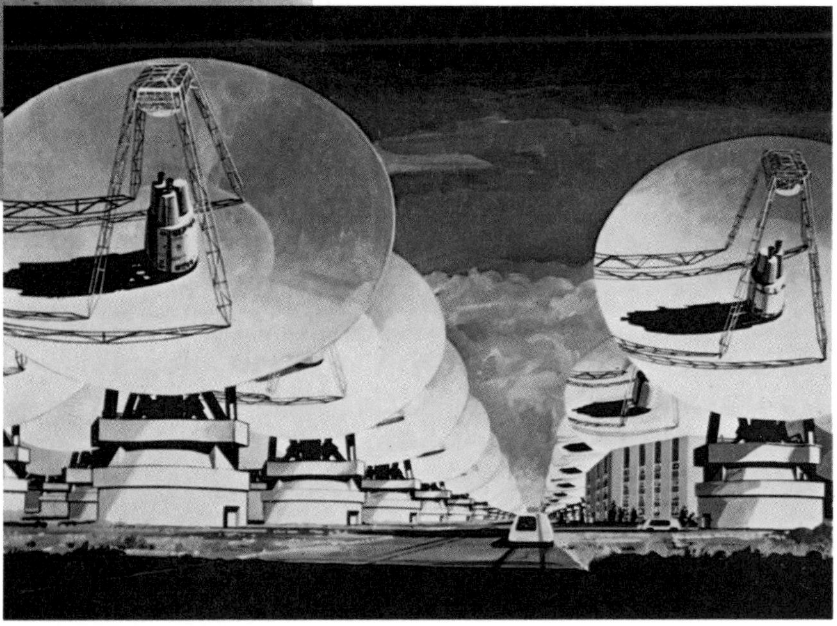

To be sure, variations in intensity seem to be quite irregular in the case of quasars, and quite regular in the case of pulsars. But in neither case do we appear to be receiving information from an intelligent source. Could the signals therefore be messages from beings so intelligent that we cannot understand them because our mental capacity is limited? This may be the case, but it seems unlikely because any advanced civilisation would no doubt appreciate the problems of interstellar discourse and would surely use the simplest possible method for establishing contact.

A more serious problem might be raised, however, by contact with less advanced civilisations than our own. How would we communicate with beings as dull-witted, say, as cows, or as primitive as Stone Age man – even supposing that we were to discover such communities? And even if we could devise some means of communication, we might wish to preserve their culture and way of life by leaving them undisturbed. (Of course, super-advanced extra-terrestrial civilisations may regard human beings as fumbling incompetents and take exactly this 'conservationist' attitude towards us.)

PROJECT CYCLOPS

But whether our neighbours in the Universe are super-brains or savages, much bigger projects will have to be set up if the search for ETI is to be carried on with any hope of success. The most famous such proposal is the National Aeronautics and Space Administration (NASA) Cyclops project, which would involve 1,000 or more radio telescopes, each the size of a football, steered in unison by a computerised electronic system. Their combined performance would be equivalent to that of a single disc 6.2 miles (10 kilometres) in diameter, virtually impossible to construct because it would collapse under its own weight.

Such an array of radio telescopes would, however, be able to detect radiation as weak as Earth's inadvertent leakage of microwaves even from a distance of 100 light years, while a message from another civilisation could perhaps be detected at a distance of at least 1,000 light years.

Project Cyclops would not be easy or cheap to construct, though it is perfectly feasible using existing technology. It has also been estimated that it would cost many billions of dollars to build and run – a considerable commitment to the search for ETI.

Our technology is capable of mounting a very effective search for extra-terrestrial signals. But is the search worthwhile? The biggest hurdle is, of course, the fact that we cannot guarantee success.

ON THE BIGFOOT TRAIL

HUNDREDS OF SIGHTINGS ALL OVER THE NORTH AMERICAN CONTINENT SUGGEST THAT THE BIGFOOT – A FABLED MAN-BEAST – EXISTS AFTER ALL. BUT WHAT EXACTLY ARE THESE STRANGE CREATURES? AND HOW HAVE THEY MANAGED TO SURVIVE?

The bigfoot riddle is not an easy one to solve. There is, of course, the question of ascertaining whether or not the creature really exists and, if it does, whether it is human or animal. But some reports, especially more recent ones, have features that seem to deepen the mystery even further.

The average height of a bigfoot seems to be between 6 and 7 feet (1.8 – 2.1 metres), though much smaller ones are sometimes reported, possibly youngsters. However, much taller ones, too, have occasionally been seen. A 15-foot (4.5 metre) creature was spotted by a USAF Staff Sergeant and two friends while they were camping at Belt Creek Canyon, Montana, in August 1977. They shot at it, but turned tail and drove away in their cars when it began to run towards them. Reports of fleeting sightings of this sort, however, can never be taken at face value: size, for instance, is easily mistaken under conditions of stress, and shape may be misinterpreted, too.

Sometimes, however, an accurate calculation of height can be made. In April 1979, 16-year-old Tim Meissner saw a bigfoot twice in three days near his rural home in British Columbia. The first time, while fishing with friends at Dunn Lake near Barriere, he heard a high-pitched screech and saw a bigfoot with its arms raised on the lake's far shore. It ran away as the youths went to investigate. Hidden there, under branches and moss, they found a deer with a broken neck.

Two days later, Tim Meissner returned with four friends, armed with a gun. They split up to search for the bigfoot; and by an astonishing stroke of luck, Meissner saw it again. His first reaction was to shoot at the tall, black, hairy creature with glaring bright eyes and shoulders, 4 feet (1.2 metres) wide. He probably hit it, since it went down on one knee; but then it got up and ran away at great speed. When Tim saw the bigfoot, it was about 50 yards (45 metres) away, standing beside a tree. Later, he returned to the tree and was able to estimate that

the creature he had seen must have been about 9 feet (2.7 metres) tall.

The Mystery Deepens

According to many accounts, some bigfeet smell revolting. During a flurry of sightings around Little Eagle, South Dakota, in the autumn of 1977, for instance, one witness reported: 'It was like a stink of a dead person, long dead. It stayed in the air for maybe 10 to 15 minutes afterwards'. It has even been suggested that they can release the smell at will, perhaps to ensure that people keep their distance. Another strange feature is that some bigfeet have exceptionally large eyes which glow. They are usually red, but sometimes yellow or green.

night in February 1974, shot into its middle from a distance of 6 feet (1.8 metres), and was astounded to see it disappear in a flash of light. Other eye-witnesses have also reported signs of insubstantiality in the bigfeet they have seen.

In the Pennsylvania case, the witness's son-in-law, who came to help on hearing the shot, saw other bigfeet at the edge of nearby woods. He also saw a bright red flashing light hovering there.

Another strange case involving a possible UFO took place on a farm near Greensburg, Pennsylvania, on the evening of 25 October 1973. When a large, bright red luminous ball was seen to come down in a field, a 22-year-old farmer's son went to investigate. He and the two 10-year-old

Bigfeet, such as the one far left, have frequently been spotted in the north-west of the American continent. Mysteriously, they seem capable of dematerialisation.

The bones, left, are claimed by the monks of Pangboche monastery to be the skeletal hand of a yeti. Although the hand seems small in comparison with the scalp, the remains have been taken as evidence to support the theory that the yeti is a form of ape, since the hands of many ape species are relatively small.

Footprint evidence is also puzzling. Five-toed prints are most commonly found, and resemble large human feet. But sometimes the prints appear to have only two toes, or three, four or sometimes six – an anomaly perhaps explicable in terms of over-eager investigators misinterpreting less than perfect footprints.

A significant number of reports, many of them made by experienced huntsmen, also tell of a particularly disturbing phenomenon: some bigfeet are apparently completely unharmed by bullets.

There seem to be three possible explanations for this: the guns used are just not powerful enough to tackle such a creature; the witness, in his excitement, did not aim properly (although some shots were fired from very close range); or bigfeet are not made of flesh and blood.

Dematerialisation

The theory that bigfeet are not composed of flesh and blood sounds incredible enough, but there is extraordinary evidence that tends to support the claim. Some bigfeet are apparently able to disappear altogether, or dematerialise. A Pennsylvanian woman, confronted by one on her doorstep one

boys he took with him saw the shining object on or close to the ground. They also saw, near the ball, two tall, ape-like creatures with green glowing eyes and long, dark hair. The creatures began to approach them.

The farmer's son fired over their heads, but they kept walking towards the witnesses. So he fired three rounds straight into the largest creature, which raised its hand. The UFO disappeared, and the 'bigfeet' turned and walked slowly into the nearby woods. Investigators were immediately called in; and although they saw neither the UFO nor the bigfeet, they did find a glowing area where the UFO had been.

Rival Killers

Such bizarre cases are by no means widespread, and generally reported in states far away from the traditional bigfoot territory in the north-west of the continent. Some veteran bigfoot hunters and investigators are sceptical of such apparently paranormal incidents, possibly feeling that they do not wish to become involved in fringe eccentricities.

Meanwhile, those hunters who feel it is their life's work to convince the world of the existence of

Tim Meissner, far left, is seen estimating the height of a bigfoot he saw and shot at near his home in British Columbia, Canada, in April 1979. The creature, about 9 feet (2.7 metres) tall, was standing beside this tree when Tim saw it.

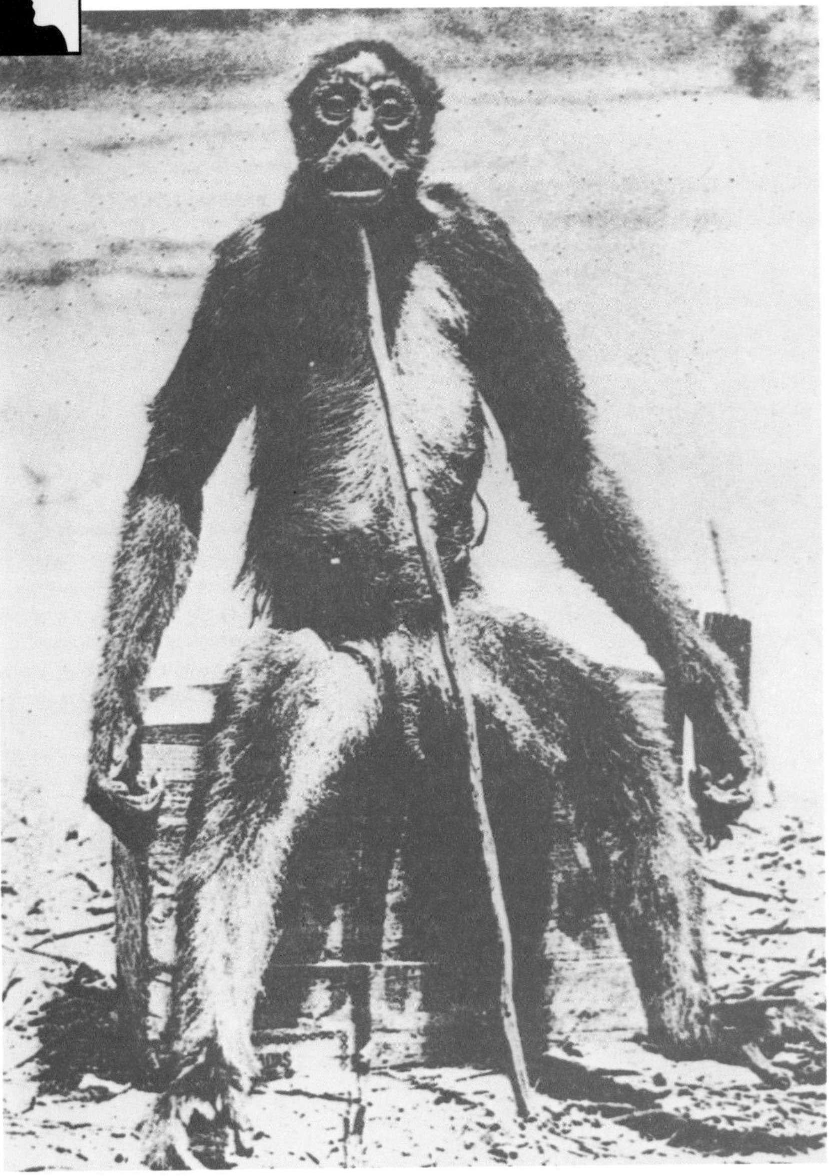

The 'man-beast'*, above, *was shot by Swiss geologist Francois de Loys on the borders of Colombia and Venezuela in 1917. It is now thought to have been a kind of spider monkey.

the bigfoot have a hard task for, despite the mass of data, few professional scientists or anthropologists will give their work a second glance. Certainly, if a bigfoot corpse was obtained, their case would be incontrovertible. Consequently there is rivalry – even open hostility – among those hunters who compete to be first to capture or kill one, and make it available for study.

In 1917, for instance, Swiss geologist Francois de Loys shot a 5-foot (1.5-metre) animal on the borders of Colombia and Venezuela, but zoologist Dr Bernard Heuvelmans believes it may have been an unknown type of spider monkey.

Of many reports from the USSR, one tells of a man-beast captured and later killed in the mountains near Buinaksk in Daghestan. A Soviet army officer, Colonel Karapetyan, saw the creature while it was still alive and later remembered it vividly:

'I can still see the creature as it stood before me, a male, naked and barefoot. And it was doubtlessly a man, because its entire shape was human. The chest, back, and shoulders, however, were covered with shaggy hair of a dark brown colour... his height was above average – about 180 centimetres [6 feet]. He stood before me like a giant, his mighty chest thrust forward... His eyes told me nothing. They were dull and empty – the eyes of an animal. This was no disguised person, but a wild man of some kind.'

FROZEN CORPSE

In December 1968, came a report from Minnesota, USA, of a bigfoot corpse, frozen in a block of ice. Dr Heuvelmans and biologist Ivan T. Sanderson saw it and, despite the difficulties of examination, were convinced that the ice contained the fresh corpse of a hitherto unknown form of human life.

But despite the number of sightings, hunters are not able simply to go into the forest and kill a bigfoot. Bigfeet are reputed to possess such intimate knowledge of the terrain they inhabit that they can travel through it far more quickly than a man and remain completely concealed. Given these alleged characteristics, the prospect for the hunter of capturing or killing one remains remote.

Most of the time, all the intrepid hunter can do is interview witnesses, examine footprints, and collect newspaper reports. Such work, carried out by dedicated enthusiasts all over the North American continent, has resulted in an accumulation of data and many intriguing theories about the nature of bigfeet – and, indeed, all man-beasts. Nevertheless, without high-quality photographs, a corpse or a skeleton, or even part of one, all that scientists can do is speculate.

What we do know for certain is that large,

human-like footprints have been found in large numbers in remote areas – not all of which are likely to be fakes – and that well over 1000 people in North America alone have reported seeing tall, hairy man-beasts. The various theories that have been put forward to explain these facts apply equally well to man-beasts seen over the world.

MAN, BEAST... OR HOLOGRAM?

On the negative side, however, it has been suggested that all man-beast reports are hoaxes. But this does seem unlikely. Another suggestion is that people may be misidentifying known animals under poor viewing conditions. This explanation could, of course, account for some of the sightings, but by no means all of them. Yet another view is that some sightings are simply hallucinations. People who have seen too many horror films have sometimes had hallucinations, claiming to have seen things that are simply not there. May not man-beast sightings be a similar case? But this theory does not account for the footprints, which appear to be real enough.

A more sympathetic view is that the man-beasts may be some form of giant ape or perhaps an early form of man-like ape, *Gigantopithecus*. This seems possible, even likely, in some parts of the world. Alternatively, man-beasts may really be men, prehistoric survivors who have managed to stay concealed against all the odds.

But some people have also argued that man-beasts are some kind of paranormal phenomenon that comes into being when certain types of energy are available (electrical, nuclear or psychic, for example). Bigfeet have certainly been reported near energy sources on occasions.

An even more remote possibility is that man-beasts come from UFOs, for reasons as yet unknown. But if UFOs and man-beasts are both paranormal phenomena, they are just as likely to have been formed in the same way – which may explain why they sometimes appear close together in time and space. Then, again, man-beasts could be holograms, three-dimensional images projected from space by an unknown intelligence. If so, who or what is doing it – and why?

Investigators differ in their interpretations of the data, and perhaps no one explanation can account for all reported sightings. All in all, it is most likely that the term 'man-beasts' covers a wide range of phenomena that, for unknown reasons, appear – or seem to appear – in similar guises. Whatever the truth, the man-beast phenomenon is an extraordinary and complex mystery – one that requires a great deal more research before any firm conclusions can be drawn.

"THE THEORY THAT BIGFEET ARE NOT COMPOSED OF FLESH AND BLOOD SOUNDS INCREDIBLE ENOUGH, BUT THERE IS EXTRAORDINARY EVIDENCE THAT TENDS TO SUPPORT THE CLAIM. SOME BIGFEET ARE APPARENTLY ABLE TO DISAPPEAR ALTOGETHER OR DEMATERIALISE."

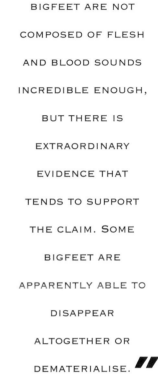

Paul Freeman is seen,* inset left, *with a number of plaster casts of the footprints of a man-beast he saw in Umatilla National Forest, Washington State, in June 1982. Some six years later, the alleged bigfoot,* left, *was photographed at Mill Creek watershed, nearby.

WHITE HOLES

AN ASTRONAUT MIGHT BE ABLE TO TRAVEL THROUGH A BLACK HOLE TO DISTANT PARTS OF OUR UNIVERSE. BUT HOW WOULD HE RETURN? WHITE HOLES, IT SEEMS, MAY PROVIDE AN INSTANT SOLUTION

In the distant future, perhaps three to six centuries from now, a fleet of 1,000 interstellar bulldozers could be setting off from Earth for a point in space one light year from the Sun – their mission, the construction of a black hole, through which astronauts would be able to travel to other parts of our Universe.

The idea may seem fantastic, but the difficulties involved in gathering the material needed to build a black hole with a total mass of more than 3 million times the mass of Earth would not be quite as great as it might seem. Each interstellar bulldozer would be capable of generating a magnetic field some 150,000 miles (240,000 kilometres) wide – a field capable of gathering matter (mainly iron, nickel and hydrogen plasma) as soon as the interstellar bulldozer is beyond the orbits of the outer planets of our solar system.

If astronauts are to travel through artificial black holes to remote parts of the Universe, vast cities in space will have to be built to act as bases for operations.

To generate this huge magnetic field, electrical energy could be supplied through a superconducting system, powered by the vehicle's main engine. The iron, nickel and hydrogen plasma, piling up in front of the magnetic field, would form a great column of matter stretching forward for hundreds of thousands of miles; and this mass would be propelled forward by the vehicle.

We can calculate that the interstellar matter would be gathered up at the rate of 35 ounces (990 grams) per second per ship; or if a fleet of 1,000 ships was at work, at a rate of 35,000 ounces (990

> "A WHITE HOLE IS NO MORE STRANGE THAN A BLACK HOLE, IT IS SIMPLY ITS OPPOSITE. A BLACK HOLE IS AN IMPLOSION, AND A WHITE HOLE IS AN EXPLOSION."

kilograms) per second – which is about 3,500 tonnes per hour.

Suppose that, because of the great distances involved in their journey (one light-year round the Sun), 20 years elapse between the time that the ships embark on their mission and the time that they begin to accumulate matter in significant quantities. After this period, their task would be made easier because there could actually be a factor working in their favour: the accumulated matter would itself ionise fresh matter, in turn caught up in the eddying forward movement.

It is not unreasonable to predict that, when this process of accumulation really begins to mount, its actual rate of increase will itself increase at a rate of perhaps one per cent every 24 hours. Now, anything that increases at one per cent per day will double, by compound interest, every 70 days. If such a rate of doubling can be achieved with the ships cruising at about seven per cent of the speed of light, or 47 million mph (76 million km/h), a black hole could in theory be constructed about 15 years after the end of the 20-year preparation period – less than 40 years from start to finish.

Gateway in Space

But having constructed the black hole, what happens to an astronaut attempting to enter it? Should he just let himself go, abandoning the controls of his spacecraft to gravitational fields, trusting that he will be safely hurled down the whirling spiral? If he did this, he would be sucked into the singularity and be crushed to pieces. Instead, he must remember the disc shape of the black hole. This disc (assuming that the black hole has 10 times the mass of the Sun) will have a circumference of just under 116 miles (190 kilometres), rotating at a velocity of 1,000 complete revolutions per second. Each part of the disc will also be revolving at a speed of 116,000 miles per second (190,000 km/s). The astronaut must match this speed precisely as he approaches the black hole. This speed, which is slightly more than 60 per cent of the speed of light, is not prohibited by any known scientific law, but could only be attained by some super-spacecraft of the future.

When the astronaut has matched his speed with that of the spinning disc, each in a sense will now be stationary. The astronaut 'looks' at the disc-edge beside him and 'sees' a long rectangular aperture with a height of about 640 yards (590 metres). This aperture is the gateway to another region in space and is the one route which passes through both event horizons (inner and outer) and avoids the crushing densities of the singularity. Diving directly into the aperture, the astronaut and his ship vanish from the sight of any outside observer. Yet they survive, vanishing only in the sense that a spectator at an airport sees an aircraft and its passengers disappear into the sky, for the astronaut and his ship will only have vanished out of the immediate region of space. They will have accomplished the miracle of vanishing in one place, reappearing, a moment later, in another, which may be separated from the point of disappearance by a vast distance.

How does this miracle occur? What actually happens in the area between the two event horizons? This region is highly mysterious, but there is one thing that can be said of it with certainty: distances within it are abridged absolutely, so the word 'distance' not only loses its present meaning, it ceases to have any meaning. By its very act of passing through the inner event horizon of the black hole, the spaceship has begun to cross what is known as an Einstein-Rosen bridge – a timeless passage that interconnects different regions of our Universe. An immeasurable fraction of a second later, it emerges in another distant part of space.

PERSPECTIVES

THE EINSTEIN-ROSEN BRIDGE

Albert Einstein and Isaac Rosen developed the simple model, *top right,* of a static black hole – the famous Einstein-Rosen bridge. They suggested that spacetime in our Universe may be curved, as shown *centre,* so a spaceship would emerge at a different time and place. But if, as astronomers now believe, spacetime in our Universe is almost flat, the shape of the bridge could look more like the wormhole, *bottom,* linking different parts of our Universe.

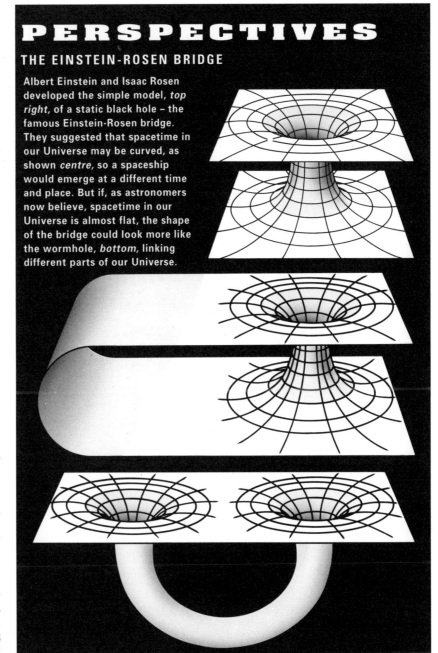

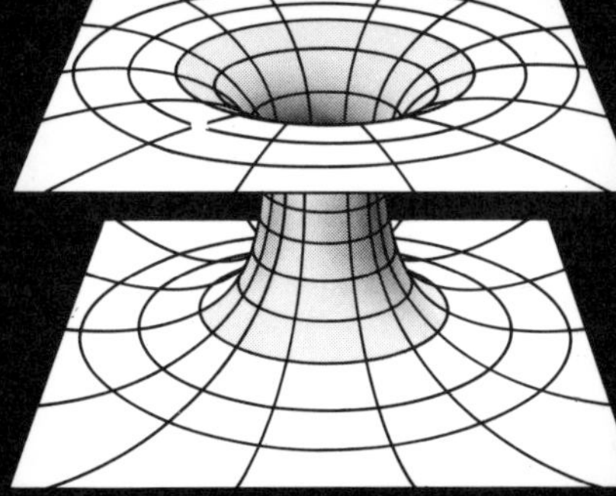

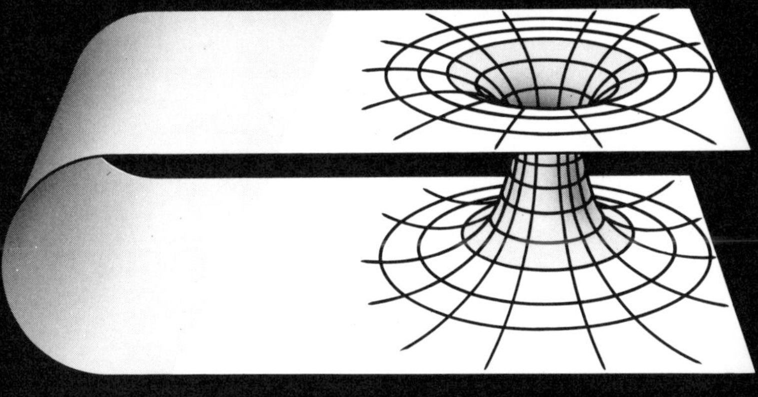

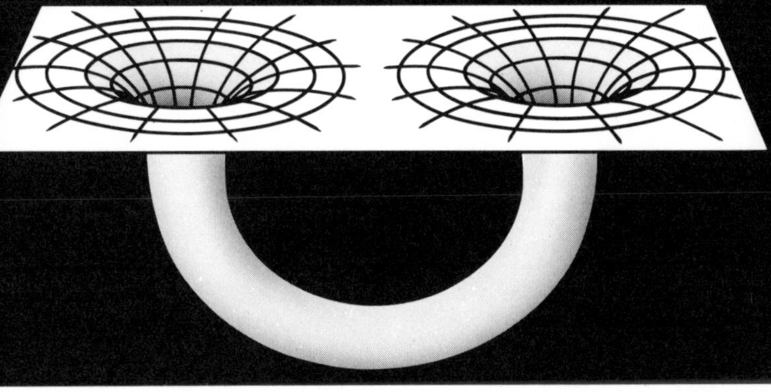

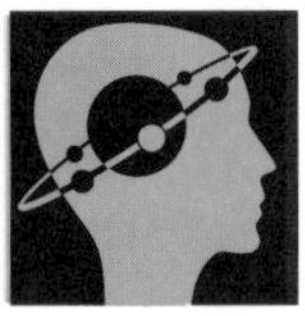

But the curious feature of entering the black hole and passing along the Einstein-Rosen bridge is that the spaceship is not only flung into another part of space, but in making this journey is propelled backwards in time. The Einstein-Rosen bridge is, in fact, a time machine.

It may seem that, in talking of time travel, we are entering into complete fantasy. But this is not so, for a time machine and a distance-abolishing machine are merely two phrases to describe the same thing. Distance simply means time travelled – or, to be more precise, it is the average speed of a journey multiplied by the time taken to achieve it. If, for example, a distance of 3,500 miles (5,630 kilometres) – the distance between London and New York – was miraculously reduced to zero, you could travel this distance instantaneously, in no time at all, because zero divided by any number equals zero. Yet to make this instantaneous journey, you would be moving backwards in time while moving forwards in space.

Return Journey

But passing through the black hole, and thereby achieving an instantaneous journey to another part of the Universe, how will our astronaut ever get back? Is he lost for ever? One theory suggests he could return to his point of departure by way of what is known as a white hole.

A white hole is no more strange than a black hole. It is simply its opposite. A black hole is an implosion, and a white hole is an explosion. Nothing can ever escape from a black hole: everything must, sooner or later, escape from a white hole.

But do white holes exist? In theory at least, white holes should be visible from telescopes on Earth, yet they have so far proved difficult to identify. A giant white hole would, in any case, be indistinguishable from an exploding galaxy; and a relatively small one of, say, 10 solar masses, would look at a great distance like an ordinary star. J.V. Narlikar and his colleague K.M.V. Apparao of the Tata Institute of Fundamental Research in Bombay have suggested that those very violent exploding galaxies (known as Seyfert galaxies (after their original discoverer, Carl Seyfert) could be giant white holes, presumably of many millions of solar masses, pouring back into the Universe matter that had been devoured by distant black holes.

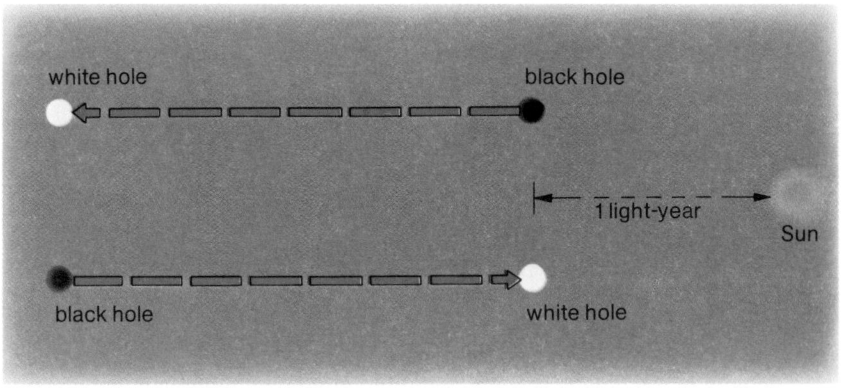

Travel between distant parts of our Universe would require two black holes, each with its corresponding white hole – one for the outward journey, the other for the return journey. The 'outward' black hole would be constructed at a convenient and safe distance (say about one light-year) from the Sun; and the black holes and their corresponding white holes would be several light-years apart. The arrows in the diagram, above, indicate the only possible directions for travel.

They propose that the physical mechanism of a white hole will be identical to that of a black hole, except that everything happens in reverse. The nature of the Einstein-Rosen bridge, the region where forward distances are reduced to zero, predicts that the white hole will come into existence at the very same instant as its corresponding black hole. So, if any astronaut can vanish down a black hole without being destroyed, then he should be able to emerge equally unscathed, a fraction of a second later, from a white hole.

Instant Travel

Yet, if instantaneous cosmic travel is to be achieved, starting from a sort of 'cosmic railway station' one light-year from the Sun, it will not be enough simply to construct a black hole. The black hole would enable astronauts to travel instantaneously to distances of many light-years, but they would have no means of coming back, except through normal space, a journey which would take them many decades. It would therefore be necessary to construct a second black hole at the distant point where they emerge into normal space, which they will use for returning to a point no further than about one light-year from the Sun.

This second black hole, in turn, will bring into existence a second white hole. The approximate positions of the four holes, two black and two white, is shown in the diagram on this page. Two parallel Einstein-Rosen bridges will have come into existence, with matter flowing through them in opposite directions, and each with a black hole and a white hole at their respective ends.

The construction of black holes as gateways to other universes will have answered one of the most formidable problems of future ages – the feasibility of travel to the stars. Failure to solve it could bring about the eventual stagnation and ruin of the human species. Yet if it can be solved, whether by the method outlined here or by any other, the prospect will instead be the establishment of a galactic community, a society in which our descendants will be scattered through millions of worlds in orbits around countless stars. Humanity will be safe for ever from the threat of extinction, and there need be no limit to the flowering of human culture that this diversity will produce.

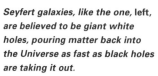

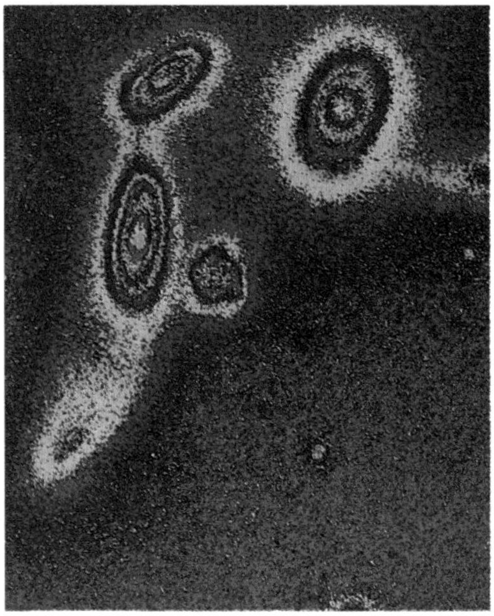

Seyfert galaxies, like the one,* left, *are believed to be giant white holes, pouring matter back into the Universe as fast as black holes are taking it out.

THE CASE OF THE COTTINGLEY FAIRIES

MOST CHILDREN ARE ENCOURAGED TO BELIEVE IN FAIRIES. BUT TWO LITTLE GIRLS ALSO CLAIMED TO HAVE MET AND MADE FRIENDS WITH THEM – AND EVEN TO HAVE CAPTURED THEM ON FILM

In the week before the end of the First World War, 11 year-old Frances Griffiths sent a letter to a friend in South Africa, where she had lived most of her life. Dated 9 November 1918, it ran:

'Dear Joe (Johanna),

I hope you are quite well. I wrote a letter before, only I lost it or it got mislaid. Do you play with Elsie and Nora Biddles? I am learning French, Geometry, Cookery and Algebra at school now. Dad came home from France the other week after being there ten months, and we all think the war will be over in a few days. We are going to get our flags to hang upstairs in our bedroom. I am sending two photos, both of me, one of me in a bathing costume in our back yard, Uncle Arthur took that, while the other is me with some fairies up the beck [stream], Elsie took that one. Rosebud is fat as ever and I have made her some new clothes. How are Teddy and dolly?'

A sharpened version of the first fairy photograph, **above right, *shows Frances Griffiths behind a group of dancing fairies. Photographic experts examined the negative and the print, but could find no trace of trickery.***

An ordinary and matter-of-fact letter from a schoolgirl to her friend, one might say, apart from the rather startling reference to fairies. But, as both Frances and her cousin, Elsie Wright, later pointed out, they were not particularly surprised by seeing fairies; indeed, they seemed a natural part of the rural countryside around the beck at the bottom of the long garden in Cottingley, near Bradford, in West Yorkshire.

The photograph enclosed by Frances – the famous one, which has since been reproduced thousands of times around the world, albeit in an improved and sharpened version – shows a little girl staring firmly at a camera. (Fairies were, it seems, frequently to be seen, but she herself was photographed not so often!) On the back of the snap was scrawled in untidy schoolgirl writing:

'Elsie and I are very friendly with the beck Fairies. It is funny I never used to see them in Africa. It must be too hot for them there.'

Elsie had borrowed her father's camera – a Midg quarter-plate – one Saturday afternoon in July 1917 in order to take Frances' photo and cheer her up; her cousin had fallen on her back and been scolded for wetting her clothes. They were away for about half-an-hour, and Mr Wright developed the plate later in the afternoon. He was surprised to see strange white shapes coming up, imagining them to be first birds and then sandwich wrappings left lying around. Elsie, behind him in the dark-room, said, however, that they were fairies.

In August, it was Frances who had the camera, when she and Elsie scaled the sides of the beck and went up to the old oaks. There she took a photograph of Elsie with a gnome. The print was underexposed and unclear, as might be expected when taken by a young girl. The plate was again developed by Elsie's father, Arthur, who suspected that the girls had been playing tricks and refused to lend his camera to them any more.

Parents Turn Sleuth

Both Arthur and his wife, Polly, searched the girls' bedroom and waste-paper basket for scraps of pictures or cut-outs, and also went down to the beck in search of evidence of fakery. They found nothing, however, and the girls stuck to their story – that they had indeed seen fairies and photographed them. Prints of the pictures were circulated among friends and neighbours, but then interest in the odd affair gradually petered out.

The matter first became public in the summer of 1919 when Polly Wright went to a meeting at the Theosophical Society in Bradford. She was interested in many aspects of the occult, having herself had what seemed to have been some experiences of astral projection and memories of past lives. The lecture that night was on 'fairy life', and

> "Elsie and Frances then took three more fairy photographs. Had they really seen these nature spirits? Or were their pictures perhaps so-called thoughtographs – figments of the imagination, somehow captured on film?"

***Sir Arthur Conan Doyle*, above, *used sharpened prints of the first two Cottingley photographs to illustrate his article on fairies, published in the Christmas 1920 issue of the* Strand Magazine.**

Polly mentioned to the person sitting next to her that fairy prints had been taken by her daughter and niece. The result of this conversation was that two 'rough prints' (as they were later called) came to the notice of Theosophists at the Harrogate autumn conference, and thence to a leading Theosophist, Edward Gardner, by early 1920.

Gardner was a precise, particular man; and his immediate impulse after seeing the fairy pictures was to improve the prints. In a letter to photographic expert, Fred Barlow, he described the instructions he had given to his assistants:

'Then I told them to make new negatives (from positives of the originals) and do the very best with them short of altering anything mechanically. The result was that they turned out two first class negatives which... are the same in every respect as the originals except that they are sharp cut and clear and far finer for printing purposes...'

It seems incredible to us, today, that he could be so naïve, not anticipating the inevitable questions from critics as to shutter speed, figure definition,

Elsie Wright and her cousin Frances*, above right, *were close companions and spent hours playing together near the beck where the fairy photographs were taken.

Polly Wright, Elsie's mother*, below, *began to take the photographs seriously after she had attended a Theosophical Society lecture on 'fairy life'.

and the suspicious resemblance of the fairies' clothes and hairstyles to the latest fashions. But Gardner only wanted the clearest pictures. (As a Theosophist, he had been studying fairy lore for years and had heard many accounts of fairy sightings, so the possible reactions of sceptics never entered his head.)

Magazine Coverage

By a striking coincidence, Sir Arthur Conan Doyle (creator of Sherlock Holmes and a fanatical Spiritualist) had been commissioned by the *Strand Magazine* to write an article on fairies for the Christmas issue, to be published at the end of November 1920. He was preparing this in June, when he heard of two fairy prints in circulation and eventually made contact with Gardner and borrowed copies.

From the beginning, contrary to later public impressions, Conan Doyle was on his guard. He showed the prints to Sir Oliver Lodge, a pioneer psychical researcher, who thought them fakes, perhaps involving a troupe of dancers masquerading as fairies. (One fairy authority told him that the hairstyles of the sprites were too 'Parisienne' for his liking.) Lodge also passed them on to a clairvoyant for psychometric impressions.

The sharpened print, **above,** *shows Elsie and a gnome, and was taken by Frances in August 1917. The original was examined by experts but, again, no evidence of trickery was found at the time.*

A Midg quarter-plate camera, owned by Arthur Wright, Elsie's father, **below,** *was used to take the photographs.*

What seems rather mysterious to us today, too, is that no one was over-anxious to examine the *original* photographs, but seemed content to analyse prints. A certain Mr Snelling (who had prepared the second batch of prints and of whom it had been said 'What Snelling doesn't know about faked photography isn't worth knowing') wrote in his first report to Gardner on the 'rough' print that he could detect movement in all the fairy figures. Kodak, by contrast, stated that an experienced photographer may have been involved – which suggests that the prints may have been sharpened ones.

A possible explanation is that Conan Doyle and Gardner may have wished to avoid any mention of improving the originals at that stage, perhaps not considering the matter important. What was vital to them was the propagation of Theosophical and Spiritualist doctrines. As far as they were concerned, clear prints showing recognisable fairies and a gnome would provide the long-sought film evidence for 'dwellers at the border' (as Conan Doyle was later to term nature spirits).

Conan Doyle despatched his 'Watson' – in this real-life case, Gardner – to Cottingley in July. Gardner reported that the whole Wright family seemed honest and totally respectable. Conan Doyle and Gardner then decided that, if further fairy photographs were taken, the matter would be put firmly beyond question. Gardner journeyed north in August with cameras and 20 photographic plates to leave with Elsie and Frances, hoping to persuade them to take more photographs. Only in this way, he felt, could it be proved that the fairies were indeed genuine.

Meanwhile, the *Strand* article was completed, and featured the two sharpened prints. Conan Doyle now sailed for Australia and gave a lecture tour to spread the gospel of Spiritualism, leaving his colleagues to face public reaction to the fairies.

NATIONAL SENSATION

That issue of the *Strand* sold out within days of publication, and reaction was vigorous – especially from critics. The leading voice among them was that of Major Hall-Edwards, a radium expert. He declared:

'On the evidence, I have no hesitation in saying that these photographs could have been 'faked'. I criticise the attitude of those who declared there is something supernatural in the circumstances attending to the taking of these pictures because, as a medical man, I believe that the inculcation of such absurd ideas into the minds of children will result in later life in manifestations and nervous disorder and mental disturbances...'

Newspaper comments were varied. On 5 January 1921, *Truth* declared: 'For the true explanation of these fairy photographs, what is wanted is not a knowledge of occult phenomena but a knowledge of children'. On the other hand, the *South Wales Argus* of 27 November 1920 took a more whimsical and tolerant view: 'The day we kill our Santa Claus with our statistics, we shall have plunged a glorious world into deepest darkness'. The Day's Thought underneath was a Welsh proverb: 'Tis true as the fairy tales told in books'. *City News,* on 29 January, said straightforwardly: 'It seems at this point that we must either believe in the almost incredible mystery of the fairy or in the almost incredible wonders of faked photographs'.

The *Westminster Gazette* broke the aliases used by Conan Doyle to protect Frances and Elsie, and a reporter went north. However, nothing sensational, or even new, was added to the story by his investigation. He found that Elsie had borrowed her father's camera to take the first picture, and that Frances had taken a picture of Elsie and a gnome. In fact, there was nothing he could add to the facts listed by Conan Doyle in his article 'Fairies photographed – an epoch-making event'. The reporter considered Polly and Arthur Wright to be honest enough folk, and he returned a verdict of 'unexplained' to his paper in London.

The case might well have faded away with the coming of spring in 1921, had not the unexpected happened: Elsie and Frances took three more fairy photographs. Had they really seen these nature spirits? Or were their pictures perhaps so-called 'thoughtographs' – figments of the imagination, somehow captured on film?

Only some sixty years later did the truth finally come to light – that the pictures had indeed been faked. But that in itself, of course, does not either prove or disprove the existence of fairies, and other forms of nature spirits.

SKETCHBOOK THE GODS

THE PERUVIAN AERIAL SURVEY TEAM COULD HARDLY BELIEVE THEIR EYES. BELOW THEM, COVERING THE DESERT AS FAR AS THE EYE COULD SEE, WAS A HUGE TWO-DIMENSIONAL ZOO – THE LINES OF NAZCA

Of all South America's many archaeological mysteries, none surpasses that of the extraordinary desert drawings at Nazca in Peru. The sheer scale, visual beauty and mystery of these enormous lines have fascinated archaeologists, scientists and adventurers alike in the 64 years since their discovery. Although as old as Stonehenge, they remained unknown to the world at large until Toribio Mexta Xesspe, a member of the Peruvian aerial survey team, first flew over them in 1927. Their discovery had to wait until the eventual coming of flight – for they can be seen only from the air.

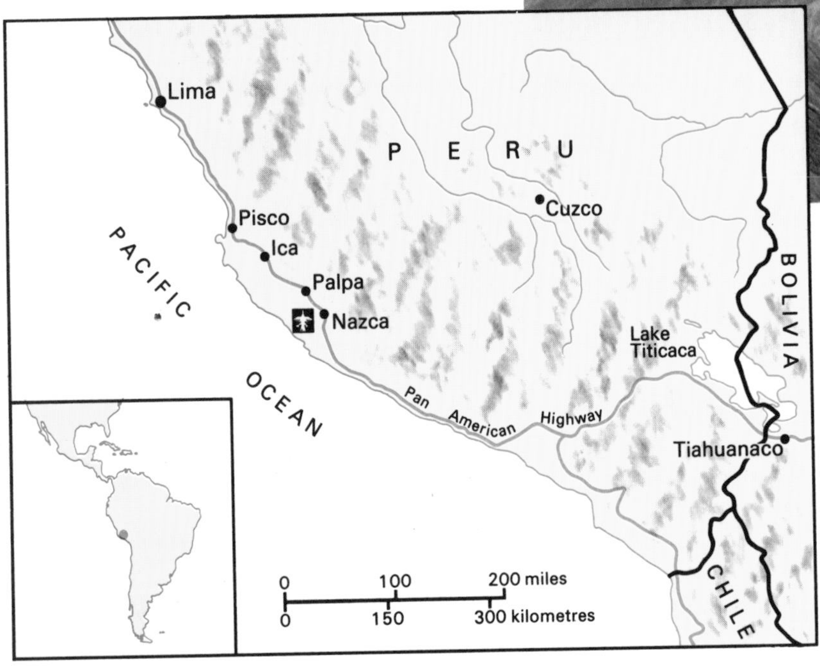

The site of the Nazca sand 'drawings', above, is marked by the symbol of the giant condor – one of the most impressive of the figures. **Inset is a map, marking** *the position of Nazca in relation to South America as a whole. Toribio Mexta Xesspe,* **left,** *first discovered the lines.*

Even today, when the lines are well-known, the sight of them from the air is staggeringly awe-inspiring. The bare plateau of Nazca – over 200 square miles (500 square kilometres) of it – is covered with starkly beautiful drawings of numerous creatues – among them, hummingbirds over 200 feet (60 metres) from wingtip to wingtip, enormous spiders, a fox, and a killer whale. Alongside are more than 100 spirals; star-shaped clusters of lines; elegant, tapering triangles; and over 13,000 perfectly straight lines.

DESERT ZOO

Yet all these drawings are 'invisible' from the ground. The Pan-American highway was even built through the 'lines' (as they are known collectively) since no one realised they were there. At ground level, all one can see of them are shallow depressions where the surface has been scraped away to reveal the yellow earth beneath. But, from the air, they show up as the brilliant yellow outlines of a desert 'zoo'.

Seen from the air – as undoubtedly they were intended to be seen – the Nazca lines give the impression that they convey some kind of important code or message. Some who have flown over them, however, see the gigantic arrows, lines and

Cuzco cathedral, **above,** *was built in the 17th century on the foundations of the Incan Temple of the Creator god. According to astronomer Rolf Müller, the Incas had a working knowledge of astronomy, often aligning their main temples with the position of the Sun at the solstices. His work on prehistoric astronomy inspired Maria Reiche to look for similar alignments at Nazca.*

The Nazca lines, **far left,** *on the Pampa San José show lines and animal figures that cannot be seen from ground level. The Pan American Highway,* **left,** *was even built straight through the desert markings, without the builders being aware of them.*

cleared spaces as landing strips – but surely not prehistoric landing strips?

Writer and archaeologist Erich von Däniken has claimed that the Nazca lines indeed acted as 'runways' for ancient astronauts; but critics have pointed out that, since the spacecraft presumably landed and took off vertically, they would not need such enormously elongated 'landing strips'; that the soil in those parts is too soft to allow any sizeable vehicle to land; and that, as the arrows often point to the sides of hills, the spaceships would probably have crashed. So if the Nazca lines were not intended to guide landing alien spacecraft, what were they created for?

Two researchers who have uncovered many clues are the late Professor Paul Kosok of Long Island University and German astronomer, Maria Reiche, whose devotion to Nazca and its mysteries has earned her the affectionate title of 'Nazca's resident archaeologist'.

ASTRONOMICAL SIGNS

Professor Kosok was the first to make a systematic study of the lines, just 12 years after their discovery in 1927. One evening in the 1940s, he saw the sun set precisely along the end of one of the lines. It was 22 June, the winter solstice in the southern hemisphere. This confirmed his theory that the lines marked astronomical alignments – that they were, in his words, 'the largest astronomy book in the world'.

Maria Reiche, meanwhile, was no stranger to the idea of prehistoric astronomy. As a governess in Cuzco (Peru's ancient Inca capital) before the Second World War, she had learnt of the work of her contemporary, the German astronomer Rolf

Müller, who had discussed the possible alignment of the Cuzco cathedral (built on the foundation of the Temple of the Creator god) and the Inca Sun Temple, concluding that the Incas had indeed set out to align the axis of their buildings with the solstice.

After the Second World War, Maria Reiche returned to South America to work with Paul Kosok at Nazca. Much of their work was severely practical, involving cleaning the lines by shuffling along them in heavy boots or dragging large stones attached to ropes behind them. Indeed, they went over that ground many times, using brooms to clean the lines and figures, and 'to brighten them for photography'.

After Professor Kosok had retired from the Nazca mystery, Maria Reiche continued her studies in the desert. At first she stayed in Nazca's one poor hotel; and then, as she became known in the area, she was given lodging in farm buildings near Ingenio – a village close to the major concentration of lines and patterns.

Clear Markers

For nearly 40 years, this German loner lived close to the mystery of the desert; and although many of her original ideas became modified, she maintained that the lines are actually a form of gigantic calendar. The Nazcans, she asserted, were first and foremost agriculturalists who needed to calculate the right season for planting and harvesting their crops. A line directed at the rising point of a star or brilliant planet would therefore act as a clear marker. Some lines may even have been directed at one end to the rising point of a star on one horizon and the setting place of another star in the opposite direction.

Professor Paul Kosok,* top, *favoured an astronomical explanation for the purpose of the lines. Maria Reiche, the astronomer,* above, *also devoted much of her life to the study of Nazca lines.

> " The lines of Nazca – probably the largest astronomy book in the world. "
>
> **Professor Paul Kosok**

Maria Reiche observed that many of those extraordinary straight lines, some over 25 miles (40 kilometres) long, had been set out with only approximately 2° deviation – even though in entirely different parts of the desert. This seems to indicate that they were built to point to the Sun, Moon or a star.

Lines of Mystery

Critics have pointed out that only some of the lines show this kind of alignment; but those lines that do are undoubtedly important. Some researchers also believe that there may have been other kinds of alignment involved in their design, alignments we know nothing about – so far.

But whatever their purpose, the precision and beauty of the lines imply a cultured and aesthetic society. Maria Reiche points to other evidence to prove this. The beautiful, finely-wrought gold objects, tightly-woven cloth, and pottery vessels

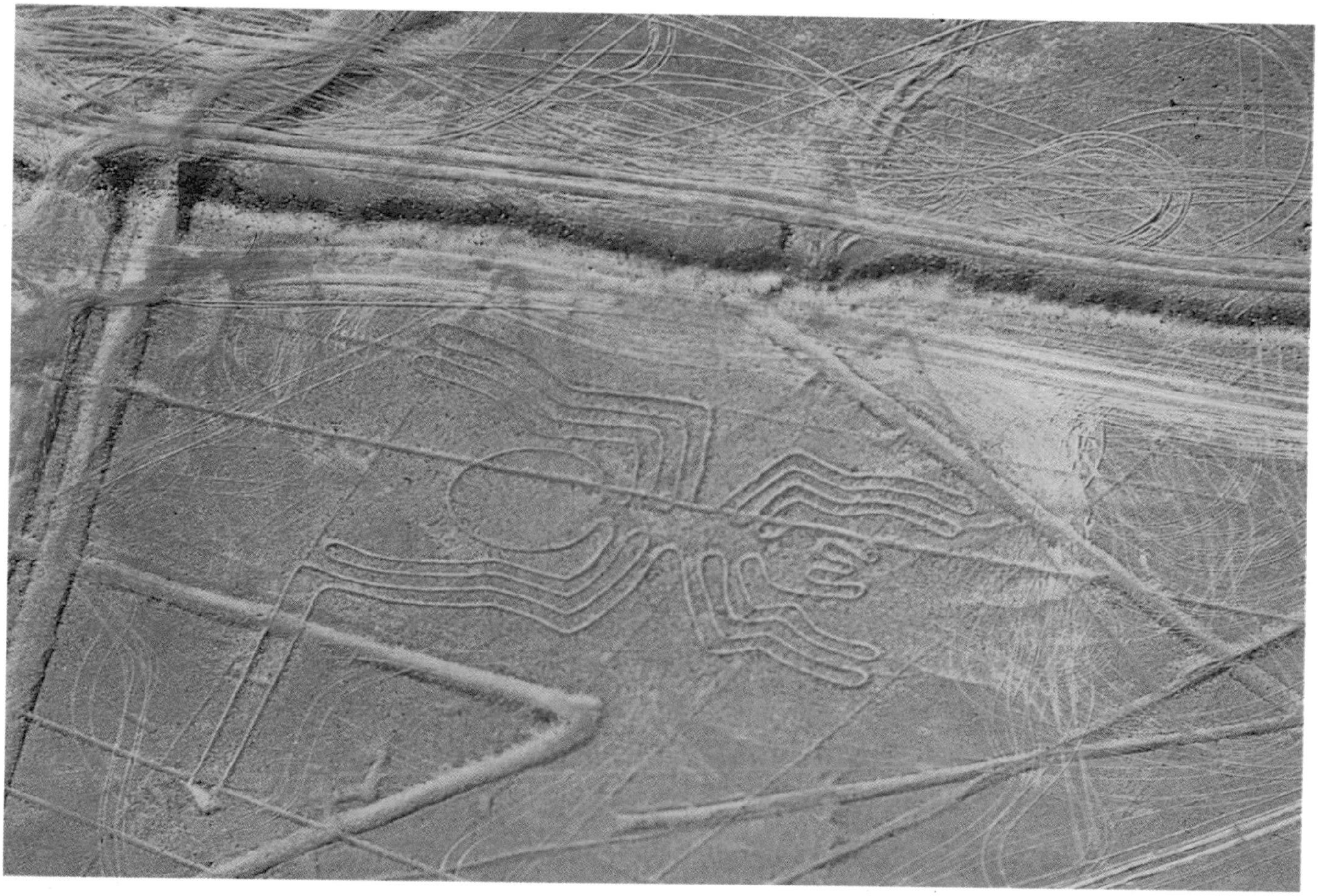

The gigantic spider design, above, on the edge of the Pampa de San José, is mingled with an assortment of triangles and straight lines.

found in the upright graves that pockmark the Nazca desert, for instance, reveal an artistically sophisticated culture.

But Nazca is not unique – even in South America. Other sites show distinct similarities to the Nazca lines. Indeed, lines, clearings and figures have been found as far as 600 miles (950 kilometres) away. And even further away, in the more remote parts of South America, there are said to be enormous lines scratched on the surface of the desert.

So are these line-making centres connected in some way? Some researchers strongly believe they are connected by ley lines or invisible channels of electro-magnetic vitality running through the Earth, on which ancient man is said to have built the pyramids, Stonehenge and other 'magical' monuments.

Down to Earth

But other, more down-to-earth connections can be made. When Maria Reiche was asked to clarify the Nazca markings in order of importance (in 1976), she put the straight lines top of the list. Although the majority of people are impressed most by the representations of animals, she insists that the very straightness of the lines – striking without deviation across difficult terrain, sometimes cutting through tough vegetation and pursuing their path over hills and through dry gulches, hundreds of yards wide – holds a fascination of its own. But if only some of them point to astronomical markers, why were they set out so straight, and so purposefully? Again and again, the 'why' of the Nazca lines comes tantalisingly close, only to recede again. But perhaps the 'how' is not so mysterious, thanks to Maria Reiche and her years of devoted research.

The wings of a large stylised bird, left, cover the desert floor; but to many Nazca researchers, the deliberately cleared areas pose questions as intriguing as those raised by the animal figures and the perfectly straight lines.

When she first arrived in Nazca in 1946, Maria Reiche was told how, within living memory, wooden posts used to stand at regular intervals along the lines. This hinted at a method of construction that fitted the limited means of the builders. She therefore concluded that the original builders worked from small scale models, transferring the designs to the desert floor, section by section, each marked in place by a wooden post. She even claimed to have located the original sections and marked each of them with little wooden pegs. The precise mathematical scale she ascribed to the use of some standardised unit of measurement, perhaps based, like the biblical cubit, on the average proportions of parts of the human body.

Visiting Britain in 1976 to examine ancient sites, Maria Reiche looked for clues as to the methods employed by prehistoric builders and the systems of measurement used. The unit used to set up Stonehenge, for example, is now widely believed to be the megalithic yard, as discovered by Dr Alexander Thom. This is equivalent to 2 feet 8⅝ inches (83 centimetres), and does seem to have been the basic unit of measurement for many prehistoric sites in Britain and in France.

But if the megalithic yard was indeed used by the builders of the Nazca lines, this in itself creates another mystery. How had it become so widely known in such 'primitive' days? And why did prehistoric communities elect to build such enduring monoliths on one side of the Atlantic, and those gigantic desert drawings, which can only be appreciated from the air, on the other?

MUSIC FROM BEYOND THE GRAVE

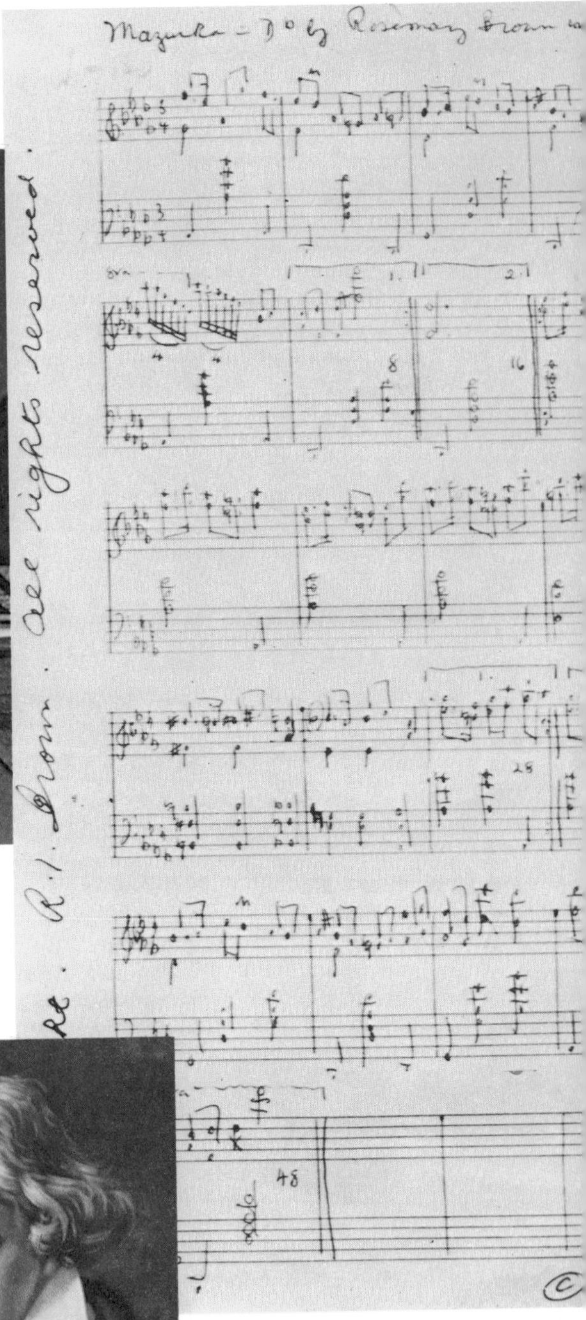

A NUMBER OF SENSITIVES CLAIM TO RECEIVE WORKS FROM LONG-DEAD COMPOSERS. BUT ARE THESE WORKS TRULY FROM THE SPIRIT WORLD, OR DO THEY COME FROM THE SUBCONSCIOUS MIND?

Beethoven is even now working on a new symphony. This extraordinary concept – that musicians and other creative beings can produce works of art years, even centuries, after their death – is as natural as breathing to many spiritualists and psychics.

The best known of those mediums who claim to be amanuenses for long-dead composers is London housewife Rosemary Brown, who in the past has acted almost as an agent for Liszt, Beethoven, Brahms, Debussy, Chopin, Schubert and, more recently, Stravinsky. She is an unassuming lady with only a rudimentary musical background, and she is the first to acknowledge that the works 'dictated' to her are beyond her everyday musical capacity. Rosemary Brown sees herself merely as the humble scribe and friend of the late composers – the ultimate polish must come from the professionals in performance.

The idea of survival beyond death is not, however, strange to this suburban housewife. As a young

Rosemary Brown,* above left, *'wrote' Mazurka in D flat,* above. *She claims to have been inspired by the spirit of Chopin,* above right, *while being filmed by an American television company in October 1980.

Beethoven,* shown left, *contacted Rosemary Brown in 1964, when he told her he was no longer deaf and again enjoyed listening to music.

Rosemary Brown sought an interview with American composer and conductor Leonard Bernstein, **below right**, on the advice of her 'spirits'. He is said to have been most impressed with the music Rosemary showed him.

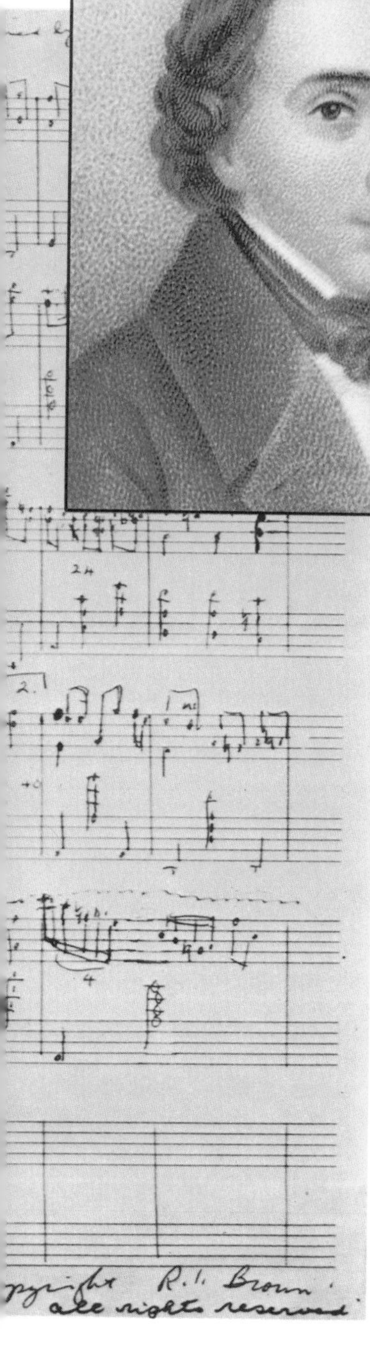

girl, she had visions of an elderly man who told her repeatedly that he and other great composers would befriend her and teach her their wonderful music. It was only many years later, when she was a widow, concerned mainly with the struggle of bringing up two children alone and on very limited means, that she saw a picture of Franz Liszt (1811-1886) and recognised him immediately as her ghostly friend.

In 1964, she was contacted by other great composers, among them Beethoven and Chopin, and her life work – taking down their 'unfinished symphonies' – then began in earnest.

The pieces transmitted to her are no mere outlines but full compositions, mainly for the piano but some for full orchestras. Rosemary Brown says the music was already composed when it was communicated to her: the musicians simply dictated it as fast as she could write it down.

Indeed, observers of the process have been amazed at the speed with which Rosemary Brown wrote the music – and the standard is far beyond her conscious capacity or even her conscious knowledge. During these sessions, Rosemary Brown would chat so naturally with her unseen guests that it is difficult to be embarrassed, despite the bizarre circumstances. Pen poised over the music sheets, she would listen. 'I see...', she would say to Franz Liszt, 'these two bars go here... no, I see, I'm sorry. No, you're getting too fast for me. If you could just repeat...' With pauses for checking and some conversation with the composer, she would write down the work far faster than most musicians could possibly compose.

But sometimes communications were interrupted, as she gently chided Liszt for becoming so excited that he spoke volubly in German or French. Chopin occasionally forgot himself and spoke to her in his native Polish – which she would write down phonetically and have translated by a Polish friend.

Recognisable Styles

So are these posthumous works recognisably those of Liszt, Chopin, Beethoven, Brahms? Concert pianist Hephzibah Menuhin put it this way: 'I look at these manuscripts with immense respect. Each piece is distinctly in the composer's style.' Leonard Bernstein and his wife entertained Rosemary Brown in their London hotel suite and were very impressed both by her sincerity and by the music, purportedly from the long-dead composers, she took to them. British composer Richard Rodney Bennett said: 'A lot of people can improvise, but you couldn't fake music like this without years of training. I couldn't have faked some of the Beethoven myself'.

Since that memorable breakthrough in 1964, Rosemary Brown claims also to have been contacted by dead artists, poets, playwrights, philosophers and scientists. Vincent van Gogh (1853-1890) has communicated current works through her – at first in charcoal ('because that's all I had') and then in oils. But Debussy has chosen to paint through Rosemary Brown, rather than compose, because his artistic interests have changed since he has 'passed over'.

Franz Liszt, **right**, first appeared to Rosemary Brown when she was a young girl. He told her that, when she grew up, he and other composers would contact her and teach her their music.

Apparently, the philosopher Bertrand Russell has also had to reconsider his atheism and disbelief in a life after death for, as Rosemary Brown points out, he is very much 'alive' these days and wants to pass on the message of hope in eternal life. Albert Einstein has also communicated, patiently explaining any difficult jargon or concepts, and reinforcing the belief in further planes of existence.

Sceptics are often quick to spot that the music alleged to come from the minds of the great composers is less than their best, and reminiscent of their earliest, rather than their mature, works. This, says Rosemary Brown, is not the point. Her first introduction to Franz Liszt was 'more than a musical break-through'. Indeed, the late Sir Donald Tovey is said to have explained the motivation behind such communications in a posthumous statement:

'In communicating through music and conversation, an organized group of musicians, who have departed from your world, are attempting to establish a precept for humanity, i.e., that physical death is a transition from one state of consciousness to another wherein one retains one's individuality... We are not transmitting music to Rosemary Brown simply for the sake of offering possible pleasure in listening thereto; it is the implications relevant to the phenomenon which we hope will stimulate sensible and sensitive interest and stir many who are intelligent and impartial to consider and explore the unknown of man's mind and psyche. When man has plumbed the mysterious depths of his veiled consciousness, he will then be able to soar to correspondingly greater heights.'

Rosemary Brown's contacts are not confined to the field of music. Vincent Van Gogh inspired the drawing,* right, *in 1975; and Debussy,* below, *now more interested in visual art, also paints 'through' her. She was contacted by Albert Einstein,* bottom, *in 1967, and by Bertrand Russell,* below left, *in 1973.

Rosemary Brown has many friends and admirers outside the spiritualist circle, notably among distinguished musicians, writers and broadcasters. Whatever the source of her mysterious music, this modest and religious lady inspires respect and affection, so obvious is her sincerity.

She is, however, not unique in her musical communications. The British concert pianist, John Lill, also claims an other-worldly inspiration for his playing. This winner of the prestigious Tchaikovsky Piano Competition had a tough beginning, playing the piano in pubs in London's East End. As he says 'I don't go around like a crazed fellow with my head in the air... I'm neither a nutter nor some quaint loony falling around in a state of trance'. But, as he has added thoughtfully, 'because something is rare it doesn't mean that it doesn't exist'.

That 'something' began for him when he was practising in the Moscow Conservatoire for the Tchaikovsky Piano Competition. He became aware of a figure watching him – someone wearing unusual clothes. He believes he was being observed by Beethoven, who later held many conversations with him. However, John Lill does not consider himself a special case. This sort of direct inspiration, he says, is available to everyone who achieves a certain frame of mind:

'It is very difficult to conceive inspiration unless it is something you receive. I don't see it as something from within a person. When I go on stage, I close my mind to what I have learnt and open it fully in the expectation that inspiration will be received.'

Concert pianist John Lill, right, is convinced that he, too, has had spiritual help in his career. He believes that Beethoven watched him practising for the Tchaikovsky Piano Competition in Moscow, and has since held several conversations with him. Beethoven has even dedicated a piece of his own music to him – the Sonata in E Minor, communicated to Rosemary Brown in 1972.

> "WE ARE NOT TRANSMITTING MUSIC TO ROSEMARY BROWN SIMPLY FOR THE SAKE OF OFFERING POSSIBLE PLEASURE... IT IS THE IMPLICATIONS RELEVANT TO THIS PHENOMENON WHICH WE HOPE WILL STIMULATE SENSIBLE AND SENSITIVE INTEREST AND STIR MANY WHO ARE INTELLIGENT AND AND IMPARTIAL TO CONSIDER AND EXPLORE THE UNKNOWN OF MAN'S MIND AND PSYCHE."
>
> **SIR DONALD TOVEY, *POSTHUMOUSLY***

***Clifford Enticknap,* below, *wrote an oratorio entitled* Beyond the Veil *'under the inspiration' of G.F. Handel, shown* bottom.**

But sometimes it is difficult to achieve this state of mind 'if it is a particularly muggy day, or the acoustics are dry. Even the attitude of the audience makes a difference. A quiet mind is essential,' according to Lill.

The composer of, among other magnificent works, the Messiah, also wrote grand oratorios through his medium Clifford Enticknap, an Englishman obsessed with Handel. The great composer taught him music in another incarnation, says Enticknap, and their relationship as master and pupil dates back to the time of Atlantis where Handel was a great teacher known as Joseph Arkos. Yet, before that, the soul we know as Handel lived on Jupiter, the planet of music, together with all the souls we know as the great musicians (and some we may never know for they will not be incarnated on Earth), Enticknap has revealed.

BEYOND THE VEIL

In his personality as 'the master Handel', the musician communicated to Enticknap a four-and-a-half-hour long oratorio entitled *Beyond the Veil.* A 73-minute excerpt of this has been recorded by the London Symphony Orchestra and the Handelian Foundation Choir, available on tape through the Handelian Foundation as 'proof' of Handel's survival beyond death.

In BBC-TV's programme *Spirits from the Past,* shown on 12 August 1980, snatches from the oratorio were played over scenes of Mr Enticknap playing the organ in Handel's favourite English church. Television critics found little fault with the music – which did indeed sound to the untutored ear to be very similar to Handel's more familiar works – but the words provoked widespread ridicule. Once critic compared them with the unfortunate poetry of William McGonagall (1805-1902) whose poetic sincerity was matched only by his total lack of talent and sheer genius in juxtaposing the risible with the pathetic. (Another critic went so far as to exclaim: 'Fame at last for McGonagall – he's teamed up with Handel beyond the veil!')

However, mediums warn against judging spirit communications in a state of flippant scepticism. As John Lill says of the difficulties that the spirits sometimes have in 'getting through': 'It's all to do with cleaning a window, and some windows are cleaner than others'.

POOL OF KNOWLEDGE

If, as many serious researchers into the paranormal have believed, the music does not in fact come from the minds of deceased musicians, then where does it come from? It is certainly not from the conscious mind of Rosemary Brown, who obviously struggled to keep up with the dictation.

Some psychics believe that our deeper inspirations are culled from the 'Akashic records' or 'Book of Life', wherein lies all knowledge. In certain states of mind, experienced by some especially sensitive people, this hidden knowledge becomes available to the human consciousness. Rosemary Brown could well be one of these remarkably receptive people; and the music she believes comes from Chopin or Beethoven may come instead from this 'pool' of musical knowledge.

The late Rosemary Rosalind Heywood, researcher into the paranormal, and author of *The Sixth Sense,* has another suggestion. Rosemary Brown is, she guesses, 'the type of sensitive whom frustration, often artistic, drives to the automatic production of material beyond their conscious capacity'.

To those who believe in the omniscience of the human subconscious, the compositions given to the world by Rosemary Brown and others like her raise more questions than they answer. But it is all so beautifully simply to the mediums: there is no death and genius is eternal.

SYMBOLS IN THE SKY

Many believe passionately that UFOs originate beyond the Earth. But the psychologist Carl Jung suggested that their true significance may in fact lie in the depths of the human subconscious

Unidentified flying objects fascinated Carl Gustav Jung, the genius of psychology who developed the idea of the 'collective unconscious'. They seemed to him to be perfect examples of his main psychological doctrines. It was therefore natural that in 1959 he should devote a short book, *Flying Saucers,* to them.

Jung was a pioneering psychologist who based much of his work on the concept of archetypes – vastly significant symbols, motifs or figures that seem to carry much the same meaning for everyone. These symbols, he said, are liable to rise spontaneously from the depths of the unconscious, manifesting themselves in any human creation and evoking powerful emotional and imaginative responses. In order to attempt an understanding of their nature and implications, Jung marshalled an astonishing array of parallels from those areas of human activity where the 'non-rational' holds sway – religion and mythology, ancient and primitive ritual, and occult systems such as alchemy and astrology, for instance. At the same time, to prove that such archetypes were alive and well in the psyche of modern Man, he showed how they emerge again and again in the dreams of his patients as well as in the art, folklore and popular myths of the 20th century.

The characteristic 'flying saucer' form is evident in the American photograph,* above, *of a UFO. This sighting was clearly not a delusion, though the possibility of a fake remains. Carl Jung,* inset, *believed that, whatever their true nature, the power of the 'saucers' over the modern mind stems from the symbolic meaning of the disc.

The eight-year-old daughter of a psychiatrist friend, for example, had a series of dreams with striking imagery of, Jung believed, great antiquity. In one of them, a horned, snakelike monster appeared, which Jung identified with a horned serpent featuring in 16th-century alchemical literature. Then, in the same dream, God 'came from the four corners' – presumably of the world, though the young girl did not make this clear. Jung relates this to ideas of a fourfold divinity, antedating the concept of the Trinity, but almost forgotten since the 17th century. The little girl was drawing, as he saw it, on 'libraries' of symbolism – the archetypes – available to all mankind through the collective unconscious.

Visions of Angels

Jung believed that one of these archetypal images was the discus, of which the UFO is a modern variant. At first, he put to one side the problematic question of whether what is seen in the sky is actually there. Certainly, people believe that they see UFOs, just as they have believed in other 'non-pathological' visions, such as the angels of Mons. Many soldiers reported having seen these apparitions during the fierce fighting accompanying the British retreat from Mons in 1914. It is an instructive parallel for, if they were imaginary, the angelic warriors were real enough in the minds of soldiers,

British soldiers in retreat from Mons in 1914 believed that angelic figures, such as those* left*, had defended them. Although this painting shows the angels as shoulder-to-shoulder with the Tommies, they were actually seen in the sky over the German forces, apparently restraining them from attacking. Soldiers on the opposing side, however, reported interventions by pro-German angels. Jung suggested that UFOs may similarly express the desires, conscious or otherwise, of those who see them.

due to the unusually powerful emotional state induced in them by the horrors of the war. Groups of people in the grip of such emotion, said Jung, will tend to see collective visions. And such visions will be projections – a key word – taking the form of some answer to their emotional needs.

In a nutshell, modern Man seems, in many ways, to be 'in search of a soul' – as stated in the title of one of Jung's most effective analyses of the world's present malaise. And that search, with all its accompanying tensions, terrors and despairs, leads frequently to collective projections – resulting in visions, rumours, mass panics, or outlandish beliefs. In them, Jung delightedly discerned the visible process of the formation of a myth. (The subtitle of his book *Flying Saucers* is: *A modern myth of things seen in the sky.*)

Projections and Portents

Jung thereby suggested that UFOs are also such myth-projections. Indeed, they may well be another herald of some current and far-reaching upheaval within the collective psyche of mankind. Interestingly, some transformations, throughout history, have always been accompanied by major upsurges – in religion, art and literature – of the most dominant and potent archetypes. And flying discs or saucers, in Jung's view, are modern versions of perhaps the mightiest archetype of all – named by Jung, the 'mandala'.

The word is Sanskrit, and the art and religion of the Hindus are filled with these symbols. But mandalas occur literally everywhere – from modern children's art to ancient circles of standing stones, from the ring featuring in the solemn marriage ritual of the Christian church to the circles of Dante's *Inferno* and the marginal scrawls and doodles of busy office workers. The mandala is basically a simple circle, though there are many variations, and it can include important additions like a central nucleus, or a quartering, or further concentric circles. It carries the meaning of a sought-after completion, totality, or wholeness.

Split Existence

That brings us abruptly back to modern Man. We live in a 'dissociated' world – split like the mind of a schizophrenic, with little or no true communication between its parts, advanced technology sustaining our lives and simultaneously threatening them with

The mandala forming the centrepiece of a 19th-century Buddhist painting from Nepal,* left*, symbolises the perfection that has been attained by the eight-armed figure at its centre. This is a bodhisattva, which has completed its series of incarnations, but delays its entry into the bliss of Nirvana in order to aid the creatures who still suffer. A mandala also appears in the 14th-century German altarpiece,* right*, where it frames another being of perfect wholeness – Christ in majesty, surrounded by the Beasts of the Apocalypse and an assembly of the blessed.

imminent holocaust. The darker, irrational impulses of human nature, disowned by reason and believed, in the 18th and 19th centuries, to have finally been vanquished by the progress of civilisation, have returned and repeatedly triumphed in this era.

Inwardly, too, we are split, to our grave cost. Materialist values have given us a high standard of living – yet they have also devalued all the areas of the non-rational: the emotions, the instincts, the imagination, religious impulses, and so on. The nominally Christian world can no longer draw strength from its religious tradition; in Carl Jung's words: 'Our myth has become mute, and gives no answers'.

But Jung does not pretend that his view of a sick world is anything but obvious. It is the effect that matters – because dissociation causes tension, illness, and monstrous deformation of the non-rational areas that have been split off and downgraded. So the dissociated mind cries out to be healed – cries out for a reunion of its parts, for a re-creation of healthy and harmonious equilibrium between them – that is, for wholeness. And out of that unconscious yearning, wretched and soul-starved modern Man projects mandalas everywhere, even into the sky.

In the broadsheet from which the woodcut, above, comes, is an eyewitness report that on 7 August 1566, in Basle, 'many large black globes were seen in the air, moving before the sun with great speed, and turning against each other as if fighting. Some of them became red and fiery and afterwards faded and went out'.

Some UFO sightings or mandala dreams, Jung said, may even carry with them elements of sexual symbolism. But he is, as always, drily dismissive of the Freudian tendency to go very little further in search of understanding, having once discerned the symbolic shape of sex organs in the spacecraft of our dreams.

Far more important, for Jung, were the unique elements of the UFO-mandala, which he found to be a variant of the archetype, highly suitable for our time. What more likely image of a healing wholeness, for this technological age, could there be than a mysterious flying machine, a piece of heavenly hardware?

Jung was especially struck by the 'unnatural' behaviour and flight patterns of UFOs in all the

"JUNG THEREBY SUGGESTED THAT UFOS ARE MYTH-PROJECTIONS AND THAT THEY MAY WELL BE A HERALD OF SOME CURRENT AND FAR-REACHING UPHEAVAL WITHIN THE COLLECTIVE PSYCHE OF MANKIND."

reports of sightings that he studied. Indeed, he had no doubt about the significance of the implication that these space-travelling mandalas are not of human origin, for those who profess to see them. And while sometimes the observer (or dreamer) may have felt threatened, more often the UFO visitation is taken to display the existence of advanced extra-terrestrials, superpowerful and friendly beings from the sky, who are watching and worrying over Man's self-destructive twitchings down on planet Earth.

Saviours From Space

Jung also noted some of those occasions when people have claimed to have had close encounters, and even to have been picked up and carried off briefly by the kindly and godlike beings. He did not give much credence to these tales, but instead concluded that here the yearning for wholeness had taken on the more precise and personalised form of a longing for and dreaming of a saviour – some being who is more than human, who will descend to help us find the respite and healing that we cannot find for ourselves.

In this part of his analysis, Jung made the illuminating point that 'things seen in the sky' existed throughout history, long before they took on the 20th-century guise of mysterious spacecraft. Indeed, unnaturally mobile flying spheres, globes and discs occur prominently in annals of strange visions and inexplicable phenomena seen during many troubled times of the past.

Again and again, Jung made the point that it matters not at all whether there actually was anything there, in the sky, nor whether there is today. If UFOs did not and do not exist in objective reality, then they can be defined as projections of all the complex and powerful emotions described earlier. And if they do exist, they can still be seen as projections – just as we unconsciously project a huge burden of symbolism, with all the potency of the archetypes, on to many real items or individuals around us (such as jewellery or weaponry, film stars or political leaders).

In the last analysis, Jung does not wholly discount the possibility that there may be some objective, physical basis for the 'symbolic rumour' of the UFO. We might forgivably dismiss as dreams or hallucinations some of the more far-fetched tales of trips into space with tall, robed beings who promise to save the world. But radar screens and cameras do not dream or hallucinate; and Jung was well aware of the solidly authenticated instances when recorded blips and photographs have seemed to

*In*Focus PATTERNS OF INTERPRETATION

Jung saw the UFO phenomenon as 'a modern myth of things seen in the sky', and believed that sightings of such craft could well be the projections of complex and powerful emotions. What we *think* we can see can indeed, in itself, be highly revealing. In the Rorschach inkblot test, (invented in the 1920s by Swiss psychiatrist Hermann Rorschach), for instance, the subject is invited to look at a series of ten cards, each featuring a bisymmetrical or mirrored inkblot pattern, rather like the one shown *right*. Responses as to colour and shape are then evaluated in order to provide information about the dynamics of the subject's emotional life.

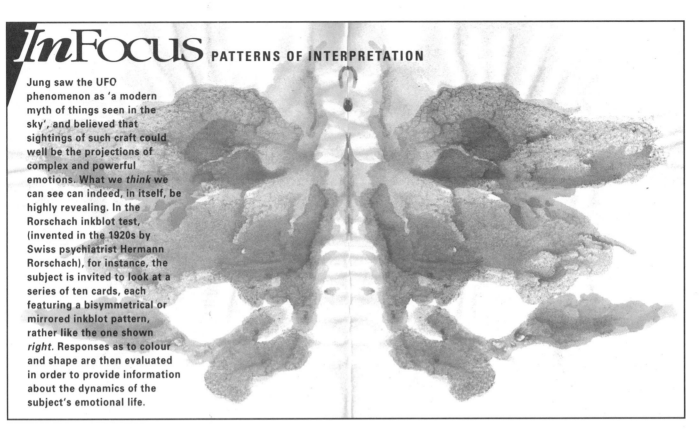

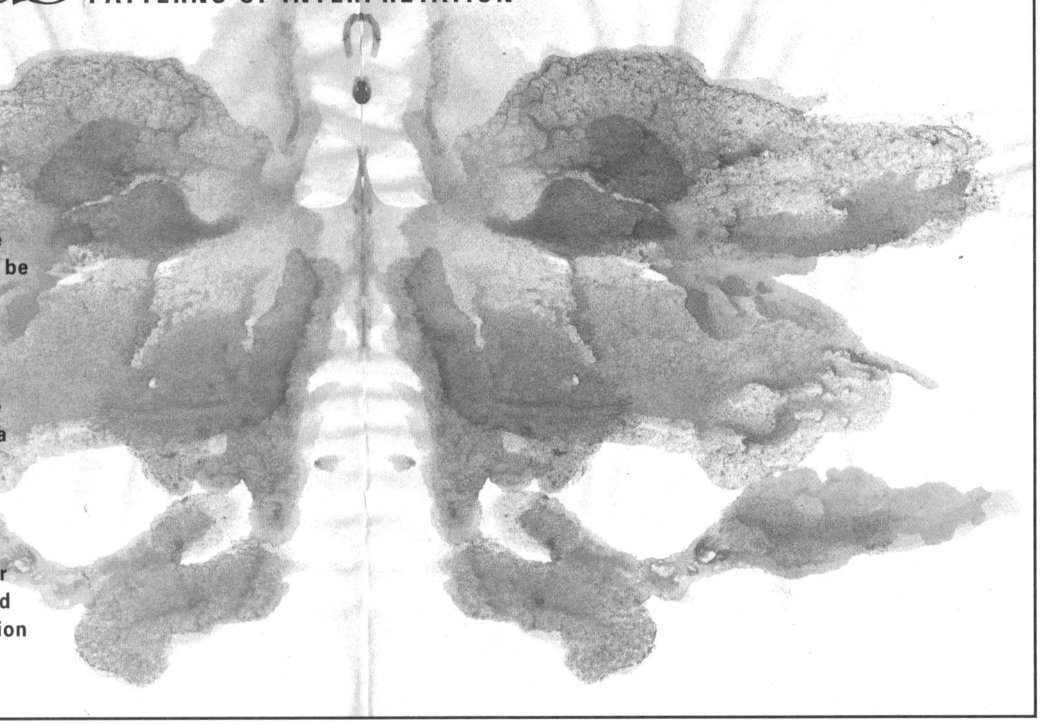

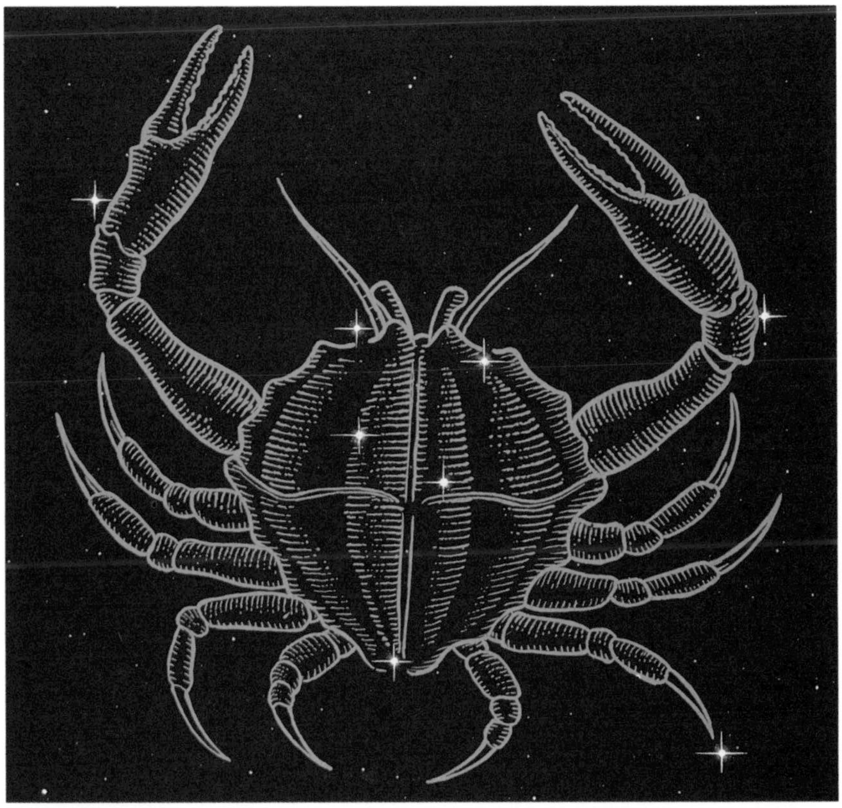

***Psychologist Carl Jung felt that unidentified flying objects could perhaps be projections from the unconscious mind – archetypal symbols in the sky, such as the constellation of Cancer, the crab, shown* above.**

confirm the existence of UFOs. As he put it: 'Either psychic projections throw back a radar echo, or else the appearance of real objects affords an opportunity for mythological projection'.

He was, of course, being ironic, and did not believe that psychic projections can affect radar screens. But the point has to be laboured because of the relentless urge, among the media and other defenders of the rationalist status quo, to take every opportunity of decrying Jung as some wild-eyed, credulous crank, hip-deep in what Freud scornfully called the 'black mud of occultism'. His critics have consistently misunderstood and misrepresented Jung's investigations of alchemy, astrology and the 'irrational' in all its forms. Inevitably, too, they have had a field day with their own inadequate comprehension of what he had to say about flying saucers.

Jung, conversely, always persisted in keeping an open mind to an enormous range of material that might in some way contribute to his understanding of the human unconscious. He perceived and analysed, towards this end, the symbolic relevance of the UFO.

He also perceived that, in all the continually amassing reports on and studies of UFOs, there remained a substantial core of 'hard' data that could only make sense if there were real objects up there, even if they were misinterpreted by those who saw them.

In the years after the publication of his book on flying saucers, Jung was often in touch with one of his nieces in Switzerland, also interested in UFO sightings. According to Gordon Creighton of *Flying Saucer Review*, Jung came to move even more firmly beyond the position that UFOs might 'merely' be symbolic projections of a powerful archetype. Whatever our unconscious wishes might make of them, whatever effects they might have upon the depths of our psyches, Jung apparently became more and more firmly convinced that there was something very real behind the phenomena.

Jung did not see himself as a prophet in any sense, but as a psychologist, and a scientific observer. Yet history is full of instances where a scientist, from objective study and observation, has 'prophetically' perceived a truth at which his blinkered contemporaries, without examining the data, continue to scoff. Jung's view of the UFO may one day prove to be another example.

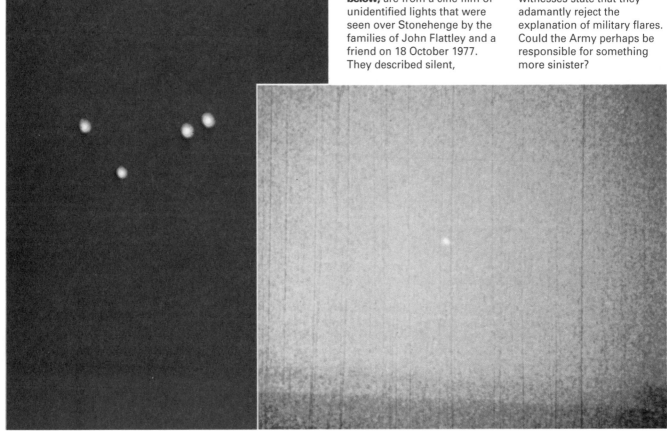

UFO PHOTO FILE

The view of the Earth's surface, **above,** shows the blue glow of the atmosphere at the horizon, cloud formations and, apparently, a small round UFO, to the right of the picture. Taken by astronaut M. Scott Carpenter from **Aurora 7,** 1,000 miles (1,600 kilometres) above the Earth, this picture has been acclaimed as conclusive evidence for rumours about the frequent 'buzzing' of NASA space capsules by UFOs. But in fact, the object following this capsule so attentively is an IFO (Identified Flying Object) – the meteorological balloon towed behind the capsule.

The two frames, **left** and **below,** are from a ciné film of unidentified lights that were seen over Stonehenge by the families of John Flattley and a friend on 18 October 1977. They described silent, erratically moving lights. Sometimes as many as seven or eight were clearly visible. At one point, the lights seemed to hang motionless in the sky for long periods. The nearby Army base has been blamed for the lights, but witnesses state that they adamantly reject the explanation of military flares. Could the Army perhaps be responsible for something more sinister?

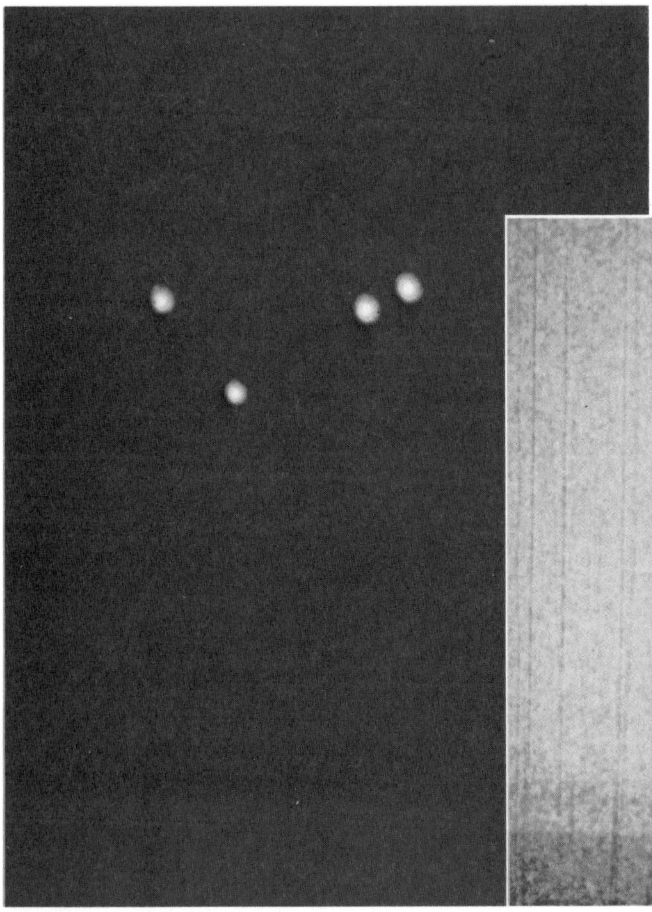

The UFO, **above** and **right,** was captured on ciné film on the morning of 11 January 1973 by Peter Day, on the road close to Cuddington (between Thame and Aylesbury, England). He had been watching the UFO for about a minute before he was able to park his car and then use his 8-millimetre ciné camera to record it. The object emerged from behind the trees and travelled horizontally from left to right at a low altitude. Peter Day said the UFO seemed to be flickering or pulsating; this is reflected in the difference in brightness of the object between the two consecutive frames of his film, shown here. He 'caught' the object for 15 seconds only as it zoomed across the tops of the trees. Although he was alone during the sighting, a number of children and teachers at a school some miles away confirmed the sudden appearance and abrupt disappearance of a UFO at approximately the same time as his sighting. The **Thame Gazette** of 16 January 1973 quoted one of the children who described the object as 'a huge blob of orange fire'. The UFO was said to have approached within a few hundred yards of the school, illuminating the ground with a bright orange glow as it passed by. One of the teachers told Peter Day that the object had hung motionless above and ahead of her for a few seconds. She noted that it looked like a ball at the top, but was flat at the bottom, and the whole object was spinning.

Ciné films of UFOs – such as those shown here – are important for a number of reasons: imagination on the part of the witnesses can be ruled out entirely; a moving object is extremely difficult to fake; and relative distances – of the object and trees, houses, the Sun or stars, for example – can be more easily estimated than from a still photograph. The usual 'explanations' – flocks of birds, the planet Venus and weather balloons – can be eliminated; and the moving pictures can be 'frozen', frame by frame, for analysis.

ARIGO: SURGEON EXTRAORDINARY

HE OPERATED ON THE DYING WITH ONLY A RUSTY KNIFE – AND APPARENTLY CURED THEM. WAS THIS HUMBLE BRAZILIAN, WHO PERFORMED MANY SUCH SURGICAL MIRACLES, WORKING 'UNDER SPIRIT GUIDANCE'?

A priest had arrived to administer to the dying woman. Candles were lit, and relatives and friends were gathered around her bedside in the town of Congonhas do Campo, Brazil. Her death, from cancer of the uterus, was expected at any moment.

Suddenly, one of those present rushed from the room, returning moments later with a large knife from the kitchen. He ordered everyone to stand back. Then, without warning, he pulled the sheets from the woman and plunged the kitchen knife into her vagina.

After several brutal twists of the blade, he removed the knife and inserted his hand into the woman, withdrawing a huge tumour, the size of a grapefruit. He dropped the knife and the bloody tumour into the kitchen sink, sat down on a chair and began to sob.

A relative rushed off to fetch a doctor; and the rest stood silently as if transfixed by the astonishing scene just witnessed. The patient was unperturbed: she had felt no pain at all during the 'operation', and what is more, the doctor confirmed that there was no haemorrhaging or other ill-effects. He also confirmed that the growth was a uterine tumour.

This extraordinary incident proved to be a turning point in the lives of the two people concerned. The woman recovered her health completely. And the man who had performed the 'surgery', José Arigo, suddenly found himself in great demand from people whose doctors had given them up as incurable. Yet he could not even remember 'operating' on the woman.

PSYCHIC SURGERY

Later, when such startling surgery became a daily occurrence in Congonhas do Campo – Arigo's home town – it was realised that he entered a trance state whenever he treated the sick. His patients also noticed he spoke with a German accent, allegedly because Dr Adolphus Fritz, who had died

Arigo is shown, **below**, *performing a delicate eye operation in his back parlour. Although it was Arigo who went into a trance, the patient felt no pain – nor, it seems, any fear – despite the unhygienic surroundings, primitive lighting and complete lack of anaesthetics.*

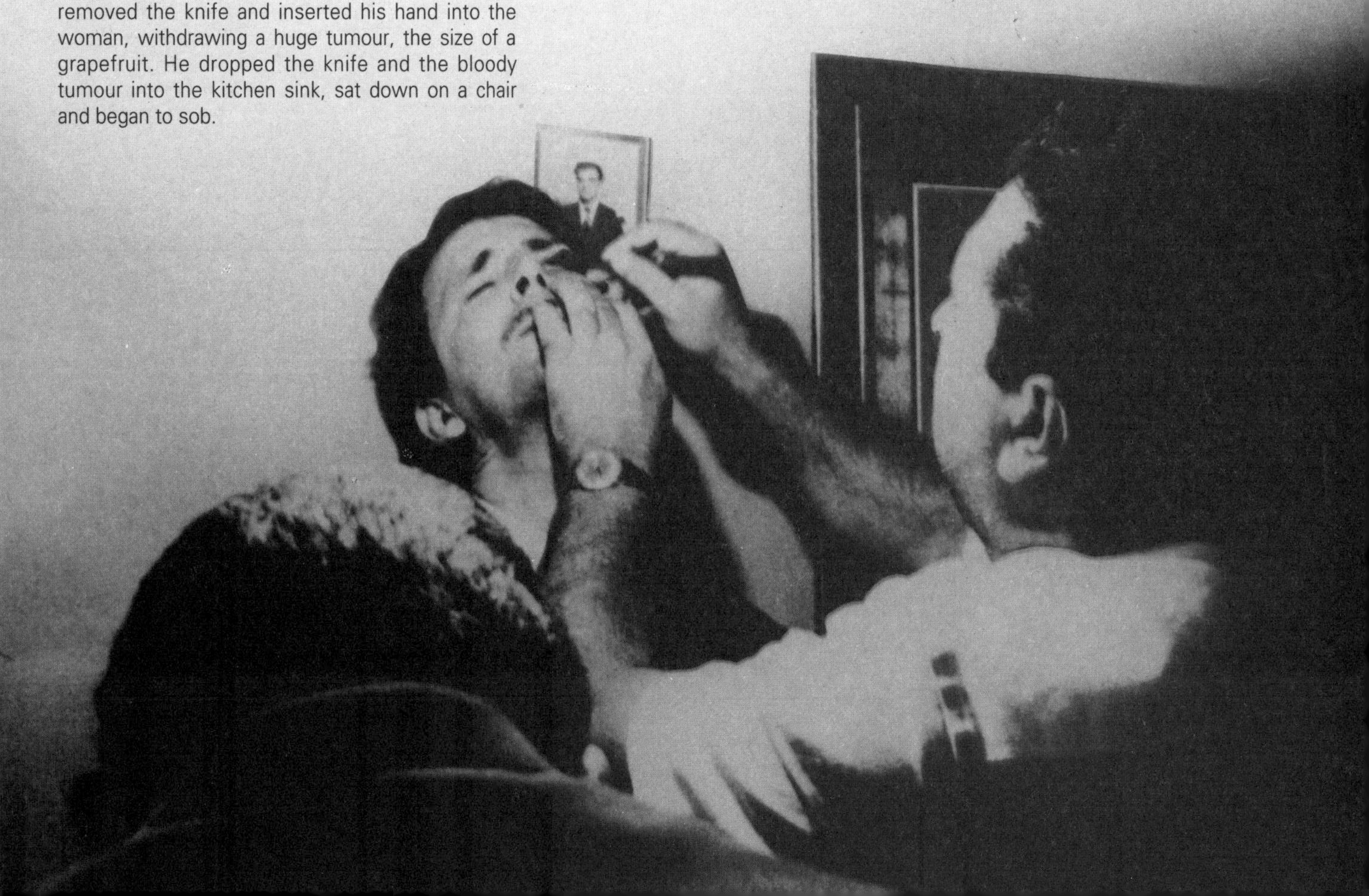

in 1918, was said still to be 'operating' directly through him.

On most days when Arigo's clinic opened at 7 a.m., there was already a queue of some 200 people waiting. Some he would treat in a rapid and often brutal fashion, pushing them against a wall, jabbing an unsterilised knife into them, then wiping it clean on his shirt. Yet they felt no pain or fear. There was very little blood, and the wound would knit together immediately, healing in days.

Not everyone received psychic surgery, however. In some instances, he would simply glance at patients, diagnose their problems without asking any questions, and then write a prescription rapidly. The medicines prescribed were usually well-known drugs made by leading companies, but in large doses and combinations that were surprising according to conventional medical knowledge. Yet they cured people.

One conservative estimate suggests that he treated half-a-million patients in a five-year period. These included people from all walks of life: rich and poor alike, it made no difference to Arigo because he never accepted money or gifts for his services.

During the 1950s and 1960s, Arigo became something of a national hero in Brazil and hardly a day passed without newspapers headlining his latest healing miracles. Patients came from all over the world. He also attracted the attention of Andrija

José Arigo is seen,* above, *in jail. During two periods of imprisonment for practising medicine illegally, his jailers secretly let him out to perform operations on the sick, as successfully as ever.

Puharich, a New York researcher with a keen interest in the paranormal who, after an initial visit, went back to Brazil with a team of doctors to investigate and film the phenomenon.

Puharich described the scene that first greeted him as 'a nightmare'. He wrote:

'These people step up – they're all sick. One had a big goitre. Arigo just picked up the paring knife, cut it open, popped the goitre out, slapped it in her hand, wiped the opening with a piece of dirty cotton, and off she went. It hardly bled at all.'

Puharich was also able to experience Arigo's extraordinary surgery for himself. He asked the Brazilian psychic surgeon to remove a small benign tumour from his arm. Arigo did so in seconds; and Dr Puharich was able to take the growth, and a film record of the surgery, back to the US for analysis.

In all the years that Arigo treated the sick by psychic surgery, there was never a single allegation that his unconventional treatment caused anyone any harm. Nevertheless, what he was doing was frowned upon by the authorities because Arigo had no medical qualifications. Eventually, in 1956, he was charged with practising illegal medicine.

Many people were willing to testify that Arigo had cured them of serious illnesses, but their testimonies only gave ammunition to the prosecution case. Arigo was given a prison sentence, which was reduced to eight months on appeal, and was fined. But just before he was put into prison, the Brazilian president, Kubitschek, gave him a pardon.

Then eight years later, he was charged again. Kubitschek was no longer president and Arigo was jailed for 16 months this time. After seven months, he was freed, pending an appeal, but eventually had to serve a further two months in prison, in 1965. During both periods, however, the warden allowed him out of his cell both to visit the sick and to operate on them.

ARIGO INVESTIGATED

The man who had to hear that appeal was Judge Filippe Immesi, a Roman Catholic with little knowledge of Arigo. But the more he studied the case, the more difficult it became for him to make a decision without seeing the astonishing psychic surgery for himself.

One day, unannounced, he visited Congonhas do Campos with a friend, who was a district attorney from another part of Brazil. Despite their anonymity, Arigo recognised them immediately as representatives of the law and invited them to see the 'operations' from close quarters. He knew that he was breaking the law, but thought the authorities might as well satisfy themselves that fraud was not taking place.

A near-blind woman with cataracts was one of the first patients they saw being treated, and Arigo asked the judge to hold her head. Though he felt queasy, he agreed to do so. John G. Fuller, author of *Arigo: Surgeon of the Rusty Knife,* quotes this testimony from Judge Immesi:

'I saw him pick up what looked like a pair of nail scissors. He wiped them on his sport shirt, and used no disinfectant of any kind. Then I saw him cut straight into the cornea of the patient's eye. She did not blench, although she was fully conscious. The cataract was out in a matter of seconds. The

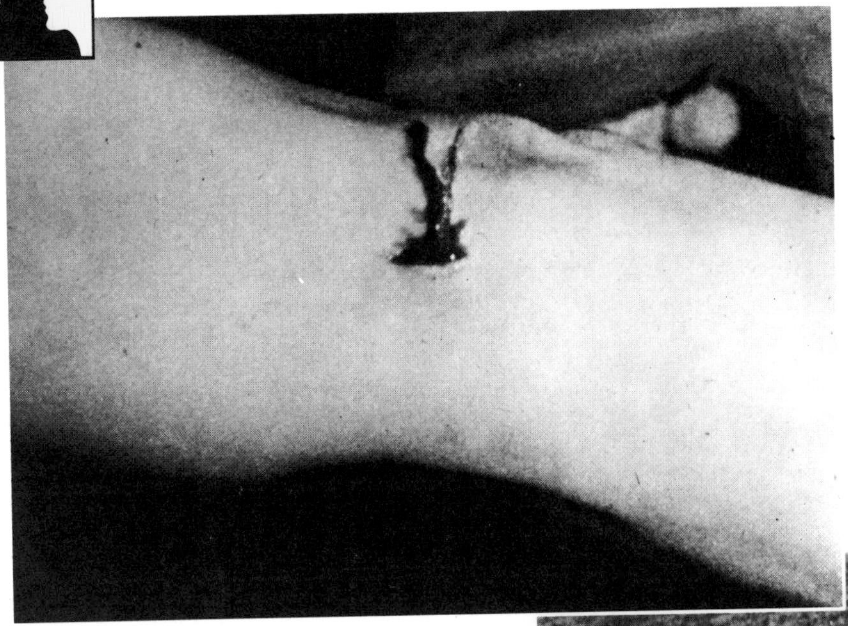

whose body was riddled with cancer. She and her husband were friends of Dr José Hortencia de Madeiros, an X-ray specialist with the State Institute of Cardiology, who took a close interest in the case. The cancer was discovered when she was rushed to a Sao Paulo clinic with symptoms of intestinal obstruction. It found that a tumour was blocking the transverse colon, and a colostomy was performed.

Later she entered the Central Cancer Hospital in the same city for another operation, where it was found that the cancer had spread dramatically. Her weight had dropped by nearly half, and the surgeon reported that she was totally beyond the resources of medical science.

So, as a last resort, she was taken to Arigo. Dr Madeiros accompanied the couple on the long trip to Congonhas do Campos, where the dying woman had to be carried into the clinic. Being an Austrian,

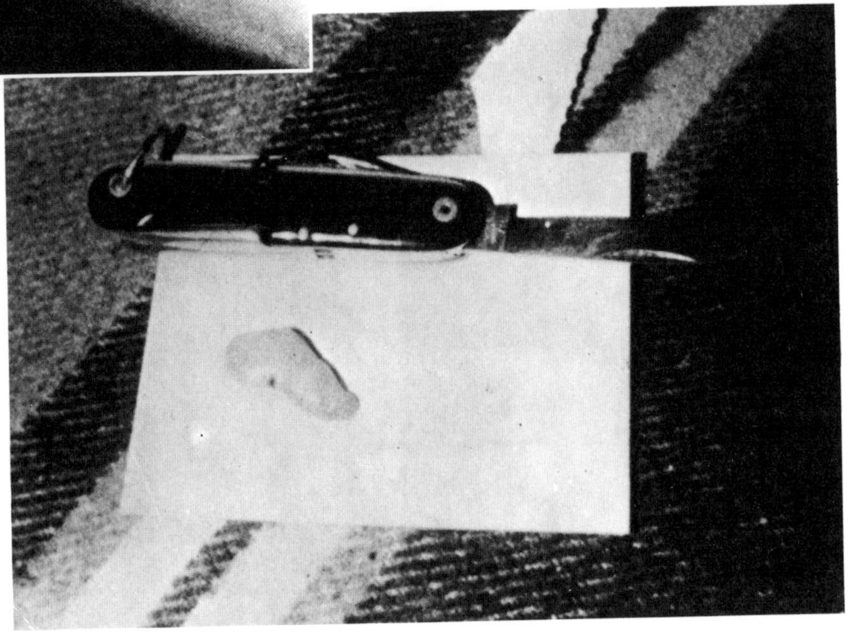

district attorney and I were speechless, amazed. Then Arigo said some kind of prayer as he held a piece of cotton in his hand. A few drops of liquid suddenly appeared on the cotton and he wiped the woman's eye with it. We saw this at close range. She was cured.'

What Judge Immesi saw convinced him that Arigo was a remarkable man who deserved to be the subject of scientific study. But the law was beyond doubt. What Arigo was doing was illegal and he would have to be punished – even though he was helping people. However, the judge looked for every possible excuse to reduce the sentence, with the result that Arigo was sent back to prison for just two months. While he was serving that sentence, Arigo's case was under review by the Federal Supreme Court, and it eventually decided to drop the charges against him. He was released on 8 November 1965.

Medical Testimony

The judge, of course, was not a medical man but he gave special attention to doctors' testimonies before reaching a verdict. There were several who had experience of Arigo's 'operations' and who were also prepared to say so in public. One of these was Dr Ary Lex, a distinguished Brazilian surgeon, a specialist in surgery of the stomach and digestive systems, lecturer at the Surgical Clinic of Sao Paulo University, and author of a standard textbook for Brazilian medical students.

Like Judge Immesi, Dr Lex was invited to hold a patient's head in his hands while Arigo operated. He witnessed four operations in half-an-hour and was satisfied that what Arigo was doing was paranormal. But he was not so impressed with the prescriptions. 'They were absolutely ridiculous,' he told author and psychic researcher, Guy Playfair. 'Some of them were obsolete medicines which were only still being made because he prescribed them.' A number of them, he said, were also dangerous in the doses prescribed, and expensive.

But however absurd the prescriptions may have seemed, their effects were frequently startling. One such case concerned a young Polish woman

***Andrija Puharich, investigator of the paranormal, paid Arigo a visit to see the 'psychic surgeon' in action. He asked Arigo to remove the benign tumour from his arm and Arigo immediately made a deep incision* (top) *and then cut out the tumour with his unsterilised penknife,* above.**

the husband spoke to 'Dr Fritz' in German and he replied in that language. Then Arigo glanced at the sick woman, scribbled a prescription, and said: 'You take this, and get well'.

Dr Madeiros administered the abnormal dosage of drugs prescribed and the patient showed signs of improvement within a week. After six weeks, her weight had returned to normal. She then visited Arigo again, who announced that she was out of danger and gave her two more prescriptions. On a third visit to the psychic surgeon, the patient was told that she was completely healed and he advised her to 'undo the operation' – a reference to the colostomy that enabled the body's waste to be passed through the abdomen into a bag. Arrangements were made for the operation to be reversed; and when her abdomen was opened, the surgeons confirmed that all signs of cancer had vanished.

Arigo was killed in a car crash in January, 1971, having told several people that he would not see them again. The techniques he used to cure the sick remain a mystery. Arigo himself offered no explanation, except to give credit to Jesus and Dr Fritz. Once, when he saw a film of himself performing operations, he had fainted.

INTO THIN AIR

THERE ARE HUNDREDS OF CASES OF PEOPLE WHO SIMPLY DISAPPEAR WITHOUT TRACE. MANY SUCH INSTANCES DEFY RATIONAL EXPLANATION UNTIL WE CONSIDER THE POSSIBILITY OF A DIMENSION WHICH EXISTS, HIDDEN BUT EVER-PRESENT, WITHIN YET BEYOND OUR REALITY

People have been disappearing mysteriously since the beginning of time; but those agencies blamed for abducting them have changed according to the spiritual preoccupations of the day. Gods, demons, fairies, and now UFOs show an astonishing predilection for the random picking up and setting down – or picking up and not returning – of perfectly ordinary people.

The fabric of space is represented below as a grid in which objects of increasing mass produce increasingly large distortions. Astrophysicists accept that such space warps may link the Universe with other dimensions.

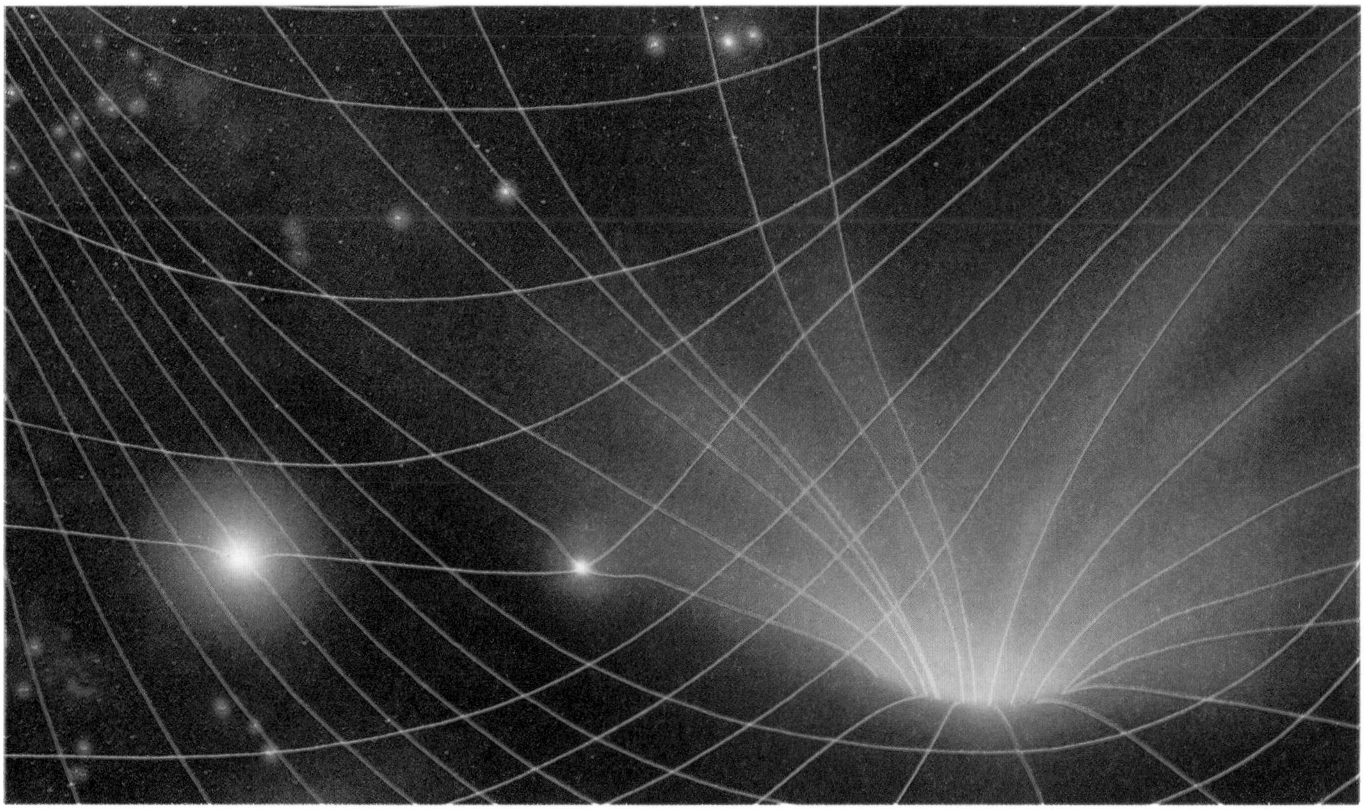

On 5 November 1975, Travis Walton, a young forester, and his five workmates were driving to work near Snowflake, Arizona when they suddenly saw a bright light hovering over their truck. As the driver, Mike Rogers, stopped the car, Travis felt an extraordinary compulsion to approach the light, jumped out and rushed towards it. There was a sudden flash, and Travis hit the ground. Terrified, the others drove off. When they had calmed down, they returned to the spot and instigated a thorough search for him that was to last for five days and cover miles of the Arizona desert and forest. Suspicion naturally fell on the five friends, but their distress seemed completely genuine and their story held up even under close questioning with the aid of a lie-detector.

TIME WARP

Five days later, a confused and shaky Walton appeared in Heber, a small town close to Snowflake. His story tallied with that of his friends – as far as theirs went – but he added some amazing details. The beam of light, he said, had knocked him unconscious and had then somehow drawn him up into a spacecraft in which he was examined by foetus-like creatures before being 'dumped' in Heber.

The late psychic and writer Wellesley Tudor Pole recounted a similar experience in his book, *The Silent Road*.

'On a wet and stormy night in December 1952, I found myself at a country station some mile-and-a-half from my Sussex home. The train from London had arrived late, the bus had gone and no taxis were available. The rain was heavy and incessant. The time was 5.55 p.m. and I was expecting an important trunk call from overseas at 6 p.m. at home. The situation seemed desperate. To make matters worse, the station call box was out of order and some trouble on the line made access to the railway telephone impossible. In despair, I sat down in the waiting room and, having nothing better to do, I compared my watch with the station clock. Allowing for the fact that this is always kept two minutes in advance, I was able to confirm the fact that the exact time was 5.57 p.m. Three minutes to zero hour! What happened next, I cannot say. When I came to myself, I was standing in my hall at home, a good 20 minutes walk away, and the clock was striking six. My telephone call duly came through a few minutes later. Having finished my call, I awoke to the realisation that something very strange had happened. Then much to my surprise, I found that my shoes were dry and free of mud, and that my clothes showed no sign of damp or damage.'

Like all such stories, there is something exasperatingly incomplete about this account. Pole told all he could remember, but inevitably the phenomenon raises questions he was unable to answer. As there were no witnesses in this case, no one will ever know how – or if – the teleportee disappeared. Was he transported invisibly? How did he reappear? But at least one thing seems certain: what triggered off the teleporting agency seems to have been no less than the writer's own will. He was desperate to get home in time for his telephone call, and his anxiety seems to have put into motion whatever it is that governs the occurrence of the phenomenon.

But in the annals of disappearing people, there is no more controversial tale nor one that is stranger than that of the alleged Philadelphia experiment. In 1943, there reportedly took place a horrifying experiment into invisibility, involving a ship and its crew. This was not a psychic test, but a top-secret experiment of the United States Navy, who created a force field around the experimental ship – a destroyer – as it lay in a special berth in the Philadelphia Navy Yard. The crew could see one another normally, but witnesses could only see the vague outline of both the ship and the men through the force field. They shimmered like a heat haze before reassuming normal shape and density. The effect on the crewmen involved was said to be appalling, and the after-effects took various horrible forms: some of the men are said to have suffered a particularly harrowing type of spontaneous human combustion – bursting into flames that burned brightly for 18 days; others went mad, while some periodically became semi-transparent or partly invisible. Some even died as a direct result of their experience.

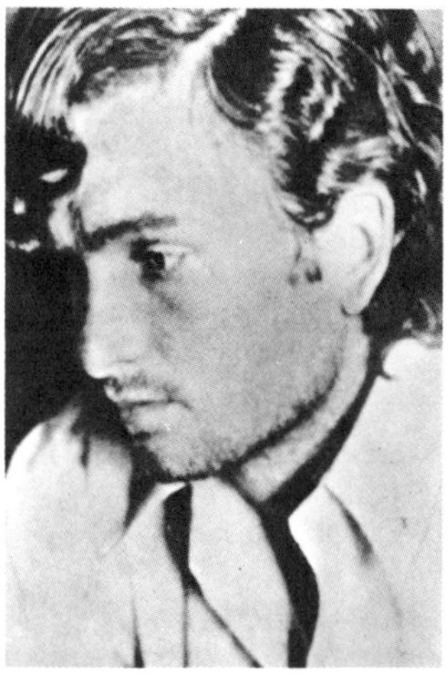

Travis Walton,* above, *a forestry worker, claims to have been abducted by a UFO while driving to work near Snowflake, Arizona, on 5 November 1975. Five days later, he reappeared, telling an amazing story of his 'flight' in a strange craft.

PROJECT INVISIBILITY

An eyewitness claimed to have seen the entire experiment take place, and even to have thrust his arm into the force field. He described it as surging 'in a counterclockwise direction around the little experimental Navy ship... I watched the air all around the ship... turn slightly darker than all the other air... I saw, after a few minutes, a foggy green mist arise like a thin cloud. I think this must have been a mist of atomic particles. I watched as [it] became rapidly invisible to human eyes. And yet the precise shape of the keel and underhull of that ship remained impressed into the ocean water... The field had a sheet of pure electricity around it as it flowed... my entire body was not within that force field when it reached maximum strength density... and so I was not knocked down but my arm and hand was [sic] only pushed backward.'

PERSPECTIVES

TIME VORTEX

Dowsers (water-diviners) are sensitive to the Earth's magnetic forces. Indeed, sacred sites, such as Stonehenge, were probably chosen because ancient priests could sense that there was something strange and powerful about the earth there.

One of the odd things about such sites is that they also seem to be able to record human emotions. One dowser, for instance, visited the Rollright Stones, near Oxford, *right,* after a black magic group had performed ceremonies there, and said that the place positively reeked of 'nastiness'.

But such 'forces' seem to wax and wane, according to the position of the moon and other heavenly bodies. It has even been suggested that some mysterious disppearances are caused by a 'time vortex' associated with powerful earth forces, and that reappearances occur once the forces start to wane.

The US Navy deny that the experiment ever took place. Yet the story is too persistent and has too much inner consistency to be dismissed. If 'project invisibility' did take place, then it made scientific history – but compared with 'natural' disappearances, it was clumsy and potentially dangerous.

The US Navy do have an interest in invisibility that can be verified, however. In September 1980, they actually made it known that they were experimenting with *radar* invisibility; but escaping a radar scan is, of course, a far cry from disappearing from human sight altogether.

VANISHING ACT

How, then, could a human being vanish into thin air? The American broadcaster Long John Nebel has a highly circumstantial account of how it happened before the eyes of an entire audience in New York's Paramount Theatre. During a Thursday afternoon matinée, his friend William Neff, a well-known conjuror, stepped into a spotlight in front of the curtain and began his patter. As Nebel watched, it seemed to him that he could see light passing through Neff's body, as if he was turning into frosted glass.

Slowly, Neff became transparent, and then disappeared completely, although his voice continued to sound quite normal. After a while, a faint outline 'like a very fine pencil sketch' began to appear: then, a few minutes later, Neff was back again, as solid as anyone else in the theatre.

The audience assumed that the vanishing was a part of Neff's act; and as soon as the show was over, Nebel rushed backstage to ask how Neff had done it. The conjurer seemed surprised. He was not aware that he had 'faded', but he admitted that the same thing had occurred three years earlier at a theatre in Chicago. It had also happened only a few evenings previously as he sat watching television with his wife, Evelyn. He was alerted to the fact that something was wrong when she screamed. When he touched her, she screamed again and cried: 'Who's touching me?'

Neff rushed from the room to get her a glass of water. When he returned, she flung her arms around him and said: 'I was so frightened – I couldn't see you for a few minutes.'

One of the most extraordinary disappearances ever allegedly took place in 1943, when the US Navy is reported to have carried out a horrifying experiment in invisibility, making a destroyer – the USS **Eldridge, *bottom,* *together with its crew – disappear for a few minutes from its berth in the Philadelphia Navy Yard, shown*** **below.**

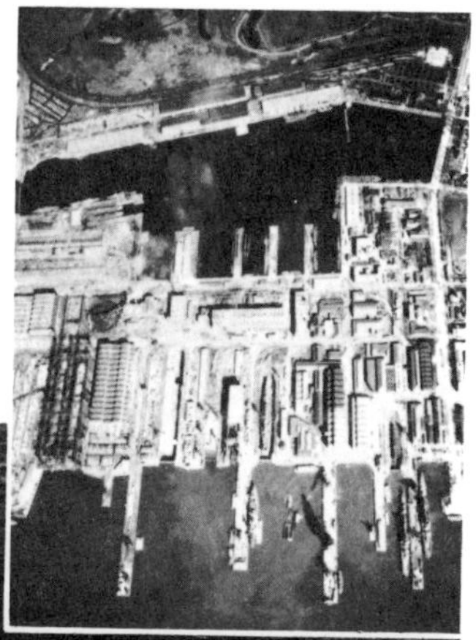

Around the turn of the 20th century, there were many who thought that they could explain such mysterious disappearances. A number of scientists even became convinced that there must exist a 'fourth dimension', at right angles to the other three (length, breadth and height), and that it is merely the limitations of the human mind that prevent us from seeing it.

HIDDEN DIMENSION

Professor Johann C.F Zollner of Leipzig University suspected that the fourth dimension theory was in fact the answer to some of the more baffling questions of psychical research – for example, how poltergeists (or 'noisy ghosts') can sometimes throw objects through solid walls. Zollner suggested that such objects do not go 'through' walls but, rather, into the fourth dimension and out again, in much the same way as a giant might step over an object that would be unscalable to a creature such as a tortoise.

The Russian philosopher, Ouspensky, became so fascinated by the idea of the fourth dimension that he devoted most of his first book to it. In *Tertium Organum,* he cites the case of a scientist named Johan van Manen, who received a vision of the fourth dimension as he lay in bed one night. 'I plainly saw before me first a four-dimensional globe', he said. 'And afterwards a four-dimensional cube...'

SLOWLY, NEFF BECAME TRANSPARENT, AND THEN DISAPPEARED COMPLETELY, ALTHOUGH HIS VOICE CONTINUED TO SOUND QUITE NORMAL. AFTER A WHILE, A FAINT OUTLINE 'LIKE A VERY FINE PENCIL SKETCH' BEGAN TO APPEAR: A FEW MINUTES LATER, NEFF WAS BACK AGAIN, AS SOLID AS ANYONE ELSE IN THE THEATRE.

Unless van Manen was deceiving himself (and he claimed to be able to recall the globe with ease, and the cube with some difficulty), then our minds are actually capable of grasping that extra dimension. Ouspensky even argued that it is the key to proper understanding of the universe. Our three-dimensional understanding cannot grasp the idea of the Universe having a beginning or an end, but insight into the fourth dimension may well solve the problem. Albert Einstein later argued that the fourth dimension is actually time, and spoke of the Universe as being a kind of 'finite yet unbounded' space which curves into the fourth dimension much like a sphere.

THE LOST RACE

THE IDEA THAT WE MAY HAVE DESCENDED FROM NEANDERTHALS ONCE SEEMED OUTRAGEOUS. TODAY, WE KNOW MUCH MORE ABOUT OUR DISTANT ANCESTORS – THOUGH ONE PUZZLE REMAINS. WHY DID THE NEANDERTHALS VANISH SO QUICKLY FROM OUR PLANET?

Though Neanderthal was broader and squatter than modern man, he was by no means the shambling brute once imagined. Indeed, some scientists believe that if he could be brought back to life today, he would hardly attract attention – apart from his remarkable psychic powers.

Neanderthal man came into the world of the Victorians like a naked savage into a ladies' sewing circle. Even the scientific community regarded him as a monstrous intrusion – half-man, half-ape, and a shameful blotch on the name of Mankind.

The Neanderthals acquired this poor reputation because they were grievously misjudged by the experts. From the discovery of their bones in 1856 to some 40 years ago, almost all palaeontologists regarded them as an insignificant – and distant – branch of the human family tree, rejecting them as candidates for Man's ancestry because they were thought to be too aberrant, too specialised, too brutishly primitive.

Only now is this misjudgement being remedied, as new research has forced scientists to upgrade their picture of Neanderthal man. Neanderthal skulls found in western Europe actually held brains larger than some belonging to modern men. Anthropologists therefore now regard Neanderthals not as dull-witted louts but as men with potentially sophisticated brains who happened to live in primitive societies. But the most remarkable about-turn in scientific thinking comes from evidence suggesting that some Neanderthals – perhaps even all of them – were our immediate ancestors.

A Horrible Embarrassment

So why did the experts originally misjudge the Neanderthals? Our knowledge of the events that occurred in the remote past will always be incomplete, and proof for any of the hypotheses can never be conclusive. But in the case of the Neanderthals, more important than evidence were the prejudices and pre-conceptions that helped to shape the intellectual climate of the time. Old ideas could not explain the Neanderthals; new ones were welcome, but they were often poorly understood.

It all started in 1856 when the flanks of the Neander valley, (*Neanderthal* in Old German), were being blasted for limestone. A number of ancient bones were found in the rubble – obviously the skeletal remains of a man – but the thickness of the limbs, and the heavy brow of the skull were unlike any seen before.

One German anatomist looked at the somewhat bowed leg bones of the Neanderthal skeleton and suggested that they belonged to a man who had spent his life on horseback. With stunning specificity, he ventured that the fossil man must have been a Mongolian Cossack of the Russian cavalry, who had chased Napoleon across the Rhine in 1814. He further guessed that the Cossack had probably deserted the Russian forces and, suffering from water on the brain, had then crawled into the Neander cave to die.

The scientific community, clearly, was not ready for the truth about the man from Neander. In 1856, they were yet to be convinced that Man had been on Earth for any substantial length of time – fundamentalists believed that Adam and Eve were created in 4004 BC – and no one would dare suggest that humans had existed in any other form. This would have been contrary to belief in the Creation.

But the idea of the Creation was soon to face a formidable challenge. Three years after the Neander discovery, Charles Darwin published *Origin of Species,* arguing that life had evolved from lower to higher forms over vast millennia of time. He said almost nothing about the possibility of humanity having evolved from such primitive forms, but the evidence for such a revolutionary conclusion was now available – Neanderthal man.

"But of all Neanderthal achievements the most significant were in the realm of spiritual beliefs. They conceived a life after death, they cared for the aged and handicapped, and attempted to control their fate through magic rites."

Still the hint fell on deaf ears. Scientists were deeply divided over the issues raised by Darwin, and none would admit that the fossils were ancient. For the fundamentalists among them, Neanderthal was a horrible embarrassment. He didn't fit into their accepted way of thinking, and so they racked their brains to come up with 'explanations' that would rationalise the whole distasteful matter.

Errors of Reconstruction

The man who originally established Neanderthal man's poor image was Marcellin Boule, a palaeontologist from the French Museum of Natural History. He had been assigned the task of making a detailed re-construction of a typical Neanderthal from a fine set of bones discovered in 1908. Unfortunately Boule committed an astonishing series of errors, and they were not corrected for decades.

He mistakenly arranged the foot bones, for instance, so that the Neanderthal would have had to walk on the outer part of his feet, like an ape. His version of the spine also lacked the flexibility that enables modern Man to stand upright. Thus, the impression was of a cross between a brutish ape and a shuffling hunchback.

Nevertheless, Boule's analysis won almost universal acceptance, and practically everyone agreed that Neanderthals could not be in any way ancestors of modern Man since they were so thoroughly ape-like. One of Boule's biographers summed up the consensus of opinion as follows:

Charles Darwin, **right**, *shattered Victorian society with his theory that 'selection was the keystone of Man's success' – not God's intervention.*

'The skeletal remains afford a clear-cut picture of the uncouth and repellent Neanderthal man. His thick-set, coarsely-built body carried upon short half-flexed legs is of peculiarly ungraceful form. The great coarse face with receding chin completes the picture of unattractiveness.'

It was not until 1957, however, that the American anthropologist William Strauss and an English professor of anatomy, A.J. Cave, re-examined the fossil evidence that had provided the basis for Boule's contentions. They discovered that Boule was entirely mistaken in his view of Neanderthal man. Not only had he reconstructed the bones quite incorrectly – to give an exaggerated ape-like appearance – but the slumped, bent-knee posture was so wrong that, by all the laws of physics, Boule's reconstruction, had it ever lived, would have fallen on its face!

Because flesh does not fossilise, anatomists have to use a degree of artistic licence when reconstructing the soft tissue that once formed the face. The Victorians, however, had used this freedom to

model Neanderthal man with the features of a chimpanzee. Strauss and Cave's work now made it seem justifiable to model the same skull with a face not too dissimilar from the one we have today. They wrote that if he could be brought back to life and 'placed in a New York subway – provided that he were bathed and shaved and dressed in modern clothing – it is doubtful whether he would attract any more attention than some of its other denizens'. Indeed, most anthropologists now favour classifying the Neanderthals as *Homo sapiens* – that is, the same as modern Man – so that ancient Man has at last been lifted out of misconceptions that had endured for nearly a century to join the ranks of humanity.

Discoveries of Neanderthal technology and rituals have added weight to this more appreciative view. About 40,000 years ago, for example, they developed highly efficient methods of making stone tools, producing them in greater numbers and with more precision than ever before.

*In*Focus

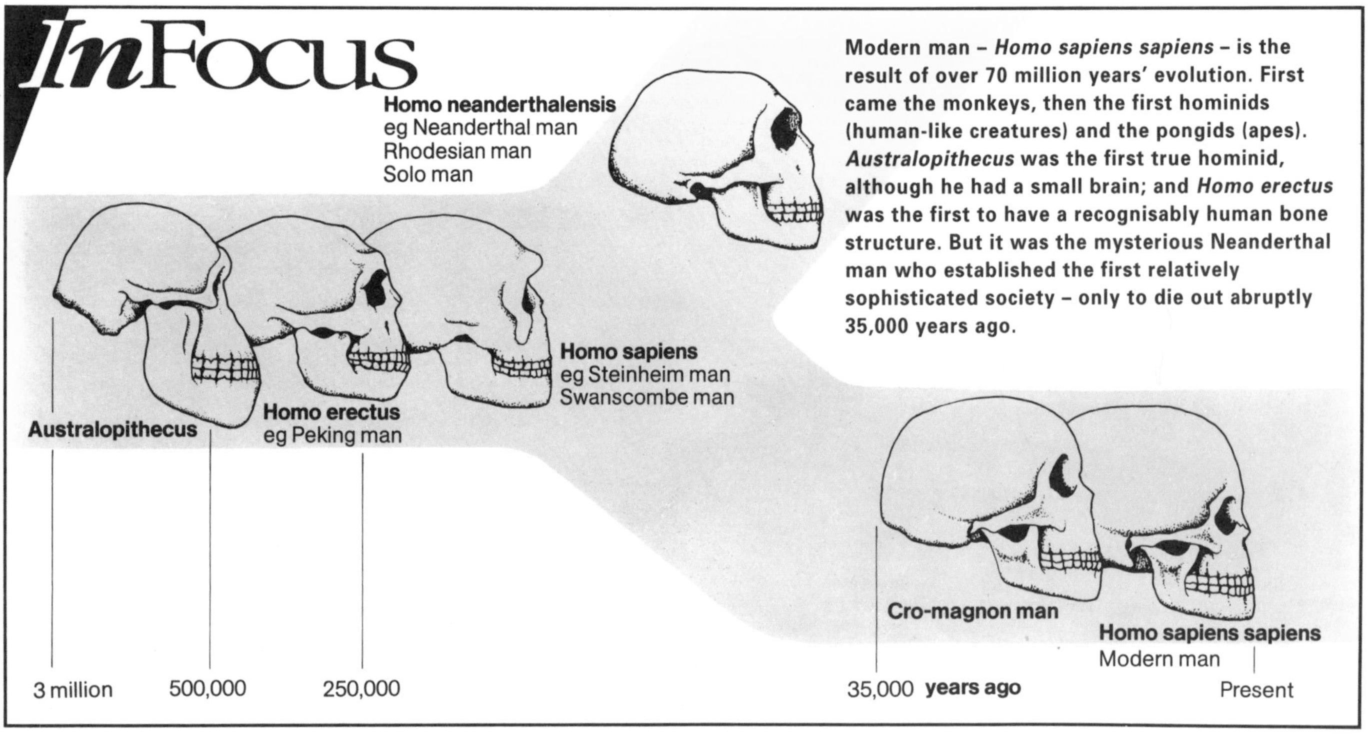

Modern man – *Homo sapiens sapiens* – is the result of over 70 million years' evolution. First came the monkeys, then the first hominids (human-like creatures) and the pongids (apes). *Australopithecus* was the first true hominid, although he had a small brain; and *Homo erectus* was the first to have a recognisably human bone structure. But it was the mysterious Neanderthal man who established the first relatively sophisticated society – only to die out abruptly 35,000 years ago.

The Neanderthals, it seems, were also pioneers, spreading outwards to penetrate new parts of the globe that had proved too inhospitable for their ancestors. They settled the European tundra, hacked their way into the Congo basin, spread across the vast plains of what is now western Russia, and even entered the semi-desert of the North African coast.

Where resources were lacking, the Neanderthals ingeniously found ways to provide them. On open plains where there were no coves they built crude shelters of saplings and animal skins – the first houses in history. And when water was scarce they used ostrich eggshells as canteens to enable them to survive between waterholes.

But of all their achievements the most significant were in the realm of spiritual beliefs. They conceived a life after death, they cared for the aged and handicapped, and attempted to control their fate through magic rites. All this we can deduce from the evidence of Neanderthal burials. Only Man refuses to accept death's finality through his belief in some sort of afterlife, and one mark of this is ritual burial of the dead.

The most remarkable Neanderthal burial site of all was discovered in 1960 at the Shanidar cave in northern Iraq. There, after digging down more than 50 feet (15 metres) and excavating more than 1,500 tonnes of earth, Ralph Solecki of Columbia University unearthed the remains of nine Neanderthals.

As a matter of routine procedure, Solecki collected samples of soil for analysis by the *Musée de l'Homme* in France. The result was quite unexpected. Pollen was present in the grave in unprecedented abundance. Only one conclusion was possible: masses of flowers had been placed in the grave by the friends of the dead men. This was a spectacular discovery for it implied a capacity for religious and aesthetic thinking that no mere animal possesses. The kind of flowers used in the burials also suggested that Neanderthals had a knowledge of the herbal and medicinal properties of plants. This view was confirmed by detailed analysis of the pollen. The majority of plants involved are still used by the people living in the area today for medicinal purposes. So it seems the Neanderthals, too, felt the flowers possessed healing qualities that would help their dead brothers in the afterlife.

Neanderthal care for the handicapped was also implied by the Shanidar remains. Some of the bones were identified as belonging to a 40-year-old man who had been deformed from birth. Yet despite his handicap, and an inability to fend for himself, he had evidently been supported until he reached what was a ripe old age for a Neanderthal.

Even the selective cannibalism that they are known to have practised can be seen as a mark of superior intelligence. They ate only the brains of their victims, suggesting that they associated brains

with the personality, in the same way that other cannibal societies believe that they can actually acquire strength and courage by eating the heart of an enemy.

But it seems unlikely that Neanderthal man had speech: most experts agree that his skull formation suggests that he was capable only of animal-like grunts. Inevitably, such lack of communication must have limited his progress. Nevertheless, psychic and paranormal powers are now considered by some to have been the norm among the mysterious Neanderthals, and they may even have been gifted telepathically.

But despite their achievements, Neanderthals did not survive. Incomplete as they are, the fossil records show that 37,000 years ago the Neanderthals mysteriously disappeared, to be replaced by a completely new breed of man, known as Cro-Magnon.

No one knows what happened to the Neanderthals. Did they suddenly evolve into Cro-Magnon? And, if so, what prompted the abrupt change? Or could it be that the Cro-Magnons were invaders, who conquered and slaughtered the Neanderthals, making them the first known victims of genocide?

CRO-MAGNON CONFRONTATION

Some anthropologists have suggested that the two varieties of man evolved separately but in parallel – Neanderthal in Africa, Cro-Magnon in India. The differences between them may be then explicable as adaptations to these two very different environments. Their isolation and limited genetic background would then explain the two distinct varieties of men that confronted each other in the Middle East some 35,000 years ago.

In his book *The Neanderthal Question,* author and psychologist Stan Gooch has pictured that first encounter.

'Neanderthal sees a group of unbelievably tall men – though these are no men of his experience. They have white skin, hair that looks like flames, and blue eyes. They must be gods come to visit Earth. Neanderthal turns round, falls to his hands and knees, and presents his raised buttocks to the gods, beseeching them meanwhile not to destroy him,' he writes.

But Gooch does not believe that Cro-Magnon destroyed Neanderthal. Rather, he theorises that the two varieties of Man inter-married to produce the crossbreed that is modern Man. If this view is correct, it may well be that not only is modern Man a hybrid – the result of mixed Neanderthal/Cro-Magnon parentage – but he may well owe all his outstanding capacities and endowments to this very ancient union.

All of us may now be carrying a part of 'Neanderthal' in our genetic make-up. An even more intriguing possibility, however, is that some Neanderthals could perhaps have avoided extinction or racial absorption, so that in eastern Europe, Siberia, and Mongolia some pure Neanderthals could have survived to this day. This suggestion inevitably makes one wonder whether the stories of wildmen or hairy monsters – common in many of the remoter parts of the world – could actually be evidence of surviving Neanderthals.

***In 1960, Ralph Solecki of Columbia University made the most remarkable Neanderthal finds at the Shanidar caves,* left, *in Northern Iraq, among them the 60,000-year-old skull,* above.**

***Neanderthals are thought to have had remarkable psychic powers, lost to us today for the most part. According to one theory, however, it could be that such abilities may be redeveloping even now, in readiness for a time when, having colonised distant planets, we will need to communicate telepathically, like Neanderthal man, but across light years, as in the artist's impression,* right.**

A BIRD, A PLANE – OR A UFO ?

WEIRD LIGHTS IN THE NIGHT SKY, STRANGE SILVERY SHAPES FLASHING THROUGH THE SUNLIGHT – THESE ARE THE STUFF OF UFO REPORTS, BUT THEY SOMETIMES HAVE A PERFECTLY RATIONAL EXPLANATION. HOW CAN YOU RECOGNISE UNUSUAL OBJECTS IN THE SKY – INCLUDING TRUE UFOs?

Allan Hendry, above, wrote The UFO Handbook, *a study of UFO identification that has become a classic of its kind.*

On 31 December 1978, two police officers in Hertfordshire, England, watched in amazement as an incredible object passed silently overhead. It had a cigar-shaped, silvery body with what looked like windows along the side. Behind trailed shimmering orange-coloured streamers. The thing then moved slowly away out of sight and, alarmed by what they had seen, the police officers radioed their headquarters.

Unknown to them, hundreds of other people, including airline pilots and coastguards, reported

Friction creates a blaze of light around the Apollo 11 space capsule, below, as it re-enters the Earth's atmosphere on returning from a mission to the Moon. Debris from satellites and other space vehicles can cause similar displays; but because they are unexpected, they are often mistaken for UFOs.

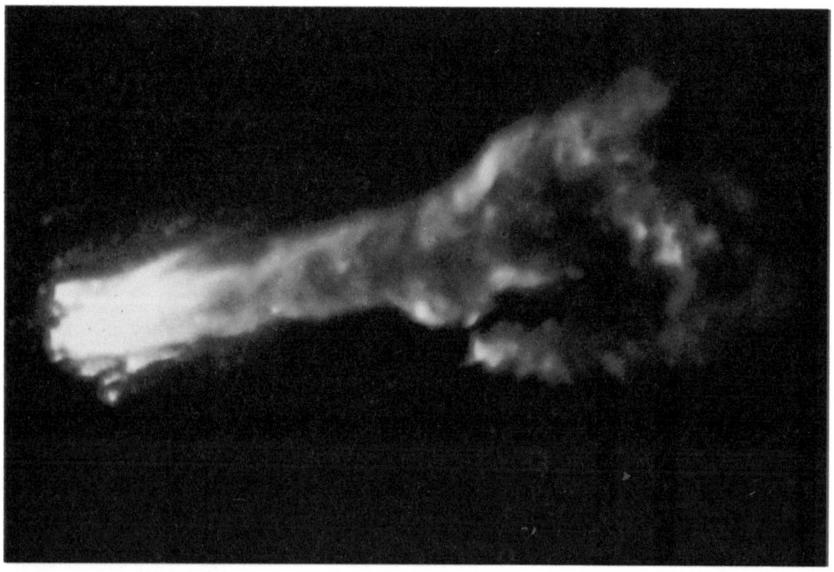

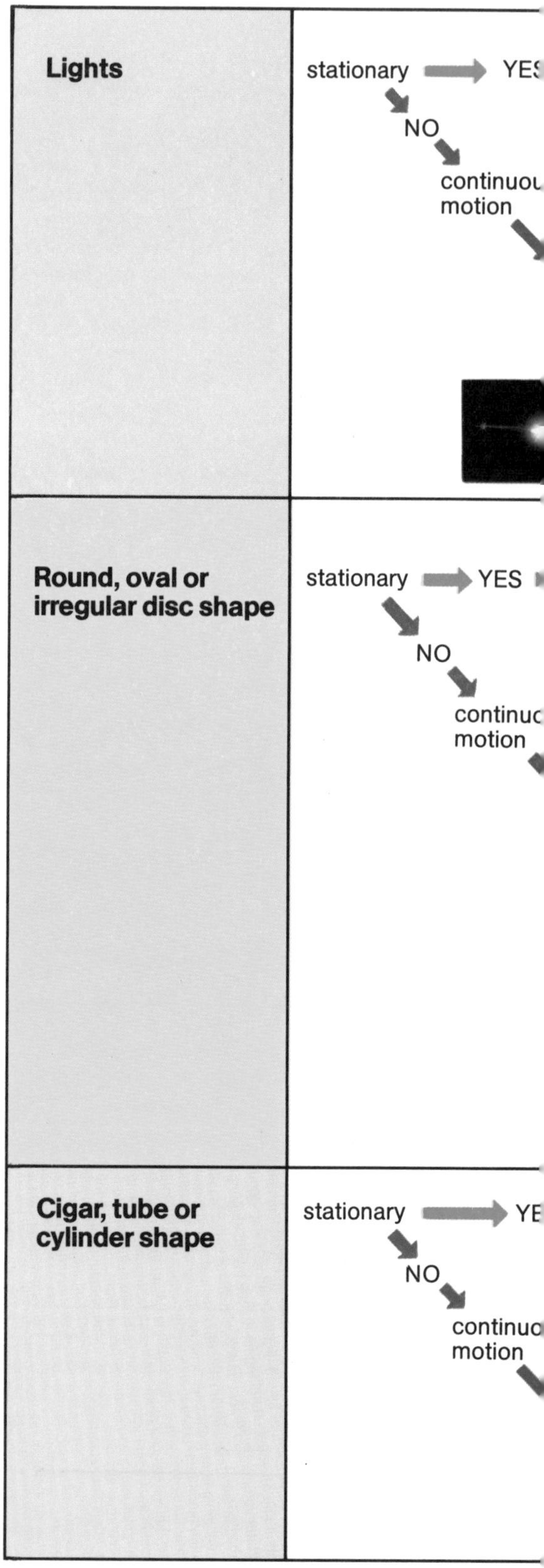

If you think you have seen a UFO, check the features of your sightings on the chart* below. *This shows the three major categories of man-made and natural objects that are most often mistaken for UFOs and will enable you to eliminate them from the investigation.

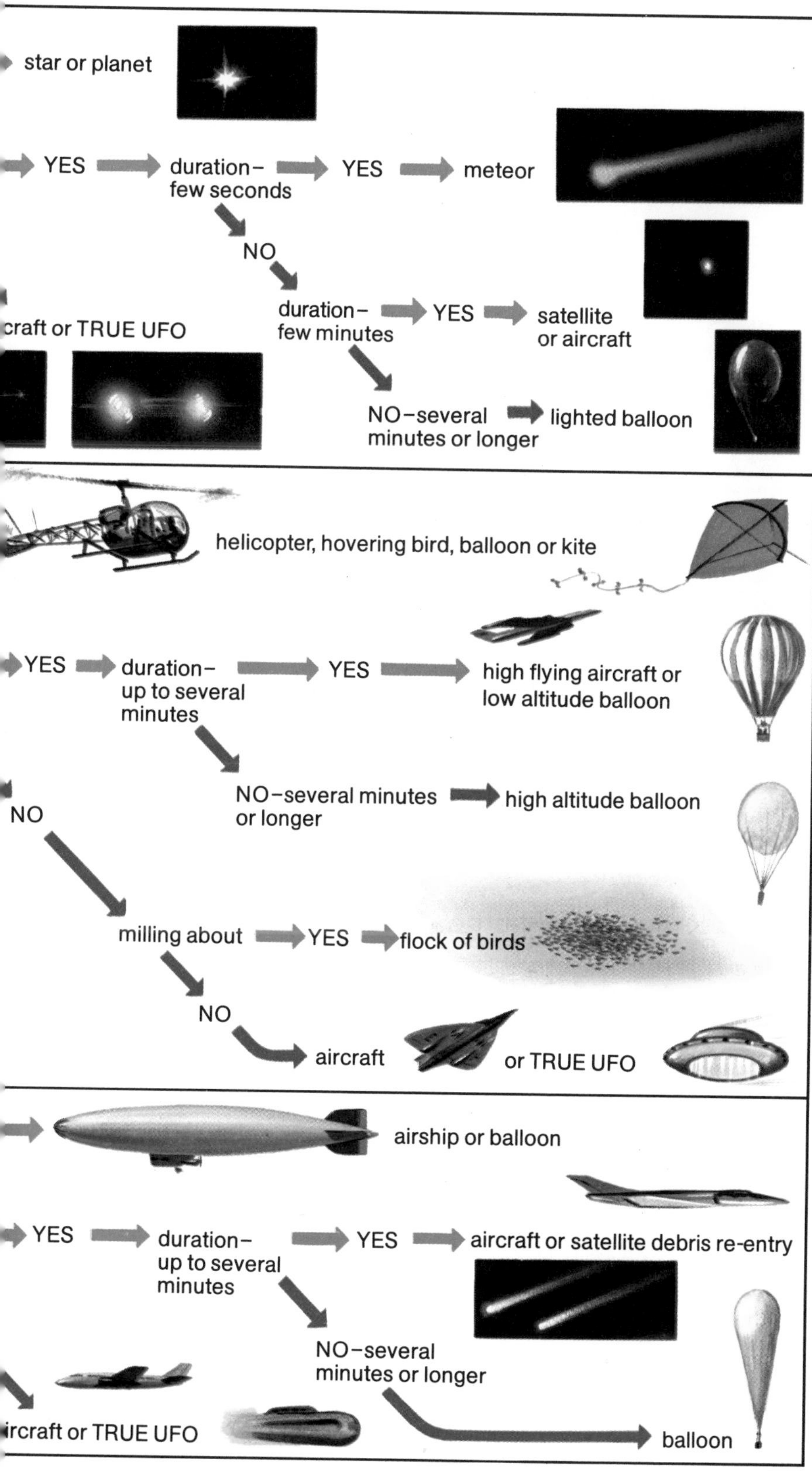

seeing the same thing in various parts of Britain. Many believed that the sighting was connected with the piece of film taken by a television crew off the coast of New Zealand the day before – film that was already receiving massive worldwide publicity; and there was widespread belief that the 'object' was definitely a UFO.

One January afternoon, thirty years earlier, a strange bright light had also been seen to hover for several hours over Godman Airfield, Kentucky, USA. In due course, a team of F-51 aircraft appeared in the area, led by Captain Thomas Mantell. Though on a routine mission, Mantell agreed to divert his planes to investigate the glittering intruder. One by one, however, the pilots were forced down, due to the lack of the proper oxygen equipment to travel above a limited height. But Mantell himself continued climbing. At 20,000 feet (7,000 metres), he reported seeing a metallic object, ahead and above him. Minutes later, the wreckage of his F-51 was found scattered over a wide area. According to a report at the time, which has persisted to the present day, Mantell had been shot down by a UFO.

On close investigation, many such cases turn out to have involved a perfectly normal object, however. Strange objects in the sky, especially when seen at night in a deserted area, can certainly be alarming. There is the case, for example, of a woman who locked herself in her bedroom and hid under the bed for an hour, terrified by an object she believed to be a UFO, but that turned out to be simply a star. Ufologist Allan Hendry has also described how one man was in such a panic after seeing a well-lit aircraft, believing it to be a UFO, that he ripped his neighbour's door off its hinges, in the attempt to escape. Such examples may sound strange, but it would be wrong to assume that those involved are idiots.

To help witnesses distinguish between what is and what is not a UFO, the term 'true UFO' is used for something that does not appear, after investigation, to be a case of mistaken identity. If the object seen turns out not to be a UFO but has a recognisable identity, then the term 'IFO' – Identified Flying Object – is used.

TELL-TALE SIGNS

Ufologists divide UFO reports into several categories. But, more often than not, reports tend to fall into one or other of two simple classes. These are often called 'low-definition' and 'medium-definition' experiences.

Low-definition experiences – 45 per cent of all UFO reports – involve seeing a light or a highly amorphous phenomenon with no distinctive shape. The colour of the light is not of great importance. In most cases, it is white; but there are many different coloured light sources, and the presence of thin cloud or smoke in the atmosphere can subtly alter what is seen. If you see an unidentified light in the sky, there are a number of things you can do.

First, note whether the light remains stationary or if it moves. If stationary, the chances are that it is a star or planet. Stars and planets are among the most common sources of UFO misidentification. Of course, they are not really stationary, but their motion is so slow relative to an observer that it is not usually noticed except over a period of hours. This is an excellent tell-tale sign. If a light is visible in the night sky for over an hour or more, and hardly moves at all, then it is probably a star. You can check by looking at a map showing the positions of stars and planets in the night sky for that particular time of year.

Venus is a common source of misidentification. It is the brightest object in the night sky, and at certain times of the year is very close to Earth. It can be seen even in daylight, as a bright white speck, if

you know where to look. But often there are good reasons why stars and planets are not immediately recognised for what they are. Optical illusion, for example, and the phenomenon known as *autokinesis,* which causes a star apparently to dart about erratically in the sky, are common causes of misidentification. Since stars do not normally dart about, this effect instills the belief that the light comes not from a star but from a UFO.

FLIGHTPATHS

If the light does appear to move, the next question is whether it follows a smooth flightpath or whether it hovers or seems to change direction dramatically. A smooth flightpath can indicate one of several things. Precisely what it is can usually be determined by the length of time for which the light is seen. If it is of very short duration, for instance, it could be a meteor – particles of dust or debris from space burning up as they enter the Earth's atmosphere. Meteors tend to glow for a second or two, leaving a trail of light.

> TO HELP WITNESSES DISTINGUISH BETWEEN WHAT IS AND WHAT IS NOT A UFO, THE TERM 'TRUE UFO' IS USED FOR SOMETHING THAT DOES NOT APPEAR, AFTER INVESTIGATION, TO BE A CASE OF MISTAKEN IDENTITY.

Occasionally, the debris is a little larger than usual and takes longer to burn up. This leads to the phenomenon known as a *bolide* or fireball, a brilliant light visible for up to 10 seconds and accompanied by a rumbling or whooshing sound. Fireballs have been seen in daylight too, although this is fairly rare. Usually, sightings of fireballs are so spectacular that they are witnessed by dozens of people over a wide area. But on the whole they are very similar in appearance to a satellite re-entry, which is another common cause of UFO misidentification.

Circling the Earth are hundreds of man-made satellites. Many are too small to be seen from the ground, but others are visible at night as points of light that may take several minutes to cross the sky. When they re-enter the Earth's atmosphere, they can present a spectacular sight. As the pieces burn away, they glow in several colours, leaving a trail through the upper atmosphere, which can take several minutes to disappear. A few parts may even survive and reach the ground, as happened to the American Skylab, for example, which landed in Western Australia in July 1979.

But by far the most common causes of UFO misidentification are aircraft. Since aircraft possess many different types of lighting, there are plenty of opportunities for strange effects. Bright searchlights, used in front of the plane, may be visible from miles away. Seen heading towards you, such lights can appear stationary for a long time before bursting into colour as the aircraft's navigation lights come into view. In many countries, aircraft are also employed for advertising by using electronic lights that flash out a computer-programmed message. The aircraft is built to fly very slowly so that the message can be read. But if the lights are seen from an angle, it is common for very weird effects to result.

Aircraft are, of course, highly manoeuvrable, – helicopters even more so. Consequently, not only might they be seen as lights on a smooth flightpath, but can also be seen to alter direction, slow down, and even stop in mid-flight. The wind, meanwhile, can carry away the sound of an aircraft's engines, leaving only a silent light in the sky.

Most of these effects would be seen only at night. But there is one object that is often seen and

It is not easy to recognise the irregular, unearthly shape silhouetted against the sun,* above left, *as a flight of helicopters.

The spectacular comet Ikeya-Seki,* left, *was seen in late 1965. Like a surprising number of heavenly bodies – including stars and planets – it was reported as a UFO.

The rare lenticular cloud formation, top, has the characteristic shape of a 'flying saucer'.

Objects such as the high-flying kite, above, glinting in the sunlight with its control wires invisible, can also take on the appearance of a typical UFO. The research balloon, right, was sent up 130,000 feet (40,000 metres) to investigate cosmic rays. Even experienced airmen have failed to recognise craft like this for what they are.

misidentified as a UFO during the day – the balloon. Weather centres release balloons at regular intervals, either to test wind direction or to carry instruments high into the sky from where they radio meteorological information back to Earth. At a high altitude, a balloon will reflect sunlight from its shiny surface while floating across the sky; and from the ground, the silvery dot, drifting across the sky, may be seen as a round or conical shape.

> " THE BELGIAN AIR FORCE HAS BEEN ON ALERT FOR THREE NIGHTS RUNNING .... SEVERAL TIMES THE UFO WAS SEEN FROM THE GROUND, BUT EACH TIME THE AIRCRAFT GOT THERE TOO LATE. [IT] TENDED TO HOVER JUST ABOVE THE ROOFTOPS, TOO LOW TO BE CONFRONTED BY AN AIRCRAFT. "
>
> THE FINANCIAL TIMES, 1990

Medium-definition experiences are those that involve the clear perception of a shape. Though they have sometimes been seen at night, they are more commonly seen in daytime. They account for a further 35 per cent of all UFO cases and, as with low-definition experiences, the most important criterion is motion. A clearly defined shape that hovers for some time is unlikely to be an aircraft, although it could be a helicopter, too distant to be heard.

Airships tend also to be a common cause of misidentification. Under certain conditions, their shape could be mistaken for a cigar-shaped UFO, hovering or moving slowly across the sky. Kites are another possible explanation. Seen at a distance, the controlling cord of a kite may not be visible, and the irregular shape of its body could easily be taken to be a UFO.

In most cases, the object believed to be a UFO is seen moving in a constant direction at varying speeds. In strong sunlight, for example, an aeroplane's wings and tailplane can be obscured, leaving just a metallic body or cylinder visible. Though really the fuselage, it can look just like a UFO. Even clouds have been mistaken for UFOs. One type, for example – a lenticular formation – looks like a structured disc. Though uncommon, its slow movement has certainly fooled more than one observer.

Flocks of birds have also caused confusion. In daylight, the reflective underbellies of certain species can shine in sunlight and may be seen as white ovals, obscuring all other detail. At night, it is even possible for street lighting to be reflected, creating different coloured oval shapes, according to the type of lighting used.

Clearly, there are many possible causes of misidentification. What Captain Mantell encountered over Kentucky, for instance, was probably one

of the 100-foot (30.5-metre) 'skyhook' balloons, which were secretly being tested in the area at the time by the US Navy. These balloons were not known to Air Force officers; and although this was the probable identity of Mantell's UFO, the case has never been conclusively proven. The 'official' explanation that what observers on the ground saw was the planet Venus is definitely not convincing to the majority of investigators.

As for the case of the Hertfordshire policemen, it was subsequently discovered that a Russian booster-rocket had re-entered the Earth's atmosphere that night. As it happened, its orbit took it over northern Europe, and it was this that many witnesses probably mistook for a UFO. The New Zealand film was not connected to the Hertfordshire incident at all. But there are still those who remain convinced that what the two policemen had seen was a true UFO.

CASEBOOK

ALIENS IN THE DARK

SIGHTINGS, SUCH AS THOSE THAT FOLLOW – IN WHICH CRAFT SHOW UP ON RADAR AND LEAVE BEHIND DEFINITE MARKINGS – CERTAINLY SEEM TO INDICATE THAT UFOS ARE A GENUINE PHENOMENON

The night of 13 August 1956 was a busy one for RAF and USAF air controllers and radar operations in East Anglia. Although some of the many inexplicable radar traces they obtained were probably spurious, others were undoubtedly from unknown objects. Indeed, the sighting described here was stated by the USAF Condon Report to be 'the most puzzling and unusual case in the radio-visual files'.

The main events began at 10.55 p.m. at RAF Bentwaters, near Ipswich, a station leased to the United States Air Force. A Ground Controlled Approach (GCA) radar operator picked up a fast-moving target 30 miles (50 kilometres) to the east, heading in from the sea at a speed of 2,000 to 4,000 miles per hour (3,200–6,440 km/h). It passed directly over Bentwaters and sped away until it disappeared from the scope 30 miles (50 kilometres) to the west. This overflight was not just a radar observation, however: a tower operator on the ground looking up saw a light 'blurred out by its high speed', while the pilot of a USAF C-47 aircraft flying over Bentwaters at 4,000 feet (1,200 metres), who had been alerted by ground control, looked down and saw the fuzzy light flash between his aircraft and the ground. The UFO was heading towards Lakenheath, another RAF aerodrome leased to the USAF, and immediate warning was given.

For the record, there was no mention of a sonic boom at Bentwaters. Ground observers at Lakenheath saw the light approach, stop dead and then move swiftly out of sight to the east. Some time after that, two white lights were seen to join up and disappear in formation.

Observers and radar operators of the Lakenheath GCA and radar traffic control centre scopes testified to having recorded objects travelling at terrific speeds, stopping, and changing course instantaneously. After some hesitation, the Americans at Lakenheath then put through a call to the RAF.

The artist's impressions,* right and top right, *show the mysterious light from an unknown object that appeared near Ipswich in 1956.

The RAF Chief Controller at Bentwaters remembers USAF at Lakenheath telephoning to say something was 'buzzing' their airfield circuit. He scrambled a Venom night fighter from RAF Waterbeach, and his interception controller, with a team of three highly trained personnel, took over. The Venom was vectored on to the UFO; and the pilot, who was accompanied on his trip by a navigator, called out 'Contact' when he could see it, and 'Judy' when

the navigator had the target fairly and squarely on the fighter's own radar scope. The Venom closed on the target, but after a few seconds, and in the space of one or two sweeps on the scopes, the object appeared behind the fighter. The pilot called out 'Lost contact, more help,' and he was told that the target was now behind him.

Meanwhile, the chief controller scrambled another Venom fighter. The American witnesses said the UFO 'flipped over' and got behind the RAF fighter, which then manoeuvred to try to get behind the UFO.

This information was given to the USAF-sponsored study of UFO phenomena under Dr E.U. Condon at Colorado University. But until the Condon Report was published in January 1969, the case remained secret. A detailed study was carried out by Dr James McDonald, working as an upper atmosphere physicist at Arizona University. This was a sighting the Condon Report could not dismiss: indeed, it had to admit that 'the apparently rational, intelligent behaviour of the UFO suggests a mechanical device of unknown origin as the most probable explanation'.

The small French village of Quarouble, not far from Valenciennes, close to the Belgian border, was also shaken by strange events during the night of 10 September 1954.

At about 10.30 p.m., 34-year-old steel worker Marius Dewilde was sitting in the kitchen of his house, situated just under a mile from the village and by a railway tract.

Suddenly his dog started to howl and, thinking there was a prowler or smuggler outside the house, Dewilde took his flashlight and ventured out into the darkness. He was instantly aware of an ill-defined shape to his left, on or near the railway line, and thought it might be a farmer's truck. Then he heard a sound to his right. He swung round, and his torch beam fell on two very odd creatures, each just over 3 feet (1 metre) tall and wearing what appeared to him to be divers' suits and huge helmets. They appeared to be shuffling along on very short legs, and both had very broad shoulders, but no arms at all. They seemed to be heading for the dark shape that he had seen close to, or on the railway line.

The close encounter depicted in the sketches,* right *and* below, *took place near Valenciennes, France, on 10 September 1954. Two very odd creatures were sighted by steel-worker Marius Dewilde, by the side of an extraordinary craft.

Recovering from his initial surprise, Dewilde ran to the garden gate with the intention of cutting off the interlopers from the path. He was about 2 yards (2 metres) from them when a blinding beam of light issued from an opening in the side of the dark shape. The beam struck him and he was stopped dead in his tracks, unable to move or shout. Then the light went out.

" HE SWUNG ROUND, AND HIS TORCH BEAM FELL ON TWO VERY ODD CREATURES, EACH JUST OVER 3 FEET TALL AND WEARING WHAT APPEARED TO BE DIVERS' SUITS AND HUGE HELMETS. "

After recovering the use of his muscles, Dewilde set off after the small creatures. All he saw, however, was what appeared to be a door closing in the side of the object, which then rose slowly from the ground like a helicopter. There was a whistling noise, and Dewilde saw steam clouding up from beneath the contraption. After rising about 30 yards (30 metres), the craft then set off towards the east, climbing and glowing red as it went.

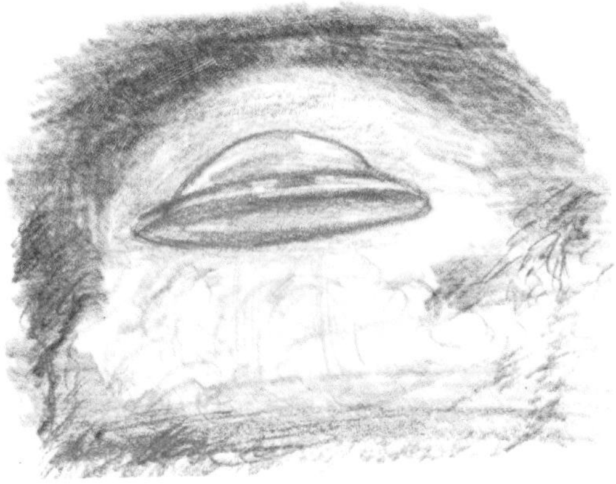

He contrived to get access to the Commissioner of Police who, after listening to his semi-coherent account, realised that this man – by now in a state of incontinence – was neither joking nor at all mad.

As a result, a detailed inquiry was set up by the regular police, the air gendarmerie and the Territorial Security Department. All became convinced that the witness had not been lying, nor suffering from an hallucination, and that the object could not have been a helicopter (carrying contraband, for example) because of the mass of telephone wires overhead which would have prevented a landing. What is more, marks – sharply and deeply cut – had appeared in the iron-hard wood of the railway sleepers where Dewilde said the object had stood. An engineer calculated that it would have taken a tremendous weight to have made the marks. It would also have taken very great heat to produce the burnt and calcined ballast stones found between the affected sleepers.

THE SECRET SENSITIVITY OF PLANTS

CAN PLANTS REALLY RESPOND TO HUMAN SPEECH? AND DO THEY HAVE SOME KIND OF NERVOUS SYSTEM THAT IS SENSITIVE TO SOUND AND VIBRATION?

The Kirlian photograph, **above,** *shows the aura surrounding a healthy leaf. In a diseased or dead plant, however, the corona effect does not show up – a phenomenon suggesting that a flow of energy probably surrounds all living things.*

Renowned nurseryman Luther Burbank, of Santa Rosa, California, spent many years developing a new variety of cactus without spines. As he worked with his plants, he spoke to them. 'You have nothing to fear,' he would tell them. 'You don't need your defensive thorns. I will protect you.'

According to Manly P. Hall, the president of the Philosophical Research Society of Los Angeles, Burbank's love produced a subtle kind of nourishment that made everything grow better and bear fruit more abundantly. As he put it: 'Burbank explained to me that in all his experimentation, he took plants into his confidence, asked them to help, and assured them that he held their small lives in deepest regard and affection... Burbank also mentioned that plants have over twenty sensory perceptions but, because they are different from ours, we cannot recognise them. He was not sure that the shrubs and flowers understood his words, but he was convinced that by telepathy they could comprehend his meaning'.

The spineless cactus, **Opuntia ficus-indica, left,** *was developed by Luther Burbank who assured the growing plant it did not in fact need its spines.*

MEASURED RESPONSES

At the same time that Burbank was pursuing plant perfection in California, a distinguished physicist on the opposite side of the world was also investigating the nature of a plant's sensitivity. Jagadis Chandra Bose, professor of physics at Presidency College, Calcutta, was a pioneer of radio research; and in the course of his work, he had been struck by the close similarities between metals and muscles in their response to stress.

Pursuing this line of thought, Bose theorised that, if such similarities of response do exist, the ideal subject of investigation would be plants – living tissue, but without a conventional nervous system and therefore, it was supposed, incapable of direct response to a stimulus.

In many respects, plants certainly appear to perform like animals, but in a remarkably economic way: they respire without the aid of a circulatory system, they metabolise their food without a digestive system, and they move (albeit slowly) without muscles. Bose reasoned that, by analogy, they might be able to respond to stimuli, even though they do not possess a nervous system as such.

Having designed and built a device in which, by means of the movement of a reflected beam of light, very small movements of plant tissue could be magnified many thousands of times, Bose was able to show that horse chestnut leaves, carrots and turnips respond to stress in much the same way as metals and muscles. He also discovered that it is as easy to anaesthetise plants as animals: chloroform renders them 'unconscious', and they can be revived with fresh air.

ELECTRICAL RESPONSE

After Bose had presented a paper to the Linnaean Society, the President of the Society wrote to him:

'It seems to me that your experiments make it clear beyond doubt that all parts of plants – not merely those which are known to be motile – are irritable, and manifest their irritability by an electrical response to stimulation...'

Five years later, Bose published the results of his experiments to date, in two bulky volumes entitled *Plant Response as a means of Physiological Investigation*. In these, he revealed a remarkable similarity in behaviour between the skins of reptiles and amphibians and those of fruits and vegetables, showing that plants can become as 'fatigued' by continuous stimulation as animal muscles. He also found a close parallel between animal eyes and leaves in their response to light.

Of course, many of these findings were ridiculed by the scientific establishment at the time. Nevertheless, Bose was subsequently knighted for his work in India, and was made a Fellow of the Royal Society. Shortly afterward, he was able to improve his instruments to such a degree that he could demonstrate the growth of plant tissue at a magnification of more than 10 million. By this

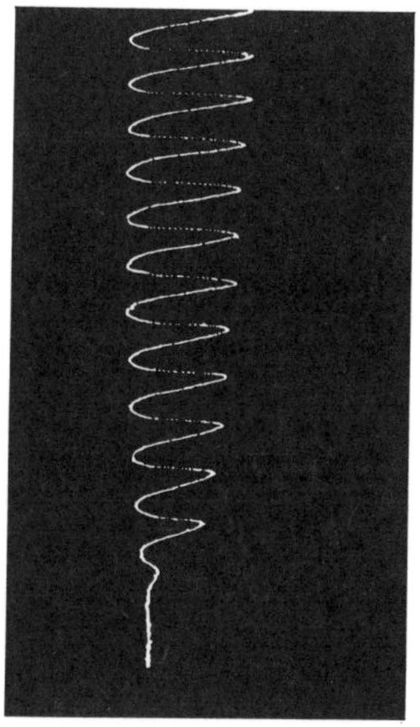

The trace produced on Sir Jagadis Bose's 'death recorder', above, shows how the pulsation from a plant steadily decreases and vanishes as the plant dies.

Two experimental plants are shown, below: one leans away from avant-garde concert music; the other is dying from heavy rock.

The original caption to the cartoon, right, reads; 'It looks as if it might have Dutch Elm Dis... ' Could it be that plants and trees are in some way able to 'tune in' to conversations at times?

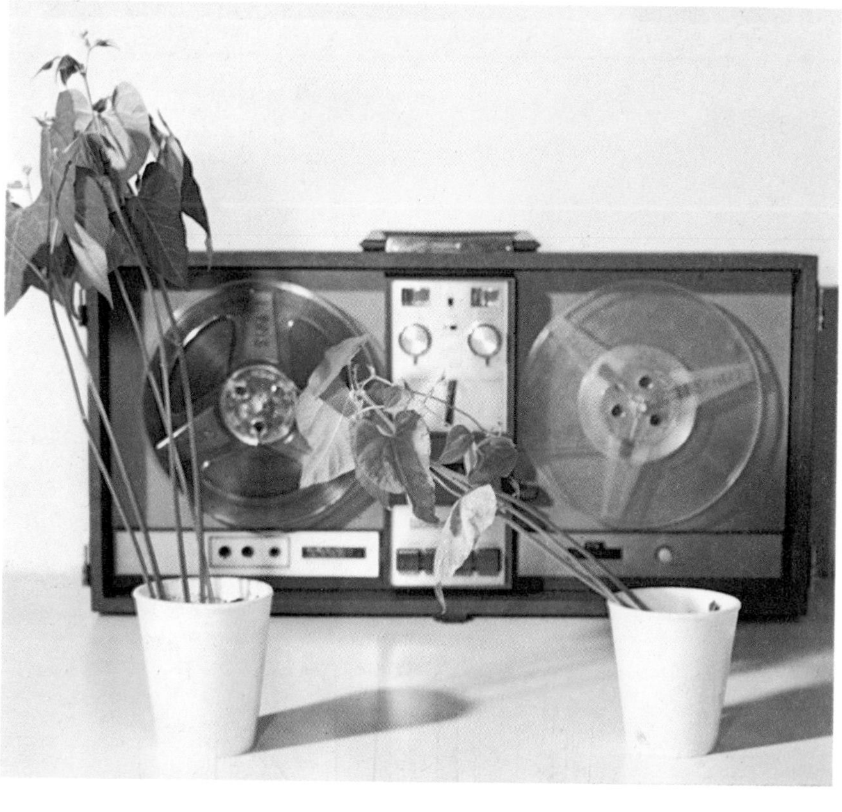

means, 'in less than a quarter of an hour', as the *Scientific American* put it, 'the action of fertilisers, food, electric currents and various stimulants can be fully determined'.

In spite of a certain amount of continued opposition, Bose continued his experiments on the responses of living plants. His findings were intriguing. As the French newspaper *Le Matin* put it, towards the end of his career: 'After this discovery, we begin to have misgivings. When we strike a woman with a blossom, which of them suffers more, the woman or the flower'?

News that the Russians were experimenting along similar lines first began to emerge in reports in *Pravda* in the 1970s. Of Professor Ivan Isidorovich Gunar – head of the Department of Plant Physiology in Moscow's Timiryazev Academy – the newspaper's correspondent reported: 'He even appears to converse with them, and it seems to me that his plants pay attention to this good, greying

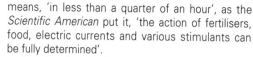

man'. A film made in the department showed how plants reacted to environmental factors, to the touch of flies and bees, and to injuries. The responses were recorded as a trace on a pen recorder attached to a galvanometer similar to a lie-detector. The film also showed how a plant immersed in chloroform would not give the usual response to an injury, such as a sharp blow.

A story in the monthly magazine *Nauka i Religiya* reported the findings of scientists at the state university of the Kazakh Republic. Here , in a region of vast apple orchards, it had been found that the trees seemed to react to the illnesses or emotional state of those who tended them. Pursuing their experiments, the Kazakh scientists conditioned a philodendron to recognise mineral ores. The plant was taught by being given an electric shock every time a piece of ore was placed beside it. In due course, it would respond in anticipation whenever ore was placed by it, but not when barren rock containing no minerals was used.

It had also occurred to the experimenters, Professor V.N. Pushkin and his assistant, V.M. Fetisor, that a hypnotised person might be able to transmit emotions more readily to plants. Working with a Bulgarian hypnotist, Georgi Angushev, they seated a young subject, named Tanya, about 2 feet 8 inches (80 centimetres) from the plant and Angushev put her into a light trance. When

Angushev suggested to her that she was the most beautiful girl in the world, the pen recorder attached to the plant's galvanometer, which had been registering a straight line, traced a series of waves.

> " IF PLANTS HAD NO SENSE ORGANS AND DIDN'T HAVE A MEANS OF TRANSMITTING AND PROCESSING INFORMATION WITH THEIR OWN LANGUAGE AND MEMORY, THEY WOULD INEVITABLY PERISH. "
>
> VLADIMIR KARAMANOV

After this, Angushev suggested a number of situations to his subject – such as that the weather had turned icy cold – and each time the plant reacted to Tanya's emotions. It was even found that the plant could detect when Tanya was lying. As Professor Pushkin wrote: 'Perhaps between two information systems, the plant cells and the nervous system, a specific link exists...These wholly different living cells seemed to be able to understand one another'.

AUTUMN DAFFODILS

In September 1964, the English trade weekly *Commercial Grower* published a letter from a nurseryman writing from the south Devon town of Brixham. He reported that he was experimenting with the conditioning of bulbs to cause spring flowers, such as daffodils, to flower in the autumn. In one of his greenhouses, where an assistant was in the habit of playing pop music on a small portable tape recorder, his success rate had been noticeably higher than elsewhere. And perhaps it was only

*In*Focus

GREEN FINGERS

Certain people seem to stimulate plant growth, and others have a depressing effect. Happiness has an especially good effect on plants, as do children at play. This certainly seems to be substantiated by the experience of several researchers and pioneers working in the field of plant physiology.

Luther Burbank, dubbed the 'Wizard of Horticulture', widely dazzled the plant-breeding profession with his extraordinary ability to create new species, calculated at around a thousand during his lifetime. Indeed, he openly attributed his success to striking up a genuine loving rapport with those plants that he intuitively recognised as sufficiently healthy and adaptable before gently persuading them into co-operating with his plan.

In the mid-1960s, Dr Bernard Grad from McGill University even proved that water held by psychic healers made a significant growth increase to barley seeds, while depressed psychiatric patients had the opposite effect. The secret of 'green fingers' therefore seems to lie in treating your plants with tender, loving care and respect – in short, much like another human being.

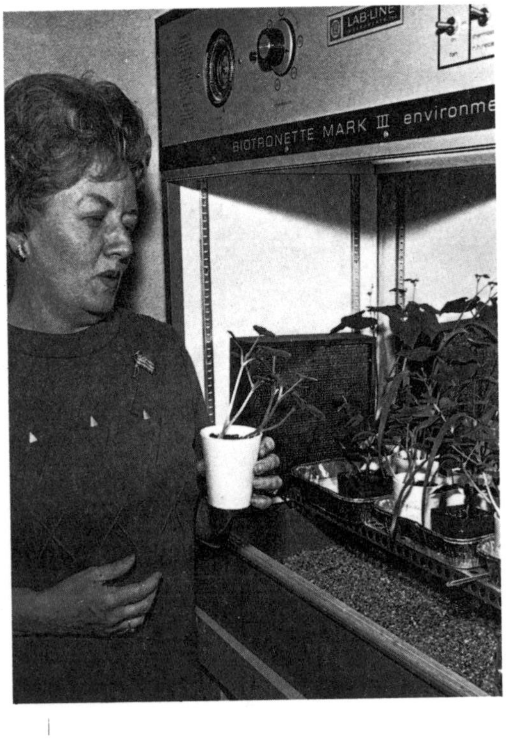

coincidence that one of the most popular groups at that time, the Mojos, had just released a record entitled *Seven Golden Daffodils*.

During the mid-1960s, a considerable number of experiments were being performed on the responses of plants to all kinds of sound. Among the first scientists to investigate were Mary Measures and Pearl Weinberger of the University of Ottawa, who showed that wheat seedlings grew most rapidly to a high-pitched note, of frequency 5,000 hertz (cycles per second).

SOUND EFFECTS

In 1968, a student at Denver, Colorado, named Dorothy Retallack, set up an experiment in which a mixed group of plants – a philodendron, corn, radishes, pelargoniums and African violets – were subjected to a tape recording of the notes B and D, played on a piano and repeated over and over again for 12 hours a day. After three weeks, all the plants, some of which had grown leaning away from the sound source as if in a strong wind, had died, with the exception of the African violets, which were flourishing. Plants in the control group, cultivated in silence, had grown normally.

With her professor, Francis F. Broman, Dorothy Retallack then pursued her investigations. She reported that rock music caused her plants to grow away from the sound source and to develop abnormally: Bach, Haydn and Indian sitar music encouraged them and caused them to lean toward the sound; folk music and 'country and western' had apparently no effect at all.

These are far from being the only experiments carried out into the effects of sound on plant growth. Lyall Watson, in his book *Supernature*, for instance, reports that bacteria are affected in much the same way, multiplying rapidly under the influences of certain frequencies, and dying when exposed to others.

There seems little doubt that a relationship has been shown to exist between humans and plants. But what form does this relationship take? Do plants respond to the sound of the human voice, and to the timbre in which they are addressed – a thesis that would appear to be borne out by experiments with music and pure sound? Or do they in fact respond to the emotional tension of the human being in the closest relationship to them?

Whatever produces such responses, what is its nature? Is the reaction of the plants merely physical, an adjustment to minute changes in their environment that are undetectable by normal laboratory equipment? Or is it the response of an undiscovered equivalent to the animal nervous system? Could it even be an aspect of something so far hardly dreamed of – a telepathic faculty that is in direct communication with the animal world?

The members of the Findhorn community in northern Scotland, seen above, have achieved remarkable results, producing magnificent plants and vegetables in previously infertile soil. Compost, they believe, is not just a physical substance but also a medium through which they can express love to what they grow.

The plants, below left, show a common response: they lean away from a speaker through which rock music is played.

Dorothy Retallack, far left, is seen observing the controlled-environment plant cabinet in which she carried out her experiments.

PERSPECTIVES

HOW TO TEST YOUR OWN PLANTS

At relatively little expense, it is possible for anybody to set up a simple piece of instrumentation to investigate plant response. A philodendron makes an excellent experimental plant, because it has large fleshy leaves that can stand up to a great deal of gentle handling. The electrodes you use for the experiment should be about the size of a shirt button, and should not be of copper or bronze, which easily corrode and affect the leaf. Ideally, two small thin discs of stainless steel should be used or, at a pinch, old coins with a silver content. A lead wire is soldered to each disc, and then the wire and the back of the disc should be covered with a small piece of insulating tape. The discs are held in contact with the upper and lower surfaces of the leaf by means of a small G-clamp. Most researchers smear a little paste that can be made of agar-agar with 1 per cent salt added between electrode and leaf. The G-clamp should be supported on a rod and stand beside the plant.

To observe the changes in resistance in the leaf, an electric test-meter, obtainable at any radio store, is quite satisfactory. These meters are provided with a range of scales to indicate electric current, voltage and resistance. The meter should be set for a range of resistance such that the needle is about halfway along the scale. Increases and decreases in the conductivity of the leaf will then show up most clearly. Those with radio experience can add an oscillator to produce a sound signal, in much the same way that a metal detector works.

TONGUES OF MEN, OR OF ANGELS?

***Religious emotion overcomes one member of the congregation during a service at a 'Holy Roller' church,* above. *The other members are unembarrassed: their church regards such displays of emotion as perfectly natural. Pentecostalists often reach a crisis of religious fervour; and when the ecstasy is at its height, speaking in tongues may occur, as seen,* left.**

FEW EXPRESSIONS OF RELIGIOUS ECSTASY ARE AS DRAMATIC OR AS BEWILDERING AS 'SPEAKING IN TONGUES' – A BIZARRE, YET SURPRISINGLY COMMON PHENOMENON

The scene is set for an extraordinary – but by no means rare – phenomenon. A Pentecostalist minister's prayers grow more fervent; and the congregation's responses correspondingly increase in enthusiasm. Cries of 'Glory be to God!', 'Jesus, blessed Jesus!', and 'Hallelujah!' resound through the church. A woman rises from her seat. Her voice then swells until it drowns all the others, which sink into a chorus of soft murmurings. Now she begins to pour out a stream of completely unintelligible sounds – yet it is clearly passionate praise for the Lord. Minister and congregation then join in exalting the Holy Spirit of God who has granted their sister the gift of 'speaking in tongues'.

This phenomenon can be witnessed by anyone who visits a Pentecostalist church – although you may have to attend more than once as it does not automatically occur at every service.

Nowadays, 'speaking in tongues' implies *unidentified* tongues (or *glossolalia*). But before they could be recorded on tape, such sounds were often considered to belong to real, if unrecognised, human languages both ancient and modern (such as Incan and Eskimo), or even to be the 'tongues of angels'.

But since the advent of tape recorders and computers, not a single case of *xenolalia* (paranormal speaking in real languages) has been recorded; and the sounds that pour out so fervently at Pentecostalist services have been proved not to be languages but language-types. A linguistics expert can tell the difference by analysing the structure of the 'tongues' spoken. A personal knowledge of every language is not required; for the rule, to the expert, is quite simple – languages follow set laws

and language-types do not. 'Tongues' have neither vocabulary nor syntax, and so it must be concluded that they are neither the language of men nor, it has been assumed, of angels.

Although speaking in 'tongues' has been called 'refined gobbledygook', it is nevertheless a genuine form of worship. Indeed, it seems that this bizarre phenomenon enables people, who normally lack the ability to express themselves in public, to give vent to their religious emotions in such a way as to convince themselves and their fellow worshippers that the Holy Spirit is among them. It seems to uplift the congregation and give the speaker a sense of euphoric psychological release. But this form of communication, by its very nature, is emotional rather than educational – a sharing of mood rather than a conveying of information.

Interpreters of Tongues

However, in almost every such congregation there is at least one 'interpreter of tongues' who sincerely believes that he or she is translating the 'tongues' into the vernacular. What is more, although the interpretation itself can help to reinforce the ecstatic mood of the congregation, it of course cannot be a translation or paraphrase of a language that does not exist.

Many Pentecostalists would deny that xenolalia has never been known in their churches, rightly pointing out that only a tiny percentage of all 'tongues' has ever been recorded or analysed. They also tell stories of numerous occasions when a foreign unbeliever, who is a casual visitor to the church, has been converted – by being preached at in his own language. Such a 'miracle' convinces the foreign sinner of the need to repent and join the Lord's church. Sometimes such a tale is told by the convert himself, sometimes by those who witnessed the alleged conversation. And since religious people are supposedly truthful, such reports are widely taken to be genuine.

Risen from the Dead

Speaking in tongues among Christians first happened, so the New Testament tells us, when the disciples gathered in Jerusalem for the annual Jewish feast of Pentecost. This occasion was just seven weeks after Christ's crucifixion. The story is told by Luke (also author of one of the Gospels) in *Acts 2.*

> " A woman rises from her seat. Her voice then swells until it drowns all the others... Now she begins to pour out a stream of unintelligible sounds – yet it is clearly a passionate paean of praise for the Lord. "

The disciples were worshipping at the Temple in Jerusalem, mingling with Jews from all over the known world, when suddenly they were seized by an ecstasy, said to have been caused by the conviction that Christ had risen from the dead. The 'Holy Ghost' is said to have descended on them, bestowing the 'gift of tongues' so that they shouted aloud their praise of God in all the various languages of the visiting worshippers, to the great astonishment of the crowd.

The 11th-century Greek Orthodox mosaic,* below, *shows the Day of Pentecost. Jesus' disciples are said to have been baptised by tongues of fire, which released such an ecstasy that they shouted praise of God in many languages unknown to them. This was the first instance of Christian 'tongues'.

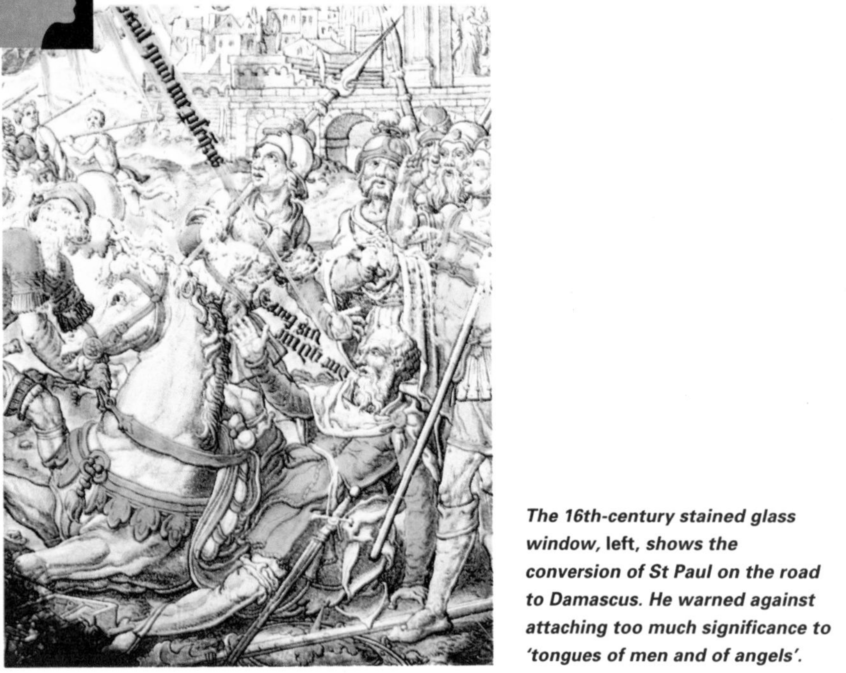

The 16th-century stained glass window, left, shows the conversion of St Paul on the road to Damascus. He warned against attaching too much significance to 'tongues of men and of angels'.

Objectively, however, the source of such xenolalia is not hard to pinpoint. Jewish religious law made attendance at certain festivals compulsory for every male adult Jew, but made allowances for great parts of the services to be spoken in the various vernaculars of the visitors present. So the disciples would often have heard what was recognisably praise of God in many languages, which they did not understand but which they probably stored deep down in their subconscious minds. Moreover, Christ had promised to send them his 'Comforter' – whoever or whatever that might be – specifically at the feast of Pentecost. This heightened sense of expectation, together with their conviction that Christ had risen, could have resulted in the first Christian 'tongues'. (The official account does not claim that the disciples understood what they were saying, nor does it mention that their utterances contained any specifically Christian message – it simply states that it happened, and astonished fellow worshippers.)

Sacred Mandate?

The disciples' experience at Pentecost might have been considered unique in the annals of the Christian Church had it not been for St Paul's statement (in *1 Corinthians* 12-14) that 'tongues' were considered part of the normal worship of the Church at Corinth and that he himself was a glossolalist. Whether the Corinthian mode of worship was typical of that of the early church is debatable, but – despite Paul's warnings against abuses of 'the gifts of the Spirit' (especially the misuse of 'tongues') and his stress on the 'more excellent way' of Christian love – these references to Corinthian glossolalia have been taken by some sects as a sacred mandate to use 'tongues' as proof of 'baptism by the Holy Spirit'.

Since the early days of the Church, the use of 'tongues' has not always found favour among Christians, however. The Roman Catholics, for example, banned it from about the end of the first century, and later regarded speaking in 'tongues' as a sign of possession (except in the case of certain saints). Mainstream Protestantism has also found no place for it. However, it was kept alive down the centuries through fringe movements and heretical sects until, in the 20th century, it became the focal point for Pentecostalism.

Spreading Hysteria

This movement started humbly, its members mainly drawn from ethnic minorities and poor people, and it was tainted at first – as its own historians admit – by hysterical behaviour and fanaticism. But it was a fast-growing movement, and quickly spread throughout the world, soon becoming by far the strongest Protestant group throughout predominantly Catholic South America, and surprisingly numerous even in countries such as Italy and Portugal, as well as in Protestant lands like Sweden.

Today, however, Pentecostal conduct and beliefs are more moderate; and in some of their churches, the emphasis on 'tongues' is not as great as it was originally. 'Tongues' now tend to be used more in private than in public worship. But possibly a much more important development in the use of glossolalia than the spread of Pentecostalism is the Charismatic Movement, which has affected almost every Christian denomination today. Small groups in individual Anglican, Baptist, Methodist, Presbyterian and even Catholic churches now meet to worship God in private, using 'the gift of tongues'. Unlike the humble members of the original Pentecostal Church, the members of the Charismatic Movement tend to belong to the professional middle-classes, and they use 'tongues' in private, in quiet, unemotional prayer. Such people do not regard 'tongues' as being real foreign languages, but take them as a sign of the Holy Spirit's revitalising effect upon the Church, often enabling members to express the otherwise inexpressible.

The use of strange 'languages' is not exclusive to the Pentecostalists nor the Charismatic Movement, however. Since the foundation of modern Spiritualism about 130 years ago, hundreds of claims of spoken and written xenolalia by sensitives and psychics have been made.

A Christian convert, above, emerges from a baptism by total immersion, crying aloud with joy. Often the climax of such baptisms results in 'tongues' being spoken by one or more of the participants.

THE FACE OF CHRIST?

Legend has it that, as Christ carried the cross to Golgotha, St Veronica – depicted left *in a detail from a 16th-century window in St John's Church, Gouda, Holland – was so moved by pity that she gave him her handkerchief to wipe his face. Later she found that the image of his face had been miraculously impressed upon it. A relic, preserved in St Peter's, Rome, was long thought to be St Veronica's cloth, but this claim is no longer taken seriously.*

The impressions of the front and back of a man's body can be clearly seen on the Turin shroud, right, for centuries the world's most holy relic.

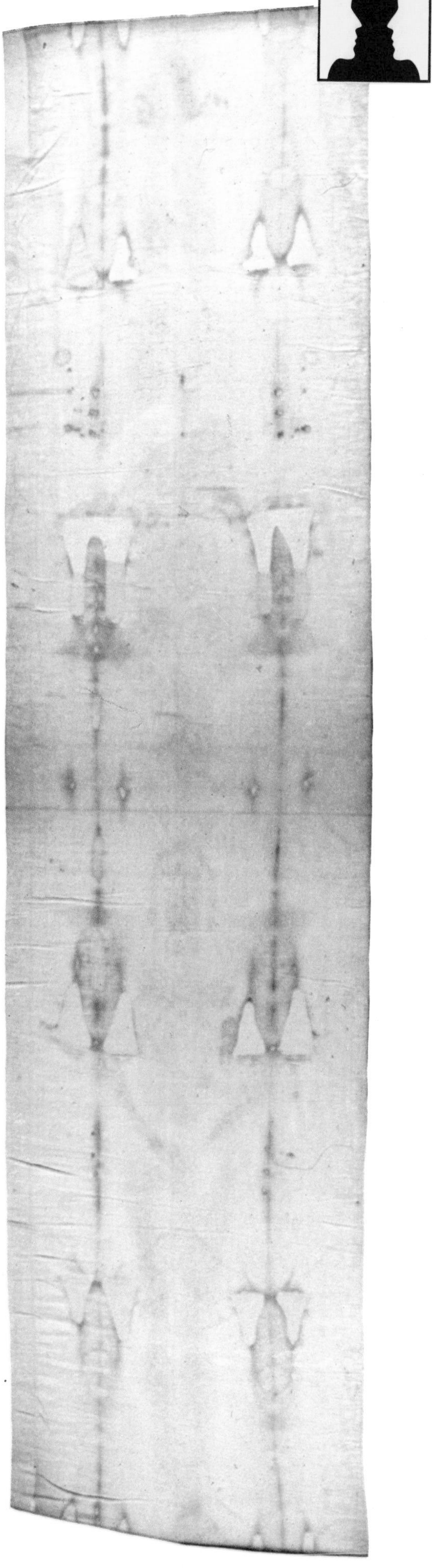

WAS THE IMAGE ON THE FAMOUS TURIN SHROUD MADE BY THE BODY OF CHRIST HIMSELF, OR IS IT SIMPLY A PAINTING – OR EVEN A PHOTOGRAPH – BY A MEDIEVAL FORGER?

The Bishop of Troyes complained to the Pope Clement VII, above, *who reigned from 1523 to 1534, that the Turin shroud was being exhibited for financial gain by its owner, Sir Geoffrey de Charnay. The Pope, however, ruled that the shroud could stay on show, but not as an authentic relic.*

During and immediately after the Crusades, mendicant friars wandered Europe, selling objects said to have come from the Holy Land – allegedly relics of the early Church. Among those recorded were the knucklebones of St Peter, the arrows that killed St Sebastian, pieces of the Virgin's gown, and lumps of dried bread from the Last Supper. So many such relics were manufactured, in fact, that the Church became a laughing stock, and ammunition was given to such reformers as Martin Luther and John Calvin. There are still said, for instance, to be enough splinters of the true cross scattered among the churches of Italy, Spain, and southern France to make a sizeable grove of trees.

Not unnaturally, the Roman Catholic Church became wary of, if not openly hostile towards, such artifacts; and at the end of the 19th century, the Vatican issued a proclamation stating that no relic, 'be it the most sacred in Christendom', could be regarded as authentic. This edict was made to counter the remarkable assertion of a French scientist and agnostic that a strip of cloth, known as the Holy Shroud of Turin, was the genuine winding sheet of Christ. Such was the standing of Dr Yves Delage, however, that science took over where superstition left off; and for 80 years, continued attempts were made to unravel the mystery of the shroud, culminating in the Shroud of Turin Research Project of October 1978. For five days, the fabric was subjected to exhaustive tests by some 40 top scientists using space-age instruments. But it soon became clear that, if the project answered certain questions, it also posed startling new ones.

Holy Imprints

The Holy Shroud of Turin is a rectangular strip of cloth, 13½ feet (4 metres) long by three-and-a-half feet (1 metre) wide. On its surface can be seen the faint, yellowish-brown imprint of a human figure, naked and bearded. Darker stains, said to be blood, are superimposed on the image, notably on the head, wrists, feet, and left side; and both back and front views of the figure appear, hinged, as it were, at the crown of the head, which seems to bear a kind of wreath.

The first probable mention of the shroud occurred in 1203, when the military chronicler Robert de Clari wrote that in the previous year he had seen a *sydoine* shroud that bore 'the figure of our Lord' during the sacking of Constantinople by Christian knights in the course of the Fourth Crusade. Unfortunately, he said, it had disappeared in the turmoil. Then, just over 150 years later, came the first certain record of the present 'Turin' shroud, and all the indications are that it was the same as that seen by de Clari. It was owned by a rather unscrupulous knight named Geoffrey de Charney, overlord of the French town of Liré.

> ACCORDING TO ONE SCHOOL OF THOUGHT, THE SHROUD MAY ACTUALLY BE A PHOTOGRAPHIC SELF-PORTRAIT OF LEONARDO DA VINCI, COMMISSIONED TO PRODUCE A FAKE FOR POSTERITY.

By 1389, the fame of the relic was such that he decided to put it on public display for money. This move caused a great deal of jealousy, for popular relics were at a premium at that time and the financial income from a good one could be considerable. Either out of pure jealousy or perhaps because he thought he was acting from honourable motives, the Bishop of Troyes complained to Pope Clement VII at Avignon about de Charney's exhibition. His story became the foundation of the most frequent accusation levelled at the shroud until the present day: that it was in fact a forgery, the work of an artist... 'cunningly painted, the truth being attested by the artist who painted it'.

But Pope Clement seems to have thought the Bishop's allegation a trifle thin, and ruled that the shroud could remain on show as an object of devotion, though not necessarily as an 'authentic' relic.

Saved from Fire

For over 60 years, the shroud continued to attract pilgrims, until in 1453 Geoffrey's grand-daughter, Marguerite de Charney, gave it – or more likely sold it, though the motive is not clear – to Louis, Duke of Savoy. The de Charneys had shown the relic in a simple setting; but Louis, either from piety or perhaps from showmanship, encased it in a silver frame and built a special shrine, Sainte Chapelle, at Chambéry, his capital.

Then, in 1532, a near-disastrous fire broke out in Sainte Chapelle. The heat melted the silver frame, and drops of molten metal burned through the cloth in several places, though water was quickly used to douse the scorching. The worst burns were neatly patched, and both the burns and the water stains proved to be of assistance during the 1978 scientific investigation.

In 1578, the shroud made its last journey across the Alps to Piedmont, where the then Duke of Savoy had set up his household at Turin. It was lodged in the cathedral, next to the Royal apartments and has remained there, apart from a spell in vaults during the Second World War, ever since.

The painting by the 19th-century French artist, Delacroix,* left, *shows Christ nailed to the cross through the feet and the palms of the hands. Research has shown, however, that the flesh of the palms of the hands cannot support the weight of the body without tearing. It is therefore highly likely that, as in the Turin shroud image, the nails were driven through the radius of the wrist. Such authentic detail of the position of the nails in the shroud image is sometimes used to support the argument that it is not a medieval forgery.

In the photographic negative of the face from the Turin shroud, above, there are clear marks around the forehead – said by some to have been made by the crown of thorns.

From the very beginning of its recorded history, however, certain observers had noted something indefinably 'wrong' about the image on the shroud. Pope Clement, for instance, is said to have felt that, if it was a forgery, far from being 'cunningly painted' as the Bishop of Troyes alleged, it was rather badly done. Albrecht Dürer, the great German artist, examined it at Ste Chapelle in the early part of the 16th century and was baffled. He made several attempts to draw it; but felt that, though the anatomical proportions were correct, the model for it must have been 'deformed'.

However, it was not until 1898 that the shroud revealed its first strange secret when taken from its silver casket to be put on rare public display. A Turin photographer, Secondo Pia, was commissioned to take the first photographs of it. As he developed his plates, there appeared not the blurred, odd image on the shroud but the perfectly formed features of a man: the shroud, it seemed, was actually itself a photographic negative. This realisation so astounded him, Pia said, that he dropped the plate he was holding in shock.

The implications of this discovery were not lost on Dr Yves Delage, a prominent physicist, zoologist and leading member of the French Academy of Sciences, who determined to find out how the image had appeared – 500 years before the acknowledged invention of photography. However, his motives were not entirely disinterested, for Dr Delage was a militantly anti-Catholic agnostic, and he had no intention of allowing the Church to make supernatural claims for the shroud.

For three years, he and a brilliant young biologist, named Paul Joseph Vignon, studied the image and also experimented with methods of reproducing it. First, they employed artists to paint an image using medieval pigments, pursuing the theory that the 'painting' might have faded in such a way that the darker areas had become highlights over the years, thus producing a 'negative' image. But none of the experiments was successful.

BURIAL TRADITIONS

Delage and Vignon then began again, working from the premise that the cloth had been 'somebody's' shroud. It was of Palestinian weave, of a type known to have been made until the fifth century AD. Crucifixion had been outlawed by the Romans in the fourth century, so the man of the shroud must have been crucified some time before then.

They also noted that, according to biblical traditions, Christ had been hastily buried on Friday to avoid the Jewish sabbath. The body had been 'anointed' but not washed. The most common form of burial ointments in use in Palestine at that time had been myrrh and aloes. Vignon was aware that sweat from a dead body produces a substance known as urea, which in decay gives off ammonia vapour. So he experimented with ammonia and cloth 'sensitised' with myrrh and aloes, and managed to produce similar brownish stains.

As far as Delage was concerned, that was the answer to the riddle. But on presenting his findings to the Academy of Sciences in 1902, he went further. He was convinced, he said, that this was indeed Christ's shroud. On the one hand, he pointed out, there was the biblical account of a man who had undergone a very uncharacteristic form of crucifixion: as well as being nailed to a cross, he had also been scourged, crowned with thorns, and finally pierced through the left side with a lance. And here was a strip of linen, apparently originating in Palestine, depicting a man who had undergone the same form of torture and death. Delage added that this conclusion did not actually affect his own anti-religious views in any way. He simply regarded the shroud as a piece of historical evidence.

Delage may have been right on this point. But the predominantly Roman Catholic Academy was nervous of the implications, and rejected his findings, refusing to print his carefully mustered evidence in their minutes. More recent research points to an even more interesting theory – not only may the shroud be a *true* photographic image, dating from centuries before the generally accepted date for the invention of photography. According to another school of thought, put forward by researcher Lynn Picknett, it may actually be a photographic self-portrait of Leonardo da Vinci, commissioned to produce a fake for posterity.

THOUGHT-OGRAPHY: FANTASY OR REALITY?

ARE THE IMAGES PRODUCED BY TED SERIOS PROOF THAT THOUGHTS CAN BE PROJECTED ON TO FILM?

One of the few colour 'thoughtographs' produced by Serios is shown, **right.** *He was aiming at a target picture of the Hilton hotel at Denver, but obtained this image of the Chicago Hilton instead.*

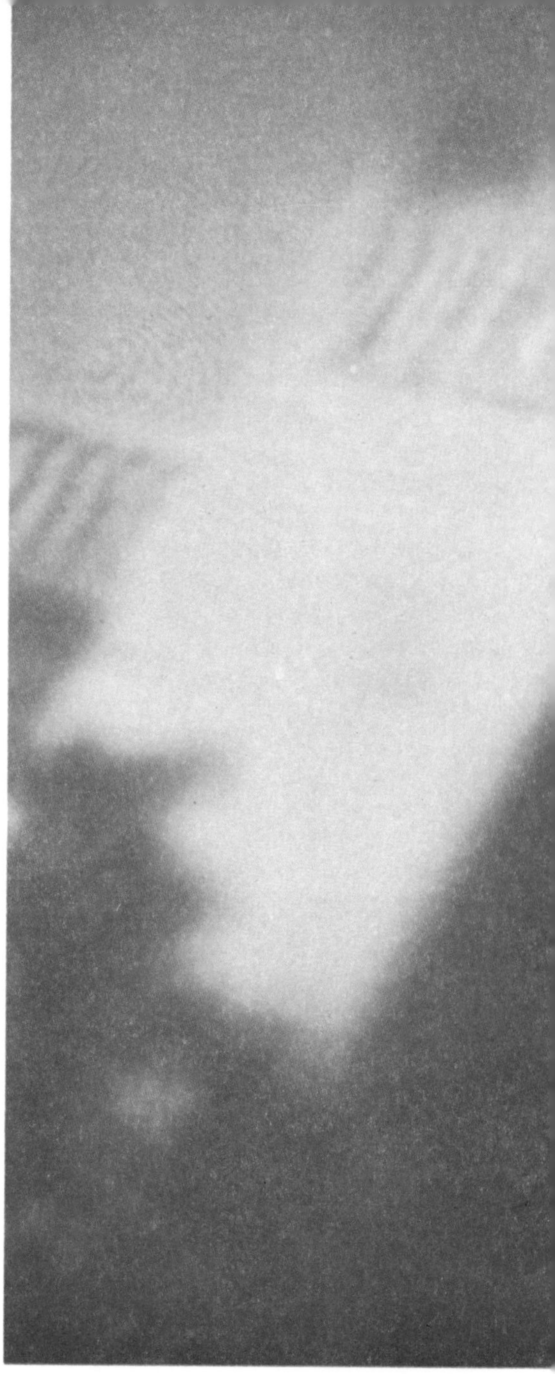

Ted Serios sat down in the hotel room and pointed a Polaroid camera at his face. The flashbulb fired. Dr Jule Eisenbud immediately took the camera from him and pulled the print from the back. Instead of Serios' face, however, the unmistakable image of a building appeared.

For Serios – a chain-smoking, alcoholic Chicago bell-hop – it was just another of his strange psychic images known as 'thoughtographs'. But for Dr Eisenbud, an associate professor of psychiatry at the University of Colorado Medical School, it was such an impressive demonstration of paranormal power that he went on to study Serios for several years and also wrote a book about him.

When Dr Eisenbud flew to Chicago for the first experimental session with the hard-drinking psychic

The picture **below** *was produced by Serios for researcher Dr Jule Eisenbud. It was immediately identified by one of the observers at the session as the Chicago Water Tower,* **below right.** *Only later was it recognised as part of the Kremlin, an image of which Eisenbud had hidden in an envelope handed to Serios.*

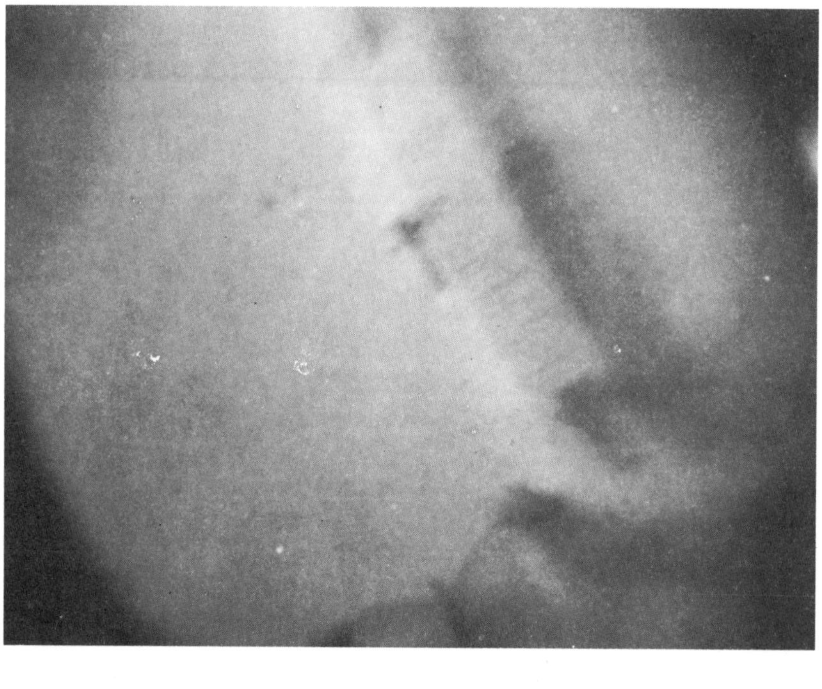

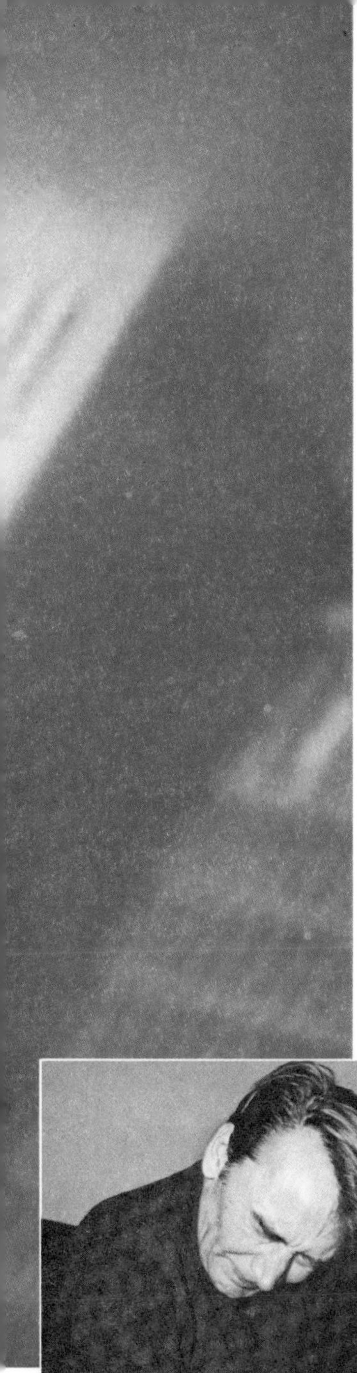

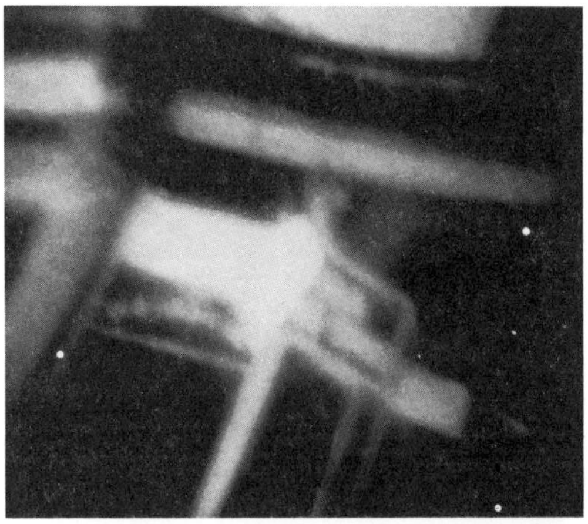

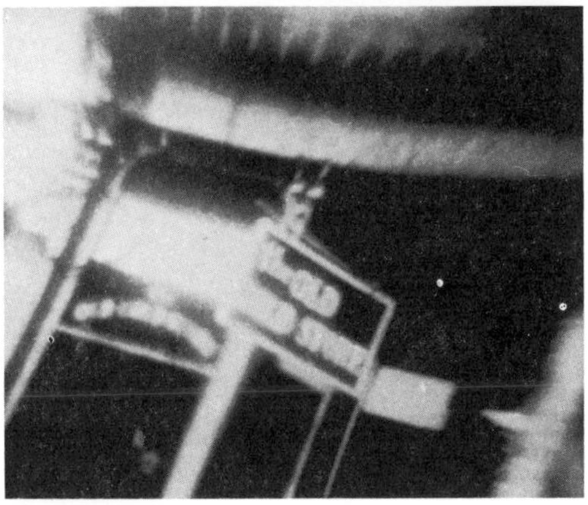

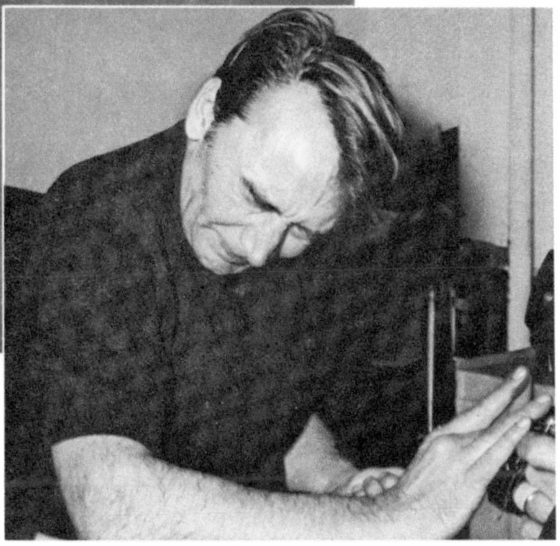

***The images** above are two of 11 views of a shop front in Central City, Colorado, produced by Ted Serios,* **left.** *At the time, the building was used as a tourist shop called the 'Old Wells Fargo Express Office'. Several years previously, however, it had been called 'The Old Gold Store', of which no photographs were known to exist.*

photographer in April 1964, he was almost certain that he was about to witness 'some kind of shoddy hoax'. Because of his interest in the paranormal, Eisenbud was aware that there had been many so-called psychic photographers over the years who had been caught cheating, usually by tampering with their film. But the appearance of the Polaroid camera had changed that, making it easier to control the production of such 'thoughtographic' prints, as well as giving results in seconds.

Investigators who worked with Serios supplied their own film and cameras; and sometimes even took the pictures themselves, with the camera pointing at the Chicago psychic. The results that emerged were frequently very strange indeed. Not all the photographs carried images, though; some were unusually white, while others were totally black, even though the room lighting and other factors remained constant. Occasionally, the image that emerged from the Polaroid covered the whole area of the print, while at other times it obliterated only a portion of Serios or identifiable items in the room where the experiment is being conducted. The Eiffel Tower, Big Ben, the White House and orbiting satellites all feature in his album of thoughtographs.

In his early days, Serios just looked at the camera to produce his startling pictures, but later he introduced a 'gismo', which he held in front of the lens while concentrating. Sometimes he used a small plastic cylinder, one end of which was covered with plain cellophane, the other with cellophane over a piece of blackened film; on other occasions, he simply rolled up a piece of paper.

Secrets of the 'Gismo'

The purpose of the 'gismo', Serios said, was to keep his fingers from obscuring the lens. His critics, however, have seen it as having a far more sinister purpose. It could very easily have concealed a 'gimmick', containing microfilm or a transparency, they argued; and, for them, its use became as suspicious as a conjuror's hat.

Two reporters, Charles Reynolds and David Eisendrath, constructed a small device that could be hidden in a 'gismo' and that produced similar-looking results to those of Serios. Their account, published in *Popular Photography* in October 1967, gave sceptics all the 'evidence' they needed.

> " Investigators who worked with Serios supplied their own film and cameras; sometimes they even took the pictures themselves, with the camera pointing at the Chicago psychic – the results were frequently very strange indeed. "

Eisenbud and other researchers, on the other hand, were satisfied that the 'gismo' contained no hidden equipment, and that Serios did not slip anything inside it just before an exposure was made. They were all aware of the hidden microfilm hypothesis, and evolved an experimental protocol to overcome it. Serios was usually given the 'gismo' when he felt he could produce a paranormal print. It was then taken from him immediately and examined. It was probably in his hands for no longer than 15 seconds at a time, and throughout that period was under close scrutiny.

At the sessions, Serios usually wore short-sleeved shirts or stripped to the waist, making it impossible for him to conceal anything close to his hands. Besides, researchers have said, they were frequently close enough to the action when Serios told them to fire the camera that they could actually

see through the 'gismo' and check that it contained no hidden devices.

On numerous occasions, images even appeared when someone else was holding the 'gismo' and the camera, and so was able to examine both freely. Two eminent American psychical researchers, Dr J.G. Pratt and Dr Ian Stevenson, who conducted numerous tests with Serios, have stated: 'We have ourselves observed Ted in approximately 800 trials and we have never seen him act in a suspicious way in the handling of the gismo before or after a trial'. Quite apart from the fact that Serios was never caught with any hidden transparencies or microfilm, Dr Eisenbud also argued that the very nature of the images that Serios produced rules out the 'gimmick' theory.

Target Pictures

On some occasions, Serios invited investigators to bring with them target pictures concealed in envelopes, which he tried to reproduce paranormally on Polaroid film. On the first occasion that Eisenbud saw Serios produce a paranormal picture, in a Chicago hotel room, the psychiatrist had taken with him two views of the Kremlin buildings, each hidden in a cardboard-backed envelope.

One of the images that Serios produced at that session was of a tall, thin building, which a witness immediately identified as the Chicago Water Tower – a landmark that would have been familiar to Serios. Though this seemed to be totally off target, Eisenbud was very impressed, partly because some of the images and symbols in the picture were relevant to a line of thought in his mind at the time.

Two years later, however, Eisenbud came across another view of the Kremlin buildings. This time, Ivan's Bell Tower, which was only partly visible in one of the original two target pictures, was prominent. It was only then that he realised that it had 'an easily discernible resemblance' to the Chicago Water Tower. Serios, it seems, had scored a hit after all.

In 1965, Serios produced 11 slightly different versions of what appeared to be the glass front of a store. On two of them, the name 'The Old Gold Store' is clearly visible in bold block lettering. Two years later, the image was recognised as a tourist shop in Central City, Colorado, which is now the 'Old Wells Fargo Express Office'. The name change, said Eisenbud, must have occurred no later than 1958 and research has failed to unearth any photographs of the store in its earlier days.

But, although Serios' paranormal picture corresponds perfectly (but for the name) with the present-day store, there is a curious substitution in one picture of the letter 'W' for 'O' so that it reads 'The Wld Gold Store'. And the 'W' is exactly where it would be if 'Wells Fargo' had been spelled out.

But even stranger things happened. One of Serios' pictures, for instance, showed two storeys of a building and some slight out-of-focus lettering that was, nevertheless, discernible. The building was ultimately acknowledged by the Royal Canadian Mounted Police as one of their Air Division hangars; but they pointed out a curious misspelling, which other observers had also noted. The words in Serios' picture read 'Air Division Cainadain Moun...'

If Serios had somehow used concealed transparencies to produce his pictures, then he was also having to tamper with the originals in an expert way in order to come up with such bizarre images.

Because of such pictures, in which Serios seems to be photographing the past (and distorting reality, too), Eisenbud and fellow researchers arranged an experimental session on 27 May 1967 at the Denver Museum of Natural History where it was hoped his powers might capture on film something that was several thousand years old.

The blurred lettering on the 'thoughtograph'*, top, *enabled researchers to identify the building as a hanger belonging to the Air Division of the Royal Canadian Mounted Police,* above. *The picture bears the stamp of Ted Serios in the misspelling 'CAINADAIN'.

The nude,* far right, *is another example of what is claimed to have been achieved by the power of thought and a single sheet of photographic paper.

*In*Focus

HIDDEN IN THE HAND?

James Randi, professional stage magician and debunker of things paranormal, has expressed the opinion that Ted Serios is a fraud and that his so-called 'thoughtographs' are produced not by the power of his mind but by means of the device that Serios calls a 'gismo'.

A 'typical Serios gimmick', described by Randi in his book *Flim-flam! – The Truth about Unicorns, Parapsychology and other Delusions,* consists of a small magnifying lens, about ½ inch (1.2 centimetres) in diameter and with a focal length of about 1½ inches (4 centimetres), fixed to one end of a cylinder about 1½ inches (4 centimetres) long. A circle cut from a colour transparency (a 35 mm slide, for example) is glued to the other end of the cylinder. To avoid detection, the device can be wrapped loosely in a tube of paper.

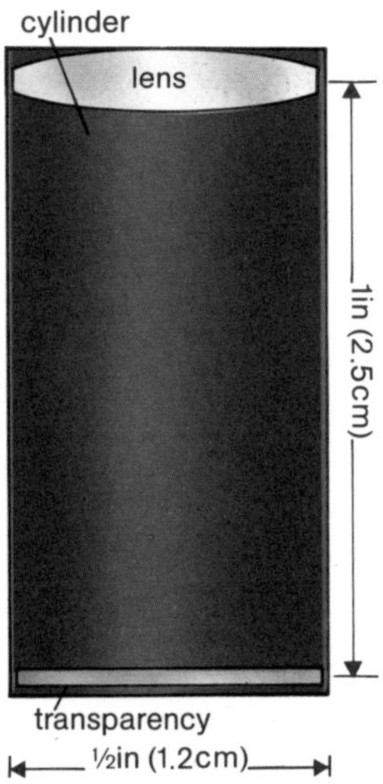

By holding the 'gismo'-lens of a Polaroid camera focused to infinity, and snapping the shutter, the image on the transparency will be thrown on to the Polaroid film. After use, Randi explains, the 'gismo' will slide easily out of the paper (presumably to be disposed of secretly later), and the empty paper tube can be offered to researchers or an audience for inspection.

It is indeed possible to take photographs in this way, although the pictures that result will usually be of poor quality. However, showing how images such as Serios' thoughtographs *could* have been produced is a very different matter from using such an optical device undetected in hundreds of demonstrations. No one to date seems to have done that.

Serios felt confident of success, and began by drawing a mental impression he had received of a man lighting a fire. Strange images were recorded on several of the pictures, the most impressive of which showed a Neanderthal man in a crouching position. But Serios' camera lens had not delved into time to record this image. It was realised immediately by one witness, Professor H. Marie Wormington, of the Department of Anthropology, Colorado College, that it resembled very closely a well-known life-size model of a Neanderthal man group in the Chicago Field Museum of Natural History, postcards of which were readily available.

THE FINAL CURTAIN?

So, did Serios actually fake these photographs? Subsequent studies show that the Neanderthal man in Serios' pictures is shown at different angles; and in the opinion of several professional photographers and photogrammetric engineers, these prints 'could not have been produced from a single microtransparency, but would have required at least several and perhaps eight different ones, most of which could not have been produced from a simple photographic copying of the Field Museum photograph or of a photograph taken by Ted himself'.

Soon after this session, Serios' psychic powers waned for a while and, within a year, although he continued to submit to experiments, all he could produce were 'blackies' or 'whities' without discernible images, leaving psychical researchers still baffled about just what paranormal forces had been at work to produce his former astonishing pictures.

Serios had previously lost his powers at other times – the longest period being for two years – and it seemed to happen without warning. As he put it: 'It is as if a curtain comes down, ker-boom, and that's all, brother'.

But perhaps there *are* warnings, and possibly even symbolic ones, for among the supervised full-frame thoughtographs he produced just prior to losing the 'gift' at one stage was a print which showed the image of a curtain.

WHAT A COINCIDENCE!

" WE THUS ARRIVE AT THE IMAGE OF A WORLD MOSAIC OR COSMIC KALEIDOSCOPE WHICH, IN SPITE OF CONSTANT SHUFFLINGS AND REARRANGEMENTS, ALSO TAKES CARE OF BRINGING LIKE AND LIKE TOGETHER.

DR PAUL KAMMERER "

EVERY ONE OF US HAS, AT SOME TIME, EXPERIENCED A COINCIDENCE. MATHEMATICIANS EXPLAIN THEM AWAY AS MERE CHANCE EVENTS – BUT THERE ARE THOSE WHO SEEK DEEPER REASONS

Shortly after British actor Anthony Hopkins had been chosen for a part in the film *The Girl from Petrovka,* he decided he ought to read the novel by George Feifer, from which the screenplay was taken. He could not find it in a single London bookshop, however. Then, while waiting for a train at Leicester Square underground station, he caught sight of a volume lying on a seat. Amazingly, it was that same novel. What is more, it had scribbled notes in the margin. As Hopkins later found out, a friend had lost Feifer's own annotated copy, and it was this very one that Hopkins had come across.

King Umberto I of Italy, **above,** ***was assassinated by the anarchist Bresci on 29 July 1900. Many important events in his life, as well as his death, were astonishingly closely paralleled by the life of another Umberto – a restaurant proprietor in a small town in northern Italy.***

Coincidences such as this certainly take one aback. Yet most of us actually have an intriguing coincidence of some sort or other to relate: bumping into a long-lost friend in some unexpected situation; suddenly thinking of someone who immediately telephones; humming a tune, and then hearing it on the radio seconds later; or even, perhaps, coming across an individual with your very own name whose life seems to run in parallel to your own.

One such occurrence involved King Umberto I of Italy who was dining with his aide in a restaurant in Monza, where he was due to attend an athletics meeting the next day. With astonishment, he suddenly noticed that the proprietor looked exactly like him. Speaking to him, he discovered that there were other similarities, too.

PERSPECTIVES

THESE FOOLISH THINGS...

The most striking coincidences often involve the most commonplace of objects or occasions. One such bizarre incident was experienced by the Chicago newspaper columnist Irv Kupcinet, *left:*

'I had just checked into the Savoy Hotel in London. Opening a drawer in my room, I found, to my astonishment, that it contained some personal things belonging to a friend of mine, Harry Hannin, then with the Harlem Globetrotters basketball team.

'Two days later, I received a letter from Harry, posted in the Hotel Meurice, in Paris, which began "You'll never believe this." Apparently, Harry had opened a drawer in his room and found a tie which had my name on it. It was a room I had stayed in a few months earlier.'

The restaurateur was also called Umberto; like the King, he had been born in Turin – on the same day in fact; and he had married a girl called Margherita on the day that the King had married *Queen* Margherita. He had also opened his restaurant on the day that Umberto I was crowned.

The King was intrigued, and invited his 'double' to attend the athletics meeting with him. But the next day, the King's aide informed him that the restaurateur had died that morning in a mysterious shooting. Even as the King expressed his regret, he himself was shot dead by an anarchist in the crowd.

Another strange coincidence connected with a death occurred on Sunday 6 August 1978, when the little alarm clock that Pope Paul VI had bought in 1923 – and that for 55 years had woken him at six every morning – rang suddenly and shrilly. But it was not six o'clock: the time was 9.40 p.m. For no explicable reason, the clock had started ringing as the Pope lay dying. Later, Father Romeo Panciroli, a Vatican spokesman, commented: 'It was most strange. The Pope was very fond of the clock. He bought it in Poland and always took it with him on his trips'.

Many such examples of coincidences seem to defy all logic, luck or reason. It is not surprising, therefore, that the 'theory of coincidence' has excited scientists, philosophers and mathematicians for more than 2,000 years. Running like a thread through all their theories and speculations is one theme. Do coincidences have a hidden message for us? But only in this century have any real answers been suggested, answers that strike at the very roots of established science and prompt the question as to whether there are powers in the Universe of which we are still only dimly aware.

HIDDEN AFFINITIES

Early cosmologists believed that the world was held together by a principle of wholeness. Hippocrates, known as the father of medicine, who lived at some time between 460 and 375 BC, believed the Universe was joined together by 'hidden affinities' and wrote: 'There is one common flow, one common breathing, all things are in sympathy'. According to this theory, coincidence could be explained by 'sympathetic' elements seeking each other out.

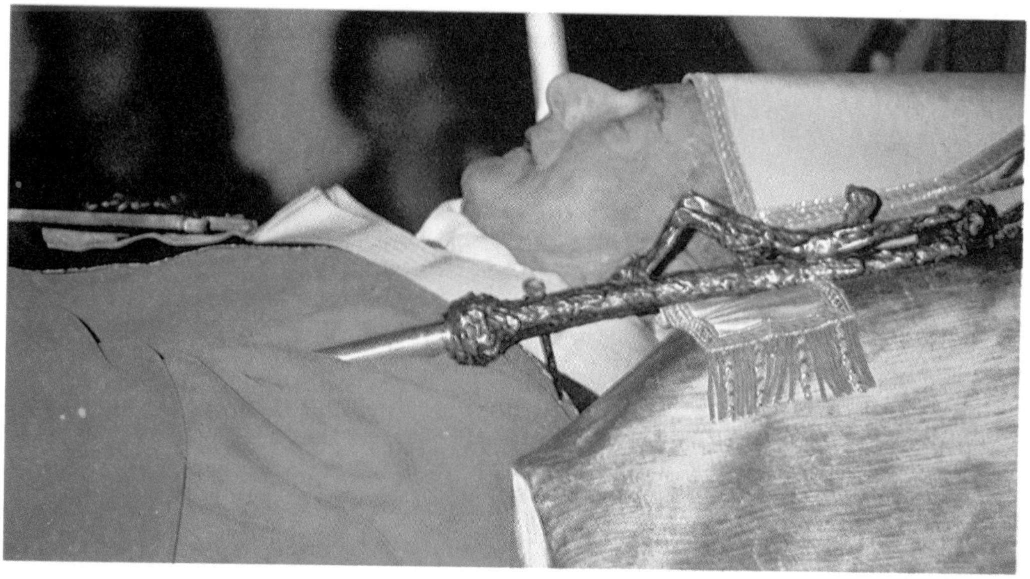

British actor, Anthony Hopkins,* above left, *was astonished to find a copy of George Feifer's novel* The Girl from Petrovka *on a bench at a London underground station, having previously searched for one in vain.

Pope Paul VI, seen* left *lying in state, experienced a strange event just prior to death. At 9.40 p.m. on 6 August 1978, his bedside alarm clock – set for six in the morning – inexplicably began to ring.

Similar beliefs have continued, in barely altered forms. The philosopher Arthur Schopenhauer (1788-1860), for instance, defined coincidence as 'the simultaneous occurrence of causally unconnected events'; and he went on to suggest that simultaneous events run in parallel lines.

These events, although links in totally different chains, nevertheless fall into place in both, he said, so that the fate of one individual invariably fits the fate of another.

Probing the Future

The idea of a 'collective unconscious' – an underground storehouse of memories through which minds can communicate – has been debated by several thinkers. One of the more extreme theories to explain coincidence was put forward by the British mathematician Adrian Dobbs in the 1960s. Dobbs coined the word 'psitron' to describe an unknown force probing, like radar, a second time dimension that was probabilistic rather than deterministic. The psitron, he claimed, was capable of absorbing future probabilities and could then relay them back to the present, bypassing the normal human senses and somehow conveying the information directly to the brain.

But the first person actually to study the laws of coincidence scientifically was Dr Paul Kammerer, Director of the Institute of Experimental Biology in Vienna. From the age of 20, he had kept a 'logbook' of coincidences. Many were essentially trivial: names that kept cropping up in separate conversations, successive concert or cloakroom tickets with the same number, or a phrase in a book that kept recurring in real life. For hours, Kammerer also sat on park benches, recording people who wandered past, and noting their sex, age, dress, and whether they carried walking sticks or umbrellas. After making the necessary allowances for factors like the rush-hour, weather and time of year, he found the results broke down into 'clusters of numbers' of a kind familiar to statisticians, gamblers, insurance companies and opinion pollsters.

Seriality

Kammerer called the phenomenon 'seriality', and in 1919 he published his conclusions in a book called *Das Gesetz der Serie (The Law of Seriality)*. Coincidences, he claimed, come in series – or 'a recurrence or clustering in time or space whereby the individual numbers in the sequence are not connected by the same active cause'. Coincidence, suggested Kammerer, is merely the tip of the iceberg in a larger cosmic principle that mankind, as yet, hardly recognises.

> "Chance furnishes me with what I need. I am like a man who stumbles along; my foot strikes something, I bend over it and it is exactly what I want."
>
> James Joyce

Like gravity, it is a mystery; but unlike gravity, it acts selectively to bring together in space and time things that possess some affinity. 'We thus arrive,' he concluded, 'at the image of a world mosaic or cosmic kaleidoscope which, in spite of constant shufflings and rearrangements, also takes care of bringing like and like together.'

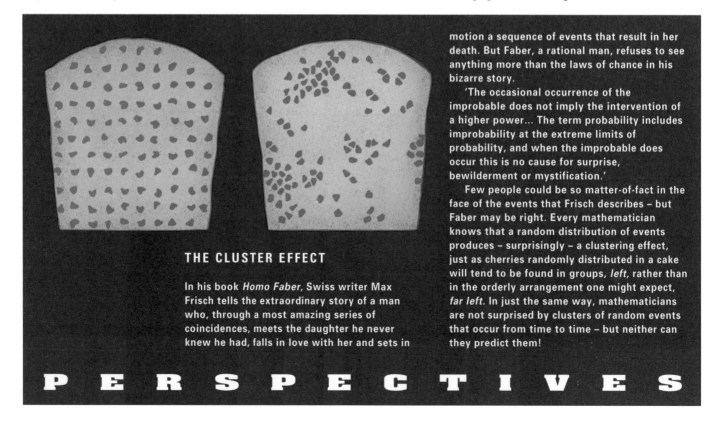

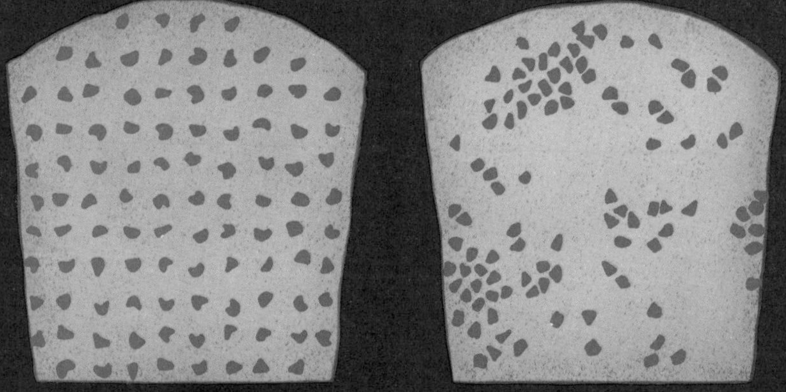

THE CLUSTER EFFECT

In his book *Homo Faber,* Swiss writer Max Frisch tells the extraordinary story of a man who, through a most amazing series of coincidences, meets the daughter he never knew he had, falls in love with her and sets in motion a sequence of events that result in her death. But Faber, a rational man, refuses to see anything more than the laws of chance in his bizarre story.

'The occasional occurrence of the improbable does not imply the intervention of a higher power... The term probability includes improbability at the extreme limits of probability, and when the improbable does occur this is no cause for surprise, bewilderment or mystification.'

Few people could be so matter-of-fact in the face of the events that Frisch describes – but Faber may be right. Every mathematician knows that a random distribution of events produces – surprisingly – a clustering effect, just as cherries randomly distributed in a cake will tend to be found in groups, *left,* rather than in the orderly arrangement one might expect, *far left.* In just the same way, mathematicians are not surprised by clusters of random events that occur from time to time – but neither can they predict them!

PERSPECTIVES

*In*Focus

THE LIBRARY ANGEL

An extraordinary number of people report amazing coincidences when searching out information in libraries, so much so that Arthur Koestler coined the term 'library angel' to describe the mysterious force that somehow leads individuals straight to the right book.

Dame Rebecca West, for example, described how she was once confronted with whole shelves of works concerning the Nuremberg Trials at the Royal Institute of International Affairs, but the method of cataloguing was of no help at all to her particular piece of research. She even complained to one of the librarians, and demonstrated her problem by pulling out a volume at random. Not only was it the actual volume she needed, but she had opened it at precisely the right page for the data that she needed for her work.

Journalist Bernard Levin had a similar experience. He had been looking for a very long while for reference to a story about a statue of Alexander the Great. This statue was said to be so large that it could hold an entire city in its hand. He happened to be looking up another reference entirely in *Plutarch's Lives,* turned by mistake to the wrong page due to a misprint, and there found the story of the statue.

Sir Arthur Conan Doyle, creator of Sherlock Holmes, was also astonished to come across a story by de Maupassant, entitled *L'Auberge,* which was almost identical in every respect to a plot which he had been developing for a book of his own. It was even set in the very same inn at the Gemmi Pass in Switzerland.

More recently, astrologer and writer Derek Walters was assisted by the library angel when researching in the Chinese section of a university library. The information he sought was not readily available; what it more, his knowledge of Chinese was somewhat limited at the time, and there was no one to assist him. Suddenly, however, a volume fell from a shelf at his feet. Picking it up, he found it contained precisely the information required.

In his book *Coincidence, A Matter of Chance – or Synchronicity,* Brian Inglis, writer and researcher into the paranormal, also describes broadcaster Alistair Cooke's experience with the library angel. Pulling down a volume from a shelf, he noticed he had unfortunately picked the wrong one. In fact, it was on a different subject altogether: the *Good Food Guide* for 1972. However, he immediately realised that it would be just what he needed for a programme on the subject of inflation that he had to record in a few days' time, and he was able to find reference to a meal costing £3-4, thought to be rather expensive at the time.

Investigators are still puzzled by the nature of the phenomenon. Does the library angel really exist? Is it pure serendipity – happy chance? Or is some form of intuition perhaps at work?

The great leap forward happened when two of Europe's most brilliant minds collaborated to produce a most searching book on the powers of coincidence – one that was to provoke both controversy and attack from rival theorists working in this area.

These two men were Wolfgang Pauli – whose daringly conceived exclusion principle earned him the Nobel Prize for Physics – and the Swiss psychologist-philosopher, Carl Gustav Jung. Their treatise bore the unexciting title *Synchronicity, An Acausal Connecting Principle;* but it was described by one American reviewer as 'the paranormal equivalent of a nuclear explosion'.

ORDER OUT OF CHAOS

According to Pauli, coincidences are 'the visible traces of untraceable principles'. Coincidences, elaborated Jung, whether they come singly or in series, are manifestations of a barely understood universal principle that operates quite independently of the known laws of physics. Interpreters of the Pauli-Jung theory have even concluded that telepathy and precognition are also manifestations of a single mysterious force at work in the Universe that is trying to impose its own kind of discipline on the utter confusion of human life.

Arthur Koestler,* above, *wrote extensively about the search for a scientific explanation that would account for coincidences, or 'puns of destiny', as he called them.

But of all recent investigators, none wrote more extensively about the theory of coincidence than Arthur Koestler, who summed up the phenomenon in the vivid phrase 'puns of destiny'.

FICTION INTO FACT

One particularly striking 'pun' was related to Koestler by a 12-year-old English schoolboy named Nigel Parker:

'Many years ago, the American horror-story writer, Edgar Allan Poe, wrote a book called *The Narrative of Arthur Gordon Pym.* In it, Mr Pym was travelling in a ship that wrecked. The four survivors were in an open boat for many days before they decided to kill and eat the cabin boy, whose name was Richard Parker.

'Some years *later,* in the summer of 1884, my great-grandfather's cousin was cabin boy in the yawl *Mignonette* when she foundered, and the four survivors were in an open boat for many days. Eventually, the three senior members of the crew killed and ate the cabin boy. His name was Richard Parker'.

Such strange and seemingly meaningful incidents abound. Can there really be no more to them than mere coincidence?

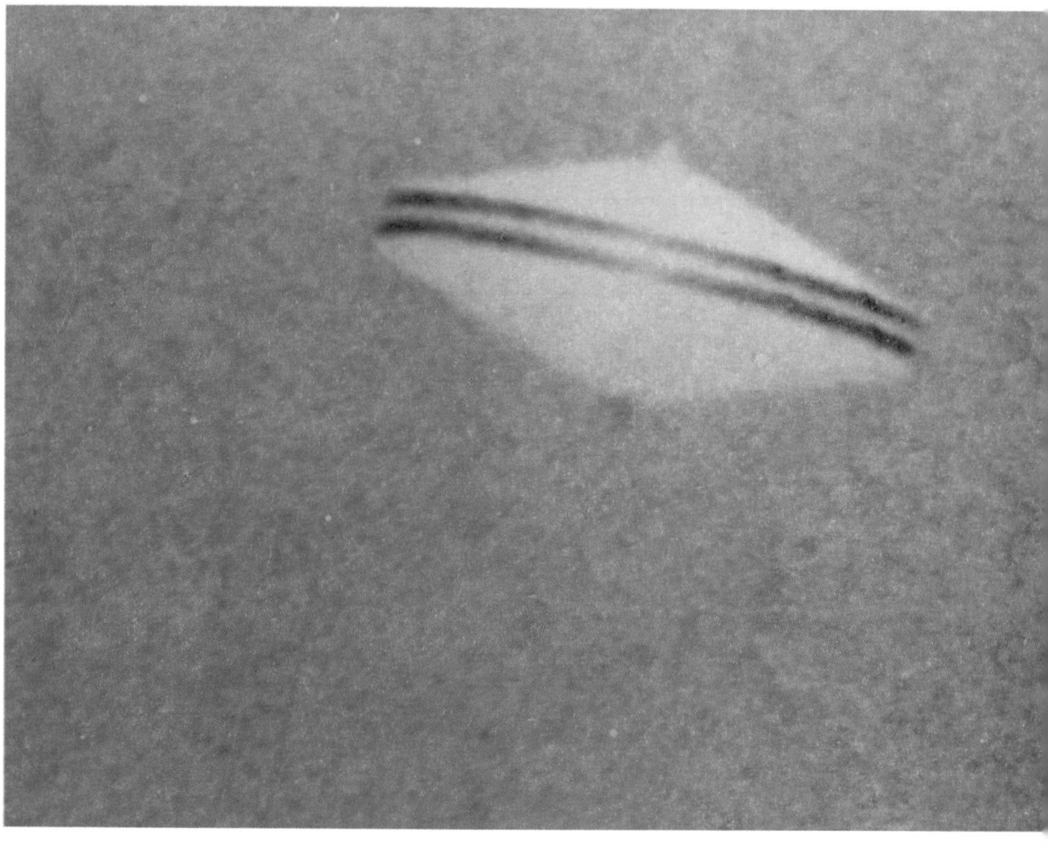

The 'long object with a hump on its back', **above,** was photographed over Bear Mountain in New York State by an anonymous witness on 18 December 1966. The sighting was reported to the US Air Force's Project Blue Book who took possession of two photographs and a negative, and also held exhaustive interviews with the witness. Although the US Air Force's own technicians could find no evidence of fraud, the file was nevertheless labelled 'Hoax'. Dr. J. Allen Hynek wrote to Major Hector Quintanilla (then Chief of Project Blue Book) saying: '... the lack of satisfactory explanation of the unidentified object does not constitute sufficient reason to declare [it] a hoax... My recommendation is... that the evaluation be changed from hoax to unidentified'. Despite this recommendation, the 'Hoax' label has remained.

The two frames, **below** and **below left,** are from a film said to be of 'an approaching UFO', and were taken by Daniel W. Fry during May 1964 near his home in Merlin, Oregon, using a 16-millimetre Bell and Howell movie camera. The UFO, described by Fry as 'spinning like a top during flight', was by no means the first alien craft Fry claimed to have encountered. It was, according to him, some 14 years previously, in 1950, that he had witnessed his first 'flying saucer' landing, and during the next four years he claims he was a contactee of beings described by him as 'the Space People'. They allegedly told him that they are the descendants of a lost super-race originally from Earth who survived a nuclear holocaust over 30,000 years ago and fled to live on Mars. Later they abandoned Mars and now live exclusively in their spacecraft.

Another 'Martian spacecraft', photographed by Daniel W. Fry, with the same movie camera, is shown **above right** and **right.** The time is May 1965 and the place, Joshua Tree, California. This craft was also described as 'spinning like a top' in the sky. Fry, a former employee of the Aerojet General Corporation (where he was 'in charge of installation of instruments for missile control and guidance'), is considered to be the most technically orientated of modern contactees. Sceptics have pointed out, however, that this technical background might also provide him with opportunities to produce fake photographs of a high standard, but there is no conclusive evidence that these two images are fakes.

CASEBOOK

SIGHTINGS AND SIDE-EFFECTS

ANIMALS AND HUMANS FREQUENTLY SUFFER PHYSICAL REACTIONS TO UFO VISITATIONS SUCH AS BUZZING IN THE EARS OR DIZZINESS. IN THE CASES THAT FOLLOW, ZOO ANIMALS STAMPEDE, SOLDIERS ARE PARALYSED, AND AN ARGENTINIAN GIRL WEEPS FOR DAYS AFTER AN EXTRAORDINARY CLOSE ENCOUNTER WITH A HUMANOID

The artists impressions, **above,** *and* **far right,** *show the sightings at Tananarive, Madagascar, in August 1954.*

One of the most spectacular of all 'light in the sky' UFO sightings took place over the city of Tananarive, capital of Madagascar (the Malagasy Republic), one day in August 1954.

Edmond Campagnac, head of Technical Services of Air France, was waiting at the time with a group of people outside the Air France office on the Avenue de la Libération for the arrival of the mail from Paris.

Suddenly, Campagnac saw a luminous green ball in the sky. It was descending, almost vertically, like a meteorite. Other people followed his gaze, and the object was seen to disappear behind mountains to the south of the city.

The time was 5.45 p.m. and dusk was approaching, although the setting sun was still visible. While the group waited outside the Air France office, they were joined by scores of others on the streets as people began their journeys home from work. They, too, were witnesses to the luminous ball.

The witnesses were still watching when an object of the same colour as that seen seconds earlier appeared over the hills near the old Queen's Palace, this time 'flying' horizontally and at a slower speed. The UFO curved past the government buildings, still appearing like a green ball. Soon it was descending even lower, almost to roof-top height, and heading along the eastern side of the Avenue de la Libération, just above the building opposite the Air France office.

Then, as the light drew level with the group, they saw that it was in fact *two* objects. A lentil-shaped device was leading the way, and this was described as having the colour of an 'electric-green luminous gas'. Following some 100 feet (30 metres) behind was a metallic-looking cylindrical object, probably about 130 feet (40 metres) in length. While described by some as a 'cigar', others said it looked more like the fuselage of the contemporary Constellation aircraft shorn of fins, elevators, wings and engines. The surface of the cylinder reflected the dying rays of the sun, while behind it there splayed a plume of orange-red flame. Eyewitnesses estimated that the objects were travelling in the region of 185 miles per hour (300 km/h).

People stopped and gazed in amazement at the phenomenon, so much so that a pall of quietness hung over the city. The giant cigar and its lenticular companion were completely silent. Then there was another shock for the observers. As the objects went over the buildings, all the electric lights were extinguished, coming on again only after the objects had passed.

The strange aerial duo continued over the city towards Tananarive airport, and then swung away to the West. Before passing from sight, they skimmed over a zoological park where the animals, which were normally quiet and undisturbed by aircraft flying into and out of the airport, went into a panic and stampeded through fences. It was several hours before soldiers and police could round them up, and before they returned to a somewhat calmer state.

Not surprisingly, there was a great furore in Tananarive over this invasion of Madagascan airspace, and an official enquiry was set up by General Fleurquin, the Air Force Commandant. This was conducted by Father Coze, director of the Tananarive Observatory. Father Coze had been at the observatory at the time of the incident and had himself witnessed the passage of the UFOs. He estimated that at least 20,000 people had seen the objects, and he and his helpers questioned more than 5,000 witnesses in all, in order to prepare a deatiled report.

It is not known what happened to his report of this remarkable encounter. If it ever reached France, it certainly failed to arouse interest. Details were known only to a handful of French researchers and to *Flying Saucer Review,* which received an account from René Fouéré of the *Groupement d'Etude de Phénomènes Aeriens* (GEPA). But not a hint of the affair was revealed to the French public until 1974, when Jean-Claude Bourret broadcast his famous series of programmes on Radio France-Inter, transcripts of which appeared in his book, *The Crack in the Universe.*

A further close encounter – with a craft like a shining egg, depicted* below *– took place in the Malagasy Republic, in May 1967.

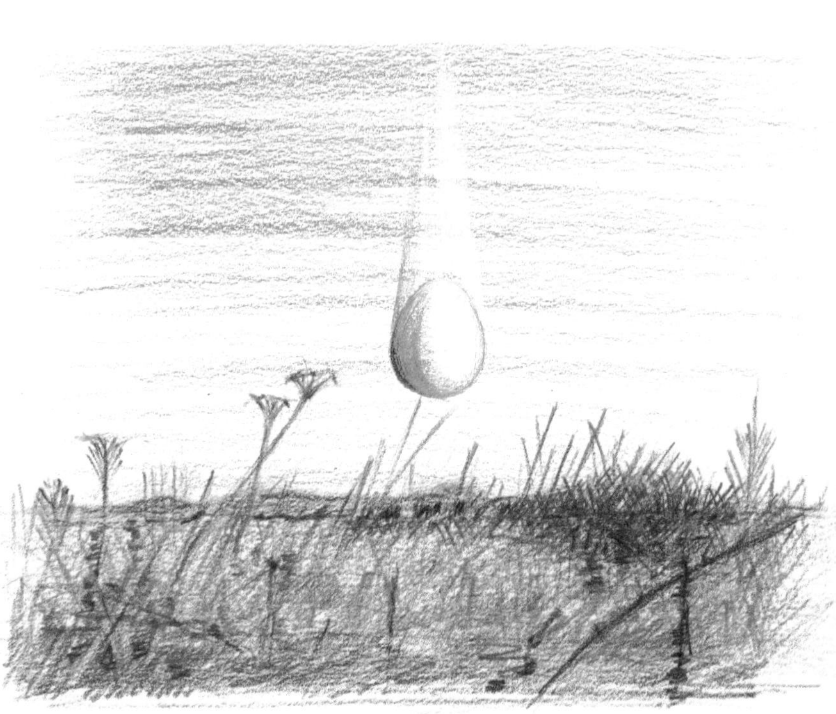

A Shining Egg

In May 1967, there was another alarming close encounter in Madagascar. But it was to take 10 years before news of the incident reached *Flying Saucer Review* from the French research group *Lumières dans la Nuit.* On this occasion, the reason for the extraordinary delay was that the witnesses were 23 soldiers, their officer and four NCOs of the French Foreign Legion, and they were forbidden to discuss the affair with anyone at all. The eventual informant was a legionnaire named Wolff.

Wolff's platoon, which was on a reconnaissance exercise, had halted at noon in a clearing in the bush country. The troops were eating lunch when they all saw a bright metallic object resembling a 'shining egg' descend rapidly from the sky like a falling leaf, accompanied by a piercing, whistling sound, before thumping on to the ground. All the soldiers were 'paralysed' and, seemingly immediately, saw the object take off. But when watches were checked, the time was 3.15 p.m., which meant that all of three hours had somehow passed.

Wolff claimed that the object was about 23 feet (7 metres) high and 10-13 feet (3-4 metres) wide at the widest part. It rose slowly at first, and then vanished at high speed, as though 'sucked up into the

CASEBOOK

A close encounter of the third kind, involving contact with a humanoid, depicted **below right**, *took place at a roadhouse in Córdoba, Argentina, shown in the artist's impression,* **above.**

sky'. It left three marks in the ground that looked as if they had been made by legs, and a 10-foot (3-metre) deep crater, at the bottom of which was a sort of vitrified ring of coloured crystals.

None of the witnesses could recall what had happened during the missing hours; but for two days afterwards, they all had violent headaches, with constant 'beating' in the region of the temples and a continual buzzing sound in the ears.

FACE-TO-FACE

The Motel La Cuesta is a well-appointed roadhouse, situated on Highway 20 – a major road that connects the town of Villa Carlos Paz, in the province of Córdoba, with eastern Argentina. The small country town is about 500 miles (800 kilometres) to the west of Buenos Aires.

The motel's proprietor, Pedro Pretzel, 39, lived at the motel with his wife and his 19-year-old daughter, Maria Eladia.

On the night of 13 June 1968, at about 12.50 a.m., Pretzel was walking home when he saw, some 55 yards (50 metres) beyond the motel – and apparently on the highway – an object that he could not identify. It had two bright red lights, but could not have been a car because it projected beams of peculiar intensity at the motel. This 'machine' was in view for only a few seconds. Puzzled and alarmed by what he had seen, Pretzel ran to his motel and found Maria Eladia lying in a dead faint, close to the kitchen door. Once revived, she had a bizarre tale to tell.

Only a few minutes earlier, she had said goodnight to her fiancé and had escorted some guests to the door. She then returned to the kitchen. Suddenly, she noticed that the lobby was flooded with light. As she had just switched off the lights, she went to investigate, and was horrified to find herself face-to-face with a 'man' some 6 feet (2 metres) tall, dressed in a kind of diver's suit that had shiny, sky-blue scales. He was fair-haired, and was holding up his left hand, on the palm of which a sky-blue ball, or sphere, appeared to be moving about of its own accord.

Maria said there was a huge ring on the fourth finger of the creature's right hand, which he moved up and down constantly in front of her. Light came from the creature's finger-tips and feet, and it seemed to Maria that she was overcome by a lethargic feeling when the light was pointed directly at her. But apart from this, the humanoid showed no signs of aggression or ill-will. Indeed, Maria remembers an impression of 'goodness and kindness' emanating from the being who, she added, smiled throughout the encounter. She said he also seemed to be trying to communicate with her; for, although his lips did not move at all, she could hear an unintelligible mumble that sounded in some respects 'like Chinese'.

After a few minutes – during which Maria stood transfixed in the presence of the humanoid – he walked, with slow, precise movements, to the side door, which was open. He went out, and the door seemed to close of its own accord. It was at that moment that Maria lost consciousness. Shortly afterwards, her father came home and discovered her on the floor.

Pretzel reported the incident to the police, who promised to investigate it. As for Maria, she became extremely nervous, and was subject to fits of weeping for some days after the affair.

The incident poses many intriguing possibilities. Had Maria Eladia Pretzel witnessed a projected image – that of a 'man' in her kitchen – that was emitted from the UFO which her father had seen on the nearby highway? Could the 'humanoid' even have been a hologram, transmitted by laser beams and projected against, say, the glass of the lobby window? The intense beams of light seemed to have been emitted by the UFO, and it was presumably this light that first attracted Maria's attention. These questions remain as yet unanswered, in spite of investigations.

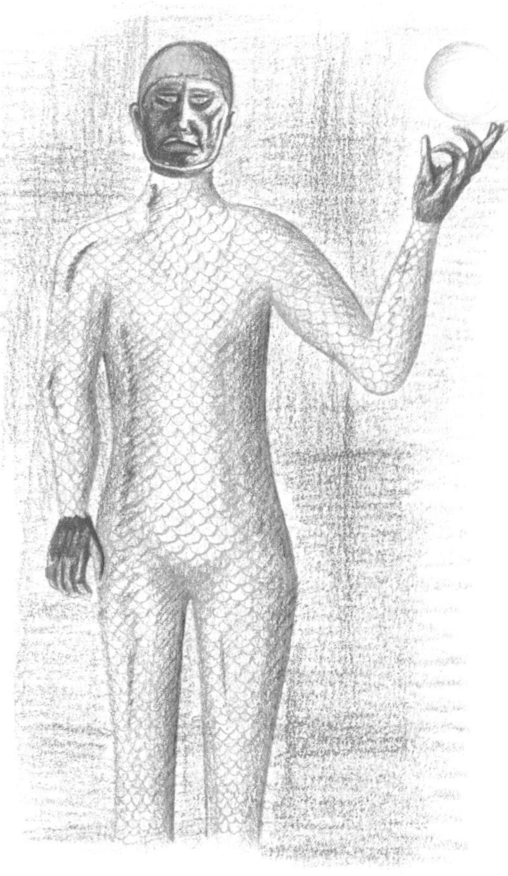

IN SEARCH OF APPARITIONS

NO TWO PHANTOMS ARE ALIKE, AND A GOOD GHOST-HUNTER WILL APPROACH EACH HAUNTING DIFFERENTLY. HOW DO SERIOUS RESEARCHERS GO ABOUT THEIR BUSINESS, AND WHAT KIND OF EVIDENCE DO THEY SEEK?

'Fear came upon me, and trembling, which made all my bones to shake. Then a spirit passed before my face; the hair of my flesh stood up. It stood still, but I could not discern the form thereof.'

This is how the experience of seeing a ghost is described in the *Book of Job* 4: 14-16. To many, including Job, encounters with ghosts have been, quite literally, hair-raising. But fortunately, some people, far from being frightened, are willing actively to seek out ghosts and investigate them.

The existence of ghosts has been accepted without question in almost all cultures throughout history. Only with the growth of a rationalist, scientific outlook in the West in the last few centuries have their existence and nature been disputed, many people responding to the idea of ghosts with an irrational blend of fear, ridicule and laughter. The tendency is to reject what we do not understand, rather than face the possibility that there are indeed more things in heaven and earth than are ever dreamed of, let alone taken seriously, by the scientific establishment.

Ghosts are even rejected by people who have actually seen them. 'I saw it, but I still don't believe it!' is a commonly reported reaction, for the human mind instinctively rejects information it cannot assimilate and interpret. Clearly, better evidence, and more of it, is needed before the ghost will ever find its way into physics and biology textbooks.

But what, to begin with, is a ghost? Dictionaries define it as the supposed disembodied spirit, or soul, of a dead person. The British Society for

Dreadful cries are said to have come from the skull, **below,** *of a West Indian slave, until his body was sent for burial in his homeland.*

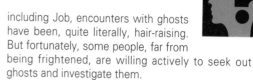

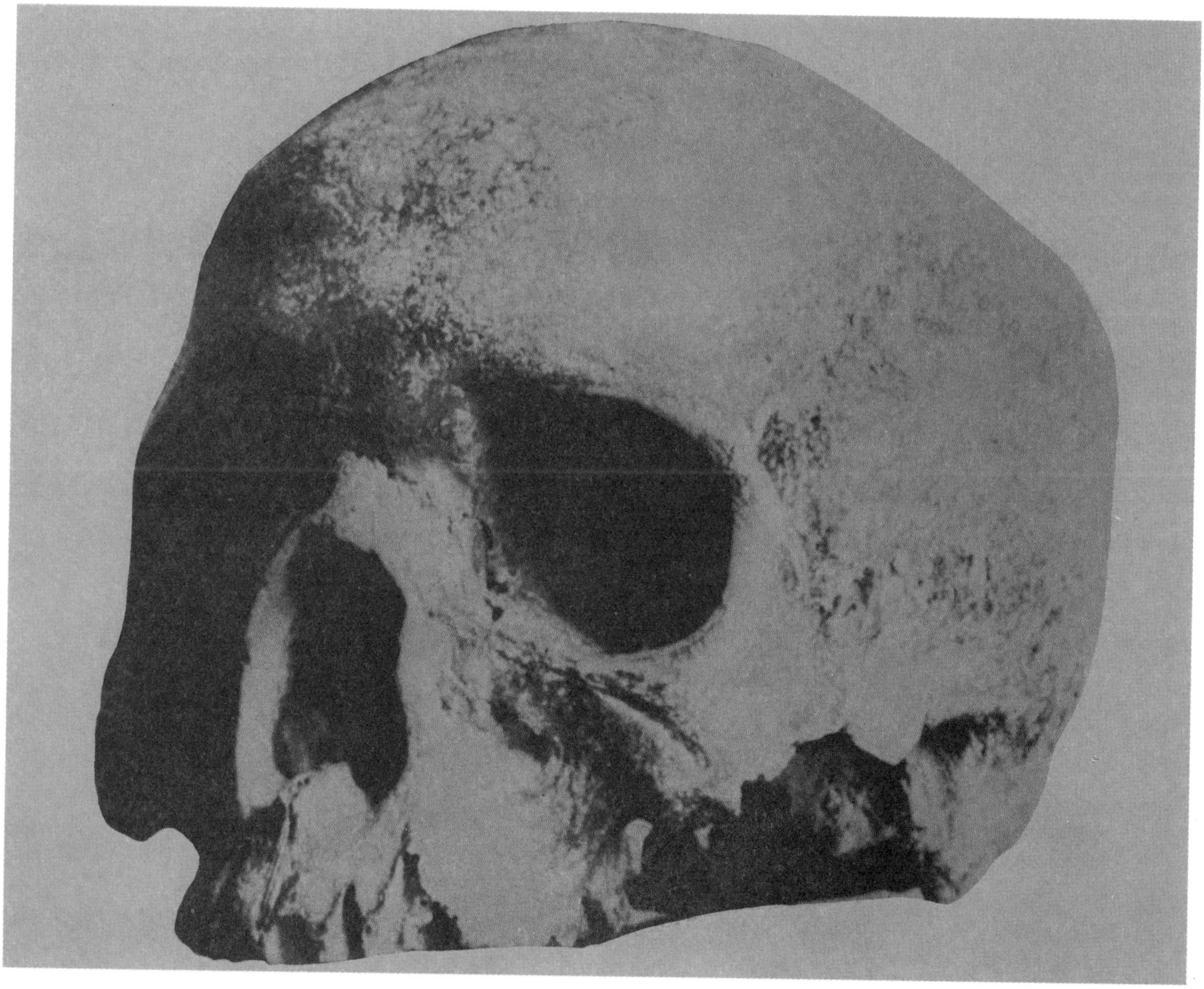

The ghost lent itself to study. Over the following seven years, six people besides the student saw the ghost, which closely resembled a known former occupant of the house, while some 20 people heard sounds apparently made by it. Sightings followed a regular pattern: the figure would walk downstairs (the resourceful student sometimes tied threads across the stairs, but they remained unbroken), enter the drawing-room and stand in the window. Then it would leave the room by the door, walk along the passage and disappear.

Cornering a Phantom

The student, who must have been exceptionally courageous, made frequent attempts to converse with the ghost; but although it seemed aware of her presence, it never replied. She also tried to touch it, but it always got out of the way. Once she saw the figure at the usual window and asked her father if he, too, could see it, but he could not. When he walked to the window, the phantom promptly walked round him.

The family's cat took no notice at all of the ghost. The dogs, however, frequently reacted as if they had seen somebody. One would run to the foot of the stairs, wag its tail and jump up as if waiting to be patted, but then back away with its tail between its legs and hide under a sofa. Another dog was often found 'in a state of terror' for no obvious reason. (This sensitivity of some animals to supernatural presences has prompted their use as 'ghost-detectors' by some investigators.)

While the nature of ghosts is still mysterious, their behaviour has actually been studied in some detail. G.N.M. Tyrrell, for instance, in his book *Apparitions*, identified four main groups by their distinct patterns of activity.

The first of Tyrrell's groups consists of apparitions that haunt certain places. These are what are now termed 'place-centred', rather than 'person-centred'. On the whole, they do not arouse fear and they sometimes come to be treated as part of the family. They rarely do any harm.

Psychical Research once conducted a large-scale survey of experiences of apparitions, asking the question:

'Have you ever, when believing yourself to be completely awake, had a vivid impression of seeing or being touched by a living being or inanimate object, or hearing a voice; which impression, so far as you could discover, was not due to any external physical cause?'

Almost 10 per cent of the 17,000 people who replied said 'yes'. Later surveys in several other countries confirm this picture.

Isolated appearances of a ghost may be undramatic; but when repeated over a long period, they become worthy of study. An example is a ghost reported by a medical student. She wrote:

'I saw the figure of a tall lady dressed in black, standing at the head of the stairs. After a few moments, she descended the stairs, and I followed for a short distance, feeling curious what it could be. I had only a small piece of candle, and it suddenly burnt itself out; and being unable to see more, I went to my room.'

***The Brown Lady of Raynham Hall in Norfolk,* above, was seen by the photographer, as well as captured on film.**

***The form of a kneeling monk,* right, appears in this picture, taken by a local solicitor in St Nicholas' Church, Arundel.**

In Focus

While Gladys Hayter sits in trance, a phantom hand appears, unseen in the darkness but captured in the infra-red photograph, right.

THE AMAZING GLADYS HAYTER

East London psychic, Gladys Hayter, frequently displayed the ability to cause phantoms to materialise, and living people and inanimate objects to dematerialise and change position. What is more, all this often took place under the gaze of the camera. Mrs Hayter, who already practised psychic healing, began photographing strange phenomena with a simple Instamatic camera. Glowing streaks of 'ectoplasm' often appeared, emerging from her body. Sometimes, her image did not even appear in the picture, although, as she insisted, she had not moved. In fact, she claimed to be unable to move when in trance during one of these sessions. The picture shown here is one of a number taken by a local photographer, using infra-red film in near-darkness. The camera on the tripod is Gladys Hayter's own.

The second category consists of post-mortem apparitions, taking place after the death of the person seen, and not related in any way to a particular place or event.

Thirdly, there are crisis cases, in which the apparition is of someone who is undergoing some profound experience at the time (often unknown to the percipient), such as an accident or illness – or, of course, death.

The last of Tyrrell's categories is the least-known type of apparition, but perhaps the most intriguing of all: the experimentally-induced apparition. Ghosts in these cases are not of dead or dying people but of individuals alive and well who have deliberately attempted to make their images visible to others at a distance. Tyrrell found records of 16 successful attempts of this type, and wondered why such evidently repeatable experiments had seemingly been ignored by researchers. It remains a neglected area of study; and, although there have been considerable recent investigations into 'out-of-the-body' experiences, reports of self-induced visibility at a distance remain rare.

Those ghosts for which evidence is most compelling, however, and that critical researchers have concluded are genuine, usually show a number of features. Such a ghost appears solid; it is visible when viewed in a mirror; and it makes sounds appropriate to its movements. It generally gives the impression of being as real as a living person, even if this is only for a limited period; and a sensation of sudden cold may be felt by those in its presence.

> THE SENSITIVITY OF SOME ANIMALS TO SUPERNATURAL PRESENCES HAS PROMPTED THEIR USE AS GHOST-DETECTORS BY SOME INVESTIGATORS.

The kneeling figure in the photograph of the altar of St Mary's Church, Woodford, below, *was not seen by the photographer at the time that the picture was taken.*

JOINT CREATIONS?

When a ghost is seen by only one person, the suspicion arises of hallucination, error or deception. But ghosts are often seen by more than one person at the same time, though not necessarily by everybody present. This is often sufficient to rule out the possibility of deception or mistake, but the true nature of the apparition remains unknown. It may not necessarily be a disembodied spirit: it could, for instance, be an 'intersubjective' phenomenon, the *joint* creation of the percipients' minds.

An apparition may also sometimes provide plain evidence of its non-physical nature. It may pass through walls; appear and disappear through phantom doors that open and close while 'real' doors stay closed; or become transparent and fade away, for instance.

These elusive wraiths can apparently be recorded on photographic film. Indeed, there are many alleged photographs of ghosts, but few are convincing; and fraud has been so prevalent in the field of psychic photography that attention has been diverted from the rare examples that may well be the real

Two ghostly forms, right, appear behind the figure of an English lady, Miss Townsend, in the Basilica at Domrémy, in France. The apparitions were unseen by her companion, Lady Palmer, when she took this photograph during a visit in 1925. The vicar of a church at Newby, North Yorkshire, the Reverend K.F. Lord, was equally amazed to find a rather strange form on his developed photograph of the altar, shown below.

thing. One impressive case took place at Raynham Hall, Norfolk, home of the Marquis of Townshend. A professional photographer and his assistant reported seeing a ghostly figure coming down the stairs. The picture taken at that time, which has been pronounced genuine by photographic experts, does indeed show a misty form. The house has a long history of haunting by a lady in brown, who was seen simultaneously by two witnesses in 1835. Later, she was seen by the author Captain Marryat, who ungallantly fired a shotgun at her. Despite this unwelcoming action, she was seen again in 1926 by Lord Townshend and two other witnesses as well.

Ghostly Worshippers

Convincing pictures of ghosts have also been taken in churches. In 1940, a local solicitor snapped an unmistakably human form in front of the altar of St Nicholas' church, in Arundel, Sussex. More solid in appearance than the brown lady of Raynham Hall, it was still partly transparent; and some have interpreted it as the figure of a kneeling priest. But the prize for technical quality of a ghost photograph must surely go to the Reverend K.F. Lord of Newby, in Yorkshire, who recorded the presence of a very clear, hollow-eyed spook before his altar, as shown below on this page.

No photographs, however, are as persuasive as the best eyewitness accounts. Cumulatively, the weight of evidence, of all kinds, suggests that ghosts do exist. But, despite a century of intensive research, what they are, and the conditions under which they manifest themselves, are questions still awaiting a definitive answer.

DEAD BUT NOT DECAYED

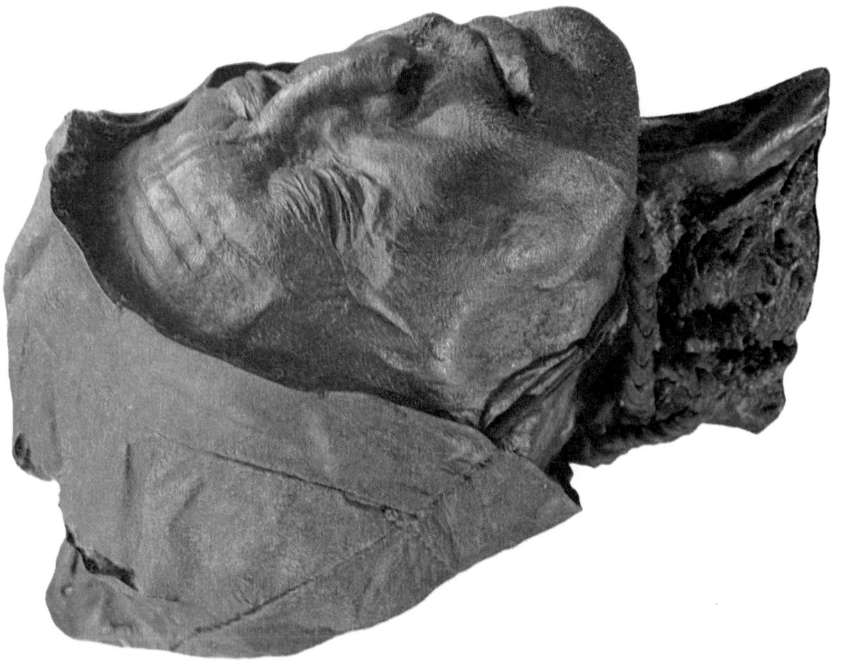

THE PHENOMENON OF DEAD BODIES THAT DO NOT DECAY MAY OFTEN BE EXPLAINED IN NATURAL TERMS, BUT THERE REMAIN MANY CASES OF INCORRUPTIBILITY THAT SEEM TO DEFY ANY FORM OF RATIONAL EXPLANATION

Records of the Saints of the Catholic church contain the greatest concentration of so-called incorruptibles – bodies of mystics who, in the words of Church historian Father Thurston, have resisted 'the horror of the tomb'. However, Roman Catholics have no monopoly of bodies that appear to defy decay: they are met with in every branch of the Christian Church, and also among many other religions. Descriptions strikingly similar to the Catholic accounts are even to be found in the Chinese annals known as *The Lives of the Buddhist Saints.*

The Iron Age head,* above, *is of a sacrificial victim. It has been perfectly preserved – if extremely discoloured – by the natural chemical processes of the bog into which he was thrown.

Below are remains, most of which have turned into adipocere, a soap-like substance.

The story of Hui Neng, one of the best known of the Ch'an (or Zen) patriarchs, is particularly remarkable. Hui Neng died in AD 712 and was buried in the Kuo-en monastery, where he had taught, in Kwantung province. During the fall of the Sung Dynasty, in 1276, Mongol troops dragged out his body to see for themselves his rumoured miraculous preservation. After 564 years, the Zen master's skin was still flexible and glossy, and there was no sign of collapsing or shrinking. The desecrators then cut open the body and were astonished to find the heart and liver in perfect condition. Completely taken aback, they decided to depart immediately without further sacrilege.

DIVINE FAVOUR

The phenomenon also occurs today. In 1977, for instance, a family grave in Espartinas, Spain, was opened to inter the body of a local man. The sexton and his helpers were shocked to find that the body of the man's son was still intact after 40 years. The boy, José Garcia Moreno, had died in 1937 of meningitis at the age of 11, and the family deny that he was embalmed. Soon the whole village had viewed the body in its rotting grave-clothes; and, believing the boy must have been a saint to be so 'favoured', they began to petition Rome for his canonisation. However, as Father Thurston has pointed out, phenomena such as stigmata, visions, levitation or incorruption are less important to the Congregation for the Causes of Saints than a life of piety and virtue; and the young boy has not been canonised in view of this.

Another case has come to light with only minimal religious colouring. In 1644, a beautiful Hungarian countess, Zofia Bosniakova, died at the age of 35, having been married twice and with one son. Her first husband had died within a year of her marriage at 17, and the brawling promiscuous ways of her second husband – Franco Wesselenyi, a renowned swordsman and diplomat – made her retreat into a simple, pious life in Strecno Castle, in northern Slovakia. During renovations of the castle in 1689, her coffin was opened to reveal her flawless beauty. According to local history, which may not be entirely reliable, 'The Lady of Strecno', although not beatified, lies in state today in a church in Teplice-Sanov, Czechoslovakia, in a robe she made herself. She is said to be still beautiful after over 300 years.

CASEBOOK

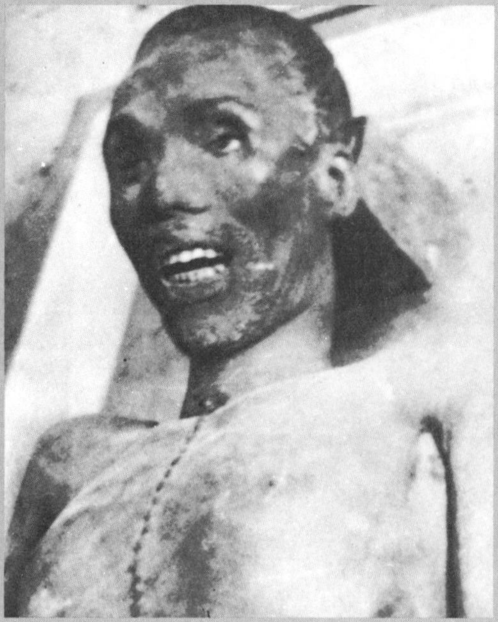

A LEGEND IN THE MAKING

At the end of 1980, in the ancient city of Kano in northern Nigeria, state troops were called in to quell a riot caused by the followers of a heretical Muslim cult, led by the self-styled prophet Muhammadu Marwa (or Maitatsine, as he was also known). Marwa established his headquarters in Kano during the 1960s and thereafter he is said to have attracted some 10,000 followers. Tension between his sect and the orthodox Muslims exploded into a riot in December 1980, during which as many as 8,000 people were killed, including Marwa himself.

At first, Marwa was buried in the bare earth in a shallow grave; but three weeks later the Governor gave orders that his body, *left*, be exhumed and placed on ice at the city mortuary. Rumour soon spread among the people of Kano that Marwa's body was miraculously incorruptible.

So what are the hypotheses most frequently put forward as alternatives to the idea of a miracle? Various kinds of embalming can safely be ignored, since in most fully authenticated cases it is clear from medical examination that no preservatives have been used and none of the viscera removed. Some bodies, however, like that of St Francis Xavier, did have internal organs removed for use as holy relics. Indeed, the incorruptible state was discovered only when the tomb was first opened to take such relics.

HOLY RELICS

Joan Cruz, author of *The Incorruptibles*, outlined three categories of preserved bodies: those preserved deliberately; the accidentally or naturally preserved; and true incorruptibles. Those that fit into the second category show effects no less wonderful for having a mundane explanation; and both Father Thurston and Cruz cite many places that have reputations for preserving human bodies (not always in a mummified form). Cruz, for instance, mentions the discovery of a natural mummy in a mountain cave in Chile in 1954, thought to be the body of a boy who had been drugged and left there to freeze as a sacrifice about 500 years previously. Bodies of Iron Age people have also been found perfectly preserved in peat bogs, but they are greatly discoloured by natural chemical processes. Preservations in alcohol, formaldehyde, honey, rum, sand, salt, and many other unusual compounds – including guano – have been known too; but such bodies are not true incorruptibles.

Certain sites have also been deliberately chosen as burial grounds because their natural conditions delay the onset or acceleration of decomposition. The Capuchin catacombs of Palermo and Malta are famous for their gruesome specimens, of which one 19th-century travel writer wrote: 'They are all dressed in the clothes they usually wore... the skin and muscles become as dry and hard as a piece of stockfish, and though many of them have been here upwards of 250 years, yet none are reduced to skeletons'. In the 18th century, burial in the lead-lined crypt of the cathedral at Bremen even became fashionable among the German aristocracy, after the discover of the astonishingly well-preserved body of a workman who had met with a fatal accident down there several years earlier.

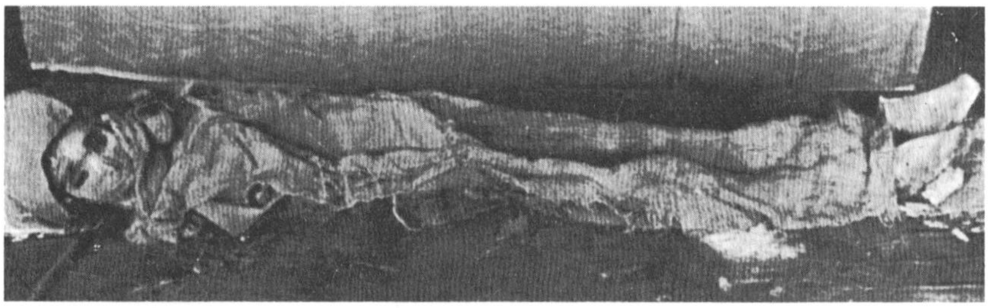

The young lady of Loulan, centre, was unearthed in China's remote Xinjiang province in 1981. Experts claim that this 6470-year-old mummy is the oldest in the world.

Julia Buccola Petta, above, was exhumed in 1927 – six years after her death. Her preservation was believed to be miraculous. This photograph was taken to be made into the plaque that now adorns her grave in Mount Carmel Cemetery, Hillside, Illinois.

DRY AIR

The vaults under St Michan's Church in Dublin have similar qualities. A survey of the church in 1901 mentions, for instance, the striking example of 'a pathetic baby corpse, from whose whole plump wrists still hang the faded white ribbons of its funeral', with the date 1679 on the coffin. The preservative effect is believed to be caused by the extreme dryness of the air and its freedom from dust – conditions that also prevail in the Russian necropolis at Kiev, in which a large number of withered bodies lie in their open coffins (now covered with glass).

Radiation, meanwhile, was suggested as the preserving agent of the 250-year-old desiccated bodies found in the Wasserburg Somersdorf Castle, at Mittelfranken, Germany. But even though tiny amounts of radiation have been detected in the castle tombs, this does not explain all odd mummifications, nor truly intact bodies.

A further consideration is the curious natural process known as *saponification*. In this, as the name suggests, the body tissues are turned into an ammoniacal soap beneath a toughened outer skin. This soap-like substance is called *adipocere* (from the Latin *adeps* for fat, and *cera,* meaning wax) – or *gras de cadavre* (French, for 'corpse fat'). It is caused by burial in damp soil in the proximity of putrefaction. Why it develops in some cases and not others is unknown. A certain Monsieur Thouret, who was commissioned to clear the cemetery of the Church of the Holy Innocents in Paris, in 1785, found that many bodies had converted to adipocere, and described them as follows:

'The bodies themselves, having lost nothing of their bulk, and appearing to be wrapped in their shrouds, like so many larvae, had, to all seeming, suffered no decay. On tearing apart the grave-clothes which enveloped them, the only change one noticed consisted in this, that they had been converted into a flabby mass or substance, the whiteness of which stood out the more clearly in contrast to the blackness in which they lay'.

Saponification is unusual but not rare: there is a saponified soldier from the United States Civil War period in the Smithsonian Museum, Washington, for instance. It even seems likely that a few cases of alleged incorruption might have been due to adipocere. The exhumation of Blessed Marie de Sainte-Euphrasie Pelletier, who died in 1868, seems to support this idea. Thirty-five years later, her lead coffin was opened to reveal the recognisable features of the foundress of the Good Shepherd Nuns.

A grisly display of dead Capuchin monks hangs, like so many broken dolls, in the catacombs in Palermo, Sicily,* below. *Most bodies left exposed to the air decay approximately eight times faster than those that are buried – but the air in these catacombs has the peculiar property of drying out the bodies and turning them into natural mummies.

'The mouth was slightly open, the eyes shut, the eyelashes intact,' wrote one examining doctor. Without unclothing the body, he was 'able to ascertain that the chest, the abdomen, the thighs and the legs were covered with a skin like that of a mummy, under which was a mass of *gras de cadavre,* resulting from the saponification of the tissues underneath'.

> FOR THOSE OF US WHO HAVE LOVED AND ADMIRED CERTAIN OF THESE SAINTS, IT IS A COMFORT OF SORTS TO KNOW THAT ... THEIR ACTUAL BODIES, WHICH WILL ONE DAY BE MADE GLORIOUS, ARE STILL PRESENT AMONG US.
>
> **JOAN CRUZ**

True incorruption triumphs over the condition of the body, the circumstances of the burial and the normal processes of decomposition, however. For some reason, a certain body stays intact while others, in the same place, rot into dust. The Catholic Church sees it as a 'divine favour' to a pious soul, although this is not, on its own, enough for beatification (except in the Russian Orthodox Church). Joan Cruz summarises the value of the relics for Catholics as follows: 'For those of us who have loved and admired certain of these saints, it is a comfort of sorts to know that they are not just somewhere in the great realms beyond, but that their actual bodies, which will one day be made glorious, are still present among us'.

SECULAR CASES

But objective researchers are not blessed with such certainty, for they see authenticated cases occurring outside the Catholic Church, and in most cultures. A secular case, typical of the form in which one might encounter it in folklore, was reported in the *News of the World* on 8 May 1977. It concerned Nadja Mattei, who died in Rome in 1965, aged two. Her mother claimed that for 12 years her dead daughter came to her in dreams, begging to be fetched from her coffin. Early in 1977, the authorities granted her request for exhumation, and baby Nadja's body was found to be quite free of putrefaction.

Authenticated true incorruption is very rare; and each story, both in a religious context and outside it, has a similar structure: an incorrupt body, an eerie persistent fragrance, and frequently attendant paranormal phenomena, such as strange lights around the grave or revelation of incorruption through a dream. The universal similarity in these accounts suggests some kind of archetypal event that transcends ordinary reality. The questions it raises, meanwhile, strike to the core of the nature of our physical and spiritual existence, and even the nature of reality itself.

WHO ARE

Bender's visitors confirmed that he had been right in his speculations as to the true nature of the UFOs – one of them was actually carrying Bender's report, and provided additional information. This so terrified him that he was only too willing to go along with their demand that he close down his organisation, cease publication of his journal at once, and refrain from telling the truth to anyone 'on his honour as an American citizen'.

But did Bender really expect anyone to believe his story? His friends and colleagues were certainly baffled by it. One of them, Gray Barker, even published a sensational book, *They Knew Too Much About Flying Saucers*; and Bender himself supplied an even stranger account in his *Flying Saucers and the Three Men* some years later, in response to persistent demands for an explanation of what had occurred from former colleagues.

He told an extraordinary story, involving extraterrestrial spaceships with bases in Antarctica, that reads like the most far-fetched contactee dream-stuff; and it has even been suggested that the implausibility of Bender's story was specifically designed in order to throw serious UFO investigators off the track.

AS UFO SIGHTINGS INCREASE, SO ALLEGEDLY DOES THE HARASSMENT OF WITNESSES – BY THE SINISTER SO-CALLED MEN IN BLACK

Albert Bender, director of the International Flying Saucer Bureau, an amateur organisation based in Connecticut, USA, once claimed to have discovered the secret behind UFOs. But unfortunately, the rest of the world is still none the wiser – for Bender was prevented from passing on his discovery to the world by three sinister visitors: three men dressed in black, known as 'the silencers'.

It had been Bender's intention to publish his findings in his own journal, *Space Review*. But before committing himself finally, he felt he ought to try his ideas out on a colleague. He therefore mailed his report. A few days later, the men came.

Bender was lying down in his bedroom, overtaken by a sudden spell of dizziness, when he noticed three shadowy figures in the room. Gradually, they became clearer. All were dressed in black clothes. 'They looked like clergymen, but wore hats similar to Homburg style. The faces were not clearly discernible, for the hats partly hid and shaded them. Feelings of fear left me... The eyes of all three figures suddenly lit up like flashlight bulbs, and all these were focussed upon me. They seemed to burn into my very soul as the pains above my eyes became almost unbearable. It was then I sensed that they were conveying a message to me by telepathy.'

Most accounts of MIBs (men in black) describe them as wearing conventional black suits, white shirts and black ties, as illustrated above. Often they are said to look strangely uncomfortable, as if unused to wearing such clothes, while the garments themselves seem brand-new, yet oddly old-fashioned.

The MIBs also have a surreal quality, as if featuring in a nightmare. Even their cars, illustrated right, are said to be disconcertingly new in appearance, yet the models are dated and the number plates, when checked, are frequently discovered never to have been issued.

THE MEN IN BLACK?

However, believable or not, Bender's original account of the visit of the three strangers is of crucial interest to UFO investigators, for the story has been paralleled by many similar reports, frequently from people unlikely to have heard of Bender and his experiences. UFO percipients and investigators are apparently also liable to be visited by men in black (MIBs); and, although most reports are from the United States, similar claims have come from Sweden and Italy, Britain and Mexico. Like the UFO phenomenon itself, MIBs span three decades, and perhaps had precursors in earlier centuries.

VISITATIONS

Like Bender's story, most later reports not only contain implausible details, but are also inherently illogical: in virtually every case, there seems on the face of it more reason to disbelieve than to believe. But this does not eliminate the mystery – it simply requires us to study it in a different light. For, whether or not these things actually happened, the fact remains that they were reported; and why should so many people, independently and often reluctantly, report such strange and sinister visitations? What is more, why is it that the accounts are so similar, echoing and in turn helping to confirm a persistent pattern that, if nothing else, has become one of the most powerful folk myths of our time.

Albert Bender, American UFO investigator, is seen* right*, with one of his many representations of a UFO landing. Bender, an occult and horror enthusiast, claimed that he was prevented from making public his insights into the nature of UFOs by the threats of three MIBs.

The archetypal MIB report runs something like this: shortly after a UFO sighting, the subject – he may be a witness, he may be an investigator on the case – receives a visit. Often it occurs so soon after the incident itself that no official report or media publication has taken place: in short, the visitors should not, by any normal channels, have gained access to the information they clearly possess – names, addresses, and details of the incident, as well as those involved.

The victim is nearly always alone at the time of the visit, usually in his own home. The visitors, usually three in number; arrive in a large black car. In America, it is most often a prestigious Cadillac, but seldom a recent model. Though old in date, however, it is likely to be immaculate in appearance and condition, inside and out, even having that unmistakable 'new car' smell. If the subject notes the registration number and checks it, it is invariably found to be a non-existent number.

The visitors themselves are almost always men: only very rarely is one a woman. In appearance, they conform pretty closely to the stereotyped image of a CIA or secret service man. They wear dark suits, dark hats, dark ties, dark shoes and

> "THE SINISTER VISITS ALMOST INVARIABLY CONCLUDE WITH A WARNING NOT TO TELL ANYBODY ABOUT THE INCIDENT, IF THE SUBJECT IS A UFO PERCIPIENT, OR TO ABANDON INVESTIGATION."

*In*Focus

THE MAN WHO SHOT A HUMANOID

One inclement evening in November 1961, Paul Miller and three companions were returning home to Minot, North Dakota, after a hunting trip when what they could only describe as 'a luminous silo' landed in a nearby field. At first they thought it was a plane crashing, but had to revise their opinion when the 'plane' abruptly vanished. As the hunters drove off, the object reappeared and two humanoids emerged from it. Miller panicked and fired at one of the creatures, apparently wounding it. The other hunters immediately fled.

On their way back to Minot, all of them experienced a blackout and 'lost' three hours. Terrified, they decided not to report the incident to anyone.

Yet the next morning, when Miller reported to work (in an Air Force office), three men in black arrived. They said they were government officials – but showed no credentials – and remarked unpleasantly that they hoped Miller was 'telling the truth' about the UFO. How did they know about it? 'We have a report,' they said vaguely.

'They seemed to know everything about me: where I worked, my name, everything else,' Miller said. They also asked questions about his experience as if they already knew the answers. Miller did not dare tell his story for several years.

socks, but white shirts: and witnesses very often remark on their clean, immaculate turn-out, all the clothes looking as though just purchased.

The visitors' faces are frequently described as 'vaguely foreign', most often 'oriental', and slanted eyes have been specified in many accounts. If not dark-skinned, the men are likely to be very heavily tanned. Sometimes there are bizarre touches: in one case, for instance, a man in black appeared to be wearing bright lipstick! The MIBs are generally unsmiling and expressionless, their movements stiff and awkward. Their general demeanour is formal, cold, sinister, even menacing, and there is no warmth or friendliness shown, even if no outright hostility either. Witnesses often hint that they felt their visitors were not human at all.

> " THE MYSTERY OF THE FLYING SAUCERS IS NO LONGER A MYSTERY. THE SOURCE IS ALREADY KNOWN, BUT INFORMATION IS BEING WITHHELD BY ORDERS FROM A HIGHER SOURCE. "
>
> SPACE REVIEW

Some MIBs proffer evidence of identity; indeed, they sometimes appear in US Air Force or other uniforms. They may also produce identity cards; but since most people would not know a genuine CIA or other 'secret' service identity card if they saw one, this of course proves nothing at all. If they give names, however, these are invariable found to be false.

The interview is sometimes an interrogation, sometimes simply a warning. Either way, the visitors, even though they are asking questions, are clearly very well-informed, with access to restricted information. They speak with perfect, sometimes too perfect, intonation and phrasing, and their language is apt to be reminiscent of the conventional villains of crime films.

MENACING ENCOUNTERS

The sinister visits almost invariably conclude with a warning not to tell anybody about the incident, if the subject is a UFO percipient, or to abandon the investigation, if he is an investigator. Violence is frequently threatened, too. And the MIBs depart as suddenly as they came.

Most well-informed UFO enthusiasts, if asked to describe a typical MIB visit, would give some such account. However, a comparative examination of reports indicates that such 'perfect' MIB visits seldom occur in practice. Study of 32 of the more reliable cases on file reveals that many details diverge quite markedly from the archetypal story: there

were, for instance, no visitors at all in four cases, only subsequent telephone calls; and, of the remainder, only five involved three men, two involved four, five involved two, while in the rest there was mention only of a single visitor.

Although the appearance and behaviour of the visitors does seem generally to conform to the prototype, it ranges from the entirely natural to the totally bizarre. The car, despite the fact that in America it is by far the commonest means of transportation, is in fact mentioned in only one-third of the reports; and as for the picturesque details – the Cadillac, the antiquated model, the immaculate condition – these are, in practice, very much the exception. Of 22 American reports, only nine even include mention of a car; and of these, only three were Cadillacs, while only two were specified as black and only two as out-of-date models.

On the other hand, such archetypal details tend to be more conspicuous in less reliable cases, particularly those in which investigators, rather than UFO percipients, are involved.

The case that comes closest to the archetype is that of Robert Richardson, of Toledo, Ohio, who in July 1967 informed the Aerial Phenomena Research Organization (APRO) that he had collided with a UFO while driving at night. Coming round a bend, he had been confronted by a strange object blocking the road. Unable to halt in time, he had hit it, though not very hard. Immediately on impact, the UFO vanished. Police who accompanied Richardson to the scene could find only his own skid marks as evidence; but on a later visit, Richardson himself found a small lump of metal which might have come from the UFO.

MIBs seem to model their behaviour on that of 'B-movie' heavies, such as Dennis O'Keefe in the 1947 film* T-men, *left.* Not only *do the MIBs resemble the 'tough guys' of the early cinema in dress, as shown in the artist's impression,* above, *but they also use cliché threats that could have been inspired by the scripts of countless indifferent gangster movies.

Three days later, at 11 p.m., two men in their twenties appeared at Richardson's home and questioned him for about 10 minutes. They did not identify themselves, and Richardson – to his own subsequent surprise – did not ask who they were. They were not unfriendly, gave no warnings, and just asked questions. He noted that they left in a black 1953 Cadillac. The number, when checked, was found not yet to have been issued.

A week later, Richardson received a second visit, from two different men, who arrived in a current model Dodge. They wore black suits and were dark-complexioned. Although one spoke perfect English, the second had an accent, and Richardson felt there was something vaguely foreign about them. At first, they seemed to be trying to persuade him that he had not hit anything at all; but then they asked for the piece of metal. When he told them it had gone for analysis, they threatened him: 'If you want your wife to stay as pretty as she is, then you'd better get the metal back'.

The existence of the metal was known only to Richardson and his wife, and to two senior members of APRO. Seemingly, the only way the strangers could have learned of its existence would be by tapping either his or APRO's telephone. There was no clear connection between the two pairs of visitors: but what both had in common was access to information that was not freely and publicly available. Perhaps it is this that is the key to the MIB mystery.

UFO PHOTO FILE

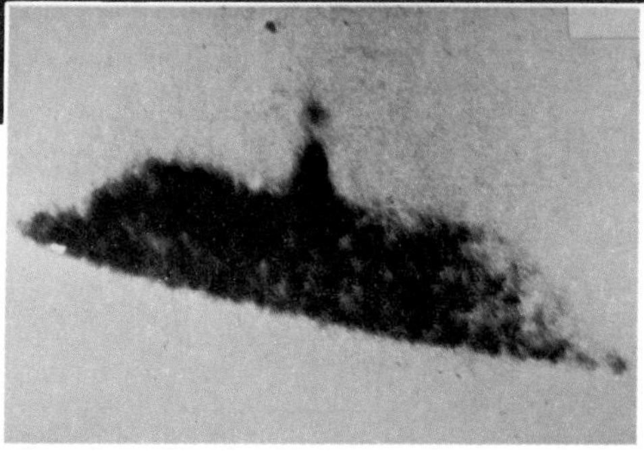

At about 7.45 p.m. on 11 May 1950 at his farm close by the Salmon River Highway, about 10 miles (17km) south-west of McMinnville, Oregon, Paul Trent and his wife claimed they saw a UFO. What is more, they took a remarkable photograph of it.

Mrs Trent was in the yard on the south side of the house, feeding the rabbits, when she saw, to the north-east, moving westwards, a disc-shaped object. She called her husband, who was inside the house. When he realised the unusual nature of the object in the sky, Paul Trent ran to his car for his camera, but his wife remembered that he had left it in the house and hurried to fetch it. It already contained a partly used film.

The object in the sky was tilted up a little as it approached, and appeared bright and silvery. It made no noise, and the Trents saw no smoke or vapour. Paul Trent took the picture, **top,** and wound on the film ready for the next frame, moving to the right to keep the object in the view-finder, and taking a second shot some 30 seconds after the first. Mrs Trent said the object seemed to be gliding, with no rotating or undulating motion. It moved off westwards and 'dimly vanished', as she later put it.

The couple said there was a 'breeze' as the object tilted before flying overhead. The Trents estimated its diameter as 20-30 feet (6-9 metres).

A few days later, when he had used up the remaining frames, Paul Trent had the film developed locally. He did not seek publicity, telling his friends he wanted to avoid being 'in trouble with the government'. However, a reporter from the local **McMinnville Telephone Register** heard of the sighting from two of his friends; and, following it up, found the precious negatives on the floor of the Trents' house, under a writing desk where the Trent children had been playing with them! The **Telephone Register's** story appeared on 8 June 1950. On 9 and 10 June newspapers in Portland, Oregon and in Los Angeles ran the story, and **Life** magazine carried the photographs a week later.

None of this publicity had been sought by the Trents; and when, 17 years after the sighting, they were visited by an investigator from the US Air Force-sponsored Colorado University Commission of Enquiry (whose findings were later published as the **Condon Report**), he found them completely unchanged by their experience, well-liked locally and known as reliable.

The McMinnville UFO, **above left,** is remarkable for its similarity to an object, **above right,** seen and photographed from an aeroplane by a French Air Marshal near Rouen, France, in March 1954.

After submitting the photographs to rigorous scientific examination, the Condon investigation was forced to admit they might be genuine. The official report concluded:

'This is one of the few UFO reports in which all factors investigated, geometric, psychological and physical, appear to be consistent.'

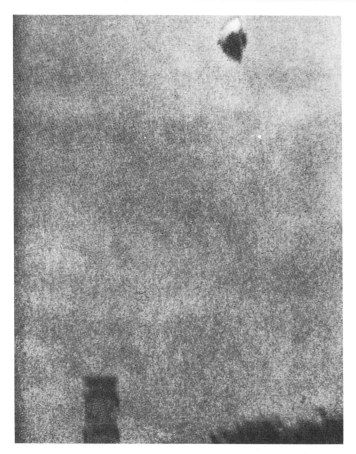

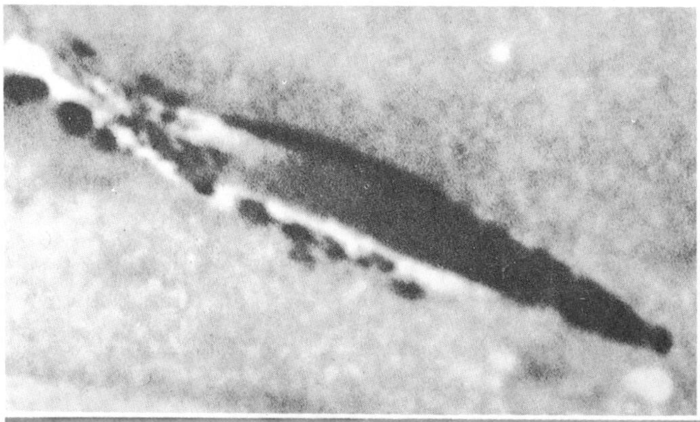

One warm, clear afternoon in early April 1966, an anonymous Australian was in his garden in Balwyn, near Melbourne, when it suddenly 'lit-up', and he saw in the sky a bright object, shaped like a mushroom, **left,** about 20-35 feet (6-10 metres) in diameter. It was about 150 feet (50 metres) from the ground and seemed to float down towards him, spinning through a 180° angle on its vertical axis, 'during which time I photographed it'. It then shot off northwards at high speed. A carpenter working in the house witnessed the object and also saw it being photographed.

The Australian is a qualified engineer, director of a large family business, and a respected citizen of Balwyn. It is difficult to believe he would perpetrate a hoax. But an American UFO organisation, Ground Saucer Watch Inc., of Phoenix, Arizona, has cast doubt on the authenticity of the photograph. Using computer techniques to analyse the photograph, GSW has claimed it is a fake. And yet GSW has been wrong in the past. The question as to who is correct in this instance thus remains unanswered.

A promotional photograph of a B-57 aeroplane in flight, **below,** found its way into a set of UFO photographs offered for sale by NICAP (National Investigation Committee on Aerial Phenomena). An unknown object appeared in the top right-hand corner of the photograph. According to UFO investigator Robert Schmidt, the object 'appeared to be streamlined, and to have dark "ports" on its lower periphery'.

Schmidt wrote to the manufacturers, the Martin Aircraft Company, asking for an enlargement, **inset left,** from the NICAP file. When questioned about the picture, the company replied that the unexplained image had been caused by a tear, a rub or an abrasion. Analysis, however, subsequently showed that, in the original negative, the emulsion grain extended over the area of the unknown object; a tear or rub would have destroyed the grain.

The Martin Company also said they had filmed another 'fly-by' to see if the same effect could be obtained again – a strange thing to do if, as they claimed, the original image had been caused by a flaw in the film.

EXORCISM HAS BEEN PART OF CHRISTIANITY SINCE ITS EARLIEST DAYS. ITS EFFICACY MAY BE QUESTIONED, BUT THE RITUAL INVOLVED CAN, IT SEEMS, BRING COMFORT TO UNFORTUNATE VICTIMS OF POLTERGEIST PHENOMENA

Among those victims of poltergeist activity who plead for, or even demand, an exorcism – and to judge from figures quoted by leading exorcists there are many hundreds – few initially have any idea at all of what is involved. Even fewer are suitable for such a rite. Indeed, there is agreement among those who have been concerned with poltergeists that only about two per cent of all reported cases genuinely involve inexplicable phenomena – that is, psychokinetic effects for which no cause can be found. But while there may be no explanation for the means whereby mattresses are slashed, or the contents of drawers or wardrobes thrown about, the source of most poltergeist activity can often be traced to some form of emotional disturbance in an individual within the afflicted household.

The real question, then, is whether the rite of exorcism is appropriate for the *person* involved – regardless of the individual's religious commitment. Even for atheists, the rite may be comforting and

CASTING OUT THE DEVIL

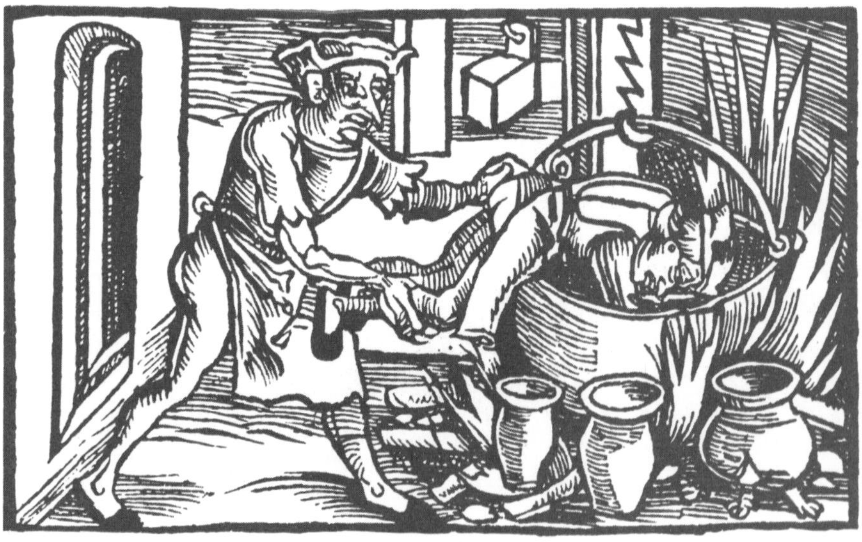

effective; while for believers, who have unwittingly engaged fanatics or incompetents to perform the rite, the results can be as terrifying as the work of the 'demon itself'.

What most victims require above all are sympathy, concern and a willingness on the part of investigators to become involved with the problem. It is very common for those affected to wonder if they are going mad; and so a warm and sympathetic investigator, who is prepared to accept the possibility that incidents of poltergeist activity are perfectly authentic, can do a tremendous amount to alleviate the acute mental distress that is often provoked in the affected individual.

Despite increasing knowledge and awareness of the diverse causes of apparently inexplicable phenomena, however, some advisers and doctors still feel unable to deal with those who fall victim and refer them instead to religious exorcists.

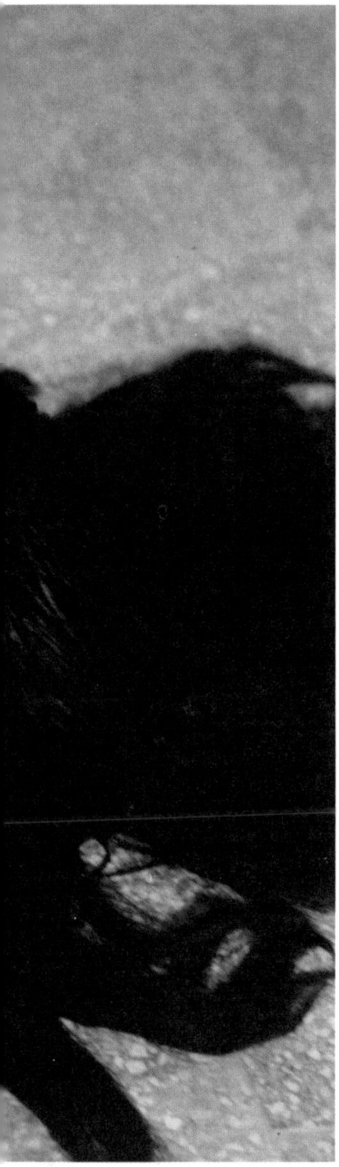

PERSPECTIVES

THE GHOST TRAPS OF TIBET

The most elaborate ceremonies of the Tibetan Buddhist calendar last for days or even weeks, and always incorporate a rite of exorcism, performed by the most distinguished Grand Lama of the region. When Buddhism first reached Tibet, it absorbed the ancient magical practices known as *Bön,* which flourished among the people of that remote country. One of the essential talents of a *Bön* priest was the power to expel demons and malevolent spirits from afflicted people or ill-omened places. Reflecting past traditions, it is still usual to find minor exorcists attached to a monastery, although they are not monks themselves. The *lha-ka* (mouth of the gods), whose role it is to expel the demons, is often a woman. But whether the ritual is performed by a local witch or the Grand High Lama, the essential features of the ritual are the same. The exorcist uses his or her energies to summon up powerful supernatural spirits through incantations, charms and magical recipes. The demons are summoned, threatened, and driven into a ghost-trap. They are then destroyed, usually by burning, or kept imprisoned in a suitably secure place.

The ghost traps themselves are made of wires which are meshed into patterns. An essential part of the exorcism ritual is the linking of this apparatus to participants by means of multi-coloured thread in order to conduct the psychic forces. Researchers have even questioned whether the *Bön* magicians of ancient times were perhaps conversant with some 'forgotten' aspect of astral physics.

Exorcism itself can take many forms. If the main object of intervention by a clergyman is to relieve an undefined 'feeling', this can often be achieved through a religious service or blessing, or by encouraging the victim to accept that the 'atmosphere' of the affected room or house in not malign. It may take a while to convince the victim; but if the exorcist is caring and patient, this approach can often eliminate symptoms.

A full exorcism cannot be authorised, however, until a thorough examination of the circumstances of the victim has been undertaken. Normally, this process involves obtaining a report from the family doctor, an assessment from the local clergyman and, often, the views of a social worker. Indicating the more balanced approach now being adopted by some responsible member of the Churches, one bishop has said that he would not consider giving his approval to an exorcism unless a medical expert were present, or had at least examined the victim and had agreed that such a service might assist. And it should be stressed that a theatrical performance, complete with bell, book and candle, is usually considered inappropriate nowadays.

Many victims of poltergeist activity obtain relief as a result of the introduction of a religious ceremony into their households, though it is by no means certain that the effects of such ceremonies are lasting. Unfortunately, just as many people endure even greater suffering in the wake of a request for an exorcism; and there is still a body of fanatics, both clerics and laymen, who have little or no knowledge of psychology or parapsychology and whose ridiculous and scaremongering activity serve merely to increase the distress of those whom they claim to be able to help.

In Hastings, Sussex, in 1979, for example, a canon so harassed a disturbed victim, who was

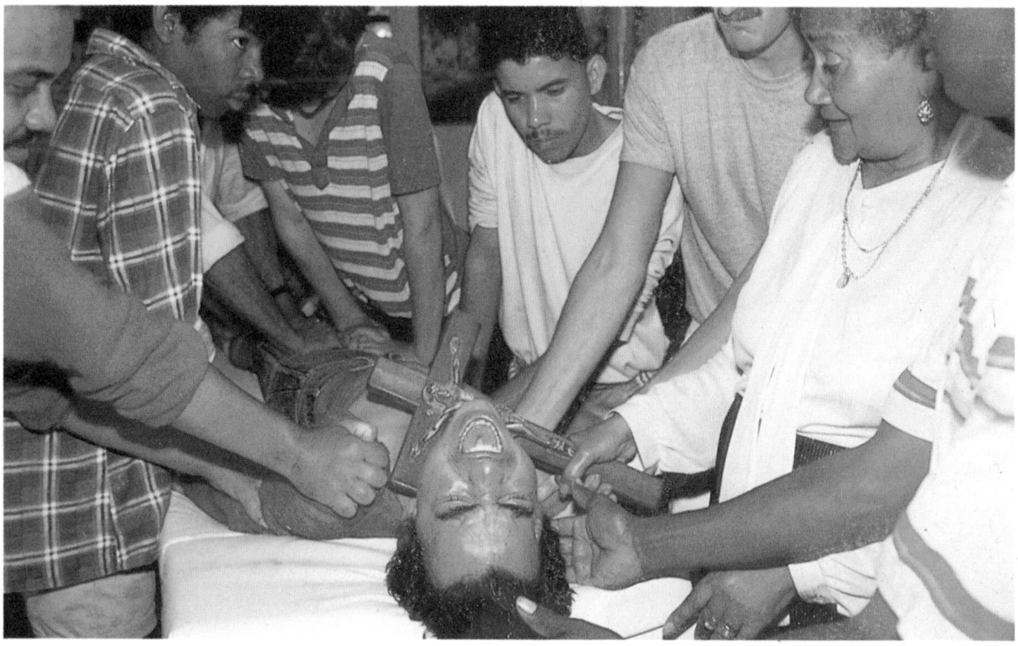

On the island of Réunion in the Indian Ocean, Firmin V.,* right, *a Creole plantation worker, reacts violently as exorcist Madame Visnelda summons an evil spirit from his body.
After an equally violent spiritual struggle, the Italian woman,* above, *lies peacefully at the end of a ceremony of exorcism.
Medieval thinkers regarded the poltergeist as a physical manifestation of the devil. In the woodcut,* left, *'The Poltergeist in the Kitchen', a cook is being pushed face-first by a poltergeist into his cauldron of boiling water.

suffering from the effects of the menopause and a drug problem, that she had to be admitted to a clinic for three months' treatment. The woman's condition could well have become far more serious if her husband had not stopped the canon in the middle of his 'treatment' and told him to leave. In 1977, a family in the Midlands was also subjected to a horrifying sequence of 'cures'. First, their house was blessed by an archbishop and a local vicar. Then, a religious group visited the victimised family (who were suffering from mass hallucinations) and held a two-hour 'stomping session'. Within a few months, two seances had been held in the house, and numerous 'spiritualist' mediums had called upon the family, each providing a different (and usually nonsensical) explanation for the imagined phenomena. One claimed that the house was haunted by the evil spirit of a tall negro; another informed the family that the incidents were to be attributed to the influence of a ginger-haired dwarf. The family was able to return to normal only after a parapsychologist had spent a few hours with the mentally disturbed wife, subsequently making arrangements for a local doctor to visit.

'I was told to bury a snail underneath an oak tree at midnight, then to walk around the tree reciting the Lord's Prayer three times,' one victim of poltergeist activity told an investigator. This remarkable piece of advice was offered to her not in 1777, as one might have imagined, but two centuries later. The woman sought treatment for a psychological ailment, and the phenomena that had been distressing her promptly ceased.

But psychological treatment is not always the correct method for dealing with such incidents. Often a simpler 'cure' will help. A woman in Hampshire, who claimed that she was 'anti-religious', was disturbed enough by a minor outbreak of inexplicable incidents to consider calling upon the services of her local vicar. Initially, however, she confided in her mother-in-law, a spiritualist, who recommended that she should attend a 'rescue seance' to try to remove the 'troubled spirit'. (This procedure has occasionally been known to help, though it is potentially dangerous if conducted by people without adequate experience.)

> "An exorcism, in fact, is no more than surrendering to God and saying 'Please Lord, clean up the mess'."
>
> **Dom Robert Petitpierre**

The suggestion made the victim somewhat apprehensive; so instead she took her problem to a parapsychologist. On his advice, she used a 'magic sign' to enable her to cope with the disturbance, and in two weeks the household had returned to normal. Needless to say, there was nothing 'magic' about the sign that she used: it was simply a device, an aid – and a successful one.

*In*Focus

THE SOLEMN RITE

Some people may view with grave misgivings the activities of certain 'professional' exorcists. In recent years, newspapers have reported a growing number of cases in which unfortunate victims have suffered severe mental (and, indeed, physical) distress; and several people have been found guilty of manslaughter and

During an exorcism in the Italian church of St Vicinius, in Sarsina, **below,** *the iron ring – a relic of the saint, who wore it about his neck, with heavy weights attached – serves as a penance.*

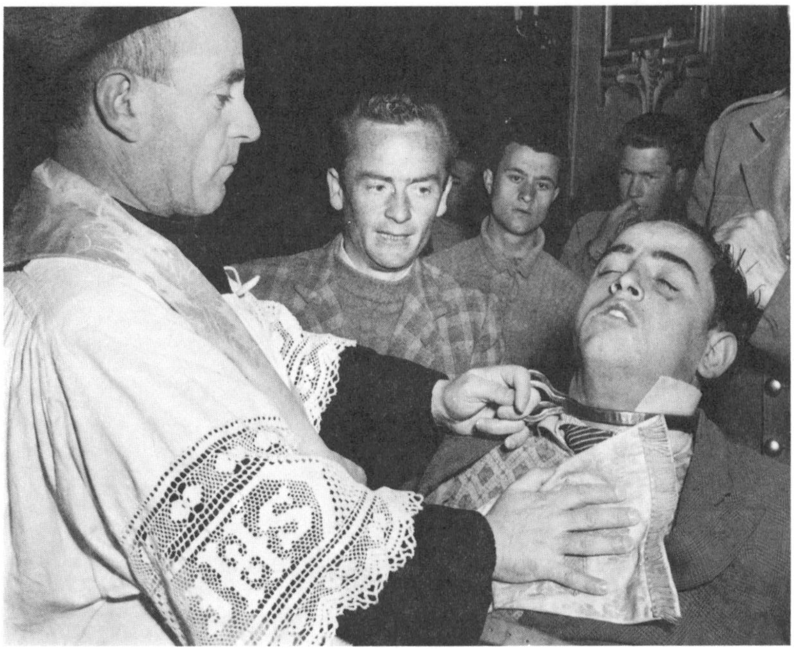

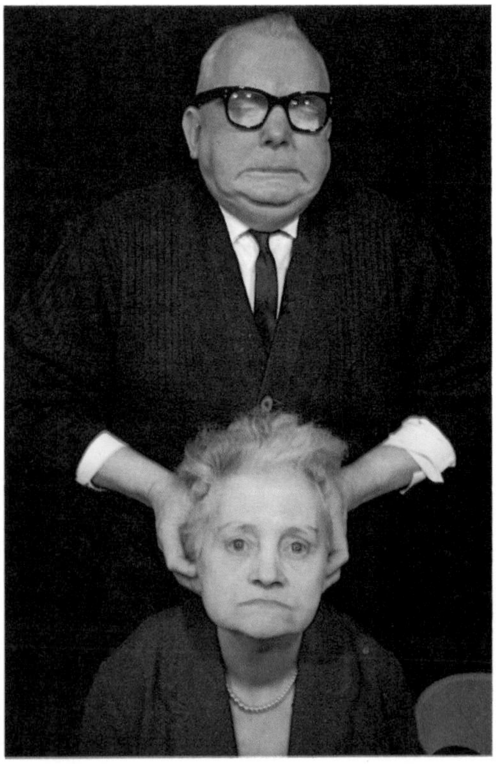

The English medium Donald Page, **left,** *is seen, carrying out an 'exorcism' on a woman patient. Whatever explanations may be put forward for the ritual and its outcome, there is little doubt that a considerable amount of physical energy is expended by the medium.*

committed to prison as a result of ignorant attempts at something of which they had no understanding or experience. Even within the ranks of the Anglican and Roman Catholic churches, there is some disquiet concerning the principles and practices that are involved.

In both churches, the ritual of exorcism is based upon the belief that a person or a place may be 'possessed' by an evil spirit or spirits, and that the appropriate words and ceremonies can be used to 'command' the evil spirit to leave. The form of the ritual is very simple, and it appears that the most important element is the strength of personality of the exorcist himself.

Since about AD 250, a ceremony of exorcism has been a part of the baptismal service in the Roman Catholic church. This does not mean that candidates are considered to be 'possessed'; rather, it is regarded rather as a ceremony to remove the effects of original sin.

The exorcism of those considered to be possessed by evil spirits is rigorously controlled in Roman Catholic canon law, and was established in the *Rituale of Pope Urban VIII.* A similar ceremony of exorcism has been retained within the canon of the Anglican church, but it is seldom performed in its original form.

In the earliest days of Christianity, exorcism was a ceremony that could be practised by anybody. Any major exorcism now requires the authorisation of a bishop before it may be performed, but many parish priests (and also certain specialist practitioners, recognised within the body of the church) have been known to carry out private exorcisms.

The form of words in the ritual varies considerably. One practitioner, for instance, begins with the traditional words: 'I rebuke thee! I abjure thee and summon thee forth from this man...' On the other hand, Dom Robert Petitpierre, an Anglican monk and Church of England authority on all psychic matters, has written of the ritual: 'An exorcism, in fact, is no more than surrendering to God and saying "Please Lord, clean up the mess".'

The Rev. Neil-Smith, of Hampstead, London, above, has been one of the most active of Anglican exorcists. At one time, he claimed to have performed over 2,000 exorcisms within a period of four years.

One young man in Richmond, Surrey, accidentally discovered his own method of disposing of an 'evil spirit', which offered – not to him, perhaps, but to a scientific observer – evidence that the phenomena he was experiencing were basically psychological in nature. After three months of suffering from 'cracking and popping noises and strange lights on the landing', he was determined to confront and eliminate the poltergeist. One morning, exhausted and irritated, he swore at the 'thing'. From then on, he experienced no further incidents. In some cases, a symbol may certainly help; and distress may be reduced to an acceptable level, depending on the state of the victim and confidence in the 'power' or 'force' of the symbol.

Yet although the number of cases of poltergeist activity reported appears to be increasing – and there are many possible reasons for this, including the stresses of modern life, and a greater willingness among victims to admit to experiences – the success rate of exorcism is apparently declining. Indeed, a mere 20 per cent of exorcisms are now considered successful, and then only after repeated visits by authorised exorcists. As the waning of religious belief gradually makes way for the scientific study of phenomena hitherto regarded as supernatural, the days of the exorcist may be numbered.

The New Testament tells how Christ himself expelled demons by a 'word of power'. The act was also said to be a sign of the coming of God's Kingdom. Evil spirits were believed to issue from the body's orifices. The decorated initial, right, *from a 12th-century manuscript in Winchester Cathedral library, shows a 'little blue devil' emerging from the mouth of a possessed man.*

THE COSMIC JOKER

THE FREQUENCY OF HILARIOUS COINCIDENCES LEADS NATURALLY TO THE IDEA THAT THEY ARE PERPETRATED BY A FORM OF COSMIC PRANKSTER. DOES SUCH AN ENTITY REALLY EXIST?

The cartoon by Cruikshank, left, *shows it raining cats and dogs, a visual interpretation of the familiar English metaphor. But there are in fact many reported incidents of extraordinary falls from the sky, perpetrated perhaps by a cosmic prankster.*

Few of us have not felt at times that our lives are manipulated by forces beyond our control and comprehension, especially when the most trivial events can take on a mysterious significance of their own. Consider the case of Essex policeman Peter Moscardi. In 1967, the telephone number of his police station was changed to 40116. But, to a friend, he inadvertently gave a wrong number, 40166. Several days later, patrolling an industrial area with a colleague, he investigated a factory. It was late at night, the door was open, and a light burned inside, but the building was empty. While Moscardi was in the office, the telephone rang – it was his friend. Moscardi looked down at the telephone, and found that the number was the one he had mistakenly given his friend. Later they learned that the manager had forgotten to lock the factory before he had left for the night, something that had never happened before.

When faced with incidents of such staggering improbability – and most of us can cite similar personal experiences – the word 'coincidence' seems almost feeble and dismissive. It explains nothing. We cling to such vague, but useful, notions as good or bad luck. But perhaps, it has been conjectured – and the idea is put forward only half in jest – such weird events are engineered by a mysterious cosmic joker, a sort of demented fairy godmother whose wand is a fool's slap-stick. In the capricious and perverse world of the cosmic joker, there are many varieties of prank. Perhaps the most spectacular of these are coincidences – especially those of name and number. The German psychologist Wilhelm Stekel spoke of the 'compulsion of the name'. We all know examples of such bizarre occurrences.

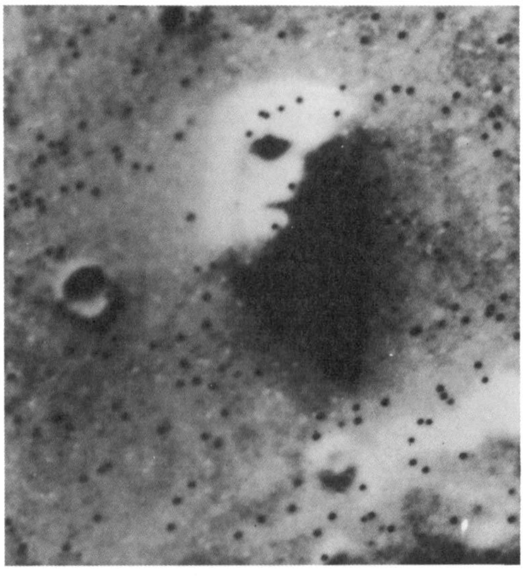

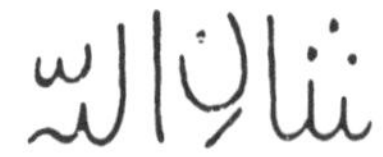

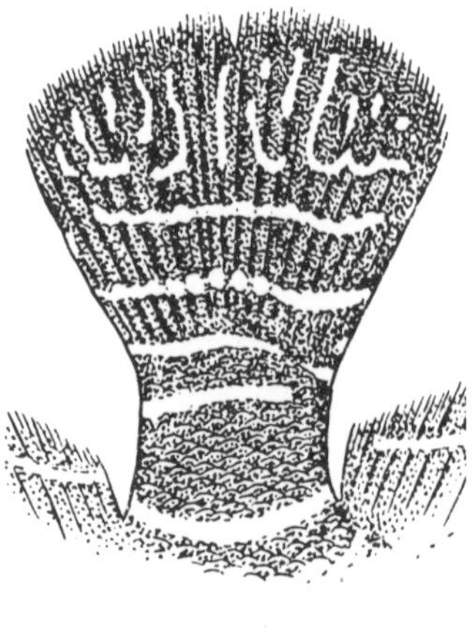

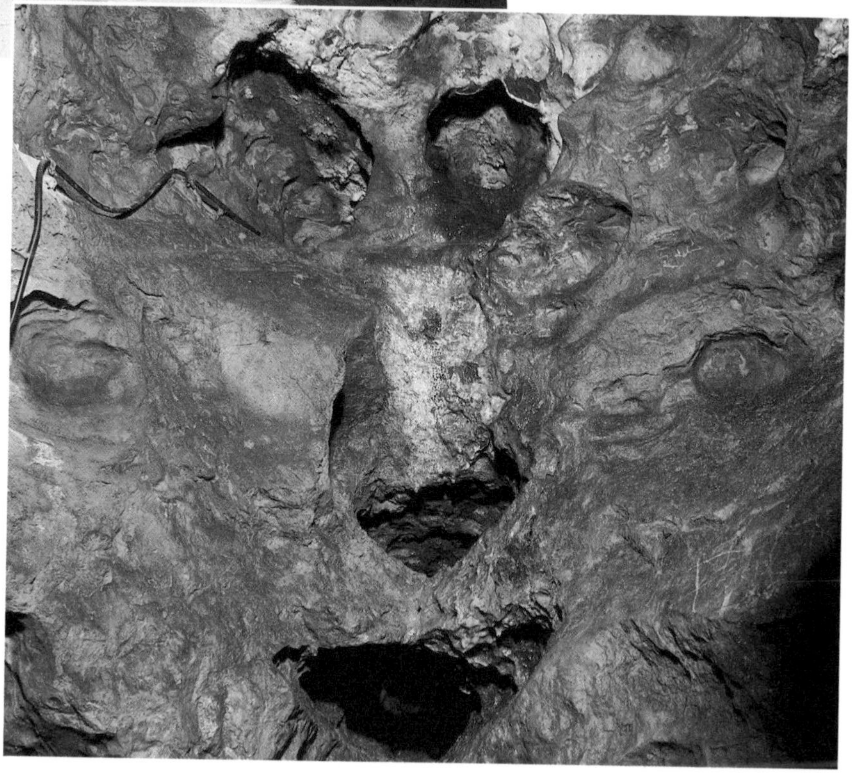

The Camel Rock,* left, *near Santa Fe in New Mexico, and the apparent image of a human face in a stalactite cave at Wiehl, near Cologne, Germany,* below, *are examples of* simulacra, *visual coincidences that occur naturally.

The photograph,* far left, *suggests that the surface of Mars, bears huge effigies of human faces; while the marks on the tail of a butterfly fish from Zanzibar,* left, *seem to read in old Arabic, 'there is no God but Allah'. The cosmic joker is once more at play.

In one, from the *Daily Telegraph* of 3 June 1982, a duck farmer in Lincolnshire found he had employed two people called Crow, four called Robbins, a Sparrow, a Gosling and a Dickie Bird. A Canadian goose also crashed through the window of a house in Derby, while the occupant was listening to a recording of *Cry of the Wild Goose.*

The serious world of science, too, comes in for the prankster's ministrations. There have, for instance, been many predictions made by astronomers that have failed miserably – such as one that the comet Kohoutek, when it passed close to the Earth in 1973, would provide the most amazing spectacle. In the event, it could hardly be seen with the naked eye.

The pranks continue. In April 1982, a New Zealand government department cancelled an earthquake alert when they found that the ominous seismograph readings they were receiving from remote stations were caused by excited wallabies hopping nearby; and a famous American university had to admit, to its great embarrassment, that for over a decade no one had noticed that one of its dinosaur skeletons was wearing the wrong head.

There is sometimes a rather dark side to the cosmic joker, however. In the *Book of Heroic Failures,* Stephen Pile tells the story of a farcical but tragic event that took place during the British fireman's strike of 1978. The army took over responsibility for firefighting operations, and on 14 January they rescued a cat that had become trapped up a tree. The old lady who owned the cat was overjoyed and invited them all in for a cup of tea. But, wrote Pile, driving off later, with fond farewells completed, they ran over the cat and killed it.

The victim of an improbable series of accidents, may be forgiven for thinking he is the victim of a curse or that 'someone up there doesn't like me'. Most of us have just enough paranoia to feel 'got at', but it usually passes and our sense of humour puts it into perspective. In paranoid schizophrenia, however, these feelings get out of hand.

THE CHESS MASTERS

The yachtsman Donald Crowhurst, who ended his life tragically by drowning himself in 1969, had fallen into schizophrenia as his vessel drifted in mid-Atlantic. Shortly before his suicide, he had begun to write a cynical parable in his ship's log. He felt our lives are manipulated by cosmic tricksters called 'chess-masters'. He believed that 'the explanation of our troubles is that cosmic beings are playing games with us'.

'God and his son were playing together in the cosmos... The game they were playing was called turning apes into gods. It was a jolly just game, and ... it was played according to one simple rule, the apes were not allowed to know anything about the gods.'

> WHATEVER THE IDENTITY OF THE COSMIC JOKER, HE IS BREATHTAKINGLY SKILLFUL AT JUGGLING WITH EVERYTHING AT ONCE. AND HE STILL MANAGES TO BE BOUNDLESSLY CREATIVE AND MAGNIFICENTLY AUDACIOUS.

A similar cynicism, but born of disillusionment rather than madness, has led to the conspiracy theory, which holds that almost every civilisation has been instigated and manipulated by powerful and insidious organisations, usually secret, of bankers, religions, cults and secret societies. A space-age variation of this is Erich von Däniken's now discredited theory that human evolution is the product of regular intervention by space-travelling aliens. In Andrija Puharich's biography of Uri Geller, we are told that Geller also claims that the source of his psychokinetic power is a group of 'superbeings',

deep in space, that have similarly manipulated human development.

A significant number of keen minds have also recognised what American psychologist Dr Jule Eisenbud has called 'subtle ordering tendencies of dispositions hidden in the very warp and woof of the universe'. The German philosopher Arthur Schopenhauer, whose ideas about the nature of the unconscious influenced Freud and Jung, believed that something more than mere physical causality influences men's lives, and called it 'the subjective connection'. The real significance of coincidence, he wrote in 1850, exists only in relation to the individuals who experience them. But to others involved in the event, people for whom it has no significance, it passes unnoticed into the background of everyday life. 'The world is indeed comic,' wrote the master of Gothic horror, H. P. Lovecraft, 'but the joke is on mankind'.

Cause and Effect

The discussion of coincidences and their meaning has attracted the likes of Carl Gustav Jung, Paul Kammerer – a scientist engaged in pioneering work on the inheritance of acquired characteristics, who committed suicide when the results of his research into midwife toads were alleged to be rigged – Arthur Koestler and Sir Alister Hardy, all of whom have concluded that the phenomenon of coincidence is somehow beyond the usual chain of cause and effect in space and time. Some contemporary researchers go so far as to suggest that these synchronistic events – as Jung termed them – might actually be arranged in some mysterious way by the collective unconscious.

In describing the subjective nature of synchronistic experiences, many writers have used the familiar simile of life being like a film, a play or a novel, directed or written by some mysterious power. Science fiction writer Larry Niven has even used the imagery of mankind as puppets in the hands of alien puppet-masters in several of his books, including *Ringworld*. The real argument among those who explain life in this way is over the identity of the puppeteer, author or director: God, angels, demons, cosmic imps, conspirators, aliens – or ourselves? It is the last possibility that provides the most interesting debate.

The Death's Head hawk-moth, top, carries the spine-chilling image of a human skull on its body. But what possible meaning can human remains have for the moth's predators?

Writing in *Psychic* magazine in October 1975, Jule Eisenbud encapsulated the proposition in the following extract:.

'Theoretically... there is nothing that would be beyond accomplishment by the most innocent-looking observer... At most he would be doing unconsciously, and with no manifest effort, what a movie director goes to great pains to do on a conscious level, that is, deploying props, natural surroundings and events, and the wide capabilities of "central casting" ... with special effects as needed. Since all... behaviour on the part of the players would be rationalized, no one would be any the wiser.'

We certainly control the 'reality' of our dreams in this way. The stumbling block of applying this idea to real life, however, is the problem of just how 'the fate of one individual invariably fits the fate of another, so that each is the hero of his own drama, while simultaneously figuring in a drama foreign to him,' as Schopenhauer put it. This, he said, is something that surpasses our powers of comprehension.

Perfect Timing

Whatever the identity of the cosmic joker, he is breathtakingly skillful at juggling with everything at once. And he still manages to be boundlessly creative and magnificently audacious. His actions are unerringly swift, perfectly timed and appropriate, as well as characterisitc of that unselfconscious state shared by somnambulists and the hypnotised, martial artists and meditators, saints and sages – and incidentally, some children, madmen and drunks. Indeed, they appear to have access to a primal, childlike, unconditioned state of mind – to the personal and collective unconscious – that reaches its perfect expression in Zen Buddhism, with celebration of the playful or comic spirit.

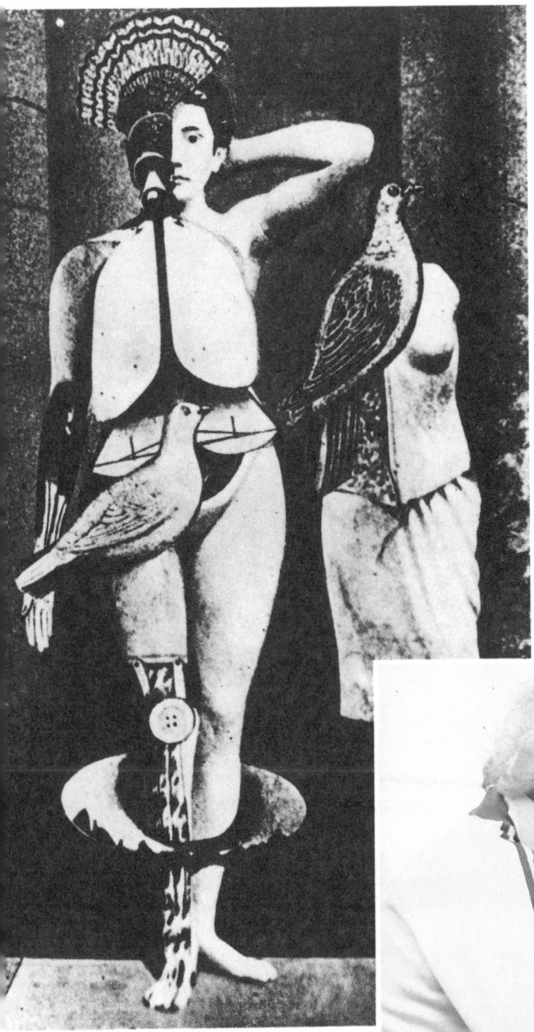

***Zen Buddhist monks on the steps of a temple in Kyoto, Japan,* right, *believe that many of the teachings of Zen are designed to be paradoxical or amusing in order to provoke laughter. Laughter they hold – whether it comes about through the abrupt release of tension or through the 'getting' of a joke – can lead, to 'sudden awakening'. The Dada movement,in the visual arts, achieves a similar effect in its use of outrageous or nonsensical images, as in the photo-montage by Max Ernst, shown* left.**

The improvisation of jazz like that of pianist Dave Brubeck,* right, *depends upon a subtle interplay between the conscious and unconscious mind – as does the appreciation of the cosmic joke.

***The black side of the cosmic joker's humour is illustrated by a story related by Stephen Pile in his* The Book of Heroic Failures. *During the 1979 fireman's strike in Britain, the army, who had taken charge of firefighting services, were called out by an old lady whose cat had become trapped up a tree. After rescuing the cat, they were invited to tea by the overjoyed owner. But as they left the house, they ran over the cat and killed it, as depicted* left.**

Of all philosophies, Zen Buddhism may be the most help to us in coming to terms with the cosmic joker, because it appears to have mastered absurdity. In his analysis of Chinese philosophy, *The Chinese Mind,* E. R. Hughes described Zen teachings as 'consciously and deliberately paradoxical, even with the intention of causing laughter, to make evident the incongruities of the human situation'. What else can one say of a school of thought that numbers among its masters the eighth-century Teng Yinfeng, who died standing on his head with the intention of turning conventional values upside down, in the hope some people would take life less seriously? The difference between a healthy appreciation of a cosmic joke and the paranoid reaction is that the former recognises its absurdity and delights in it, while the later imbues it with a deadening seriousness.

As M. Conrad Hyers points out in *Zen and the Comic Spirit,* the child, the madman, the fool and the sage share a common ground in which they transcend the limits on behaviour and imagination accepted by the majority. The child has not yet learned to carve up the world into neat but arbitrary categories, nor is he governed by them; the madman cannot help himself as he confuses categories; the fool confuses categories deliberately, as do those great fools of art, the Dadaists and surrealists; while the sage has gone beyond our need for categories and thus returns to the childlike state.

SUDDEN AWAKENING

The Zen masters have always taught by exploiting the parallels between the instant in which we get the point of a joke, and the 'sudden awakening' of *satori* ('enlightenment'). Laughter is an explosive response to a situation that has suddenly been plunged into contradiction or reduced to absurdity, says Hyers; and it is this abrupt relief of tension that takes us by surprise, precipitating laughter in the 'getting' of a joke.

Whatever the ultimate origin of cosmic jokes, we certainly perceive them as an example of wit. It seems reasonable, too, to draw another parallel, this time between *koans* – the paradoxical riddles given to Zen students for meditation – and anomalous phenomena of any kind. The pranks of the cosmic joker, unexplained or inexplicable, like *koans,* challenge our presumptions and expectations, and make us reflect on the mysteries of our existence.

Cosmic jokes are phenomenological, specially formulated, perhaps, by our collective unconscious, for the enlightenment – and enjoyment – of those with eyes and minds open enough to perceive them. It is an exquisite irony that a phenomenon so all-pervading and universal should have its origins in the trivial. As the great Zen master of the West, W. C. Fields said: 'It's a funny old world. You're lucky to get out of it alive'.

MANY OF THE WORLD'S GREAT LEADERS – ABRAHAM LINCOLN, WINSTON CHURCHILL AND FRANKLIN ROOSEVELT, AMONG THEM – ALL BELIEVED IN PSYCHIC POWER. TO WHAT EXTENT MIGHT INTERNATIONAL POLITICS HAVE BEEN INFLUENCED BY ESP?

OBEYING THE INNER VOICE

Winston Churchill was entertaining three of his ministers at 10 Downing Street during World War II, when he suddenly had a premonition. An air-raid had begun, but the dinner party continued without interruption, as the British Prime Minister rose and went into the kitchen where the cook and maid were working next to a high plate-glass window.

'Put dinner on a hot-plate in the dining room,' Churchill instructed the butler. Then he ordered

Winston Churchill is seen, left, on one of his many visits to anti-aircraft batteries in 1941. During the Second World War, his 'inner voice' served him well; and by heeding its advice, he managed both to escape serious injury himself and to help others to do the same.

everyone in the kitchen to go to the bomb shelter. The Prime Minister returned to his guests and his dinner. Three minutes later, a bomb fell at the back of the house, totally destroying the kitchen.

Churchill's intuitive powers were evident throughout his life and he learned to obey them. But it was during wartime that their influence was most dramatic.

In 1941, for instance, Churchill made a habit of visiting anti-aircraft batteries during night raids. Once, having watched a gun crew in action for some time, he went back to his staff car to depart. The near-side door was opened for him because it was on that side that he always sat. But for some reason, he ignored the open door, walked round the car, opened the far-side door himself, and climbed in. Minutes later, as the car was speeding through the darkened London streets, a bomb exploded close by. The force of the blast lifted the Prime Minister's vehicle on to two wheels, and it was on the verge of rolling over when it righted itself. 'It must have been my beef on that side that pulled it down,' Churchill is said to have remarked.

Later, when his wife questioned him about the incident, Churchill at first said he did not know why he had sat on that side of the car that night. But then he added: 'Of course I know. Something said "Stop!" before I reached the car door held open for me. It then appeared to me that I was told I was meant to open the door on the other side and get in and sit there – and that is what I did'.

What the British prime minister had done was to listen to the 'inner voice' that we usually refer to as intuition or a hunch, and heed its advice. He knew from experience that he could trust it, just as many top executives have learned to be guided by ESP in making business decisions.

PERSPECTIVES

A STAR-STRUCK FIRST LADY

While some world leaders have based decisions purely on hunches, others in the corridors of power believe they are guided by higher forces. Nancy Reagan, wife of the former US President, Ronald Reagan, believes fervently in the value of astrology. In her early days as a Hollywood film actress, she often consulted astrologers, even attending evening astrology classes.

She found support for her occultish interests in her actor-husband, Ronald. Taking advice from an astrologer on the most propitious time for his installation as governor of California in 1967, Reagan insisted on taking the oath of office in the middle of the night – at 12.16 a.m. to be exact – while facing west.

Governor Reagan continued to show an interest in things astrological. Whenever he flew to Washington, DC, for example, he met with the well-known astrologer Jeane Dixon who repeatedly promised him that he would eventually get to occupy the White House. (The Reagans dropped Dixon when she – correctly – refused to predict Ronald as President in 1976.)

Nancy Reagan's reliance on the stars reached its zenith during her husband's presidency (1980-1988). As America's First Lady, she would secretly spend hours each week on a three-way telephone link-up with San Francisco astrologer Joan Quigley and a presidential assistant, coordinating the President's movements in and out of the White House according to a zodiac chart. If the stars predicted a good day, Reagan's appointments could be kept; if a bad day was in store, and there was a chance the President could be harmed, an alternative date would be proposed.

Sometimes, however, much to Nancy's fury, Reagan's advisers could not deter him from going out spontaneously – say, to a baseball game – when the stars advised against it. So great a trust did she have in astrology that she even had President Gorbachev's chart drawn up during the 1985 Geneva summit.

In 1987, the stars were again brought in to direct the President's schedule. After he had undergone prostate surgery in January, astrologers told Nancy that her husband should stay out of the public eye for 120 days. Said Joan Quigley: it was the 'malevolent movements of Uranus and Saturn' which 'were in Sagittarius' that kept Reagan hidden in the White House.

Abraham Lincoln often attended seances. At one, for instance, a piano was seen to levitate while he sat on it with his bodyguard. But his interest in the paranormal also served worthier ends, such as the Emancipation Proclamation of 1863, illustrated in A.A. Lamb's allegorical painting,* above left. *It is even said that Lincoln first decided to abolish slavery after a trance-lecture from a medium.

PARANORMAL INFLUENCE

Other statesmen, too, have at times been guided by intuition, or have allowed the psychic talents of others to guide them. Indeed the influence of the paranormal may well have shaped the destinies of many of the world's nations.

Many believe, for instance, that American slaves owe their emancipation to the intervention of a teenager, Nettie Colburn Maynard, who gave spirit messages to Abraham Lincoln. While in trance, young Nettie is said to have lectured the President for an hour on the importance of freeing the slaves. Lincoln also attended other seances, at one of which he and his bodyguard are reported to have climbed on to a piano. Despite its load, it then lifted off the ground, until the tune being played by a medium, Mrs Miller, was finished.

When a newspaper, the Cleveland *Plain-dealer,* published a story about some of Lincoln's alleged psychic experiences, he was asked if it was true. 'The only falsehood in the statement', said the President, 'is that the half of it has not been told. This article does not begin to tell the wonderful things I have witnessed.'

The Canadian statesman W.L. Mackenzie King, left, *often visited leading mediums, such as Geraldine Cummins,* above.

The pandas which Richard Nixon, right, *took back to America in 1972 created a huge demand for replicas – a market that toy-maker Herbert Raiffe had predicted the year before.*

No one knows how much the paranormal influenced the great Canadian statesman, William Lyon Mackenzie King, but his diaries certainly show that he had very distinct beliefs and was convinced that the spirits of dead politicians were in touch with him. When he visited England, he always consulted top mediums – among them Geraldine Cummins who was particularly well-known for her automatic writings.

Franklin Roosevelt also consulted a psychic – Jeane Dixon, known as the 'Washington seer'; and Nancy Reagan, of course, frequently consulted an astrologer for guidance on behalf of her husband during his presidency.

There are times, too, when ordinary citizens have premonitions about what presidents are going to do. In 1971, for example, a Brooklyn, USA, toy manufacturer, Herbert Raiffe, had a hunch that toy pandas were going to be good-sellers. There was no logic behind the decision he made. Nevertheless, he ordered that panda production should be increased severalfold at his factory.

In February of the following year, President Nixon visited China, toured the Forbidden City, and returned to America with a gift of two much-publicised pandas. No one was better placed to meet the sudden and unexpected demand for cuddly replicas than Raiffe, whose intuition seems to have tuned into an aspect of the President's China mission, long before the visit had even been arranged.

In America and Europe, the police use psychics at times to help them solve serious crimes or find missing people. Psychics have even been able to guide archaeologists to the sites of long-buried ancient remains. And around the world, the ability of dowsers to locate subterranean water supplies and other resources is well documented. So why should we find it so odd that eminent men in the political arena are also prepared to open their minds to information which comes to them in a way that by-passes normal sensory channels?

Franklin Roosevelt and Winston Churchill, above, were both firm believers in the power of ESP.

Not that it is always helpful to know what the future holds. Abraham Lincoln, for example, awoke one day, having had a vivid dream. In it, he had heard the sound of sobbing and had followed it, through the White House, until he reached a room where he found a coffin that was draped with the American flag. Lincoln, in his dream, asked a soldier who had died. 'It's the President,' came the reply. 'He has been assassinated'.

Days later, Lincoln was dead... killed by an assassin's bullet. The President's dream, it seems, had been a truly prophetic one.

CAN PEOPLE REALLY BE BURIED ALIVE AND SURVIVE, OR WITHSTAND FREEZING TEMPERATURES? IS IT POSSIBLE TO DEMOLISH A PILE OF BRICKS WITH JUST A HAND? THERE IS EVIDENCE THAT THE ASTOUNDING POWER OF THE MIND CAN BE USED TO PUSH THE HUMAN BODY TO NEW LIMITS

EVERY MAN A SUPERMAN

It can give you the strength to demolish a pile of bricks, the means to kill people without touching them, the ability to raise your sports performance to new heights or the will to regain your health: it is the formidable power of the mind. Over recent years, research has shown that the mind-body relationship, or 'psychosomatic link' as medicine calls it, is deeper and more active than once realised in the West. Indeed, studies of meditation, deep relaxation and other forms of mind-expansion have yielded new information that is helping us towards greater understanding of this mind and body inter-relationship. It is a slow process of exploration, however. We in the West still have no commonly accepted definitions of mind and consciousness, and no philosophical basis for beliefs about their interplay. Small wonder, then, that science has often felt uneasy, not to say downright uncomfortable, when confronted with reports or even actual demonstrations of some of the mind's more spectacular feats.

Dr James Braid, a Scottish ophthalmic surgeon, ran into just such scientific bias in the 1840s when he suggested that people could undergo painless surgery, and proposed the use of hypnosis. His medical colleagues scoffed and sneered: this was, after all, prior to the discovery of anaesthesia. And even after hypnosis had been successfully used over a considerable period of time, many doctors

In a peaceful application of a deadly martial art, karate is used,* above*, to demolish a building.

Meditation, as demonstrated in an eastern setting,* below*, is a discipline recognised as effective against stress and in attaining new spiritual heights.

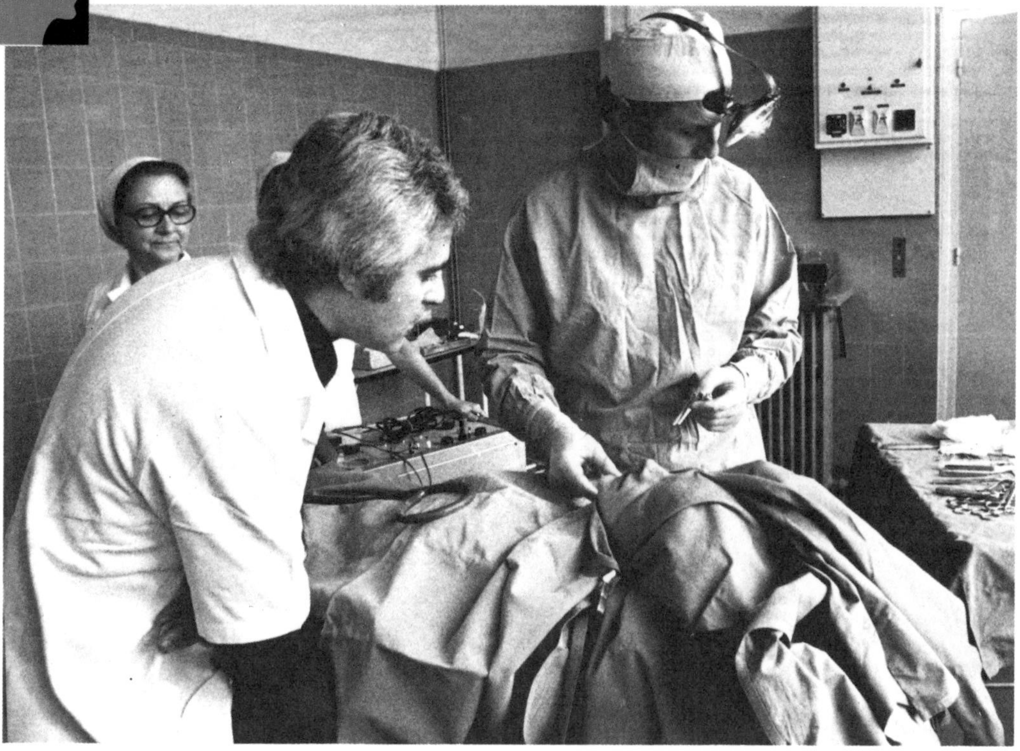

simply refused to believe it was possible to control pain through the mind. But hypnotism is by no means the only condition under which the mind can induce physical changes, as certain discoveries have since shown.

Western scientists have now investigated and validated many claims made for meditation and other Eastern disciplines, even measuring the extent to which disciples can control heart rate and other autonomic functions, for example. And, not unexpectedly, scientific proof of such control actually adds to the amazement inspired by some such feats, as we begin to see how far the human body can be pushed. In order to show how finely they are able to regulate their autonomic functions, for instance, some yogis have stayed buried alive in air-tight boxes for a period of days. While anyone else would have suffocated within hours, they managed to eke out the available air supply by reducing their heart rate and breathing to a barely detectable tick-over level. Such a level of control is gained only after years – and sometimes nearly a lifetime – of disciplined training.

Internal Fire

The Tibetan practice of *tumo* is another source of wonderment. The goal is to allow disciples to withstand the intense cold of their climate, and training includes a long programme of meditation and breathing exercises. Part of this training involves the visualisation of an internal fire as the only source of warmth during meditation in the icy Tibetan climes. How effectively this art of self-heating internally has been mastered is tested in the most demanding way.

On a given cold and windy night, each student is draped in a sheet that has been soaked in icy water. The initiate is required to dry out this sheet with his own body heat, not once but three times in succession. After this test, the final one of the training, the adept wears nothing more than a single cotton garment, regardless of the season or the harshness of the conditions.

Superhuman prowess is also associated with many of the schools of Eastern martial arts, which cultivate the same kind of self-awareness and self-mastery as religious and spiritual schools. The principle object of martial arts is to enable practitioners to perform feats of strength and acts of combat beyond ordinary limits. According to some accounts, martial arts training creates the ability to tap into some secret power source. But this energy source is seen as accessible to everyone through techniques of training that aim to unify the mind and body. The Japanese call this extraordinary energy *ki*.

A surgeon,* above, *operates on a hypnotised patient while the hypnotist looks on. The mind-over-body technique of hypnotism has today gained widespread respectability among many orthodox doctors.

A group of Japanese Buddhists,* below, *pour icy water over themselves in the bitter cold of a Tokyo winter. Mental training enables them to do this without any visible signs of ill effect.

In his film **Enter the Dragon**, *Bruce Lee smashes an enemy with a* **kung fu** *blow.* **Kung fu** *is one of many martial arts that develop physical powers through mental training.*

Methods for developing ki may differ in detail, but in general they all have in common the five elements of relaxation, concentration, breathing exercises, emptying the mind of thought, and rhythmic activity. Some teachers say that there are three stages towards mastery of the energy *ki*. In the first stage, the individual achieves a centralisation of *ki*. In the second, the influence of the energy can reach out beyond one individual to touch others. Then, in the final stage, the master gets in touch with what is believed to be the very centre of life – a stage rarely reached by anyone.

KUNG FU MASTERS

As more and more is written on the martial arts, many stories of paranormal feats come to light. Some of these have been witnessed by observers who testify to their truth. In a public demonstration, Bruce Lee – *kung fu* master and international film star – showed remarkable powers that went nearly beyond the believable. Standing with his right foot forward and his right arm almost fully extended to within an inch (2.5 centimetres) of a man, he struck. Yet, though it is generally accepted that it is physically impossible to generate enough power to hurt someone from this position, Lee sent the man flying.

Moreshei Uyeshiba, founder of *aikido,* is reputed to successfully have moved a boulder that had defeated the efforts of 10 labourers. Explaining this and similar feats, he said: 'I taught myself that an extraordinary spiritual power or soul power lies within a human body'. Such demonstrations of strength might appear pointless to many, but the karate expert's demolition of a pile of bricks cannot but impress.

The mind can even kill while a person under attack remains untouched, working its own lethal effect so that people quite literally think or worry themselves to death. This direct effect can be clearly seen in the placing of a curse; for in cultures where witchcraft is practised, a curse is almost always effective because the victim believes so strongly in the magic being worked.

In dismissing beliefs of this kind as mere superstition, the sophisticated Westerner overlooks the most important lesson implicit in witchcraft: namely, that suggestion, thought and imagination are unquestionably powerful weapons. But if they can be used to kill, can they not be used to produce beneficial effects?

POSITIVE THINKING

Emile Coué, a French psychotherapist, was convinced that people could make themselves better by simply exerting their minds, and so advised patients to say every morning: 'Every day, in every way, I am getting better and better'. His theories enjoyed a vogue in the 1920s, and his methods can be seen as a forerunner of the visualisation and positive thinking techniques used today by those healers who try to tap the power of the mind in order to aid recovery from illness.

Such new approaches have also been used with some success in the fight against diseases such as cancer; and among the techniques used are relaxation and visualisation exercises designed to help individuals mobilise their resources to conquer their condition.

It is difficult, if not impossible, to identify objectively those changes that result from mental techniques. A notable exception, though, is deep relaxation. A great deal of research has been carried out into transcendental meditation (TM), Zen and other meditation practices in several countries; and studies have shown that the definite, measurable

*In*Focus

IRON IN THE SOUL

There are many stories of superhuman feats in sports – of achievements that go way beyond the physical prowess achieved by exercise and practice, and that instead are put down to unexplained forces. So far, no systematic study of the paranormal in sports has been made, but there is mounting evidence that success is often due to psychological factors and maybe more. Famous golf professionals in particular often talk about the importance of 'will' in helping them win. It was once said of Arnold Palmer that 'more than anything else, you get the feeling that he actually willed the ball into the hole'. In his book on the game, American golfer Johnny Miller also wrote about Bobby Nichols' special ability to come through in the crunch. Describing a contest between himself and Nichols, he said: 'When he hit the ball, I thought to myself, "There's no way that ball will get to the hole". It was going so slowly, it looked as if it would be a foot [30 centimetres] short. Then I heard Bobby say, "Get in", and it did'.

Jack Nicklaus is also credited with special powers of will. Many observers felt that he could win 'whenever he wanted to', one going so far as to say he 'could will the ball into the cup if he needed a birdie at the 18th'. Can these consistent winners have powers of PK? Until further study is done, nobody can say at this point – but players themselves often seem to feel that there is something quite outside the ordinary that affects the way a game sometimes goes.

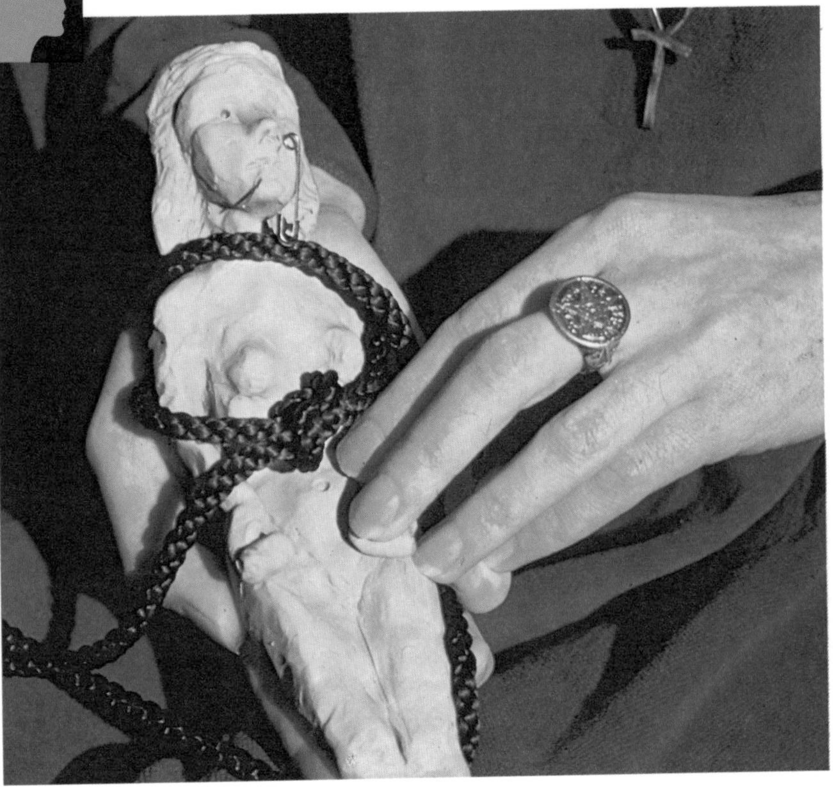

changes occurring during meditation can have tremendous therapeutic value. In general, such measurable physiological alterations are associated with the autonomic life support functions that lie beyond normal conscious control.

Natural Antidote

Some researchers believe that meditation offers a natural antidote to the stresses and strains of everyday life because it gives the body a chance to dissipate unwanted build-up of effects resulting from the fight-or-flight response. This response was identified in the 1950s as a legacy from the distant past when our ancestors faced dangers calling for rapid, spontaneous action. Self-preservation dictated that – under threat – people either turn tail and run or stand the ground and fight. Either way, the body needs to gear itself up to unleash the necessary energy. In the Western world, running or fighting is unnecessary except in the most extreme circumstances. But the body does not discriminate between the threat posed by, say, an unjust tax demand or a car heading for a collision. They are threats of a different dimension, but they trigger the same kind of response. And the constant physiological process of keying up, without the release of physical reaction, can take its toll.

Meditation provides what has been dubbed the 'relaxation response' by Dr Herbert Benson of the Harvard Medical School. This relaxation response is a quietening down of pulse rate, blood pressure and other physiological regulators. Once the body has been calmed, the mind can purposefully counteract the adverse effects of the fight-or-light response.

One of the more revolutionary developments growing out of the study of meditation is biofeedback. Its purpose is to make people conscious of physiological functions (of which they are not usually aware) through machines that monitor these internal processes and give visual or auditory signals of changes. The theory is that it will then be possible for the individual to control those physiological processes associated with psychological states such as breathing and heart rate. Biofeedback is particularly useful for those who want to reduce high levels of stress or deal with 'blocks' – caused, for instance, by pre-exam anxiety.

Effigies, such as the one above, are sometimes used to harm a victim by witchcraft. Here a pin has been passed through the doll's mouth with the intention that the victim will be hurt in her mouth, too. The mind, it is believed by some, can be used to kill in this way.

Like the eastern adept, seen right, we can all, it seems, learn to control bodily functions such as heart rate, through the technique of biofeedback.

Mastering Control

Once you have been connected to a machine that records the heart rate, the speed of the beat will produce a specific sound tone, heard through a pair of headphones. As you relax, slowing down the heart, you can hear the tone and pitch fall. By concentrating on something calming, you can bring your heart rate down to an acceptable level.

Biofeedback can also help reduce brain activity, inducing a feeling of relaxed – almost meditative – well-being. Electrodes placed on the scalp are connected to an electro-encephalograph (EEG) machine, which detects electrical activity in the brain. As you relax, the normal functioning of the brain slows down and the EEG machine begins to reflect a pattern of so-called 'alpha waves' coming from the cortex (the outer layer of the brain). Knowing when the brain is putting out alpha rhythms will allow you to control thoughts that produce alpha activity, thereby producing greater peace of mind.

Maxwell Cade, an expert on biofeedback and who described his work in *The Awakened Mind,* is a scientist who was also trained in Zen and who has carried our research in the field of healing, as well as self-healing. Biofeedback, he has said, provides a quicker route towards self-awareness and the technique has therapeutic value as well. Biofeedback, Cade claims, is as effective as hypnotherapy in producing 'almost miraculous relief of symptoms' but gives more lasting results. Indeed,

there is clinical evidence that those with hypertension (high blood pressure) can be taught to relax and thereby relieve their condition by watching a machine that gives continuous visual feedback.

Arguably, the preventive and therapeutic aspects of techniques such as meditation, self-help, biofeedback and similar practices are sufficient to command much wider interest among the medical community. But it is in other areas, most especially sport, that their potential has been most avidly seized on, and nowhere more enthusiastically than in Eastern Europe.

Here,a branch of applied psychology, called psychic self-regulation (PSR), has developed. It is a blend of hypnosis, yoga and the martial arts, leading to control of various physiological and psychological functions. Some athletic training programmes, for instance, specifically include meditation, hypnosis and other related techniques.

MENTAL TRAINING

Although the United States has not in general embraced such techniques, the United States Olympic Committee has included biofeedback and mental training courses in some of their programmes. In baseball, the Detroit Tigers are known to have used biofeedback, and the Philadelphia Phillies have tried TM.

Many individual competitors, meanwhile, have used mental techniques to help themselves perform better, among them tennis star Billie Jean King, Olympic 400-metres champion Lee Evans, bodybuilder Arnold Schwarzenegger, and high jumper Dwight Stone. They visualise themselves in advance in the winning position, playing the perfect stroke or extracting the maximum effort. We do not yet fully understand how mental techniques actually help to improve sports performance or conquer disease. But there is no reason why people should not expose themselves to mind-over-body systems. It is a generally known that most of us live well below our physical and mental potential. So there certainly seems to be a case for considering those techniques that might stretch us to reach new levels of self-awareness and ability.

Arnold Schwarzenegger,* right, *world-famous bodybuilder and film star, is one of the few Westerners to use mental techniques in training and performing. In contrast, most athletes from the East receive psychological as well as physical training.

An experienced meditator can choose any quiet place to meditate, indoors or out. Many prefer to sit in a yoga posture, such as the 'lotus', shown above.

RELAXATION FOR MIND AND BODY

Meditation has become increasingly popular in the West in recent years, both as a way to cope with the stresses of daily life and as a medical treatment. The many techniques all have in common the attainment of a deep relaxation – almost suspension – of the mind and body. The following is just one method.

First, find a comfortable seat in a quiet room where you will not be disturbed for at least 15 minutes. It is best to keep your feet flat on the floor and your hands clasped loosely in your lap. Wear something loose.

Now close your eyes and relax your body completely. Do this gradually, starting with the toes and working up little by little to the top of the head.

Breathe in and out of the nose, concentrating until respiration becomes soft, smooth and regular. If your mind begins to wander, pull it back to your breathing.

Empty your mind of all thought. One way to do this is to direct your mind to a spot on your own body, and keep it there. Your breathing will soon become almost imperceptible. Aim to remain in this relaxed state for between 15 and 20 minutes.

Open your eyes gently and come out of the relaxed state very slowly. Enjoy the peaceful feeling that should now have been induced for a few minutes before standing up. Then stretch slowly from head to toe.

PERSPECTIVES

THE WOUNDS OF CHRIST?

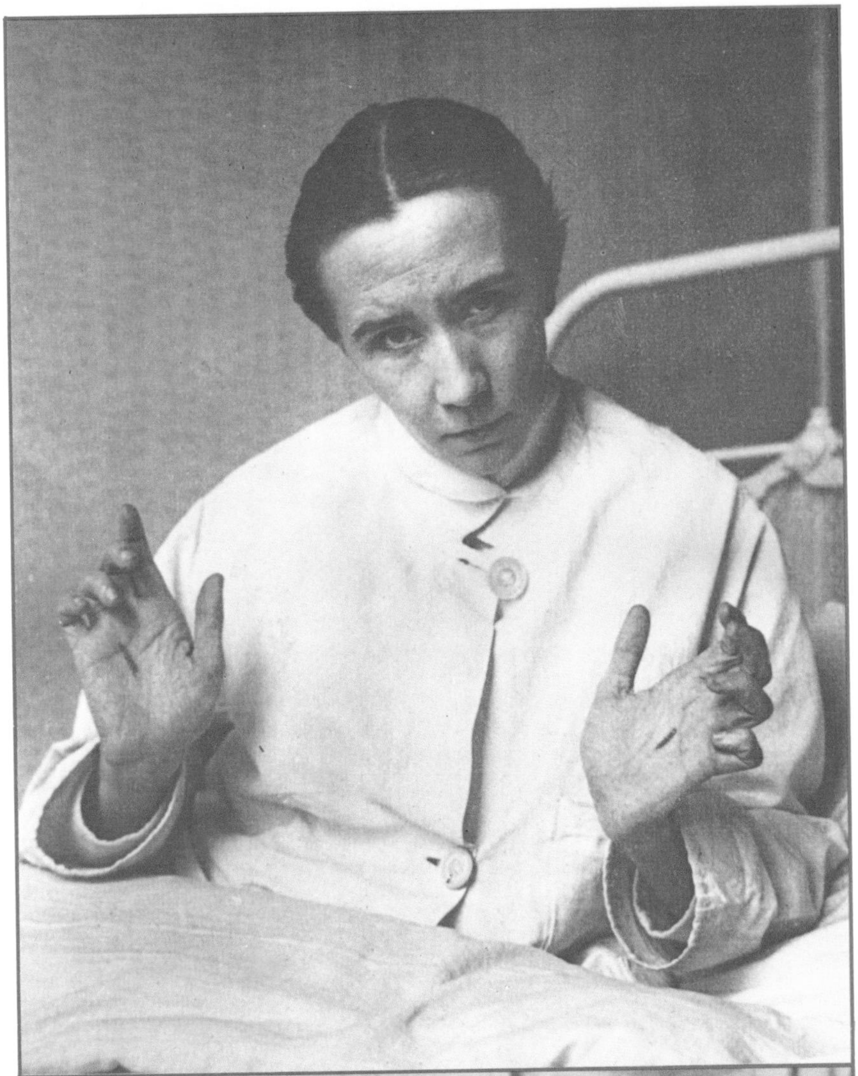

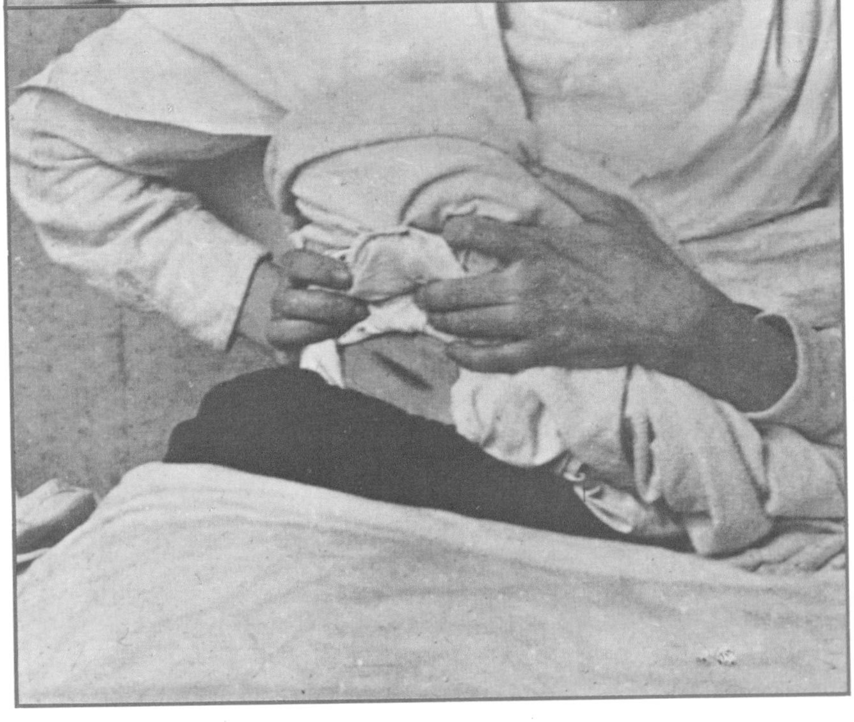

WHAT CAUSES THE PHYSICAL PHENOMENON OF STIGMATA? IS IT, AS MANY BELIEVE, THE RESULT OF MEDITATION ON CHRIST'S SUFFERINGS BY A SAINTLY PERSON? OR IS IT A CLINICAL CONDITION, PERHAPS EVEN SOME FORM OF HYSTERIA?

The curious phenomenon of stigmata – the mysterious appearance of wounds resembling, as far as one can tell, those that were suffered by Christ on the cross – is almost exclusively found among members of the Roman Catholic faith. Church records, therefore, contain all essential information for researchers in this field. Yet the Church cannot be said to be objective about the phenomenon, for it allows for the occurrence of both 'divine' and 'diabolical' stigmata, depending in theory on the saintliness or otherwise of the individual stigmatic. One criterion has been consistently applied, however: stigmatics who exploit their wounds for fame or wealth are said to be demonstrably 'diabolical'.

If such ostentatious display is indeed a factor in determining the 'divine' or 'diabolical' origin of

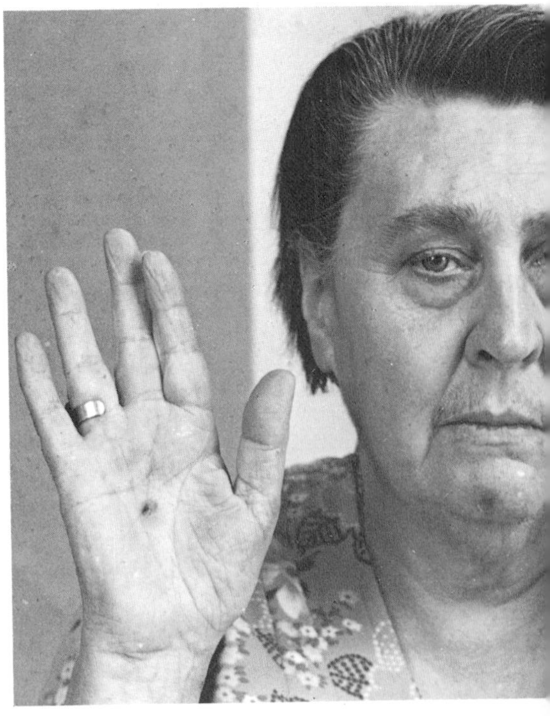

stigmata, then Elizabeth of Herkenrode should have been damned long ago. This 13th-century nun spent most of her life in almost continual trance, enacting the whole of the Passion every 24 hours, often portraying Christ and several of his tormentors by turns. Father Thurston, the Roman Catholic historian, described the scene, drawing on contemporary accounts as follows:

'Catching hold of the bosom of her own dress with her right hand, she would pull herself to the right; and then with the left hand she would drag herself in the opposite direction. At another time, stretching out her arm and raising her fist threateningly, she would strike herself a violent blow on the jaw so that her whole body seemed to reel and totter under the impact'.

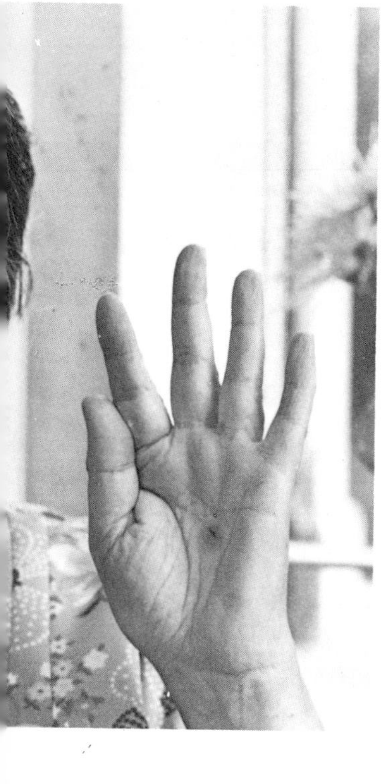

***Georges Marasco*, far left, *was stigmatised during Holy Week in 1923. Here he shows shows the wounds in his hands, and in his side*, below left.**

Mortado, the music hall performer*, right, *was billed as 'the only man with marks of crucifixion'. The origin of his stigmata is obscure, but his ostentatious display of them left Roman Catholics in no doubt: he was quite simply a puppet of the Devil.

The English stigmatic Ethel Chapman*, below, *who died in the late 1970s, shows the hand-wounds that occurred every Easter, as she felt nails were being driven into her palms.

She was, apparently, dramatising scenes and actions experienced in her visions; and at appropriate moments, scourge marks – those of the 'crown of thorns' – and stigmata would open up on her body and gush blood.

Self-Inflicted Blows

Not all stigmata occur in the same way. Domenica Lazarri (who died in 1848) and the English stigmatic Teresa Higginson (whose 'blessed death' came 50 years later), for instance, beat themselves mercilessly with their own fists. Domenica's self-inflicted blows were so loud, it is said, that they were heard out on the street, and Teresa believed firmly that her beatings were administered by the Devil himself. The revered mystic and stigmatic, St Mary Magdalen de'Pazzi, was undoubtedly motivated by the ecstatic union with God that was to inspire her writings; but the relish with which she exhorted her superiors to flog her and with which she, too, whipped her novices is hardly edifying. One can sympathise with Father Thurston's perplexity concerning the phenomenon, as he wrote:

'There are many instances of stigmatisation where imposture is out of the question but in which many of the details recorded are suggestive rather of disease than of that showing forth of the divine attributes which we associate with the idea of a miracle.'

Sceptical scientists, often prefer to dismiss these stories and their frequently unimpeachable witnesses as the subjects of hoaxes, delusions or wishful thinking. There are many, meanwhile, who believe that the 'stigmatic complex' corresponds to certain psychoneurotic conditions, particularly one known as 'hysteria'. To the majority of people – including most Catholic theologians – the term conjures up an image of highly excitable neuropaths or weak-minded, pathological liars, who are given to tantrums and excessive scenes with the express purpose of getting their own way.

Call someone hysterical, and almost inevitably it is taken as an insult. The clinical meaning of the term is, however, quite different. Before the 20th century, hysteria was believed to be exclusively a woman's complaint. (The word 'hysteria' derives from the Greek for 'womb'.) But psychiatrists dealing with the effects of extreme stress on soldiers in the trenches discovered that men can suffer from 'hysterical' symptoms, too. Indeed, there is even said to be a hysterical personality type.

Hysterical Symptoms

Such an individual may sometimes indulge in the dramatic and exaggerated behaviour commonly associated with 'hysteria', but the symptoms can afflict anyone in circumstances of stress, heightened emotion or inner conflict. Indeed, they may actually be useful to us when we are in danger. There are even cases on record of soldiers in action who are suddenly smitten with inexplicable paralysis or blindness. Tests show that they are not malingering – the symptoms are real enough – but the cause is discovered to be hysterical. The soldier cannot face the battle any longer; but because of his training and a fear of being labelled a coward, he cannot give in to his terror and run away. Instead, his brain resolves the conflict for him, causing his body to cease functioning.

There are also cases where symptoms are revealed – under hypnosis, for example – to be literal translations of everyday sayings. 'I can't go on', for example, may be 'translated' by the brain into hysterical lameness; 'I can't face it' into blindness; and even 'it's all a pain in the neck' into the matching physical symptom. So certain allegedly holy manifestations – such as the appearance of a wedding-ring-like ridge or indentation around the appropriate finger of a nun (or 'bride of Christ') – may also be a form of hysteria.

Hysterical symptoms are, most psychiatrists agree, not incompatible with ordinary lives nor with those of the highest sanctity. So hysteria does not 'explain away' stigmata, as many Church apologists fear, but in fact could well describe the mechanism of this bizarre phenomena.

Yet most Roman Catholics still regard a 'hysterical' explanation of stigmata as an insult and a blasphemy, pointing out that stigmatics such as St Gemma Galgani, Padre Pio or St Teresa of Avila were humble, quiet and distinctly unexcitable. But a closer look at the lives of such 'quiet' stigmatics often reveals a history of mysterious maladies and an abnormal physical sensitivity. They were frequently subject to a range of inexplicable illnesses, including black-outs, fits, paralysis, blindness and so on. Many were also victims of tuberculosis, which heightens suggestibility. And, interestingly, the visions that stigmatised them also often marked the end of their many mystery illnesses.

Many stigmatics also develop the sort of behaviour associated with the shaman (or witch doctor) of more primitive societies: going into trances, having visions, exhibiting the ability to heal, levitate, prophesy, or even immunity to fire. Many also reveal multiple personalities – Teresa Higginson, Constante Mary Castreca (a 17th-century Italian nun), Mother Beatrice Mary of Jesus, and Teresa Neumann, who also spoke in tongues, for instance. It may well be that stigmatics are the Catholic Church's equivalent of shamans; but even so, multiple personality is now recognised as a hysterical symptom, and it could be that many of the 'gifts' displayed by such people, including stigmata, have the same cause.

Reliving the Crucifixion

Teresa Neumann, a Bavarian stigmatic who was investigated by many doctors as well as researchers into the paranormal during the course of her lifetime (1898-1962), would bleed every Thursday or Friday when experiencing what has been described as 'religious ecstasy'. In 1925, she had been miraculously cured of blindness and paralysis, following the beatification of St Theresa of Lisieux; and it was soon after this that the mysterious bleeding first began.

Waking from a deep sleep, she would suddenly sit up and stretch out her hands. As she did so, her eyes half-closed, blood-stained tears would appear running down her pale cheeks, before clotting on her face. On each occasion, it seems, she would relive in her mind the entire story of the Crucifixion, and while she meditated, the stigmata would appear on her hands, feet and forehead. Sceptics have pointed out the possibility of self-inflicted wounds; but several witnesses remain convinced that these were indeed those of Christ.

Another clue to a possible hysterical foundation for stigmata comes from the component of suggestibility. The wounds of St Veronica Giuliani (who died in 1727) opened and bled at the command of her confessor, just as the Belgian stigmatic Louise Lateau and others could be recalled instantly from their highest ecstasies by the command of their superiors. The side-wound of Anne Catherine Emmerich was known to resemble the unusual Y-shaped crucifix in the church at Coesfeld in Germany where she meditated as a child. And the scourge marks of St Gemma Galgani apparently reproduced exactly those on her favourite crucifix.

This subjective element in the patterning of stigmata, and the great variety of forms it takes, also seems to argue for a hysterical foundation. Wounds have been known to range from simple red spots to cross-shaped fissures, and round, oblong or square holes in the hands; 'nail-heads' have marked the backs of hands or the palms of feet, even the soles, and side-wounds have shown similar variations, according to how the stigmatic imagines Christ was crucified. Significantly, perhaps, there are no known examples of wounds occurring in the wrists, the site of the wounds suggested by certain researchers into the Turin Shroud. But now that this is quite common knowledge among the devout, it is thought that future stigmatics could well exhibit wrist wounds.

Holy Anguish

From autumn 1911 until 1968, the most famous of 20th-century stigmatics, Padre Pio, bled regularly from his hands and feet.The wounds were exceedingly painful; his sore hands would have to be bandaged and then covered by mittens; and his shoes – now preserved as relics – had to be especially enlarged in order to make room for thick dressings.

In a letter dated 8 September 1911 to Father Benedetto, his spiritual guide, Padre Pio wrote

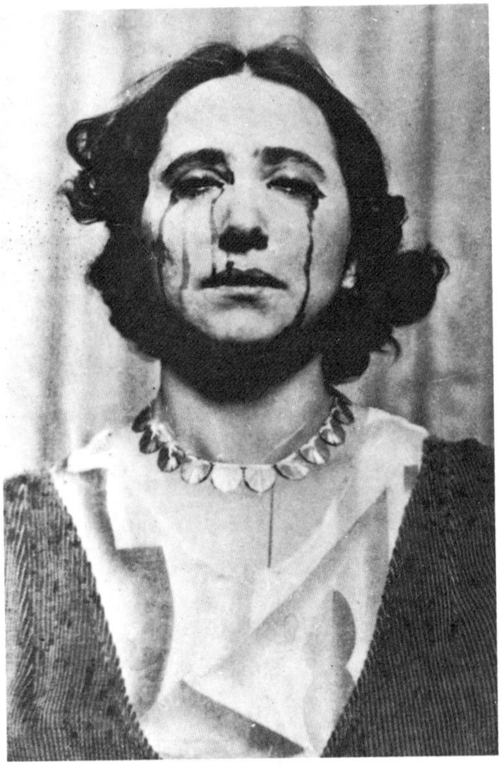

Weeping blood,* right, *is a rare phenomenon, closely related to true stigmata and equally mysterious.

Padre Pio,* far right, *experienced stigmata for well over 50 years, in the form of bleeding hands and feet, while on his chest was a wound resembling an inverted cross.

describing the affliction: 'Yesterday evening something happened to me that I can neither explain nor understand. Red marks appeared in the middle of the palms of my hands; they are about the size of a cent; and in the centre of the red part, I feel a very acute pain... At the altar, sometimes, I feel as if my whole being is on fire... my face particularly seems to be ablaze'.

But it was on 20 September 1918, shortly after celebrating the feast of St Francis (who was also a stigmatic), that Padre Pio – while alone and praying, at the chapel of the village of San Giovanni Rotondo – experienced the wounds that were to mark him for the rest of his life, and which never ceased bleeding, yet never became infected. These stigmata marked his hands, front and back, and both his feet. On his chest, meanwhile, was a wound resembling an inverted cross. Intriguingly, he bled most copiously from Thursday evenings to

*In*Focus

THE MARKS OF EASTER

Cloretta Robertson was just 12 years-old in 1974 when she first experienced the stigmata she went on to suffer every springtime as Easter approached. There were many witnesses, too; for the bleeding emanating from her forehead and dripping right down her face, started in the classroom at her Oakland, California school, in the middle of a maths lesson.

The case of this highly religious black girl is somewhat unique: for Cloretta is not in fact a Catholic, but a Baptist. The bleeding also occurs not only on her forehead but at all the traditional sites of Christ's wounds.

Several doctors have examined her. However, as the blood is wiped away, there is never any sign of an actual wound, merely discolouration. What is more, analysis has shown the blood from the stigmata to be her own. Since this time, Cloretta has also demonstrated an ability to heal. The New Light Baptist Church, meanwhile, has experienced delight at one of its members being 'chosen' in this visible and quite remarkable way.

" THE VISION OF THE PERSON FADED AND I SAW THAT MY HANDS, FEET AND SIDE HAD BEEN PIERCED AND WERE DRIPPING BLOOD. IMAGINE THE AGONY I FELT AT THAT MOMENT AND CONTINUE TO FEEL, NEARLY EVERY DAY; THE WOUND IN MY BREAST BLEEDS COPIOUSLY, ESPECIALLY FROM THURSDAY EVENING UNTIL SATURDAY ... I'M AFRAID I'LL DIE THROUGH LOSS OF BLOOD IF THE LORD DOES NOT HEAR THE CRIES OF MY POOR HEART AND STOP DOING THIS TO ME... "

PADRE PIO

Saturday, and was always fearful that he might die through loss of blood.

Noted, too, for his prophecies, healing gifts and facility of 'bilocation' (being in two places at once), this remarkable man was visited by many thousands of pilgrims in the course of his life. Yet the Vatican expressly forbade him to write about his stigmata or even to leave his monastery. He was even prevented from celebrating Mass in public and hearing confessions. Financial contributions from visitors, however, enabled him to build a magnificent hospital right by the monastery.

Those who knew Padre Pio well were only too aware of the extent of his suffering. His greatest anguish, however, is said to have been caused by those who claimed his stigmata were actually self-inflicted wounds.

There have been many attempts to reproduce stigmata by hypnosis, but the only results have been a short-lived reddening of the skin, or sporadic bleeding. This pales in comparison with the dramatic piercings and copious bleedings of 'genuine' stigmata which have defied normal healing processes and stayed with the stigmatics for most of their lives. Outside the religious context, where there is no need for stigmata to take the form stylised by the crucifixion of Christ, there are many kinds of paranormal and even psychological phenomena where spontaneous formations or lesions of the skin may develop. One such case was that of Eleonore Zugun, a famous poltergeist victim, studied by Harry Price the 1920s, whose skin showed weals, bite marks and even raised lettering when she believed she was being attacked by a devil that only she could see.

In many, if not all, cases of stigmata, the effects seem somehow to stem from the subconscious mind of the stigmatic. In time, we may begin to understand the process involved. But in that case, the miraculous would become the mundane; and for the devout, such a loss could be hard to bear.

THOUGHTS MADE FLESH

In a photograph taken in the 1930s, below, pilgrims approach the holy city of Lhasa, the forbidden capital of Tibet. The modern photograph, below right, testifies to the continuing practice of this arduous form of religious devotion. One of the most remarkable pilgrims to have undertaken this journey was Alexandra David-Neel, seen right with a companion, the lama Yongden. During the 1920s, she travelled throughout Tibet and learned many of the secrets of the Tibetan Buddhists, including the art of making thought forms materialise.

APPARITIONS, MANY PEOPLE BELIEVE, EXIST ONLY IN THE HUMAN MIND. BUT WHAT OF THE ART ALLEGEDLY PRACTISED BY TIBETAN ADEPTS – THAT OF MAKING THEIR THOUGHT FORMS MATERIALISE SO STRONGLY THAT THEY CAN ACTUALLY BE SEEN BY OTHER PEOPLE?

Conditions on the road from China to Lhasa, the forbidden capital city of Tibet, were even worse than usual in the winter of 1923 – 1924. Nevertheless, small numbers of travellers, mostly pilgrims wishing to obtain spiritual merit by visiting the holy city and its semi-divine ruler, the Dalai Lama, struggled onwards through the bitter winds and heavy snow. Among them was an elderly woman who appeared to be a peasant from some distant province of the god-king's empire.

The woman was poorly dressed and equipped. Her red woollen skirt and waistcoat, her quilted jacket, and her cap with its lambskin earflaps, were worn and full of holes. From her shoulder hung an ancient leather bag, black with dirt. In this, were the provisions for her journey: barley meal, a piece of dried bacon, a brick of compressed tea, a tube of rancid butter, and a little salt and soda.

With her black hair coated with grease and her dark brown face, she looked like a typical peasant woman. But her hair was really white, dyed with Chinese ink, and her complexion took its colour from oil mixed with cocoa and crushed charcoal. For this Tibetan peasant woman was in reality Alexandra David-Neel, a French woman who, 30 years before, had been an opera singer of note, warmly congratulated by Jules Massenet for her performance in the title role of his opera *Manon*. In the intervening years, Mme David-Neel had travelled to many strange places and had undergone even stranger experiences. These included meeting a magician with the ability to cast spells to hurl flying rice cakes at his enemies, and learning the techniques of *tumo*, an occult art that enables its adepts to sit naked amid the Himalayan snows. Most extraordinary of all, she had constructed, by means of mental and psychic exercises, a *tulpa* – a phantom form born solely from the imagination, and yet so strongly vitalised by the adept's will that it actually becomes visible to other people. A *tulpa* is, to put it another way, an extremely powerful example of what occultists term a thought form.

To understand the nature of the *tulpa,* one has to appreciate that, as far as Tibetan Buddhists (and most Western occultists) are concerned, thought is far more than an intellectual function. Every thought, they believe, affects the 'mind-stuff' that permeates the world of matter, in very much the same way as a stone thrown into a lake makes ripples upon the water's surface. A thought, in other words, produces a 'thought ripple'.

Lasting Ripples

Usually thought ripples have only a short life. They decay almost as soon as they are created and make no lasting impression. If, however, the thought is particularly intense, the product of deep passion or fear, or if it is of long duration, the subject of much brooding and meditation, the thought ripple builds into a more permanent thought form, one that has a longer and more intense life.

Tulpas and other thought forms are not considered by Tibetan Buddhists to be 'real' – but neither, according to them, is the world of matter that seemingly surrounds us and appears solid enough. Both are illusory. As a Buddhist classic from the first century AD expresses this firm belief: 'All phenomena are originally in the mind and have really no outward form; therefore, as there is no form, it is an error to think that anything is there. All phenomena merely arise from false notions in the mind. If the mind is independent of these false ideas, then all phenomena disappear.'

If the beliefs about thought forms held by Tibetan Buddhists, mystics and magicians are justified, then many ghostly happenings, hauntings, and cases of localities endowed with a strong 'psychic atmosphere' are easily explained. It seems plausible, for example, that the thought forms created by the violent and passionate mental processes of a murderer, supplemented by the terror stricken emotions of a victim, could linger around the scene of the crime for months, years or even centuries. This could produce intense depression and anxiety in those who visited the 'haunted' spot and, if the thought forms were sufficiently powerful, 'apparitions', such as a re-enactment of the crime, might at times be witnessed by people possessed of psychic sensitivity.

Sometimes, it is even claimed by students of the occult, that those 'spirits' that haunt a particular spot are in fact *tulpas,* thought forms that have been deliberately created by a sorcerer for his own purposes.

The existence of extremely potent thought forms that re-enact the past would, of course, also explain the worldwide reports of visitors to old battlefields 'witnessing' military encounters that took place long before. The sites of the battle of Naseby, which took place during England's Civil War, for instance, and of the 1942 commando raid on Dieppe, are among battlefields that enjoy such ghostly reputations.

A *tulpa* is no more than an extremely powerful thought form, no different in its essential nature from many other ghostly apparitions. Where, however, it does differ from a normal thought form is that it has come into existence, not as a result of an accident, a side-effect of a mental process, but as the result of a deliberate act of will.

The word tulpa is a Tibetan one, but there are adepts in almost every part of the world who believe they are able to manufacture these beings by first drawing together and coagulating some of the mind-stuff of the Universe, and then transferring to it some of their own vitality.

Creative Power

In Bengal, home of much Indian occultism, the technique is called *kriya shakti* ('creative power'), and is studied and practised by the adepts of Tantrism, a religious magical system concerned with the spiritual aspects of sexuality and numbering both Hindus and Buddhists among its devotees. Initiates of so-called 'left-handed' Tantric cults – that is to say, cults in which men and woman engage in ritual sexual intercourse for mystical and magical purposes – are considered particularly skilled in *kriya shakti*. This is because it is thought that the intense physical and cerebral excitement of the orgasm engenders quite exceptionally vigorous thought forms.

Many Tibetan mystical techniques originated in Bengal, particularly in Bengali Tantrism, and there is a very strong resemblance between the physical, mental and spiritual exercises used by the Tantric yogis of Bengal and the secret inner disciplines of Tibetan Buddhism. It thus seems likely that Tibetans originally derived their theories about *tulpas,* and their methods of creating these strange beings, from Bengali practitioners of *kriya shakti*.

Students of *tulpa* magic begin their training in the art of creating these 'thought beings' by adopting one of the many gods or goddesses of the Tibetan pantheon as a 'tutelary deity' – a sort of patron saint. But while Tibetan initiates regard the gods respectfully, they do not look upon them with any great admiration. For, according to Buddhist belief, although the gods have great powers and are, in a sense 'supernatural', they are just as much slaves of illusion, just as much trapped in the wheel of birth, death, and rebirth, as the humble peasant.

The student retires to a hermitage or other secluded place and meditates on his tutelary deity, known as a *yidam,* for many hours. Here, he combines a contemplation of the spiritual attributes traditionally associated with the *yidam* with visualisation exercises, designed to build up in the mind's eye an image of the *yidam* as portrayed in paintings and statues. To ensure that every waking moment is dedicated to concentrating on the *yidam,* the student continually chants traditional mystic phrases associated with the deity he serves.

The rigorous mental and physical discipline taught by Buddhism enables some of its followers, such as the monk seen,* below, *with drum and incense stick, to attain paranormal powers. In her book* Initiations and Initiates in Tibet, *Alexandra David Neel even tells of a man* (right, *standing on* left) *who was reputed to be able to hypnotise a subject and cause death at a distance.

Protective Circles

He also constructs the *kyilkhors* – literally circles, but actually symbolic diagrams that may be of any shape – believed sacred to his god. Sometimes he will draw these with coloured inks on paper or wood, sometimes he will engrave them on copper or silver, sometimes he will outline them on his floor with coloured powders.

The preparation of the *kyilkhors* must be undertaken with care, for the slightest deviation from the

*In*Focus

WOLF AT THE DOOR

In her book **Psychic Self Defence,** the occultist Dion Fortune, **left,** related how she once 'formulated a were-wolf accidentally'.

She had this alarming experience while brooding about her feelings of resentment against someone who had hurt her. Lying on her bed, she was thinking of the terrifying wolf-monster of Norse mythology, Fenrir, when suddenly she felt a large grey wolf traditional pattern associated with a particular *yidam* is believed to be extremely dangerous, putting the unwary student in peril of obsession, madness, death, or a stay of thousands of years in one of the hells of Tibetan cosmology.

It is interesting to compare this belief with the idea, strongly held by many Western occultists, that if a magician engaged in evoking a spirit to visible appearance draws his protective magical circle incorrectly, he will be torn in pieces.

Eventually, if the student has persisted with the prescribed exercises, he 'sees' his *yidam,* at first nebulously and briefly, but then persistently and with complete – and sometimes terrifying – clarity.

But this is only the first stage of the process. Meditation, visualisation of the *yidam,* the repetition of spells and contemplation of mystic diagrams is continued until the *tulpa,* in the form of the *yidam,* actually materialises. The devotee can feel the touch of the *tulpa's* feet when he lays his head upon them; he can see the creature's eye following him as he moves about; he can even conduct conversations with it.

Thoughts Made Visible

Eventually, the *tulpa* may be prepared to leave the vicinity of the *kyilkhors* and accompany the devotee on journeys. If the *tulpa* has been fully vitalised, it will by now often be visible to others besides its creator.

Alexandra David-Neel tells how she 'saw' a phantom of this sort which, curiously enough, had not yet become visible to its creator. At the time, Mme David-Neel had developed a great interest in Buddhist art. One afternoon, she was visited by a Tibetan painter who specialised in portraying the 'wrathful deities'. As he approached, she was astonished to see behind him the misty form of one of these much feared and rather unpleasant beings. As she approached the phantom, she stretched out an arm towards it and felt as if she were 'touching a soft object whose substance gave way under the slight push'.

The painter told her that he had for some weeks been engaged in magical rites, calling on the god whose form she had seen, and that he had spent the entire morning painting its picture.

Intrigued by this experience, Mme David-Neel set about making a *tulpa* for herself. To avoid being influenced by the many Tibetan paintings and images she had seen on her travels, she decided to 'make' not a god or goddess, but a fat, jolly-looking monk whom she could visualise very clearly, and began to concentrate her mind.

She retired to a hermitage, and for some months devoted every waking minute to exercises in concentration and visualisation. Soon she began to get brief glimpses of the monk out of the corner of her eye. He became more solid and lifelike in appearance; and eventually, when she left her hermitage and started on a caravan journey, he included himself in the party, becoming clearly visible and performing actions that she had neither commanded nor consciously expected him to do. He would, for instance, walk and stop to look around him as a traveller might do. Sometimes Mme David-Neel even felt his robe brush against her, and once a hand seemed to touch her shoulder.

Mme David-Neel's *tulpa* eventually began to develop in an unexpected and unwished-for manner. He grew leaner, his expression became malignant, and he was 'troublesome and bold'. One day, a herdsman, who brought Mme David-Neel a present of some butter, saw the *tulpa* in her tent, and mistook it for a real monk. It had got out of control. Indeed, her creation turned into what she called a 'day-nightmare' and she decided to get rid of it. Eventually it took her six months of concentrated effort and meditation to do so.

If this, and many similar stories told in Tibet, are to be believed, the creation of a *tulpa* is not a matter to be undertaken lightly. It is, in fact, yet another fascinating example of the remarkable powers of the human mind.

Tibetan Buddhists regard their gods, such as the representations above, with reverence but believe that they are no less trapped in the cycles of birth, death and rebirth than any human being. They even attempt to make the gods materialise by a sustained effort of concentration.

materialise beside her, and was aware of its body pressing against hers.

From her reading about thought forms, Fortune knew she must gain control of the beast immediately. So she dug her elbow into its hairy ribs and pushed the creature off the bed. The animal disappeared through the wall.

The story was not yet over, however, for another member of the household said she had seen the eyes of the wolf in the corner of her room. Dion Fortune realised she must destroy the creature. Summoning the beast, she saw a thin thread joining it to her and began to imagine she was drawing the life out of the beast along this thread. The wolf faded to a formless grey mass, and ceased to exist.

CASEBOOK

THE FISHERMEN'S TALE

The account of a close encounter that follows is one of the classics of UFO literature – and deservedly so, if the story told by the witnesses is true. But is it? The case is typical of many UFO reports: there were few witnesses, the bulk of the information coming from one man, as the second witness lost consciousness at the beginning of the incident. In such circumstances, even when sophisticated techniques, such as lie detector tests, are used, only the personal integrity of the witnesses can substantiate their story.

The six-month period from October 1973 to March 1974 was a remarkable one for UFO sightings, particularly in the United States, north-west Europe, Italy and Spain. One of the most outstanding reports in the USA came from Pascagoula, county town of Jackson County, in the state of Mississippi. This town, with a population of just under 30,000 at the time, is situated at the south of the Pascagoula River on the coast of the Gulf of Mexico, about 100 miles (160 kilometres) to the east of New Orleans.

There were two witnesses, both of whom worked locally at the Walker Shipyard: Charles E. Hickson aged 45, a foreman, and Calvin R. Parker Jr, 18, who alleged that, on 11 October 1973, they experienced a close encounter with a UFO and its occupants, and subsequent abduction, while fishing from the pier of the Shaupeter shipyard on the Pascagoula River.

It was about 9 p.m. when Hickson turned to get fresh bait. He says it was then that he heard a 'zipping' noise. Looking up, he saw an elongated, oval, bluish-grey craft, which in a later interview he was to refer to as 'a spacecraft'. It had very bright, flashing, 'blue-looking' lights. This object was hovering some 2 feet (60 centimetres) off the ground; and when the next move came, the witness was a trifle puzzled, for he said: 'It seemed to open up, but really there wasn't a door there at all . . . and three creatures came *floating out* towards us. I was so scared, I couldn't believe it was happening'.

The creatures were said to be pale, 'ghost-like', and about 5 feet (1.5 metres) tall. Their skin seemed to be wrinkled, and was a greyish colour, while in place of hands they had 'crab-like claws' or pincers. According to the witness's first report, these entities may have had slits for eyes, but he did not see them. They did have two small cone-shaped ears and a small pointed nose, with a hole below in the place of a mouth. They approached the two flabbergasted fishermen and floated just off the ground without moving their legs. A buzzing noise was heard from one of them and, said Hickson, 'they were on us before we knew it'. The older man was paralysed with fear, and Parker passed out when, apparently, he was touched by one of the creatures.

Meanwhile, two of the entities lifted Hickson from the ground, and they glided motionless into the craft. Hickson claims he had lost all sensation of feeling and weight. He was taken into a very brightly lit room which, however, had no visible light fixtures. His friend was led into another room by the

The artist's impressions show the spacecraft and its strange occupants that appeared in Pascagoula, Mississippi, in October 1973.

third entity. Hickson says he was placed in a reclining position and suspended in such a way that he did not touch any part of the craft. His limbs were completely paralysed; only his eyes were free to move. An instrument that looked like a big eye floated freely backwards and forwards about 9 inches (25 centimetres) above his body, and the creatures turned him so that all parts of his body came under the instrument's scrutiny. After some time, Hickson was guided back outside the craft and was 'floated', together with Parker, back to his position on the pier, landing upright on his feet. He says he was so weak-kneed that he fell over.

Calvin Parker was unconscious throughout the incident, so all the evidence comes from Charlie Hickson. In his first interview, he said the UFO was about 10 feet (3 metres) wide, and something like 8 feet (2.5 metres) high. When it left, he said, it disappeared from sight in less than a second. The occupants were like robots; they 'acted like they had a specific thing to do, and they did it. They didn't try to communicate with us.... I know now that they didn't intend to hurt us physically, but I feared they were going to take us away. I would like to emphasise that they didn't mean us any harm'.

Calvin Parker,* below, *was 18 years old at the time of the close encounter at Pascagoula. He apparently fainted when one of the humanoids touched him and remained unconscious throughout the incident. It was reported that he later suffered a nervous breakdown.

That statement was made in an interview with the *Mississippi Press* a week after the incident. On the day of the encounter, Hickson and Parker had called at the paper's offices, and found them closed. They then went to the sheriff's office, at 11 p.m., to make a report. Richard W. Heiden gave details of what took place in a report to *Flying Saucer Review.* Sheriff Fred Diamond and Captain Glen Ryder interrogated the witnesses, doing everything they could to break the stories, but to no avail. Ryder commented: 'If they were lying to me, they should be in Hollywood'. The interviews were taped. Then the two officers left the witnesses alone and unaware that the recorder was still running. They spoke agitatedly about their experience, and Calvin Parker was so emotionally overcome that he started praying when Hickson left the room. The sheriff was convinced the two fishermen were telling the truth.

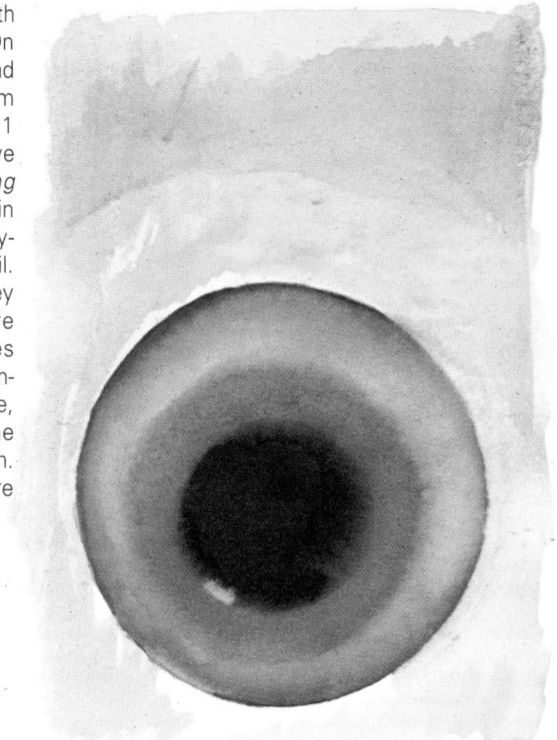

" THE OCCUPANTS WERE LIKE ROBOTS. THEY ACTED LIKE THEY HAD A SPECIFIC THING TO DO, AND THEY DID IT. "

Next morning – Friday 12 October – detective Tom Huntley from the sheriff's office drove Hickson and Parker to Keesler Air Force Base at Biloxi, Mississippi, where they were checked for radiation. There was no evidence of contamination. While there, they gave details of their experience to the head of intelligence at the base, who 'acted as though he'd heard it all before!'

On Sunday, 14 October, the witnesses were interviewed by Dr J. Allen Hynek of Northwestern University, Evanston, Illinois, former civil scientific consultant on UFO reports to the US Air Force, and Dr James Harder of the University of California, Berkeley. Dr Harder hypnotised the men individually, regressing them to the time of the experience. They each relived the terror of the occasion to such an extent that Dr Harder said: 'The experience they underwent was indeed a real one. A very strong feeling of terror is practically impossible to fake

The artist's impression, **above right,** *shows the strange instrument, looking like a big eye, that was said to have floated freely, scanning Hickson's body.*

Charlie Hickson, **right,** *was the principal witness at the scene of the Pascagoula incident. But doubt was cast upon his reliability since details of his story varied substantially with each retelling.*

Dr James Harder, **above left,** *and Dr J. Allen Hynek,* **above right,** *interviewed Charlie Hickson and Calvin Parker shortly after their alleged abduction. Dr Harder hypnotically regressed the men to the time of their experience and both scientists later agreed that the witnesses had been subjected to some very terrifying experience – although they were unable to say precisely what it involved.*

under hypnosis'. Dr Hynek was more reserved: 'There is no question in my mind that these men have had a very terrifying experience'.

On 30 October, Hickson – but not Parker who was apparently suffering from a nervous breakdown – underwent a polygraph examination (lie detector test) at the Pendleton Detective Agency in New Orleans. It was reported that the polygraph operator, Scott Glasgow, was forced to admit after 2½ hours of exhaustive tests that Hickson was telling the truth.

If this is true, it was a very strange remark for a polygraph operator to make. Polygraph tests are not sufficient to establish that a subject is lying; and any polygraph operator would have been well aware of this. In his book *UFOs Explained,* Philip J. Klass claims that his own investigations have shown that Scott Glasgow was not, in fact, qualified as a polygraph operator. So it seems that, in spite of the newspaper publicity given to the fact that Hickson's story stood up to the lie detector test, it must remain inconclusive.

Hickson's experiences brought him considerable publicity; he appeared on television shows and even wrote a book. But unfortunately, his story often changed in the telling. Originally, for instance, he claimed that the UFO was some 10 feet (3 metres) long; but in subsequent interviews, he said it was 20 or 30 feet (7 or 10 metres) long – quite a difference.

Hickson's descriptions of the alien creatures also varied on different occasions. In his original account, Hickson claimed they had two small, cone-like ears, possibly slits where the eyes should have been, and a small sharp nose with a hole below it. Later, again on a television show, he said there were no eyes and that the hole below the nose was a slit. And more than a month after the incident, he disclosed for the first time that the light inside the spacecraft had been so bright that he had suffered severe eye injury, which had persisted for about three days.

These discrepancies, of course, tend to cast doubt upon the entire story – although they do not disprove it. But there are reports that possibly corroborate the evidence. Although no one but Hickson and Parker saw the UFO – despite the fact that the incident happened close to Highway 90, a busy road – many owners of television sets in the Pascagoula area reported interference.

On the same day, 11 October, 450 miles (700 kilometres) away near Hartwell, Georgia, a former Methodist minister was driving along when he saw a UFO land on the road in front of him. He also saw silver-suited, white-haired occupants.

On the same night, too, Police Chief Greenhaw of Falkville, Alabama, was telephoned by a woman who claimed that a 'spaceship' had landed in a field near her house. He raced to the location, armed with a Polaroid camera. There was nothing at the alleged site, but Greenhaw said he was confronted by a silver-suited creature on a side road. He took four Polaroid shots – which indeed show a silvery creature, obligingly turning to face the camera. The entity bolted, and Greenhaw gave chase in his patrol car, but failed to catch up with it – an inconclusive end to an intriguing series of events.

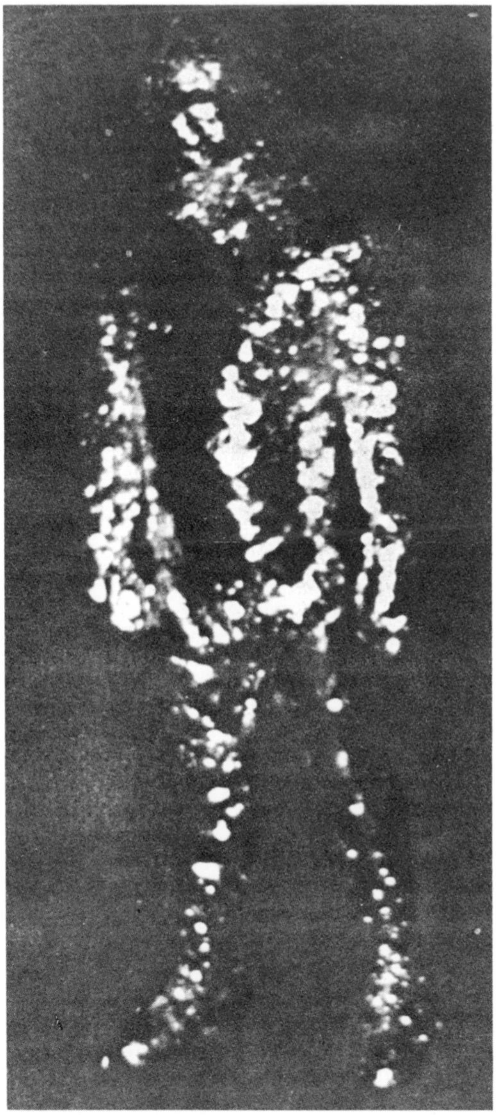

The 'UFO entity', **right,** *was photographed with a Polaroid camera by Police Chief Jeff Greenhaw at Falkville, Alabama, on the night of the Pascagoula encounter. The entity reportedly bolted. Greenhaw drove after it in his patrol car, but did not succeed in catching it.*

BACK INTO THE FUTURE

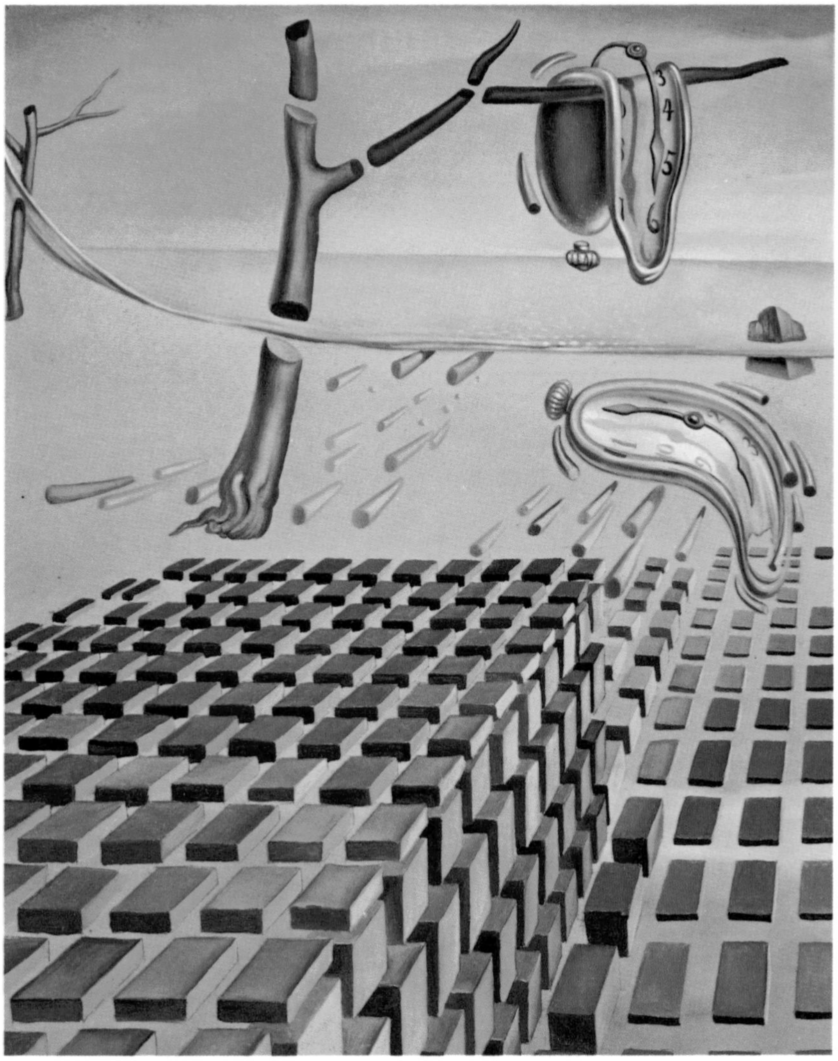

Reports of sudden leaps in time are intriguing. What is it that triggers such events? Have we perhaps already experienced everything to come?

To most people, timeslips are firmly relegated to the realm of 'the supernatural' and left at that. Some, however, would argue that the 'supernatural', as such, cannot exist, since any event arising in the natural Universe in which we live must have natural origins. So even if we cannot explain a particular phenomenon in terms of the known laws of nature, this must be because current knowledge is incomplete. Who, for instance, could explain the mechanism of an eclipse before the true motions of the planets were known?

The mechanism of timeslips eludes us still. So all we can do is sift the evidence and search for common denominators among reputed experiences, and possibly some relationship with known laws of physics. What we do know, however, is that some sort of a trigger factor usually appears to set the occurrence in motion. There is generally an abrupt onset of the experience; and a sensation of living in two time zones at once, either past and present or future and present. There is, too, almost always a feeling of being an integral part of the experience or a participant in the action; an absence of sound from beginning to end of the timeslip; and a marked difference at times between normal light conditions and those experienced during the timeslip. Indeed, a 'silvery light' is often described by those who travel in time this way.

The nightmare scene in the detail from **Disintegration of the Persistence of Memory** *by* **Salvador Dali, above,** *is festooned with melting clocks that seem to represent the concept of journeys in time.*

In a 19th-century mandarin's court, **right,** *an astronomer observes an eclipse through a telescope, while the superstitious fearfully hide their faces – as many still do from reports of timeslips, the precise mechanism of which still eludes us.*

Electric Experiences

It seems that certain physical effects often take place, too, the subject seeing and hearing abnormally and experiencing a feeling of disorientation or detachment. Occasionally, people have also reported a tingling sensation or nausea immediately before they experience a timeslip, just as particularly sensitive people may react to an impending earthquake or thunderstorm. (It is interesting that several of these sensations also herald hauntings or other paranormal happenings.)

One subject wrote describing a tingling in her arms and legs, and a feeling of being 'plugged in'. She may have been much nearer the truth than she realised, for there are indications that some form of electrical activity may well play a part in many paranormal experiences.

This sort of trigger was a major factor in the case of Anne May, the Norwich teacher who, in May 1973, at Clava Cairns in Scotland, experienced a slip into what appeared to be the remote past of the area. Significantly, it was not until she leaned back against one of the standing stones that her extraordinary transition into the past took place, as

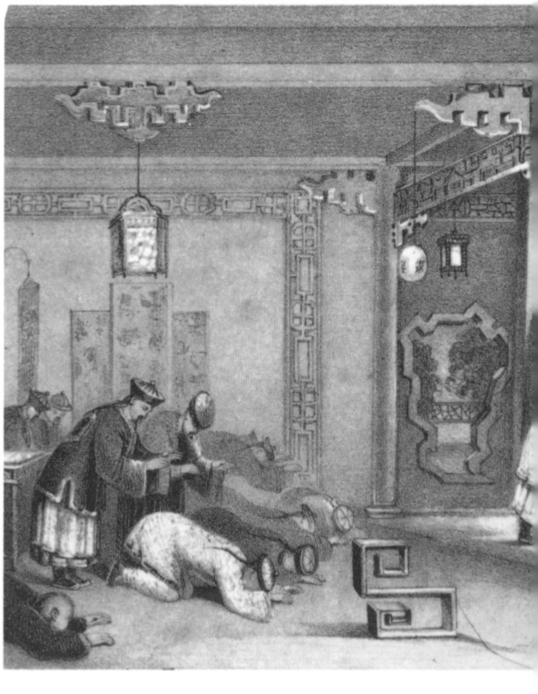

brain was alone in being in the necessary state to receive the information and transform it into pictures and sound?

WAVE PATTERNS

Particularly fascinating is the theory that if the operation of timeslips is due to the transmitting of information from past or future into the present, then that information must already be in existence somewhere. Indeed, perhaps every single component of the world in which we live is continually broadcasting information about itself (form, colour, texture, situation, and so on) by means of 'waves', as yet unknown to science.

> THE MECHANISM OF THE TIMESLIP ELUDES US STILL ... THERE IS GENERALLY AN ABRUPT ONSET OF THE EXPERIENCE; AND A SENSATION OF LIVING IN TWO TIME ZONES AT ONCE, EITHER PAST AND PRESENT OR FUTURE AND PRESENT.

Captain Flowerdew,* inset, *picked up a pink pebble from a beach as a child and instantly 'remembered' a desert city built of pinkish stone where 'he' had died in a battle centuries ago. However, detailed as the memory was, it was not until he saw a television programme about the ancient site of Petra,* above, *that he remembered the city's name.

though a switch had been thrown. Several correspondents have also used that very phrase to describe their individual timeslips. The immediacy of the slip is always pronounced, too. It is as though the trigger object (in Anne May's case, the stone) itself contained the power to evoke the time dislocation she experienced.

PART OF HISTORY

Several people have reported finding themselves actively involved in some historical occasion. One woman, while walking near Bootham Bar, York, for instance, suddenly found herself in the past when a shaft of sunlight struck a coat of arms on the medieval city gate. At once, her awareness of the present dissolved and she discovered herself standing in the midst of a medieval scene, where there were milling barrows, carts and a great crowd of people. She also saw mounted horsemen clearing the way for some great personage who followed them. Then the sun went in, and the whole glowing picture disappeared. There seems little doubt that she 'saw' an actual historical scene and was herself briefly a part of it.

Here, again, the trigger factor is present – in this case, the sudden shaft of light on the coat of arms on the city gate. It may even be possible that the Bar itself had 'recorded' this scene from its own past, and that the particular conditions of light provided by the sudden flash of sunshine 'switched on' the 'playback'. But if that were so, why did the Bar 'choose' to replay this scene out of all its millions of recorded moments? And why was the scene not witnessed and reported by everyone else present in the modern precincts of Bootham Bar in 20-century York? Perhaps that particular scene had some special significance, such as a spontaneous memory of a past life? Or could it be that this woman's

In theory, some of this information may be received and absorbed by surrounding material and, when conditions are appropriate, rebroadcast. Any human being then in the area, whose brain is at the time operating on the same frequency as the transmitter, could – at least in theory – register an audio or visual impression of the original 'wave' pattern sent out by the first broadcaster. Thus, in moments of high emotion or stress, you may yourself be sending out signals into the air that will be received years hence by some sensitive individual. Most (though not all) hauntings are attributed by some to this type of mechanism.

The human brain operates electrically and uses several frequencies. But there is some variation from brain to brain, and not all operate on exactly the same frequencies. So it may be possible that persons sensitive to psychic phenomena are merely tuning in to existing wave patterns (either past or future) by accident, their own brain activity being on the correct frequency for reception at the time.

TOMORROW'S WORLD

What, then, are these mysterious waves that seem to have the power to carry pictures and sounds through time? We do not know as yet. But it is a physical fact that all objects radiate electromagnetic waves. Light waves, which enable us to perceive the world around us, are just one example; and radio waves, infra-red and ultra-violet waves, X-rays and gamma rays are all electromagnetic. Most of these invisible forms of radiation were discovered only within the last century; so other types of radiation may well still await discovery.

The fascinating branch of physics known as quantum mechanics presents the concept of electrons in atoms moving backwards and forwards in time equally easily. Perhaps, therefore, it could be

*In*Focus

THE GIRL FROM SCOTLAND

One afternoon in 1950, Brigadier K. Treseder and colleagues from the British and American embassies in Oslo, Norway, went skiing.

On preparing to return to their base, the Brigadier, his wife and a friend became separated from the others and were suddenly confronted by a tall, old lady dressed in Edwardian clothes who demanded to know why they were trespassing on her land. She spoke English with a Scottish accent and was obviously very angry with them. The three apologised profusely, even though they were utterly mystified by her appearance and outburst, but she continued to complain, adding some bitter comments about modern manners.

A shouted enquiry from the others made the three look round; and when they turned back, the old lady was no longer to be seen: she had vanished. Later it transpired that none of the others had seen her at all.

Local enquiries revealed that, although no eccentric Scottish lady lived there at the time, the local landowner's great grandfather had married 'the girl from Scotland' at the turn of the century.

Was the figure a curiously talkative ghost or a shared hallucination? Or could it be that the skiers actually held a real conversation with a woman from the past?

possible for information from the future to be returned us by some mechanism. So, if such information can indeed be returned from the future, then that future must already exist 'somewhere', in some form. What is more, it may be that we ourselves – and indeed all atomic material – carry within us the seeds of our own future.

The behaviour of individual atomic particles is unpredictable, but it is possible to predict how they will behave en masse. In other words, by cause and effect, all events may perhaps be predetermined. The idea of destiny may even have arisen from an instinctive knowledge of this very fact.

> IN MOMENTS OF HIGH EMOTION OR STRESS, YOU MAY YOURSELF BE SENDING OUT SIGNALS INTO THE AIR THAT WILL BE RECEIVED YEARS HENCE BY SOME SENSITIVE INDIVIDUAL.

Bootham Bar, above, is one of York's medieval city gates, where a pedestrian experienced a slip-back into the city's past when a sudden shaft of sunlight struck a coat of arms on the Bar.

If this were always and wholly true, we and the whole of human history would indeed be predestined and our futures would be laid down for us inescapably. Do we therefore actually have the power to alter and modify our destiny – at least occasionally – by the exercise of will?

When we encounter precognitive experiences, whether dreaming or waking, it may be that we are actually receiving from matter already existing (people, animals, or buildings) information about the future. In the short term, it seems possible that such information is likely to prove true; in the long term, less so – for over a longer period of time, there is greater likelihood of human will being used to intervene in the cause and effect process. With more time available, in theory there should be more opportunities for action, and therefore more opportunities for change.

However, there are exceptions. Occasionally, precognitive experiences will come to completion accurately several years after they have been initially encountered .Indeed, there are cases where there has been a full 20-year lapse between the precognitive experience and its accurate fulfilment. This is, however, unusual.

The view is also sometimes expressed that many bizarre time experiences can be explained as hallucinations. Memory is incompletely understood, and the subconscious mind has proved to be very complex, dreams and hypnosis revealing a level of creativity inaccessible to the conscious mind. The full scope of the human mind has by no means been fathomed, leaving the possibility that time-slips may perhaps be the result of imaginative responses, hysteria, drug usage or even illness at times. However, even when all these factors have been considered, there still remain experiences that cannot be accounted for – or which can only be accounted for by analogies that relate to the electromagnetic force field every human possesses, and through which we doubtless give and receive information. If electrical data fed into the brain from outside sources is indeed capable of being translated by the brain into terms of pictures and sound, then many psychic phenomena, including timeslips, may thereby be explained.

THE RISE AND FALL OF THE INDIAN ROPE-TRICK

ONE CONJURING TRICK THAT HAS FIRED THE IMAGINATION FOR CENTURIES AND CAUSED ENDLESS SPECULATION IS THE INDIAN ROPE-TRICK. IS IT, AS SOME CLAIM, JUST A MYTH? OR PERHAPS A HYPNOTIC ILLUSION?

For centuries, European travellers in India have brought back tales of the incredible conjuring tricks performed by Hindu street magicians, but one trick in particular has seized the imagination – the famous Indian rope-trick. Many stories have grown up around it, including the assertion that it is mere myth since it was impossible to find anyone who had seen it himself. One thing is sure: the Indian rope-trick has prompted more heated debate than any other piece of conjuring. So did it ever happen? And if so, how was it done?

The answer perhaps lies partly in the training of those who performed the trick. Many Indian magicians (or *fakirs* – an Arabic word meaning 'the poor ones') are quite capable of achieving genuinely remarkable feats, such as controlling their nervous systems at will, an ability developed through yogic training. But fakirs tend also to be excellent showmen with a gift for creating illusions and performing conjuring tricks. Much of their repertoire, however, has been dismissed by Westerners as 'mass hallucination' or 'mass hypnosis'. What is more, there is said to be no one left living who knows the real trick and no one living who remembers seeing it performed. Seemingly doomed to extinction, the Indian rope-trick is likely to be remembered – if at all – as a mass delusion or merely a highly colourful myth. It is neither. But one may be forgiven for thinking so, for it has a long and sensational history.

It is unlikely that the West would have heard of the rope-trick, let alone taken it seriously, if it were

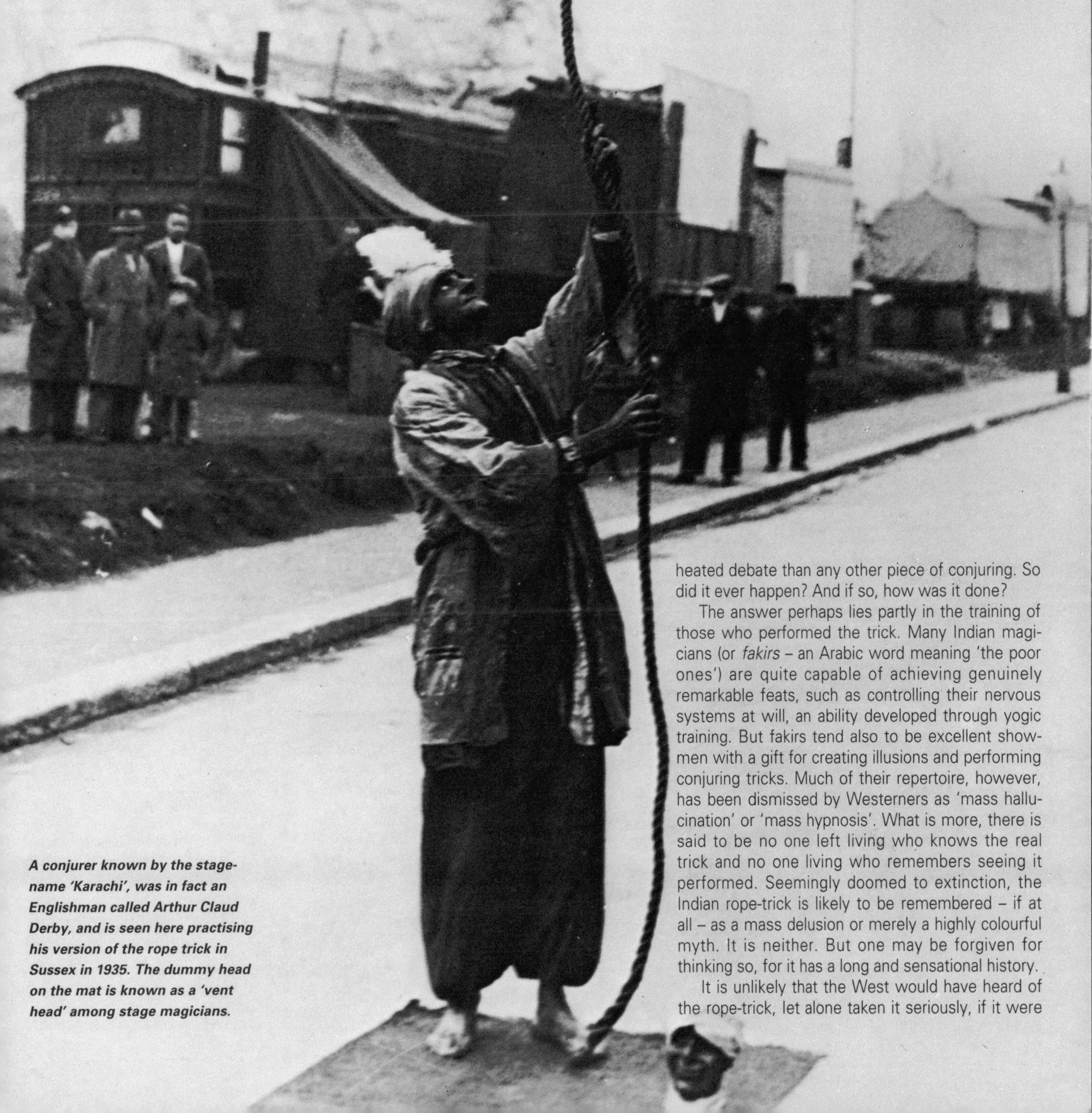

A conjurer known by the stage-name 'Karachi', was in fact an Englishman called Arthur Claud Derby, and is seen here practising his version of the rope trick in Sussex in 1935. The dummy head on the mat is known as a 'vent head' among stage magicians.

The photograph, left, is said to be of the famous rope trick, and was taken by an anonymous English soldier in India. It seems, however, that this was merely one of the many rope 'suspension tricks' ,common in the East.

not for the writings of the great Moroccan explorer and medieval author Ibn Battutah. One evening in the year 1360, he dined with Akbah Khan and a number of honoured guests at the Royal Court in Hang-Chou in China. After an enormous meal, the Khan invited his sated guests to join him in the palace gardens where he had arranged a special surprise entertainment. Ibn Battutah noted in his journal that:

'When the feast was over, one of the entertainers took a ball of wood in which there were several holes. Through these he passed a rope. He threw it into the air and it went up to a point where we could no longer see it, finally to be held there without visible support. When there was only a little end of the rope in his hand, the entertainer told one of his assistants to hang on to the rope and climb into the air, which he did, until we could no longer see him. The entertainer called him three times with no response. Then he took his knife in hand, as if he were angry, grabbed the cord and disappeared also.

'Next, the magician threw on the ground the hand of the child who had climbed the rope, then a foot; after that the other hand, then the other foot, the body and, finally, the head. He came down out of breath, his clothes tinged with blood . . . the entertainer took the limbs of the young boy and put them on the ground in their original position. He then gave the mutilated body a slight kick and there was the child, who got up and stood quite straight, completely whole.'

Since there is no rational explanation for such outrageous feats as levitating ropes and miraculous resurrections, succeeding generations looked upon Ibn Battutah's report, and any subsequent accounts, as tall tales or blatant chicanery, intended to extract a few coins from the purses of the credulous. It is small wonder, then, that medieval scholars dismissed the rope trick as a complete tissue of lies. The Victorians, on the other hand, sought to explain it in terms of the new, fashionable science of hypnosis. During the 1890s, the British public enjoyed a flirtation with all things psychical and mysterious, and laymen and scientists soon began to argue over the rope-trick, often quite bitterly.

HINDU HOAX?

An enterprising American newspaper, the *Chicago Daily Tribune*, suffering at the time from a decline in sales, threw its hat into the ring of debate by sending S. Ellmore, a writer, and a painter called Lessing to distant India with a bold mission to fulfil. They were to photograph, sketch, and ultimately prove that the trick was a Hindu hoax.

Although it was common knowledge that the Indian rope-trick was seldom performed, the two Americans soon managed to return to Chicago with several sketches and photographs that, it seemed, gave the death blow to the trick by proving that it was, as suspected, a 'mass hallucination'. When the film was developed, the photograph showed only a baggy-trousered Hindu surrounded by an apparently hypnotised crowd. There was no sign of an erect rope, let alone a boy clinging to the top. It was therefore concluded that it was all caused by collective suggestion. The article was printed, and it was clear that yet another triumphant debunking

The engraving, below, shows a Chinese suspension trick in which performers climbed up ropes, fell down, apparently dismembered, and were reassembled by 'magic'.

had been achieved by the efforts of the *Tribune's* sagacious journalists.

A few months passed and another 'daring trick' came to light, but this time one that the *Tribune* had not bargained for. The Lessing-Ellmore illustrations were exposed for the outright fakes they were. Lessing had never set foot on Asian soil and had certainly never witnessed the much-maligned Indian rope-trick. What was worse, journalist 'S. Ellmore' did not even exist. Under pressure, the newspaper's publisher was forced to print a retraction, confessing the elaborate hoax, the object of which was to increase sales.

Thirty years on, the rope-trick became news again as a certain Colonel Elliot addressed the London Magic Circle in an attempt to settle the matter once and for all. In March 1919, the Colonel put up a prize of £500 to anyone who could perform the trick under carefully controlled scientific conditions. Because of the marked absence of London-based fakirs, an advertisement was placed in the *Times of India,* offering the fabulous prize to any rope-climbing Hindu able to perform the elusive feat. But the worthy challenge went unanswered.

Much to their frustration, the poor Colonel and his colleagues concluded that the trick must therefore be, as rumoured, a myth. It had never occurred to them that fakirs are not the sort of chaps who pass a quiet afternoon at the local gentlemen's club reading English-language newspapers. The fakirs of the period were, for the most part, illiterate even in their own language, and could not speak, let alone read, English. The dour gentlemen of the Magic Circle therefore gradually came to agree with the supporters of parapsychology and reached the tidy conclusion that the Indian rope-trick was the product of 'collective hallucination'.

However, some years after the attempts of the Magic Circle to investigate the rope-trick, a group of Irish and English soldiers stationed in India witnessed a performance that was almost identical to the feats that had been reported by Ibn Battutah in China in the 14th century.

The Magic of Words

The rope-trick has often been explained away as a form of hypnotic suggestion. But if you imagine the situation reversed and assume that *you* are a hypnotist touring India and giving demonstrations of your skill to native audiences, it is logical to assume the following. Your audience comprises, say, 50 Hindus from New Delhi (who almost always speak English) and 50 lamas – Buddhist priests (who rarely speak English) from Sikkim in far northern India. Unable to speak either Hindu or Tibetan, you begin to make hypnotic suggestions in English to your audience, and your skills soon take effect. You instruct them to fall into a deep sleep and to

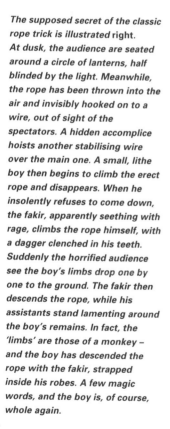

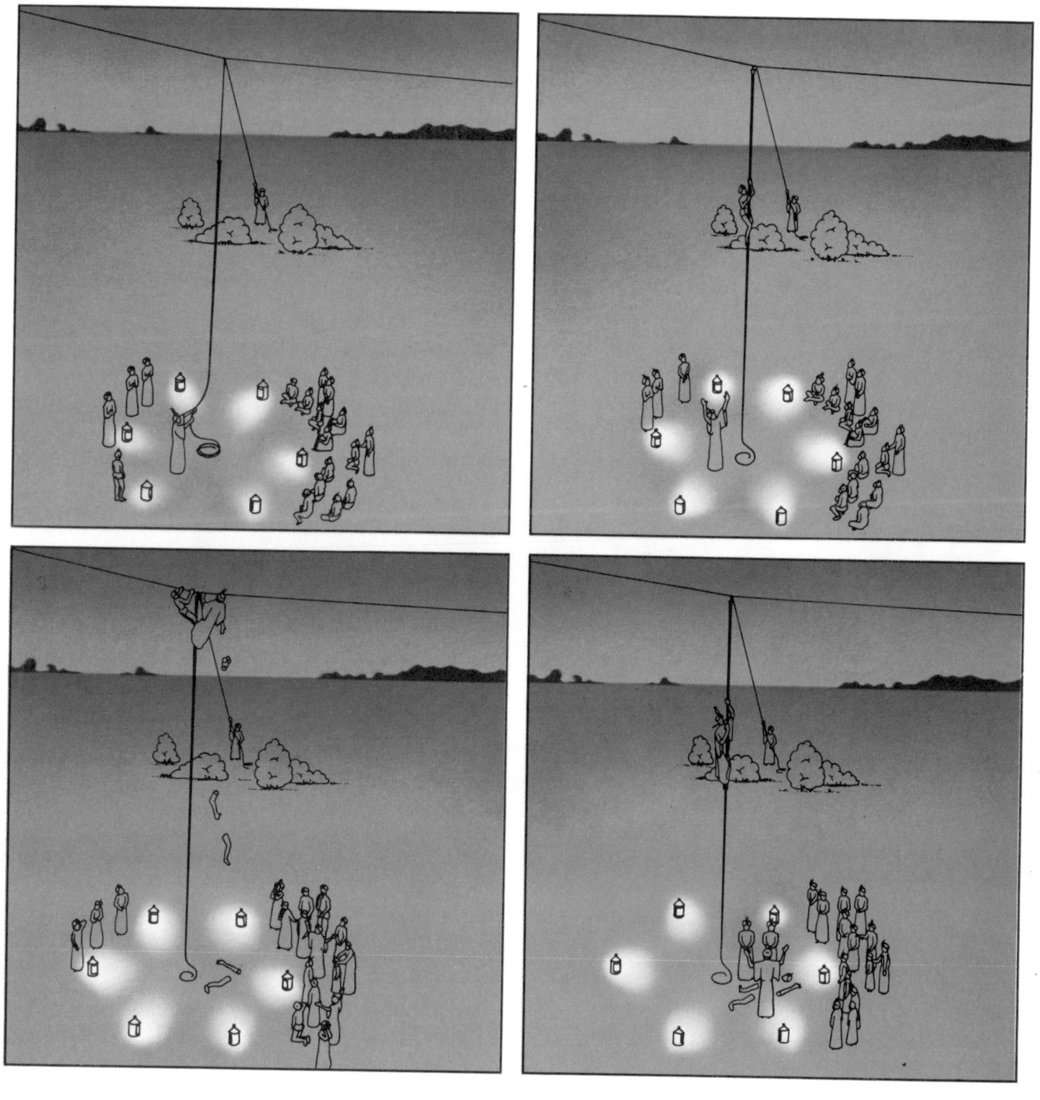

The supposed secret of the classic rope trick is illustrated right. At dusk, the audience are seated around a circle of lanterns, half blinded by the light. Meanwhile, the rope has been thrown into the air and invisibly hooked on to a wire, out of sight of the spectators. A hidden accomplice hoists another stabilising wire over the main one. A small, lithe boy then begins to climb the erect rope and disappears. When he insolently refuses to come down, the fakir, apparently seething with rage, climbs the rope himself, with a dagger clenched in his teeth. Suddenly the horrified audience see the boy's limbs drop one by one to the ground. The fakir then descends the rope, while his assistants stand lamenting around the boy's remains. In fact, the 'limbs' are those of a monkey – and the boy has descended the rope with the fakir, strapped inside his robes. A few magic words, and the boy is, of course, whole again.

'see' a dragon with gold wings. You are bound to notice that your English-speaking Delhites are busily looking at mythical beasts, while there are 50 wide-awake lamas sitting in front of you, waiting for something to happen.

The principle seems clear enough. Hypnotic suggestion is, as far as we know, always a verbal procedure; and if the subject cannot understand the language of the hypnotist's suggestions, then that person cannot be hypnotised at all. But if mass hypnosis is not the answer, how can we explain the rope-trick and the reason why it is so seldom seen?

> ONE THING IS SURE – THE INDIAN ROPE-TRICK HAS PROMPTED MORE HEATED DEBATE THEN ANY OTHER SINGLE PIECE OF CONJURING.

The nature of the trick has been a closely guarded secret that was handed, like a family heirloom, from father to son. At any given time, the number of people who knew how to perform it could be counted on one hand since very few fakirs had the skill or the courage to stage the trick successfully, especially when failure would inevitably have resulted in a broken neck. It is even said that by the mid-1940s all the old-time performers were far too old, or too unsure of their audiences, to bother with the Indian rope-trick. But if it was not a myth, how was it actually done?

UP IN THE AIR

It might reasonably be suspected that the secret is in the rope itself and that joints (metal or bone) hold it erect, or that the magician works some sort of hidden device on the ground. But the true secret is, quite literally, up in the air.

When the trick was first planned – long before the advent of invisible wires used by today's stage magicians – a long, fine and remarkably strong cord was skillfully woven from black hairs. Since this was not completely invisible, the trick was always performed at dusk when the cord would be concealed against a darkening sky. Moreover, it was necessary to perform this version of the trick against a carefully chosen background – never, for example, in a desert or an open space. The only way to avoid detection was to perform in a valley between two hillocks or knolls. The cord was stretched from one hill to another, spanning the valley so that it was concealed by the foliage in the background, in the same way that modern telephone wires are obscured by a woody countryside but visible against clear sky. Ever careful to avert the suspicious eye and to win the confidence of his audience, the fakir always began the magic show at dusk and 'warmed up' the crowd with juggling, story-telling and a few banal tricks until the sky was at last black.

It was at this point that his assistants would come forth with several lanterns and place them at specific points around the seated performer. As this was being done, the magician performed a routine 'patter', deliberately inducing a state of mild boredom and distraction in his audience.

Imagine the scene: as he is chattering to the audience – who are seated some 12 feet (3.5 metres) in front of him – the fakir removes a length of hemp from a wicker basket and throws it up in the air many times to show that it is just an ordinary rope. Most fakirs will not attempt to slip the wooden ball into the rope in front of their audience but will have concealed it in the rope beforehand. Still chattering, he throws the rope once more into the air. The spectators are now bored, so they fail to notice that, on the final handling, the magician has slipped a sturdy metal hook into a special hole into the concealed wooden ball. This hook is attached to an extremely fine hair wire, which cannot be seen against the inky sky. The wire leads up to, and over, the main horizontal cord suspended some 60 feet (18 metres) in the air. As members of the audience look up to watch the rope rising into the air by some seemingly magical force, they are compelled

Stills from a film purporting to show the classic rope-trick, taken in the 1920s by a European in India, are reproduced here. The fakir shows the crowd that the rope is just an ordinary length of hemp, **bottom,** ***and then throws it into the air where it remains rigid,*** **below.** ***The boy begins to climb up it,*** **right,** ***and is clearly seen at the top,*** **right.** ***Was this a tame version of the fabled trick or just another clever balancing act?***

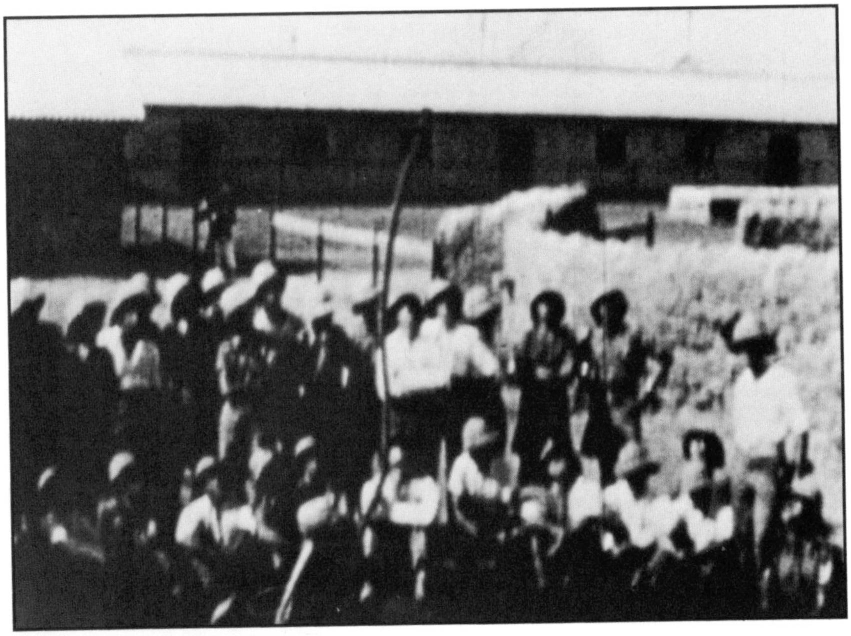

to stare into the bright lanterns. This creates a partial nightblindness so that the rope appears to be levitating, reaching up 200-300 feet (60-90 metres) into the heavens – given that the perspective is cunningly faked. What the audience does not know is that the rope is being hoisted up with the help of a hidden assistant.

From where the audience is sitting, it is impossible to see the top of the rope, and when the magician's young assistant refuses his command to climb the rope, they can quite see why. The small boy – usually aged eight or nine – protests fearfully. Of course, he eventually gives in and climbs up the rope, which begins to sway dramatically. Then, suddenly, he appears to vanish into thin air. The 'miracle', however, is the result of natural camouflage, since the boy is no longer within the range of the lanterns after he has climbed as far as 30 feet (10 metres) or so. When he reaches the top, he takes another hook from his dark robes and adds further support to the rope by slipping it in the wooden ball and over the main wire.

Suddenly the fakir shouts out something to the boy, who gives an insolent answer. Apparently seething with anger, the fakir takes up a cruel-looking knife and, placing it between his teeth, he proceeds to climb the rope. In a few moments, he vanishes, too. The audience below then hears a bitter argument, followed by screams of mortal agony. And, horribly, one by one, the poor lad's limbs fall to the ground with sickening thuds. But these are really only the shaved limbs of a large, freshly slaughtered monkey, wrapped up in cloth to match the boy's clothing and hidden in the fakir's commodious robes. The conjurer merely removes them and sprinkles them with a little blood that he keeps in a glass phial. Finally, the boy's severed head – a carefully painted wooden model in a turban – falls to the ground. The audience is in no mood to inspect it.

Four assistants rush to the butchered body, noisily lamenting. Meanwhile, at the top of the rope, the boy slips into a harness inside the fakir's loose clothing, pressing himself against the trickster's stomach, while his legs and arms fit into four well-concealed loops. The magician then climbs down the rope with the boy hidden in his robes, and with a noticeably bloodied blade between his teeth. On the ground, the magician feigns sorrow as he stares at the hacked-up remains of the lad that are laid out before him. The assistants gather around the grief-stricken fakir and attempt to console him. While this is being staged, the boy slips out of his master's robes and the accomplices hide the butchered monkey's limbs in their costumes. The assistants' backs form an effective screen that prevents the audience seeing the boy as he lies down on the ground in place of the gory pile. The fakir's confederates then step back as the magician utters words of power and gives the little fellow a good, swift kick that – lo and behold! – brings the butchered boy back to life.

Is there trick photography involved? Or could this indeed be the Indian rope-trick, as supposedly demonstrated by Karachi and his son Kyder in 1935?

FUTURE LIVES

IF WE CAN BE HYPNOTISED TO RELIVE PAST LIVES, CAN WE ALSO BE HYPNOTISED TO 'SEE' INTO POSSIBLE FUTURE INCARNATIONS?

The discovery by hypnotists that subjects could be taken back to adolescence, childhood, infancy, and even, it was claimed, back into the womb, was followed by regression to alleged previous lives. Ian Wilson's book, *Mind out of Time*, appears to show that one day most, if not all, of such lives may be explicable by what will be seen as normal principles.

But if it is possible to regress subjects into previous lives, and if time is not the simple progression that it normally appears to be, providing 'slips' into the past, should it not then be possible to project hypnotic subjects into *future* lives? Such an idea raises complicated philosophical questions, but there are known experiments that have attempted to progress as well as regress hypnotic subjects.

Early work in this field was carried out by a pioneer of past-life regression, the Frenchman Colonel Albert de Rochas. In the first decade of the 20th century, he progressed no fewer than 10 subjects – all female – into the future, sometimes of their present lives, and sometimes apparently through their deaths into existences yet to begin.

He used a system of 'longitudinal passes' (waving his hand up and down in front of the subjects) to take them into the past and 'transversal passes' (sideways gestures) to return them to the present. By continuing, he also managed to carry them forward by a series of stages to future years.

The subjects seemed, at a subconscious level, eager to please de Rochas by incorporating him into their accounts of the future, his presence being, apparently, the only comfort in singularly unpleasant lives. Details of these future existences seemed to be based largely on fears of what was to come, which the subconscious then dramatised as having already happened.

Dr Rochas began his experiments with Josephine, an 18-year-old servant working at Voiron, whom he regressed normally. After a number of sessions with her, he had occasion to go to Paris in 1904 and renewed experiments with a former subject, Madame Lambert, aged 40. Having regressed her and returned her to the present, he continued the transversal passes under the pretext of waking her more completely, but in reality to find out what would happen. After a time, without questioning her for fear of in some way implanting a suggestion, he asked her to look at herself in a mirror and tell him what colour her hair was. She described it as grizzled, whereas at the time it was still completely black.

After further passes, she found herself growing very feeble and complained that every day she was losing strength. She said she had decided to live with her younger brother who, she was convinced, was going to marry. (Actually, she went on to live alone, not with her brother.) She also saw herself aged 45, looking after an old man in the country and found this tedious.

De Rochas did not dare continue the ageing process without warning the subject, and suggested to her, in her normal state, that he might bring her to the moment of her death, a proposal she vehemently rejected, although she had remembered nothing of either past or future life under hypnosis. Experiments with Madame Lambert were finally discontinued because de Rochas left Paris.

The painting,* below, *dates from around 1596, is by an anonymous artist and shows scenes from the entire life of Sir Henry Unton, an English aristocrat. According to one theory, our future lives may be similarly laid out, so that in certain circumstances – such as being put into an hypnotic trance – we can see and describe scenes from them.

Back home, he renewed his experiments with Josephine, using the same method to take her into her future, as he had with Madame Lambert. The composite result of seven sessions was as follows. Further progression showed she entered de Rochas' service (later proving true) for six weeks while awaiting a position as a salesgirl at a Grenoble store, Les Galeries Modernes (false). She also gave entirely fictitious details of her lodgings while supposedly working there. She left the store after three months and was asked by de Rochas to return to Voiron for further experiments (false). As she was about to set out, however, she said that her mother died (inconsistent) and she heard no more from de Rochas. At the age of 25, she was living with her parents, having left domestic service three years before. Further passes caused her to show signs of great suffering, writhing in her chair, averting her head, burying her face in her hands, weeping and showing such agony of spirit that her mistress, who was present, was so moved that she withdrew to another room.

Josephine, overwhelmed by grief and shame, went on to reveal that she was now 32 and that two years earlier she had been seduced under promise of marriage by a young farmer whose name she refused to give until later, when she said it was Eugène F. De Rochas. Josephine apparently had a child by Eugène and she saw her seduction as punishment for wrong that she done in a previous, regressed, life.

Progressed to the age of 35, she revealed that her father had died by then but her mother and her child were still alive. At 40, she was still at her village, Manziat, and very sad, her child having died a short time before. (Eugène had married someone else.) Still wretched at 45, she earned her living by cutting out breeches for a tailor. She had no news of her old employers at Voiron, and Louise, her best friend there, had only written three times. In old age, Josephine's sight weakened, owing to her tailoring work, but she forgot some of her miseries. Asked if she would like to know what would happen to her when she left this life, she hesitated and then said, 'Yes'. More transversal passes resulted in her falling back in her chair with an expression of intense suffering, after which she slid to the ground. She was nearly 70 when she 'died'.

A Happy Release

Continuing the passes, de Rochas then questioned her about the afterlife. She said she was without suffering, but saw no spirits. She said she had witnessed her own funeral and heard people at it say that her death was a happy release for a poor woman who had nothing to live for. The priest's prayers had meant little to her, but his circling the coffin had driven away evil spirits. She then entered a state of almost complete darkness, lit from time to time by gleams of light in which she saw around her more or less luminous spirits with whom she found she was unable to communicate. She felt a need to reincarnate and signalled her desired entry into her new mother's womb by adopting the familiar foetal position.

> "Some of Dr Wambach's subjects told of an apocalypse, with the globe's population reduced to a twentieth of its present size. Indeed, such widespread disasters occurred in the 21st century that, by the year 2100, the Earth was barren ... and what was left of the population had to live in domed cities, eating artificial foods."

Her voice then became that of a two-year-old child, called Lili, a contraction of Alice or Elise, daughter of Claude and Françoise. The child, who could not give her surname nor the district in which the family lived, died aged three or four (both ages were given at different sessions). She was not, she said, completely 'in' her body, and saw around her spirits, both good and bad. After this particular death, she wandered happily in space, no longer seeing the Earth but shining spirits who did not speak to her, and among whom could not recognise her parents or friends. She remembered her past experiences little by little but could not account for the purpose of all these incarnations.

Nevertheless, she entered yet another existence as Marie, daughter of Edmond and Rosalie Baudin, bootsellers at St Germain-du-Mont-Or. She was 16 in 1970, wrote her name – but in Josephine's handwriting – and lived in a France that was a republic.

De Rochas found, to his surprise, that at his third session with Josephine, longitudinal passes took her into the future, not the past, and transversal passes brought her back again. Yet, at other sessions, his original method had its expected results. After his final sitting with her, he took her through all her previous prophecies and, by pressing her forehead, he was able to remind her of them.

A certain Mademoiselle Mayo, aged 18 – another of de Rochas' subjects – could not see beyond her twentieth year. She foresaw a future in which she left home at Aix with sadness at the age of 19. She had gone with her step-father to a land where the inhabitants were black and naked, and she had glimpses of being in a house near a railway station, the name of which she could not read. Later, in the same country, she saw herself playing at a theatre, but in what production she could not say. The girl did, in fact, leave her home-town of Aix in obscure circumstances, telling her friends nothing. Indeed, de Rochas commented that her vision of the future so frightened her that she vehemently refused to reveal it entirely.

Albert de Rochas' first hypnotic subject, Josephine, an 18-year-old domestic servant, lived in Voiron, France, above, in the first years of the 20th century. Under hypnosis, she seemed troubled by a deep sense of insecurity about what the future held.

Sixteen-year-old Juliette, an artists' model, saw her future life in far more detail, and told de Rochas, advancing three years, how she had previously left Grenoble for Geneva because her step-father could find no work, and had now started to pose for a sculptor by the name of Drouet. She even described what she ate and gave specific information about her daily routine. Eventually, however, she caught cold whilst posing and had to give it up, moving to Nice where she died from a serious illness at only 25. Reborn into a well-to-do family, she said she then became Emile Chaumette, and was eventually ordained as a priest. When de Rochas tried to follow up details of the life of Juliette, however, he found that she did indeed leave Grenoble with her mother, but was unable to make other details tally to any meaningful degree.

INTO THE FUTURE

Dr Helen Wambach, an American, began her researches into future lives in the early 1980s, and has since offered workshops at which subjects can be progressed to the years 2100 or 2300. The intention was not specifically to investigate individual cases, but rather to assemble a compendium of rather mundane facts on ordinary people. She had discovered that it was not constructive to ask questions that might be disturbing or damaging to the subject's self-awareness. Indeed, emotive questions such as 'how did you die?' were found to block the flow of responses.

Usually, she chose a year and a date which would most likely be remembered, such as a birthday. The replies dealt with everyday matters, children, credit card worries, or career plans; and the same pattern was followed year after year. Then the pattern would change. After being progressed forward several decades, many subjects reported being in a blissful state of lightness, and floating freely. Dr Wambach's view was that the subjects were reporting an existence between incarnations. Other subjects, progressed to the same period, gave a very dismal account of life then. After correlating the accumulated reports, Dr Wambach came to the depressing conclusion that some universal cataclysm had overtaken the planet. Some 'souls' were able to find bodies to inhabit, while others floated in limbo, or perhaps faded from existence altogether.

In the hypnosis technique used by Dr Wambach, subjects are asked to visualise their own front doors as clearly as possible. They are then taken, in imagination, to the rooftop, and asked to view the surroundings. Then they are to imagine themselves feeling light, and gently taking off, flying swiftly over land to a favourite beach. Wambach would next ask them to visualise a white cloud, on which they could relax and ride backwards or forwards in time. Rather than take them to a specific date which might provoke anxieties, she would invite them to choose a period in the past or future which they found pleasant.

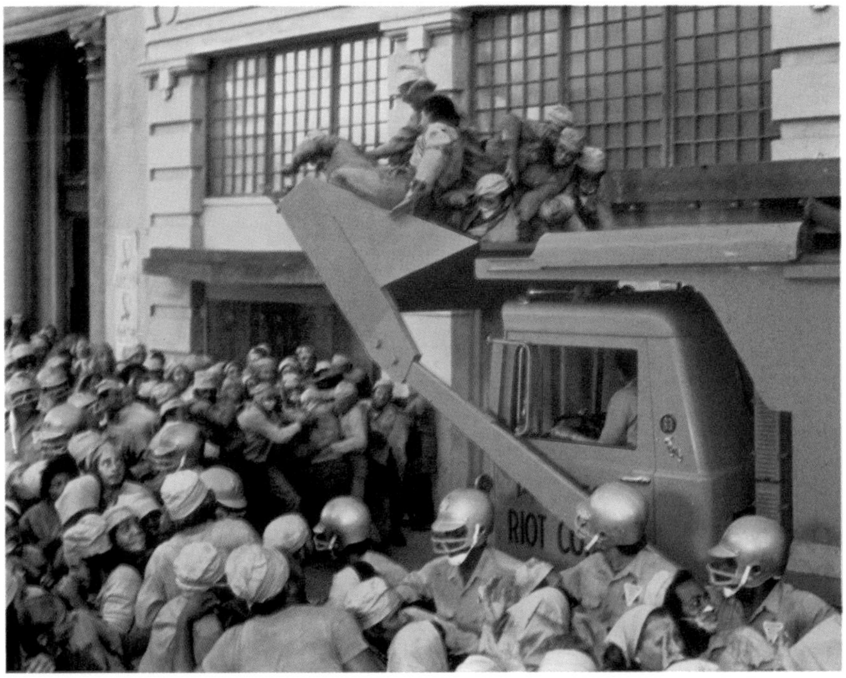

Few people view the future with equanimity. Films like* Metropolis, *above, which was made in 1927, and* Soylent Green, *below, made in 1973, share the vision of a soulless future where individualism is ruthlessly suppressed. Similarly, future 'lives', described under hypnosis, often seem to be dramatisations of our deepest fears and anxieties.

Some of Dr Wambach's subjects (as reported in *Mass Dreams of the Future*) told of an apocalypse, with the globe's population reduced to a twentieth of its present size. Indeed, such widespread disasters occurred in the twenty-first century that, by the year 2100, Earth was barren, the soil poisoned and what was left of the population had to live in domed cities, eating artificial foods. More happily, progressions to the year 2300 have revealed that our planet seems to regenerate itself: there are fresh vegetables again, and the population had doubled, re-colonising not just this planet, but others in the solar system as well.

GOLDBERG'S VARIATIONS

Curiously, another hypnotherapist, Dr Bruce Goldberg, conducting research along similar lines, found that his subjects also reported a future global disaster – but not until the 25th century. In his book, *Past Lives, Future Lives,* the dossier of blessings and calamities awaiting future generations includes information pills, geographical changes, and underwater cities.

As a public test of the validity of hypnotic progression, on 2 February 1981, Dr Goldberg put a Baltimore newsreader, Harry Martin, into hypnosis, and then asked him to read the news for the following week. Checking a week later with the actual newscasts, there were a number of notable successes, a detailed description of a road accident being the most remarkable. Further experiments took Harry Martin into a future life in the 22nd century, where he discovered he was employed as a researcher into thought transference, working with 300 other people in a solar-powered glass pyramid. But, of course, only when the requisite time has elapsed can such claims possibly be substantiated.

MASS HYSTERIA

ITS SYMPTOMS ARE OFTEN SIMILAR TO THOSE OF SERIOUS ILLNESS – BUT HYSTERIA SPREADS FASTER THAN ANY KNOWN DISEASE. HOW CAN THIS BE POSSIBLE? IS THERE PERHAPS A LINK WITH SOME FORM OF ESP?

Reports of outbreaks of mass hysteria in places throughout the world, together with the limited amount of research that has been done on the subject, strongly suggest that certain long accepted assumptions about the phenomenon should be revised. Three aspects, in particular, need reconsidering.

Firstly, it is unwise to think of hysteria simply in terms of self-indulgent shamming. A better description would be a 'breakdown' which, whether nervous or physical, may provide a form of protection from an intolerable situation by removing the victim from it. Thus, it can at times perform the same valuable function as a fuse-wire in an electrical circuit.

Secondly, the symptoms of hysteria are not necessarily always those we tend to associate with the term. In general, they will tend to manifest themselves in whatever form is associated with breakdown of normal behaviour by the society in which they occur.

Thirdly, the diagnosis of 'hysteria' should not be regarded as a sign that there was nothing really wrong with the victim. On the contrary, the prevalence of such outbreaks suggests that they should definitely be carefully investigated in order to find out precisely how displays of mob hysteria occur and for what reasons.

So what is the force that takes over a group of people and, in effect, breaks them down, inducing a range of symptoms that may vary enormously in different circumstances, but that are generally quite consistent within a single outbreak? What, in other words, is the nature of 'psychic' contagion, a phenomenon that results in scores or even hundreds of people breaking down at, or around, the same time, in much the same way – even when they are not all within sight of one another, so that simple imitation can be ruled out?

When dealing with such problems, it is always worth looking back over Man's evolutionary past, to see if there are any parallels. In this case, there are.

*In*Focus

> COULD IT BE THAT MASS HYSTERIA IS A RELIC OF A COLLECTIVE HUMAN INSTINCT – AN EVOLUTIONARY DEVICE THAT HAS BY THIS POINT IN TIME LARGELY OUTLIVED ITS USEFULNESS?

Indeed, many species appear to use methods of communication that biologists have yet to explain.

At its most basic level, this communication seems to take place between cells. In his book *Supernature,* Lyall Watson describes the remarkable capacity of the common or bathroom sponge – a colony of cells in its natural ocean habitat – to reconstitute itself in similar form if destroyed. 'Some sponges grow to several feet in diameter,' Watson observes, 'and yet, if you cut them up and squeeze the pieces through silk cloth to separate every cell from its neighbour, the gruel soon gets together and organises itself and the complete sponge reappears'.

THE JONESTOWN MADNESS

Late in November 1978, a horrified world learned of the appalling mass suicide at Jonestown in the jungles of Guyana, on the northern coast of South America. The victims – over 900 of them – were members of a California-based religious sect known as the People's Temple, led by the psychopathic Reverend Jim Jones. They had killed themselves by drinking potassium cyanide mixed with a sweet, fizzy drink.

Many theories have been advanced as to how so many people could be induced to disregard their own instinct for self-preservation to the extent of killing themselves on the order of a madman. It is a clear case of mass hysteria – that strange vestige of the instinct that, in animals, enables the will of the group to triumph over that of the individual.

The thousands of termites,* above, *that live inside each mound, such as the one in picture,* top, *organise their highly specialised activities in such a way that everything contributes to the welfare of the entire community. They have developed a special instinct to do this; mass hysteria may be produced in human beings in a similar way.

It has been suggested that the weird human behaviour that we call mass hysteria is a vestige of the instinct that keeps flocks of birds, such as the one* above opposite, *together – in other words, a kind of collective mind.

In his book *The Soul of the White Ant,* the South African scientist Eugène Marais describes his experiments with colonies of ants. These revealed that, although groups of ants and even individual ants were engaged in separate pursuits at any given time – feeding the queen, collecting the food for her, storing it, building larders for it, or fighting off intruders – the activities of all of them were dictated by what, for want of a better word, he felt bound to call a 'soul'.

BIRDS OF A FEATHER

The behaviour of starlings is a good example of such collective behaviour on a larger scale. Thousands of starlings roost in London, but they spend their days in the countryside, where food is more plentiful. At a certain time in the evening, starlings all round London – as far away as Essex and the Home Counties – will begin to make the same inward journey, so that day after day the flocks can be tracked on radar, spreading outwards in the morning, moving inwards in the evening.

Even more remarkable is the group behaviour of these starlings as they fly out and back. They do not follow a leader; rather, it is as if, in their whirlings, they are directed by what Marais termed a 'soul'.

The most plausible explanation for this kind of behaviour is that it depends on a form of communication that developed early in the evolutionary process. In the case of ants, it was a form of diversification, enabling the community as a whole to survive while various groups within it performed their various tasks. In birds, it developed into a mechanism for the protection of the group, providing large flocks of birds with collective guidance for their movements.

Could it be, therefore, that mass hysteria is a relic of a similar collective human instinct – an evolutionary device that by this point in time has largely outlived its usefulness?

This seems a likely hypothesis: but we are still no nearer an explanation of the way in which the symptoms are transmitted in an outbreak of mass hysteria. The most promising line of research in this connection has been into *pheromones,* free-floating scent molecules, the discovery of which has helped to account for the way in which, for example, males of a species will come clustering round a female who is on heat.

In her novel *The Group,* Mary McCarthy claimed that women living in close contact with each other tend to menstruate at the same time; and research at Harvard and elsewhere has since shown that this is correct. Room-mates' periods do tend to move into synchronisation; and so do those of close friends who spend a great deal of time together. Pheromones are currently front-runners in the search for an explanation. But if pheromones are the channel of communication in this case, may they not serve the same purpose in other epidemics that hitherto have been thought to be spread solely by infection?

In a fascinating research project, the astronomers Fred Hoyle and Chandra Wickramasinghe demonstrated that, contrary to common assumption, influenza does not necessarily spread by person-to-person contact – a fact that had already been established globally, as large-scale epidemics do not follow the course that would be expected if person-to-person infection were the sole agent of the spread of the disease. The same phenomenon has been confirmed at the Common Cold Research Unit at Salisbury in England. Coughs and sneezes seem to be the obvious suspects, but they are not always guilty.

The cells of the common sponge, above, seem, in some mysterious way, to be able to communicate. If dispersed, they will regroup in a similar form.

The Pheromone Connection

So in what other way might epidemics spread? An alternative theory is that viruses are constantly here, there and everywhere, but that we can resist them unless, and until, an epidemic is signalled – by pheromones.

Pheromones, however, take us only part of the way on this voyage of discovery. Eugène Marais, who knew nothing of pheromones but had convinced himself that the secret of ant communication must lie in scent, was imaginative enough to recognise that the kind of scent involved was not quite the kind we generally think of. It was misleading, he argued, to assume the existence of a gas, or microscopic particles. 'Perfume is not entirely a physical substance. You may scent a large room for ten years with a small piece musk, and yet there will not be any loss of weight.' Scent, he felt, should be thought in terms of 'waves in the ether'.

Much of Marais' work has been superseded by subsequent research, but it remains stimulating. In *Tuning in to Nature,* Philip S Callahan, of the University of Florida, followed up Marais' idea, and came to the same conclusion: the sensory mechanism involved in ant communication is not 'straight' smell. Insects, he claims, 'smell' odours electronically, by tuning into the narrow band infra-red radiation. If this turns out to be correct, and Callahan presents impressive evidence for his theory, then the traditional assumptions about the way in which epidemics of all kinds are spread will need to be re-examined.

The origin of a number of serious conditions is still uncertain: these include epilepsy, Legionnaire's disease, Parkinsonism and multiple sclerosis. To date, the whole weight of research into their causes and spread has been on the quest for some common biological factor – germs, a virus, biochemical mix-up, or toxic substances. But so far, this research has achieved little.

Sometimes, researchers find what they believe at the time to be the cause – and it is triumphantly paraded. But soon, other contributory factors are identified – or the suspected virus is also found in the bodies of perfectly healthy people. The whole idea that illnesses are always caused by viruses is, in fact, beginning to fall into discredit in many respects. Instead, it is now thought likely that their role is more like that of looters, who come out on the rampage only when law and order – in this case, the orderly and healthy functioning of the human body – have broken down.

But what causes this sort of breakdown, and resulting epidemics? The answer, of course, is that

Iranians in Tehran mourn the death of their Ayatollah,* below. *Outbreaks of mass hysteria often occur at moments of heightened emotion.

CASEBOOK

A LINK WITH ESP?

In 1944, an epidemic of strange incidents took place in the small town of Muldoon in the United States. It began when a woman reported to police that, for no reason at all, a man had approached her and then sprayed her legs with gas, leaving them paralysed. The incident was reported in the local press. Suddenly, a spate of similar events began all over the town, and a single culprit was thought to be at the root of this strange crime. Police were unable to catch the 'phantom anaesthetist of Muldoon', remarkable for being able to spray several different women simultaneously in different parts of the town and the perpetrator of these extraordinary attacks seemed still to be at large.

When it was suggested that the epidemic was not one of paralysis but of mass hysteria, the flood of reports ceased. This was followed by a period during which reports of all kinds of unusual phenomena fell below average – perhaps as a result of the suggestion of mass hysteria.

The story bears a remarkable resemblance to accounts of many paranormal phenomena. In general, those who report such incidents state that they have no knowledge at all of other similar cases. Nevertheless, the knowledge seems to spread, as in other outbreaks of mass hysteria, by a mysterious 'psychic contagion' that may perhaps have something to do with the mysterious method of communication that must be involved in telepathy and mind-reading.

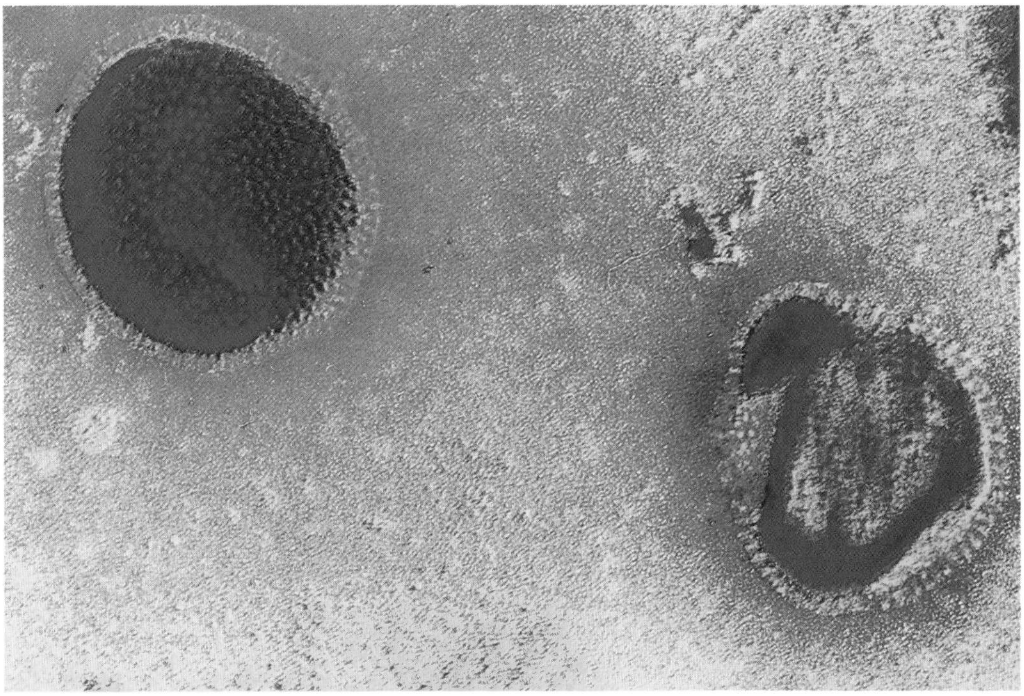

According to one theory, the influenza virus, **left**, *is not automatically spread by person-to-person contact: at times, epidemics may be triggered off by pheromone action.*

When lemmings, **below**, *make their suicide leaps into the sea, they are responding to an instinct that in many ways is equivalent to human mass hysteria. Lemmings kill themselves in this way when the population has grown to such numbers that their habitat can no longer support them.*

we do not know as yet. However, a detailed study of mass hysteria might perhaps bring us closer to an explanation.

Do pheromones elicit the responses that result in an epidemic? Or could it be that pathogens from outer space, falling to Earth, are responsible for disease, as Hoyle and Wickramasinghe have also suggested? Or is there perhaps some as yet undiscovered psychokinetic force – as reported so often in accounts of hauntings or poltergeist activity – that can affect groups?

More serious and systematic investigation of mass hysteria could provide the answers not merely to these questions, but to much that is imperfectly understood, or misunderstood, about disease in general. It might also help solve many of the problems that have baffled biologists in their study of animal, bird and insect behaviour, and psychologists in their study of the ways in which men and women communicate when no contact through the ordinary senses seems possible.

PERSPECTIVES

OF ONE MIND

In 1980, while a brass band competition was underway in the heart of the Nottinghamshire countryside, some 250 people suddenly collapsed, suffering from symptoms of vomiting, dizziness and shaking. The possibility of food poisoning was ruled out; and an official diagnosis of mass hysteria was finally declared. Most amazing of all, however, was the fact that small babies had also been affected.

At times, it seems, such apparent epidemics may be due to unconscious imitation. In Florida, for instance, on one afternoon, more than 70 pupils – mostly girls – at an elementary school suddenly fell ill, experiencing headaches, stomach pains and shortness of breath. A few were even taken to hospital. Once again, no identifiable virus could be found. An investigator, however, discovered that the 'epidemic' had started shortly after an 11-year old girl, who had fainted, had been taken out on a stretcher. The reaction of her fellow-pupils could, he decided, be put down to mass hysteria. Perhaps not unexpectedly, however, the majority of parents reacted quite dramatically to this rather unusual diagnosis, suggestive as it was of mental instability on the part of their offspring. Gustave le Bon, author of *The Crowd,* suggested that, in crowds, our intellectual control becomes weaker, while instincts, passions and feelings become strengthened. This, he maintained, is why many people behave in mobs in ways that few would be likely to behave as individuals. This could provide, at least to some degree, an explanation of so-called psychic epidemics.

THE CLOSEST ENCOUNTER EVER

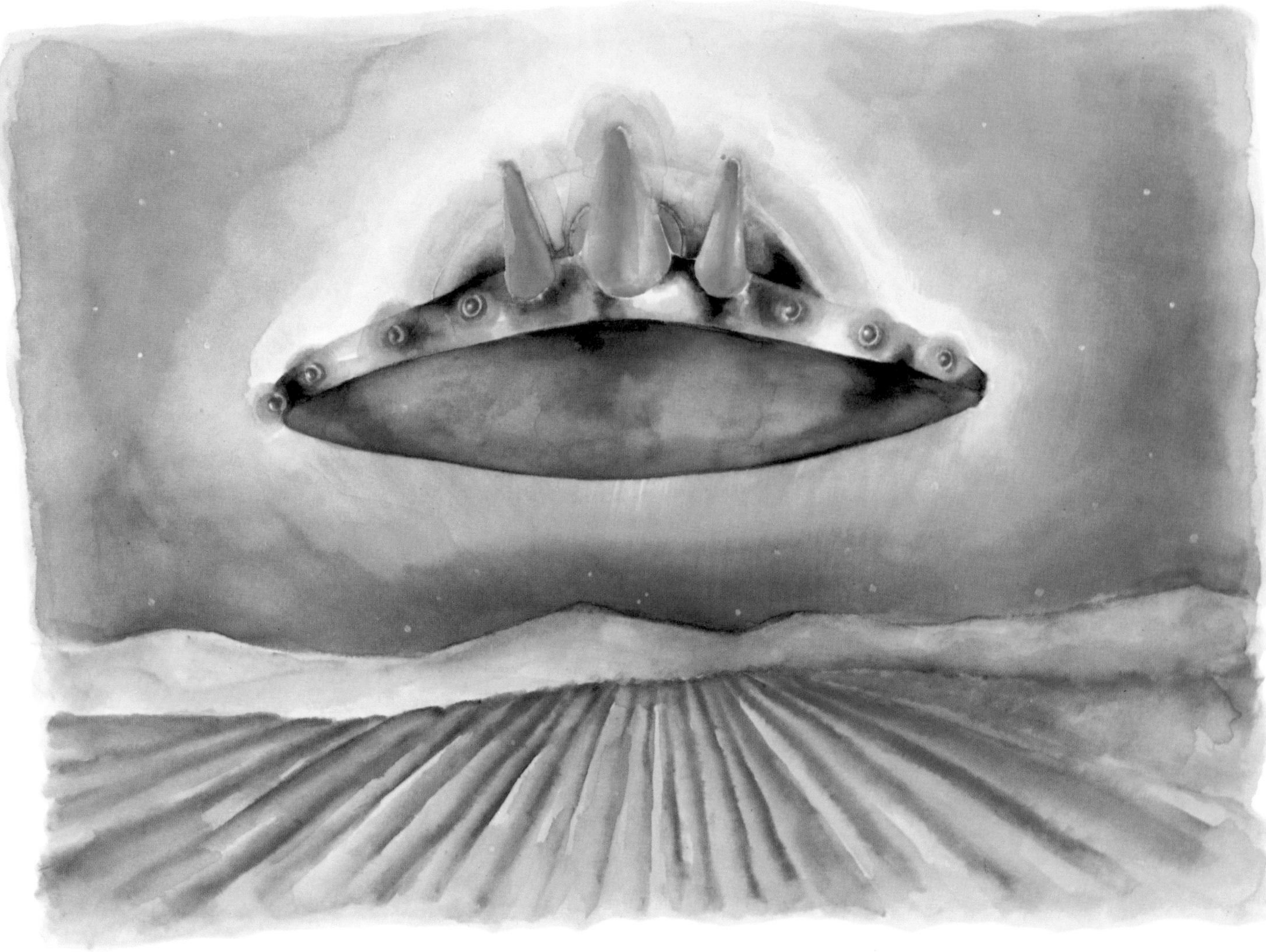

ONE OF THE PUZZLING FEATURES OF SO MANY UFO INCIDENTS IS THEIR APPARENT POINTLESSNESS. YET A BRAZILIAN FARMER WAS ALLEGEDLY ABDUCTED BY HUMANOIDS FOR A STARTLING PURPOSE: TO HAVE SEX WITH A BEING FROM ANOTHER PLANET

One of the earliest reports of an alleged abduction by humanoids was kept secret for over three years because it was deemed too 'wild' by those who first interviewed the abductee. This amazing case first became known when the victim, known only as A. V. B. to preserve his anonymity, wrote to João Martins, a Brazilian journalist, and his medical friend, Dr Olavo T. Fontes, towards the end of 1957. The man with the strange story was a young farmer who lived near the small town of São Francisco de Sales in Minas Gerais, Brazil. Intrigued, Martins and Fontes sent the farmer some financial aid so that he could make the long journey to the city of Rio de Janeiro, where the investigation began on 22 February 1958 in Dr Fontes' consulting room.

The story that unfolded was, the investigators felt, so astonishing that they decided to 'keep it on ice' in case a similar incident occurred that might corroborate any of the details. They also feared that if the account became widely known, there would be a rash of 'copycat' cases, which would end up invalidating the story. But a few details did leak out – fortunately in the right direction for the outline of the tale reached the ears of Dr Walter Buhler in 1961. As a result, he began to make his own detailed investigation.

The Buhler report eventually appeared as a newsletter and this, translated by Gordon Creighton and supplemented with editorial comments, appeared in *Flying Saucer Review*, in January 1965. Very soon after, João Martin's account was published in the Spanish language edition – not the Portuguese, as might have been expected – of the Brazilian magazine *O Cruzeiro*. Finally, the full case, including the results of various detailed clinical reports, was included in *The Humanoids*, a collection of accounts of encounters with UFO occupants, in 1969. At last, the story that had been thought too 'wild' to be made known to the public was in print and 'A.V.B.' was revealed to be 23-year-old Antônio Villas Boas.

***Antônio Villas Boas*, above, had a remarkable experience, at first concealed by UFO researchers because they considered it too wild to publish.**

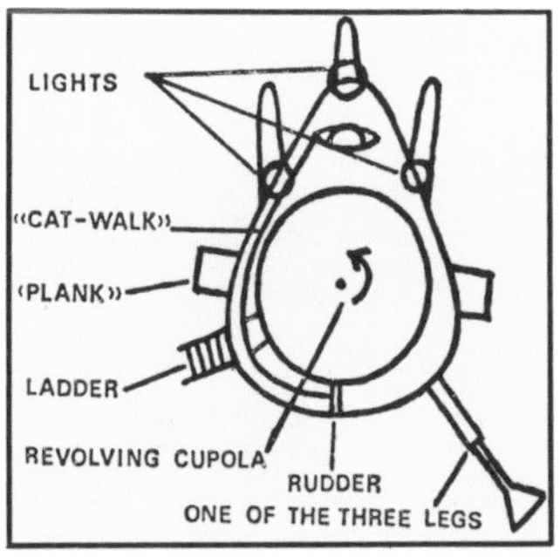

Sketches of the UFO were made by Villas Boas in February 1958 – above, for Dr Olavo Fontes, and in July 1961, below, for Drs Buhler and Aquino of the Brazilian Society for the Study of Flying Saucers.

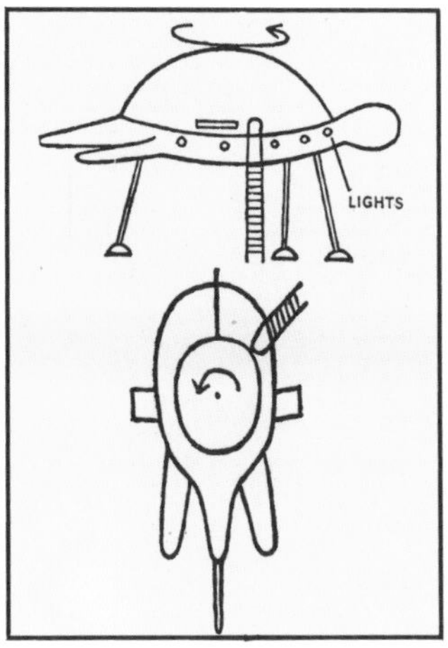

UNIDENTIFIED LIGHTS

The actual abduction of Antônio Villas Boas was heralded by two unusual events. The first took place on 5 October 1957, when he and his brother were retiring to bed at about 11 p.m. after a party. From their bedroom window, they saw an unidentified light in the farmyard below. It moved up on to the roof of their house, and together they watched it shine through the slats of the shutters and the gaps in the tiles (there was no proper ceiling) before it departed.

The second strange incident occurred on 14 October at about 9.30 p.m. when the Villas Boas brothers were out ploughing with their tractor. They suddenly saw a dazzling light, 'big and round', about 100 yards (90 metres) above one end of the field. Antônio went over for a closer look, but – as if playing games with him – the light moved swiftly to the other end of the field, a manoeuvre it repeated two or three times. The young farmer tried to get a closer look at it. Then the light abruptly vanished.

The following night, 15 October, Antônio was out in the field again, ploughing alone by the light of his headlamps. Suddenly, at about 1a.m., he became aware of a 'large red star' that seemed to be descending towards the end of the field. As it came nearer, he saw that it was in fact a luminous egg-shaped object. The UFO's approach brought it right overhead, about 50 yards (45 metres) above the tractor. The whole field then became as bright as if it were broad daylight.

Villas Boas sat in his cab, transfixed with fear as the object landed about 45 feet (15 metres) in front of him. He saw a rounded object with a distinct rim that was apparently clustered with purple lights. A huge round headlamp on the side facing him seemed to be producing the 'daylight' effect. There was a revolving cupola on top, and, as he watched, fascinated, he saw three shafts – or 'legs' – emerge and reach for the ground. At this, the terrified farmer started to drive off but after a short distance, the engine stopped, despite the fact that it had been running smoothly. Villas Boas found he could not restart it and, in a panic, he leapt from the cab and set off across the heavily ploughed field.

HELMETED ALIENS

The deep ruts proved a handicap to his escape and he had gone only a few paces when someone grabbed his arm. As he turned, he was astonished to see a strangely garbed individual whose helmeted head reached only to Villas Boas' shoulder. He hit out at the humanoid, who was knocked flying, but he was quickly grabbed by three other aliens who lifted him from the ground as he struggled and shouted. He later said, when revealing details about the extraordinary experience:

'I noticed that, as they were dragging me towards the machine, my speech seemed to arouse their surprise or curiosity, for they stopped and peered attentively at my face as I spoke, though without loosening their grip on me. This relieved me a little as to their intentions, but I still did not stop struggling'.

As he was carried to the craft, a ladder descended from a door, and his captors hoisted him up with great difficulty, especially as he tried to resist by hanging on to a kind of handrail. But, in the end, they succeeded.

Once inside the machine, Villas Boas found himself in a square room with metallic walls, brightly lit by small, high lamps. He was set down on his feet, and became aware that there were five small beings, two of whom held him firmly. One signalled that he should be taken through to an adjoining room, which was larger, and oval in shape, with a metal column that reached from floor to ceiling, together with a table and some swivel chairs set to one side.

A 'conversation' then ensued between his captors, who made sounds like dogs barking. As Villas Boas put it:

'Those sounds were totally different from anything I had heard until now. They were slow barks and yelps, neither very clear nor very hoarse, some longer, some shorter, at times containing several different sounds all at once, and at other times ending in a quaver. But they were simply sounds, animal barks, and nothing could be distinguished that could be taken as the sound of a syllable or word of a foreign language. Not a thing! To me it all sounded alike, so that I am unable to retain a word of it... I still shudder when I think of those sounds. I can't reproduce them... my voice just isn't made for that.'

HANDLED BY HUMANOIDS

This strange communication ceased abruptly, when all five set about him, stripping him of his clothing while he shouted and struggled – but to no avail. (Apparently they stopped to peer at him whenever he yelled; and, strangely, although they seemed to be using force, at no time did they hurt him.)

> THE ALARMED VILLAS BOAS WATCHED THE CHALICE FILL WITH WHAT WAS PRESUMABLY HIS OWN BLOOD. THE CREATURES THEN LEFT HIM ALONE, CONTEMPLATING THE NIGHTMARE SITUATION.

The beings were all dressed in tight-fitting grey overalls and large, broad helmets, reinforced at back and front with bands of metal. There were also apertures through which Villas Boas could see light-coloured eyes. Three tubes emerged from the top of each helmet, the central one running down the back and entering the clothing in line with the spine; the other two, curved away to enter the clothes, one beneath each armpit. The sleeves ended in thick gloves, which seemed stiff at the fingers. The trouser part fitted closely over seat, thighs and lower legs, and the footwear seemed an integral part of this section, the soles being very thick – about 2 inches (5 centimetres). On his chest,

The artist's impressions,* left and below, *show one of the humanoids seen by Villas Boas, and the inscription above a door in the humanoids' craft. In the statement he made to Dr Fontes, Villas Boas said it was a sort of luminous inscription – or something similar – traced out in red symbols which, owing to the effect of the light, seemed to stand out about 2 inches (5 centimetres) in front of the metal of the door. The naked female humanoid,* below right, *seduced Villas Boas aboard the craft.

each being had a kind of breastplate or 'shield', which was about the size of a slice of pineapple. It reflected light, and was joined to a belt at the waist by a strip of laminated metal.

The naked and shivering farmer – it was a chilly night outside, and no warmer in the craft – stood there quaking and 'worried to death'. He wondered what on earth was going to happen to him now. One of the little creatures approached him with what seemed to be a sort of wet sponge, which he rubbed all over Villas Boas' skin. As he later put it: 'The liquid was as clear as water, but quite thick, and without smell. I thought it was some sort of oil, but was wrong, for my skin did not become greasy or oily'.

He was now led to another door, which had an inscription in red over it. He tried to memorise this, although it meant nothing to him, since it was in unknown characters. In yet another room, one of the beings approached with a sort of chalice from which dangled two flexible tubes. One of these, with a capped end like a child's suction 'arrow', was fixed to his chin, while the other tube was pumped up and down. The alarmed Villas Boas watched the chalice fill with what was presumably his own blood. The creatures then left him alone, as he sat on a soft couch contemplating the nightmarish situation in which he found himself.

Suddenly, he smelt a strange odour, which made him feel sick. He examined the walls and saw metallic tubes at just below ceiling level. Grey smoke was coming through perforations in the tubes. Villas Boas rushed to a corner of the room and vomited, after which he felt a little less frightened. Moments later, there was a noise at the door, which opened to reveal a creature just like a woman. As Villas Boas gaped, the woman walked towards him. Flabbergasted, he suddenly realised she was naked, too.

The woman, said Villas Boas, was more beautiful than anyone he had met before. She was shorter than he, her head reaching only to his shoulder – he is 5 feet 5 inches (1.65 metres). Her hair was smooth, and very fair, almost white, and as though bleached. Parted in the centre, it reached halfway down her neck, with ends curling inwards. Her eyes were large, blue and elongated, 'slanted outwards'. Her small nose was straight, neither pointed nor turned up. She had high cheekbones, but – as Villas Boas discovered – they were soft and fleshy to the touch. Her face was wide, but narrowed to a markedly pointed chin. Her lips were thin, and her mouth like a slit. The ears were normal, but small.

The door then closed, and Villas Boas found himself alone with this woman, whose slim, lithe body was the most exquisite he had ever seen. She had high, well-separated breasts. Her waist was slender, her hips wide and her thighs large, while her feet were small and her hands, long and narrow. He saw, too, that the hair in her armpits, and her pubic hair, was a strange blood red. He smelt no perfume on her, 'apart from the feminine odour', which he noticed specifically.

> IF VILLAS BOAS' STORY IS TRUE, IT MAY WELL BE, THAT, SOMEWHERE OUT THERE IN THE UNIVERSE, THERE IS A STRANGE CHILD ... THAT MAYBE IS BEING PREPARED TO RETURN HERE.

She approached the farmer and rubbed her head against his (presumably by standing on tip-toe). Her body felt as though glued to his, and she made it quite clear what she wanted. His excitement welled up. The sexual act was normal – as was the one that followed – but then she tired, and refused further advances.

Villas Boas recalled that she never kissed him while they made love, nor were caresses exchanged, but she once gently bit him on his chin. Although she never spoke, she grunted, and that 'nearly spoiled everything, giving the disagreeable impression that I was with an animal'.

When she was called away by one of the other beings, she turned to Villas Boas, pointed to her belly, and then to the sky. These gestures instilled a great fear in Antonio – a fear that was with him years after the event – for he interpreted them as meaning she would return to take him away. (Dr Fontes later calmed him by suggesting that she meant: 'I am going to bear our child, yours and mine, there on my home planet'. This led to speculation by the farmer that all they wanted was 'a good stallion' to improve their stock.) Then Villas Boas was told to get dressed, after which he says he was taken on a conducted tour round the craft. During this time, he tried to steal an instrument merely for a keepsake, only to be rebuffed, angrily, by one of the alien crew. Eventually, he was invited by the humanoids to go down the ladder, and back on to solid ground. From there, he watched the ladder retract, while the metal legs and the lights began to glow. The craft rose into the air, its cupola turning at great speed. With lights now flashing, it listed slightly to one side, then suddenly shot off just like a bullet.

By now it was 5.30 a.m., so the abductee's extraordinary adventure must have lasted over four hours in all.

Villas Boas returned home, hungry and weakened by his spell of vomiting. He slept through to 4.30 p.m. and awoke feeling perfectly normal. But when he fell asleep again, he was restless, and woke up shouting after dreaming of the incident. Next day, he was troubled by dreadful nausea and a violent headache. When that left him, he found that his eyes began to burn. Unusual wounds, with infections, appeared on parts of his body; and when these dried up, he noticed that they left round, purplish scars.

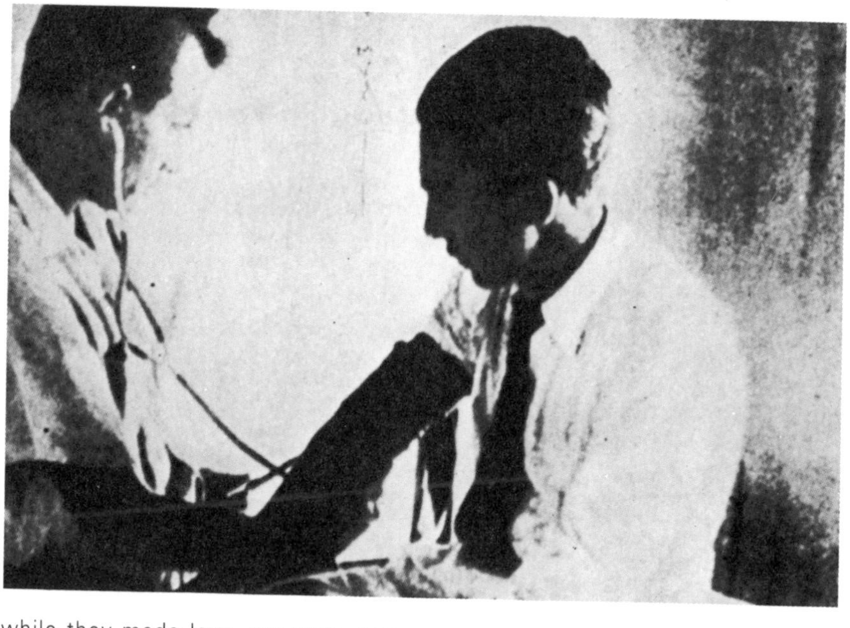

Villas Boas was examined by Dr Fontes, below, in February 1958, four months after the alleged abduction. The symptoms he described suggested either radiation poisoning or exposure to radiation, but it was too late by this time for this diagnosis to be confirmed.

MYSTERIOUS SCARS

When Dr Fontes examined Villas Boas, he observed two small patches, one on each side of the chin. He described these as 'scars of some superficial lesion with associated subcutaneous haemorrhage'. Several other mysterious scars on his body were also noted.

In a letter to *Flying Saucer Review,* Dr Fontes suggested that the symptoms described pointed to radiation poisoning, or exposure to radiation. As he wrote: 'Unfortunately he came to me too late for the blood examinations that could have confirmed such a possibility beyond doubt'.

On 10 October 1971, João Martins was at last officially cleared to write about the case for the Brazilian public. His account eventually appeared in the Rio de Janeiro Sunday review *Domingo Illustrado.* An abridged account concluded with a fascinating statement confirming that:

'A.V.B. was subjected by us [Martins, Dr Fontes, and a military officer – whose presence was not revealed in the earlier reports] to the most sophisticated methods of interrogation, without falling into any contradictions. He resisted every trap we set to test whether he was seeking notoriety or money. A medical examination . . . revealed a state of completely normal physical and mental equilibrium. His reputation in the region where he lives was that of an honest, serious, hardworking man.'

Martins also revealed that the interrogation to which the abductee had been subjected at times bordered on harsh and cruel treatment, just short of physical violence, but Villas Boas never veered from his original story in any detail. The journalist therefore reached the rather intriguing conclusion that: 'If this story is true, it may well be that, somewhere out there in the Universe, there is a strange child ... that maybe is being prepared to return here.'

BURIED ALIVE

In Dahomey, West Africa, certain tribesmen are drugged, wound in a sheet, as shown left, and buried for long periods. During this time, they are supposed to be in touch with magical or archetypal forces that will benefit the whole tribe. In December 1953, a yogi named Count Ostoja, shown below, put himself into a self-induced cataleptic state, so that he could endure being buried alive in a coffin. It took him just a minute to go into a deep trance, and he duly survived the ordeal.

HOW CAN A MAN – EVEN A TRAINED ADEPT, SUCH AS AN INDIAN YOGI – SUSPEND HIS BODILY FUNCTIONS IN SUCH A WAY THAT HE IS ABLE, IN EFFECT, TO SIMULATE DEATH?

It seems almost impossible to Westerners that men can deliberately put themselves in a state of suspended animation – by controlling their autonomic bodily functions, in a way not understood – and remain buried underground for hours, days, or – so it is rumoured – even years, and emerge alive. Yet, for centuries, reliable witnesses have reported many such incredible feats performed by Indian fakirs or yogis. Why, though, do they choose to engage in such an extreme form of self-mortification?

The yogi develops such disciplines to minimise inner and outer distractions in a quest for the attainment of higher consciousness. The Indian fakir, however, uses them simply to control his body rather than to reach some nebulous *samadhi*, or ecstasy. To him, live burial becomes the supreme demonstration of his power over his body and mind. But according to author and researcher Andrija Puharich, the fakir is never unconscious in the ordinary sense, since one of his aims is to maintain full control of four states – waking, sleeping, dreaming and the biological shutdown of the 'false death' of catalepsy, which in the fakir's case is often self-induced. During the period of burial, he does not lose actual consciousness but enters a deep state of meditation.

Just how and why the practice first originated is lost in the mists of time, but the physician James Braid was sure of its antiquity. In his *Observations of Trance, of Human Hibernation,* he cites a passage from the *Dabistan,* a Persian classic on Indian religion: 'It is an established custom amongst the yogis that, when malady overtakes them, they bury themselves'. This implies that self-inhumation may have its origin in attitudes towards illness, and that

Among other accounts of suspended animation from Africa, mention must be made of the 'walkers for water', who were first drawn to the attention of Ivan Sanderson in 1932 by a British representative, N. H. Cleverley, in Calabar, British Cameroons. He had a senior official and a sergeant of the Native Bush Police investigate the refusal of several villages in the Ibibio tribal territory to pay their taxes. The villagers were nowhere to be found on their large swamp-surrounded islands, until the native sergeant doffed his uniform and went 'under cover'. Then he made a most startling discovery.

Peering over a 6-foot (1.8-metre) cliff, the sergeant saw 'the entire community (over a hundred souls, men, women and children, and their pets, which were confined in openwork baskets and appeared to be asleep) sitting motionless at the bottom of the water with their backs to the bank'. The sight of his sergeant shaking with fear – and failing to 'wake up' the villagers, in 8 feet (2.4 metres) of water – was too much for the European official, who fled back to Calabar. His report was not dismissed by his superiors, who were 'old Coasters' and well acquainted with the bizarre practices of the region. A second, more experienced team was dispatched; but by the time they arrived, village life was back to normal and the sergeant had collected the taxes. This was not 'a yarn', Cleverley assured Sanderson: the incident had been soberly recorded at the court in Calabar.

This story is not unrelated to the live burial of fakirs. Either the African villagers could suspend their vital functions spontaneously, or they prevailed upon the services of some shaman skilled in techniques akin to hypnotism. But there is a record of at least one yogi who performed a very similar phenomenon by an act of his own will in Bombay, on 15 February 1950, according to a report in *The Lancet* for that year, signed by a Dr R. J. Vakil. Before a huge crowd, and under Dr Vakil's supervision, an emaciated middle-aged *sadhu* called Shri Ramdasji was sealed into a small underground cubicle for 56 hours. The chamber measured 5 by 8 feet (1.5 by 2.4 metres) and was made of concrete

the technique was learned from survivors who undoubtedly reported that this extreme form of isolation hastened their cure or enhanced their ecstasies to a marked degree.

Whatever the origins of live burial, instances similar to those of India also occur in other countries where they may be associated with ritualised trance – as described in M. Eliade's *Shamanism*. In *More Things,* Ivan Sanderson tells of the burial of an unnamed fakir for 24 hours under two truckloads of gooey earth in Belize, supervised by five doctors, including a British Senior Medical Officer.

FAST DEATH

In Japan, meanwhile, there existed a strange cult of self-mummification, described in Carmen Blacker's *The Catalpa Bow.* Apparently, some Buddhists would vow to complete fasts lasting up to 4,000 days, beginning with a severely restricted diet and gradually diminishing it to a total fast with the goal of dying. At least two members of this interesting and now extinct group are recorded as entering their tombs alive.

According to the South African *Pretoria News* in late 1974, a Togolese jujuman, named Togbui Siza Aziza, was buried for three hours in Accra in an ordinary coffin. Stone slabs covered the box, then a layer of mortar, topped with more slabs. After two hours, the crowd began to panic and pleaded with Aziza, whose muffled voice could still be faintly heard. Finally, the ground shook and Aziza burst through the mortar, easily shoving the slabs aside. But the coffin was found naïled shut. Interestingly, Aziza, who subsequently toured with a group promoting African mysticism, Afrika Azzeu, said that he gained his magical powers, which include the ability to heal the sick, understand animals and be impervious to pain of any kind, by meditating while buried underground.

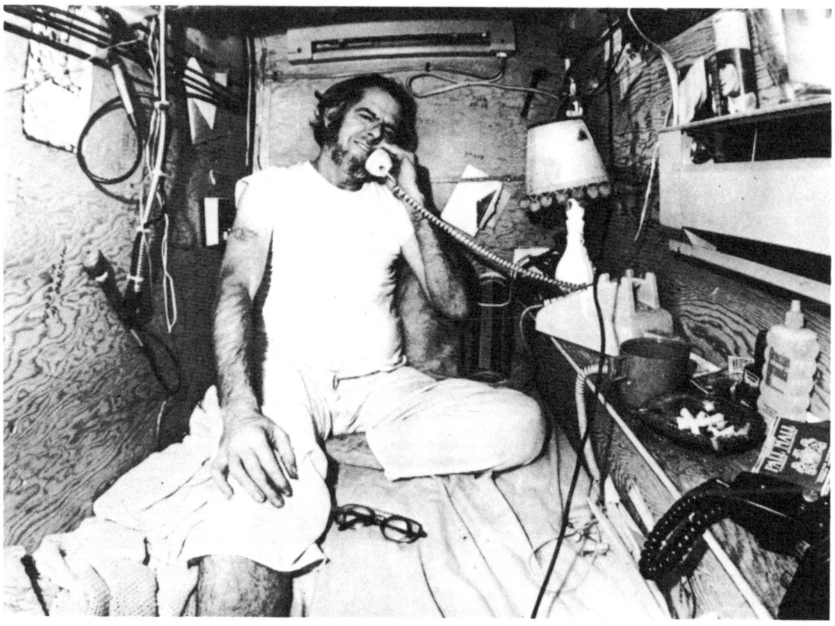

In 1974, an Indian yogi,* top, *buried his head in earth for many long minutes, with a pulse rate of just two beats per minute, and survived. American stuntman Bill White,* above, *also attracted attention by staying underground for 134 days, two hours and five minutes in 1978, passing the time by telephoning the press – including the public relations officer of* The Guinness Book of Records *(in which he found a place).

The legendary feats of Indian holy men include being buried alive with arms protruding from the ground, left.

studded with large nails, and plugged with more concrete. After 56 hours, a hole was bored in the lid, 1,400 gallons (6,400 litres) of water poured in through a firehose, and the hole re-sealed. The watery tomb was broken open nearly seven hours later. The *sadhu* had survived.

For 15 years after hearing the story of the Ibibio villagers, Sanderson tried to find out more. 'Trouble is,' he wrote, 'I can't find anybody in our world who will even discuss the matter sensibly and from a scientific point of view. One would have thought that this would be a golden opportunity for liars and other storytellers. Perhaps they just don't have the imagination... Perhaps, however, it is the truth...'

PERSPECTIVES

DEATH, WHEN IS THY STING?

Stephen Pile's bestselling *Book of Heroic Failures* includes 'The most unsuccessful lying in state' and 'The funeral that disturbed the corpse'. The first concerns the Bishop of Lesbos who, in 1896, after two days lying in state, suddenly sat up and demanded to know what the mourners were staring at. He was, it seems, not dead after all. In the second story, a missionary called Schwartz, who 'died' in New Delhi in the 1890s, joined in the hymn singing from his coffin during his funeral.

In the context of Pile's book, both are hilarious stories, yet premature burial was – and still is – a grim business. In the days when doctors merely felt the pulse or held a mirror to catch the mist of breath, cataleptic patients had a horrifyingly high chance of being certified dead and duly buried – alive. In primitive areas, meanwhile, knocking sounds emitting from freshly dug graves might be taken as ghostly manifestations and therefore ignored.

Such errors were most probably unintentional. But the ability to simulate death is not unknown in the West, too. St Augustine, for example, wrote of a priest who could deliberately stop his pulse and respiration during a trance state, when he was also insensitive to pain.

But, despite today's medical sophistication, the actual moment of death is a subject of hot debate. Are we 'dead' only if our hearts stop beating or when our brains cease to register electrical activity?

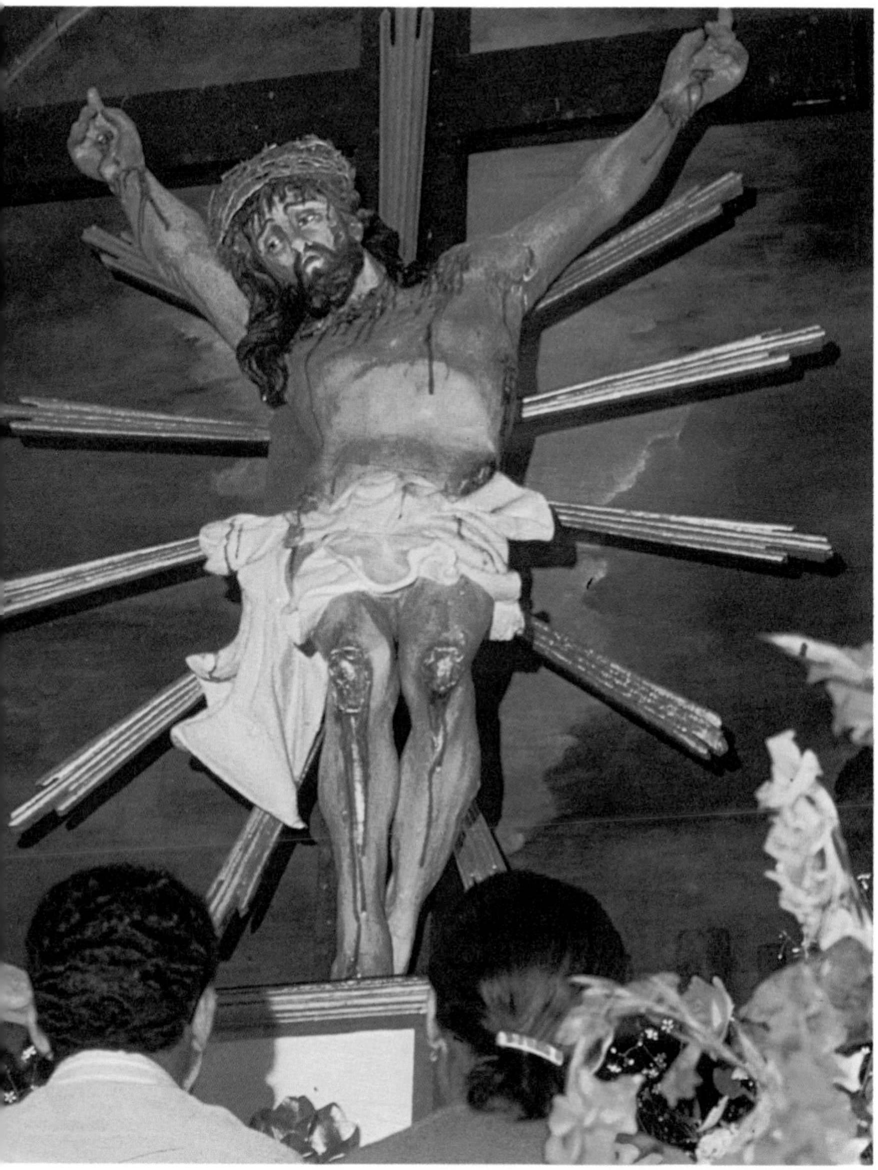

BLOOD AND TEARS

HOW CAN A PLASTER STATUE OF CHRIST SHED REAL BLOOD, OR A PAINTING OF THE VIRGIN CRY? THESE PHENOMENA HAVE BEEN RECORDED MANY TIMES, CONTINUING TO INSPIRE – AND ALSO PERPLEX – TODAY

One day in April 1975, just after Easter, Anne Poore of Boothwyn, Pennsylvania, USA, was praying for those who had turned away from the Church. She was kneeling in front of a 26-inch (66-centimetre) plaster statue of Jesus, given to her by a friend the year before. 'Suddenly I looked up at the statue,' she later told reporters, 'and my heart stopped beating. Two ruby-red drops of blood had appeared over the plaster wounds in its palms. I was terrified. I could see it was real blood. Since then, I've seen blood flow from the statue dozens of times.'

It is fashionable today to disbelieve in such things – or rather, to prefer to believe that such things do not happen. The closed or frightened mind characteristically takes refuge behind an exaggerated rationalism. To such entrenched sceptics, accounts of statues, paintings and other objects of religious worship seen weeping tears or issuing blood are evidence of the deplorable survival into this scientific age of primitive and superstitious beliefs. But there is evidence that proves such things do indeed happen at times, as the following stories show.

> "IT BEGAN ON THE EVENING OF 16 MARCH 1960, WHEN A TINTED PORTRAIT OF THE BLESSED VIRGIN MARY BEGAN TO WEEP TEARS INSIDE ITS GLASS FRAME. THE TEARS DID NOT COLLECT BUT VANISHED."

In the 1950s, an Italian physician, Dr Piero Casoli, made a prolonged study of weeping Madonnas. There was no shortage, for he concluded that they occurred on average about twice a year in Italy alone. And the records of the British *Fortean Times* show that such occurrences have been recorded throughout modern history, reports being received from all over the world. In 1527, for instance, a statue of Christ in Rome wept copiously and was taken as an omen of the fall of that city. In July 1966, a crucifix owned by Alfred Bolton of Walthamstow, London, shed tears on at least 30 occasions. In December 1960, a statue in a Greek

The 300-year-old wooden crucifix, above, in the church at Porto das Caixas, Brazil, began to bleed in 1968. The carving then became the focus for many miraculous cures.

The crucifix, right, in the church of St Ignatius in Rome, was also seen to ooze drops of blood in 1959.

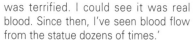

Orthodox church at Tarpon Springs, Florida, streamed 'little teardrops'. And in January 1981, a statue of the Virgin Mary at Caltanisetta, Sicily – said first to have wept in 1974 – began to bleed again from the right cheek.

Faced with such seemingly 'impossible' occurrences, we are prompted to ask the rational question: can these stories be dismissed as 'mass hallucinations'? There are certainly records of people gathered around a religious image said to bleed or weep, their anticipation fired by rumour, who have 'seen' the miracle, possibly when the most suggestible person present cried out: 'Look, the Madonna is weeping!' The American psychical researcher Raymond Bayless himself discovered just such a case.

It began on the evening of 16 March 1960, when a tinted portrait of the Blessed Virgin Mary began to weep tears inside its glass frame. It was owned by Pagora Catsounis of New York, who immediately called in her priest, Father George Papadeas, of St Paul's Greek Orthodox Church, Hempstead. He said:

'When I arrived, a tear was drying beneath the left eye. Then, just before our devotions ended, I saw another tear well in her left eye. It started as a small, round globule of moisture in the corner of the eye and slowly trickled down her face'.

At the bottom of the frame, the slow but steady trickle did not collect, as expected, but appeared to vanish before it had a chance to form a puddle.

WEEPING MADONNAS

In the first week, 4,000 people filed through Mrs Catsounis' apartment to stare and to pray, while tears flowed intermittently. The painting was subsequently transferred to St Paul's. Then, almost beyond belief, another weeping Madonna turned up in the family. It was owned by an aunt of Mrs Catsounis, Antonia Koulis. The circumstances seemed suspicious, but the phenomenon was vouched for by the Archbishop himself. The portrait was said to weep copiously; and when Father Papadeas let reporters handle it, the picture was still damp. Samples of the fluid were taken for analysis and found not to be human tears. This painting was also enshrined in St Paul's. Mrs Koulis was given a replacement, and this too began to weep.

It was at this point that Raymond Bayless began his investigations, as reported in the magazine *Fate* in March 1966. Close examination of the surface of the painting revealed stains below the eyes that consisted of crystallised particles, something like those of a serum. The accumulations, being dried, had not moved downwards. When Bayless examined the image a second time, these raised 'tears' were still in the same place. He found no pinholes or other openings through which liquid could have been introduced into the central area of the painting, and stated:

'During our first visit . . . one woman, who was acting as interpreter, suddenly cried out that a new tear was descending from an eye. I looked immediately but in my opinion such was absolutely not the case.Some viewers and worshippers were convinced they saw tears appear and move on the surface of the icon while my friend and I were both present. On the other hand, we both were convinced, because of our careful examination, that . . . the tear was not liquid and did not flow or even descend a fraction of an inch'.

The plaster statue,* above, *began to bleed from its hands in April 1975 in the home of Anne Poore of Boothwyn, Pennsylvania, USA. Thereafter the hands bled every Friday and the statue became the centre piece of a shrine.

Archbishop Takovos, of the Greek Orthodox Church of America, is seen* below, *inspecting an icon of the Virgin Mary, reported to have shed tears in the home of the Catsounis family in 1960.

Another weeping Madonna,* below right, *was discovered in the Catsounis' home within weeks of the first. This was found to shed an 'oily' substance.

The case of Anne Poore's bleeding statue is quite different. When she recovered from her shock at its sudden bleeding, she made the statue the centre piece of a shrine on her front porch where a great many people saw it. On Fridays and holy days, the flow of blood was particularly strong, streaming downwards, in a cyclical recurrence that parallels the regular bleedings of some stigmatics. Eventually, the statue was moved to St Luke's Episcopalian Church at Eddystone, Pennsylvania, and installed on a platform 10 feet (3 metres) above the altar. Father Chester Olszewski, pastor of the church, said: 'It has bled as long as four hours. I know there can be no trickery. I have seen the palms dry, then, minutes later have observed droplets of blood welling out of the wounds.... Incredibly the blood seldom runs off the statue. Its robes are now encrusted with dried blood'. Another priest, Father Henry Lovett, said he came to see it as a sceptic and went away convinced it was a miracle. 'I've personally taken the hands off the statue – they are held in place by wooden dowels – and examined them. They're solid chalk. And the statue has bled profusely even as I watched.'

The Blood of Christ?

In this case, there is no doubt that a blood-like liquid flowed mysteriously from the sites of Christ's wounds on the statue. But was it actually blood? Dr Joseph Rovito, a respected Philadelphia physician, conducted his own investigation. X-rays revealed no trace of a reservoir or other trick mechanism concealed in the statue, but the result of the blood tests was not so straightforward. Although identified as human blood, the low red cell count was curious, and indicated great age. The fact that the

> I was astounded. The photo of Bob's grandmother was soaking wet, dripping with a small pool of water ... the photo didn't dry quickly ... when it did dry, the area about the face remained puffed, as though the water had originated there and run downwards from the eyes.

blood flowed quite a distance before coagulating indicated that it was fairly fresh, but fresh blood contains millions of red cells. Father Lovett, and other Catholics, jumped to the conclusion that this was actually the blood of Christ.

Such images are almost always objects of worship, and so the mysterious appearance of liquids on or near these images is bound to be interpreted in a religious context. But outside this context, there are almost identical accounts of a variety of related phenomena: bleeding tombstones, for instance; persistently wet or recurring bloodstains in a few haunted houses (evidence of a legendary murder, perhaps); or the constant distillation of substances such as clear oils or blood-like fluids that appear to come from the relics of some saints.

Once trickery and natural explanations, such as condensation, have been discounted, and the flow of blood has been established as not coming from inside the statue, then we have to accept that the liquid is appearing on the surface of the object, materialised there from an unknown source by the mysterious phenomenon of teleportation. The same probably applies to the appearance of tears on statues or icons. Yet appearances of these liquids are not random; in fact, they are remarkably consistent, for they restrict themselves to sites where either faith or legend leads us to expect miraculous happenings. Further consistency is observed in the association between bleeding and images of Christ, and weeping and images of the Virgin Mary. This regular association suggests either that the teleportative force is created by an unknown intelligence or that it acts automatically in response to especially powerful images in the human mind, on an instinctive or unconscious level.

A

B

C

D

In September 1911, a portrait of Christ in the church at Mirebeau-en-Poitou in France began to ooze blood (A). By Christmas of that year, blood was flowing from both palms, from the head and from the stylised heart (B). By March 1912, the blood was flowing copiously (C). The phenomenon seemed in some way connected with the parish priest, Abbé Vachère. Consecrated hosts bled as he blessed them and a nearby statue of the Virgin Mary wept. Much to his superiors' displeasure, he revelled in the attention of the pilgrims who flocked to witness the ever-increasing bleeding (D). Abbé Vachère was eventually excommunicated. Mysteriously, the portrait stopped bleeding at his death in 1915.

American parapsychologist, D. Scott Rogo, told the story of the Reverend Robert Lewis who, on the day of his ordination, recalled how his grandmother – his first spiritual mentor – had wept with joy the day he said he wanted to join the ministry. However, she died before his ordination and he deeply regretted not being able to share the happiness of his success with her. He glanced at her photograph on his dresser, and suddenly accused his companion of playing a joke. The friend, the Reverend William Raucher, later wrote:

'I went over to see what was troubling him. I was astounded. The photo of Bob's grandmother was soaking wet, dripping with a small pool of water spreading on the dresser under it. Examining the picture we found that it was wet inside the glass.... The back of the picture, made of dyed imitation velvet, was so wet the velvet had streaked and faded. Removed from its frame, the photo didn't dry quickly. When it did dry, the area about the face remained puffed, as though the water had originated there and run downwards from the eyes'.

Tears of Joy

Rogo suggested that Lewis had unconsciously used a telekinetic ability to project a strong emotion into his immediate environment. 'Lewis underwent a mini-trauma when he passed his ordination exams,' wrote Rogo. 'His grandmother often wept with joy... He wanted to share his joy with [her]; he wanted to see her cry with happiness, so he used his psychic ability to stage the event.' Rogo made the further suggestion that this was not a freakish power of one individual, but that we all may possess this ability to cause dogmatic changes in our environment by projecting outside ourselves powerfully felt or suppressed emotions.

This type of paranormal projection, in which events are related to the spiritual or psychological tensions of those involved, takes two classic forms: overtly religious phenomena, and the disturbances known as poltergeist activity. In both cases, contemporary theorists relate the outburst of activity, or sudden manifestation of phenomena, to some inner crisis. Such a crisis may take many forms, such as the onset of puberty and its attendant physical and emotional complications, or the mounting pressures of illness, frustrations and inadequacies.

In May 1979, in New Mexico, for example, an ordinary plastic-coated, postcard-sized portrait of Jesus wept tears of seemingly genuine blood. The religious memento had been bought in 1972 by Kathy Malott for her grandmother, Willie Mae Seymore. On 25 May, Mrs Malott and her husband Zach were visiting Mrs Seymore when Mr Malott noticed a small dark drop forming on the picture, just under the right eye. It quickly turned into a steady stream, forming a puddle at the bottom, where it was tucked into the frame of a larger painting. 'The blood was running from the picture just as if I had cut my finger,' said Mrs Seymore. Mrs Malott went to wipe it off but, somewhat awed by the occurrence, other members of the family stopped her and decided to call a priest. One declined to come.

As the news spread, and reporters came to the house, many examined the postcard portrait and could find no cut or hole through which a liquid could appear. The blood seemed to flow directly from the surface of the plastic. Later the substance was given a standard blood test – a 'hematest' – at the Eastern New Mexico Medical Center Hospital in Roswell. A spokesman said: 'Yes, it was honest-to-gosh bona fide blood'. An even more bizarre note was added when the blood was discovered still to be uncongealed after 24 hours.

Perhaps the most intriguing fact, however, was that the flow had only just begun when Zach Malott noticed it. It was almost as though the phenomenon was waiting for attention before it began in earnest.

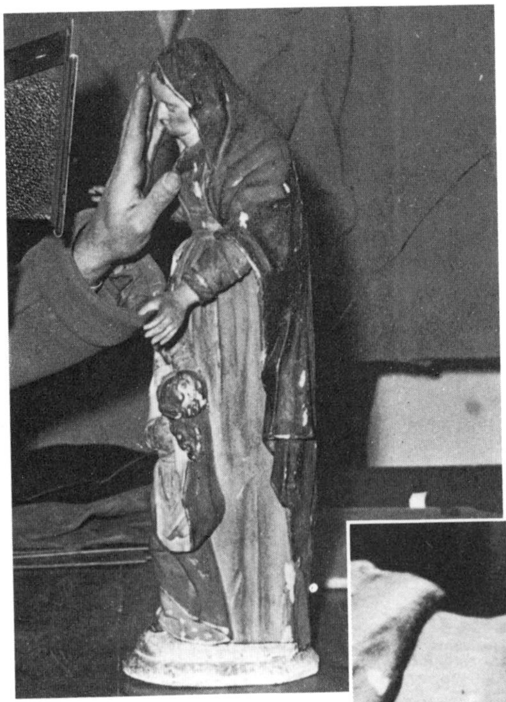

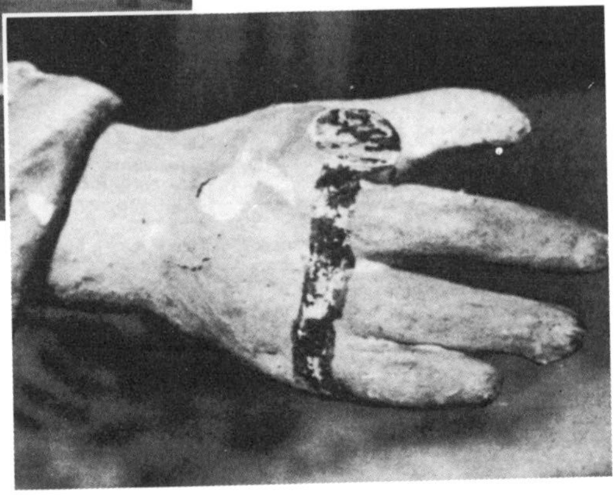

A finger of the statue of St Anne,* left, *belonging to Jean Salate, a hotel owner of Entrevaux in France, began to ooze blood,* below, *after Salate had broken it in a fit of anger in 1954. The finger bled 30 drops during the day and again the next morning. Crowds of the pious and the curious gathered to venerate the statue. Although chemical analysis proved that the blood was real, rumour soon spread that Salate had faked it.

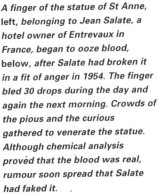

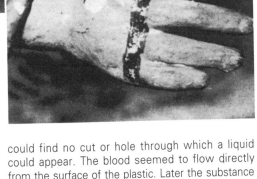

The bronze statue of an aristocratic Japanese lady,* below, *owned by Allen Demetrius of Pittsburgh, USA, began to cry just 10 days before the nuclear accident at Three Mile Island, Pennsylvania in 1979. She had been known to weep only once before, on 6 August 1945, the night that an atomic bomb was dropped on Hiroshima. Demetrius said: 'It was like she was crying about the bombing'. Thousands of people travelled to witness the oxidised stains on the face of 'the weeping bronze of Hiroshima'.

Second Coming

There is an interesting sequel, too: four nights later, Zach Malott had a vivid dream in which Christ appeared and told him that the blood was a sign of his Second Coming. Prior to this, Malott had told reporters his family were 'not too religious'. Now, he said, his whole outlook had changed. 'I was sinner. Now I'm going to follow Jesus Christ.'

A more demonstrable case of bizarre cause and effect involves the celebrated weeping Madonna of Syracuse, Sicily. The statue was owned by Antonietta Janusso and was in fact a small plaster bust of the Virgin Mary in the style known as 'The Immaculate Heart of Mary' – a wedding gift, and a mass-produced ornament bought locally.

The couple were desperately poor and sharing accommodation in an extremely run-down quarter of the city. Suddenly, Mrs Janusso began to suffer mysterious illnesses. Some months into pregnancy, she experienced fits and convulsions, with alternating periods of blindness, deafness and dumbness. Doctors thought it was some kind of toxaemia but could find no cause. (However, similarity between her symptoms and those of clinical hysteria have been noted by some researchers.)

The bedridden girl, in a sorry state, looked up one day to the shelf above the bed where the statue rested, and saw it begin to cry. It continued to do so for many days and was seen by impeccable witnesses. But at the end of the first day, despite the excitement and strain of people crowding into the small room to see for themselves, Mrs Janusso felt considerably better, and by the time the statue had stopped crying, she had completely recovered.

> THE FLOW HAD ONLY JUST BEGUN WHEN ZACH MALOTT NOTICED IT. IT WAS ALMOST AS THOUGH THE PHENOMENON WAS WAITING FOR ATTENTION BEFORE IT BEGAN IN EARNEST... FOUR NIGHTS LATER, HE HAD A VIVID DREAM IN WHICH CHRIST APPEARED AND TOLD HIM THAT THE BLOOD WAS A SIGN OF HIS SECOND COMING.

To the faithful, it was a miracle: to others, though, it seemed to be confirmation that her illnesses, genuinely debilitating though they were, had a hysterical origin. Indeed, perhaps the unconscious mind stages such apparently mystical or magical events in order to break a vicious circle of depression and self-pity. As has been said about the Catsounis case: 'The tears stopped when the reasons for self-pity were removed by blessing and return to health'.

The Madonna of the Sicilian village of Caltanisetta, left, was seen to shed tears in 1974 and bled from a cheek in 1980. These 'flows' persisted under rigorous scrutiny.

Mrs Antonietta Janusso, above, is seen lying on her sickbed in Syracuse, Sicily, in 1953 while her mother wipes away the tears shed by the plaster Madonna. She recovered completely after the statue stopped crying.

Many of those unfortunate enough to be the focus of poltergeist phenomena also suffer from similar traumas, crises or changes. Mary Jobson, a 13-year-old poltergeist victim investigated in 1839 by Dr Reid Clanny, suffered patches of anaesthesia on her skin, as well as swellings, and convulsions, while her bedroom furniture moved, and while music and voices came from mid-air, and raps emanated from the walls. At times, quantities of water were also seen to fall, apparently from nowhere, on to the floor.

Many more cases could be cited, but one particularly worthy of mention seems to display overlapping characteristics of both the religious and the poltergeist type of projection. It centred on a devout 16-year-old Irish boy, James Walsh, of Templemore, Tipperary, in whose home all the holy pictures and statuary began to ooze blood. A hollow in the earthen floor of his room also kept filling with water, no matter how many times it was emptied. It was said that thousands of people took away containers of the water that was found there. The family was also tormented by mobile furniture and other forms of unexplained psychokinesis.

Such phenomena undoubtedly occur – but we can only guess at how or why. The facts are suggestive of a teleportation of liquids, but from where remains a mystery at present. Intriguing, too, is the difference between certain types of paranormal projection and the way in which they affect those who are troubled by them. As researcher Dr Nandor Fodor observed: 'Religious ecstasy of the weeping Madonna type restores, whereas the poltergeist senselessly frightens and destroys'.

SECRETS OF THE SEX CULTS

IS THE CULT OF TANTRA SIMPLY AN EXCUSE FOR SEXUAL EXCESSES, AS CLAIMED BY ITS CRITICS? OR ARE ITS RITUALS INDEED THE KEY TO ULTIMATE SPIRITUAL SALVATION?

The entire universe is in perfect equilibrium, its two primary polarities precisely balanced – like a god and goddess locked together in divine and intimate union. The highest spiritual goal, therefore, is for humanity to attain resonance with that unsurpassable state through sexual rituals. So say the followers of Tantra, a cult that originated in

Shiva, the major male god of Tantra, is seen above, dancing upon a dwarf demon and encircled by symbols of creation, destruction and rebirth. Tantrism has a whole pantheon of deities and a complex ideology of spiritual fulfilment.

the ancient East and that has enjoyed popularity among Western occultists and mystics since at least the end of the 19th century. It continues to flourish – largely in secret – today.

To the outsider, its rites may seem nothing more than an indulgence in promiscuous and apparently obscene sex. Even worse, perhaps, the rituals seem to smack of utter depravity and black magic. But in its purest sense, Tantrism is nothing of the kind. Tantra, from which the cult's name is derived, is a Sanskrit word meaning 'warp'. It signifies a body of written teaching – the warp – through which are threaded the supplementary oral and physical training and preparation – the weft – needed for the attainment of personal and direct experience of God, the gods, the Universal Essence, the Ultimate – however the seeker after wisdom and salvation chooses to envisage this awesome goal.

In fact, the sexually explicit, erotic and, to some, disgusting aspects of Tantric rites take up only a small percentage of the entire written texts. Yet it is probably true to say that these practices, and the powers they are supposed to confer, are the main factor in the cult's appeal to Westerners.

Tantrism has almost always been practised in secret. And, in spite of the increased sexual freedom and permissiveness of the late 20th century, it is still a secret cult. Although the oldest texts date back only to around the end of the 10th century, it is said that there were many more ancient ones, which were destroyed by successive invaders of the Indus Valley and by orthodox Hindus who tried to stamp out Tantra. Libraries of Tantric scripts were burned, the cult's monasteries were razed, and priests were put to death. Not surprisingly, surviving teachers and followers went into hiding. Tantra, however, has much to offer besides the sexual practices that offended the persecutors and that appal modern critics.

In Tantric philosophy, the two major gods, who personify the balanced polarities of the cosmos, are

Shiva and his consort Shakti. But it is the female, Shakti, who is regarded as the superior of the two because she is seen as the primal, creative, active force – the Mother Goddess, Great Mother or Great Goddess. The Tantrics have no caste system, consider women completely equal to men and, in many rites, envisage the female partner as the physical vehicle of the goddess Shakti herself.

Occult Philosophy

The range of subjects that Tantrism treats is so broad that it covers almost all areas of occult philosophy including the creation and ultimate destruction of the world; an entire pantheon of deities; yoga and meditation; astral travel and heightened consciousness; prolonged longevity – and, of course, the sexual rites by which, it is believed, many powers and profound insights may be obtained. Indeed, more than one commentator has noted that the medieval grimoires and rituals of Western magic and sorcery seem to have been borrowed from eastern Tantrism and dressed it up in western trappings.

Long and difficult periods of preparation and training are essential for any form of attainment in the Tantric system. There are complex breathing exercises, gestures and postures, designed to lead to control of body temperature, pulse rate and other automatic physical functions. Intense and profound mental exercises are also performed, calculated to give total control to the will.

Successful adepts should ultimately be raised mentally, bodily and spiritually to attune their highest, inner essence to the Universal Spirit. This is often a religious goal, but there are many who would insist that Tantra is not a true religion.

The texts that describe the necessary techniques of Tantra are couched in highly allegorical and abstruse symbolism, designed to veil inner meaning. The sections dealing with spiritual alchemy, for example, at first sight appear to be describing nothing more than the physical effort of attempting to transmute base metals into gold. But they are actually intended to be applied internally.

Despite such open display in art as the erotic sculptures on the Khajuraho temple in India, **top and above,** *the Tantrics have nearly always practised their sexual rites in secret to escape persecution.*

> " THE SUCCESSFUL TANTRIC IS, IN FACT, A PART OF – AND ABLE TO MANIPULATE AT WILL – ANY SEGMENT OF THE COSMOS. IT IS A CASE OF SALVATION THROUGH SEX. "

Shakti-yoga is the key to the real alchemical process indicated, and its exercises are based on the concept of the chakras, which might be defined as centres. Another name used almost synonymously with chakras is *padmas,* meaning 'lotuses'. Chakras are said to be located inside the body, but are not envisaged as physical organs. Rather, they are subtle physical centres of energy, located at each plexus (nerve centre) of the body.

There are seven major chakras in the human body, we are told. The lowest of these is called the *muladhara,* which is said to lie near the base of the spine. It is here that the feminine, active principle, the goddess Shakti herself, is believed to lie dormant. She is symbolised as a sleeping serpent, known as the *kundalini* – from *kundala* meaning 'coiled' – and she waits to be awakened and eventually conjoined with her counterpart Shiva, who is the male, passive principle.

Shiva, meanwhile, supposedly inhabits the *sahasrara* chakra – the 'thousand-petalled lotus' – that is to be found in the crown of the head. The way to bring these deities together, say the Tantrics, is to awaken Shakti and then cause her to move gradually up through the five intervening chakras of the body. These are the *svadhisthana,* above the genital region; the *manipura,* near the navel; the *anahata,* in the heart area; the *akasa,* in the throat; and the *ajna,* somewhere in the region of the pineal gland. The *ajna* is the so-called 'third

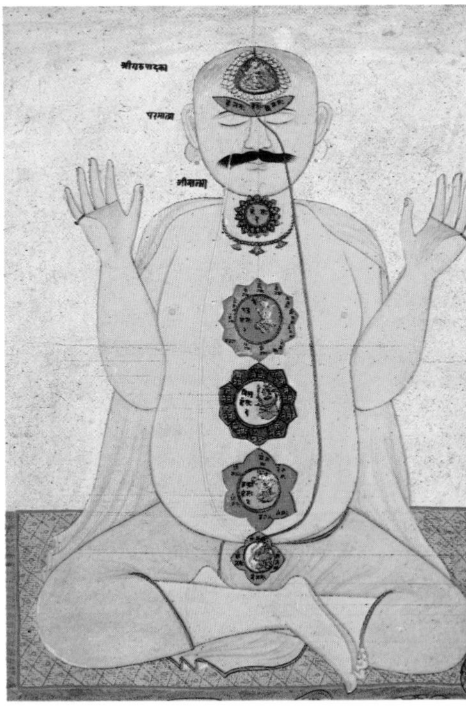

The 19th-century drawing, **right,** *shows the seven chakras (centres of energy). The lowest chakra is at the base of the spine, and here lies the kundalini, a snake symbolic of the goddess Shakti. Tantrics seek to awaken her and make her move up the body to the god Shiva, the highest chakra in the crown of the head. When this 'divine union' takes place, the Tantric has achieved his final goal, which takes years of rigorous training.*

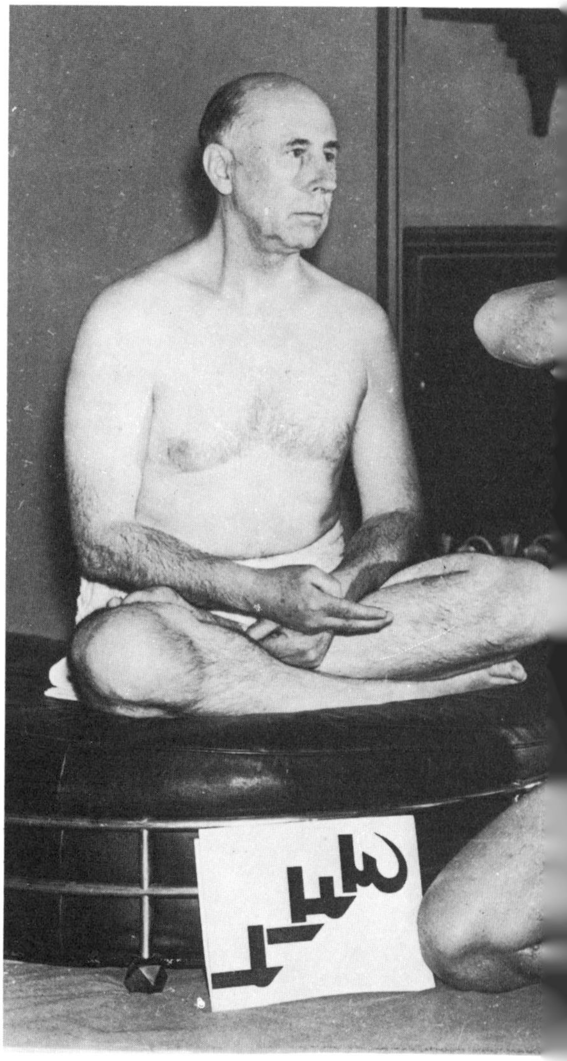

" If not undertaken properly with the aid of a knowledgeable master, dangers are very real. It is even said ... madness and death can result. "

eye', beloved of eastern and western mystics alike as an organ of occult vision.

When the *kundalini* has reached the seventh chakra, Shakti and Shiva are united. The successful adept is then perfectly attuned to the Universe itself. This puts the enlightened one in a superior position to the rest of 'unawakened' mankind, leading as it does to the highest order of wisdom and power. The successful Tantric is, in fact, a part of – and able to manipulate at will – any segment or entity of the entire cosmos. It is, so it would appear, a case of salvation through sex.

But there are many pitfalls in this long, complex and arduous process of Tantric enlightenment and, if not undertaken properly with the aid of a knowledgeable master, dangers are very real. It is even said that if the *kundalini* force, which is likened to a kind of occult fire, gets out of control, madness or death can result.

The Tibetan bronze, above, is of the god Hevajra with his goddess Shakti. According to Tantric belief, such divine union keeps the Universe in perfect balance. The cult's sexual rituals aim to bring the cultists into resonance with this divine equilibrium.

Another of the dangers along the way is that aspirants could be diverted by mundane desires, born of their weaknesses and fanned by some of their achievements. The desire for wealth, longevity, or power over others, for instance, may seduce them away from the ultimate goal of divine union. And the sexual rites themselves, if not undertaken in the spirit of discipline that is intended, can obsess the practitioner to the point of bodily and mental collapse.

These rites – so often the target of the severest external criticism – involve nudity, group sex, incest and adultery. But although Tantrism has been described as a cult of ecstasy, it is not merely physical, sensual ecstasy that is paramount. Tantric rituals are deliberately designed to make the selection of a partner arbitrary. There is no emphasis on youth, beauty or mutual attraction.

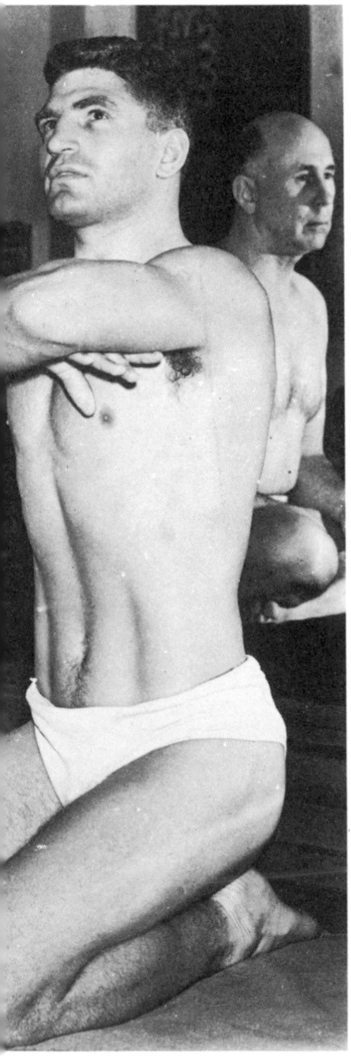

Lou Nova, above right, a boxing champion, is seen preparing for a major fight by taking muscle control instructions from Oom the Omnipotent, founder of an American cult with roots in Tantrism. Oom had a wealthy patron who established a permanent home for the cult in Nyack, New York.

"ALTHOUGH TANTRISM HAS BEEN DESCRIBED AS A CULT OF ECSTASY, IT IS NOT MERELY PHYSICAL, SENSUAL ECSTASY THAT IS PARAMOUNT. TANTRIC RITUALS ARE DELIBERATELY DESIGNED TO MAKE THE SELECTION OF A PARTNER ARBITRARY."

At higher levels of attainment, there are even claims of sexual intercourse with goddesses, elementals and female demons. One testimony to this has come from Stephen Jenkins, an English history teacher who was initiated into Tantric sexual ritual in Mongolia. In his book *The Undiscovered Country,* Jenkins explains that there are two stages in advanced Tantrism; one in which the female partner is an ordinary human being, and another in which she is 'a being of another order altogether'. The latter, he says, can take the form either of a 'skywalker' – spirits said to haunt western India and Ladak – or even of the Great Goddess Shakti herself. 'At the highest level of this particular method, the experience is indistinguishable from normal human intercourse at its intensest and most refined. I do not pretend to know how this works: I can only testify that it does,' he has said.

ELEMENTAL INTERCOURSE

It should be noted here that there are two different schools of Tantric sexual rites, known as the Right-Hand and Left-Hand Paths. It is believed that many of the cults that flourish secretly in the West today adhere to the Left-Hand Path. In Tantrism, this simply means that, in rites involving actual physical sex, the prospective female partners sit on the left-hand side of the male practitioners as the rite begins. In the Right-Hand Path, the sexual rites that take place are purely symbolic.

Francis King, a historian of ritual magic, wrote in *Sexuality, Magic and Perversion* that Edward Sellon (1818-1886) introduced Tantrism to Britain, although a few English and French academics had shown an interest in Hindu sex religion in the 18th century. Sellon – soldier, fencing master and pornographer – became acquainted with Tantric sexual rites in India, and his *Annotations on the Sacred Writings of the Hindus* appeared in 1865.

In the United States, possibly the first person to study and practise a form of sexual magic with some Tantric links was Paschal Beverley Randolph (1825-1871). He established various secret groups, one of which is believed to survive in France today. Like some Bengali practitioners of Tantra, Randolph used hallucinogenic drugs in his rites to attain heightened states of consciousness.

Another cult with distinctly Tantric overtones emerged in New York around 1919 under the name of the Brae Burn Club. It was headed by Pierre Bernard, who styled himself 'Oom the Omnipotent', and his wife, 'Mademoiselle de Vries', a vaudeville dancer whom he had taught the art of oriental dancing and the basics of Tantrism. Mlle de Vries also promoted a so-called 'health system of Tantrism', attracting a succession of society people. Among these was a member of the Vanderbilt family, one of the wealthiest in the country. It was she who arranged for the Bernards to buy a mansion and estate at Nyack, New York, as a permanent home for the cult.

SECRET ORDER

The inner sanctum of this club was the 'Secret Order of Tantrics', whose members came to regard Bernard as a kind of man-god. Bernard and his wife aimed 'to teach men and women to love, and make women feel like queens' – a clear echo of the Tantric belief in the superiority of Shakti. One Tantric aphorism actually says: 'Shiva without Shakti is a corpse'.

Other occult groups had already adopted some of the sex magic associated with Tantra. During the late 19th century, for, instance, Karl Kellner, a wealthy German industrialist, had established an occult order based upon the sex magic he claimed he had learned while travelling in the East. This group developed into the Ordo Templi Orientis (OTO), branches of which spread throughout Europe and parts of Scandinavia. Occultist Aleister Crowley became the leader of the British OTO in 1922, but moved away from Tantric ideas and introduced elements such as 'magical masturbation' and homosexuality, adding degrees of adeptness of his own invention. He also used sex magic for temporal gain, which is not commensurate with traditional Tantric teaching. However, branches of the OTO continued to be established, and many still exist today, in the USA as well as Europe – evidence that western links with Tantric sexual ritual have survived into the late 20th century.

The 17th -century Tibetan cloth painting, right, is of the Tantric Buddhas, including the Knowledge Holder, the Peaceful Buddhas, the Wrathful Buddhas and those presiding over the realms of reincarnation.

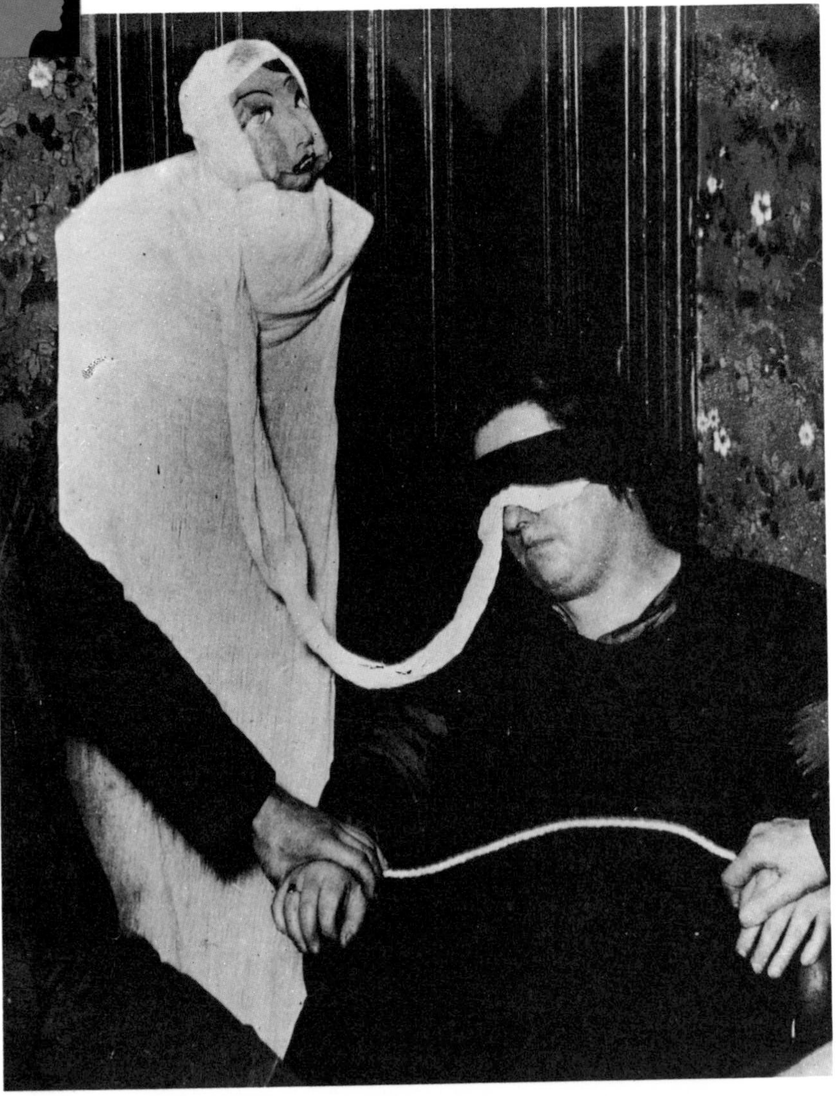

'It is my wish that this takes place for the sake of my little girl,' the materialisation of Mrs Woodcock told the couple. A year later, they were married. At a subsequent seance, a further materialisation of the dead woman told the newly-weds how happy she was they had complied with her wishes.

This touching story of true love was later recounted by Vincent Woodcock in court when he appeared as a witness for the defence in an astonishing trial at London's Old Bailey. In the dock was the medium whose astonishing psychic powers had made possible his wife's return from the spirit world: Helen Duncan.

Back From the Dead

Helen Duncan had been born in Scotland in 1898. She married at the age of 20, and her psychic talents were much in demand in the 1930s and 1940s, when she travelled around the country, holding seances in private homes and Spiritualist churches. She convinced thousands of people that the dead could return in physical form. But there were also sceptics who believed Helen Duncan's materialisations were in fact produced by trickery. She was said to have a spirit child, 'Peggy', who played an important role in her seances. But, in a court case in Edinburgh in May 1933, it was claimed that 'Peggy' was, in reality, nothing other than a woman's undervest that a policewoman succeeded in grabbing during a seance. The medium was found guilty of fraud and fined £10.

However, the verdict did not interfere with her career of mediumship. Indeed, during the Second World War, Helen Duncan's mediumistic powers were much in demand by the relatives of those who had died on active service, and she held many seances in Portsmouth, Hampshire, the home port of the Royal Navy. One of these seances, held on

A SPIRITED DEFENCE

The conviction of a leading physical medium on a charge of conspiracy caused a storm of protest in Spiritualist circles. Was Helen Duncan guilty or not?

The curtains of the cabinet in the darkened seance room parted and out stepped the figure of a woman. Vincent Woodcock recognised her immediately; it was his dead wife. In all, the young electrical draughtsman from Blackpool was to see the materialised spirit of his wife on 19 occasions during seances given by the medium Helen Duncan; but it was this particular occasion that changed his life.

Vincent Woodcock had brought his wife's sister with him to this seance; and when the spirit of his wife appeared from the curtained cabinet, she asked them both to stand. Then, with difficulty, the materialisation removed her husband's wedding ring and placed it on her sister's wedding finger.

At a seance held at her home in 1933, the physical medium Helen Duncan, shown above and right, produced the materialised form of her spirit guide 'Peggy'. Psychical researcher Harry Price claimed it was constructed out of cheesecloth and a rubber doll. However, reputable witnesses, such as the Glasgow medical officer for health, testified at Mrs Duncan's trial in 1944 to seeing many genuine spirit forms at her regular seances.

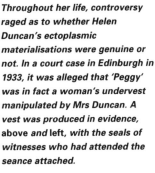

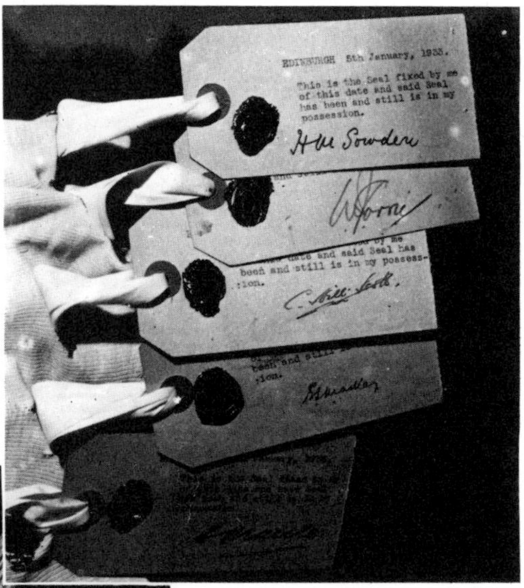

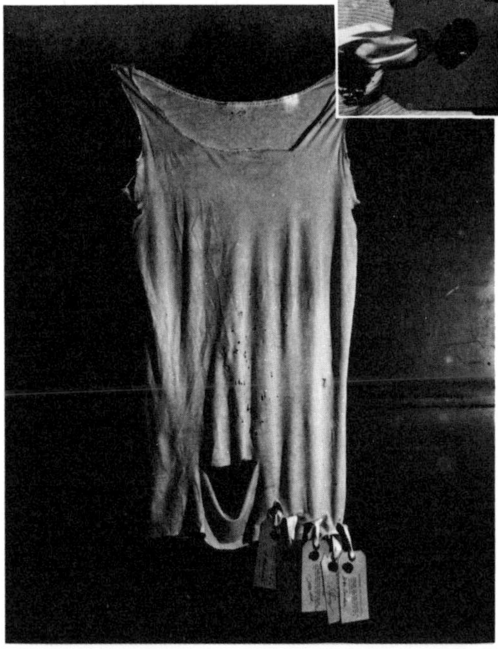

Throughout her life, controversy raged as to whether Helen Duncan's ectoplasmic materialisations were genuine or not. In a court case in Edinburgh in 1933, it was alleged that 'Peggy' was in fact a woman's undervest manipulated by Mrs Duncan. A vest was produced in evidence,* above and left, *with the seals of witnesses who had attended the seance attached.

19 January 1944, was raided by the police. A plain-clothes policeman who was present blew a whistle to give the signal, and his colleagues burst in. A grab was made at the ectoplasm issuing from the medium and the seance ended abruptly in commotion. Although nothing incriminating was found, Helen Duncan, together with three others who were said to have arranged the seances, Ernest and Elizabeth Homer and Francis Brown, subsequently appeared at Portsmouth magistrates' court on a charge of conspiracy.

At the preliminary hearing, the Portsmouth court was told how Lieutenant R. H. Worth of the Royal Navy had attended Mrs Duncan's seances and suspected fraud. He bought two tickets for 25 shillings (£1.25) each for the night of 19 January and took a policeman with him – War Reserve Cross. Cross made a grab for the ectoplasm, which he believed to be a white sheet, but he was unable to retain it. No sheet was found by the other police officers when they entered the seance room. After the hearing, bail was refused, and as a result the medium was remanded in Holloway prison in London for four days before the case was resumed in Portsmouth.

The prosecution seemed to be uncertain on what charge the four accused should be indicted. On their first appearance at Portsmouth, they were charged under the Vagrancy Act of 1824; but the charge was then amended to one of conspiracy. When the case was eventually transferred to the central criminal court at the Old Bailey – where it was dubbed the 'trial of the century' by some newspapers – the Witchcraft Act of 1735 was cited.

Under this ancient act, the defendants were accused of pretending 'to exercise or use a kind of conjuration that through the agency of Helen Duncan spirits of deceased persons should appear to be present....' Other charges were brought under the Larceny Act and they were accused of taking money 'by falsely pretending they were in a position to bring about the appearances of the spirits of deceased persons and that they then, *bona fide,* intended so to do without trickery'.

Spiritualists were dismayed by the use of the Witchcraft Act to bring a prosecution against such a famous medium. Under this Act, it appeared that Helen Duncan could be proved guilty whether or not her powers were genuine.

The prosecution clearly believed Helen Duncan was a fraud, and were not deterred by the absence of any props. During the trial, prosecuting Counsel John Maude produced a long piece of butter muslin and referred repeatedly to the theory put forward by a psychical researcher, Harry Price, that Helen Duncan achieved her results by swallowing muslin and then regurgitating it. Defence witnesses offered to produce a doctor's statement as well as X-rays to show that Mrs Duncan had a perfectly normal stomach, incapable of hiding any props that would produce the effect of materialisation. But these were not admitted in evidence.

A ONE-EYED SPIRIT

The trial took place a few months before D-Day and lasted seven days. Numerous witnesses testified to events during Helen Duncan's seances that must have shaken many sceptics. Several people said, for example, they had seen the medium – who weighed all of 22 stone (140 kilograms) – and her tall, thin spirit guide, Albert Stewart, simultaneously. Kathleen McNeill, wife of a Glasgow forgemaster,

SPIRITUALISTS WERE DISMAYED BY THE USE OF THE WITCHCRAFT ACT TO BRING A PROSECUTION AGAINST SUCH A FAMOUS MEDIUM. UNDER THIS ACT, IT APPEARED THAT HELEN DUNCAN COULD BE PROVED GUILTY WHETHER OR NOT HER POWERS WERE GENUINE. THE PROSECUTION CLEARLY BELIEVED HELEN DUNCAN WAS A FRAUD AND WERE NOT DETERRED BY THE ABSENCE OF PROPS.

told how she had attended a seance at which her sister appeared. This sister had died just a few hours earlier, after an operation, and news of her death could not have been known to Helen Duncan at that time. Yet Mrs Duncan's guide, Albert, announced that the sister had just passed over. At another seance some years later, Mrs McNeill's deceased father strode out of the cabinet and came up to within 6 feet (1.8 metres) of her. She testified that he had only one eye, as indeed he had when alive.

Some of the most impressive evidence was given on the sixth day of the trial. Alfred Dodd, an academic who had written books on Shakespeare's sonnets, told the court that he had attended Helen Duncan's seances on several occasions between 1932 and 1940. At one of these, his grandfather had appeared – a tall, corpulent man with a bronzed face, wearing a smoking cap just like the one he always used to wear. His hair, as always, was in a donkey-fringe style. After talking to his grandson, he turned to Dodd's friend, Tom, who had come with him to the seance. 'Look into my face, look into my eyes and you will know me again,' he said. 'Ask Alfred to show you my portrait. It's the same man.' The spirit then walked back to a curtained cabinet, clapped his hand on his leg three times and said: 'It's solid, Alfred, it's solid'.

Two journalists, H. Swaffer and J. W. Herries, were also called by the defence. The flamboyant Swaffer told the court that anyone who described ectoplasm as butter muslin 'would be a child': under a red light in a seance room, it would look yellow or pink, whereas the spirit forms had a living whiteness. Herries, chief reporter of *The Scotsman* newspaper and a justice of the peace, affirmed that he had seen Sir Arthur Conan Doyle materialise at one of Helen Duncan's seances. He had noted Doyle's rounded features and moustache, and had identified his voice. He maintained that the idea that the spirit form of 'Peggy' could have been an undervest was ridiculous, and that the cheesecloth regurgitation theory was absurd.

Apart from the testimony of witnesses, the defence offered the jury an actual demonstration of Helen Duncan's mediumship. At the start of the trial, the judge declined this offer and suggested instead that Mrs Duncan should be called as a witness. The defence replied, however, that Mrs Duncan could not testify, as she was in a trance during seances and unable to discuss what transpired. On the final day, the judge changed his mind about the demonstration, and asked the jury if they would like to have one. After some discussion, they turned down the offer.

The jury took 25 minutes to consider their verdict: they found the four defendants guilty of conspiracy to contravene the Witchcraft Act. They were discharged from giving verdicts on the other counts. The chief constable of Portsmouth then

Even with her hands held by witnesses and her feet bound, Helen Duncan,* below, *succeeded in materialising her spirit guide 'Peggy', apparently from ectoplasm issuing from her nose. She also had a male spirit guide, Albert Stewart, who was tall and thin, and several people testified to having seen Albert and the solid, generously proportioned form of Mrs Duncan simultaneously.

described Mrs Duncan's background. She was married to a cabinet-maker, had a family of six ranging in age from 18 to 26, and had been visiting Portsmouth for the past five years. In 1941, she had been reported for violating the security laws when she announced the loss of one of His Majesty's ships before the fact was made public. 'She is an unmitigated humbug and pest,' he said.

The judge deferred pronouncing sentence until after the weekend, and Mrs Duncan was led downstairs weeping, declaring in her broad Scots accent: 'I never heard so many lies in all my life'.

Appeal Rejected

When he came to pass sentence, the judge said that the verdict had not been concerned with whether 'genuine manifestations of the kind are possible . . . this court has nothing whatever to do with such abstract questions'. The jury had found this to be a case of plain dishonesty, and he sentenced Mrs Duncan to nine months' imprisonment. The medium cried out, 'I didn't do anything,' and was led away moaning and crying. Of the other defendants, Mrs Brown was given four months (she had two previous convictions for larceny and shop-lifting) and the Homers were fined £5 and bound over to be of good behaviour for two years. An appeal for the case to go to the House of Lords was rejected.

Helen Duncan served her sentence in Holloway prison. The Spiritualist movement, shocked by the verdict, called for a change in the law to prevent such prosecutions. Many of Mrs Duncan's supporters believed she had been prosecuted to stop her leakage of classified war-time information.

When she was released from prison on 22 September 1944, Helen Duncan announced that she would not give any more seances; but it was not long before she changed her mind. In fact, she was soon giving so many that Spiritualists became concerned that she was over-sitting. The quality of the manifestations in her seances was said to have deteriorated, and the Spiritualists' National Union even withdrew her diploma.

Song and Dance Act

But other reports suggested that her powers were in fact far from weakened. In the home of medium Susie Hughes, in Liverpool, for instance, Susie's spirit guide, 'Bluebell', was said to have appeared together with 'Peggy', Mrs Duncan's child guide. The two even sang and danced together in front of many witnesses. At another seance, Susie Hughes' father materialised. He greeted his wife and insisted that they walk into the brightest part of the room so that she could be sure that it was him. He then led her back to her chair and, with outstretched hands, took her in his arms and lifted her high above his head.

Alan Crossley, who wrote *The Story of Helen Duncan,* attended a seance with Mrs Duncan in 1954 at which he saw both the medium and Albert, her male spirit guide. He also saw the spirit of a man who had died just a few days earlier. The man's wife and son, present at the seance, were overcome with emotion when they recognised him.

In 1951, the Witchcraft Act of 1735 was repealed and replaced with the Fraudulent Mediums Act. Mrs Duncan's trial had certainly prompted this change in the law, but Spiritualist hopes that mediums would no longer be subjected to police harassment were short-lived. In November 1956, police raided a seance taking place in Nottingham.They grabbed the medium, searched her and took flashlight pictures. They shouted that they were looking for beards, masks and a shroud. They found nothing. The medium conducting that seance was Helen Duncan.

***Wrapped in black from neck to toe, medium Helen Duncan materialised a spirit hand that bears a remarkable resemblance to a rubber glove,* right. *But more than a quarter of a century after her death in 1956, Mrs Duncan spoke with her daughter Gina for over an hour through the direct-voice mediumship of Rita Goold of Leicester,* below.**

The interruption of a physical seance is always regarded as extremely dangerous by Spiritualists, because the ectoplasm is said to return to the body too rapidly. In this case, it caused Mrs Duncan great discomfort. A doctor was called, she was treated for shock, and two burns were later discovered on her stomach. She was so ill that she returned to her family in Scotland and was admitted to hospital. Five weeks after the police raid, she left the hospital; and two days later she was dead.

The story of Helen Duncan is one of the most tragic and remarkable in the history of Spiritualism. She was either a brilliant fraud, able to make people see what they wanted to see by manipulating articles in the dark, or she was one of the most outstanding physical mediums of all time. Her story does not end with her death. Her daughter Gina revealed in *Psychic News* on 4 September 1982 that her mother had spoken to her for more than an hour through the direct-voice mediumship of Rita Goold of Leicester.

Most of the conversation was of a highly personal nature; and at the end of the seance, Gina declared: 'Yes, it is my mother. There is no doubt about it'. Some 26 years after her death, it seems that Helen Duncan was still working to prove that life does continue beyond the grave.

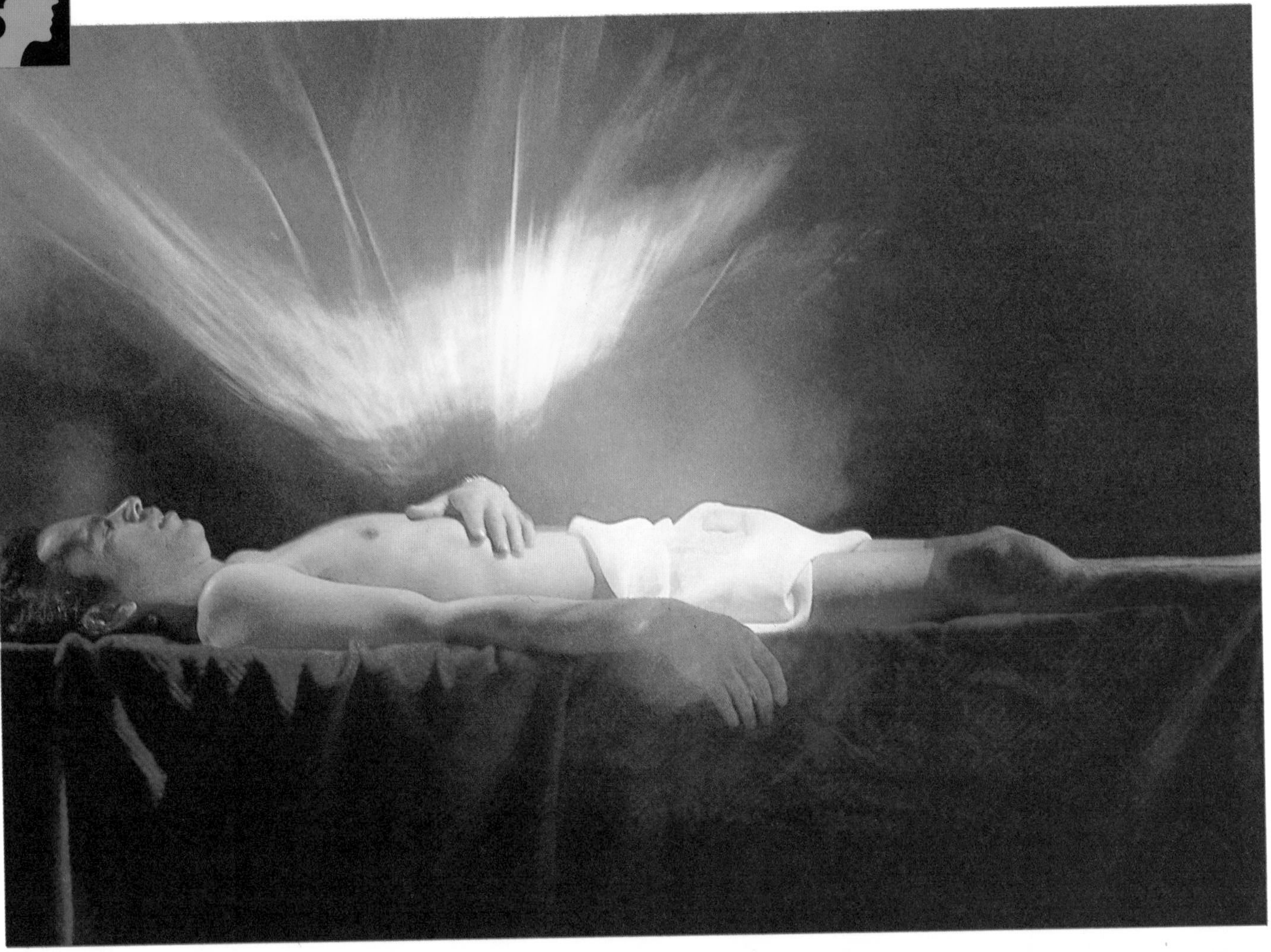

ELECTRIC PEOPLE

THERE ARE THOSE WHO CAN DELIVER AN ELECTRIC SHOCK WITH THEIR TOUCH, MAKE ELECTRICAL APPLIANCES STOP WORKING, OR ATTRACT OBJECTS TO THEIR BODIES. INVESTIGATIONS HAVE SHED SOME LIGHT ON THE PHENOMENON OF SUCH 'ELECTRIC PEOPLE'

Mrs Antoine Timmer went to New York with high hopes of winning a $10,000 prize offered, in 1938, for demonstrating a psychic phenomenon that could not be reproduced by trickery. The demonstration was organised by the Universal Council for Psychic Research, headed by the famous stage magician Joseph Dunninger. Mrs Timmer, seeking to understand her singular ability herself, showed how spoons and other small objects stuck to her hands and could only be removed by a vigorous tug. But her claim was dismissed because Dunninger said that he could do what she did with a concealed thread. Nonetheless, there were no allegations of trickery against Antoine Timmer – and she no doubt went away as puzzled by her magnetic hands as she had been when she came. On their part, the Council missed a chance to explore what seemed to be a truly unexplained phenomenon.

People with unusual magnetic or electrical abilities are not all that rare. These 'human magnets' and 'human spark plugs' may attract objects to their bodies, create disturbances in electrical machines, or shock other people with their touch. But whatever their behaviour, 'electric people' still make the news at the end of the 20th century just as they did in the 19th when interest in all kinds of curiosities was particularly high.

The photograph, above, simulates the sort of discharge believed to be emitted by so-called 'human spark-plugs'.
The electric eel, above right, is an example in nature of an animal able to store and use electricity. It can deliver a shock of up to 500 volts.

1889 and concerned Frank McKinstry, of Joplin, Missouri, USA, a man with a reputation as a good dowser. He was plagued in a peculiar way: his charge was so strong in the early morning that he had to keep moving. If he stopped even for a second, he became fixed to the ground and had to wait until a helpful passer-by would be asked to pull one of his legs free.

The second case cited by Gaddis concerned 17-year-old Caroline Clare of London, Ontario, Canada, who underwent a strange undiagnosable debilitation in 1877. Her weight fell dramatically to about 6½ stone (40 kilograms), and she suffered spasms and trances. These passed after 18 months; but then the electrical phenomena began. Metal objects would jump into her hand when she reached for them and, if she held one for any length of time, it stuck to her until someone pulled if off. She shocked those she touched, in one experiment passing the shock along 20 people holding hands in a line. The electrical phenomena lasted for several months and, once gone, never returned.

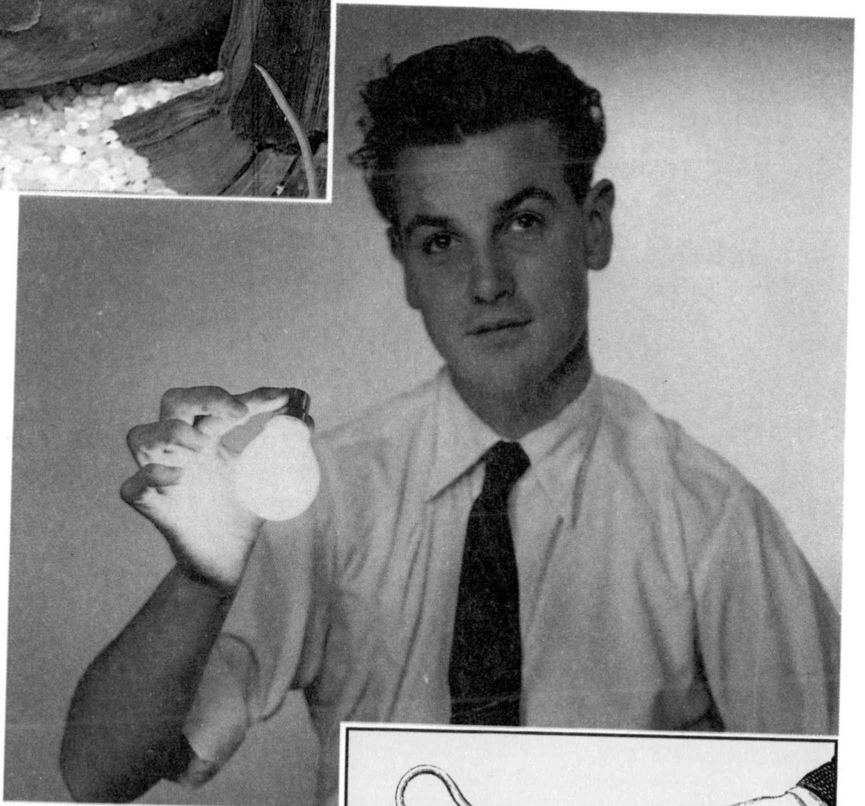

The *Daily Mirror* of 2 March 1967, for example, told the story of Brian Clements, known to his friends as 'Flash Gordon' Clements, who was so highly charged that he had to discharge his voltage into metal furniture before he touched anyone. The previous week, the *Sunday Express* reported the miserable life of a certain Grace Charlesworth, who had been tormented by electric shocks in her house for a period of over two years after having lived there uneventfully for 40 years. She said: 'Sometimes they have swung me round bodily and in the night my head has started to shake as though I was using a pneumatic drill. One day sparks ran up the walls'. Curiously, it was only Mrs Charlesworth who was affected.

Shocking Birth

Not surprisingly, many instances of electric people have been noticed or recorded by doctors. In January 1869, the doctor who delivered a baby in St Urbain, France, said the infant was charged up 'like a Leyden jar' (a type of electrostatic condenser). The baby shocked all who touched him, and luminous rays emanated from his fingers. This peculiarly endowed baby had a brief life, dying in his ninth month. Douglas Hunt recorded two similar but non-fatal cases in *Prediction* magazine for January 1953. In the first instance, a doctor received a sharp shock while delivering a baby. The baby's 'electrification' lasted 24 hours, during which time he was actually used to charge a Leyden jar, and sparks issued from him. The second infant gave off a 'feeble white light' and caused 'vibrations' in small metal objects brought near his hands and feet.

Other 19th-century cases are even more spectacular. Vincent Gaddis mentions three in his book *Mysterious Fires and Lights.* The first occurred in

Brian Williams of Cardiff,* above, *made news in 1952 as a human so full of electricity that he could light a lamp simply by rubbing it with his hand.

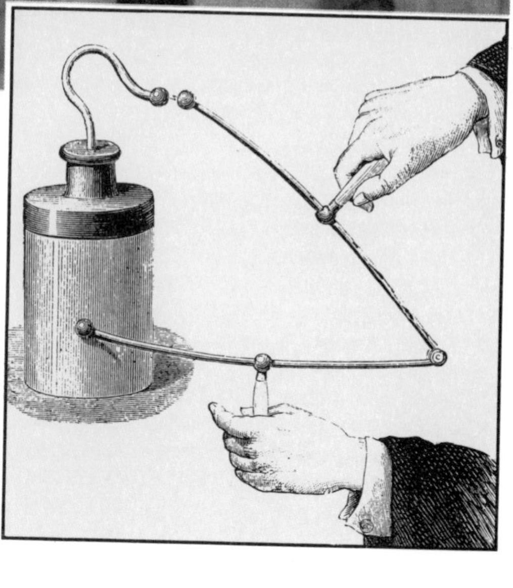

The Leyden jar,* right, *is a device used for storing electricity. It produces a spark when its inside and outside metal foil coatings are connected by a wire. One doctor has reported delivering a baby so 'electrified' that the child was actually used to charge a Leyden jar.

Gaddis also mentions 16-year-old Louis Hamburger who, in 1890, was a student in Maryland, USA. When his fingertips were dry, he could pick up heavy objects simply by touching them. Pins would dangle from his open hand as though from a magnet, and only a vigorous shake would send them flying. His favourite demonstration was to place his fingers against a glass beaker full of iron filings and pull the filings up the inside of the beaker by moving his fingers on the outer surface of the container.

> THE BABY SHOCKED ALL WHO TOUCHED HIM, AND LUMINOUS RAYS EMANATED FROM HIS FINGERS ... A DOCTOR EVEN RECEIVED A SHARP SHOCK WHILE DELIVERING THIS BABY.

Both humans and animals have nervous systems that generate electricity, and some animals are able to store and use this potential. For example, electric eels – which are really fish – have an organ in their tails that produces an electric current. This current passes from the tail to the front, and enables the fish to discharge a hefty shock of up to 500 volts, depending on the animal's size and health. The biggest jolt is delivered when the fish's head and tail touch well-separated parts of the victim's body, thereby allowing the current to travel some distance. The human body can accumulate about 10,000 volts when a person walks across a thick carpet but, unlike the electric eel's shock, any jolt given is harmless. This is because the body can develop only a small electrical charge, which means in turn that the current discharged is small. In contrast to this, 'electric people' seem able to utilise their electrical potential, although they may not even want to do so. Their physiological state appears to have something to do with it, just as an electric eel's health is known to influence its electrical power.

The Disease Factor

But what makes a person electric? According to one theory, disease may play a part – not in itself, but through its effect on the metabolism and other physiological functions. An astonishing report was made in 1920 by Dr Julius Ransom, chief physician at a state prison in New York, after 34 inmates developed a form of poisoning. During convalescence, one of them screwed up a piece of paper and tried to throw it away, but the paper stuck fast to his hand. Investigation showed that the man was carrying a high static charge, and so were all of his fellow sufferers. They found they could deflect compass needles and also make a suspended steel tape sway simply by moving their hands towards and away from it. These phenomena apparently ceased when the men recovered from their food poisoning.

There is some evidence to indicate that atmospheric and geomagnetic conditions may play a part in the strange phenomenon of electric people. Consider the case of 'a lady of great respectability', reported in the *American Journal of Science* by her physician. She was aged 30, of a nervous temperament and sedentary habits, and the wife of a prominent man in the town of Orford, New Hampshire. For two years, she had suffered from acute

Angélique Cottin*, bottom, *was one of the most famous 'electric girls' of the 19th century. However, her powers seemed to wane when she was investigated by a hostile team appointed by the French Academy of Sciences and led by the physicist Francois Arago*, below. *But she was not accused of fraud.

PERSPECTIVES

A HIGHLY-CHARGED SUBJECT

In many respects, electricity behaves like, and is described in terms of, a fluid. We speak, for instance, of an electric *current*, a stream of electrons that carry negative electric charge and are constituents of atoms. The rate of *flow* of the current is measured in amps. The 'pressure' that drives the current is electrical potential, measured in volts and more often simply called voltage. The quantity of electric charge is measured in coulombs, one coulomb being the amount of electric charge that flows when one amp passes for one second.

When electricity accumulates on the human body as a result of friction – say, of a nylon shirt rubbing on car upholstery – it may be at a potential of thousands of volts. But the quantity of charge is tiny, so that it can do little harm when discharged. This can be compared with the jet of water from a water pistol – it is delivered at a high pressure, but in too small a quantity to do any damage. Dangerous shocks, such as those from electric mains, are caused by large currents flowing at a high voltage for a relatively long period.

Usually we are unaware of the electrical nature of matter because negative and positive charges exist in equal quantities, and their effects cancel out. Only when the two are separated are their effects seen.

Rub a plastic comb on a sleeve and it will take up electrons, which are negatively charged and can move about, from the cloth. It can then attract a small piece of paper. This is because there is a fundamental electrical law that 'likes repel, unlikes attract'. The paper's negative electrons move away and leave the surface of the paper that is closest to the comb with a surplus of positive charge. The 'positive' paper is then attracted to the 'negative' comb. There is a similar effect when a balloon is rubbed on clothing: it will gain a charge that causes it to stick to things.

Her hair standing on end, science teacher Anthea Sothcott, below, demonstrates the phenomenon of static electricity to her students. The Van de Graaf generator she is touching is producing 500,000 volts; but she is standing on a deep pad of insulation which cuts the current so drastically that no damage is done. This is not an experiment we recommend readers repeat.

rheumatism and a strange ailment called 'unseated neuralgia'. The electrical phenomena began one January evening when she was feeling distinctly odd. She happened to pass her hand over her brother's face and, as she did so, sparks shot from her fingers, to the astonishment of both. When she stood on a thick carpet, the sparks could be seen, and heard, discharging near her hands. They were brilliant and shocking, and felt not only by the woman but also by anyone she touched. The conditions favourable to bringing this about included hot weather with temperatures of about 80°F (27°C). Under these conditions, the sparks would be about 1½ inches (4 centimetres) long, coming at the rate of four a minute.

Thinking the woman's silk clothes were generating the charges, her doctor had her wear only cotton apparel. As a control, her sister wore silk. The woman's electricity was not reduced, and her sister remained normal. The electric charges, which caused her much discomfort, lasted for about six weeks, after which she was 'relieved of most of her neuralgia and other corporeal infirmities, and was in better health than she had been for many years'.

The doctor had also observed that 'a crimson aurora of uncommon splendour' was lighting the heavens and exciting scientific interest at the time of the Orford woman's strange attack. Her charges began on the same evening as this heavenly display of electricity, and the doctor felt it was no mere coincidence. Interestingly, a theory put forward by Livingston Gearhart relates instances of spontaneous human combustion to moments of change in the intensity of the Earth's magnetic field.

One of the most famous 19th-century 'electric girls' was Annie May Abbott, who toured the world as 'The Little Georgia Magnet' in the late 1880s and early 1890s. On the stage in London in 1891, she raised a chair, with a heavy man seated in it, merely by touching it with the palm of her hand. Though she weighed only 7 stone (45 kilograms), groups of men could not lift her in a chair when she resisted it. In Japan, she even overcame the attempts of the huge and skilful Sumo wrestlers to budge her from where she stood, just as she could 'neutralise' their strenuous efforts to lift any small object on which she had lightly rested her fingers. Another 'immovable' was Mary Richardson, who gave performances in Liverpool in September 1921. She was easily lifted one minute, and then six men would fail to move her even slightly. Her touch could also knock men across the stage. A.C. Holms, the Scottish psychical researcher, put his hand on Mary's shoulder while a line of 13 men pushed against her and his hand, and he felt no pressure at all from their push. He was convinced that the force exerted against her was somehow neutralised or shunted, perhaps into another dimension.

But the classic 'electric girl' must be Angélique Cottin, a 14-year-old from Normandy, France. Her ordeal began on 15 January 1846 and lasted 10 weeks. The first manifestation occurred when the weaving frame, on which she and three other girls were making gloves, twisted and rocked. Within a short time, the girl's parents exhibited her in Paris, where she came to the attention of a certain Dr Tanchou.

Dr Tanchou reported to the Academy of Sciences that the girl could identify the poles of a magnet, agitate a compass and alternately attract and repel small objects like a magnet. He also said that he could feel a sensation 'like a cold wind' in her vicinity during these activities. Objects were violently propelled away from her at her slightest touch: her bed rocked violently; chairs twisted away from under her when she tried to sit down; and a 60-pound (25-kilogram) table rose into the air when her apron brushed against it.

An Empty Performance

The Academy appointed a research team, led by the famous physicist François Arago. Although Angélique performed as best she could, the phenomena seemed to have deserted her, which also tends to happen when modern poltergeist children and 'spoon-benders' face a sceptical enquirer or the starkness of a laboratory. The committee had ignored Dr Tanchou's observations that the girl performed best when she was relaxed. Poor Angélique was extremely frightened by the situation and the manifestations that occurred, and frequently left the room. The committee reported that they could not corroborate any claims made for Angélique, but refrained from calling her a fraud.

Dr Tanchou had found that Angélique's force was strongest in the evening, especially after a meal, and that it radiated from her left wrist, inner left elbow and spine. From his experiments, Dr Tanchou believed the cause was an undiscovered form of electricity. But Arago's team was not convinced. Besides, the Academy was waging a 'holy war' against Mesmerism at the time and could not accept phenomena similar to those claimed by the detested practitioners and advocates of 'animal magnetism'. Arago recommended that the Academy treat the case of Angélique Cottin 'as never having been sent in'. And so another chance for the scientific world to discover what causes electrical phenomena in people slipped away.

CASEBOOK

A LOGIC OF THEIR OWN

TWO TERRIFYING INCIDENTS FROM JAPAN, TOGETHER WITH ONE FROM ITALY, OFFER INTRIGUING CLUES ABOUT UFO POWER

One of the most curious categories to be found in files of reported UFO sightings consists of isolated reports of UFOs landing on rivers or lakes and siphoning up considerable quantities of water. We report on two cases, widely separated in both space and time: the first is from Japan; the second, from northern Italy in 1952. In both instances, the amount of water taken on board by the UFOs suggests that it was not intended merely for scientific analysis – yet what else was it for? Are we to believe that UFOs are powered or cooled by water, or that their occupants need water for drinking or cooking? A third case is one of the weirdest ever to have been reported in Japan. Yet no UFO was observed during the incident.

If some alien entities can survive without spacecraft, why are others so apparently vulnerable that they require regular supplies of water? Reports simply do no add up to a coherent picture of the perplexing phenomenon.

The artists' impressions, **below and above opposite,** *are of a close encounter at Tomakomai, Hokkaido, Japan, in July 1973.*

Some years ago, *Flying Saucer Review* received an exciting account of one of the occasional sightings of UFOs taking on water. It came from a Japanese UFO investigator, Jun-Ichi Takanashi of Osaka. Shadowy humanoid beings were also said to have been observed. The event took place at Tomakomai, a small industrial town on the southern coast of Hokkaido, the northernmost island of Japan, in July 1973. The eyewitness was Masaaki Kudou, a university student, then aged 20. He was home on vacation, and had taken a temporary job as a night security guard at a timber yard.

After patrolling the premises in his car, Kudou returned to the prescribed place from which he could observe the premises – as well as the waters of the bay beyond – and settled back to listen to his radio, light a cigarette, and relax. It was a still night, with the stars clearly visible. Suddenly he saw a streak of light flash across the sky, a spectacular 'shooting star' that suddenly stopped in its tracks, vanished, and reappeared. Remaining stationary, the light now expanded and contracted alternately at high speed, growing until it reached the apparent size of a baseball held at arm's length. It darted about and Kudou found himself dizzily trying to follow its gyrations. Then, as it began to descend towards the sea, the young student felt a surge of alarm, especially when the light halted near a distant cement works, and began to direct a beam of intermittent pulses of green light towards the north.

> " AROUND HIS CAR, EVERYTHING WAS LIT UP AS THOUGH BY DAYLIGHT, AND HE SAW WHAT APPEARED TO BE WINDOWS AROUND THE DIAMETER OF THE SPHERICAL OBJECT. IN THE MIDDLE OF ONE OF THESE, THERE WAS A SHADOWY HUMAN-SHAPED FIGURE. "

Next, the object continued its descent towards the sea, this time sweeping in an arc until it was in a position much closer to the student observer. It halted its descent at about 70 feet (20 metres) from the sea, and the student was amazed to see a transparent tube emerge and lower itself towards the water. A soft *min-min-min-min* noise could be heard as this was happening, and the pitch of the noise lowered as the tube descended. When the tube touched the water, its lower edge glowed, and it seemed that water was being sucked up into the object above.

Masaaki Kudou wondered if he was dreaming or if his imagination was playing tricks with him. He lowered his gaze for a minute or so; and when he looked up once again, the water-suction operation seemed to be over, as the tube had been withdrawn from the water. No sooner had he registered this fact than the hovering UFO began to move menacingly towards him. He feared he was about to be attacked in some way, and probably killed.

The object moved into a position some 160 feet (50 metres) above Kudou's car. By leaning forwards and looking up, he could keep it in view. He says its surface was as smooth as a table-tennis ball and, emitting its own glow, appeared to be white. Around his car, everything was lit up as though by daylight, and he saw what appeared to be windows around the diameter of the spherical object. In the middle of one of these, there was a shadowy human-shaped figure, while to the right there were two smaller shapes in another of the windows, but Kudou could not see whether or not these were similar to the first. All this, plus a sudden feeling that he was bound hand and foot, was too much for the witness, who began to rock his head in his hands, with his chin on the steering wheel, moaning to himself.

Nevertheless, Kudou still felt an urge to look upwards and, straining to do this, he saw in the sky above the car three or four newly-arrived glowing objects, similar in all respects to the first one. There was also a large, dark brown object, in silhouette, which he said looked like 'three gasoline drums connected together lengthwise' and which hovered noiselessly.

Suddenly the whole phenomenal spectacle came to an end. The glowing spheres swiftly manoeuvred into position and disappeared into one end of the large 'gasoline can' objects. This in turn shot off to the north, rather like a shooting star. The witness sat motionless, numb all over. He slowly became aware that his car radio was giving forth meaningless sounds, and that he himself was suffering from a severe headache. He was later able to estimate that the whole terrifying incident had lasted for only about 12 minutes in all.

Water-Sampling

Another incident involving water occurred at 3 a.m. on 25 July 1952, when a keen fisherman named Carlo Rossi was walking alongside the River Serchio, opposite San Pietro a Vico in Lucca, northern Italy. Puzzled by the appearance of an unusual light from an unseen position on the river below, he climbed the high embankment, and looked down to see a huge circular craft with a transparent cupola on top, and a shallow turret underneath from which three legs protruded, supporting the body of the craft above the water. There was also a ladder, and a long tube by which, apparently, the craft was taking in water. Suddenly, a port opened in the upper part of the turret, and Carlo saw a 'human' figure look out. This figure pointed at the fisherman, who scrambled down the embankment. A green ray passed over his head, and he threw himself down. Looking up, seconds later, he saw the craft rise above the embankment and move off at high speed towards Viareggio.

The illustration, **below,** *depicts another close encounter of the third kind, at Lucca, Italy, on 25 July 1952.*

Rossi was badly shaken by the incident but something that happened a few weeks later worried him much more. To the outsider, the incident seems trivial – although it is a classic example of a 'man in black' encounter: a strange man approached Rossi and offered him, Rossi said, a 'bad' cigarette. Rossi was terrified. He used later to say: 'I wonder if they want to do me harm, maybe, because of the thing I saw in the river?'

The circumstances of Rossi's subsequent death seem to lend substance to his suspicion. He was riding home on his bicycle one day when he was knocked down by a car. The driver, however, was never identified.

Other aliens, however, seem to show no interest in water, but the purpose behind their actions can be just as mysterious. One particularly alarming experience occurred on the evening of 3 October 1978, when Hideichi Amano, using his mobile unit

CASEBOOK

Hideichi Amano, **right,** *victim of the Sayama encounter, recounted his experience on a television programme.*
An artist's impression of the strange humanoid creature seen by Mr Amano, is shown **below.**

radio car, drove up a mountain outside Sayama City, Japan, at about 8.30 p.m. with his two-year-old daughter, Juri. Amano, who owned a snack bar and was also a keen radio ham, made the trip so that he could get unrestricted radio transmission and reception for a conversation with his brother, who lived in a distant part of the country. When their hook-up was finished, and a few other local calls had been made, Amano was about to drive back down the mountain when the interior of the car suddenly became very bright. A light ten times brighter than normal was coming from the fluorescent tube he had fitted inside the car. He observed that this light was confined to the car's interior: none, he said, was passing through the windows. Moments earlier, Juri had been standing on the passenger seat beside him, but now her father was aghast to see the child lying on the seat and foaming at the mouth. At the same instant, he became aware of a round patch of orange light that was beamed through the windscreen and on to his stomach, and he saw that this was coming from a point in the sky. Then his alarm turned to terror when he sensed something metallic being pressed against his right temple.

Amano glanced sideways and saw an unearthly humanoid creature standing there with a pipe-like device in its mouth, and it was this that was being pressed against Amano's head. From the tube came an incessant babble, as if from a tape being played too fast. Was the humanoid somehow reading Amano's brain waves, or perhaps acquiring a form of electrical power in this way?

The witness said the creature had a round face, but no neck, two sharply pointed ears, two small, motionless eyes that glowed bluish-white, and a triangular depression on its forehead. The mouth was clamped round the pipe, and no nose could be seen. While the babble continued, Amano says he found it difficult to move, and his mind became strangely 'vague'.

The terrified radio ham tried to start the car to flee the place, but there was no response from the

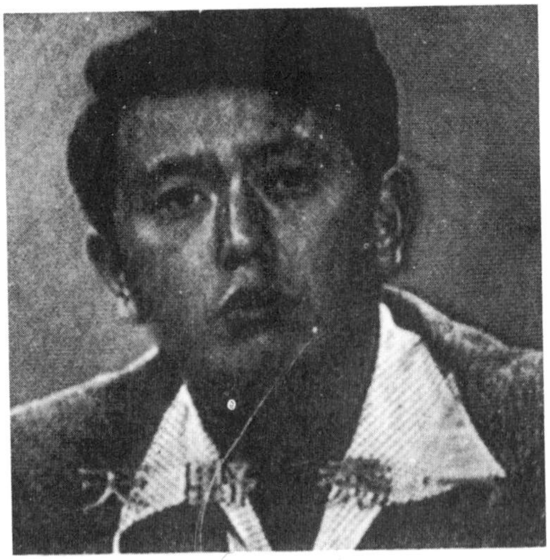

engine, and the lights would not work either. Then, after four or five minutes, the creature began to fade and slowly vanished. The orange light disappeared, the interior lighting returned to normal, and other equipment that had previously been switched on now began to function again. When the headlights returned, Amano switched on the starter and got an instant response. Still in a confused state, he roared away down the hill, and it was only when he reached the lower slopes that he remembered little Juri's condition. As he stopped, however, the child stood up and said: 'I want a drink of water, papa.'

> " THE WITNESS SAID THE CREATURE HAD A ROUND FACE ... AND A TRIANGULAR DEPRESSION ON ITS FOREHEAD. WHILE THE BABBLE CONTINUED, AMANO FOUND IT DIFFICULT TO MOVE. "

The witness decided to report the experience to the police, but they only poked fun at him, so he went home and retired to bed, still suffering from a severe headache.

Researchers for a television programme heard of the affair and eventually arranged for Amano to be questioned under hypnosis in front of the cameras. One piece of information retrieved was that the creature was alleged to have told him to return to the meeting place at a certain time. To avoid a stampede by the curious, this was not revealed to viewers.

Investigator Jun-Ichi Takanashi, however, seemed to have little faith in the regression session because the 'hypnotist's insistence on more information was far too severe'. He even suspected that the idea of a second meeting with the humanoid was a creation of the witness's subconscious mind. The fact that no second meeting was ever reported seems to lend weight to this. Yet, despite his reservations, Takanashi considered the encounter, as originally reported, to be 'the strangest ever to have taken place in Japan'.

WINDOWS ON ANOTHER WORLD?

WHY IS IT THAT CERTAIN AREAS OF THE WORLD SEEM TO BE FOCAL POINTS FOR MYSTERIOUS HAPPENINGS SUCH AS THE SIGHTING OF UFOs OR HAUNTINGS? ARE THESE 'WINDOW AREAS' GATEWAYS TO THE UNKNOWN?

'It has been observed, on more than one occasion, that there exist peculiar haunted regions upon the face of this planet. These enigmatic "window areas", which serve as focal points for UFOs, mystery animals, and all manner of unusual phenomena, are often as puzzling as the "Things" they host.' So wrote American phenomenologist David Fideler as he opened a major survey of one such 'window', in Michigan, USA, for the magazine *Fortean Times*.

The possibility of windows, doorways, gateways or portals into the unknown has long been discussed; and local legend sometimes associates

Ancient sites, such as Stonehenge, are often associated with strange phenomena. Do they perhaps provide a gateway to other dimensions?

A giant explosion, the cause of which was never explained, occurred on 1 January 1970 at Pullman, below, a suburb of Chicago, left, on the shore of Lake Michigan. This, added to the many other reports of strange events in the region, led the Michigan Anomaly Research Group study team to conclude that Lake Michigan is a window area.

paranormal happenings with certain spots. Knowes, or Neolithic burial mounds, for example, are often regarded as such magical places. One story tells of two Orkney fiddlers who were walking past a knowe when, suddenly, in the middle of a sentence, one disappeared. Years later, the remaining fiddler was passing the mound when suddenly his companion was back, his eye still as bright and his beard still as black as before, and on his lips the end of the very sentence he had been uttering at the point when he disappeared.

Space Warps

A favourite science-fiction theme is of the man who suddenly steps through a time or space warp into another world. The famous movie *2001 – A Space Odyssey* shows star travellers reaching their destination by just such a route. Even modern music ensures that this concept remains in our consciousness. The rock group The Moody Blues, for instance, had a hit with a song called *Slide Zone,* describing the effects of falling through a window in the framework of space. So clearly this is a familiar idea. But just what evidence is there for the existence of such windows?

David Fideler, a member of the Michigan Anomaly Research Group, which was set up to investigate the window concept scientifically, cited the following as examples of the kind of case that the team has on record, and which they believe suggest that Lake Michigan may well constitute a window area.

On 31 March 1897, a brilliant white light appeared in the sky over Galesburg, Michigan, accompanied by a strange crackling sound. Ten days later, fishermen at Pine Lake observed an 'alien' animal, something like a panther – but panthers are not indigenous to Michigan. It made a 'terrible noise' and was blamed for the slaughter of local livestock.

Other strange events occurred in the Lake Michigan area, too. On 6 February 1901, a mysterious fall of dust-like material descended on the town of Paw Paw on a perfectly calm day. In May 1954, a motorist at La Porte (a pleasingly suitable French name that means 'the door') observed three oval UFOs that gave out beams of light. His car engine and radio failed while the UFOs flew by overhead. Five years later, a young mother was the first to experience what became a wave of sightings of gorilla-like 'furry' humanoids, similar to the bigfoot or sasquatch, again in the Lake Michigan area.

On 1 January 1970, a gigantic explosion rocked Pullman, a lakeside suburb of Chicago, just after midnight. Windows were broken, things fell from shelves, and a mysterious large hole appeared in the frozen surface of the lake, 200 yards (180 metres) from the shore, throwing great chunks of ice high into the air. The unexplained blast was felt 4 miles (7 kilometres) away.

Then, in August 1976, several witnesses at New Buffalo saw a misty white object floating over a field. It was interpreted by one witness as a ghost, and by another as an angel.

All these, and many other weird experiences in the vicinity of Lake Michigan, certainly indicate that there is something strange about the place. Sceptics may claim that any populated area would reveal a similar catalogue if researched thoroughly enough, but there is sufficient evidence to prove that certain areas definitely record far more than their fair share of mysterious phenomena.

Interestingly, language sometimes provides a clue to the discovery of window areas. For if an area has always experienced a large number of strange events, this may be reflected in its name. Loren Coleman, an American writer on the paranormal, has conducted a study of locations with names that refer to the Devil, or the equivalent in the local language. He theorises that these places often received their names because of their reputation, since rumours of terrifying encounters would, in ancient times, have been directly linked with the Devil. Coleman analysed a large number of such places throughout the USA, and found that very often they were rich in a wide variety of peculiar events. He concluded: 'Geographical "Devil names", worldwide, may indicate locales high in Fortean energy and strangeness. These places deserve some extra attention...'

David Fideler agrees, and points to an area around Draguignan in France (the name is possibly derived from 'dragon') and a nearby hill, known as *Le Malmont,* which translates into English as 'the evil mountain'. Several strange incidents are reported to have taken place there – including the appearance of mysterious floating balls of light, and the mountain-top confrontation between a car and humanoid figures that emerged from a 'glow'.

Light ball phenomena have been reported at two localities in France – the town of Draguignan at the foot of Malmount hill, **above,** *and the district of Aveyron,* **below.** *Such anomalous events are considered to be a strong characteristic of a window area.*

NORTHERN GHOSTS

There are many 'Devil names' in Britain, although sometimes they are of a local nature and not readily found on maps. Boggart Hole, Clough, in north Manchester, for example, is so named because of frequent meetings here with the 'boggarts' – a northern name for spirits or ghosts.

One of Britain's most frightening close encounter events took place at the Devil Garden, a secluded spot beside the River Weaver, near Frodsham in Cheshire. The date was 27 January 1978. At 5.45 p.m., four men in their late teens were wandering through some meadows close to a weir. They had to admit that they were poaching, which meant that they were rather unwilling to discuss their story. But on this night, they were to bag rather more than they had bargained for, when they saw a strange object floating along the surface of the river from the direction of Weaverham. It was about 20 feet (7 metres) above the ground, and at first they took it to be a satellite that was out of control. (A Soviet satellite had crashed in Canada a

> **"** SUDDENLY, A SMALL SAUCER-SHAPED OBJECT FLEW TOWARDS HIM ... IT HAD TWO SMALL DOMES ON TOP; AND INSIDE, SURROUNDED BY A GREENISH HAZE, WERE TWO HUMANOID FIGURES. **"**

few weeks earlier, so this was a natural assumption.) The 'satellite', a round silvery object with a small skirt underneath, floated down into the nearby undergrowth, emitting flames as it did so. It then sat there, immobile and eerie, making a sound like rushing wind.

The men were very scared, of course, but well hidden in the bushes, so they felt reasonably secure. They gazed in amazement as a peculiar bluish glow, which may have been ultra-violet light, emanated from the object; it hurt their eyes to stare at it. Just as they were about to run, with thoughts of radioactivity now uppermost in their minds, a 'man' appeared around the side of the object. He surveyed some cows in a nearby field, which were standing unnaturally still, perhaps through fright. A moment later, he went back round the craft and returned with a colleague; between them, they were carrying a frame-like structure, not unlike a cage.

The humanoids wore silver suits and helmets that bore lamps. They placed the large frame-like structure, which appeared to be very light, around one of the cows, and they then proceeded to take measurements by moving some struts up and down. The four men had by now had enough and fled the scene, no doubt thinking that they might be next on the list for inspection, and not relishing the thought. They ran until they reached the village. One of them felt a strong 'pulling' sensation tugging him backwards by his genitals. These were sore for some days afterwards, and red as if sunburned – out of the question in an English winter!

'Light ball' phenomena are in fact the commonest occurrence in an apparent window area. The similarity to ball lightning is obvious. Ball lightning, however, occurs in well-defined meteorological conditions, whereas there appears to be no restriction as to when and where window area light balls can appear. It seems likely that the light balls, like ball lightning, are electrical effects; but whereas ball lightning is thought to be caused by a static electrical charge in the atmosphere, light balls may be caused by a charge in the ground itself, produced by some kind of magnetic anomaly.

The catalogue of events that have occurred in Aveyron region of France is typical of experiences at a window area. François Lagarde was the author of an excellent study of the affair, as covered in *Flying Saucer Review* and the French UFO journal *Lumières dans la Nuit*.

Clearly, the balls of light that seem so often to invade window areas are very odd things indeed, and are capable of inducing quite disturbing effects.

The story concerns a farming family who had lived in the depths of the countryside for many years. On 15 June 1966, they saw a series of light balls, which were about 4 feet (1.2 metres) in diameter, floating about their large farmyard, climbing over hedges and seemingly inspecting things. They disappeared by 'blending into' a large opaque vertical cylinder of light in a nearby field. Over the next few years, these light balls were seen frequently, the cylinder always appearing with them. It was on the night of 11 January 1967, however, that the family experienced what appears to have been the most bizarre phenomenon of all.

Devil's Garden, below, *in Cheshire, is the scene of a frightening close encounter that took place on 27 January 1978. The secluded spot lives up to Loren Coleman's theory that place names with 'Devil' in them have a high incidence of weird occurrences.*

Boggart Hole, bottom, *is another of Britain's place names that indicate a history of mysterious encounters. 'Boggart' is a northern name for ghosts.*

one a sense of the macabre. It is hard to handle the idea of his characters being real, so it is comforting to think of them as roles for horror movie stars such as Vincent Price or Christopher Lee. But Keel undoubtedly means us to take very seriously indeed what he has to say.

MACABRE HORROR

One window Keel claims to have found is in West Virginia. For months during 1967, local citizens were plagued by an horrific apparition, a winged humanoid dubbed 'Mothman'. There were also cold spots, space messages and meandering light balls. Warnings were received telepathically from mysterious aliens, that the current Middle East situation might escalate into a third world war, and that a nationwide power failure was imminent. Few people took any notice of these reports, but Keel knew better. On 15 December 1967, he sat watching the television news, sure that something was about to happen.

Over in West Virginia, it was the busy evening rush hour. At Point Pleasant, an old steel bridge carried the road across the Ohio River. Under the abnormal load of a traffic snarl-up, it creaked and groaned, tottered and swayed. Then, suddenly, it snapped. Cars and screaming people were plunged to their doom. Bodies and wreckage floated on the icy surface as the night set in. Thirty-eight people were dead. Meanwhile, local residents who had been spared the disaster looked into the sky and saw, bobbing up and down above the river, meandering balls of light.

Point Pleasant, it has now been generally recognised, is right in the middle of John Keel's West Virginia window.

The farmer's son decided to take his car and pursue one of the light balls. He saw some of them blend into the cylinder, only one of them remaining outside it. As he approached the object, which was hovering above the road, his car lights and engine cut out. Desperately he tried to restart the car and turn on the internal light – but nothing happened. He had no power at all, and felt unable to move. Suddenly, a small saucer-shaped object flew towards him, straight across the fields. It had two small domes on top, and inside, surrounded by a greenish haze, were two humanoid figures wearing green overalls. The UFO came closer, and then departed with a blast of heat. The metallic road sign close to him began to vibrate visibly as the UFO flew away.

Eventually, the witness recovered and was able to return home, but he suffered strange reactions for some time afterwards. At first, he could not sleep; then he slept for 20 hours or more. At times, he found himself floating as if out of his body; he also experienced temporary limb paralysis on several occasions.

Undoubtedly the major proponent of the window area theory was American journalist and collector of oddities, John Keel. His restless pursuit of the myths and monsters, falling frogs and flying saucers that haunt his native land is pervaded by the wry humour that also characterised the writing of Charles Fort. But to read John Keel's work gives

The two silver-suited figures,* above, *emerged from a shiny round object at the Devil's Garden in Cheshire and took measurements of a cow in the nearby meadow. They were seen by four youths, one of whom was left with a painful reminder of the close encounter.

The twisted wreck of the Silver Bridge at Point Pleasant in West Virginia, USA, is shown* right. *On the night the bridge collapsed without a known cause, balls of light were seen in the sky.

Joan of Arc, as shown in the painting, right, was inspired by an angel to lead the French to victory against the English. 'The Maid', as she was known, heard voices that urged her to forsake the normal life of a peasant girl and become a soldier. On at least one occasion, she claimed to have seen St Michael himself. Her voices, however, seemed to let her down badly for her victories were few and transitory, and she died horribly at the stake. For this reason, some commentators have even suggested that her inspiration may have been diabolical in origin.

VISIONS OF THE VIRGIN

FOR CENTURIES, BELIEVERS – AND EVEN SOME NON-BELIEVERS – HAVE REPORTED THE EXPERIENCE OF A VISION OF THE VIRGIN MARY. MIRACLES OF PROPHECY AND HEALING HAVE FREQUENTLY FOLLOWED, TOO

History is full of accounts of visions – some that have led great men to do great things, and some, evil men to do evil things. Visitations from non-material figures, for instance, led Joan of Arc to fight for France in the 15th century, and more recently allegedly caused the Yorkshire Ripper to murder prostitutes. A researcher who looks for long enough can find references to visions of almost every kind – angels, demons, cities, monsters, heaven, hell, elves, fairies, flying saucers, saints, lovers, the dead and dying, and many more.

At the grotto at Lourdes, above, *Bernadette Soubirous,* right, *had a vision of a girl who later said: 'I am the Immaculate Conception'. Although Bernadette herself died in agony from a tubercular knee in 1879, Lourdes has become a major place of pilgrimage. The sick and dying flock in great numbers,* far right, *to bathe in the healing water of the grotto.*

Most such visions are unique – seen once only, or rarely repeated. They relate only to the person who sees them, to the place where they are seen, or to an individual combination of circumstances that is unlikely ever to occur again. Few conclusions can be drawn from cases that vary so widely. There are, though, a few kinds of vision that are reported again and again, and show marked signs of consistency. There may be a variety of reasons for this; but if a large number of unconnected individuals claim a similar experience, we must begin to take them seriously, and wonder whether there is more to it than illusion or imagination. Does the figure or person that is reportedly seen indeed have some independent reality of his or her own?

The vision most frequently seen and experienced in the West in the past 800 years is that of the Virgin Mary, Mother of Christ. There have been

numerous variations in detail – age, exact appearance, clothing, and companions – but the overall picture is remarkably consistent. Consistent, too, are the reports of healing and prophecy that often accompany the visions. Clearly, a pattern has been established, and some elements of the reports must be seen as the consequence of expectation and belief. But it does seem that there may be more to it than that: certainly, people's lives have frequently been changed, often for the better, by what is said to have been seen.

The number of visions reported must run into thousands, and is constantly increasing. The cases that follow – some famous, some less so – occurred in Europe and the USA in the last 150 years, and give a general impression of this fascinating field.

The Weeping Woman

La Salette is a small village in the French Alps, in the region of Grenoble. Here, on 19 September 1846, something of a pattern was set for visions of the Virgin. Two children, 15-year-old Melanie Calvat and 11-year-old Maximin Giraud, tending their herd of cows in a remote spot, saw a weeping woman, who seemed to be resting on the bed of a dried-up stream. She rose and said: 'Why do you not come nearer, my children? Be not frightened. I have come to tell you some great news'. The two children described the woman as utterly radiant, 'brighter than the sun, but not to be compared with it'. She wore a long, sequined, white robe, with a white, patterned scarf, a yellow apron, and white, pearl-studded shoes. She wore a cross on her breast that shone with its own brilliance. Rays of light darted from her. Overcoming their fear, the children listened to the radiant figure. She predicted famine, and illness before it; and that the grape and potato crops would rot. She complained bitterly of the distress caused her by the sins of the people, and is said to have given secret information, which was passed to Pope Pius IX in 1850.

As was often the case, priests and the general population alike were unwilling to believe the children's story at first, and they suffered threats and physical injury. But they did not retract their claims, and argued plausibly for what they had seen. The stream that the children had seen to be dry flowed with water the next day; but, as predicted, the potato crops failed, causing famine in France and Ireland; and *phylloxera,* a plant-louse, destroyed the vineyards. The claims of the children at La Salette have never been completely refuted.

Our Lady in White

The events at Lourdes, in south-west France, where a 14-year-old girl experienced 18 visions of the Virgin, are far better known. Films, plays, books and television have dealt repeatedly with the story of the small French town that has become the centre of so many hopes – and, sometimes, of seemingly miraculous healings. Images of the religious peasant girl, Bernadette Soubirous, collecting driftwood, seeing the Virgin, speaking with her, and watching the healing spring burst forth from the ground are now the stuff of legend. But it is interesting to look a little closer at the vision itself, through a translation of Bernadette's own account.

'I looked up and saw a cluster of branches and brambles underneath the highest opening of the grotto, tossing and swinging to and fro, although nothing else stirred.

'Behind these branches and inside the opening, I saw at that moment a girl in white, no bigger than myself, who greeted me with a slight bow of her head... She was wearing a white dress right down to her feet and only the tips of her toes were showing. The dress was gathered high at the neck from which there hung a white cord. A white veil covered her head and came down over her shoulders and arms, almost to the bottom of her dress. On each foot, I saw a yellow rose. The sash of her dress was blue and hung down below her knees. The chain of the rosary was yellow, the beads white and

By the mid-19th century, visions were becoming increasingly common all over mainland Europe. But at Knock, County Mayo in the Republic of Ireland, a vision seen on the evening of 21 August 1879 took on a somewhat different form. The scene on the outer wall of the chapel in this remote village was described by the local *Tuam News:*

'The first person who saw it passed on, but others soon came and remained, and these saw, covering a large portion of the gable end of the sacristy, an altar, and to its sides the figures of St John the Evangelist, the Blessed Virgin, and St Joseph .... the altar was surrounded by a brilliant golden light through which, up and down, angels seemed to be flitting ... To St John's right, the Blessed Virgin, having her hands extended and raised towards her shoulders, the palms of her hands turned towards the people, and her eyes raised up towards heaven ... These figures remained visible from 7.30 p.m. to 10 p.m., witnessed during that time by about twenty persons... '

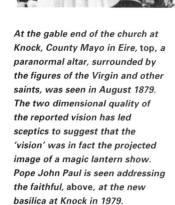

big, and widely spaced. The girl was alive, very young and surrounded with light. When I had finished my rosary, she bowed to me smilingly. She retired within the niche, and suddenly disappeared.'

This was all the communication that took place during the first vision on 11 February 1858; and not until 25 March 1858 did the figure pronounce itself to be 'The Immaculate Conception' – a description and doctrine, oddly enough, defined by the Pope only four years previously.The visions continued until 16 July 1858, although the first healing miracle apparently occurred as early as 7 April. Clearly, some confusion has arisen as to facts. Bernadette declared the figure she saw was 'no bigger than myself' – that is, a child far from full-grown. Bernadette did not at first give the figure a religious title, but referred to it merely as 'Aquero', meaning 'this thing'. As she had contact with a priest who believed strongly in the vision at La Salette, it is perhaps not surprising that, in time, she identified the figure as Mary, and that history has turned the child seen by Bernadette into the full-grown Mother of Christ. But this does not detract from the significance of the original experience, nor from the subsequent healings at Lourdes that seem to have been a direct result of Bernadette's vision.

"THE FORM WAS OF A WOMAN, A VEIL HUNG OVER THE HEAD AND FACE. THE HANDS WERE BOTH RAISED AS IF IN BLESSING ... ITS APPEARANCE WAS LIKE THE PICTURES OF THE IMMACULATE CONCEPTION."

At the gable end of the church at Knock, County Mayo in Eire,* top, *a paranormal altar, surrounded by the figures of the Virgin and other saints, was seen in August 1879. The two dimensional quality of the reported vision has led sceptics to suggest that the 'vision' was in fact the projected image of a magic lantern show. Pope John Paul is seen addressing the faithful,* above, *at the new basilica at Knock in 1979.

In this vision, the Virgin is said to have worn a white dress and golden crown, but the physical nature of the Knock visions – flat, two-dimensional against a wall, statue-like and motionless in all essentials, surrounded by light, and growing brighter as night fell – has led to suspicions that the 'vision' was, in fact, an image cast by a magic lantern, or even phosphorescent paint on the wall. Such rationalisations would seem unlikely to fool so many people for so long; but no other wholly conventional explanation has been put forward. Whatever the vision may have been – and we shall almost certainly never know now – it was clearly believable and convincing for those who saw it, and it had a tremendous effect. It occurred at a time of poverty, hardship and dispute; and regardless of its source, it met a need.

A scene of regular papal visits, the shrine at Knock now attracts over a million visitors a year. The vision communicated nothing, but a 'limestone broth' was made of plaster from the church wall and mixed with holy water; it was administered to the sick, and there were many claims made for its healing properties.

Apparitions at Gwent, in Wales, are perhaps the most outlandish and occurred in the grounds of the monastery at Llanthony Abbey, between 30 August and 15 September 1880. The community was very varied in composition, and was founded and led by the eccentric and remarkable Joseph Leycester Lyne, known as Father Ignatius. Following the appearance of a ghostly sacrament to a Sister Janet that morning, in the twilight of the evening of 30 August 1880, four boys of the community, aged between 9 and 15, claimed to have witnessed a vision of the Virgin.

'A halo of glory shone out from the figure all around in an oval form. The form was of a woman, a veil hung over the head and face; the hands were both raised as if in blessing. It approached very slowly. Its appearance was like the pictures of "The Immaculate Conception" ... the beautiful form entered the hedge, and after remaining there in the light for a few minutes, passed through the bush and vanished.'

On Saturday, 4 September, in response to the singing of the *Ave Maria,* a light in the same bush developed into 'the form of a woman surrounded by light ... the face and head covered with the veil'. Then, 'in the light appeared the form of a man, unclothed save a cloth round the loins ... as the forms met, both vanished'.

The climactic event of the series occurred on 15 September, when four persons had a brief but remarkable experience.

'We had no sooner begun it [an *Ave Maria*] than the whole heavens and mountains broke forth in bulging circles of light, circles pushing out from circles – the light poured upon our faces and the buildings where we stood, and in the central circle stood a most Majestic Heavenly Form, robed in flowing drapery. The Form was gigantic, but seemed to be reduced to human size as it approached. The figure stood sideways, facing the Holy Bush. The vision was most distinct and the details were very clear; but it was 'in the twinkling of an eye'.

The accounts and claims of the Llanthony residents have at times been criticised, but they have never been disproved. There have also been reports of healing that was apparently effected with leaves from the Holy Bush, which is actually wild rhubarb.

The attitude of the Roman Catholic Church towards these and other apparitions of the Virgin Mary is fairly straightforward. To retain credibility, the Church maintains a prudent distance, refusing to pronounce on them until they have been fully investigated. In the case of Lourdes, for example, a Medical Bureau subjects scientifically inexplicable cures to a rigorous investigation; the result is that very few are acknowledged as miraculous. And while apparitions such as the Virgin of Guadelupe in Mexico (of 1631) and Fatima in Portugal (of 1917) are now officially accepted, those at Medjugorje in Yugoslavia – still apparently occurring – are not. Individuals are welcome to believe in visions, but it takes time, so it seems, for the Church to approve.

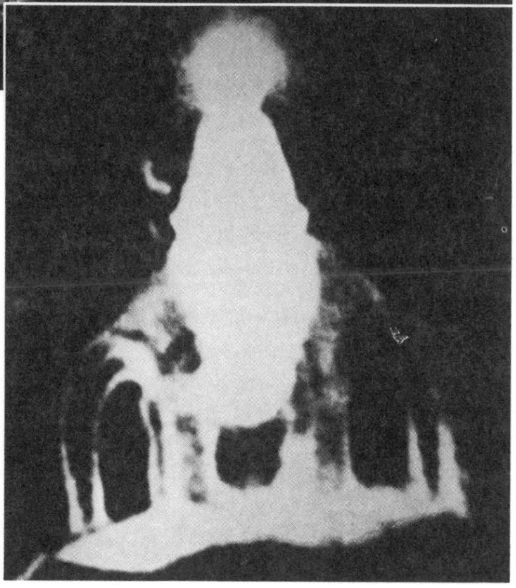

Strange lights,* above *and* right, *were seen over the Coptic orthodox church of St Mary at Zeitoun, Egypt, in 1968. Some believe it to have been a vision of the Virgin Mary.

PERSPECTIVES

HOLY HAPPENINGS

Apparitions of the Virgin Mary have continued to occur in recent years. In 1933, 11-year-old Mariette Beco from the impoverished village of Banneux near Liège, Belgium, claimed to have seen the Virgin eight times between January and March. When asked her identity, the apparition replied she was 'the Virgin of the Poor', come to help the sick and suffering. Today, thousands flock to Banneux annually, to pray at the chapel built in the Becos' small garden where the Virgin had stood, or be healed at the local hospital for pilgrims.

Other visions have occurred in more far-flung places. In Rwanda, in Central Africa, for instance, between 1981 and 1986, the Virgin appeared regularly to seven children, including a pagan, illiterate boy; and in Australia, in 1979, she appeared before a 54-year-old Anglican, Robert de Caen who, while recovering from a stroke in hospital and a near-death experience, saw the Virgin wearing a crown and regarding him with outstretched arms.

In the New World, Nicaraguan tailor, Bernado Martinez of Cuapa, saw a vision of Mary while returning from a day's fishing in 1980. A flash of lightning from the clear sky drew his eyes to a white, radiant cloud on which stood a beautiful, bare-footed woman, wearing a long, white dress and a veil that was edged with gold embroidery. It was the first of several visions that has made the town of Cuapa a pilgrimage centre for thousands, including Mother Teresa of Calcutta.

The Yugoslav town of Medjugorje is also a major goal of pilgrims. Here, on 24 June 1981, six local children witnessed the first of a series of appearances of the Virgin Mary which are apparently still continuing 10 years later.

MORE DEAD THAN ALIVE

THE DEAD CAN BE RESTORED TO A SEMBLANCE OF LIFE – AS ZOMBIES, THE MINDLESS SLAVES OF EVIL MAGICIANS – SO THOSE STEEPED IN VOODOO TRADITION BELIEVE

'Near her, the black fingers of one silent guest were clutched rigidly around the fragile stem of a wine glass, tilted, spilling. The horror pent up in her overflowed. She seized a candle, thrust it close to the slumped, bowed face, and saw the man was dead. She was sitting at a banquet table with four propped-up corpses...'

This is the vivid account of a voodoo wedding breakfast held in the 1920s, as recounted to the American journalist, William Seabrook, by friends who had been present. The propped-up corpses were intended to be turned by sorcery into zombies – half-animate bodies living a twilight existence as the slaves of the magician who was the banquet's host. (In fact, according to Seabrook, the magician's intention was thwarted, he fled and the corpses promptly disappeared.)

There is only one country in the West where such a ghastly celebration might have taken place: Haiti, birthplace of voodoo. But do voodoo sorcerers really have the power to reanimate newly-dead corpses? Or is the notion of the zombie pure self-deception on the part of voodoo practitioners?

The word *zumbi* appears in many African languages. In the Congo, it means a fetish; in Benin, it refers specifically to the python god. In modern voodoo, it seems that a snake deity is called upon to animate the zombie at the whim of the sorcerer who has become the corpse's master. The rites involved combine aspects of African magic and religion, with elements derived from both western occultism and popular Catholicism.

The role of a zombie is acted out by participants in a voodoo street festival,* above. *The whitened face and shroud-like wrappings suggest a newly-buried corpse.

The structures over the Haitian graves,* below, *are intended to make them secure homes for corpses. Even the poor spend large sums on fortifying their graves in this way.

Voodoo actually played a part in the revolution in which Haitians threw off French rule. In August 1791, France was in the throes of the turmoil that had begun some two years previously. The King and Queen were prisoners, the nobility and clergy had seen their power torn from them, and Liberty, Equality and Fraternity had been adopted as the watchwords of the new order.

Little seemed at first to have changed in St Domingue, the western third of the Caribbean island of Hispaniola, the brightest jewel in the French colonial crown. There, 40,000 Frenchmen controlled half-a-million black slaves and 30,000 mulattos, growing crops of cotton, sugar, coffee and indigo. The first effect of the disturbances in France had been to improve the lot of the mulattos. Then the darker-skinned Haitians grew restless, helped by the agitation of a mysterious priest-sorcerer, named Boukman, who had found his way to St Domingue from the British colony of Jamaica. On 14 August 1791, Boukman summoned those who wished to follow him to a rendezvous deep in the forests. According to contemporary accounts, thousands of slaves slipped away along secret forest trails to the meeting, during a colossal tropical storm that must have lent extra terror and awe to the proceedings that followed.

Blood Ritual

Boukman then conducted a blood ritual, sacrificing a pig and asking all who wished to be free to drink of the still-warm blood. The ceremony ended with a wild dance of 'divine inebriation', after which the participants melted away again, into the forests. The whole ritual closely resembled the activities of the Mau Mau during the Kenyan war of independence of the 1950s – and it had a similar result. During the next few days, most of the great plantations were overrun and their owners killed. Although the stronger French colonists clung on for a further 12 years, the final result of the nocturnal gathering was the complete defeat of the French and the establishment, under the leadership of President Toussaint l'Ouverture, of the independent black republic of Haiti – home of voodoo. According to the beliefs of the Haitian peasantry and, often enough, of the educated élite, it was also the home of the zombie, that sinister, animated, but reputedly soulless corpse.

A dark hat and suit, draped over a gravestone, represent the funeral clothes of Baron Samedi, a voodoo god of death, **bottom.** *The image of the zombie,* **below,** *is ever-present at Haitian celebrations, and often involves elaborate costumes and make-up.*

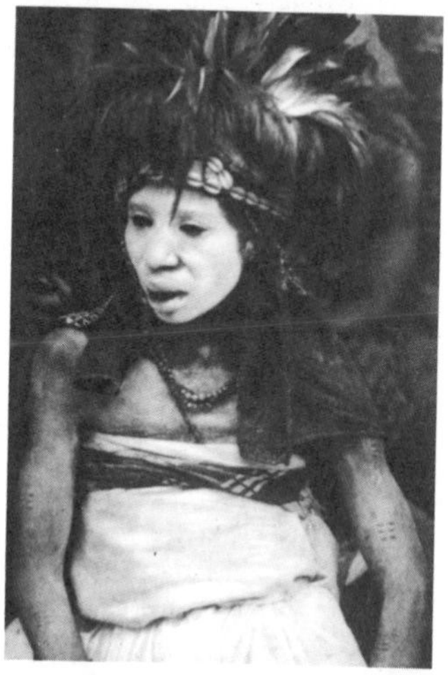

The zombie is the slave of an evil sorcerer, known as a *bokor,* who has removed a newly dead body from its grave and, by means of spells, endowed it with the shadow of life. It is an incomplete existence. Although the zombie eats, breathes, excretes, hears and even speaks, it has no memory of its previous life and no understanding of its own true condition. In other words, a zombie is a fleshy robot, a biological machine.

The Haitian peasant, ever alert for evil or dangerous aspects of voodoo, has several signs by which he can spot a zombie. It tends to lurch from side to side as it walks, to carry out other physical actions in a mechanical way, to have glazed and unfocused eyes, and to have a nasal quality in its voice. This characteristic is particularly associated with death in Haitian folklore, probably because it is the local custom to plump out the nostrils of a corpse with cotton wool. The *Guédé* – sinister, lecherous gods of death in the voodoo pantheon – are notable for speaking in this way. When a voodoo devotee is possessed by one of the *Guédé,* he or she always speaks with a strongly nasal intonation. A further link between zombies and the death gods is suggested by the fact that one of the most prominent of the latter, Captain Guédé, is often given the title 'Captain Zombie'.

Almost all Haitians fear the possibility of deceased relatives being transformed into walking cadavers, and the various preventive measures taken to avoid this possibility are readily noticeable, even in present-day Haiti. Even the poorest

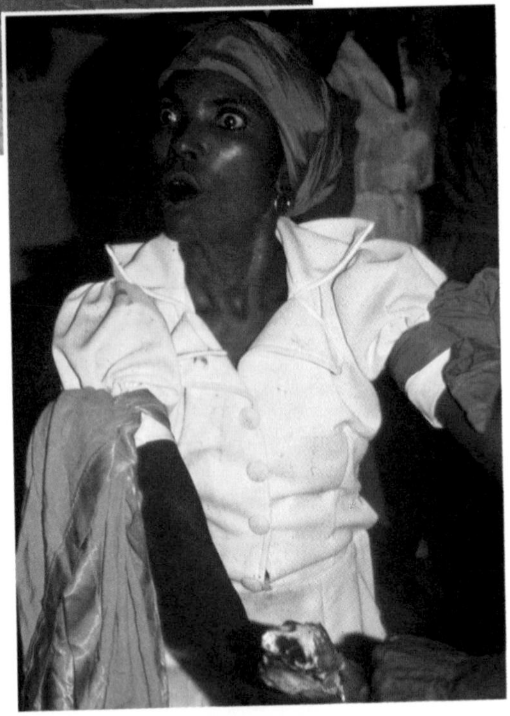

The headless body of a sacrificial goat lies on the floor of a hut in Benin, Africa, above left. The young woman possessed by the goat's spirit imitates it by going on all fours. Identical rituals are also performed in Haiti.

A voodoo priestess, left, her eyes staring, is seen in the grip of religious frenzy. She has just bitten the head from a chicken: its blood stains her dress.

The American writer, William Seabrook, below left, stands with a machete and a Haitian national flag which featured in a ceremony held in his honour in the 1920s.

peasants will borrow money to build heavy stone coverings over the graves of their immediate relatives. In rural areas, graves are dug as near as possible to a public road or footpath, so that sorcerers will be unable to go about their nefarious work, for fear of prying eyes. Sometimes, a bereaved family will watch over a new grave for night after night until they are certain that the body is sufficiently decomposed to be useless for the purposes of a *bokor*. On occasions, the dead are buried in the safety of a peasant farm's compound.

Some carry out even more extraordinary precautions to prevent their dead entering the misty half-world of the zombie. They have been known to inject poison, for instance, into the body, mutilate it with a knife, or even to fire a bullet into it, thus 'killing' it twice over.

Impossible Tasks

A less drastic measure includes placing eyeless needles and balls of yarn in the grave, along with thousands of tiny sesame seeds. It is thought that the spirit of the deceased will be so busy with the impossible tasks of threading the needle and counting the seeds that it will be unable to hear the voice of a *bokor* calling it from the tomb. Alternatively, a knife, with which it can defend itself, may be placed in the corpse's hand.

Sorcerers sometimes control whole troops of zombies and on occasion have gone so far as to hire them out as labourers. One such alleged case was recorded by William Seabrook. During a bumper sugar crop in 1918, Hasco – the Haitian-American Sugar Corporation – offered a bonus for new workers on its extensive plantations. Soon, little groups of villagers, including whole families, made their way to the company's labour office. It was customary for such village groups to work collectively, and the pay for the entire work force would be given to a foreman who would share it out when the party returned home.

One morning, an old village headman, Ti Joseph, and his wife Croyance, led a band of nine ragged and shuffling men into the Hasco office. They were, explained Joseph, backward and ignorant hill farmers from the trackless mountain area near Haiti's border with the Dominican Republic. They spoke only an obscure rural dialect and could understand neither Creole nor French. In spite of this disadvantage, he continued, they were excellent workmen, strong and healthy, who would labour happily at whatever tasks they were given.

Hasco's labour manager took on the gang, agreeing with Joseph's suggestion that they should work far from other groups: the head man explained that they were so primitive that they would become shy and confused near others. But his real reason for insisting on his workers' isolation was his fear that one or other of them would be recognised by a relative or former friend. For every one of Ti Joseph's work gang was a zombie.

Ti Joseph's labourers worked steadfastly through the hours of daylight, stopping only at dusk for their meal of unsalted millet porridge. (Voodoo tradition holds that if a zombie tastes meat or salt, it becomes conscious of its true condition and, weeping bitter tears, makes its way back to its grave.)

One Sunday morning, Ti Joseph left his wife Croyance to look after the zombies while he took the day off. Croyance led them into the nearby town: there was to be a church festival and she

"The eyes were the worst... It was not my imagination. They were in truth like the eyes of a dead man, not blind but staring, unfocused, unseeing. The whole face ... seemed not only expressionless, but incapable of expression."

apparently thought that the zombies would be pleased to witness a religious procession. But the zombies were as unmoved by the spectacle as by anything else that happened around them. Dumbly and vacantly, they continued to stare into space.

Croyance, pitying them, decided that sweetmeats might please them. She bought some *tablettes,* which are made of brown sugar, coriander and peanuts, and put a piece into each zombie's mouth. But the peanuts had been salted before the *tablettes* had been made. As they chewed the delicacy, the zombies realised that they were dead, and that they did not belong to Haiti's bright sunlit world, but to the darkness of the tomb.

With an appalling cry, they rose and shuffled out of the town into the forests, towards their home village in the mountains. When at last they arrived there, they were recognised by the relatives and friends who had buried them months before. As they reached the graveyard, each approached its own grave, scrabbled away the stones and earth that covered it, and then fell to the ground, a mass of decomposition. Ti Joseph's power, which had preserved their bodies from decay, had vanished.

The villagers inflicted their revenge on Ti Joseph and paid a local sorcerer to cast a spell on him. But before it could take its effect, some of the men had ambushed him and cut off his head.

EXPRESSIONLESS FACES

Seabrook was told this tale by Constant Polynice, a Haitian farmer who claimed to disbelieve the superstitions of his countrymen – but the zombies, he explained, were plain fact. Shortly after telling this story, he showed Seabrook a group of three supposed zombies. They were digging with machetes, under the supervision of a young woman. Seabrook looked into the face of one of the men and said:

'And what I saw then, coupled with what I had heard previously, or despite it, came as a rather sickening shock. The eyes were the worst. It was not my imagination. They were in truth like the eyes of a dead man, not blind, but staring, unfocused, unseeing. The whole face ... seemed not only expressionless, but incapable of expression.'

In the Haitian temple,* above, *an altar carries such Christian images as the Virgin Mary, a crucifix and the Ten Commandments. It is also adorned with drums, swords and ritual drinking cups – implements used in voodoo ceremonies.

The woman,* shown left, *was believed by the photographer to have been a zombie for 29 years, and was identified by at least two people as a relative, Felicia Felix-Mentor who had died in 1907. She was being cared for in a hospital when the journalist, Zora Hurston, took the picture.

Seabrook reassured himself that these men were 'nothing but poor ordinary demented human beings, idiots, forced to toil in the fields'. But his Haitian friend was not convinced.

Writing in the 1950s, the French anthropologist Alfred Métraux heard a good deal of evidence both for and against the existence of zombies. But when he was shown one in the flesh, he concluded that she was 'a wretched lunatic'. Indeed, the following day, the person he had seen was identified as a mentally deficient girl who had escaped from the locked room in which she was usually kept.

A writer who was perhaps less credulous than Seabrook concerning Haitian voodoo was Zora Hurston, another American. She met and photographed a girl who was alleged to have been a zombie for no less than 29 years. In 1907, Felicia Felix-Mentor had died of a sudden illness, and was buried by her husband and brother. In 1936, a girl dressed only in a thin, torn cotton smock was found wandering in the roadway near the brother's farm. She appeared to have lost the power of speech completely. Felicia's father and brother both identified her as the long-dead girl. Taken to a hospital, she cringed fearfully when anyone approached, as if expecting ill-treatment. It was there that Zora Hurston took her picture and tried to speak to her. Afterwards she wrote:

'The sight was dreadful. That blank face with the dead eyes. The eyelids were white all around the eyes as if they had been burned with acid. There was nothing you could say to her or get from her except by looking at her, and the sight of this wreckage was too much to endure for long.'

Was the girl who had been found merely a wandering lunatic? The firmly entrenched belief of the Haitians that relatives and loved ones have been seen after their burial, living the half-life of the zombie, throws doubt on this comforting theory. There must surely be something deeper to the legend of the zombie.

THE CARDS THAT SPEAK

In a 15th-century reading of the Tarot cards, above, a man throws up his hands after learning something unexpected. The earliest known Tarot pack dates from 1390. The cards probably originated in the East, and were spread to Europe by gypsy fortune-tellers and Moorish invaders.

USING TAROT CARDS TO PREDICT FUTURE EVENTS HAS LONG BEEN ONE OF THE MOST POPULAR FORMS OF DIVINATION. BUT THE WAY IN WHICH THE CARDS ARE CONSULTED AND THE INTERPRETATION OF EACH IS VERY MUCH DEPENDENT ON THE INDIVIDUAL PRACTITIONER

Some methods of divination are aleatory – that is, they are based upon chance and involve a random selection of elements. The word 'aleatory' comes from the Latin for 'dice-player', one of the simplest divinatory methods being the throwing of dice.

However, numerous experiments in psychokinesis have suggested that an experienced dice-thrower can actually influence results; and it may well be that the subconscious mind, or some transcendental aspect of it, is able to calculate implications and select the most suitable answer to the question posed, then subconsciously causing the appropriate figure to be generated.

Some process of this kind also seems to be at work with the Tarot – probably nowadays the most popular of all divinatory methods.

The use of a pack of cards for divination is definitely not aleatory, since each of the elements selected – namely, the cards – is distinct, and has a particular significance all of its own. There are a number of packs of specially designed cards available for divination – the French firm of Grimaud, for example, markets such sets as the cards of 'Mademoiselle Le Normand', or 'The Parlour Sybil' – but some diviners are able to make do with an ordinary pack of playing cards. In this respect, it is important to remember that the Tarot pack is also an ordinary pack of playing cards. Although some of the images of the Tarot pack may appear bizarre to north-western Europeans familiar only with the standard 52-card bridge and whist pack, they do not embody any intrinsic occult significance. Indeed, for 500 years, Tarot cards have been the standard pack for a variety of common card games that go under the generic name of *tarok* or *tarocchi*.

Modern Tarot packs have 78 cards, and consist of the Minor Arcana (56 cards, divided into four suits: buttons, cups, swords and coins), and the Greater or Major Arcana (22 cards with distinctive images, each having a particular significance.) There are very many ways of 'consulting the cards', and there is no reason to suppose that any one way is more correct or successful than any other. All that is important is that the practitioner should be completely confident about his or her method and the way in which the cards are to be interpreted. Easier methods only make use of the 22 cards of the

The Tarot cards, opposite, are from the Major Arcana, and date from the 15th to early 20th century. They are 'Strength' (La Force) right and 'The Fool' (Le Fou), above right. The Major Arcana cards are numbered I-XXI: only 'The Fool' has no number, and may have been an early equivalent of the joker in today's standard pack of 52 playing cards.

Major Arcana, while more complicated methods employ all 78 cards; but even experienced practitioners often find it necessary to resort to textbooks in order to remind themselves of the accepted significance of the numbered suit cards.

The same kind of divinatory process can be carried out with a pack devoid of Major Arcana, such as a common 52-card pack, but in this case interpretation is commensurately more difficult.

There are two ways in which Tarot cards are used in divination: either a select number of cards is chosen for interpretation, or the complete pack is disposed according to a precise formula, producing a pattern of distribution in which it is the position of the card that determines its part in the divinatory process.

As in all other methods of divination, the process comprises a questioner, who asks for advice by proposing a particular question, and the diviner, who interprets the answer. The cards may be dealt out either by the questioner or by the diviner. No two authorities agree on this, and it may also depend upon the particular method employed – but it is essential that both parties should concentrate fully upon the question because a frivolous question, or one that is idly put, will provoke an answer that may be equally facetious or, possibly, quite frightening in its implications.

Cult film-maker Alejandro Jodorowsky, whose cinematic creations have included *El Topo* and *Santa Sangre*, is a dedicated reader of the Tarot. Every Wednesday, he drives from his house in Vincennes, in east Paris, to an Arab café in the rue Saint Jacques, where he gives free public readings of the cards.

The weekly event draws a large crowd, and in the space of two hours, Jodorowsky may do over 20 sittings. Like many Tarot readers, he does not predict the future. Once the shuffled cards are spread out on the table, he gives his total attention to the here-and-now problems of his enquirers, although each is allowed only one question. Around him, the café crowd listens, fascinated, to the problems aired and Jodorowsky replies. He accepts no money, but requires that the questioners merely trace the word *'merci'* (thanks) on to his palm.

The following is an example of how the Tarot cards are laid out in a pattern, and then used for divination. The questioner in this instance is a young woman, who has been married for several years. She has a full-time professional job. Due partly to the tastes and partly the ambitions of her husband, she finds herself compelled to live in a district that she finds unpleasant. Her question is whether she should she endeavour to make her present home as comfortable as possible, or whether she should try to persuade her husband to move elsewhere.

The account book of the treasurer to Charles VI of France records a payment in the year 1392 to the painter Jacquemin Gringonneur for three packs of cards 'in gold and various colours, of several designs, for the amusement of the said King'. The three cards seen here – 'Death', left, 'The Sun', right, and 'The Fool', below right – are from 17 that survive in the Bibliothèque Nationale in Paris, and that were long believed to be the original Gringonneur cards. They are now, however, thought to be from the 15th century and of Italian origin.

The particular arrangement of cards used is one known as the 'Celtic cross'. Only the 22 cards of the Major Arcana are required for this.

1. A card is chosen to represent the question. This is known as the significator. In this particular case, 'The Star', representing 'new beginning; pleasure; salvation', was the card selected.

2. The questioner then shuffles the remaining cards, cuts them, and places them in a pile, face down, to the left of the significator.

3. The top card of the pile is now turned over from left to right (so that it remains as it was in the pile, either upright or reversed) and placed directly on top of the significator. This card represents the present conditions in which the questioner lives or works. The card chosen happens to be 'The World' (card 1). In spite of the nature of the question asked, it therefore appears that the questioner, on the whole, feels a sense of achievement in her work, and perhaps also in her home.

4. A second card is placed across the first, to represent any immediate influences that may affect the interests of the questioner. The card in this instance is 'Temperance': in other words, whatever decision is reached, it is likely to be controlled by reason.

5. A third card is placed above the first group of cards, to represent the ultimate aim of the questioner. This turns out to be the 'Fool', reversed. Since it is reversed, it signifies the opposite of luck or fate, and implies a rational outcome.

6. A fourth card is placed below the first group to represent influences from the past that have affected the questioner and also the question she now asks. The 'Empress' is chosen , telling us that she is a woman of considerable understanding.

7. A fifth card is placed to the right of the central group to represent the recent past. The 'Hermit' suggests that the passage of time has brought wisdom and further understanding.

8. A sixth card is placed to the left of the central group to represent influences that may come into play in the near future. The 'Hanged Man' represents adaptability and change; it brings knowledge of the future and new understanding of the past. It also advises the questioner to face up to whatever changes may come.

These first six cards drawn have presented a picture of the questioner and her problem, as well as revealing small details that she did not provide. The final four cards, placed one above the other to the right of the table, supply divinatory advice.

9. The next card represents the present position of the questioner, and may answer the question directly. This is 'Death', but is not to be taken literally, for it represents transformation.

10. The next card chosen represents people and factors that may have an influence upon the answer. It is the 'Wheel of Fortune' which, though also signifying change, counsels prudence.

*In*Focus

SIGNIFICANCE OF THE TAROT TRUMPS

1 Magician	**Man in search of knowledge; the answer that he seeks**
2 Woman Pope	**Intuition, inspiration; subconscious memory, lack of foresight**
3 Empress	**Human understanding, femininity, sensuality, beauty and happiness**
4 Emperor	**Masculinity, independence, creativity, action**
5 Pope	**Advice; justice; healing**
6 Lovers	**Choice, decision**
7 Chariot	**Achievement, success; danger of defeat**
8 Justice	**Caution in taking advice; control of one's fate**
9 Hermit	**Time; wisdom; withdrawal**
10 Wheel of Fortune	**Change; prudence; the eternal return**
11 Fortitude	**Strength of purpose, coming danger**
12 Hanged Man	**Adaptability; desire to learn; violent change and sacrifice**
13 Death	**Change by transformation, rebirth**
14 Temperance	**Moderation, mercy; modification**
15 Devil	**The adversary; caution**
16 The Tower	**Punishment; pride; divine inspiration**
17 The Star	**New beginning; pleasure; salvation**
18 The Moon	**Uncertainty; changeability**
19 The Sun	**Splendour, health, wealth, affection; treachery**
20 Judgement	**Punishment or reward; final achievement**
21 The World	**Fulfilment, completion on a material level**
0 The Fool	**Fate; luck; the end**

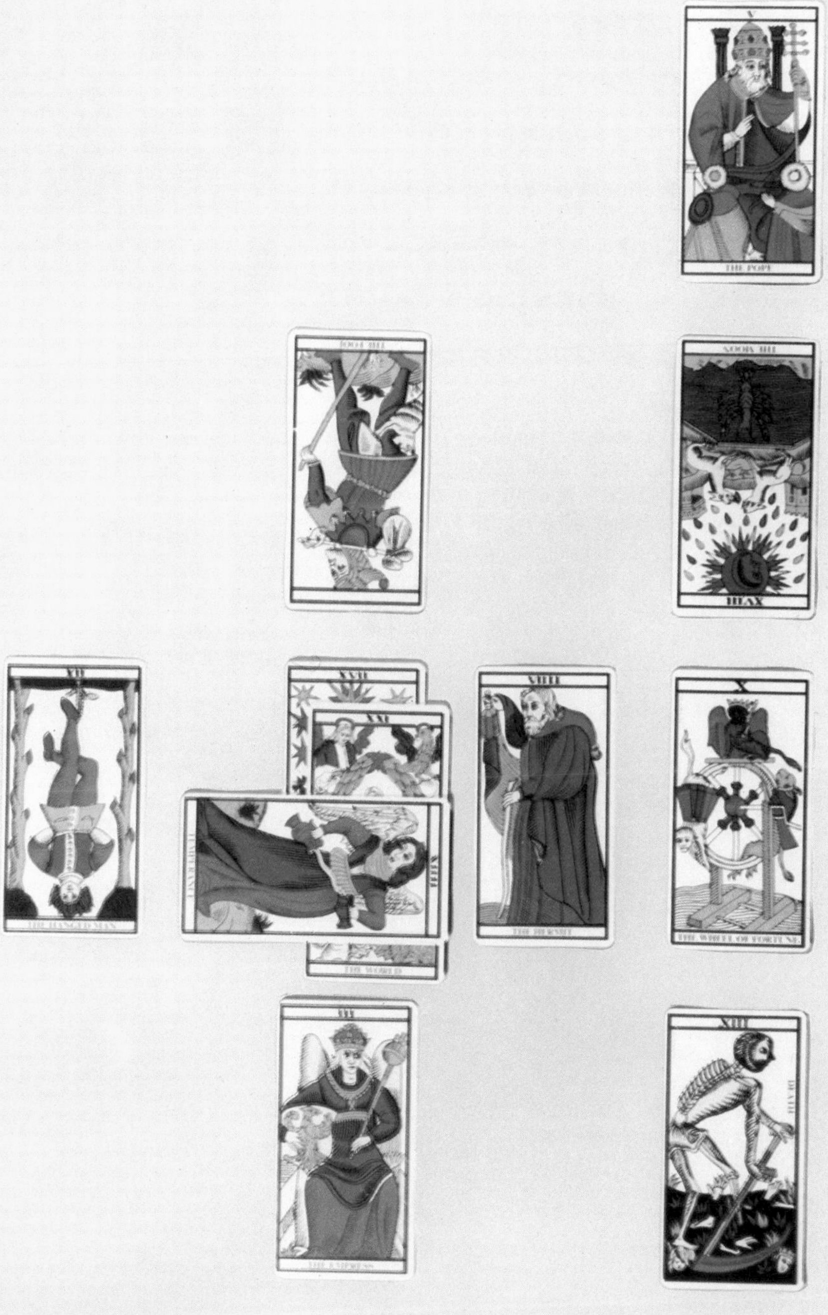

The Tarot cards, above right, have been laid out in the spread known as the Celtic Cross. The significator (here, The Star) represents the questioner and lies in the centre of the cross, largely hidden by two other cards – The World and Temperance. Note that The Fool is reversed. The four cards to the right of the cross provide an opportunity for divinatory advice.

11. The following card chosen reveals the inner feelings of the questioner, which she may well have kept hidden. It is the 'Moon', reversed. This suggests very strongly that the questioner does not really want to make the change that she has said she is considering.

12. The final card represents the end result of everything indicated by the preceding cards. It is the 'Pope' – representative of the firm foundations of our lives, and concepts of natural law and justice. This card, appearing in this position, suggests that the questioner and her husband have a mutual sympathy and understanding; that their marriage appears to be a successful one; and that it would be dangerous to threaten its stability by pursuing the change that was the subject of the question.

The number of possible sequences is virtually infinite; and even if only the 22 cards of the Major Arcana are used, as in this example, there are over a thousand million million million different layouts.

CRAZY NIGHT IN MAINE

EYES THAT TURNED ORANGE, A DETAILED MEDICAL EXAMINATION BY ALIENS AND SUBSEQUENT THREATS MARKED AN AMAZING EVENING'S JAUNT FOR TWO YOUNG AMERICANS

While Dr Herbert Hopkins, an American medical practitioner living in the state of Maine, was investigating a UFO case, he was allegedly visited by a weird 'man in black'. Subsequently, his son and daughter-in-law were also visited by a bizarre couple.

The case under investigation by Dr Hopkins at the time was a most extraordinary occurrence, involving two young Americans.

"THE CREATURE HAD HANDS AND FEET, WITH THREE WEBBED FINGERS AND A THUMB ON EACH HAND. THE HEAD WAS MUSHROOM-SHAPED, ITS LARGE, WHITE EYES WERE SLANTED ... AND NO MOUTH WAS VISIBLE. IT WORE A FLOWING BLACK SHEET-LIKE GARMENT."

While these young men watched what seemed to be hovering UFOs for several hours one night, they both experienced strange distortions of reality. Through the use of hypnosis, Hopkins subsequently elicited from one of the witnesses memories of having been being taken aboard an alien spacecraft and subjected to a medical examination of the kind that is common to so many reports of UFO contacts and close encounters.

The paranormal phenomena in the case were similar to those reported in many other sightings. The witnesses experienced obscure promptings that seemed to guide them to the encounter; and they thought that nearby farm animals – cows, ducks and geese – were also involved in the strange events. The psychic aspects of the case had been pursued by another investigator, Dr Berthold Schwarz, but without success.

The witnesses were terrified after their experience – to the point that they mistook stars and planets in the night sky for other UFOs. The two men were sincere, and investigating ufologists could find

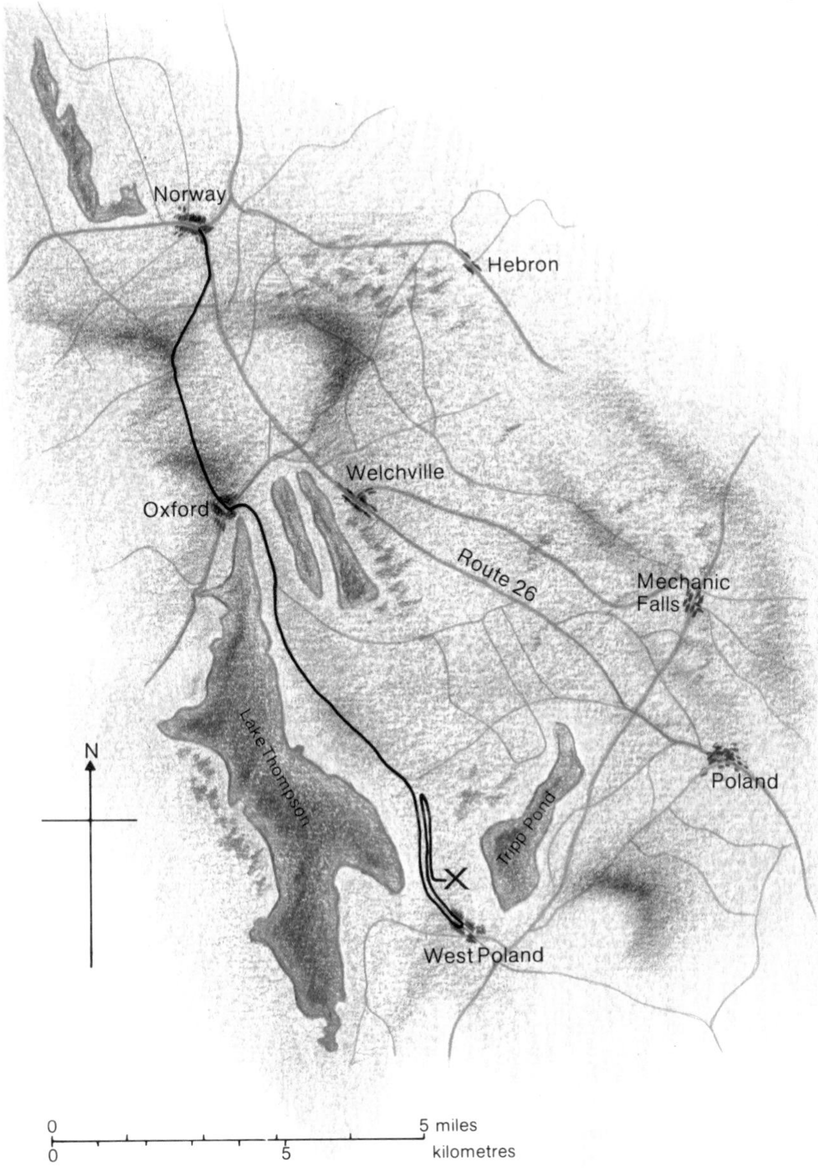

no explanation for the events of this crazy night, recounted here.

In October 1975, David Stephens, aged 21, and a friend aged 18 were sharing a trailer home in Norway, Maine, in the eastern United States. The two young men originally requested anonymity, but Stephens' name was subsequently revealed by an American UFO magazine. His friend's name was not revealed, however, so he will be referred to here as 'Paul'. They had known each other only a few weeks and had been struck by the fact that similar paranormal experiences had occurred to both of them.

Both David and Paul were working late shifts – David at a poultry processing plant, Paul at a wool mill – which is why they were both awake in the early hours of 27 October. They were listening to music at about 3 a.m. when they heard what sounded like an explosion. They rushed outside, but saw nothing unusual. While they were standing there,

On the map, above, 'X' marks the point where David Stephens and Paul watched UFO aerobatics over Tripp Pond during the night of their UFO encounter. The artist's impression,* left, *shows the strange spheres and cubes which they both sighted.

David suggested it would be a good night for a drive. Paul recommended a run down to nearby Lake Thompson. So they began driving southwards down Route 26. Their intention was to stay on that road until they were about 2 miles (3 kilometres) east of the town of Oxford. Then they would cut across to Oxford and go south alongside the lake.

RAPID JOURNEY

However, things did not work out like that. According to their subsequent statements, the car made a right turn on to a back road, against their will and with Paul gripping the steering wheel firmly. The road was a more direct route to Oxford, and was about 5 miles (8 kilometres) long. The ride was unusually smooth and they covered the distance very quickly, taking only about two minutes in all – implying that they were travelling at a speed that must have been in the region of 150 miles per hour (240 km/h).

After passing through Oxford, they continued down the eastern side of Lake Thompson where they noticed that cows in a field that they passed were shaking their heads from side to side. Just after that, they saw two beams of white light shining from a cornfield on to the road. Expecting to see a truck emerging, Paul slowed down. They were surprised to see the source of light rising from the ground. Coming to a halt, Paul switched off the car engine and they wound down the windows, expecting to see a helicopter. There was no sound. They saw instead a cylindrical shape rising behind the trees that fringed the field. It was surrounded by multicoloured lights that went out as the object lifted above the trees.

Alarmed, the two men restarted the car and accelerated away, closing the windows and locking the doors. Driving southwards, they then became aware of a beam of extremely bright light but had no conscious recollection of what happened next, until they found themselves in the car, parked on a track leading off from the tarred road on which they had been travelling, and close to the cornfield of the original sighting. The car windows were now partly opened, the doors were unlocked and they made an alarming discovery: David saw that Paul's eyes were 'all just orange', while Paul saw that David's were orange, except for the dark area of the pupils.

ENCOUNTER ON IMPULSE

The UFO still visible in the sky, David and Paul decided to drive on towards the town of West Poland. There they turned round and headed back along the same road. When they had gone about 2 miles (3 kilometres), the UFO was no longer visible. They turned back yet again, so that they were now travelling south. On an unexplained impulse, Paul again turned off the intended route, on to a gravel road leading down to Tripp Pond. As they completed the turn-off, they then saw the cylindrical object at an elevation of about 30 degrees from the horizontal and at an estimated distance of 150 to 200 yards (135 to 180 metres).

Suddenly, the car engine died and could not be restarted. The radio fell silent. Then the object moved 'in an up-and-down fashion' and took up a position at about 80 degrees of elevation in the

CASEBOOK

south-east, at an estimated distance of 500 yards (450 metres).

David and Paul had been sitting in the immobile car for some 45 minutes when two disc-shaped objects appeared. They carried red, green and blue lights, and each was about a quarter of the size of the cylindrical craft. The discs then put on an 'aerobatic display', descending with a rocking motion, skimming the surface of Tripp Pond and rising swiftly, 'as though climbing a staircase'.

While all this was going on, the witnesses had the feeling that the pond, which in reality was half-a-mile (800 metres) distant, was only 20-30 feet (6-9 metres) away and immense, like an ocean. It seemed to them that there was an island over which the 'aerobatics' were taking place: but in fact, Tripp Pond has no such island.

Now fog began to form above the water. It approached and enveloped the car, but the cylinder was still visible. Meanwhile the radio burst into life – with a weather forecast, announcing that a bright and sunny day was in store.

At 6.30 a.m., Paul tried again to start the car. This time he was successful, and by 7 a.m., they arrived at the home of David's family in Oxford. The dreamlike quality of the experience and the ominous significance that seemed to invest every small incident are brought out in remarks made by David:

'What was weird was when the big one went straight up, the clouds seemed to follow it. It just took off, and all this time not a car went by. We didn't see a person, or an animal, or a bird ... nothing! And when the cloud disappeared, two ducks went by and then two geese went by and then two ducks again went by. They were going in twos, and we noticed the cows were getting up in twos'.

Surprisingly, the pair made a return journey to Tripp Pond at 4 p.m. on 28 October, when what seemed like snowflakes began to fall around them and strange cubes and spheres apparently 'whizzed in all directions'.

THREATS FROM A STRANGER

The following morning, David Stephens was alone in the trailer when he was disturbed by a loud knocking on the door. When he opened it, he found himself face to face with a stockily built man who sported a crew-cut hairstyle, sunglasses and dark blue clothing. He asked David if he was the one who had seen a 'flying saucer'. When David confirmed this, the stranger said: 'Better keep your mouth shut if you know what's good for you'. He then scurried away around an adjacent building, and no more was seen of him.

The Stephens family reported the UFO encounter to the Androscoggin County Sheriff and then to the *Lewiston Daily Sun*. After making initial enquiries, a UFO investigator, Shirley Fickett, taped interviews with the witnesses on 11 November. She was interested in the time that was 'lost' after the intense beam of light had struck the car and rendered its occupants unconscious. She wanted to have the witnesses questioned under hypnosis and learned that Dr Herbert Hopkins sometimes used hypnosis in the treatment of his patients. In a spirit of scientific adventure, Dr Hopkins offered his services free of charge.

The artist's impression,* above, *shows one of the strange creatures who took blood from David Stephens and subjected him to a thorough medical.

Dr Berthold Schwarz,* below, *studied the contact witness David Stephens, finding him to have much in common with other contactees and with gifted psychics – energy, individualism and pent-up tension.

David Stephens was the first to be questioned. His parents, Mrs Fickett and Paul were present. But Paul later refused to attend any further sessions and withdrew completely from the investigations. Eight hypnotic sessions were conducted from December to March 1976. Under hypnosis, David described standing outside the car after the light beam had struck it: he felt that he was standing on a 'floor suspended above', watching through a window as the car slid sideways, with Paul still in it. He was in a room with curved walls. At first he was alone, but he was joined after a while by what appeared to be a non-human being. The creature had hands and feet, with three webbed fingers and a thumb on each hand. The head was mushroom-shaped, its large, white eyes were slanted, its nose was small, and no mouth was visible. The creature wore a flowing black sheet-like garment. It communicated not by voice but by 'brain waves' with David, whose name it somehow knew.

BLOOD SAMPLES

David was then taken into another room where there were four similar beings. It was like a 'hospital room with an operating table'. Blood – enough to fill two syringes – was taken from near his right elbow. When the beings tried to persuade him to lie on the table for a medical examination, David became violent and struck one of them. They did not retaliate, and eventually he relented. He was divested of his clothes and thoroughly examined, from head to toe, with a box-like device. The creatures seemed to want to be friendly. When David was at last returned to the car, Paul seemed unaware that he had ever been away.

In the final hypnotic session, David seemed to suffer great emotional conflict when he was questioned about a statement made by the beings, to the effect that they would return. He could not, or would not, disclose anything on this point, and the questioning was discontinued because of his obvious distress.

When Dr Berthold Schwarz conducted his psychiatric-parapsychological investigation, he concluded that there had been no previous interest on David Stephens' part in flying saucers, or detailed knowledge of any classic cases, in spite of an interest in the paranormal. He also concluded that David was still frightened and puzzled by the events, that there were no contradictions in his story, and that there was no history or evidence of dishonesty or loss of memory before these events.

Concerning the medical examination, Dr Schwarz stated that it seemed so absurd technically that 'one wonders if this wasn't staged by the UFO forces in order to create a particular impression'. He noted, in connection with the orange colour of witnesses' eyes at one point, that an ophthalmologist had said that, when he used a substance known as *fluorescein* in the course of his work, the eyes became transiently orange.

Using their 'brain wave' system of communication, the entities had told David Stephens that they would return. Did they perhaps do so, in the guise of the weird 1930s-style character who attempted to scare off Dr Herbert Hopkins – an investigator who had perhaps learned too much?

CURSES HAVE ALWAYS BEEN FEARED – WITH JUSTICE IT SEEMS, FOR DISEASE, LOSS OF LOVED ONES AND DEATH HAVE OFTEN BEFALLEN VICTIMS OF SUCH INVOCATIONS

A curse is an invocation of destruction or evil, part of the accustomed armoury of the priest, magician, shaman or ill-wisher. But do curses work and, if so, how? Swearing at someone gives vent to pent-up feelings; and most psychologists would say that ritual curses do nothing more – unless, that is, the victim is expecting trouble. Sandford Cohen, a psychologist at Boston University, USA, became convinced from field research that curses can be lethal, because of the feeling of utter helplessness they can inspire. Indeed, he saw a striking similarity between western Man dying from a fear of some disease generally believed to be fatal and primitive Man dying from a witch doctor's curse.

Another explanation involves the 'tape recording' theory – that a thought can imprint itself on an object or person, and also be transferred to others. If the thought is malevolent, so is the effect. There are, however, numerous cases of victims who were totally sceptical of supernatural 'mumbo-jumbo', but this did nothing to save them from the effects.

The Mycenaean funeral mask, above, represents Agamemnon – according to Greek legend, one of the many sufferers from the ancient curse on the House of Atreus by Hermes. Agamemnon, the grandson of Atreus, was forced to sacrifice his daughter and was himself killed by his wife's lover.

NOTHING BUT TROUBLE

Take the case of Robert Heinl Junior, a retired colonel in the US Marine Corps. From 1958 to 1963, he served in Haiti as chief of the US naval mission, while his wife studied the voodoo religion. Afterwards, back in the United States, they wrote *Written in Blood*, a history of Haiti that was openly critical of the ruling dynasty of François 'Papa Doc' Duvalier. Then they learned from a newspaper published by Haitian exiles that a curse had been placed on the book, probably after Papa Doc's death in 1971, by his widow, Simone.

Initially, the Heinls were flattered that their book was thought to be worth cursing, but amusement soon turned to fear. First, the manuscript was lost on the way to the publishers, then it turned up four months later in a room that the publishers never used. Meanwhile, the Heinls prepared another copy of the manuscript and sent it off for binding and stitching, but the machine immediately broke down. Next, a *Washington Post* reporter who was preparing to interview the authors was struck down with acute appendicitis. The colonel then fell through a stage when he was delivering a speech, injuring his leg. And while walking near his home, he was suddenly – and severely – bitten by a dog.

Accidents continued, two involving the number 22, which Papa Doc considered magical. Finally, on 5 May 1979, the Heinls were on holiday on St Barthélémy Island, east of Haiti, when the colonel

Robert and Nancy Heinl, *left, fell foul of the Haitian dictator, François 'Papa Doc' Duvalier and his wife Simone,* below, *while researching their book* Written in Blood, *which was openly critical of Duvalier's regime. The Heinls believed that Simone Duvalier had cursed them, causing a chain of events that culminated in the sudden death of Robert Heinl. Nancy Heinl was in no doubt that a curse was responsible for their string of bad luck.*

dropped dead from a heart attack. His widow mused: 'There is a belief that the closer you get to Haiti, the more powerful the magic becomes'.

Rod of Light

Curses, precisely laid down in many rituals, are still cast by priests in many of the world's major religions. In September 1981, for example, Rabbi Moshe Hirsch, leader of the Neturei Karta, an orthodox Jewish sect, threatened to invoke the 'Rod of Light' against the Israeli archaeologist Yigal Shilo if he persisted in excavating the biblical city of David. This, the rabbi maintained, involved desecrating a medieval Jewish burial ground. Archaeologists, meanwhile, denied the very existence of such a cemetery.

The Rod of Light ceremony involves the reading of a text based on Kabbalistic writings. The participants burn black candles, sound a ram's horn and invoke the name of the cursed man's mother. 'This ceremony is an absolute last resort', said the rabbi. 'It has only been invoked twice in the last 30 years, both times with horrible consequences. There are many ways of dying, some that are less pleasant than others.' Interestingly, the rabbi claims he failed to discover Shilo's mother's name.

In the Church of England, too, spiritual contracts are occasionally put out on church thieves. Since the 1970s, in Gloucestershire alone, two vicars have performed the commination (or divine threat) service – the Reverend Harold Cheales of Wych Rissington in 1973, and the Reverend Robert Nesham of Down Ampney in 1981. The commination service contains 12 curses and leaves room for more. It first appeared in the 1662 *Book of Common Prayer;* but in the 1928 revision, the word 'curse' was replaced by 'God's anger and judgement'. It was traditionally used against enemies of the Church on the first day of Lent, or whenever a church or churchyard had been desecrated. Christian curses seem to be, on occasions, just as effective as demonic ones: the old abbeys that Henry VIII seized from the monks after the dissolution of the monasteries in the early 16th century, for instance, often bedevilled their new owners over generations with the dreadful curses laid by angry monks.

A Heart of Stone

There is a widespread ancient belief that no good will come from disturbing old stones or buried treasure: folklore worldwide is full of such tales, and the theme continues in the enduring popularity of the idea of a mummy's curse. Some researchers even believe that such deep-seated and widespread beliefs, as part of the collective unconscious, can exert a material influence, bringing myths to life and also reinforcing them.

The old castle of Syrie in Aberdeenshire, Scotland, is one such building plagued by a legendary curse. A group of stones in the local river is known as the Weeping Stones, one of which is missing. It is said that no heir to Syrie will ever succeed until that stone is found.

In 1944, when a 2-tonne 'Witch's Stone' was shifted from a crossroads at Scrapfaggot Green, Great Leighs, Essex, England, in order to widen the

PERSPECTIVES

BY FIRE AND WATER

Battle Abbey in Sussex, *below,* was the scene of a grim curse laid on the descendants of Sir Anthony Browne, 'Esquire to the Body of

road, psychic havoc broke out. A great boulder was found outside the local pub, chickens were found locked up in rabbit hutches, rabbits ran loose in the garden, the church bells chimed irregularly, 30 sheep and two horses were found dead in a field, and a village builder's scaffolding poles tumbled about 'like matchsticks'. The 'Witch's Stone' was replaced and peace duly restored.

More recently, in 1980, a 30-tonne boulder was removed from the Devil's Marbles to a park in Tennant Creek, an isolated mining town in the Australian outback. Aborigines of the Warramungu tribe believe the Marbles are a relic from the so-called 'Dream Time' – when ancestral spirits created the world – and that any interference with such relics will lead to sickness and death. After the boulder's removal, a number of Aboriginal children fell ill with sores on their legs, and a tribal elder, Mick Taylor, warned that 'someone would get killed' if the stone was not returned. In March 1981, Mick Taylor died from meningitis at the age of 50. The town then agreed to return the boulder.

Rocks of Wrath

Curses that are inflicted as result of moving sacred stones are found in the New World, too. During the summer of 1977, airline vice-president Ralph Loffert, of Buffalo, New York state, USA, his wife and four children visited the Hawaiian volcano, Mauna Loa. While there, they collected some stones from the volcano despite a warning from the locals that this would anger the volcano goddess, Pele. Some claim to have seen Pele, who traditionally appears to warn of imminent eruptions. Shortly after they returned home, Mauna Loa erupted, and Pete certainly seems to have been angered, for within a few months, one of the Loffert boys, Todd, developed appendicitis, had knee surgery and broke his wrist; another son, Mark, sprained an ankle and broke his arm; his brother, Dan, caught an eye infection and had to wear glasses; and the daughter, Rebecca, lost two front teeth in a fall. In July 1978, the Lofferts sent the stones to a friend in

Henry VIII, Master of the House and Justice in Eyre', in 1538. Sir Anthony was cursed at the feast held to celebrate his ownership of the abbey by a monk who was angry at the seizure of Church lands during the dissolution of the monasteries.

The curse was specific: the family would die 'by fire or water'. It seems, however, that the curse went awry. Sir Anthony's other property, Cowdray House – which he had inherited from his half-cousin, the Earl of Southampton – was burned down; but this was much later, in 1793, after the property had passed into the hands of another family.

Antony Hippisley Coxe, compiler of the book *Haunted Britain,* records that the curse came into force yet again, in 1907, when the Duchess of Cleveland – renting Battle Abbey briefly – drowned in its grounds on her way to church.

A 788-year-old curse was ritually lifted by the former Chief Rabbi at the consecration of Clifford's Tower in York,* above, *on 31 October 1978. On the night of 16 March 1190, 150 Jews fled to the tower where they died by their own hand rather than fall into a mob's hands. The last to die was the rabbi whose final act was to curse the city of York. Until well into the 20th century, York was avoided by Jews, even though nearby Leeds has always had a thriving Jewish community.

'The curse has come upon me,' cried the Lady of Shallott, Tennyson's doomed heroine who is seen,* right, *preparing to meet her fate.

granddaughter had a bad fall and broke her arm in two places.

Morris also admitted that he had broken the rock in two and given a piece to a friend, adding: 'He brought the rock back to me after he wrecked four cars in less than two years'. Morris later sent the rocks back.

Jon Erickson, a naturalist at the Volcanoes National Park in Hawaii, at one time received up to 40 packages of rock a day from tourists who felt they should return them to avoid further disasters.

Skulls, too, frequently take revenge on those who move them. Lieutenant Commander 'Buster' Crabbe dived with the Royal Navy in 1950 in Tobermory Bay, Isle of Mull, in search of the Duque de Florencia, a payship of the Spanish Armada, which had been sunk in 1588 with a reputed 30 million pounds of gold on board. One of the trophies with which he surfaced was a skull that medical experts said had belonged to a North African

Hawaii who was asked to return them to the volcano. But the disasters continued: Mark then hurt his knee, Rebecca broke three more teeth, Dan fractured a hand bone, while Todd dislocated an elbow and fractured his wrist again. Mark then confessed that he still had three stones. They were returned – and the trouble ceased.

HEAD-ON CRASH

Allison Raymond of Ontario, Canada, and her family also took some stones away from the volcano. She told reporters: 'My husband was killed in a head-on car crash and my mother died of cancer. My younger son was rushed to hospital with a pancreas condition that's slowly getting worse. Then he broke his leg. My daughter's marriage nearly broke up and it was only when I posted the rocks back that our luck improved'.

Despite warnings, Nixon Morris, a hard-wood dealer from El Paso, Texas, took home a Mauna Loa stone in 1979. After returning, he fell off his roof, lightning struck an aerial, ruining several home appliances, and his wife fell ill.

Then Morris broke a hip and thigh when he fought with a burglar in their house. The family cat was sleeping under the bonnet of his wife's car when she started the engine: as a result, the cat was stripped of its fur down one side. Then Morris'

The Devil's Marbles in northern Australia,** above, **is a sacred Aboriginal site. In 1980, after one of the boulders was removed, Mick Taylor – a tribal elder – warned that this would lead to sickness and death. Several children fell ill, and Taylor himself died the next year at the age of 50.

At the Mauna Loa volcano of Hawaii,** below, **the Loffert family, on holiday in 1977, picked up some stones from the volcano – despite a warning that this would anger the local deity, the goddess Pele. Just as had been predicted, a series of disasters struck the family, ceasing only when the last stone had been sent back to Hawaii. Other tourists have reported similar runs of bad luck after taking away stones.

woman. Six years later, Crabbe disappeared, some maintain mysteriously, while on an underwater mission in Portsmouth harbour. The following year, a coroner decided that the headless body of a frogman washed up at Chichester, Sussex, was that of Crabbe himself.

The skull that had been found on the wreck was kept in the Western Isles Hotel, Tobermory, Scotland. One day, the barman accidentally caused it to fall and break. That same same day, he crashed his motor scooter and cracked his skull. He never returned to the island. The hotel owner, Donald Maclean, stored the skull away in a cupboard. In 1970, Richard Forrester, the new English owner of the hotel, drilled a hole in the skull so that he could hang it up in his cocktail bar.

'I was using an ordinary electric drill. The first odd thing that happened was that the metal bit of

*In*Focus

THE CURSE OF THE PHARAOHS –

Archaeologists can be said to be modern grave robbers – and, as such, often seem to have paid the price, for many ancient Egyptian tombs apparently carry curses for any who dare to desecrate them.

According to the American journalist Webb Garrison, Professor S. Resden opened an Egyptian tomb in the 1890s that was thus inscribed: 'Whosoever desecrates the tomb of Prince Sennar will be overtaken by the sands and destroyed'. Resden knew he was doomed, it is said. He left Egypt by ship and died on board, a victim of suffocation with no discernible cause. Small amounts of sand were found clutched in his hands.

The poetic neatness of this story is, it must be said, rather suspicious and should perhaps be taken with a pinch of salt – or even sand.

But the 'curse of the pharaoh' continues. In September 1979, George LaBrash had a stroke while guarding the Tutankhamun mask, *left*, in San Francisco. In January 1982, he sued the city authorities for disability pay, claiming that the stroke was a job-related injury caused by the alleged curse on the tomb' s desecration. The case was dismissed. The question remains as to whether this in itself was a refinement of the curse.

Film star Jayne Mansfield was killed in the appalling crash, above, on 29 June 1967. This was widely rumoured as being no accident. Jayne was said to have been cursed by her former friend, Anton LaVey, head of the Church of Satan.

Lance Sieveking, above right, broadcaster and father of author Paul Sieveking, demonstrated an unusual immunity to a curse laid by black magician Aleister Crowley by living 30 years longer than the curse allowed.

the drill, after piercing the bone, bent inside at an angle of 45 degrees. I found this surprising but thought nothing more about it. Two hours later, I was struck by excruciating pain in the back of the head. I was completely incapacitated for two days. Since then, I have been taking prescribed pills but the searing pain continues and never leaves.'

The only other person to handle the skull since the drilling had also experienced searing headaches.

RELATIVELY SPEAKING

The notion of a curse affecting a whole family is as old as civilisation. The ancient Greeks were firm believers in the efficacy of curses – the most celebrated affecting the house of Atreus. Atreus himself had killed the son of the god Hermes in a love contest, and as a result the deity put a curse on the murderer 'and all his house'. Atreus killed his own son by mistake; another son, the hero Agamemnon, was killed by his wife's lover; and she in turn was murdered by her son.

In Britain, several aristocratic families are believed to be afflicted by family curses. In the 18th century, the Scottish Earl of Breadalbane moved a graveyard to build the castle of Taymouth. According to tradition, a lady whose grave was disturbed laid a curse on the family whereby no two earls of this line would succeed each other. The prophecy apparently came true.

Even researching the subject of curses might be considered hazardous. In 1928, the occultist and magician Aleister Crowley ('The Beast'), met the young radio producer, Lance Sieveking, on the French Riviera. They spent many hours in conversation, and Crowley subsequently cast Sieveking's horoscope. It contained a number of predictions that were later fulfilled. One, however, was not. Crowley wrote: 'By the way, you will oblige me personally by dying at the age of forty-five'. Sieveking was then 32, but he disobligingly lived to be 75.

Crowley's curses, however, often claimed victims. The last was Dr William Brown Thompson, who withheld the addicted Beast's supply of morphia. In a rage, Crowley put a curse on him, saying that when he died he would take the doctor with him. Crowley died on 1 December 1947, aged 72. Thompson was dead within 24 hours.

> "Two hours later, I was struck by excruciating pain in the back of the head and was completely incapacitated for two days. Since then, I have been taking presribed pills, but the searing pain never leaves."
>
> RICHARD FORRESTER

CRASHED TO EARTH?

Ever since the term 'flying saucer' was coined in 1947, there have been rumours that the US government has one or more crashed UFOs – complete with alien pilots – in its custody. What evidence is there for this intriguing idea?

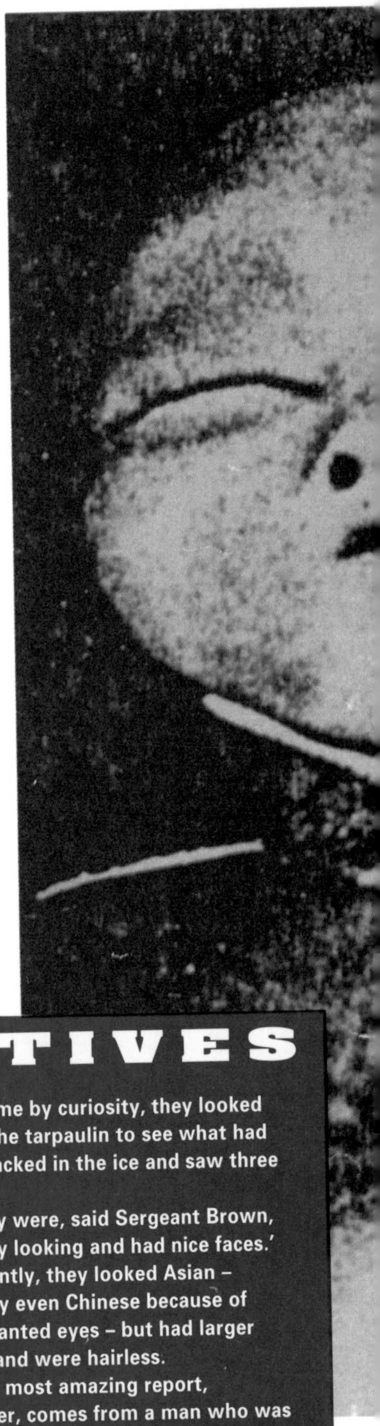

Towards the end of 1988, a group of Soviet military men, flying in a helicopter near Dal'negorsk in the far east of the USSR, noticed a strange object on the ground. After landing to investigate, they found a cylindrical object about 19 feet (six metres) long, which did not look like any part of a conventional aircraft. Unable to lift it, they decided to return the following spring, but by then the object had vanished.

Reports of crashed UFOs have made news ever since the first reports of 'flying saucers' in 1947. At that time a rumour circulated that a UFO had crashed and was under examination by American scientists. It was logical enough: given the great number reported to be around, it seemed statistically certain that sooner or later one of them would suffer an accident, or be shot down.

Such reasoning assumed that the UFOs were solid, material objects, liable to physical accident or mechanical malfunction. In those early days, there was little question in anyone's mind that the UFOs were as solid as terrestrial aircraft: the only question was as to where they originated.

What threw the crashed saucer legend into disrepute was, paradoxically, a book that set out to establish it as fact. In 1950, an American writer named Frank Scully brought out *Behind the Flying Saucers,* a bestseller in both the USA and Europe. Something of the contemporary climate of opinion comes over in the dust-cover blurb: 'It is typical of the whole extraordinary and delightful business of the flying saucers that the first person to attempt a serious book about them should be the show business magazine *Variety's* ace columnist.' (The point could have been made even more strongly by mentioning that Scully was also the author of *Fun in Bed* – not a sex manual, but a collection of diversions for the bedridden – which was sufficiently successful to be followed by *More Fun in Bed* and *Junior Fun in Bed.*) True, there were few serious ufologists around in 1950; but Scully's credentials did nothing to enhance the credibility of his story.

The story Scully had to tell needed all the support it could get. In the course of his professional writing, he claimed, he had come across a Texas oilman named Silas Newton who, in turn, told Scully of his colleague 'Dr Gee' – who, he alleged, had first-hand knowledge of three UFOs that were held in the custody of the United States military, along with 16 dead occupants, about 3 feet (1 metre) tall. No supportive evidence was produced: it all

PERSPECTIVES

ALIENS, DEAD AND ALIVE

Most descriptions of aliens recovered from crashed UFOs conjure up creatures that are very human-like. A crash in the New Mexico desert, west of Socorro, in July 1947, has given rise to several extraordinary reports about the craft's occupants. A civil engineer who encountered the 'disc-shaped aircraft' described the dead aliens as having round heads that were larger in proportion to their bodies than in humans, small eyes that were oddly spaced, and no hair. 'Their clothing,' he said, 'seemed to be one-piece and grey in colour. You couldn't see any zippers, belts or buttons...'

The New Mexico aliens were also claimed to have been seen by a Sergeant Melvin E. Brown while at Roswell Army Air Field in the same year, 1947. Some of the materials collected from the site of the crash were put in refrigerated trucks and Sergeant Brown and another were ordered to guard one of the vehicles. Overcome by curiosity, they looked under the tarpaulin to see what had been packed in the ice and saw three bodies.

They were, said Sergeant Brown, 'friendly looking and had nice faces.' Apparently, they looked Asian – possibly even Chinese because of their slanted eyes – but had larger heads and were hairless.

The most amazing report, however, comes from a man who was in the area of the crash at the time; then, he was but a five-year-old searching for moss agate stones together with members of his family. He claims to have come across three aliens lying underneath a silver disc on the side of a hill.

Measuring about four feet long, with unusually large heads and 'almond-shaped, coal black eyes', they lay quite still. One had trouble breathing, while a fourth alien sitting nearby 'recoiled in fear, like it thought we were going to attack it.' The man and his family were eventually hustled away by US soldiers.

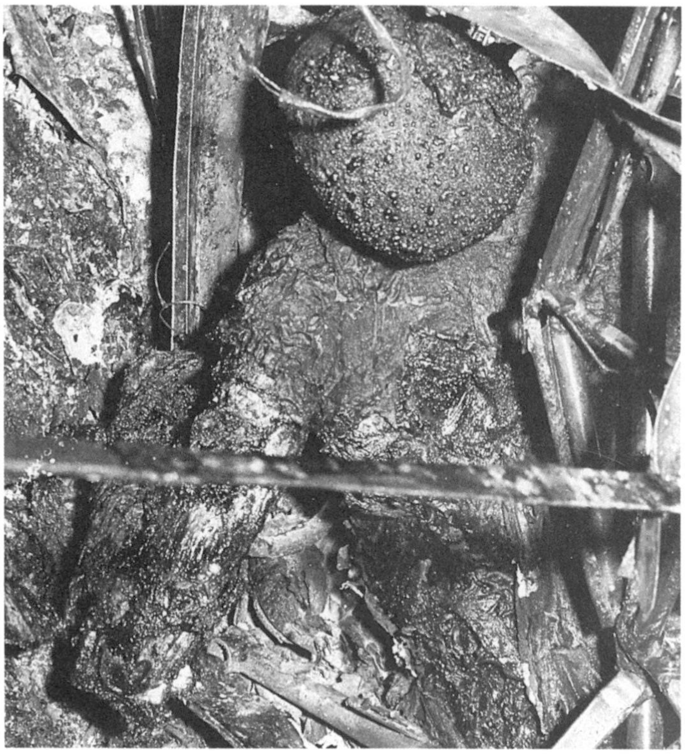

The photograph, left, is of an alleged dead alien, retrieved from a UFO that crashed in New Mexico on 7 July 1948.

A model of what is believed to be an alien corpse that was recovered in New Mexico in July 1947 and placed in a zippered body-bag, is shown above.

depended on the word of 'Dr Gee', who claimed to have been one of the scientists called in by the authorities to examine the UFOs.

This drawback did not prevent Scully's book selling more than 60,000 copies; but it did mean that when, two years later, journalist J.P. Kahn wrote an article pointing out the weaknesses of Scully's story, he found it easy enough to persuade the world that it was a total fabrication. The fact that Kahn's exposé was itself full of exaggerations and inaccuracies was overlooked: it made its point, namely that Scully had taken the story on trust and done virtually no independent research. Newton and 'Dr Gee' were labelled frauds.

It was not until some 25 years later that the crashed saucer legend surfaced again. In April 1976, there appeared in the pages of *Official UFO* (at that time, a fairly serious journal) an article entitled 'What about crashed UFOs?', by the widely respected investigator Raymond Fowler. Instead of serving up again the vague rumours of the past, he produced dramatic new evidence in the form of a technician's sworn statement that he had personally examined a crashed UFO at Kingman, Arizona, on 21 May 1953.

The Roswell Incident

From then on, interest in the subject became very serious and intense. Another investigator of repute, Leonard Stringfield, dedicated himself to the search for further evidence; and while he ranged far and wide in his quest, two other men, William Moore and Stanton Friedman, in conjunction with Charles Berlitz, concentrated on a single case that was soon to become famous – the Roswell incident.

The story, in outline, is as follows. Sitting outside their home on the night of 2 July 1947, a couple at Roswell, New Mexico, saw a glowing object streak across the sky. The next morning, about 75 miles (120 kilometres) further on in the direction of its path, a rancher found extraordinary debris scattered over his ground. A further 150 miles (240 kilometres) or so away, an engineer and some archaeologists came across the remains of an unidentifiable flying object, together with several strange bodies. The authorities took control, announced that the object was simply a weather balloon, and nothing more was heard of the matter – until Moore, Friedman and Berlitz took up the case, that is.

Other incidents, uncannily similar in some respects, abound. On 7 July 1948, near Del Rio, Texas, USA, for instance, unusual radar sightings led to the suspicion that an unidentified flying

A flying saucer collides with the Washington Monument in a still, below, from the 1956 movie Earth vs Flying Saucers. *However advanced the technology of UFOs, there is surely no reason why they should not sometimes crash. And if they do, then surely it is natural for the military to take an interest?*

In 1953, a metallurgist named Daly, who worked at the Wright-Patterson Air Force Base in Ohio, was sent on a secret mission to examine what appeared to be a flying saucer. After carrying out tests on the craft – as shown in the artist's impression,* right *– he concluded it must be of extraterrestrial origin.

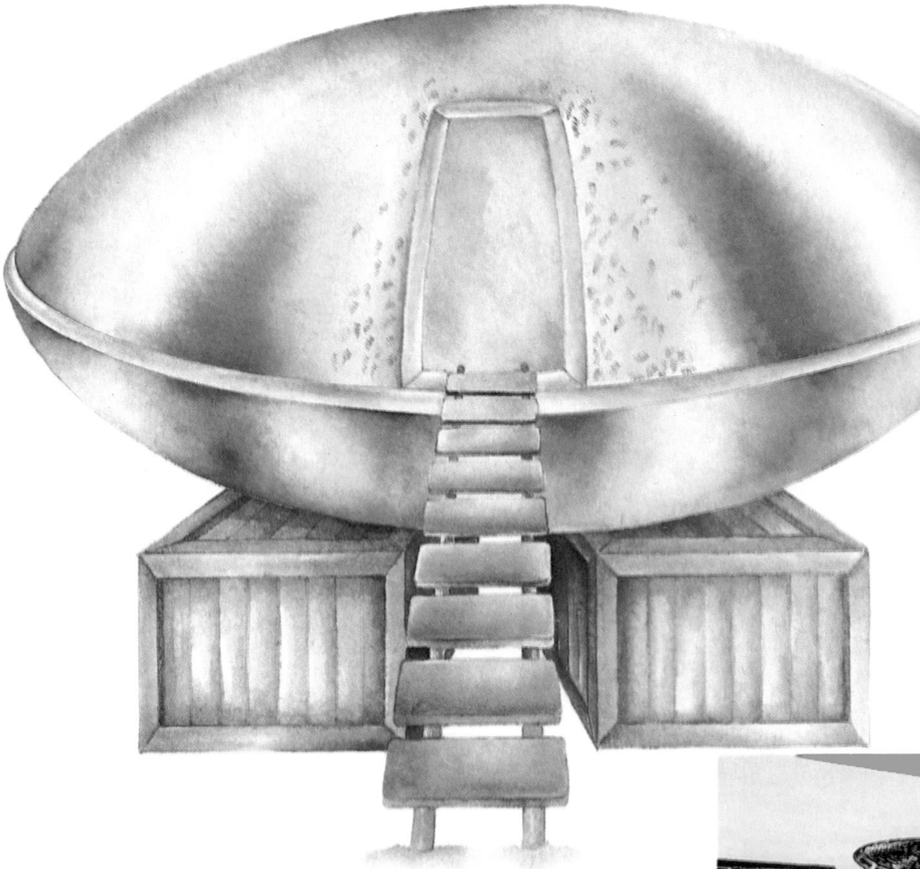

A crashed UFO in the Arizona desert is shown illuminated by the glare of spotlights in the sketch,* centre right. *A civilian engineer, known by the pseudonym Fritz Werner, brought in to calculate the object's speed of impact, noticed the body of a small humanoid figure in a metallic suit. In 1973, Werner signed an affidavit testifying that this incident had occurred to him 20 years before.

object had crashed some 30 miles (50 kilometres) across the Mexican border. With permission from the Mexican government, US troops went to investigate, and found a metallic disc, together with the burned bodies of the crew, more or less human-like beings about 5 feet (1.5 metres) tall. The object, which had been clocked at 2,000 miles per hour (3,200 km/h) by radar, had been seen simultaneously on radar by USAF Colonel Whitcomb in an F94 jet fighter. He landed at his home base and immediately took off for the scene in a borrowed light aircraft. Here, he found Mexican troops in control, and the object hidden from sight. But a naval intelligence officer arrived in time to see the crash area roped off and some objects being loaded on to trucks.

The troops taking part had apparently been warned that, if they spoke of the matter, they would be 'the sorriest people around'. Photographs, allegedly of the bodies of the occupants, were circulating clandestinely some years later, and continue to be the subject of controversial debate.

Official reaction was no less threatening when, in 1952, at the Muroc (now Edwards) Air Force Base in California, a USAF radar operator tracked an object descending towards Earth at great speed. After a crash had been confirmed, he was instructed: 'You didn't see anything'. Later he learned that a UFO, more than 17 yards (16 metres) in diameter, had crashed in a desert area not far away. It was metallic, and badly burned; and it contained bodies of beings about 5 feet (1.5 metres) tall. The debris was kept for a while at the base, then allegedly shipped to the Wright-Patterson Air Force Base at Dayton in Ohio. There is strong evidence that some object was indeed secretly shipped to the Wright-Patterson base.

Possibly relating to the same incident is a five-minute film that was shown the following spring, apparently by the military authorities, to a select group, including a radar specialist with security clearance, who was working at the time for the army and air force, stationed at Fort Monmouth, New Jersey. The movie showed a silver disc-shaped object embedded in the sand in a remote desert area. It had a dome on top, and an open hatch or door. Some 10-15 military personnel could be seen standing near the craft. Its diameter, based on a comparison of its size with that of the human figures, appeared to be 6-8 yards (5-7 metres). The film also showed the bodies of three

CASEBOOK

FRAGMENTARY EVIDENCE

In June 1952, six Norwegian army jets on summer manoeuvres over the inhospitable islands of Spitzbergen, *right,* in the Arctic Ocean, spotted wreckage in a mountain area near the Hinlopen Straits. Within hours, using ski-planes, Norwegian investigators – among them, an expert on rocketry – were on site. No doubt, a Soviet vehicle or missile was suspected, but instead they found the wreckage of a disc-shaped object, with 46 jet-like orifices on the rim. The object

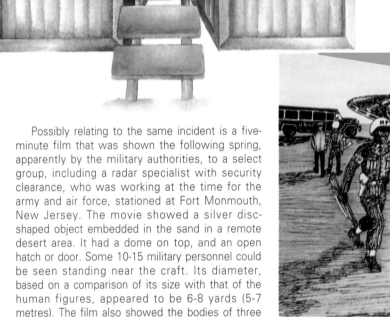

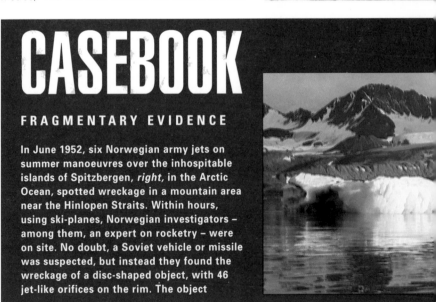

dead occupants: they were small and human-like, with over-large heads. The group was told to think about the film but not to tell anyone about it. Two weeks later, they were told it was a hoax. This seems strange, for there is a certain amount of evidence that the film was shown to officers at a number of military bases. Clearly someone, somewhere, felt that it was important for them to see it. Quite apart from the poor quality of the film – which, paradoxically, tends to suggest it is genuine – the cost in time and effort of setting up such an elaborate fake must have been formidable.

> "If UFOs have crashed, and aliens ... are in custody, it is surely time that the authorities let us into such secrets."

Perhaps the most explicit item of evidence in the entire crashed UFO saga is an affidavit signed in 1973 by a certain Fritz Werner – a pseudonym, although his true identity is known – who swore that he had assisted at the investigation into a crashed unknown object. While serving as project engineer on an air force contract near Kingman, Arizona, in 1953, he was given an assignment. Along with some 15 others, he was taken early one morning under strict security conditions in a blacked-out bus on a five-hour journey. He and his companions were then told that a super-secret air force craft had crashed, and that each of them was to investigate the crash in terms of his specific field of expertise.

Werner described the object as like two deep saucers, one inverted on the other, about 11 yards (10 metres) in diameter, made of dull silver metal, with an open hatch to the interior. His particular task was to calculate the object's impact velocity from the traces. He found no landing gear, and no dents or scratches. In a tent nearby, he saw a dead humanoid, about 4 feet 3 inches (1.3 metres) in height, on a table. Not only were the investigators instructed to tell nobody of the incident, they were not even allowed to discuss it among themselves.

Another incident from 1953 that seems to confirm the Fritz Werner report is the case of a metallurgist named Daly who worked for the air force at the Wright-Patterson AFB, Ohio. He described being taken to a location, unidentified but abounding in hot sand. (For the last part of his journey, he was blindfolded.) For two days, he was required to examine the structure of a silvery metallic craft lying undamaged in the sand. He concluded it was not of earthly origin; what is more, he saw no sign of occupants.

Despite obvious discrepancies, these two reports may relate to the same incident. Relevant, too, may be the evidence given by the wife of a guard at Wright-Patterson. She alleged that, at about this time, her husband had witnessed scientists examining the bodies of large-headed humanoids, about 3 feet (1 metre) in height.

Another incident, two years later, at the Wright-Patterson base, also appears to confirm that pilots of crashed spacecraft were taken there for examination. A woman, whose duty was to catalogue all incoming material relating to UFOs, stated that she had seen the bodies of two dead humanoids, about 5 feet (1.5 metres) tall, with large heads, being transferred from one location to another.

South American Mysteries

In March 1964, it was reported that a round, flat UFO, giving off a bright blue and orange light, had crashed high on Mount Chitpec, Mexico. Officials wanted to take it to the nearest town, San Cristóbal de las Casas; but the local tribe, the Chalulas, insisted it was a gift from God and the Virgin, and refused to allow its removal.

Some years later, in May 1978, many people in Tarija, in the most remote and inaccessible part of Bolivia, saw a glowing object cross the afternoon sky. It was generally described as a metallic cylinder, some 8 or 9 yards (7 or 8 metres) in length, without windows or structural details, and closely followed by another, smaller object. A few seconds later, there was the sound of a great explosion, accompanied by an 'earthquake' that registered on seismic equipment over some 77,000 square miles (200,000 square kilometres). After the crash, the smaller object was seen to fly away.

The object's rate of travel was far too slow for it to have been a meteor, and investigation subsequently ruled out the possibility of a satellite returning to Earth. But while speculation bubbled in the press, a security blackout was officially imposed. Reporters saw the object removed by technicians, and asserted that it had been taken by the United States Air Force back to the USA. NASA denied any knowledge of this – as, of course, it would have done even if it had been involved.

The evidence presented in such incidents is often far from convincing; yet it is hard to discount it altogether. To assert that every one of these reports is a lie, or a misinterpretation of some simple event, is to call into question a great number of witnesses, unknown to one another and wholeheartedly trusted by experienced investigators. If UFOs have indeed crashed, and aliens – dead or alive – are in custody, it is surely time that the authorities let us into such secrets.

seemed to be made of an unknown metal, and there was no trace of occupants.

What is perhaps the most remarkable aspect of this incident is the comment made by a high-ranking army officer, Colonel Gernod Darnbyl of the Norwegian general staff, who later said: 'The crashing of the Spitzbergen disc was highly important. Although our present scientific knowledge does not permit us to solve all the riddles, I am confident that these remains from Spitzbergen will be of utmost importance. Some time ago, a misunderstanding was caused by saying that this disc probably was of Soviet origin. We wish to state categorically that it was not built by any country on Earth. The materials used in its construction are completely unknown to the experts who took part in the investigation'.

SMELLS CAN EXERT A SURPRISING POWER, INDUCING FEELINGS OF ELATION, DEPRESSION AND EVEN FEAR AT TIMES. SOME FRAGRANCES, IT IS BELIEVED, MAY EVEN HAVE A MYSTICAL ORIGIN

PERFUME POWER

Even unbelievers sometimes feel religious stirrings when, for the first time, they witness a Greek or Russian Orthodox celebration of the Easter Eucharist. As they inhale the heady aroma of incense smoke blended with the fumes given off by flickering beeswax tapers, so they may sense unfamiliar, mystical impulses in their own inmost depths.

Indeed, the sense of smell has often been underestimated in the study of human behaviour – though the power of odours to trigger off memories is a common experience. One promising line of research has even shown a relationship between body odours, in the form of substances known as pheromones, and the emotional excesses of mass hysteria.

The civet cat, **above**, *can produce a musk-like odour, probably used during mating as a sexual attractant. The musk scent is also thought to attract humans sexually and is therefore used in the manufacture of perfume.*

The smell of incense, **left**, *as used in the Church, is meant to turn our thoughts towards the divine. Aromatherapists say that they have also used incense smoke successfully in treating chronic headaches.*

Pheromones are even known to influence the timing of the menstrual periods of women working or living in close proximity. Martha McClintock of the University of Chicago discovered this when she collected perspiration from the armpit of a volunteer who did not shave or use a deodorant. The experiment involved dissolving the perspiration in alcohol and placing a drop on the upper lips of a test group over several weeks. A control group was given drops of pure alcohol only.

At the start of the experiment, participants' menstrual patterns varied consideraby. But after some four months, approximately 80 per cent of those who had smelled the perspiration began to menstruate to coincide with the original volunteer. Scent, it seems, plays a far greater role in our lives than is imagined.

The Greeks believed that by breathing in the scent of the poppy, right, *a person would become brave, like Ares, their god of war, shown* below.

The aroma of the violet, below, *is used by aromatherapists to bring about feelings of calmness.*

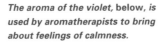

Dion Fortune, an occultist who was also a trained psychotherapist, commented upon the link between smells and the emotions. 'A man attending Mass,' she said, 'will find his mind turning towards the Divine as he savours the sweet smell of incense; if he suddenly gets a breath of musk or patchouli from the woman in the next pew, his thoughts will turn in quite a different direction'.

There can be little disagreement with this assertion. Most of us find that smells, pleasant and unpleasant, affect our psychological states, particular aromas inducing feelings of elation, depression, erotic stimulation, and even fear.

Social Links

To some extent, this link between odours and the emotions is 'all in the mind', the product of an association of ideas. It may be only because of the customs of our society that, for instance, our minds associate the scents women wear with feminine sexuality. If customs were different and only celibate nuns used perfumes, it is possible that we would associate these fragrances with such attributes as chastity.

But the association theory cannot be the whole truth because smells never previously encountered can also exert a physical effect on both animals and humans. A kitten, for example, will begin to salivate the very first time it encounters the smell of cooking fish, and most of us retched when we first experienced the stench of rotten eggs.

Interestingly, too, it has been discovered that the odour of certain substances can only be recognised clearly by women at the time of ovulation. Men and girls are only able to detect this scent if they are given large doses of oestrogen, the female hormone, Lyall Watson reveals in his natural history of the supernatural, *Supernature*.

Some smells are even said to have mysterious origins: Padre Pio – the Italian friar who is known to have experienced stigmata (wounds on his hands and other parts of his body that correspond to those of Christ on the cross) – was said to give off a strong perfume of violets, roses or cyclamen. The faithful of his parish came to refer to as this the 'odour of sanctity'.

An Ancient Art

Since the 1930s, practitioners of fringe medicine have become sufficiently interested in the psychophysical effects of smells on ill people to revive the ancient art of aromatherapy, and it is now an increasingly popular form of alternative healing. Practitioners maintain that odours can change moods, and that such changes are powerful enough to be harnessed for therapeutic use. The aim of the aromatherapist, then, is deliberately to induce emotional alterations that will help improve a sufferer's mental as well as physical state. The healer decides on the exact nature of the desired changes in mood by considering both the physical condition and the individual personality of the patient. On this basis, a perfumed oil considered appropriate for one depressive, for example, will not necessarily be suitable for another depressive. Often, too, aromatherapy is used in association with other alternative treatments, such as chromotherapy, which involves shining coloured lights on the patient.

Aromatherapists do not, of course, believe that scents can actually cure infectious diseases. They do, however, believe that complaints associated with stress – illnesses in which the relationship between the body and the mind plays an important part, such as asthma and some forms of backache – can be alleviated substantially by using aromatherapy. They also aim to offer relief from various common ailments including such conditions as migraine, menstrual problems and bronchitis.

Sacred Scent

The fragrance of fresh flowers – as found in the plant's essential oils – is important in this respect. The Greeks assigned a flower or flowers to each deity in their pantheon and believed that, by inhaling the scent of a plant sacred to a certain god or goddess, they could share in the attributes of that particular deity. If, for example, they breathed in the scent of the red poppy, one of the plants sacred to Ares, god of war, they would become brave. The Romans shared this belief.

> "A man attending Mass will find his mind turning towards the Divine as he savours the sweet smell of incense; if he suddenly gets a breath of musk from the woman in the next pew, his thoughts will turn... "

Modern aromatherapists maintain that each flower scent has its own specific effect, good or bad. These attributions are mostly based on the medieval 'doctrine of signatures', which holds that the shape, colour, aroma or other quality of a plant is a sign of its secret qualities. Reading the 'signature' tells the healer for which part of the body or what particular disease the plant is suitable. The lungwort, liverwort and kidneywort, for instance, are namesakes of the human organs they vaguely resemble in shape, and are therefore said to be efficacious in treating related ailments. In aromatherapy, the violet is considered a 'shy' plant because of the way it hides its flower heads among its leaves. So the scent of violets is believed to bring feelings of calmness and modesty as good effects.

Secret Benefits

Chrysanthemum scent is said to inspire mysticism, otherworldliness, and psychic abilities. The aroma of cornflowers induces sobriety, and so is helpful in overcoming a hangover. The scent of gentian is believed to be a powerful but harmless anti-depressant, and – some believe – an excellent substitute for some of the powerful drugs used in orthodox psychiatric treatment. The slightly peppery odour of nasturtiums, meanwhile, is held to be an aphrodisiac. The scent of red roses inspires the 'poetic impulse', while that of verbena arouses a more general artistic creativity.

Fruits, as well as flowers, have been employed by ancient and modern aromatherapists to beneficial effect. Indeed, the odours of all citrus fruits are considered to have health-giving and psychologically stimulating qualities, as do the more delicate scents of ripe apples and pears.

Sometimes the more powerful odours of spices are also employed. In medieval times, for example, it was customary during outbreaks of the plague to sniff a 'pomander' – originally no more than an orange studded with cloves – as an antidote to the 'toxic effluvia' permeating the atmosphere.

Modern aromatherapists rely on essential oils extracted from a wide range of plants, including cinnamon and eucalyptus. These are taken from the plants' leaves, bark, roots and seeds, as well as the flowers themselves. Today, aromatherapists also buy ready-distilled oils – and there is a huge range – through small, specialist shops and then blend the oils themselves according to a patient's needs.

CASEBOOK

THE SCENTED TOUCH

The following case histories (in which names are withheld to assure privacy) give some indication of how aromatherapy can work to relieve illness. Massage with essential oils is the principal technique used by aromatherapists. The massage acts on the body, and the wafted fragrance acts on the mind and the emotions.

The first case is that of a 28-year old woman. When the therapist first met the patient, he was immediately conscious of two things. One was the extraordinary rigidity of her bearing and movements, 'like somebody encased in cardboard'; the other was the unhappiness of her face. She was also extremely shy and found it difficult to communicate. It transpired that she had been withdrawn and unhappy ever since early childhood, and that she was, as a result, perpetually tense.

The therapist decided to give general body massage with essential oils derived from agrimony, which lessens anxiety, and clematis, which inspires courage. He also massaged the area around the base of the spine, for some therapists believe that there is an important 'psychic centre' associated with this part of the body. After four treatments over a month, the patient was less physically rigid. She also found it easier to talk to people and even began to face social situations with confidence.

Another case concerns a man, whose symptoms were almost exactly the same as

Body massage with fragrant essential oils, right, is the principal technique used in aromatherapy.

Clematis, below, has a scent is believed to inspire courage.

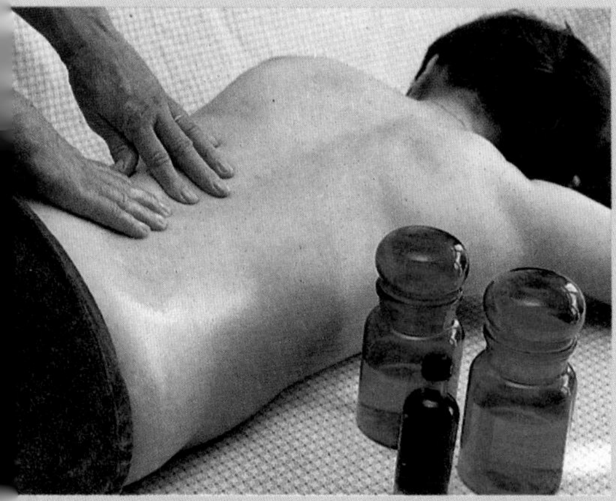

those of the previous patient. The therapist tried a similar course of treatment; but after six sessions, his health showed no improvement at all. The therapist attributed the failure to the patient's age: he was approaching retirement.

A third case involves a 42-year-old man who had for many years suffered from intermittent back pain, sometimes of great severity. Orthodox doctors had been unable to find any cause for the pain and had given no help. Resort to osteopathy, chiropractic and acupuncture had proved equally unhelpful in bringing him any lasting relief.

The aromatherapist decided that there was nothing physically wrong, but that he was too active for his own good, his body producing back pain to force him to slow down.

The therapist also sought to slow him down, administering essential oil of cornflowers – for staidness – and zinnias – for caution – through massage. After six months, the patient had become less hyperactive, and his pains had diminished in both severity and frequency.

Aromatherapists, like herbalists and other unorthodox practitioners, emphasise that they are 'treating a patient, not a disease'. They maintain that they are concerned with guiding the sick to heal themselves by helping them to bring the mind and body into a natural equilibrium. To put it another way, aromatherapists while not denying the physical reality of stress-related diseases, emphasise that the psychological state of the sick person is of primary significance in causing such diseases. By changing that state, by restoring the natural flow of psychic energy, it is believed that the patient can be brought back to health.

Few people today would utterly deny the importance of psychological factors in physical illness: even in cases of infection or accident, the individual's will to survive plays an important part in recovery. But some doctors find it is difficult to accept the validity of claims made by aromatherapists. No controlled trials of the techniques have been made as yet, and the 'evidence' that the practitioners themselves provide is not considered adequate by critics. It may be said, for example, that 'Patient A' had suffered from backache for nine years and had been cured in four months by a combination of spinal manipulation and aromatherapy; or that 'Patient B' was relieved of chronic headaches by acupuncture and incense smoke. Such testimonies are of much interest, but from a factual point of view, they are valueless – especially since it is known that spontaneous remission, and even spontaneous disappearance, of sickness, organic or otherwise, is surprisingly frequent. There is no form of fringe medicine, from bee sting therapy to osteopathy, that does not produce a crop of 'unsolicited testimonials' from those who have benefited and who want to share their experience with others.

Some of these testimonials may well be the product of self-delusion, but others are probably genuine. Indeed, there is increasing evidence that if people believe, consciously or unconsciously, that a certain course of action or treatment will benefit their health, that belief may actually produce physiological changes.

In the woodcut **below**, ***a doctor holds a sponge soaked with vinegar and spices to his face as he treats a plague patient. Many people in the medieval period believed that sweet or pungent scents protected them against the dreaded plague by fighting off 'effluvia' (unpleasant exhaled substances) in the air.***

Pleasant Treatment

There seems to be no reason to discount totally reports of those who claim to have been successfully treated by aromatherapy – to have been relieved of crippling back pain, for example, by massage with perfumed essential oils. From the point of view of the patient, it does not matter that the old 'doctrine of signatures', on which the attribution of various odours to different psychophysical states is based, may be superstitious nonsense. All that matters to those who were sick is that they have undergone a pleasant and comparatively inexpensive process that has relieved them, to a certain extent at least, of a troublesome and long-standing physical or mental ailment.

So should people who are interested in the unexplained elements of life and consciousness be prepared to experiment with aromatherapy? There seems no reason why not. Indeed, it is possible for people to analyse the influence of different perfumes and flower scents for themselves, and to employ those that seem to exert a beneficial psychological effect. As far as more serious illness is concerned, there is also no reason why people should not try aromatherapy as an adjunct to more orthodox treatment– as long as their own doctors have no objection.

The connection between aromas and the plague has come down to us in the form of the line 'a pocket full of posies' from the ring-a-ring-a-roses game (depicted **left**, ***in an illustration by Arthur Rackham). It is a reminder of how people carried posies – bunches of fragrant flowers – in their pockets or hands in the hope of keeping away the plague.***

THERE ARE, IT SEEMS, SKULLS THAT CREATE SUPERNATURAL DISTURBANCES SIMPLY BECAUSE THEY WANT TO STAY IN A FAVOURITE PLACE

SKULLS THAT SCREAM

In the quiet village churchyard of Chilton Cantelo in Somerset, England – picturesque in both name and setting – a lichen-covered tombstone dated 1670 marks the last resting place of a certain Theophilius Broome – or at least the resting place of most of him. For over 300 years, his skull, polished like old ivory, has lain in a cupboard at his former home, Chilton Cantelo Manor. This fulfils a deathbed wish that his head should remain in residence. Not unnaturally, his heirs were uneasy about the idea. But they quickly discovered that attempts to bury the skull with the rest of the body only created problems for everyone.

According to the inscription on Theophilus' tombstone, 'horrid noises, portentive of sad displeasure' were heard throughout the village when attempts were made to re-bury his head. These ceased only when the bony relic was disinterred and once more returned to its cupboard.

Another skull, kept at Wardley Hall near Manchester, is said to be that of a Roman Catholic priest, executed for treason in 1641. After having been displayed on the tower of a Manchester church, it was recovered by a Catholic family and taken to Wardley. Like its Somerset equivalent, it would make noises whenever it was removed from the premises. Moreover, it was said to have caused violent thunderstorms and refused to remain buried. In the chilling words of ghost-hunter Eric Maple, it 'always managed to find its own way back [to the house] again'.

Burton Agnes Hall, a beautifully restored Elizabethan mansion in Humberside, contains the skull of Anne Griffith, daughter of Sir Henry Griffith, who built the residence in 1590. Like Theophilius Broome, Anne made the deathbed request that her head be cut off after she died and kept in the house, and the wish was granted. The skull, known locally as 'Owd Nance', was removed on several occasions. Each time, it screamed horrifyingly until it was returned to the house. To prevent any further outbreak of such supernatural annoyances, 'Owd

Nance' was bricked into the walls of the house itself in 1900 – and Burton Agnes has mercifully been tranquil ever since.

'Screaming skull' legends form a small but curious part of British folklore. One suggestion is that such stories have their roots in the Romano-British practice of making 'foundation sacrifices' – burying a human or animal victim in the foundations of a house to ensure good luck and to propitiate the gods. It was perhaps with some knowledge of such practices in mind that Anne Griffith and Theophilius Broome made their strange requests.

BROKEN VOWS

Another theory suggests that the stories arose from the rumoured custom of walling up monks and nuns as punishment for breaches of their chastity vows, though in fact such 'executions' were probably very rare indeed. A third source could be the Celts. They revered the head in their religion and often preserved severed heads as family treasures or offerings to the gods. Celtic cult heads of stone have been found in many places in Britain. But whatever their origins, 'screaming skulls' show a uniform objection to being moved from their chosen niches.

One such skull resides in Bettiscombe Manor, near Sherborne in Dorset. Bettiscombe, a fine building of mellow brick and white stone, dates

CASEBOOK

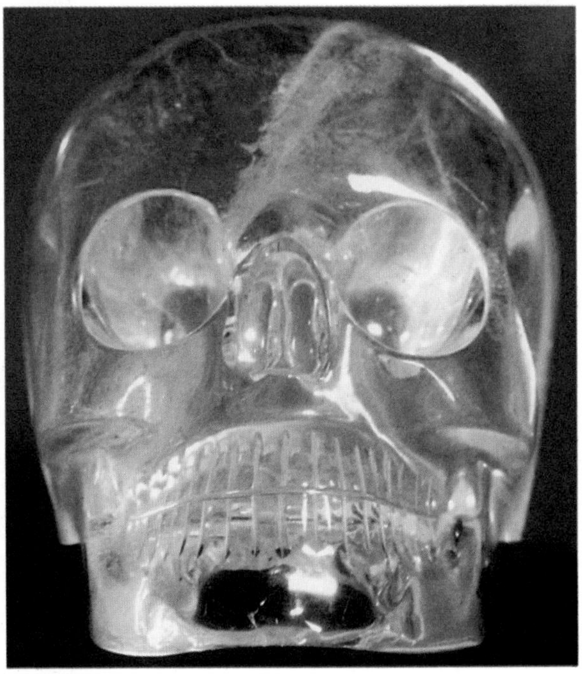

SKULLS OF DOOM

Magnificent crystal skulls of mysterious origin – such as the one *above*, currently housed in London's British Museum – are often said to trigger spectacular reactions, and could well have had important mystical significance. The Mitchell-Hedges skull, for instance, said to have been found in British Honduras beneath a Mayan temple, is thought to be some 3,600 years old and to have been carved from a single block of rock-crystal – a task that must have taken all of 150 years or more, experts say. Some claim to have seen images within it, or to have heard growling noises or chanting emanating from within. Oddly, too, the skull frequently causes extreme thirst. Equally, however, it is acknowledged to have remarkable healing powers, and many who have been in its presence have claimed miraculous cures.

Anna Mitchell-Hedges, owner and custodian of the skull, has asserted that some people find it terrifying even to be in the same room as the skull. Anton LaVey, the notorious Satanist, has even claimed it was created by Satan himself. Others, meanwhile, consider the skull may be possessed by a spirit or poltergeist – perhaps not that far-fetched since crystals are widely believed to absorb living energies. Explorer and adventurer F. A. Mitchell Hedges, who claimed to have found the skull, asked that it be buried with him on his death, but this was a request not finally granted.

The resident skull at Wardley Hall near Manchester,* left, *is supposedly that of a Catholic priest. It not only screamed but also caused wild thunderstorms when removed from the premises.

The screaming skull of Bettiscombe Manor in Dorset,* far left, *rests on a table The skull is said to have taken revenge on someone who tossed it out of the house it loved. Family tradition has it that the relic is the head of a West Indian slave.

principally from the early 17th century. Parts of it are much older, however, and the land on which it stands has been inhabited since pre-history. The house was built by the Pinney family.

Earliest written accounts of the skull date from the early 18th century, but the story itself starts in 1685. At that time, Azariah Pinney, the squire of Bettiscombe, took part in the Monmouth rebellion against King James II. On the losing side, Pinney was exiled to the West Indies. As it turned out, his family flourished there, and his grandson, John Frederick Pinney, was able to return to Dorset in style, moving back to the lands of his ancestors. With him came a black slave who became part of the household. The slave had been promised that, on his death, his body would be returned by his master to Africa, from where he had been taken by slavers as a child.

John Pinney, however, died first. When the slave died shortly afterwards, no one kept the promise made to him and his body was buried in the local churchyard, near that of his master. It did not rest content and a mournful wailing seemed to emanate from the grave. Crop failure, cattle disease and storms also accompanied the months of moaning. Finally, the body was disinterred and the skull taken back to its adopted home in the manor house. There it has remained, fulfilling the double role of family heirloom and harbinger of doom to any that remove it. According to Michael Pinney, a direct descendant:

'It is said to scream and cause agricultural disaster if taken out of the house, and also causes the death, within a year, of the person who commits the deed. A photographer once carried it as far as the open doorway to take pictures of it, but my wife snatched it back indoors again without anything untoward occurring'.

Terrifying Vengeance

Local lore has it that the last time the skull was 'interfered with', it took its vengeance just as the legend says it would. At the beginning of the 20th century, a tenant who had leased Bettiscombe prior to moving to Australia, had a boisterous Christmas party at the manor. During the party, he took the skull and hurled it into a horse pond that lay at the side of the house.

The following morning, the skull was found not in the pond but on the doorstep. How did it get there, when it had to go up a flight of stairs and across a paved patio? One theory, according to Michael Pinney, was that 'it had been blown there by the wind, but it must have been a very strange and powerful wind. In the Thirties, however, I had an unannounced visit from three young Australians. One of them said that he was the son of the former tenant. His father had indeed died suddenly in Australia within a year of the incident, and his mother had always told him that the skull had brought a curse on them'.

Skulls placed in the niches of a French Celtic sanctuary,* above, *were offerings to the gods. Such heads may be a source for stories of skulls that scream.

Until alterations were made to the attics of Bettiscombe after the Second World War, the guardian skull had traditionally been kept in a small attic room. The remains of this room can still be seen today, among the chimney stacks and thick oak rafters under the roof. There is an alternative tale to the black slave legend connected with the attic. This version says that a young girl had been kept prisoner there, bedded on straw like an animal and fed through a grille in the door. Although there is no historical evidence to support the claims for this story, as there is for John Frederick Pinney and his slave, there is a strong family tradition that the skull's 'place' for many years was under the rafters.

InFocus

A GRISLY EXHIBIT

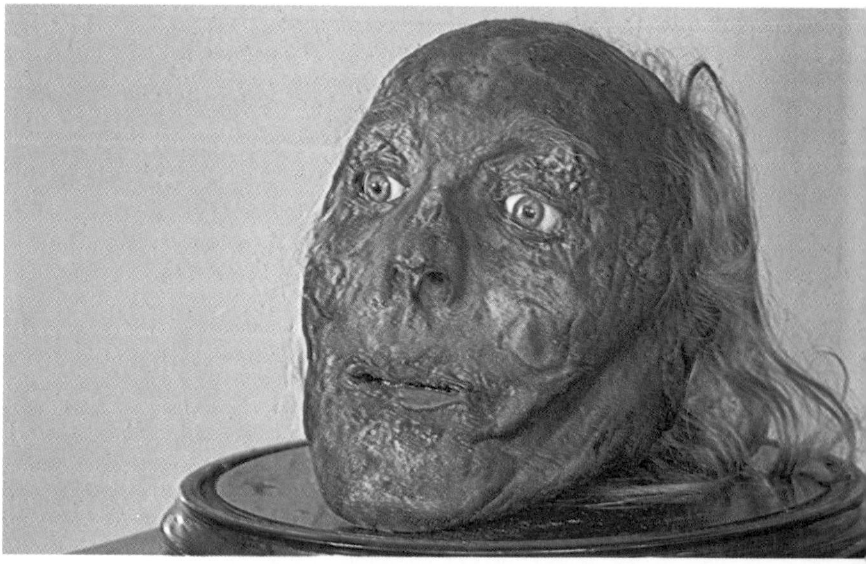

Jeremy Bentham, philosopher and political theorist whose reforming zeal helped to improve 19th-century life in Britain, shared with the screaming skulls a desire to remain in a favourite place after his death. And he went to elaborate lengths to do so.

Bentham arranged that, when he died, a surgeon friend was to embalm his head and place it upon his skeleton after the body had been dissected for the teaching of medical students. The skeleton, according to the fun-loving sage's instructions, was dressed in the

In the early 1960s, on the track of the Bettiscombe skull, researcher and author Eric Maple interviewed an old farm worker who claimed to remember 'hearing the skull screaming like a trapped rat in the attic'. Other locals claimed that during thunderstorms a rattling could sometimes be heard in the upper rooms – a rattling made by 'them' playing ninepins with the ancient relic. Exactly who 'they' were was left to the imagination.

Other snippets of lore about the skull seem to have been added over the years. Michael Pinney and his wife, for instance, are said to have been rather startled when a visitor asked if the skull had 'sweated blood in 1939 before the outbreak of the war, as it had in 1914'.

In fact, the 'screaming skull' of Bettiscombe Manor is probably neither that of the slave nor the girl who is the subject of the strange legend. In the 1950s, at Pinney's specific request, it was examined by Professor Gilbert Causey of the Royal College of Surgeons. Surprisingly, he pronounced it to be much older than anyone had suspected. It was, he said, the skull of a pre-historic young girl with delicate features who probably died between 3,000 and 4,000 years ago. So how did it come to be kept at Bettiscombe Manor, and why did such weird legends come to be associated with it?

DEATH BY THE SWORD

There is some evidence of a Roman-British settlement on the Bettiscombe site, which points back to the idea of a foundation sacrifice. But if Professor Causey's estimate is correct, the skull pre-dates any house that could have been built there by several hundred years.

An interesting parallel can be drawn with the screaming 'ghosts' of Reculver in Kent. For many years, a legend had persisted that screams and cries heard in woodland around this site of an early Roman settlement were made by the ghosts of children who had been murdered there. In 1964, important archaeological excavations were begun, during the course of which a number of children's skulls and bones were indeed unearthed. One of these even bore marks indicating that it had died by the sword. The skeletons were rather older than the Roman site, however, some dating from between 1000 and 500 BC.

Michael Pinney himself came up with a plausible, if unusual, explanation of the skull's arrival at Bettiscombe Manor: it is possible, he said, that it made its own way there.

Behind the manor, the steep slopes of wooded Pilsdon Pen stretch up far beyond the house's tall chimneys. The tor shows signs of prehistoric fortifications, dating from about the same period as Maiden Castle, the great earthworks fortress that lies some miles away to the south-east. Besides containing the remnants of hut circles, the tor is also studded with small burial mounds and cairns. Pinney excavated some of them through professional interest as an archaeologist. As he has explained:

'I can't prove it, of course, but I rather suspect that the skull was worked loose from the soil at the top of the hill, tumbled into the stream and rolled down the sloping bed of the brook and down into the outhouse here. Such a find would have been traumatic to say the least in a superstitious age. The finder may well have tried to get rid of it, only to feel uneasy about the event – perhaps odd things did occur which convinced him that the skull wished to stay where it had landed. Then the stories began to grow as news of the skull's arrival spread.'

The story of the skull at Bettiscombe might easily have reached the ears of old Theophilius Broome at Chilton Cantelo in the adjoining county of Somerset. Indeed, perhaps it influenced his decision to arrange that his own head should stay above ground.

For their part, the Pinneys have prospered despite the bizarre relic. So far, however, they have refused to allow the family 'heirloom' to be taken outside the walls of the old manor. Meanwhile, other apparently man-made skulls, carved from crystal, also make noises and display extraordinary powers, it is said – some even exerting supposed evil influences over those who mock them.

Professor Gilbert Causey of the Royal College of Surgeons,* top, *was called in to give an expert opinion on the Bettiscombe skull. He said it was that of a young prehistoric woman – a far cry from the slave of the traditional story.

The ruins of Reculver church in Kent,* above, *are connected with local legends about children's ghosts that scream pitifully. Skulls dug up on the site proved to be from an earlier time than the stories had indicated – suggesting that screaming skull stories may have origins deep in ancient tradition.

clothes he had liked best. It was then seated in a glass-fronted upright mahogany box. This was placed in University College London, of which Bentham was a founder and constant supporter. It has remained on a landing of this building ever since Bentham's death in 1832.

A wax model has replaced the deteriorated head, but the figure still wears the genial philosopher's straw hat and holds his trusty walking stick. A number of witnesses have said that Bentham's ghost, tapping the stone flags with the cane, often walks the corridors near his curious coffin. According to Bill Grundy, the television producer who made a film of Bentham, the ghost 'seems to appear most in times of trouble' – during the 1940 Blitz, for example. It is as though the philosopher had appointed himself the 'guardian of University College'.

Freda and Greta Chaplin, **above,** *are twins who, since early childhood, have exhibited 'mirror-imaging' to an uncanny degree.*

TWIN SOULS

SOME IDENTICAL TWINS BEHAVE SO SIMILARLY THAT THEY SEEM TO SHARE ONE IDENTITY, THE SAME PERSONALITY. IS THIS REALLY POSSIBLE?

Strange though it may seem, identical twins who are reared apart often exhibit more similarities of behaviour than those who grow up together. When they reach their early teens, however, most twins begin to develop a desire to assert individuality, even if this is expressed only by dressing differently. A few, however, fail to do this, and grow up as if they were one person.

One of the most striking examples of this phenomenon emerged in 1980 when the 38-year-old Chaplin twins, Greta and Freda, were brought before magistrates in York, England, charged with having behaved in a manner likely to cause a breach of the peace.

They had, it was asserted, been harassing Ken Iveson, once a neighbour of theirs, for 15 years, following him about, waiting for him outside the glassworks where he was employed as a lorry driver, shouting abuse at him, and even hitting him with their handbags. This extraordinary fixation, however was not the reason that psychiatrists, social workers and journalists were so fascinated by the case: it was the fact that the twins spoke in what appeared to be precise synchronisation that intrigued everyone.

ACTING IN UNISON

Greta and Freda also exhibited other signs that seem to indicate that they were effectively one person – speaking, moving and dressing identically. Children in York even believed them to be witches, throwing stones at them in the street, while adults spat in their faces.

They once had identical grey coats, but as one originally came with green buttons and one with grey, they cut off two buttons each, so that both coats had two green and two grey. When given two different pairs of gloves, they simply took one from each pair. Similarly, a gift of two differently coloured bars of soap caused them real anguish. They burst into tears, then solved the problem by cutting the bars in half and sharing them. Once, when Greta got a prescription for bronchitis, Freda demanded the same medicine.

The twins have also be seen to eat in unison, slowly raising forks and spoons together, and both finishing up one item of food before starting on the next. But most uncannily, they appear to speak the same words at the same time, especially when excited or under stress. Careful listening, however, reveals that the words of one come out a split second later than those of the other.

They also exhibit 'mirror-imaging' which is characteristically found in twins that develop from a single split fertilized egg. In typical cases, one twin is right-handed, the other left-handed; the whorls of the hair grow clockwise in one and anti-clockwise in the other; and the left thumbprint of one almost matches the right thumbprint of the other.

The Chaplins also generally dress in mirror image of each other, although a casual observer would say they dress identically, and eccentrically, in their long skirts, clashing colours and headscarves. When Greta wears a bracelet on her left wrist, Freda might wear one on her right; and if one breaks a shoelace, the other has been known to pull out a lace from her opposite shoe.

Although the twins have been difficult and unpredictable to interview, some journalists have managed to talk to them. Some years ago, one writer elicited this telling statement from them: 'We're so close that we're really one person. We know exactly what each other is thinking because we're just one brain'. This journalist later remarked: 'You go gently for fear they'll disappear and leave you thinking you dreamed them up, like something from Alice in Wonderland'. She must have gained their confidence, however, because she did find out that they wear different underclothes.

The Chaplin twins first achieved national notoriety in 1980, when they were brought before York magistrates, charged with persistently hounding Ken Iveson, right, for 15 years. Their fixation with him became intolerable: they would lie in wait for him and shout abuse or hit him – this, it seemed, was their way of showing affection. It was their appearance in court that finally revealed the extent of their simultaneous behaviour. For many years, the twins, below, were the focus of many newspaper and magazine articles, and the centre of a medical controversy.

The twins have also been seen to argue, sometimes hitting each other lightly with their identical handbags, then sitting sulking together for hours. But, if they believe they are the same person, then how can an argument happen?

A closer examination of their history shows that their extraordinary togetherness was actively fostered by their parents, especially their mother, who dressed them identically and allowed them no friends. They were not mentally abnormal and attended a secondary school near their York home. Teachers and fellow pupils remember them as neat, clean and quiet; and although among the slowest students, they could read and write as well as the others in their class. The deputy headmaster of the school had no doubts about what turned them into the disturbed adults they later became: 'It was clear that they had a doting mother who never allowed them any separate identity.... The other kids just saw them as a bit quaint. I don't think they were acutely isolated then or maladjusted'. They had not, at that point, begun to speak simultaneously.

Their mother's attitude towards them seems to have triggered off a pattern of abnormal behaviour, perhaps aided by their biological affinity. Both parents seem to have been uncommunicative and friendless, and Mrs Chaplin was known to be obsessively houseproud. This emphasis on cleanliness may explain why at one time the twins' only apparent pleasure was bathing together, grooming each other, and washing each other's hair. They were said to use an average of 14 bars of soap and three large bottles of shampoo each week.

ACUTE HARRASSMENT

Ken Iveson – the subject of their harrassment – had grown up next door to the Chaplins, and married when the twins were two years old, continuing to live at his parents' home with his wife and children. Neither he nor his parents had ever set foot inside their neighbours' house; they were never asked in and never saw anyone else pay social calls. Iveson would, however, occasionally pass the time of day with the girls who, isolated from the outside world, obviously took this as some kind of romantic encouragement. They rapidly became a nuisance and, eventually, after 15 years, Iveson could take no more of it. Their case came to court.

The twins' parents had, it transpired, forced them to leave home. When asked about this, Freda and Greta reply as one: 'Something must have happened. Yes, yes, yes. Something strange. Must have happened'.

Mr and Mrs Chaplin refused to talk to the press, and exactly why the twins left is not known. They now live near London.

Curiously, local psychiatrists, called in by the court as expert witnesses, were baffled by the twins' case, describing it vaguely as 'a personality disorder'. Yet their behaviour towards Ken Iveson matches the textbook symptoms of *erotomania*, a form of schizophrenia in which there is delusion of being loved by a particular person. It has been recognised as a clinical condition since the mid-1960s. Dr Morgan Enoch, of the Maudsley Hospital

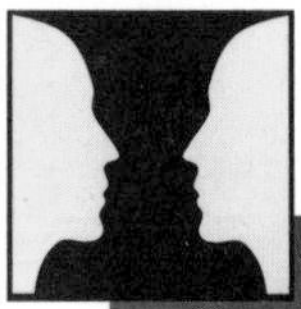

"IDEOGLOSSIA, THE PHENOMENON IN WHICH TWO INDIVIDUALS, MOST OFTEN TWIN CHILDREN, DEVELOP A PRIVATE LANGUAGE, USUALLY INVOLVES HIGHLY ORIGINAL VOCABULARY AND SYNTAX."

in south London, has also discovered that if one identical twin is schizophrenic, then the other is also likely to suffer from the disease.

But does *erotomania* – or any form of schizophrenia – entirely explain the Chaplins' behaviour, especially their strange way of speaking? In their case, there seem to be many highly influential factors – genetic, environmental and social.

PRIVATE TONGUES

The Chaplins' peculiarity of speech is just one aspect of the way twins sometimes communicate with one another. Better known is *ideoglossia,* the phenomenon in which two individuals, most often twin children, develop between them a unique and private language. It usually involves highly original vocabulary and syntax.

It is, however, commonly confused with a subcategory, twin speech – a private collection of distorted words and idioms used, it is estimated, by 40 per cent of all twins because they feel isolated, or secretive, or both. Most twins tend to give it up at the age of three, although as twin Robert A. Nelson wrote to the *New York Times* in 1932: 'It is a matter of record in my family that when my brother and I first started to talk, and until we were well past six, we conversed with each other in a strange tongue of our own'. The only other person who could understand their particular speech was their brother, who was eight years older.

Identical twins, Grace and Virginia, were born in 1970 in Columbus, Georgia, USA, to Tom Kennedy and his German wife Christine. The day after the girls were born, Grace suddenly raised her head and stared at her father. Virginia did the same thing the next day. These strangely precocious acts, labelled 'convulsive seizures' by doctors, continued periodically for six months, in spite of treatment. At 17 months, they apparently developed *ideoglossia,* beginning to speak rapidly in a language of their own – their only concession to English being 'mommy' and 'daddy'. They called each other 'Poto' and 'Cabenga'.

'Snap aduk Cabenga, chase die-dipana': at this mysterious command from one of the Kennedy twins,* left, *they both began to play with the doll's house. Grace and Virginia were believed to be mentally retarded until it was discovered that they had developed a language of their own, complete with extensive vocabulary and syntax. 'Poto' and 'Cabenga', as they called themselves, were investigated by speech therapist Anne Koenecke at the Children's Hospital in San Diego, California. She finally coaxed them into speaking a little English and eventually discovered that their private language comprised both made-up and mispronounced words. It was clearly a vocabulary designed to exclude others.

When the twins were two years old, the family moved to California, but there were very few other children in the neighbourhood with whom Grace and Virginia could play. So they were left to themselves or entrusted to their maternal grandmother, Paula Kunert, a stern disciplinarian who still spoke only her native German.

In 1977, the speech therapists at the Children's Hospital in San Diego, California, began to study the twins, taping their conversation in the hope of learning something about the mysteries of developing language. Is it, they wondered, predominantly a product of genetic programming or a learned response to the world around them? A typical conversation between the girls would run:

'Genebene manita.'
'Nomemee.'
'Eebedeebeda. Dis din qui naba.'
'Neveda. Ca Baedabada.'

When the study began, the twins spoke no English, but gradually the therapists coaxed some out of them – which they spoke with a curious high-speed delivery. Someone even tried to talk to them in their own language, but they just looked at her as if she were crazy.

'Snap aduk, Cabenga, chase die-dipana,' said 'Poto' masterfully. Having apparently issued a command, she and 'Cabenga' instantly began to play with a doll's house.

Analysis of tapes showed that their communication was something less than true *ideoglossia.* Many apparently new words turned out to be mispronounced words and phrases from German and English, jammed together and said at high speed. However, a few words, such as 'nu-nukid' and 'pulana', remain unidentified. As the twins grew older, they suddenly began to speak English – but they remain silent about the meaning of their once private language.

DIVINING BY NUMBERS

USING NUMBERS IN ORDER TO DIVINE THE FUTURE OR INTERPRET CHARACTER OFTEN ANSWERS A DEEP-SEATED HUMAN NEED TO SEEK MEANING IN COMMONPLACE EVENTS. LEARN HOW TO CALCULATE YOUR OWN PERSONAL NUMBER, AS HIDDEN IN YOUR NAME, AND FIND OUT THE SECRETS THAT NUMEROLOGISTS BELIEVE IT HOLDS

Can the study of numbers reveal the future? Can they be used to reveal hidden aspects of a person's character? Practitioners of the ancient art of numerology believe they can.

Numerology is a method of making names, dates or events correspond to numbers – generally between one and nine, although sometimes 11 and 22 are included in the system. Each number has a certain significance: William Shakespeare, for instance, corresponds to five, the number of versatility and resourcefulness.

The correspondence is established by a very simple identification of the letters of the alphabet with numbers according to the 'Hebrew system', as numerologists call it, and as illustrated in the table below..

To find your number, simply write down the number corresponding to each letter of your name, and add them together. If the resulting number is over nine, add up its digits and keep doing this until the result is less than 10. For instance, the letters of the name Charlotte Brönte add to five. (Charlotte = 3 + 5 + 1 + 2 + 3 + 7 + 4 + 4 + 5 = 34; Brönte = 2 + 2 + 7 + 5 + 4 + 5 = 25; 34 + 25 = 59; 5 + 9 = 14; 1 + 4 =5.)

If the digits corresponding to your name add up to one, you are probably a dominant kind of person, a leader. 'Ones' are pioneers, inventors, designers – but they often put their plans into practice with little regard for the way they will affect those most directly involved. They tend to dominate everyone they meet, rarely have close friends and are sometimes, despite their confident appearance, very lonely people.

Two is interpreted by modern numerologists as the number of passive, receptive people. 'Twos' are quiet, unambitious, gentle, kind, tidy and conscientious. They often get their own way, however, by gentle persuasion rather than force. They are inclined to be hesitant, and to make problems for themselves by putting off decisions for no good reason. This quality can sometimes lead them into difficult situations.

THE 'HEBREW' NUMEROLOGICAL SYSTEM

1	2	3	4	5	6	7	8
A	B	C	D	E	U	O	F
I	K	G	M	H	V	Z	P
Q	R	L	T	N	W		
J		S			X		
Y							

In Albrecht Dürer's engraving Melencolia I *(1514)*, below, *the artist has included a magic square in the upper right-hand corner, its rows, columns and diagonals of numbers all adding up to the same total. Such squares, epitomising the mystical properties of numbers, have often been used as talismans.*

The table, below left, *is that most generally used by numerologists to calculate the number corresponding to a particular name or word.*

Traditionally, three is one of the most extrovert numbers, belonging to intelligent, creative and witty people, who generally make friends easily and seem to succeed at anything to which they turn their hands. They are proud, ambitious and pleasure-loving, but their great weakness lies in an inability to take anything – ideas or people – seriously for very long.

Four, like two, is a number corresponding to dependable, down-to-earth people. They are born organisers. They lack the volatility of 'ones' and 'threes', but they make up for this by fairness and meticulous attention to detail. They may be subject to sudden irrational rages or depressions that seem extraordinary in people who are usually models of calmness. Four has also long been regarded by numerologists as the number of ill-luck; indeed, those whose number is four often seem to pay dearly for any success they achieve in life.

Five is the number of bright, fast-moving, clever, impatient people. They live on their nerves, and love meeting people and seeking out new experiences. They are often physically attractive but rather feckless, hating to be tied down. Five is the number that represents sex (the digits of which also add up to five), and people whose number is five often have varied and exciting love-lives that can be problematic. Sometimes the sexual side of their nature may even show itself in excesses or perversions.

People whose number is six are among the happiest of the whole numerological system. They are happy, tranquil, well-balanced and home-loving. They are affectionate, loyal, sincere and conscientious. They are often creative, and many of them are successful in the performing arts. The negative aspect of their character is a tendency to be rather fussy, conceited and self-satisfied.

Seven is the number of the loner, the introspective scholar, philosopher, mystic or occultist. These people tend to stand aside from the mainstream of life, content to observe it. They are dignified, self-controlled and reserved. They tend to be indifferent to worldly wealth but, while they may seem aloof and stand-offish, make loyal friends. Despite their powerful intellects, they are often surprisingly bad at putting their thoughts into words, and may even dislike discussing them if they feel their own ideas are being challenged.

Eight represents worldly success, people who have this number often making successful businessmen, politicians or lawyers. Their success is, however, often built on a great deal of hard work, likely to be done at considerable expense to their warmer, more human qualities. They often seem to be hard, egocentric and grasping; but behind the unsympathetic exterior, there can be a whimsical streak that endears them to other people.

Nine stands for the height of intellectual and spiritual achievement. People whose number is nine are the idealists, the romantics, the visionaries – poets, missionaries, doctors, religious teachers, brilliant scientists. Their great qualities are unselfishness, self-discipline and determination and their idealism is concerned with mankind as a whole. In their everyday lives, they may be inclined to seek the limelight, and to be fickle friends or lovers, however.

Some numerologists also employ the numbers 11 and 22. They believe that these represent a higher plane of experience than the numbers one to nine. Eleven is the number of those who experience revelations and suffer martyrdom; those with names that add up to this number are often people with a strong vocation for their work – preachers, doctors, nurses or teachers. They tend to be idealists in many respects.

Twenty-two, meanwhile, is the 'master' number; and people whose names add to 22 combine the best qualities of all the other numbers.

The number of New York, seen below, is three – representing pride, ambition and love of pleasure, but an inability to take ideas and people seriously for long. Some would find this an apt description of the USA's glittering capital of finance and fashion.

PERSPECTIVES

MYSTICAL NUMBERS

In the 16th century, the Western esoteric tradition – witchcraft, alchemy and astrology, for example – began to be influenced by a complex Jewish mystical system known as the *Kabbala* (Hebrew for 'tradition'), much of it concerned with the power and meaning of numbers in the Hebrew scriptures.

Since, in Hebrew, each letter also represents a number, Kabbalists would, for example, take a Hebrew word from the Bible, translate each letter into a number, add them up and then find another word with letters adding up to the same total. These words, they claimed, had a mystical connection with each other.

Kabbalists also enjoyed speculating on biblical passages containing actual numbers. The measurements of Noah's Ark, for instance, was thought to be imbued with meaning as to God's nature, even reflecting the anatomy of Adam Kadmon, the archetypal human in whose image mankind was supposedly created.

The ground-plan at the heart of the Kabbalistic system is the Tree of Life – a geometrical arrangement of ten spheres, the so-called *sefirot,* each of which is associated with a divine attribute (such as Wisdom and Mercy), and 22 paths connecting the spheres.

The study of the Hebrew letters, with their corresponding numbers, their inner meaning and position on the 22 paths of the Tree of Life, is said to give Kabbalists a key to understanding how the creation originally came about.

Eleven is the number of those with a strong sense of vocation – such as Churchill,* left, *and Florence Nightingale,* far left. *Albert Einstein,* below left, *even called himself a 'lone traveller'. What Pablo Picasso,* below, *was told by his mother could be said of any of them: 'If you become a soldier, you'll be a general. If you become a monk, you'll end up as the Pope'.

Apply this procedure to the name you were given at birth and you find, numerologists claim, the characteristics you were born with and that will underlie your personality throughout your life; apply it to the name you give yourself, or would like to have, and you will discover how your experiences in the world have moulded your personality. Using a nickname, you will be able to ascertain what your friends think of you. Comparing her maiden and married names, a married woman can find out how married life is likely to have changed her.

Hidden Numbers

The total of vowel numbers in your name is your heart number, which shows your inner character. The total of consonants is your personality number, which indicates your outward personality, or the impression you make on the people around you. (This distinction is derived from Hebrew, in which only the consonants of any word are actually written down; the vowels are therefore 'hidden', and represent the aspects of the personality that are not outwardly apparent.)

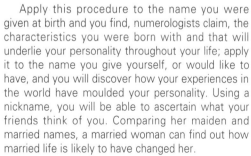

Like the character types suggested by the sign of the zodiac under which you were born, the traits indicated by these numbers are to be regarded as indicating a general type, not a detailed description. But that people whose names add to the same number share certain personality traits can be supported with numerous examples. The letters of the names Winston S. Churchill, Einstein, Pablo Picasso and Florence Nightingale, for instance, all add up to 11 – the number belonging to those with strong vocations in life.

The same technique can be applied to the names of cities, and many of the results seem to confirm the beliefs of numerologists. London adds up to five, indicating many-sidedness and resilience; New York to three, indicating brilliance and glitter. The ancient cities of Oxford and Cambridge both have the number seven – the number of the aloof, inwardly-turned scholar.

Numerology can also be used to assess the characteristic of a year, decade or century. The 1920s, depicted* top*, the third decade of the century, had the number three – the number of the pleasure-loving and fickle; but the 1930s,* centre*, corresponded to four, representing unstable moods and ill-luck. (The decade began with the Depression – a Christmas Day dole queue is shown here – and ended with the Second World War.) After VE Day,* above*, the 1940s saw the return of prosperity and renewed experiment in fashions and life-styles – in character with the decade's number five ('bright, clever, impatient').

Numerologists believe that numbers can also be used to suggest beneficial courses of action. If your number is seven, for example, you should be sure to make difficult decisions or perform important tasks on days of the month that add up to seven: that is, the seventh, the 16th and the 25th. Certain years, too, can be good or bad for an individual. To find your year-number, add your month and date of birth to the current year: 1992, for instance, is a 2-year for someone born on 24 February (24 + 2 + 1992 = 2018; 2 + 0 + 1 + 8 = 11; 1 + 1 = 2), indicating it is a year for quiet reflection and gentle action, rather then forcefulness.

Why, though, should the system work? Numerologists are quick to point out instances that seem to show the importance of number, such as in the career of Louis XIV of France. He came to the throne in 1643, which adds up to 14; he died in 1715, which adds up to 14, at the age of 77 – which adds up to 14. But is it just coincidence?

Numerologists counter this question by claiming that there is no such thing as coincidence. They believe the Universe is like a vast harp with countless strings, each vibrating at a certain rate, characterised by a number. Number, they believe, is at the root of all things. They point out, too, that science has found that light, sound, atomic structure and many other things are dependent on frequency, or number. But what of the objection that, even if this view of the Universe is correct, basing the system on a person's name must be wrong, since the naming of a child is largely a matter of the personal tastes and whims of the parents? The numerologists have their answers ready, as Florence Campbell, an American, explains:

'The Soul has taken many journeys in the past and knows its present needs. The Soul wants progress upwards on the Great Spiral and chooses for the incarnating ego the vowels whose total shall accomplish this purpose... There is a long "Dark Cycle" before the child is born, and during this Dark Cycle the vibrations that are to label the new life are so impressed upon the subconscious minds of the parents that they are compelled to carry out the plan.'

In other words, the numerologist believes that the name each person carries is no accident, and that it tells something significant about its bearer, in a code to which the numerologist has the key.

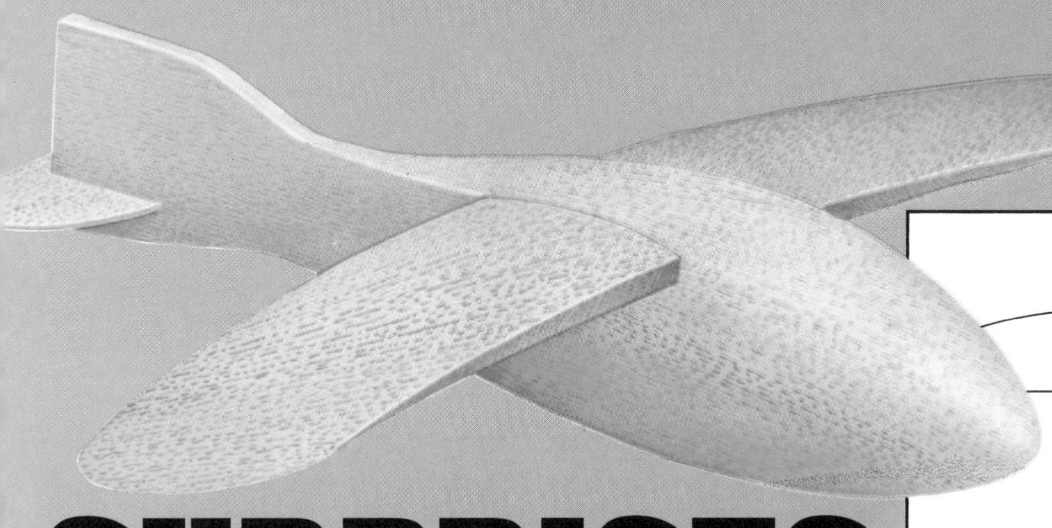

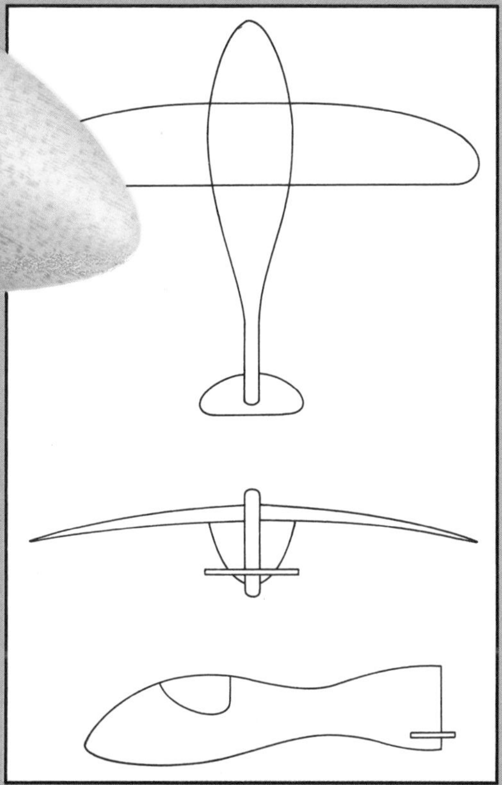

SURPRISES FROM THE PAST

MODERN RESEARCH SUGGESTS THAT OUR ANCIENT ANCESTORS MAY HAVE HAD TECHNOLOGIES FAR MORE ADVANCED THAN OUR OWN

In a museum in Cairo, Egypt, a small wooden model was on display. No one could mistake what it was: one glance showed the wings, fin, tailplane and deep, bulky body of some kind of aircraft. The body of the model was just under 6 inches (15 centimetres) long, and its wingspan extended to just over 7 inches (18 centimetres). Made of light sycamore wood, it would glide a short distance when thrown from the hand.

It would not have been a great surprise to see a model like this in a science museum. But this model had pride of place as an exhibit in Cairo's Museum of Antiquities, and it probably dated from around 200 BC.

This ancient model is a glaring challenge to our ideas about the development of technology. And it is only one of innumerable oddities and enigmas that fuel speculation about the scientific knowledge and engineering skill of our ancestors.

No one had connected the wooden model with the idea of artificial flight when it was first found in 1898 – five years before the Wright brothers had even made their first successful powered flight – in a tomb in the ancient Egyptian city of Saqqara. It had been stored there in a box together with figurines of birds. Dr Kahlil Messiha, who rediscovered it in 1969, was astounded by its evident resemblance to a modern aircraft.

A committee of archaeological and aeronautical experts studied the model, and they pointed out the cambering of its wings – that is, the curve of the upper surface, which generates lift – and the 'anhedral' or downward droop of its wingtips, which provides stability. They conjectured that the craft was a model of a full-sized aircraft. It would have been a 'powered glider', designed to carry heavy loads at very low speeds – probably less than 60 miles per hour (95 km/h). It could even have been propelled by an engine mounted at the rear, at a point where the model's tail is now broken.

The committee was sufficiently convinced of the importance of their find to devote a special display to it in Cairo, and the discovery prompted a fresh look at 'bird models' in other collections. Over a dozen similar 'gliders' were found in other tombs. Could they really be models of ancient aircraft?

The idea of ancient aeronauts is possibly almost as surprising as that of ancient astronauts, but aero-modellers may have been at work in South America as early as the first millennium after Christ.

The working model glider,* above, *was made in Egypt in 200 BC. Some experts believe it is a model of a full-sized 'powered glider': others, however, have pointed out that it could be a weather-vane.

Gold ornaments from South America, made some time between AD 500 and 800, are shown* below. *One of them,* left, *bears a striking resemblance to a modern delta-winged jet.

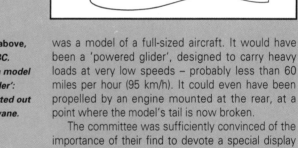

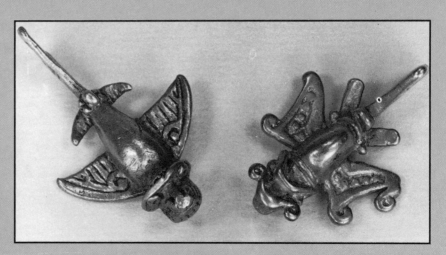

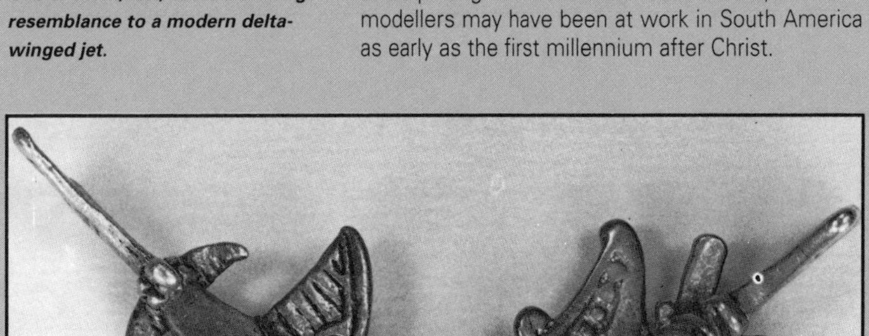

The supposed aircraft models that have come to light are a number of small gold ornaments that have been found in Colombia, Costa Rica, Venezuela and Peru. Aeronautical experts and biologists have compared these ancient objects with the forms of bats, sting rays and birds. One example was spotted in a collection of ancient art objects from Colombia by Ivan T. Sanderson, head of the Society for the Investigation of the Unexplained in the United States. It was a pendant, 2 inches (5 centimetres) long, intended to be worn on a necklace or bracelet. The Colombian archaeologists had classified it as 'zoömorphic', or animal-shaped; but it looks much more a delta-winged jet fighter than like any animal or bird. It has triangular appendages that look just like the wings of several types of modern supersonic aeroplane, a small straight tailplane, a tail fin – and there are even what appear to be insignia on one side of the fin. Yet the ornament is attributed to the early Chimú (who are also called Mochica), a pre-Incan society that flourished in South America from about 200 BC to 800 AD.

Being so very small, and made of solid gold, the model does not, of course, fly, but the resemblance to certain advanced aircraft built since World War II is so remarkable that one is inevitably left wondering whether it was indeed produced as a replica.

***One of the most impressive pieces of evidence for the highly advanced states of some early technologies is the so-called 'Baghdad battery',* below. *It was made during the Parthian occupation of Iraq at some time between 140 BC and AD 224 – and, astonishingly, could have been made to generate electricity. A West German Egyptologist, Dr Arne Eggebricht,* below left, *has proved, using a model that the battery could have been used for electroplating small figures with gold,* bottom.**

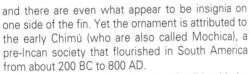

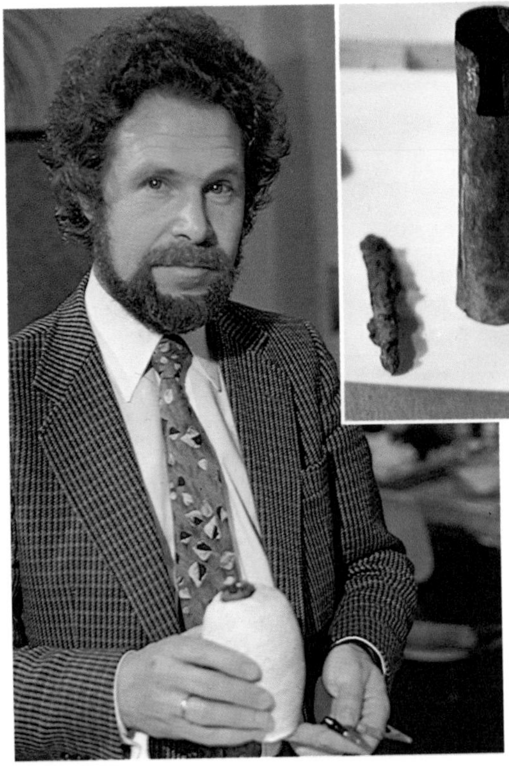

However, although these objects look like jets, how safe a guide is that? Curiously, the symbol on the Colombian ornament's 'tail fin' clearly resembles the Semitic 'beth', or letter B. Some researchers have therefore jumped to the conclusion that the aircraft perhaps originally came from the Middle East.

Over-enthusiastic interpretation may lead some people to regard all extravagant claims for ancient objects with suspicion, but it becomes necessary to pay serious attention when a functioning device from an 'impossible' date is discovered. The Saqqara glider is one example; and an equally impressive one is the 'Baghdad battery'.

Externally, the battery is a clay pot under 6 inches (15 centimetres) tall. It is stoppered with bitumen, in which is mounted a copper cylinder that runs down about 4 inches (10 centimetres) inside the pot. The cylinder is made from strips of copper soldered together, and is closed with a copper cap. Inside the cylinder is an iron rod that been heavily corroded, probably by acid. The pot was found in Baghdad, and dates from some time during the Parthian domination of this part of Iraq, which lasted from 140 BC to AD 224.

Ancient Electricity

When the archaeologist Wilhelm König came across the 'Baghdad battery' in a museum in Iraq in 1937, he immediately saw how it could have been used to generate an electric voltage. Experiments made with modern replicas some years later confirmed König's belief that it could indeed have served this purpose. To generate a voltage, it would be necessary to pour a suitable liquid into the cylinder. A large variety of fluids could have been used, including acetic acid or citric acid (these are the main constituents of vinegar and lemon juice respectively), or copper sulphate solution. This arrangement will generate between 1½ and 2 volts between the copper cylinder and the iron rod. If a series of such cells were to be linked (forming a 'battery' in the proper sense of the word), the available voltage could be increased substantially.

The most likely use for electricity among the Parthians would have been the electroplating of figurines, an advance on the art of gilding which dated back centuries before them. The battery could have been used to apply a voltage between a metal statuette and an ingot of gold while both were immersed in an electrolyte. Gold would have been transferred through the liquid to be deposited as a thin film on the figure's surface.

Similar clay pots have been found at other sites near Baghdad. They are a salutary reminder that our conceptions of mankind's historical development are often based as much on ignorance as on knowledge of skills of a particular period.

Static electricity was known to the ancients: they knew, for instance, that when amber (in Greek, *elektron*) was rubbed, it would attract light objects such as dust and hairs. So the technique of generating electrical current – which is electric charge in motion – could have been an equally haphazard, isolated discovery centuries before its generally recognised initial use. Neither finding seemed to lead to further technological development or insight into the causes of the phenomenon, however, although

" IT BECOMES NECESSARY TO PAY SERIOUS ATTENTION WHEN A FUNCTIONING DEVICE FROM AN IMPOSSIBLE DATE IS DISCOVERED. "

some enthusiasts have claimed that the Parthians – and, before them, the ancient Egyptians – used electric light.

There are, indeed, enough soberly accredited anomalies of technology from the past to keep us well aware that some of our ancestors did develop their technology – to astonishingly high levels.

TREASURE SHIP

In 1900, sponge divers found the wreck of a treasure ship, almost 2,000 years old, off the Greek island of Antikythera, between the Peloponnesian peninsula and Crete. It was laden with bronze and marble statues, and may have been sailing to Rome when it went down in about 65 BC. In its cargo was found a mass of wood and bronze, the metal so badly corroded that it could just be made out as the remains of gearwheels and engraved scales. Only in 1954 did Derek J. de Solla Price of Cambridge University finally deduce that the mechanism was a kind of astronomical clock, far ahead of anything that was to be seen in Europe again for hundreds of years. In fact, the mechanism, when new, must have borne a remarkable resemblance to a good modern mechanical clock.

The device consisted of at least 20 gearwheels, supported on a number of bronze plates, the whole mounted in a wooden box. When a shaft that passed through the side of the box was turned, the pointers moved at different speeds over dials, which were protected by doors. Inscriptions in Greek explained how to operate the machine and how to read the dials.

> **"** THERE ARE ENOUGH SOBERLY ACCREDITED ANOMALIES OF TECHNOLOGY FROM THE PAST TO KEEP US WELL AWARE THAT SOME OF OUR ANCESTORS DID DEVELOP THEIR TECHNOLOGY – TO ASTONISHINGLY HIGH LEVELS. **"**

Among the treasures recovered in 1900 from a ship wrecked some 2,000 years ago off the Greek island of Antikythera were the remains of bronze scientific objects,* above, *so badly corroded that it was almost impossible to make out what they were. After decades of speculation – and cleaning by the Greek National Archaeological Museum in Athens – the objects were identified as 'arithmetical models of the solar system... which evolved into the orrery and the planetarium'. Nothing so complex would be seen again until the clocks of the Renaissance, such as the one,* right, *made in Germany in the 15th century.

The device was a working model of the celestial bodies – Sun, Moon, and the planets then known to the Greeks. Their relative positions in the sky were shown with great accuracy. The time of day was also indicated by the pointers.

In Price's words: 'Nothing like this instrument is preserved elsewhere. Nothing comparable to it is known from any scientific text or literary allusion'. He goes on to say that: 'It seems likely that the Antikythera tradition was part of a large corpus of knowledge that has since been lost to us, but was known to the Arabs'. Mechanical calendar devices were indeed made by them centuries later, and they are said to have inspired the clock-makers of medieval Europe.

But what other remarkable inventions might such a body of knowledge have contained? What forces, benevolent or malevolent, might the ancients have commanded that did not stay alive in the memory of their descendants? That, of course, remains a mystery.

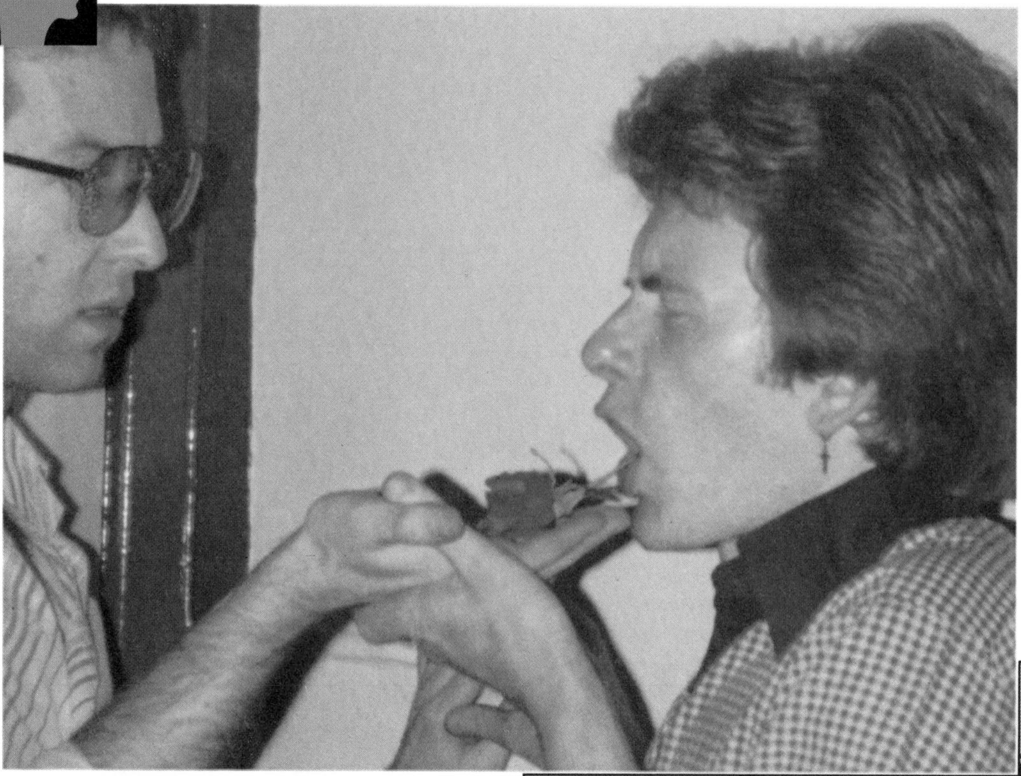

OUT OF THIN AIR

FLOWERS, FRUIT, ORNAMENTS AND EVEN LIVE ANIMALS HAVE SUPPOSEDLY BEEN MATERIALISED THROUGH SOME ESPECIALLY GIFTED MEDIUMS. THE PRODUCTION OF SUCH OBJECTS, CALLED 'APPORTS', IS SURROUNDED BY MUCH CONTROVERSY – AND SOMETIMES THE CRY OF 'FRAUD'

Former medium Paul McElhoney, top, *seems to be producing an apport of a fresh flower from his mouth. There were no signs that it had been regurgitated. Flower apports,* above, *were not all that allegedly appeared at his demonstrations. The cast metal model of Cologne Cathedral,* right, *landed in the palm of SPR council member Anita Gregory 'from nowhere'. Ceros, McElhoney's spirit guide said it was a gift from her dead father. Mrs Gregory discovered later that her father had spent his honeymoon in a hotel overlooking Cologne Cathedral.*

The problem about those who claim to produce apports is seen in the case of one-time London medium, Paul McElhoney, who frequently held demonstrations at his home in the 1970s and 80s. Like many mediums, he performed his apport-producing displays in a darkened room – something that would normally arouse the suspicions of believers as well as non-believers.

In McElhoney's case, however, several observers reported that flowers did indeed appear to have apported from his mouth. In November 1981, spiritualist Michael Cleary told *Psychic News* of an experience he had at the medium's home circle. He said he had searched McElhoney and the seance room before the proceedings began. During the seance, the medium was entranced by a spirit called Ceros. 'When Ceros brought the first flowers, the lights were on,' said Cleary. 'I looked into Paul's mouth. There was nothing there. Then a [fresh] flower began to fall from his mouth. Carnations are very significant in my family. I had previously asked my mother in the spirit world to bring that kind of flower. When Ceros apported a carnation for me, he said it was a present from a woman in the spirit world.'

Another witness to this phenomenon was author and investigator Guy Lyon Playfair, who also received a carnation. When home, he put it in his mouth and tried to talk as the medium had done. 'The stalk stuck in my throat. I nearly threw up. Paul talked easily and then produced the carnation.'

Although Cleary said he had searched the medium and the room before McElhoney began his demonstration, he failed to look in the tape-recorder which McElhoney was using. During one demonstration, a reporter – determined to establish the truth – switched on the light and found a bunch of flowers inside the recorder itself. It was a discovery that marked the end of McElhoney's career.

Planted Flowers?

Flowers have been common apports for well over 150 years. One of the earliest investigators of this phenomenon was a Frenchman, Dr G. P. Billot, who witnessed the production of flower apports by a blind woman medium way back in October 1820.

One of the most extraordinary accounts of an apport concerns a famous English medium, Madame d'Esperance, in whose presence a materialised spirit named Yolande was said to appear. At a seance in 1880, Yolande took a glass carafe that had been half-filled with sand and water and placed it in the centre of the room, covering it with a thin piece of drapery. The sitters then watched in amazement as the drapery began rising and Yolande came out of the cabinet, in which Madame d'Esperance was seated, to inspect what was happening. When she removed the drapery, it was seen that a perfect plant had grown in minutes.

Yolande told the sitters to sing quietly for a few minutes; and when they inspected the plant again, they found it had burst into bloom, with a flower 5 inches (12.5 centimetres) in diameter. It had a thick woody stem, which filled the neck of the carafe, was 22 inches (56 centimetres) high and had 29 leaves. It was subsequently identified as a native of India, *Ixora crocata,* and lasted for three months.

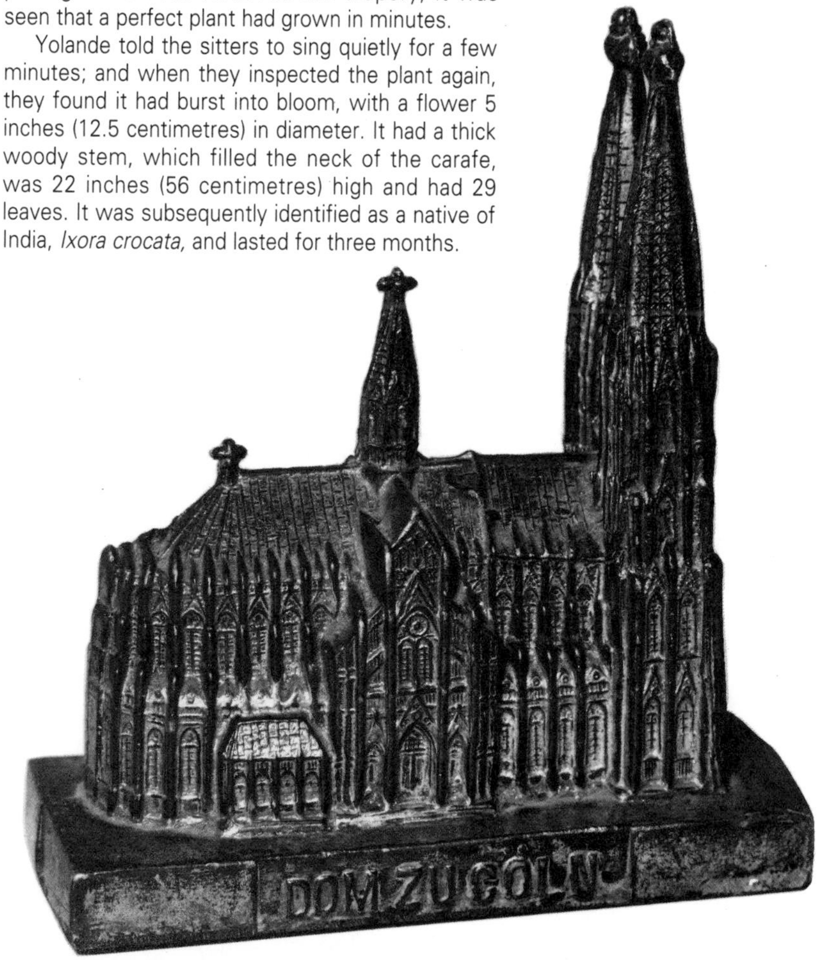

Madame d'Esperance,* right, *was one of the foremost physical mediums of the late 19th century. She is seen with the golden lily that – through the agency of her materialised guide Yolande – literally grew in front of her sitters on 28 June 1890 to a height of 7 feet (2 metres). Exuding a strong fragrance and with five flowers in bloom, it seemed solid enough – yet at her next seance, Yolande dematerialised it in seven minutes. All that remained was this photograph and a couple of the flowers.

Ten years later, the same medium was responsible for an equally spectacular apport. This time – on 28 June 1890 – a beautiful golden lily with an overpowering perfume grew before the eyes of the sitters to a height of 7 feet (2 metres). Five of its 11 flowers were in full bloom; and in photographs taken at the time, it was seen to tower above the medium. Yolande told the sitters, however, that it could not remain and became quite upset when she found she could not dematerialise it. She asked them to keep the plant in a darkened room until the next session, on 5 July, when it was placed in the centre of the room. Its physical presence was recorded at 9.23 p.m., but by 9.30 p.m. it had vanished. The only proof of its existence were the photographs and a couple of the flowers.

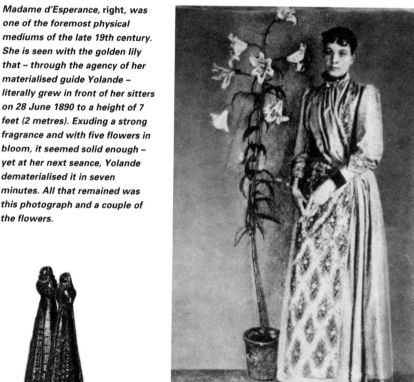

Even with such large apports, more hardened sceptics could probably suggest ways in which they might have been produced fraudulently. But fraud is difficult to accept in cases where mediums materialise items at the request of sitters. A friend of Agnes Nichols (later, Mrs Samuel Guppy), one of the most gifted apport mediums during the 1860s and 1870s, once asked for a sunflower, and the medium complied with its immediate production, in a darkened seance room. It was a 6 foot (1.6-metre) specimen, which arrived on a table with a mass of earth around its roots. At another seance, each sitter was asked to name a fruit or vegetable: the apports that were received included a banana, two oranges, a bunch of white grapes, a bunch of black grapes, a cluster of filberts, three walnuts, a dozen damsons, a slice of candied pineapple, three figs, two apples, an onion, a peach, a few almonds, three dates, a potato, two large pears, a pomegranate, two crystallised greengages, a pile of dried currants, a lemon and a large bunch of raisins.

Doves and other birds are as popular with apport mediums as they are with magicians, but their materialisation is achieved under very different conditions. An Australian boot-maker, Charles Bailey, is even credited with apporting an entire menagerie during his many years as a medium. To rule out trickery, he allowed himself to be stripped, searched and dressed in clothes supplied by investigators. Dr C. W. McCarthy, an eminent medical man in Sydney, imposed even more stringent test conditions. Having searched Bailey, he then placed the medium in a sack with holes for his hands, and tied him up.

On occasions, the sitters were searched as well and the medium would be placed inside a cage covered with mosquito netting. The door to the room was locked or sealed, the fireplace was blocked and paper pasted over the window. The only furniture allowed in the room was a table and chairs for the sitters. Yet, after a few minutes of darkness, when the lights were put on, Bailey was found to be holding apports, such as two nests with a live bird in each. At other seances, he produced a live, 18-inch (46-centimetre), shovel-nosed shark and a crab dripping in seaweed. Many of the live apports produced at his seances disappeared as mysteriously as they had arrived.

Later in his career, however, Bailey's mediumship was found to be far from convincing by a number of investigators who produced evidence to show that he had purchased the 'apports' from animal dealers. But others remained entirely convinced that some, even if not all of his phenomena were genuine.

Stolen Items?

Intriguingly, the 'spirit control' of a famous medium, Mrs Everitt, refused to produce apports. 'I do not approve of bringing them,' she explained cryptically, 'for they are generally stolen.' There have certainly been well-corroborated cases where an apport has been an object that has been dematerialised from one place and rematerialised in another, sometimes at a sitter's request. The following account was written by Ernesto Bozzano, an eminent Italian psychical researcher:

'In March, 1904, in a sitting in the house of Cavaliere Peretti, in which the medium was an intimate friend of ours, gifted with remarkable physical mediumship, and with whom apports could be obtained at command, I begged the communicating spirit to bring me a small block of pyrites which was lying on my writing table about two kilometres [1.2 miles] away. The spirit replied (through the medium) that the power was almost exhausted but that all the same he would make the attempt.

'Soon after, the medium sustained the usual spasmodic twitchings which signified the arrival of an apport, but without our hearing the fall of any object on the table or floor. We asked for an explanation from the spirit operator, who informed us that although he had managed to disintegrate a portion of the object desired, and had brought it into the room, there was not enough power for him to ... re-integrate it.

'He added, "Light the light". We did so, and found, to our great surprise, that the table, the clothes and hair of the sitters, as well as the furniture and carpets of the room, were covered with the thinnest layer of brilliant impalpable pyrites. When I returned home after the sitting, I found the little block of pyrites lying on my writing table from which a large fragment,about one third of the whole piece, was missing.'

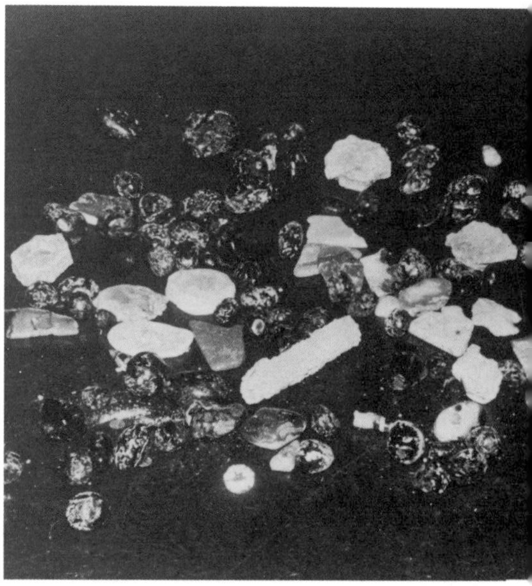

The American medium Keith Milton Rhinehart,* above, *held public demonstrations in London in the 1960s, which provoked a guarded reaction from some of the audience. He produced numerous objects,* above right, *from his mouth, including a prickly sea horse; but there is some evidence to suggest that he had merely regurgitated them.

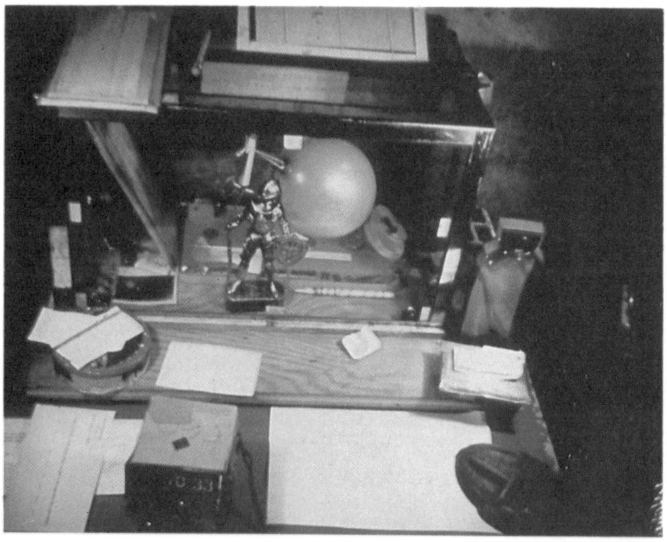

Two frames from a controversial films taken at Rolla, Missouri USA,* below, *allegedly show the paranormal movement of objects through the glass wall of a minilab. Despite several years of research, none of the minilab pioneers has managed to induce PK on a scale comparable to that of the physical mediums.

Apport mediums seem to use different psychic techniques to produce the phenomenon; but, with some, the object seems to materialise out of their bodies. T. Lynn, a miner from the north of England, was photographed producing apports in this way. Small ectoplasmic shapes were often seen extending from his body, usually near the solar plexus. Hewat McKenzie and Major C. Mowbray tested Lynn at the British College of Psychic Science, London, in 1928. The medium was put in a bag, and his hands were tied to his knees with tapes. Flashlight photographs taken by the investigators showed luminous connections between his body and the apports.

Another miner, Jack Webber, was photographed some years later producing an apport in a similar way. Webber, a Welshman, was famous as a physical medium at whose seances trumpets would levitate and spirit voices would speak to those present. At a seance in 1938, Webber was searched thoroughly by a policeman in front of all the sitters, and then tied to a chair. This account of the seance is taken from Harry Edwards' book, *The Mediumship of Jack Webber:*

'The red light was on, sufficiently bright for all to see the medium with his arms bound to the chair. Trumpets were in levitation ... one of these turned round, presenting its large opening to the solar plexus region and an object was heard to fall into it. It then came to the author who was asked to take out of the trumpet the article within – an Egyptian ornament. After a minute or two, the trumpet again travelled to the solar plexus and another object was heard to fall into it.'

In November of the same year, at a seance in Paddington, London, Webber's guide announced his intention of trying to materialise a brass ornament from an adjoining room. He asked for a photograph to be taken at a particular moment and said that this ought to record the production of the apport. The sitters then heard the sound of an object falling to the floor. When the plate was developed, the small ornament – a bird weighing 2 ounces (57 grams) – could be seen apparently emerging in a white substance from the medium's solar plexus.

The Indian guru Sai Baba,* above left, *worshipped as a modern Hindu saint, holds one of his many apports.

The ex-miner Jack Webber,* above, *produces a cord-like string of ectoplasm from his mouth. On several occasions, small ornaments,* top, *were seen to take shape in a white cloud over his solar plexus; but when handled, they were perfectly solid.

> AT OTHER SEANCES, BAILEY PRODUCED A LIVE SHARK AND A CRAB DRIPPING IN SEAWEED. MANY OF THE LIVE APPORTS PRODUCED AT HIS SEANCES DISAPPEARED AS MYSTERIOUSLY AS THEY ARRIVED.

American medium, Keith Milton Rhinehart, demonstrated apport mediumship in London in the 1960s at the Caxton Hall. In a well-lit area, before a capacity audience, he successfully produced a number of items from his mouth, including a very prickly sea-horse. Semi-precious stones were also 'apported' through his body: they were found embedded in his skin and were plucked out by witnesses. Some members of the audience, however, were distinctly unimpressed: the stones were never seen to emerge through his skin, they claimed, and seemed to have been deliberately implanted in his flesh. Similarly, a number of witnesses thought some of his supposed apports had merely been regurgitated.

But a comparison of the best apport mediums does provide some striking similarities, and some believe that this indicates that it is a genuine phenomenon. At the turn of the century, Henry Sausse recorded many instances of apports produced by an entranced woman medium. Her method was to form her hands into a cup, in full light. A small cloud would then be seen to form inside. This would transform itself instantly into an apport, such as a spray of roses, complete with flowers, buds and leaves. There are countless similar stories of physical mediumship; but the fact remains that apports are rare today.

DO COUGHS AND SNEEZES ALONE SPREAD DISEASES? OR COULD IT BE THAT SOME EPIDEMICS ARE SPREAD, NOT BY CONTAGION, BUT BY MEANS OF INFECTIOUS ORGANISMS FALLING INTO THE EARTH'S ATMOSPHERE FROM PASSING COMETS?

BUGS FROM OUTER SPACE

Every now and then, the Earth is struck by diseases such as the Black Death, depicted in the manuscript illumination, below right, *or Legionnaire's disease, which first attacked delegates to an American Legion convention in 1976. Legionnaire's disease baffled doctors for some time, and extensive research was carried out, as seen* below left, *before the bacillus responsible for the disease,* below, *was isolated. Sir Fred Hoyle and Professor Chandra Wickramasinghe believed such diseases are brought to the Earth by comets. Try as we might to eradicate them, they said, we cannot succeed: sooner or later they will be reintroduced into the atmosphere.*

Invasion of the Earth by life-forms from outer space has long been a staple theme of science fiction (SF). But it seems there may be more truth in the idea than SF writers have realised. For, according to two eminent scientists – Sir Fred Hoyle and Chandra Wickramasinghe – there is a regular influx of extraterrestrial organisms on to the Earth, and these breed in our bodies. Such 'space invaders' are not monsters like those in the film *Alien,* but tiny bacteria and viruses that cause diseases – not only colds, influenza and measles, but great epidemics of the past and present, such as the bubonic plague, and perhaps even AIDS.

Professors Hoyle and Wickramasinghe proposed that the organisms that cause disease are seeded into the Earth's atmosphere from passing comets, which carry the organisms through space. Once these organisms reach Earth, they then float down through the atmosphere and are inhaled or ingested to produce illness.

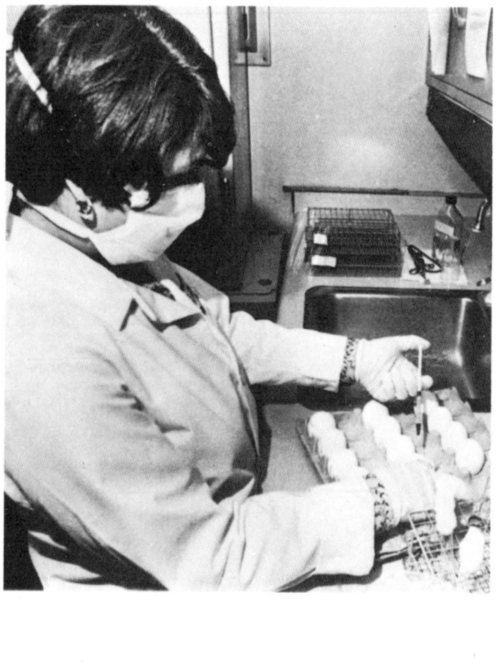

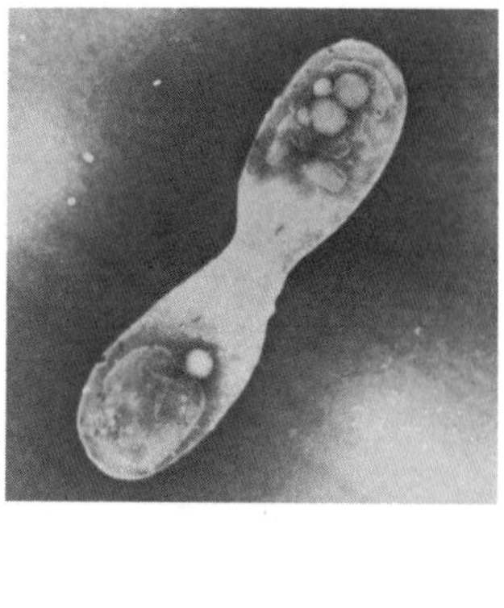

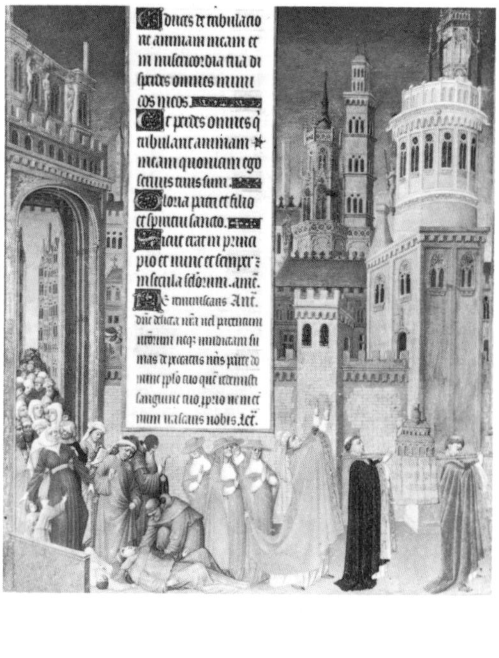

Comets, such as Comet West,* top left, *are at the centre of a controversial theory proposed by Sir Fred Hoyle,* top, *and Professor Chandra Wickramasinghe,* top right. *They claimed that epidemics of diseases, such as influenza, may originate in outer space, in the tails of comets.

The Orion Nebula,* above, *is a region of clouds of gas and interstellar dust that may signify stars-in-the-making. It is in such clouds, Hoyle and Wickramasinghe believed, that life first formed.

If this startling and controversial theory is correct, then campaigns to eradicate certain diseases such as polio must inevitably fail, because they will be periodically reintroduced into the atmosphere from space. What is more, other new diseases may strike without warning, these scientists claimed.

Hoyle and Wickramasinghe's ideas about diseases from space stem from their theories concerning the origin of life. They claimed that life, in the form of single-cell organisms such as bacteria, is widespread in the clouds of gas and dust that astronomers observe in space. But how did living cells get out there? They were formed there, said Hoyle and Wickramasinghe. Furthermore, it was the sprinkling of such cells on to the Earth that brought life to our planet. Since, according to their hypothesis, this process would be repeated on other planets, life could well be widespread throughout the Galaxy. They also claimed that evolution on Earth has progressed by the continuing input of genetic information in the form of biological material from space.

Controversy surrounds these views, but on one thing astronomers are agreed: complex molecules – many of them containing carbon, the chemical backbone of life – exist in the gas and dust clouds of space. The densest clouds, where most molecules are found, are the sites of star formation, such as the famous Orion Nebula. So it seems that stars and their planets come into being enveloped in a rich smog of chemicals, many of which are believed to be important in the formation of life.

However, while most astronomers and biologists have traditionally assumed that the complex chemical processes that led to life took place in the atmosphere and oceans of the primitive Earth, Hoyle and Wickramasinghe proposed that life arose in comets – ghostly balls of dust and ice that shuttled through the cloud surrounding our embryo solar system.

Hoyle and Wickramasinghe challenged the belief that conditions on the young Earth were suitable for life. Instead of our primitive planet having a dense atmosphere and extensive oceans, they maintained that the Earth formed as a dry, airless ball, like the Moon, and that our present-day atmosphere and oceans were imported by the arrival of comet-like objects from the outer solar system. About four billion years ago, life also arrived via a comet; by then, conditions had become sufficiently favourable for life to persist and develop, they concluded.

CLUES FROM THE CLOUDS

An important feature of this argument is that the dust clouds of space contain a great deal of cellulose, which is the most abundant organic substance on Earth, forming the cell walls of plants and trees. Evidence to support this contention concerns the infra-red spectrum of the clouds. If they are right – and it is certainly true that some organic chemicals have been identified out there – then the most important structural parts of living cells are lying around virtually ready-made in space, waiting to be swept up into the chemically rich, water-bearing interior of a comet, where they remain dormant until a chance encounter with a suitable planet.

Hoyle and Wickramasinghe claimed that living cells still exist in the comets of our solar system, and that these cells reach Earth – to cause disease – when our planet passes through swarms of cometary dust.

Hoyle and Wickramasinghe focused on colds and influenza as examples of diseases arriving from space. The cold you had last winter, they proposed, may have come from space by the same process that originally brought life to Earth four billion years ago. Ironically, the name 'influenza' originated in the 15th century because the disease was thought to arise from the 'influence' of the stars! Could a medieval superstition really be receiving 20th-century scientific support?

It may seem a little incongruous to test such a wide-ranging theory on the incidence of colds among Welsh schoolboys, but that is what Hoyle and Wickramasinghe did. They began by studying medical records of the 1978 influenza outbreak in Welsh schools, and found that influenza victims in dormitories showed no tendency to infect their close neighbours. From this surprising result, they concluded that influenza is not a transmitted disease, and they used the result to support their contention that viruses do indeed reach us from the atmosphere.

The professors also noted that the famous Asian influenza epidemic of 1957 and the so-called Hong Kong influenza of 1968 seemed to be due to the reappearance of viruses that had hit the Earth respectively 77 and 78 years previously. Now, Halley's comet has an orbital period around the Sun of between 75 and 78 years, and Hoyle and Wickramasinghe's contention was that the epidemics could have been caused by debris travelling in the wake of the comet. (This, incidentally, is the only attempt that Hoyle and Wickramasinghe made to link a given disease with a specific comet.)

The incidence of influenza in the four dormitory houses of Howell's School, Wales, is illustrated* above. *The geographical location of the houses is shown in the map,* right. *Hoyle and Wickramasinghe argued that the distribution of disease could not possibly have been brought about by contagion: the pupils must have been infected directly by comet debris. Interestingly, there are two number 13 victims; this results, presumably, from a typographical error in Hoyle and Wickramasinghe's data.

The orbit of Halley's comet relative to the Earth is shown* below. *The comet has an orbital period around the Sun of between 75 and 78 years. Hoyle and Wickramasinghe linked the influenza epidemics of 1957 and 1968 with viral infections that appeared on the Earth 77 and 78 years previously, and concluded that they must have been caused by debris travelling in the wake of Halley's comet.

Diseases other than influenza also show sudden resurgences that could be due to a regular input of viruses from space. The most feared of these is smallpox, which reappears throughout history at intervals of several centuries. Hoyle and Wickramasinghe took this as evidence that smallpox comes from a comet, at present unknown, that orbits the Sun every few centuries. In the 1990s, much of the developing world still suffers from many other diseases; and technologically advanced countries, too, are of course suffering from the major epidemic of AIDS.

Meteor Showers

But if diseases really do come from space by the mechanism proposed by Hoyle and Wickramasinghe, one would expect certain diseases to peak each year following one of the annual meteor showers, for such showers are the densest swarms of cometary dust that the Earth encounters. Yet no correlation between meteor showers and disease has been offered. What is more, two meteor showers – the eta Aquarids, which occur each May, and the Orionids of October – are both believed to be debris from Halley's comet, the very comet that Hoyle and Wickramasinghe linked with Asian and Hong Kong influenza. Why, then, do these two types of influenza not recur whenever the Earth passes through debris from each comet?

The diseases-from-space theory aroused a storm of controversy among the medical profession, who did not take kindly to such a total overthrowing of conventional ideas concerning medical microbiology. But significantly enough, the most

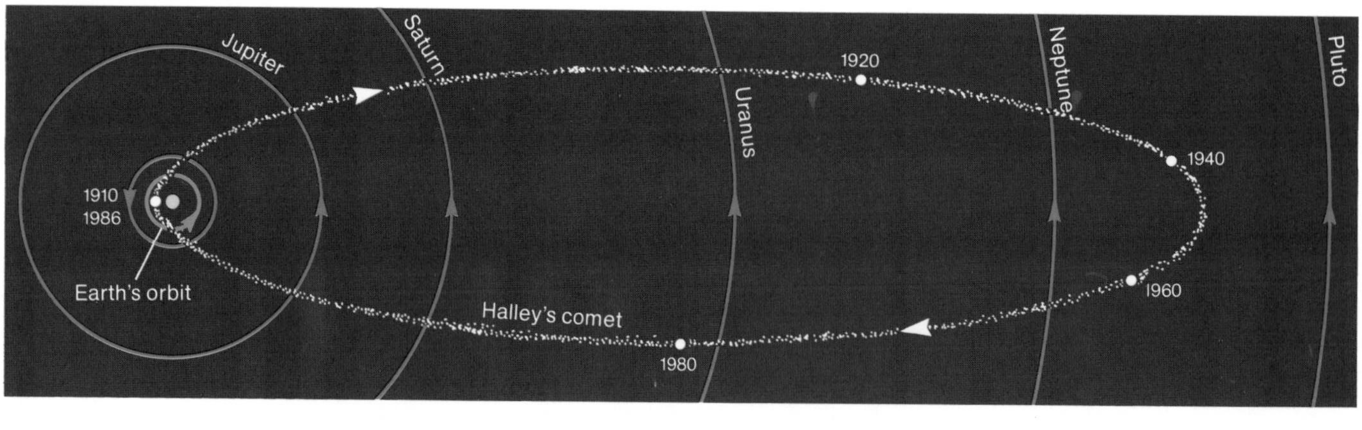

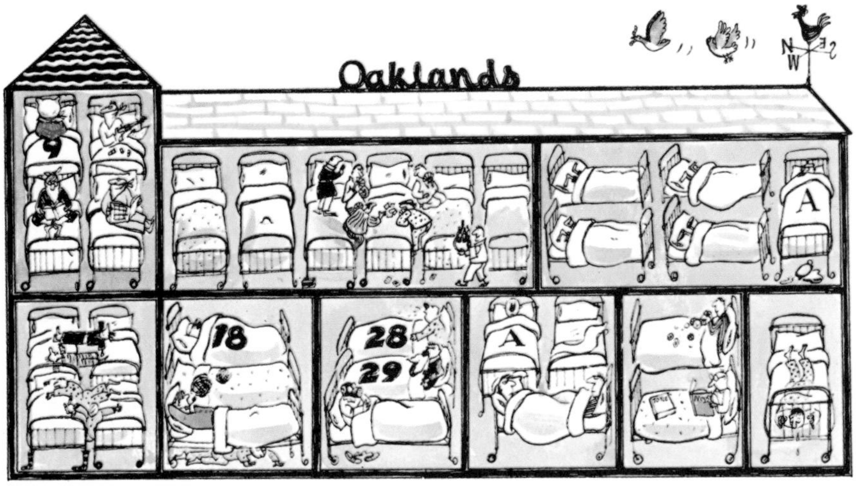

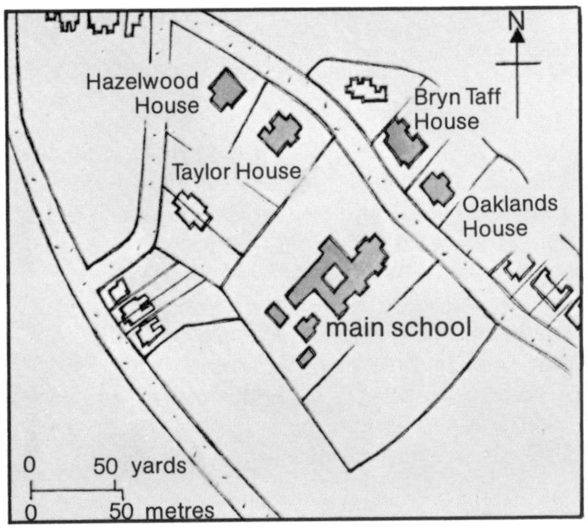

An artist's impression, shown **right**, *is of the European Space Agency's probe* Giotto *which, in 1986, flew past Halley's comet. Although it provided us with much useful information, perhaps only the arrival of a meteorite carrying living organisms from outer space will be able to tell us whether or not comets actually support life.*

telling criticisms came from the champion of life-out-there, Carl Sagan, and his colleague, Bishun Khare of Cornell University. Sagan and Khare contested the interpretation that cellulose or other biologically significant molecules must exist in space. Instead, they said, the infra-red 'fingerprint' of interstellar dust can be closely matched by grains of a complicated tarry substance formed in laboratory experiments when a mixture of gases known to be abundant in interstellar clouds – notably methane, ammonia and water – is bombarded with an energy source such as ultraviolet light. Sagan and Khare stated that the resulting brown residue, which has no particular biological significance, is distributed in the form of tiny grains like smoke particles throughout interstellar clouds.

STAR TAR

Particularly damaging to Hoyle and Wickramasinghe's case was Sagan and Khare's contention that organic compounds, including cellulose, show a strong dip in their infra-red spectrum at around 3.4 micrometres because of bonds between hydrogen and carbon atoms. But infra-red observations of the dust in several interstellar clouds show no such dips. So it seems that cellulose, viruses and living cells must be ruled out on the basis of this evidence. However, Sagan and Khare's 'star tar' contains very little hydrogen and shows scarcely any such dip, so it could well be a component of interstellar dust clouds.

Sagan and Khare dismissed the Hoyle-Wickramasinghe hypothesis with the argument that, even if life originated in outer space, the fact that the evolutionary process on Earth is bound to have differed from that in outer space means that it is 'highly improbable that the biochemistry of extraterrestrial organisms will resemble very closely the biochemistry with which we are familiar on Earth'. In particular, they said organisms such as the influenza virus, if they came directly from outer space, would be unlikely to be compatible with life forms as they have evolved on Earth.

In 1986, the European Space Agency's probe *Giotto* and the US *Galileo* flew past Halley's comet: what they found in the tail were organic molecules that could represent the building blocks of living matter, but no sign of life as such. Perhaps only a further sample-return mission to a comet will end the controversy.

" IF THIS THEORY IS CORRECT, CAMPAIGNS TO ERADICATE CERTAIN DISEASES MUST FAIL, BECAUSE THEY WILL BE PERIODICALLY REINTRODUCED FROM SPACE. "

UFO PHOTO FILE

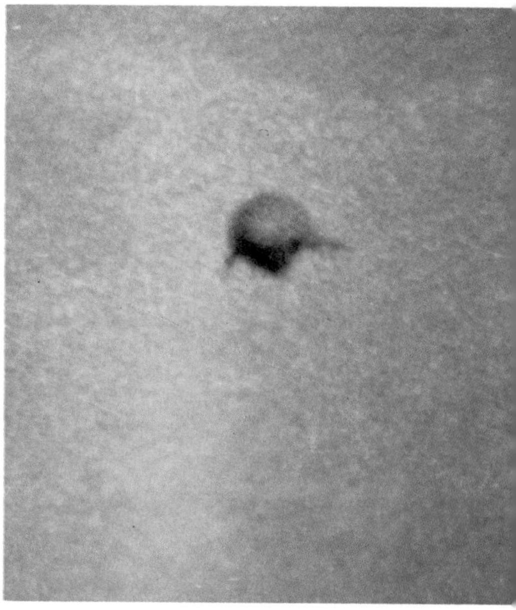

One of the two photographs taken of a daylight disc by a Mr Smith in Calgary, Canada, on 3 July 1967, is shown **left.** Both photographs were analysed by Ground Saucer Watch (GSW) but some time apart. The first photograph passed the tests with flying colours and was publicly announced to be 'genuine'. However, on analysing the second, GSW concluded that the film 'depicts the crudest attempt at a hoax that we have ever seen'. This contradictory analysis illustrates the limitations of GSW's computer analysis technique at the time.

The photograph, **below,** of what appears to be 'a slow moving fireball' was taken in Piedmont, Missouri, USA, on 22 March 1973. There was no known conventional or astronomical explanation for the sighting.

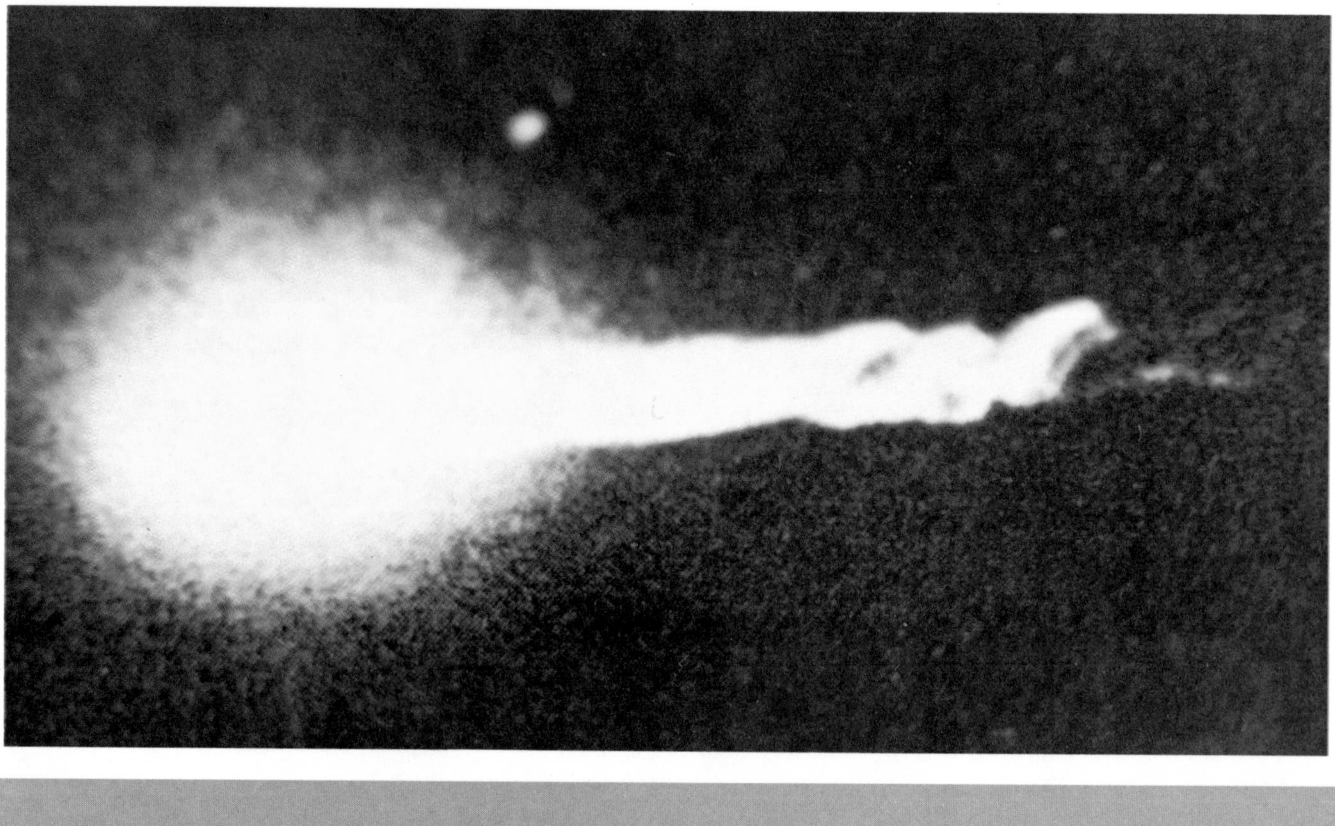

The airship-shaped object, **left,** was photographed near the small colonial town of Cocoyoc, south-east of Cuernavaca, Mexico, on 3 November 1973. Witnesses noted that it was about 30 feet (10 metres) across and Ground Saucer Watch concluded that the UFO must have been a military 'drone', used for meteorological purposes. Most people are unfamiliar with modern military hardware, which frequently results in mistaken reports of UFO sightings.

The disc-shaped UFO, **right,** photographed high over Namur, Belgium, on 5 June 1955, moved erratically and emitted a vapour trail.

The daylight disc, **above,** was photographed by W.N. Henry during mid-August 1978 over the Dolomite Mountains, Italy. Henry, a New Zealander on holiday in Europe, had been involved in the photographic field for eight years and, although intrigued by the object – which he described as being silver and spherical – he thought it might have been a hot air balloon. Yet, as in the case of so many UFO pictures, the object was not seen by Henry when he took the photograph.

Photographer Bill Burson caught the phenomenon, **below** – a bright streak – as it hovered over Pelham, Georgia, USA, on the night of 31 August 1973. The other streaks are stars, the effect being caused by the movement of the Earth during the photographic exposure. Although many explanations were put forward, the object that caused the large streaking remains unidentified. There were many witnesses, including several police officers of the South Georgia cities over which it was seen.

THE OLD BELIEF THAT A CORPSE WILL REACT TO THE PRESENCE OF ITS MURDERER SEEMS TO HAVE FOUND HORRIFIC EXPRESSION IN THE STRANGE CASE OF A ROTTING CORPSE THAT WINKED

Once dead and buried, few people have shown signs of life – but those who have, or are rumoured to have been reanimated, naturally enough have inspired witnesses with awe and fear.In the case of Joan Norkot, who died in 1629, her brief moment of posthumous glory did more: it was enough to point the finger of accusation – almost literally – at her murderers, and subsequently to secure their conviction.

The strange case of Joan Norkot was rediscovered in 1851, when it became one of the legal and

WITH A NOD AND A WINK

The Long Parliament of 1640, in which John Mainard, above, *had sat, living long enough to see William III come to the throne in 1688, is seen* top. *His intellect remained as sharp as ever, and he was considered an impeccable witness to the bizarre case of Joan Norkot.*

The resuscitation of Margaret Dickson, a murderer who was hanged in 1728, is depicted left. *But Joan Norkot's body had begun to decompose. So how could she have revived?*

historical occurrences that were selected from the day books of Dr Henry Sampson for inclusion in the July edition of *The Gentleman's Magazine* and *Historical Review*. In 1851, pragmatism,fact and scientific evidence were the order of the day, as this Victorian journal's prefatory remarks on the Narkot case clearly show:

'The next extract contains a narrative of a very singular legal case, which comes down to us upon the most unquestionable authority – that of the old Serjeant who, after having been an original member of the Long Parliament of Charles I, lived as father of the bar to congratulate King William on his accession in 1688... It would be difficult to parallel the following relation of superstition and miserable insufficiency of legal proof... '

The 'old Serjeant' in question was one Sir John Mainard, 'a person of great note and judgment in the law', whose version of the Norkot incident was recorded in a manuscript 'fair written with his own hands' and discovered among his papers after his death at the age of 88 in 1690. A copy of it was taken by a certain Mr Hunt of the Temple (one of London's Inns of Court), who gave it to Dr Sampson for his records.

Joan Norkot lived in Hertfordshire – it is not known exactly where – with her husband, Arthur, her infant son, her sister Agnes and brother-in-law John Okeman, and her mother-in-law Mary Norkot. By all accounts a cheerful, good-looking woman, happily married and a good mother, Joan was well-known to the locals, who expressed surprise and horror when it was revealed that one morning she had been found with her throat cut, still clutching her child in her arms, apparently the victim of a violent attack. Her family claimed that her death was certainly suicide.

EXHUMATION

On the night of her death, said Mary Norkot and the Okemans, Joan's husband had been away visiting friends. They further claimed that there had been 'a deal of trouble' between Arthur and Joan of late, and that on her last evening alive she had been 'in a sour temper and some despondency'. So maybe, in a fit of despair, she had indeed plunged the knife into her throat. But this was not good enough for Joan's friends and neighbours. In the weeks following the inquest, rumour grew to such an extent in the village that it directly challenged the legal verdict. With new evidence coming to light from investigations at the Norkot cottage, it was widely believed that Joan could not have killed herself. Acting on popular opinion, 'the jury, whose verdict was not drawn into form by the coroner, desired the coroner that the body, which was buried, might be taken up out of the grave, which the coroner assented to, and thirty days after her death she was taken up, in presence of the jury and a great number of the people'.

It was at the exhumation, according to the testimony later given in court by the local clergyman, that the test of touch, decreed by superstitious custom, was made. It was believed that the body of a murder victim would acknowledge the touch of the assassin, and this was admitted as binding legal evidence if it did so. Mainard takes up the story:

The portrait, **left,** *is said to be of Sir Nicholas Hyde, the Lord Chief Justice at Hertford Assizes,* **below,** *in 1629 when Joan Norkot's family were tried for her murder. At first, it was thought that Joan had committed suicide, but the local people suspected foul play and her body was exhumed. Each member of Joan's family was compelled to touch the grisly remains, which then winked and raised a finger – damning evidence in those days. Once the case was brought to court other more conventional evidence came to light, and the accused were convicted of Joan's murder and duly hanged – except for her sister-in-law Agnes, who was reprieved because she was pregnant. The motive for the murder remains obscure.*

'The four defendants present, they were required, each of them, to touch the dead body. Okeman's wife fell on her knees and prayed God to show token of their innocence, or to some such purpose.... The appellers did touch the dead body, whereupon the brow of the dead, which was of a livid or carrion colour (that was the verbal expression in the terms of the witness) began to have a dew or gentle sweat [which] ran down in drops on the face, and the brow turned and changed to a lively and fresh colour, and the dead opened one of her eyes and shut it again, and this opening the eye was done three times. She likewise thrust out the ring or marriage finger three times and pulled it in again, and the finger dropt blood from it on the grass'.

This, in 1629, was irrefutable proof of homicide, and once the furore that necessarily accompanied Joan Norkot' s sudden return to the land of the living (and equally abrupt return to eternal sleep) had died down, the jury altered its verdict.

There are many legends of mysterious rappings coming from such altar tombs, as the one below, and of skeletons found bent and twisted inside them. Premature burial was common in earlier centuries when comatose or cataleptic people were often thought to be dead and were duly buried, only to die of asphyxiation, thirst or horror. Yet it seems that Joan Norkot was certainly dead when her body was exhumed, so premature burial can definitely be ruled out as an explanation for her brief reanimation.

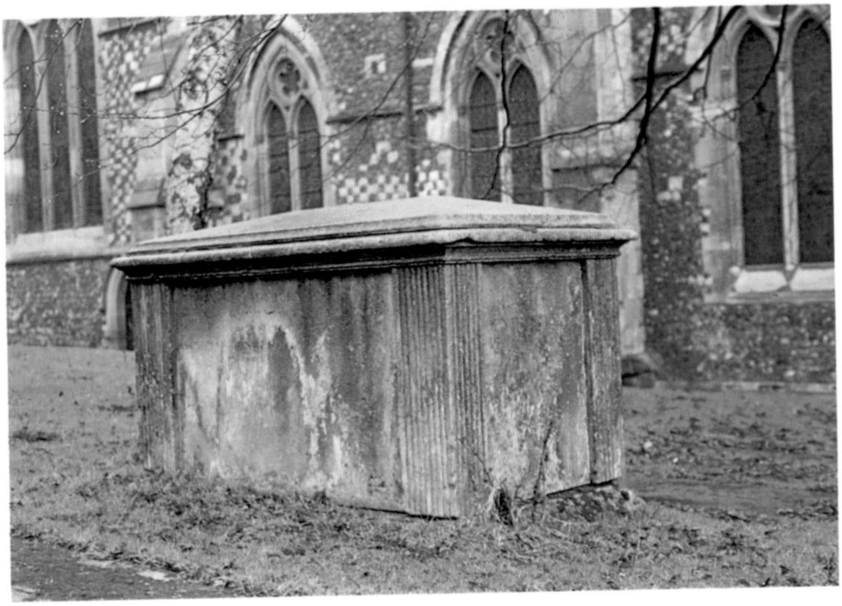

Although it was now declared that Joan Norkot had been 'murdered, by person or persons unknown', the eye of suspicion had come to rest firmly on Arthur, Mary, Agnes and John, and they were subsequently tried at Hertford Assizes. At first, they were acquitted, but the evidence weighed so heavily against them, that presiding Judge Harvy suggested 'that it were better an appeal were brought than so foul a murder should escape unpunished'.

Joan Norkot's orphaned son became the plaintiff in the appeal, which was duly lodged against his father, grandmother, aunt and uncle. As Mainard said himself: 'Because the evidence was so strange, I took exact and particular notice of it'. In the trial, the touch test was soberly recounted by the local parish minister, described by the chronicler as a 'grave person', but one whose name has not survived.

Not surprisingly, the officiating judge, Chief Justice Nicholas Hyde, doubted the old cleric's evidence. 'Who saw this beside yourself?' he asked the witness. 'I cannot swear that others saw it,' replied the minister, 'but my Lord, I believe the whole company saw it, and if it had been thought a doubt, proof would have been made of it, and many would have attested with me ....'

Further, less fantastic evidence was then brought against Mrs Norkot senior and the Okemans, adding to the argument that if no one had gone into the cottage between the time when Joan retired for the night and when she was found dead, then they must be her murderers. Joan had been found lying in her bed with the bedclothes relatively undisturbed, and her child with her. Her throat was cut from ear to ear and her neck broken. How, if she first cut her throat, could she have possibly broken her neck while she was lying in the bed, or vice versa?

Murder Most Foul

It seemed the dead body had been moved and there had been a half-hearted attempt to conceal the evidence. Moreover, the bloody knife had been firmly embedded in the floor at some distance, its point towards the bed, the handle towards the door. However violent her death throes, there is no way that Joan Norkot – had she actually taken her own life – could have thrown the blade into that position. There was, too, the bloody print of a left hand on top of Joan's own left hand, an item of evidence that Chief Justice Hyde questioned but that he eventually accepted.

The four prisoners were then brought forward but they had no defence to offer. Arthur Norkot's alibi collapsed when it was revealed that he had not actually visited the friends with whom he had claimed to be staying for several years. The jury retired and when it returned found Norkot, his mother and Agnes all guilty of murder. Okeman was, however, acquitted. The three guilty persons each cried out: 'I did not do it! I did not do it!' Nevertheless, judgement was passed. Norkot and his mother were sentenced to death and duly hanged, but Agnes Norkot was reprieved when it was discovered she was pregnant.

In his reconstruction and discussion of the case in *Unsolved Mysteries,* Valentine Dyall suggests a possible – though speculative – reason for the murder of Joan Norkot:

'The motive for the crime remained obscure, though it was generally supposed that Arthur Norkot had believed his wife unfaithful. The other two women of the family, known to be jealous of Joan's good looks and position as mistress of the house, probably made willing accomplices – while John Okeman, a simple fellow, was bullied into silence.'

But there is no logical explanation for the incredible scene that took place when Joan was disinterred. We can toy with the notion of premature burial, but there can be no doubt that Joan Norkot was well and truly deceased when she was laid to rest. Perhaps exposure to the elements had an immediate chemical effect on her decaying flesh, explaining the 'lively and fresh colour' of her brow. But how did Joan's eye wink, and her finger move and yield fresh blood? Maybe, some have ventured to suggest, it was just that Joan Norkot, in the course of divine retribution, awoke fleetingly from death to ensure that justice was done.

MAGICAL RITUALS HAVE BEEN PERFORMED SINCE TIME IMMEMORIAL AND ARE STILL USED TODAY – NOT JUST IN TRIBAL CULTURES BUT IN THE WEST, TOO – FOR GOOD AND FOR EVIL

The performing of rites – that is to say, ceremonial observances – probably plays a bigger part in our lives than most of us realise. Even people who have never, for example, been present at a *barmitzvah*, the Jewish 'rite of passage' that marks the transition from boyhood to manhood, or witnessed a celebration of the Christian Eucharist, have probably attended a twenty-first birthday party – the 'ceremonial observance' of the attainment of an adulthood that, in purely legal terms, is now reached some three years earlier in some parts of the western world.

Indeed, from prehistoric graves, it is clear that our Stone Age ancestors carried out elaborate funeral rituals, and most primitive communities that

Young girls of the Caraya tribe of Peru, above, perform a dance for the Sun to mark the onset of puberty. If they did not take part in this age-old ritual, they would not be considered truly adult.

RITES AND WRONGS

Aubrey Beardsley's illustration for the text of Oscar Wilde's play **Salome, left,** ***inspired Aleister Crowley to perform one of his more repulsive and risible ceremonies. He solemnly baptised a cockerel with the name of John the Baptist and then beheaded it, in a manner loosely based on the corresponding scene in Wilde's play. This ceremony was supposed to undermine the influence of Christianity.***

out a similar rite with a toad, baptising it 'Jesus of Nazareth' and then crucifying it. Both rites seem to have been singularly ineffective.

If a clay doll, a wax image, or – as in the two strange Crowleyan rites mentioned above – an animal, is supposedly given the inner qualities of a particular living being by means of baptism or some other ceremonial observance, it is believed that a 'magical link' is established between the image and the living being. In some way, they have become mystically identified with one another, and anything that affects the image or animal will, so it is argued, affect its 'psychic twin' in a similar way.

In medieval times, if a peasant wanted to kill an enemy, he would make a realistic image of him and baptise it with the enemy's name. To make the psychic identification of image and enemy as close as possible, he would endeavour to obtain some hair and/or nail clippings of his intended victim and incorporate them into the statuette. He would then hammer nails or pins into the image or slowly destroy it, melting it over a slow fire, if it was made of wax, or putting it in a wet place, if it was made of clay. As the fire or water wasted away the image, so the body of the enemy would also, it was thought, waste away.

have survived into modern times seem to practise highly formalised and complex ceremonies to mark birth, puberty and death.

While it is impossible for us to know exactly what beliefs our early forbears held, it is likely that ritual was always associated with magic and the supernatural. A ceremony not only marked a particular event in life but in some way was often seen actually to produce that event. If, for example, a man or woman had not undergone the appropriate rituals associated with the attainment of adulthood, he or she was not considered a 'real adult', in spite of all appearances to the contrary.

Indeed, it was only a short mental step from thinking that sexually mature individuals were not adult humans because they had not been made adults by the appropriate rite to believing that certain ceremonies could also be used to turn some non-human entity (a tree or a clay image, for example) into a sort of honorary human being.

Taste of Deception

Strange as such a mode of thinking may appear, it has persisted throughout history and has even survived into comparatively recent times. In the late medieval period, for instance, an abbot who yearned to eat meat during Lent was accused of adopting the ingenious device of baptising a sheep with the name of 'Carp', butchering it, and then eating it during the fast under the pleasant conviction that whatever appeared to be on his plate, it was in substance fish, not mutton.

During the 1930s, the fanatically anti-Christian occultist Aleister Crowley employed baptism in much the same way. He had a cockerel baptised with the name of John (the Baptist) and then solemnly beheaded it, in an elaborate ceremony based on Oscar Wilde's play *Salome*. This was supposed to destroy, in some mysterious way, the influence of Christianity upon the world. He carried

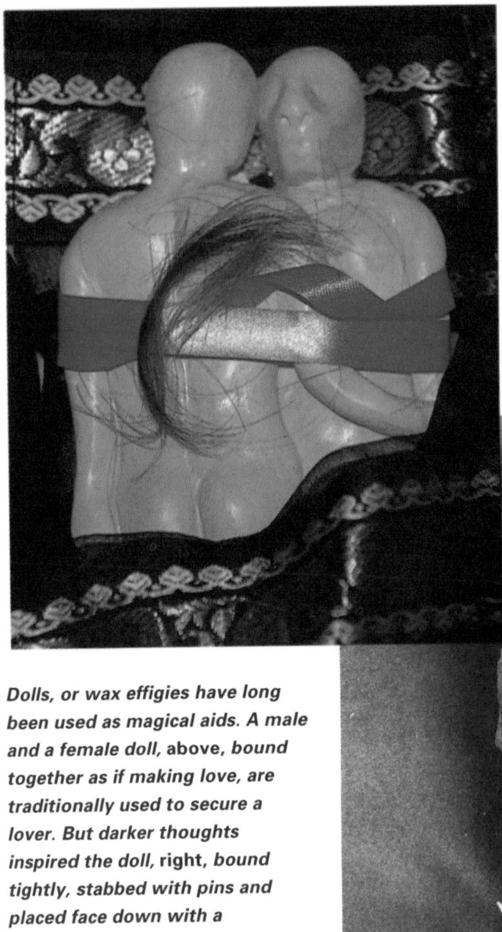

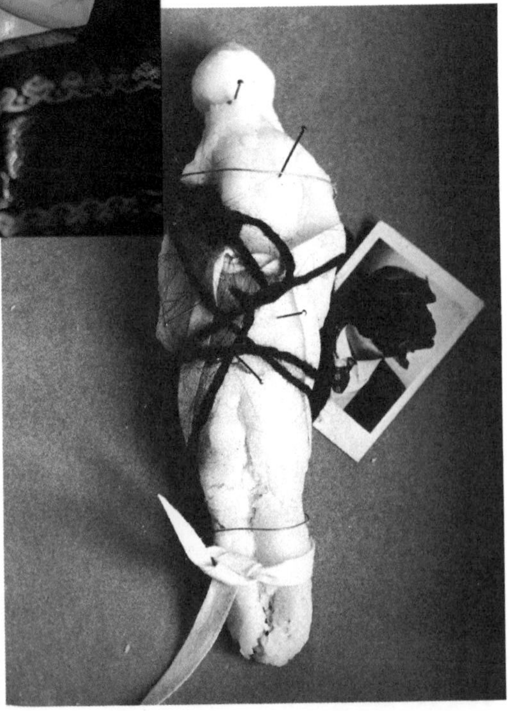

Dolls, or wax effigies have long been used as magical aids. A male and a female doll, **above,** ***bound together as if making love, are traditionally used to secure a lover. But darker thoughts inspired the doll,*** **right,** ***bound tightly, stabbed with pins and placed face down with a photograph and strands of hair of the intended victim. A sick mind may have devised it, but there is evidence that such 'games' can at times be deadly.***

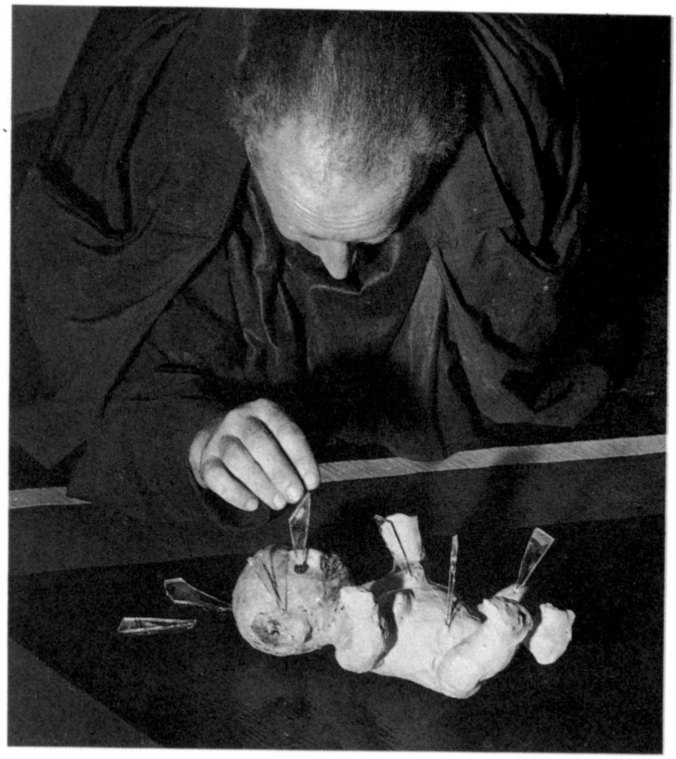

A similar, if more kindly intentioned process was often employed for sexual ends. A girl who desired a man would make images of herself and her beloved, incorporating, when possible, hair, nails, and bodily secretions and endowing the figures with prominent genitals in a state of sexual excitement. The images would be baptised with the appropriate names and then tied together with thread (usually red – a colour psychologically associated with sexual excitement), as though energetically copulating. Soon, it was hoped, the man's sexual desires would be directed towards the sorceress who, by this simple magical rite, would manage to capture his love.

Magical Links

But were such magic rites actually effective? Sometimes, so it seems so, for there are well authenticated cases even in modern times, of the mysterious and medically inexplicable deaths of those who have been attacked by ritual magic involving the use of images. Exactly why these victims die is uncertain. It may be that there really is some 'magical link', created by ritual, between image and victim. Or it may be that the concentrated hate that the sorcerer pours out upon the image of his enemy telepathically exerts some form of destructive influence. More probably, it has been suggested, the victim is aware, or very strongly suspects, that ritual magic is being used by an enemy and kills himself by auto-suggestion – dying, quite literally, of fright.

Two stories from the 1930s that give support to this idea, but involving injury rather than death, were told by the American journalist William Seabrook. The first concerned a certain French concert pianist. (Seabrook called him Jean Dupuis to disguise his real identity.) A student of Rosicrucianism, astrology and other aspects of occultism, he had become involved with a dubious

A woman who sent a curse in the form of a letter to the Witches' Kitchen coven at Castletown, Isle of Man, provoked Cecil Williamson, the group's leader, to respond with all his painstaking art. First he made a 'poppet' to represent the woman who had cursed the coven; then he appealed to the spirits for power. Next, he breathed 'life' into the doll through a straw in its mouth, **above left.** ***Symbolically and, magicians believe, in some way actually, the doll had become the woman. Then Williamson inserted glass splinters into various parts of her body,*** **above right.** ***As long as the candles burned, she would 'feel torment sharper than the sting of needles'. In ritual magic, it is often the person with the greater hate – and ingenuity – who wins the psychic battle.***

'esoteric group' with which he subsequently quarrelled. The group, angry at his defection, decided to destroy his ability to play by using a combination of ritual magic and applied psychology.

Five-finger Exercise

The magic came first. A doll was made in the image of Dupuis, baptised with his name and then clad in evening dress such as he wore on the concert platform. Its hands were then placed in a vice that was slowly tightened each day.

The psychology followed. Supposed friends of the victim – but in actuality, members of the group that was working against him – began to make comments and ask questions. His finger-work seemed less dextrous than usual, they remarked. Perhaps he was in need of a few days rest? Had he sprained his wrist, they enquired, or was he suffering from neuritis?

Within a week or two, these sly suggestions began to take effect. Jean Dupuis became excessively aware of his fingers, and his playing began to degenerate. Then, a few days before a concert, he received an anonymous note, beginning: 'I can tell you what is wrong with your hands, but it is so frightful that I am almost afraid to tell you'. The letter then proceeded to go into occult theories about magical links between images and men – matters that the writer knew the pianist had studied – and concluded by giving details of the doll with its hands held in a vice. On the night of the concert, a second note arrived: 'The handle of the vice will be slowly turned tonight, until your hands are crushed'.

The concert was a disaster: 'a false note, then a succession of jangling chords, followed by worse fumbling ... whispers and hisses from the outraged audience ... the young man half-turned to the audience, resumed desperately; and, after a ghastly parody of the next few bars ... fled from the stage in shame and confusion.'

William B. Seabrook is seen above with the Ivory Coast forest people, including a young witch called Wamba. Seabrook travelled widely in the 1920s and discovered the universality of magical rites.

In this case, the victim was a student of the occult, a believer in ritual magic and its powers to hurt or kill. The other story told by Seabrook does, however, illustrate the fact that such sinister rites may sometimes exert an equally strong influence upon those who do not consciously believe in their efficacy, and would probably deny their power, if questioned.

In this instance, the victim was Louis, a French motor mechanic, the lover of a young girl whose peasant grandmother, a woman locally reputed to dabble in witchcraft, had taken an intense and unreasonable dislike to him. One day, Louis and the old woman quarrelled violently and almost came to blows. As the two parted – Louis to set off along a well-marked mountain path, the grandmother to return to her nearby cottage – the supposed witch began to chant an incantation:

'Tangled mind will twist and turn,
And tangled foot will follow . . .
So tangle, tangle, twist and turn,
For tangling webs are woven.'

By nightfall, Louis had not returned from his walk and a search party was sent out to hunt for him. He was found some distance from the path, entangled in briars, unable to walk, his legs paralysed. He said that he had wandered off the path, having become dizzy and increasingly confused, and he claimed that he had suffered some sort of stroke. He was ill, he continued to assert, even after the local doctor had been unable to find any physical injury to account for his condition.

Eventually Seabrook, convinced that ritual magic was responsible for Louis's condition, raided the old wine cellar in which the grandmother practised her witchcraft. On the floor, he found laid out a miniature landscape, 'a tangled labyrinth of thorns and briars'. In its midst lay an image of Louis, with its eyes bandaged, and its feet tied and enmeshed in thorns and brambles.

Seabrook took the doll and showed it to Louis, who was annoyed that the old woman had attempted to harm him but still refused to accept that her activities had in any way been responsible for his paralysed state. 'I don't believe any of it,' he said, 'I've had a stroke.' His conscious mind, paradoxically enough, was lacking in the imaginative ability to understand the real cause of his paralysis. If he had been able to understand that primitive beliefs in sorcery and the supernatural lurked in the hidden depths of his own mind, he would probably once again have been able to walk.

These two cases represent only the most primitive strand in ritual magic, for the rites employed were extremely simple. As long ago as classical times, however, far more complex forms of ritual magic were evolved. The formulae, techniques and secrets of such elaborate occult systems are enshrined in the *grimoires* – textbooks of ceremonial magic.

" IT MAY BE THAT THERE REALLY IS SOME MAGICAL LINK, CREATED BY RITUAL, BETWEEN IMAGE AND VICTIM ... MORE PROBABLY, THE VICTIM IS AWARE OR VERY STRONGLY SUSPECTS THAT RITUAL MAGIC IS BEING USED BY AN ENEMY AND KILLS HIMSELF BY AUTO-SUGGESTION. **"**

Exactly when and where the first *grimoires* were compiled is uncertain. But something very like them existed in ancient Egypt; while magical works, many of them of Jewish origin, were circulated widely in the later centuries of the Roman Empire. It is probable that the European *grimoires* of the medieval period were derived from these, for they too show much evidence of Jewish influence. The authorship of many of them was attributed to King Solomon. According to legend, he was such a master of magic that he had dominion over men, demons, and even the angels of heaven.

The *Clavicula Salomonis* (Key of Solomon) and other magical works attributed to the great Jewish

The extract, below, *is a medieval magical incantation from the* Key of Solomon *– one of the most important of all grimoires.*

SALOMONIS
(CITATIO)

XYWOLEH.VAY.BAREC
HET.VAY.YOMAR.HA.ELOHE
ELOHIM.ASCHER.TYWOHE
HYTHALE.CHUABOTAY.LEP
HA.NAWABRA.HAMVEYS.HA
HAKLA.ELOHIM.HARO.HE
OTYMEO.DY.ADDHAYON
HAZZE.HAMALECH.HAGO
ELOTYMYCCOL.RAH.YEBA
RECH.ETHANEA.TYM.VEI
KA.REBA.HEM.SCHEMVE.EEL
SCHEMABO.TAY.ABRAHAM
VEY.SCHAK.VEYYD.GULA
ROBBE.KEREBHAARETZ.
CHAY.SEWAH.ANOCHY.YA
HEL.PARYM.BEWO.WYKAR

HIER NENNE DER GEISTER NAHMEN MIT IHREN (HEBRÆ) RUF, DIE DU HABEN WILLST, ZU DIENSTEN, AUS (DENEN) (NB) AMULETEN, UND NIMM IHR AMULET, LEGE ES VOR DICH HIN AUF DIE ERDE.

king display, like almost all the *grimoires,* a notable moral ambivalence. The hard core of the ritual magic of these works is the 'raising to visible appearance' of spirits, good and bad, with the object of obtaining benefits of one sort or another – usually wealth, power or knowledge.

The processes used fall into three stages: first, the preparation of the materials and implements to be used in the ceremony; secondly, the preparation of the magician's own mind and body; and thirdly, the actual performance of the rite.

The first of these stages involves the experimenter in compounding incense, moulding candles, and first manufacturing and then consecrating a variety of 'magical weapons', including a wand, a sword, and even a sickle. These processes are often extremely complex. One *grimoire,* for example, instructs the magician to forge his sickle one hour after sunrise on a Wednesday, bring it thrice to a red heat and then to immerse it in a mixture of herbal extracts and the blood of a magpie.

Another text tells the experimenter to build a stone altar on a river bank before dawn, behead a white cockerel at the moment of sunrise, throw its head in the river, drink its blood and burn its body. He must then jump into the river, climb out backwards, don new clothing and return to his dwelling.

Once the first two stages have been successfully accomplished, the magician can proceed to the ritual itself. He stands within a circle inscribed with names and symbols which are designed to protect him from demons who might wish to destroy him, and burns incenses, brandishing his magical implements, and chanting the lengthy and sonorous incantations given in the *grimoires.* Eventually, the spirit appears and gives the magician the things he desires, or so some occultists believe.

On the face of it, many of the processes involved in the ritual magic of the *grimoires* are so absurd – and often so repellent – that no normal person would wish to carry them out. This has led some modern occultists to deny that the texts of the *grimoires* are to be taken literally. These works, so it is argued, are written in a code only fully understandable by initiates. Thus, one *grimoire* teaches a method of giving someone a sleepless night: 'Pick a June lily under a waning moon, soak it in laurel juice and bury it in dung. Worms will breed therein. Dry them and scatter on your enemy's pillow'. This means, say those who believe the *grimoires* to be written in code, invoke the demons Lilith (the June lily) and Q'areb Zareg (the laurel), both of whom are reputed to give bad dreams.

Similar interpretations are employed by modern practitioners of ritual magic, who also take oaths to work in secret. There are, it is claimed, a surprising number of such exponents.

A common, if melodramatic, image of the ritual magician summoning demons while standing in his magic circle is shown* right. *Essentially, the image is correct: a devoted magician will use ancient texts to summon up spirits and will often stand for hours inside a magic circle. He may indeed succeed in producing some entity – but it may be only an hallucination, visible just to him and owing its appearance more to the result of fasting and meditation than to the use of 'words of power'.

The photograph,* left, *shows one of the images carved on the wall of a house at Bunbury, Cheshire, by a poacher who had been deported by the squire. On his return, the poacher carved three images to represent the squire and his two henchmen, and cursed them daily as witches do with dolls. The three men did indeed soon die.

"IF A CLAY DOLL OR WAX IMAGE IS SUPPOSEDLY GIVEN THE INNER QUALITIES OF A HUMAN BEING BY MEANS OF SOME CEREMONIAL OBSERVANCE, IT IS BELIEVED THAT IN SOME WAY THEY HAVE BECOME MYSTICALLY LINKED WITH ONE ANOTHER, AND ANYTHING THAT AFFECTS THE IMAGE WILL AFFECT ITS 'PSYCHIC TWIN' IN A SIMILAR WAY."

SOUNDS MYSTERIOUS

WHY DO SANDS AROUND THE WORLD PRODUCE WEIRD BOOMS, ROARS, SQUEAKS AND WHISTLES, WHILE COASTAL WATERS SOMETIMES ECHO TO MYSTERIOUS EXPLOSIONS? SOME OF THE INTRIGUING SOUND EFFECTS CREATED BY NATURE ARE ANALYSED HERE

The British physicist, R. A. Bagnold was travelling on a field-trip in the desert area of south-west Egypt when he and a companion had a strange and unnerving experience.

'It happened on a still night – suddenly a vibrant booming so loud that I had to shout to be heard by my companion. Soon other sources, set going by the disturbance, joined their music to the first with so close a note that a slow beat was clearly recognized. This weird chorus went on continuously for more than five minutes before silence returned and the ground ceased to tremble.'

The phenomenon of booming sands is only one of the weird sound effects nature can produce. Sands that sing, bark, roar, squeak and whistle have cropped up in travellers' tales for over 1,500 years. Earliest references are in chronicles from the Middle and Far East. Marco Polo, for instance, described an example of the phenomenon that occurred in the Gobi Desert in medieval times, and Charles Darwin remarked upon a case in Chile in the 19th century.

A seventh-century account taken from the *Tun-Huang-Lu* manuscript, preserved in the British Museum, gives a description of a rumbling dune that appears to have been used as a kind of fairground side-show at festivals in the oasis town of Ho-t'ien (Khotan) in north-west China. In Khotan is a sand hill that at certain times gives out strange noises. The account reads as follows:

'The hill of sounding sand stretches 80 *li* [25 miles or 40 kilometres] east and west and 40 *li* [13 miles or 20 kilometres] north and south, and it reaches a height of 500 feet [150 metres]. The whole mass is entirely constituted of pure sand. In the height of summer, the sand gives out sounds of itself, and if trodden by men or horses, the noise is heard 10 *li* [3 miles or 5 kilometres] away. At festivals, people clamber up and rush down again in a body, which causes the sand to give a loud rumbling sound like thunder.'

In a desert landscape, such as that below, one would expect to find profound silence. Yet such places can be wildly noisy even, according to some accounts, making it necessary to shout to be heard by someone nearby.

A similar example was reported by an early investigator, A D. Lewis. He described a rumbling dune in the Kalahari Desert of South Africa in 1935 in this way:

'By sliding down the slope in slow jerks on one's "sit-upon" ... a very loud roar is produced. In the still of the evening and early morning, natives were kept sliding down the slope in this way, and the noise was easily heard at a distance of 600 yards [550 metres], like the rumbling of distant thunder.'

But what causes sands to boom? It is known that the continuous internal movement of sand within the dune, whether it occurs naturally or as a result of intervention, can – under certain conditions – produce a low-frequency vibration. This is audible as a hum which can sound like the pure note of an organ or a double bass. The presence of overtones, meanwhile, can produce a sound more reminiscent of the rumble of thunder, the drone of bumble-bees or low-flying aircraft. Seismic waves accompanying the sound have also been recorded; and these ground vibrations may even manifest themselves as mild electric shocks.

The actual mechanism that produces such vibrations is, however, far from completely understood. It has been conjectured that the hum may originate as an oscillation of individual grains caught between sliding masses of sand. But the key to the phenomenon is sometimes said to lie in the way in which the grains are packed together. Windy conditions and dryness are essential for producing booming sand, a fact giving rise to the suggestion that booming sand may also be common on the windy and waterless deserts of Mars.

Mist Pouffers

Sand dunes are generally found in remote regions, far from what might be called the 'noise pollution' of the 20th century. Acoustic phenomena that occur in more densely populated areas, meanwhile, are often more difficult to isolate, and run the risk of being misidentified. So it is with certain seemingly distant explosions, heard all around the European coast and as far into the Atlantic Ocean as Iceland. These so-called 'mist pouffers' are also heard on the North American and Asian coasts. The most famous example, found in Barisal, now in Bangladesh, is known as the Barisal guns because of the nature of its sound. G.B. Scott gave this report in *Nature* magazine in 1896:

'I first heard the Barisal guns in December 1891, on my way to Assam from Calcutta through the Sunderbans [tidal forests]. The weather was clear and calm, no sign of any storms. All day the noises

The 13th-century manuscript, above, shows Marco Polo arriving at the court of Kubla Khan. One of the great travellers of history, Marco Polo described in an account of his Asian journeys the mysterious phenomenon of 'singing sands'.

Along the south-west coast of Bangladesh, near the city of Barisal, left, are heard the Barisal guns, so named because the sound over the water is much like the firing of heavy artillery.

Some scientists say that the windy and almost waterless conditions on Mars, **right,** *are ideal for booming sands. But no one has yet had the opportunity to hear them.*

on board the steamer prevented other sounds from being heard; but when all was silent at night . . . the only sounds the lap of the water or the splash of earth, falling into the water along the banks, then at intervals, irregularly, would be heard the muffled boom as of distant cannon. Sometimes the reports would resemble cannon from two rather widely separated opposing forces, at others from different directions but apparently always from the southward, that is seaward.'

Suggested explanations for the Barisal guns have been many and varied. They could result, perhaps, from explosions of vast methane bubbles rising from the ocean floor. They could be caused by seismic activity on the ocean bed – although, curiously, there is no correlation between the mysterious detonations and seismic records. They may be caused by the sonic boom of meteorites falling through the atmosphere faster than the speed of sound. The explanation remains elusive: and the question, for some reason, has become one of those curiosities of the natural world that are generally overlooked.

A quick explanation was sought with urgency, however, when a series of mysterious explosions hit the east coast of North America in December 1977. Residents of New Jersey and South Carolina in the United States and Nova Scotia in Canada reported mysterious booms accompanied by explosions. Mrs Hattie Perry, of Barrington, Nova Scotia, who monitored the reports of the phenomenon, described the occurrence as follows:

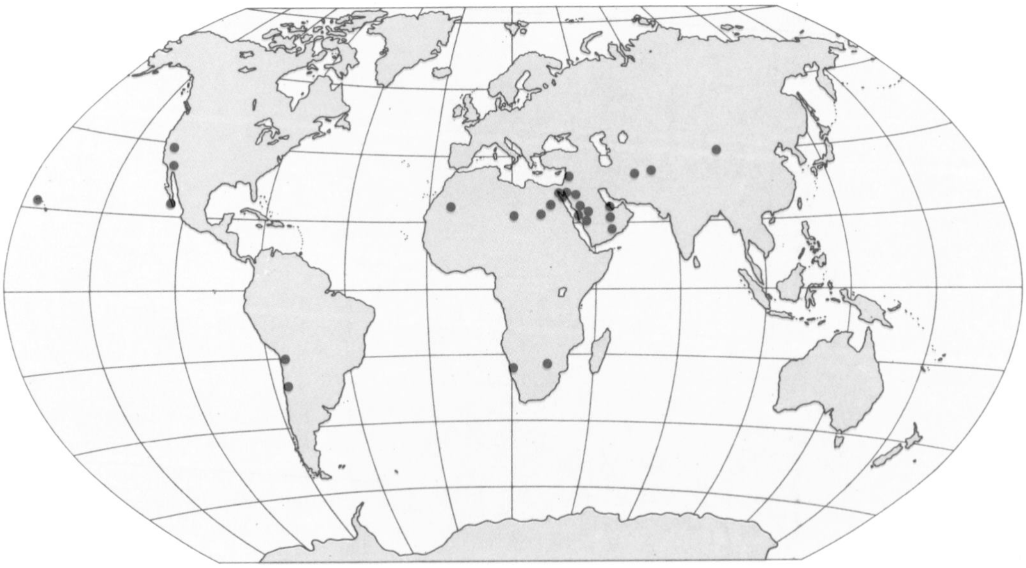

The map, **left,** *shows the location of booming sands throughout the world. The noise normally occurs at the crests of large dunes.*

'Some say it sounds as though a car has hit the side of a house. Others think that some missile has landed on the roof. One woman, lying in bed, was terrified to see the tiles on her ceiling pull apart, then close together again.'

The booms were registered on sensitive seismic equipment at Columbia University's geological observatory, which is situated just outside New York City, and the explosions were estimated as equivalent to the detonation of between 50 and 100 tonnes of TNT.

So what caused the blasts? One explanation was that deposits of methane gas hidden under the continental shelf or along the shore, suddenly ignited. Another was that they could have been due to the sonic boom created by Concorde as it flew close to the North American seaboard. True, the blasts were not heard at the time that Concorde flew over; but, it was argued, in the extremely cold weather conditions that prevailed at the time, it would have been possible for the sonic boom wave, travelling upwards, to be reflected from a boundary between layers of cold and warm air. The reflected sound wave could then have reached ground level some considerable time after Concorde had flown over the spot. A third suggestion was that the sonic wave came from unscheduled military test flights in the area.

Few scientists were prepared to lend support to the methane theory, and the Pentagon quickly denied any supersonic activity by military aircraft at the time. That left the possibility that the culprit was indeed Concorde.

The Canadian government, however, took this idea seriously enough to request the British and French air authorities to change Concorde's route: there had been reports of Concorde flying as close as 20 miles (32 kilometres) to the Canadian coast. As a result, from 17 February 1978, Concorde pilots were instructed to maintain a minimum distance from the Canadian coast of 50 miles (80 kilometres). But reports of booms heard in the region of Nova Scotia still persisted.

What, then, are we to make of such evidence? It is, of course, perfectly possible that the booms were caused by military aircraft engaged in supersonic manoeuvres; and, interestingly, the Naval Research Laboratory, which was commissioned by the United States government to investigate the phenomenon, remains evasive on this particular point. All one can do for the moment is to agree with the comment of Ernest Jahn, a scientific investigator for the National Investigations Committee on Aerial Phenomena (NICAP), who said: 'It is some kind of physical phenomenon which we simply don't understand'.

In Focus

ANGER OF THE GODS

The inhabitants of the small town of East Haddarn, Connecticut, USA, are used to hearing mysterious noises.The rumblings – known to the local American Indians long before the Europeans came – have shaken buildings, rattled crockery and even, on one occasion, allegedly thrown someone out of bed. Variously likened to cannon fire, a heavy log falling, thunder, or the passing of a lorry, the sound was believed by the original inhabitants to be the ragings of the god Hobbamock. This god supposedly lived inside Mount Tom, which is situated to the north-west of the town; and in the 17th century, the Indians would inform newly-arrived European colonists that the god was expressing his anger at them as unwelcome settlers. The area in which the noises are most often heard is the hilly part called Moodus, which takes its name from the Indian *Matchitmoodus* ('place of bad noises').

Intriguing though these noises are, they rarely appear to harm people or property. 'There's nothing to be afraid about; we're so used to it', Frances Kuzaro, the town librarian has said. 'Usually, your dishes will rattle and you might think it's the furnace in the cellar ready to blow up.' Other locals are equally dismissive. James Meyer, a high school biology teacher who devoted his thesis to the noises, commented: 'A lot of people don't bother listening to them any more. You hear a noise and assume it's something else – sonic boom, traffic'.

The noises do, however, definitely exist; and their origin has been studied by a group of seismic experts headed by Dr John E. Ebel. Ebel placed a network of five seismometers within a 10-mile (16-kilometre) radius of Moodus. This 'net', which was extremely sensitive, showed tiny earthquakes that matched reports of noises recorded by listeners whom Ebel employed in Moodus. 'Every one I've heard has been verified' said Cathy Wilson, one of Ebel's volunteer listeners, 'except one, which turned out to be a gunshot.'

Ebel concluded that the noises are the result of shallow, low-magnitude so-called 'micro-earthquakes'. 'The surprising and unexpected result of my study', Ebel commented, 'is the fact that the micro-earthquakes are so very, very shallow that they shake the surface in a way that makes it act like a loudspeaker, sending off the boom.'

This explanation seems more likely than previous ideas, which ranged from gaseous and chemical reactions far below the surface of the Earth to exploding gemstones. But how exactly does it happen? And why only at Moodus? Scientists are puzzled; and the precise way in which the geology of the area allows the Earth's crust to act as a sounding board remains unknown.

According to the so-called biorhythm theory, there are three unvarying cycles that govern the physical, emotional and intellectual aspects of every single person. Can we improve our quality of life by taking note of them?

RHYTHMS OF LIFE

On 11 November 1960, the guest on the Long John Nebel all-night radio programme in New York was George Thommen. His topic was what he defined as 'the application of mathematics to the biological scheme of things' – or what is now popularly called biorhythms.

On that same date, one of America's best-loved screen actors, Clark Gable, was making a seemingly successful recovery from the heart attack he had suffered six days previously. The heart machine that had saved his life had been removed, and there were hopes that the popular star of *Gone with the Wind* would soon be back on his feet.

Thommen made some calculations during the programme and announced that Gable's heart attack had taken place on a 'critical' day in his biorhythm cycle. He urged the hospital to watch the patient carefully on his next critical day, which was according to him in five days' time. On that very day, the 16th, Clark Gable suffered another heart attack. According to press reports, doctors believed he might have been saved if the heart machine had been on hand – but it was not, and the actor died. Unusual as Thommen's theories on biorhythms may have seemed – and to many, still do seem – he had apparently made a correct prediction regarding Gable's health based on them.

Biorhythmic theory owes much to the work of Dr Hermann Swoboda (1873-1963), a psychology professor at the University of Vienna. He published the first of his six books on the subject in 1904, under the title *The Periods of Human Life*. According to his theory, there are two such periods or cycles that regulate people's lives: one of 23 days, which governs the physical state, and the other of 28 days, which concerns the emotions. Each cycle begins at birth and recurs throughout the whole life span, and each is divided into two equal parts, one 'positive' and the other 'negative'. The first day and the day in the middle of each cycle were designated by him as 'critical' days, when the human body or mind undergoes a change over from positive to negative, or 'up' to 'down', or vice versa. Swoboda's

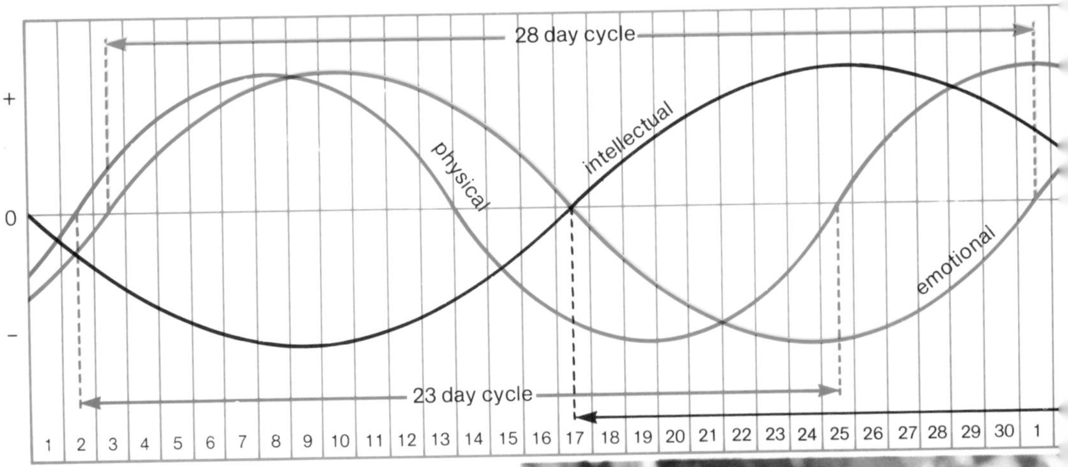

Benny 'Kid' Paret,** far right, **lies unconscious after being knocked out in the boxing ring. The fight took place on a critical day for Paret.

Dr Hermann Swoboda,** above left, **a psychologist, was one of the originators of biorhythmic theory.

The chart,** above, **shows the three biorhythmic cycles.

Arnold Palmer is shown,** right, **in a tense moment of play. This champion golfer once lost an important tournament when all three of his biorhythms were at a low point.

conclusions were based on his own observations of cyclic fluctuations in both the physical symptoms and the emotional moods of his patients.

Biorhythms were identified and described independently, and almost simultaneously, by a Berlin physician named Wilhelm Fliess,(1859-1928), who later became president of Germany's Academy of Sciences. His first book on biorhythms, *The Course of Life,* was published in 1906. Like Swoboda, he based his conclusions on a study of his own patients. But he took the idea a stage further by associating the two cycles with his theory of the bisexual nature of humans. He identified the 23-day cycle as 'male', or physical, and the 28-day cycle as 'female', or emotional. The similarity of the latter to the average length of the menstrual cycle lent the theory a greater semblance of logic.

'All life,' Fliess wrote, 'follows an internal regulated pattern, a mechanism which is alike in man, animal and plant: one that regulates the hour of birth with the same accuracy as the hour of death.' He reasoned that, since people are the result of the development of both male and female cells, it is logical to suppose that a bisexual periodicity would continue to govern the behaviour of the organism.

It would be wrong to accuse Fliess of making unsubstantiated claims, as he supported his theories with a huge mass of statistical evidence. In fact, there is so much mathematics involved that even his disciple, George Thommen, admits he overdid it – to the point of frightening off scientists as well as ordinary people. One of Fliess' earliest admirers was Sigmund Freud, who wrote no less than 184 letters to him over a 16-year period, and underwent two nose operations at his hands.

Biorhythmic theory was later altered by an Austrian engineer, Alfred Teltscher. He came up with a third cycle of 33 days. This, he claimed, applies to human intellectual activity. Unfortunately, he left no published material at all. It is supposed that his work was based on a study of the performance of a group of Innsbruck students, whose

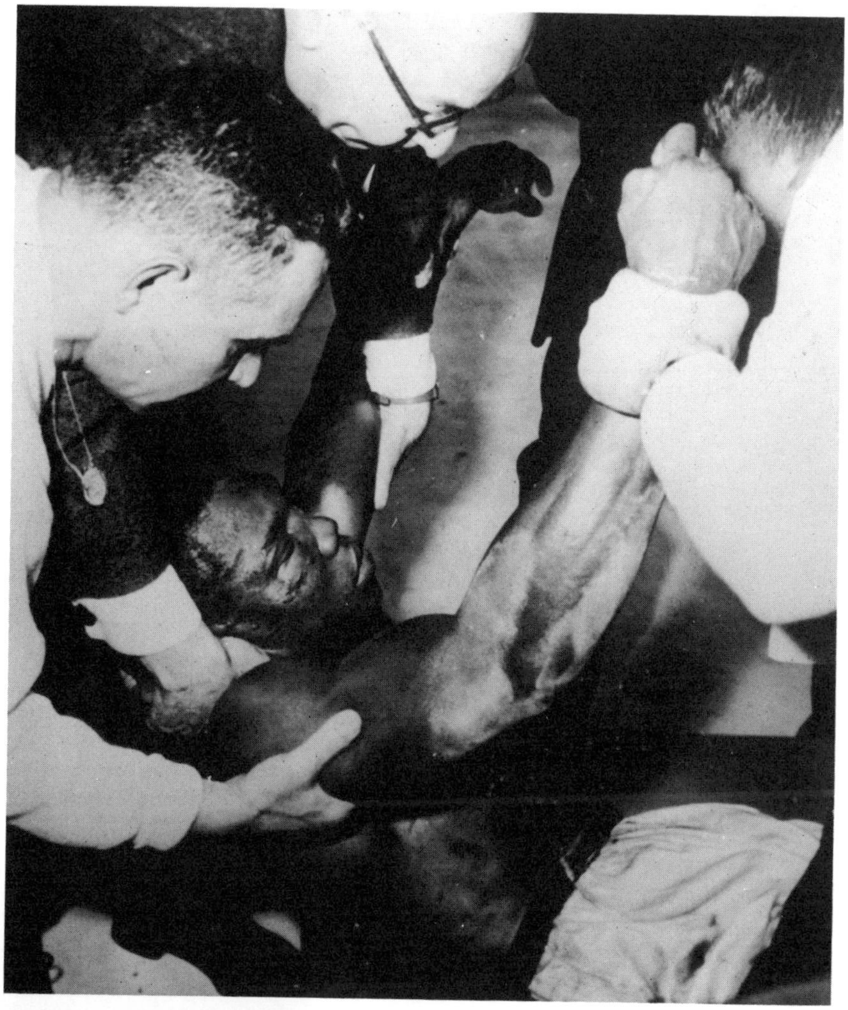

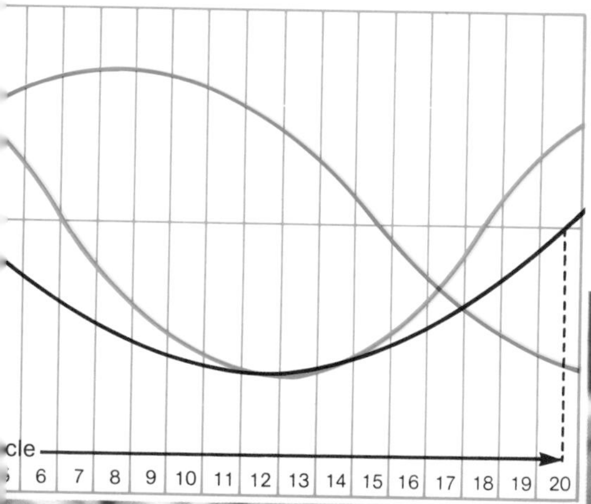

"ALL LIFE FOLLOWS AN INTERNAL REGULATED PATTERN, A MECHANISM WHICH IS ALIKE IN MAN, ANIMAL AND PLANT: ONE THAT REGULATES THE HOUR OF BIRTH WITH THE SAME ACCURACY AS THE HOUR OF DEATH."

WILHELM FLIESS

Clark Gable,* left, *died on 16 November 1960 – one of his critical days. George Thommen, a biorhythm exponent, had warned of the actor's extreme danger in a radio programme five days earlier after calculating Gable's biorhythmic cycles.

Astronaut Scott Carpenter,* below, *is seen rehearsing part of the re-entry procedure for his planned space flight in 1962. The actual flight took place on 24 May, a critical day in Carpenter's emotional cycle, and he overshot his target landing site on the scheduled re-entry.

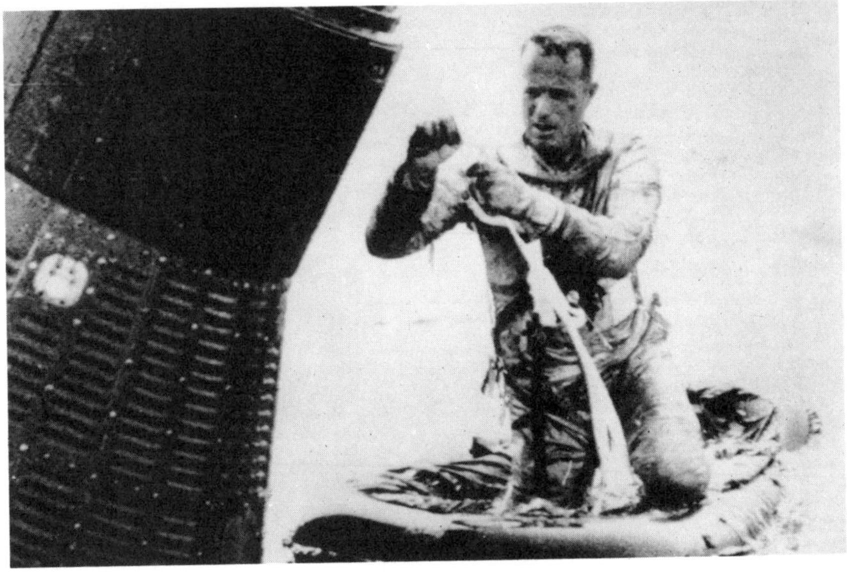

ability to grasp and absorb new material seemed to show peaks and troughs within a 33-day period. By the 1920s, it appeared that a new science, based on the direct observations of three independent researchers, had come into being.

But what are the main principles of biorhythmic theory? At the moment of birth, a baby undergoes a sudden and drastic change both in its environment and in its internal processes. It begins to exist as an individual, deprived of its mother's life-support system with the severing of the umbilical cord. At this time, all three internal clocks are set at zero.

From now on, three separate cycles of 23, 28 and 33 days will run throughout the individual's life. Each cycle in turn consists of a half-cycle of positive activity followed by one of negative activity. The first and middle days of each full cycle are believed to be critical days.

The three cycles will restart all together at zero only after 23 x 28 x 33 days – a total of 21,252. This makes 58 years and 66 or 67 days, depending on how many leap years have followed the individual's birth. However, any two of the three cycles will show simultaneous critical days quite frequently. When the midpoints are included in the calculations, it can be seen that there will be at least four double critical days in any given year, and one triple critical day in every period of just over seven-and-a-quarter years. As for single critical days, there will be at least five in every month, and sometimes as many as eight. The result is that we are never more than a few days away from one.

The 23-day physical cycle has two halves, each of 11½ days. In the first half, we reach peak physical condition and are in tiptop shape during the fifth and sixth days, the midpoint of the half-cycle. Then, in the second half-cycle, we subside to recharge our batteries and recuperate from the exertions of the first half.

In the first half of our 28-day emotional cycle, we likewise enjoy a fortnight of optimism, creativity and good feeling. Then we have to go through 14 days of emotional subsidence and recharging. This is when we are most likely to think negatively, becoming annoyed easily, and experiencing what might be termed 'bad days'. The midpoint days in each half-cycle bring an increased probability of accidents.

The third cycle of 33 days offers us 16½ days of lucid thinking, good memory and mental alertness, and is followed by the characteristic half-period of lower intellectual activity and output. We are advised not to take important decisions on these intellectually low or critical days.

Critical days are not dangerous in themselves, Thommen insisted. They are merely 'switch-point days' when we change from one state to another. Our biorhythms, he said, do not predict accidents. 'The way a person acts depends on what is happening to him, as well as on the condition he happens to be in physically, emotionally and intellectually at a particular time.'

There is a certain amount of evidence that events do take place as proponents of biorhythmic theory would expect. Celebrities other than Clark Gable who died on critical days have included Pope John XXIII, the conductor Bruno Walter, Queen Wilhelmina of the Netherlands, the poet Robert Frost, General MacArthur, Senator Estes Kefauver and the actress Marilyn Monroe. C.G. Jung died on a double critical day. The boxer Benny 'Kid' Paret had the misfortune to enter the ring on a triple critical day. He was knocked unconscious and subsequently died – on his next critical day.

Similarly, critical days in the emotional cycle have coincided with mishaps in the lives of well-trained professionals. Astronauts Virgil Grissom and Scott Carpenter, for example, each suffered accidents on re-entry into the atmosphere on critical days. Grissom almost sank along with his capsule, while Carpenter overshot his target landing site by 250 miles (400 kilometres) after coming in at the wrong angle.

> **"** CRITICAL DAYS ARE ... MERELY SWITCH-POINT DAYS FROM ONE STATE TO ANOTHER. THE WAY A PERSON ACTS DEPENDS ON THE CONDITION HE HAPPENS TO BE IN PHYSICALLY, EMOTIONALLY AND INTELLECTUALLY. **"**

Employees of the Ohmi taxi company in Japan, above left, are seen plotting the biorhythms of drivers. By assigning rotas accordingly, the company claims to have reduced accidents by 30 per cent.

Japanese telegram messengers, left, are warned of a coming critical day by a yellow flag placed on their motorcycles. The critical day itself is announced by a red flag – and the safe period by a green one.

For golfer Arnold Palmer, too, July 1962 may have seemed like a month when biorhythmic theory was proving uncomfortably correct. He was enjoying a triple-high period when he won the British Open four strokes ahead of the runner-up. He was in good humour throughout the match, even claiming that the heat, which bothered other players, was doing him good. Yet just 10 days later, in irritable mood, he trailed into 17th place in the US Professional Golfers Association tournament. By then, all three of his biorhythms were close to the bottom of their negative half-cycles.

These are isolated incidents, of course. Yet there is also evidence in support of the biorhythm theory from surveys of large samples. For his 1939 doctoral dissertation, Hans Schwing examined 700 accidents and 300 deaths. He found that nearly 60 per cent of the former and 65 per cent of the latter fell on critical days. However, these represent no more than 20 per cent of the days in our lives when all three cycles are included, and only 15 per cent when the intellectual cycle is omitted, as it was in Schwing's survey.

In 1954, Reinhold Bochow of Humboldt University, Berlin, published the results of a survey of 497 accidents caused by agricultural machinery. His findings were remarkable: 24.75 per cent took place on triple critical days; 46.5 per cent on double critical days; and 26.6 per cent on single ones. Only 2.2 per cent took place on non-critical days. Two years later, the Hanover Sanitation Department published a report, showing that 83 per cent of certain accidents were related to critical days in the biorhythmic cycle.

A Swiss surgeon, Dr F.Wehrli, has claimed a total of 10,000 successful operations after scheduling them to coincide with non-critical days. Researching a smaller sample, George Thommen found that one third of 28 patients who had undergone surgery on a critical day had died. The normal death rate following operations in the New York hospital he studied was actually much lower.

Commercial organisations that have reportedly started to use biorhythms as a means of reducing accidents among employees include America's United Airlines and Swissair. In Japan, telegram messengers find little red flags on their motorcycles to warn them to take more care on a critical day. The Ohmi taxi company of that country also claimed at one time to have reduced accidents by 30 per cent since adopting a biorhythmic early warning system.

Knowing when we are likely to be at our best or worse – physically, emotionally and intellectually – allows us to structure our lives more efficiently. Yet, there are competing theories, such as the effects of the natural cycles of the sun and moon, and the magnetic field of the earth. These, in the end, possibly have an equally strong effect on us as the biorhythmic theories put forward by Swoboda, Fliess, Teltscher and their followers.

THE GENERAL BELIEF IS THAT TIME FLOWS ALONG STEADILY 'LIKE AN EVER-ROLLING STREAM'. BUT MODERN SCIENCE IS DISCOVERING THAT THE REALITY MAY IN FACT BE FAR MORE COMPLEX. INDEED, THE ENDURING FANTASY OF TIME-TRAVEL MAY WELL BE PHYSICALLY POSSIBLE AFTER ALL

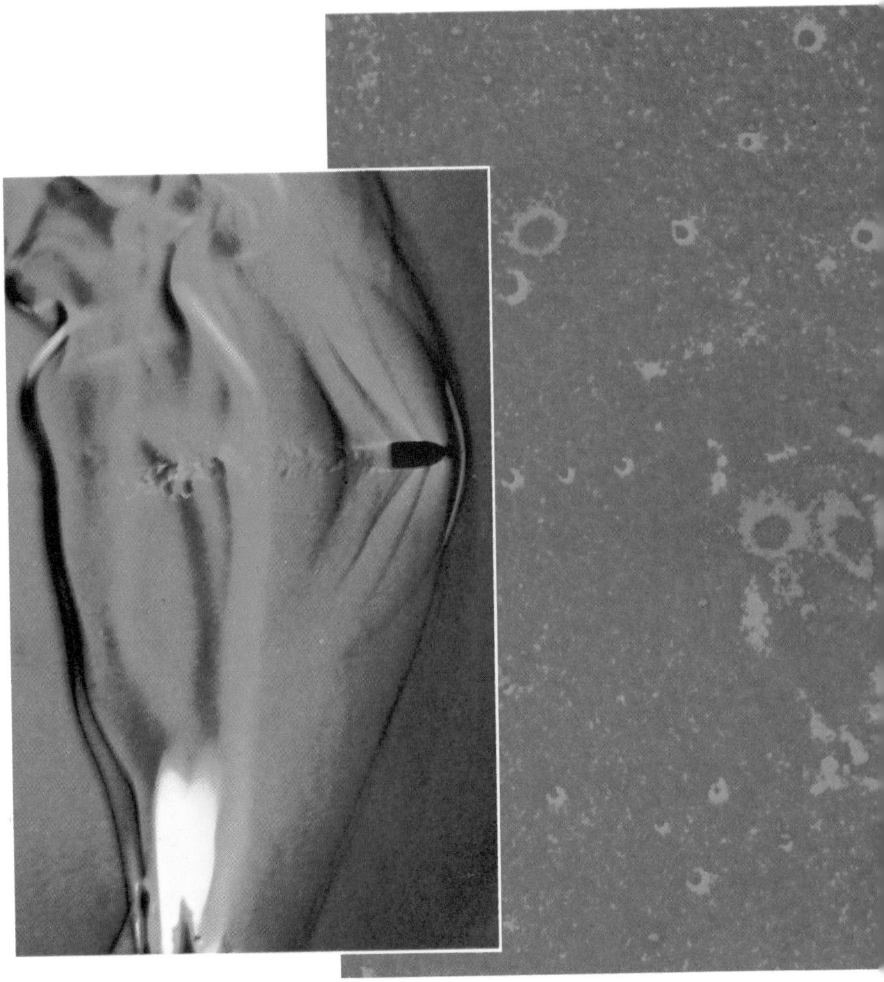

TIME-TRAVEL

We are all time-travellers, moving a certain distance in time with every full rotation of the Earth – a distance that is shared by everyone else. That is the reality of our everyday lives. But who has not speculated on the possibility of varying this steady progress, so that either we speed up while everything around us seems to move more slowly, or we somehow drag our feet so that everything hurries by as we are left behind? And what of the possibility of travelling backwards down that same road, to visit the past and even, perhaps, to alter it? Even if physical time-travel is impossible, could we perhaps communicate across time, through dreams and visions?

Surprisingly, perhaps, science acknowledges the possibility of physical time-travel in certain circumstances. This, however, demands a new way of looking at reality. To provide a bridge between our everyday experience of time and the bizarre possibilities that stem from abandoning this view, it is best to look first at some of the paradoxes inherent in the very concept of time-travel. The discovery of a paradox, to the unimaginative, demonstrates impossibility. To the truly imaginative, however, a paradox is actually a challenge to find a more radical solution.

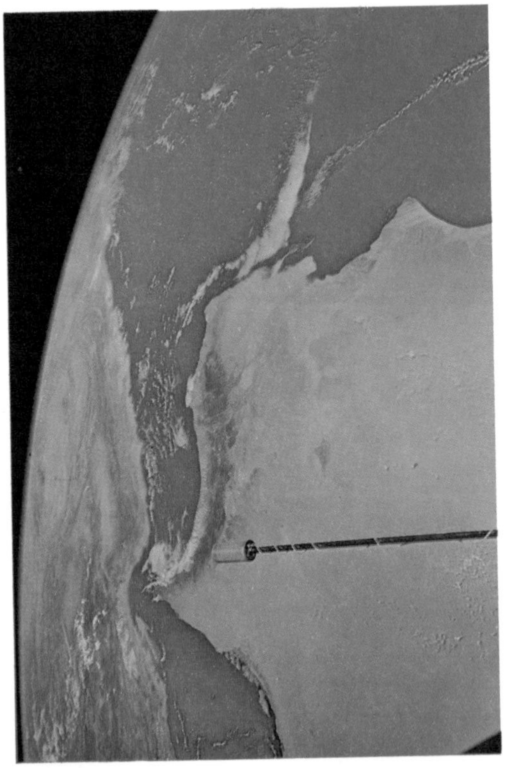

A bullet leaves the gun after you pull the trigger. But what if, seeing the bullet in flight,* above, *you were able to travel back in time and prevent the trigger being pulled? For now, it seems that only the invention of a working time machine would refute denial of the possibility of time-travel, just as the photograph,* left, *does of the idea, held by most medieval scholars until the 13th century, that the Earth was flat.

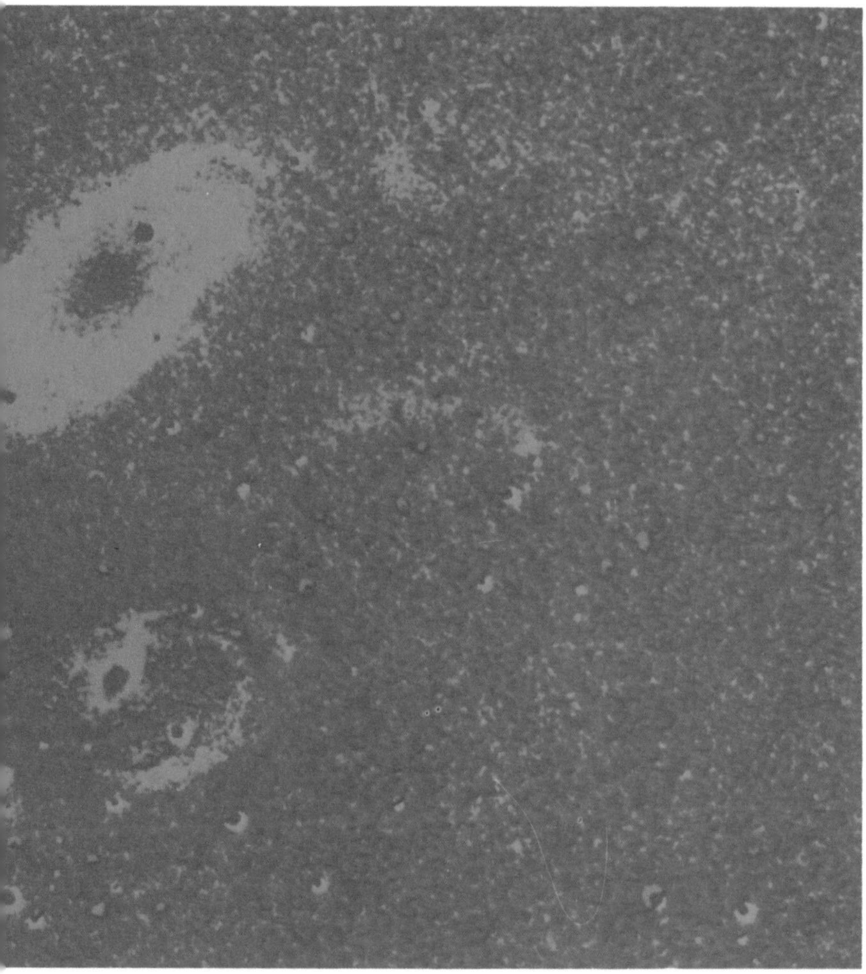

An image-processed photograph of the Stephan's Quintet group of galaxies is shown above. Scientists believe that time becomes distorted near large, dense masses such as stars or black holes, making time-travel possible.

The idea of a steady flow of time is already outmoded by experiments involving particles that travel at speeds close to that of light, under conditions where Einstein's theory of relativity, far removed from our usual perception of the world, provides the best description of how the Universe works. Time, like space, is elastic, not rigid; and Einstein's description involves a blending together in which time and space are seen as two sides of the same coin – a coin dubbed 'space-time'. Both time and space can be stretched and squeezed, depending on circumstances, and time can be traded for space as long as the total balance is maintained. This is all solid, sober scientific fact.

ACCELERATION

Relativity theory is confirmed by the direct measurement of what happens to sub-atomic particles that are whirled at huge speeds inside modern 'atom-smasher' machines – accelerators. It is fact, not mere speculation, that such a particle has a longer lifetime than a stationary counterpart; and it is fact that an astronaut travelling at a speed that is a sizeable fraction of the speed of light – 186,000 miles per second (300,000 kilometres per second) – ages less rapidly than the rest of us who are left behind on Earth.

Another way in which we can stretch time, entirely within accepted modern scientific thinking, involves sitting in a strong gravitational field – the sort of gravitational field you might find near a sizeable black hole. This does not necessitate travelling through the back hole, just sitting in its gravitational field and watching the Universe go by, seemingly at a speeded-up rate. Both tricks are forms of time-travel – and they get the intrepid astronaut into the future 'faster' than the usual rate. If, however, the astronaut does not like what he finds there, he faces a problem for there may be no way home. Whether or not time is a steadily flowing stream, within the framework of modern science, it is usually regarded as a one-way street. Hurrying forward may, just, be possible; bucking the stream and swimming back into the past is probably not.

The key to the discussion is causality – the seemingly logical assumption that events always follow their causes in an orderly procession. A bullet leaves the gun *after* the trigger is pulled, not before; the results of the 3.15 at Ascot reach us only *after* the race is run, not in time for us to be able to rush round to the betting shop and make a killing. The logical implication is therefore that, if time-travel involves violation of causality, it must be impossible. Logically, a theory that tells us we can commit suicide, and *then* go to a restaurant and enjoy a good dinner, must be suspect. But the Universe may yet hold a few surprises for logicians.

Science-fiction writers have their own answers to this paradox and highlight two possibilities – branches and loops in time. The hoariest example of a time-travel paradox concerns a traveller who goes back in time and, wittingly or unwittingly, prevents the birth of the person who would have been his grandfather. But if so, he could never have been born himself. So how could he go back in time if he had never been born? The very existence of the

The Van de Graaff electrostatic accelerator at the Atomic Energy Research Establishment at Harwell, Oxfordshire, England, right, is used to speed subatomic particles to high velocities. Experiment has shown that such particles have longer lives than their stationary counterparts, so that, for them, time actually passes more slowly.

In his novel **Behold the Man,** ***Michael Moorcock describes a fanatical Christian who journeys back to the time of Christ. He finds no sign of the Jesus described in the gospels, nor evidence for Christ's triumphal entry into Jerusalem, depicted*** **above.** ***As he tries to tell people the gospel story, he finds himself playing out the role of Christ – thus making it possible, 2,000 years later, for a religious fanatic to become inspired by the story and, travelling back in time, to re-enact a story he himself has created.***

paradox is seen by many people as proof that time-travel is impossible. Just as nature was once said to 'abhor a vacuum', now we might say that she 'abhors time-travel'. But it is very easy to imagine a resolution to the paradox whereby the grandfather is both born and not born, and the grandson both exists and does not exist. The simplest answer is that the effects of a time-traveller's activities are already rooted in the fabric of time and space. Quite simply, his visit to the past cannot change the present because that visit is already part of history.

Michael Moorcock developed the theme in his novel *Behold the Man*. In this, the time-traveller is a disturbed individual with a tendency to religious mania, who journeys back to the time of Jesus to view the crucifixion. His time machine is destroyed beyond repair, and he finds no trace of the Jesus described in the Bible. Inexorably, as he attempts to tell people about the Jesus he came to see, he is drawn into the role of Jesus, playing out events he remembers from the Bible, up to and including the crucifixion. So history is created, and in 2,000 years time a certain individual travels back in time to close the loop, like the snake that eats its own tail.

This resolution of the paradox sees time as fixed in some greater fabric, with ourselves merely actors who are playing out predetermined roles on the stage of space-time. The alternative resolution of the paradox sees space-time as infinitely variable. It

> THE LIGHT THAT WE SEE FROM DISTANT GALAXIES LEFT THEM MILLIONS OF YEARS AGO, AND IN THE CASE OF THE MOST DISTANT OBJECTS THAT WE HAVE SEEN, THE LIGHT LEFT THEM SOME 8,000 MILLION YEARS AGO. THUS, WHEN WE LOOK AT THE UNIVERSE, WE ARE SEEING IT AS IT WAS IN THE PAST.
>
> STEPHEN W. HAWKING,
>
> A BRIEF HISTORY OF TIME

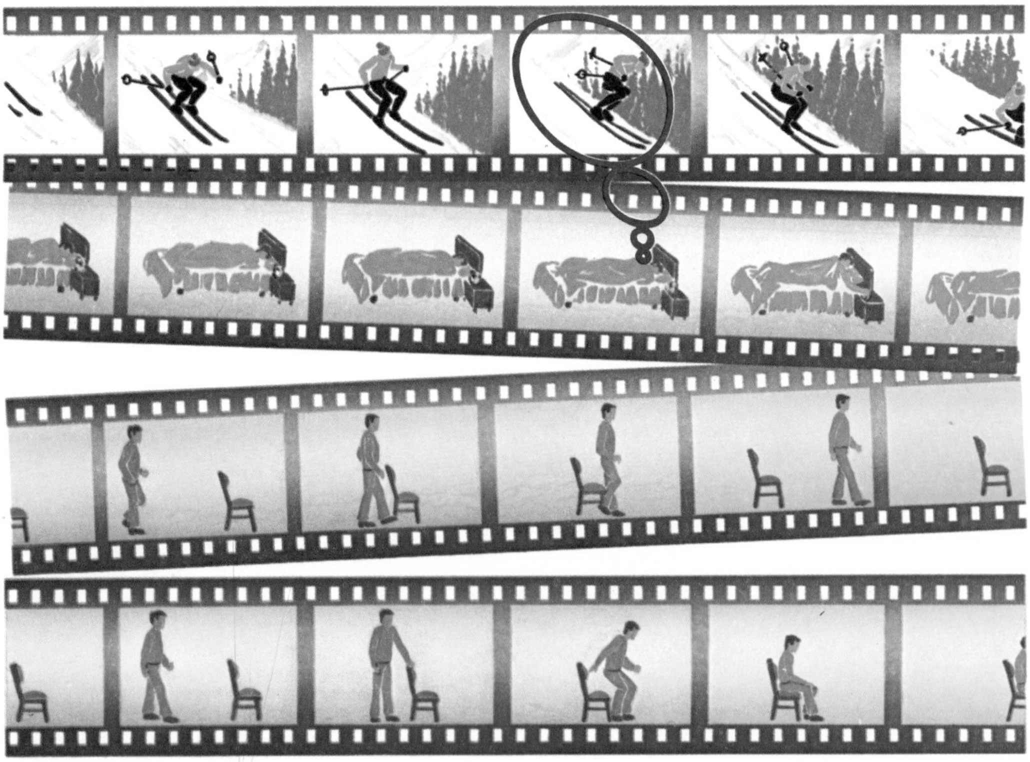

One philosophical theory of time sees all possible combinations of events as somehow running parallel to our own, as in the filmstrips, shown **right.** ***Thus everything that can possibly be imagined to happen does happen – somewhere along the infinite array of parallel worlds. Some of these may differ from our normal, everyday existence only by a single detail; others may be quite fantastic. It has been suggested by some theorists that both dreams and paranormal events – such as the psychic warning of a mining disaster to Andrew Jackson Davis, depicted*** **far right** ***– could be 'leaks' of information from parallel worlds into our own.***

also sees each of us master of his or her own destiny to an extent few people ever realise. Again, an example from science fiction makes the point. In *Lest Darkness Fall*, L. Sprague de Camp's hero is a 20th-century man who is mysteriously deposited in sixth-century Italy and averts the Dark Ages single-handed. The story is hokum but author's explanation is that, having 'slipped down the trunk' of the tree of history, the hero has created a new branch, a new line of history growing out as a result of his introduction of 20th-century ideas into a sixth-century environment.

With only slight modifications, this idea becomes a respectable philosophical concept, whereby there may exist parallel universes, worlds running alongside one another in some sense, with an infinite number of variations. If you go back and kill your grandfather, the argument runs, you have also slipped 'sideways' into a parallel reality where the grandfather always was killed by an intruder from elsewhere (and elsewhen). So when you come home to find history unchanged, you should not be surprised: in your 'timeline', nothing has happened to change history at all!

Taken to its logical conclusion, this view of reality argues that we have complete control over our destiny, because literally anything is possible, and also actually happens somewhere among the infinite array of parallel universes. All we have to do is find a way to travel across the time barrier, not forwards or backwards but *sideways* in time. It is, of course, much easier said than done; but if physical time-travel remains at the very least an unlikely prospect for us, there remains the intriguing possibility that dreams, ghosts and other mysterious phenomena generally classified as paranormal experiences could be just as well explained in terms of information somehow leaking into our world from parallel worlds of time.

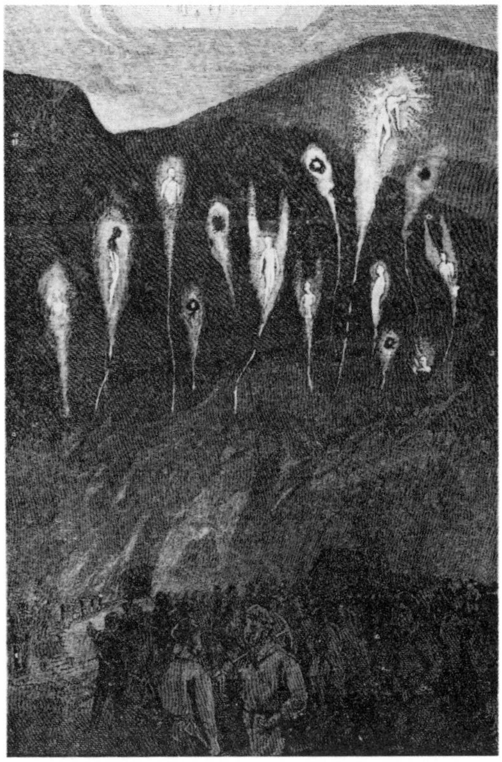

One of the most startling philosophical theories sees everything as being in the mind. Sir Fred Hoyle, an eminent astronomer who had a penchant for speculation and science fiction, mentioned this idea in a serious scientific book, *Ten Faces of the Universe,* and elaborated on the theme in his science-fiction novel, *October the First is Too Late*. In these, he suggests that all the events that we imagine making up the flow of time exist in a kind of infinite sorting office, with each event, or state, in its own pigeon hole. Hoyle explains:

'Suppose that in each of these states your own consciousness is included. As soon as a particular

A lassooed Rod Taylor,* above, *stars in the 1960 MGM film* The Time Machine, *based on the novel by H. G. Wells. Such stories raise an exciting question: could it be that mankind will one day be capable of building a working time machine to take us both into the future and back into the past?

state is chosen, as soon as an imaginary office worker takes a look at the contents of a particular pigeon hole, you have the subjective consciousness of a particular moment, of what you call the present. Think of the clerk in an office taking a look, first at the contents of one pigeon hole, then at the contents of another. Suppose he does this, not in sequence, but in any old order. What is the effect on your subjective consciousness? So far as the clerk himself is concerned, he's jumping about all over the place among the pigeon holes. So your consciousness jumps all over the place. But the strange thing is that your subjective impression is quite different. You have the impression of time as an ever-rolling stream.'

We may all, in fact, be experiencing time-travel, as well as travel between different possible universes; but, because one of the rules of the game is that the clerk in the office can look at only one pigeon hole at a time, we never know it.

True or not, theories such as these show that there is more to time than we may suppose – and that there are, philosophically speaking, ways round the paradoxes of time-travel. And if there are ways round the paradoxes, there seems to be no logical reason why it should not be possible one day for us to build an actual time machine.

WHEN LIGHT BEAMS BEND

THE ABILITY OF UFOS TO DEFLECT LIGHT BEAMS, THEREBY DEFYING ALL KNOWN PHYSICAL LAWS, ARE REPORTED IN THE TWO CASES PRESENTED HERE, FROM AUSTRALIA AND FRANCE

***Sullivan's headlight beams bent sharply and mysteriously to the right, as depicted in the artist's impression,* above.**

Newcomers to ufological research, accustomed to conventional physics, often throw up their hands in incredulity when they are confronted with reports of the extraordinary phenomena that sometimes occur during UFO sightings. Among the most remarkable of these are accounts of beams of light that stop short or make abrupt bends, without any evident absorbing, refracting or reflecting agencies to bring this about. In the two cases discussed here, beams from torches and car headlamps seem to have been manipulated in an equally 'impossible' way.

The London *Daily Express* of 12 April 1966 carried a story in which it reported that a motorist, 38-year-old Ronald Sullivan, had been cruising along near Bendigo in southern Australia under a moonlit sky when he noticed that, inexplicably, his headlight beams suddenly bent to the right. In a statement made to the police at Maryborough, near Melbourne, he said that he avoided a crash only with difficulty and, as he drew to a halt, saw a display of 'gaseous lights' of all colours of the rainbow in a field alongside the road. The display, he said, was followed by the appearance of an object that rose vertically to a point about 10 feet (3 metres) in the air and then just disappeared.

When Sullivan returned to the scene a few days later, he found that another motorist, Gary Turner, had been killed in a crash at the same spot the previous evening. Meanwhile, the police had made their investigations and found, in a freshly ploughed field 50 feet (20 metres) from the fence, a circular depression about 5 feet (1.5 metres) across, and varying from 2 to 5 inches (5–13 centimetres) in depth. The police regarded Sullivan – a highly respected businessman – as a reliable witness, and noted that he professed not to believe in UFOs.

The *Daily Express* story ended there. The corresponding Associated Press message was more detailed, however: apparently, Sullivan's encounter took place on 4 April 1966; he returned to the site on 8 April, and it was then that he learned of the fatal accident that had taken place on 7 April. A report in the *Melbourne Herald* added that he had driven to nearby Wycheproof where he had had his headlights checked – they were found to be in perfect working order – before going on to the police.

It was also revealed that the bent beam incident and the fatal accident occurred on a long straight stretch of road between Bendigo and St Arnaud, at a point 9 miles (15 kilometres) east of Bealiba, a small town nearly 130 miles (210 kilometres) north-west of Melbourne.

The information that was available left it a matter of speculation as to whether the bending of the headlight beams was accidentally caused by Sullivan's car running into the UFO's 'force field' or whether, if the incidents of 4 and 7 April were connected in some way, the bending was the result of a deliberate action by a hostile agency – whether it be human or alien.

FREAK REFLECTIONS

In a commentary in *Flying Saucer Review,* scientist Stephen L. Smith deplored the absence of important detail such as the make of Sullivan's car, the kind of dipping mechanism employed in its headlights, and the exact position on the beams at which they were bent. He pointed out that there were three possible explanations: that the beams were bent at source, that the bending occurred somewhere along the beams, or that the beams appeared bent through illusion or hallucination. Smith wrote that his colleagues of the Cambridge University Investigation Group had suggested how an illusion might be brought about by the sudden extinguishing of the left-hand component of the headlight beam which 'through its divergent character would seem to have been bent to the right . . . [due] to a freak of reflection caused by the absence of dust particles by which headlight beams are normally seen'.

***The Centre for Ecumenical Meetings, Taizé, close to the landing point of what seemed to be an alien craft, is seen* below.**

A map of the 1972 Taizé encounter,* below, *shows:
A *Position of the UFO*
B *Position of the witnesses*
C *Position of the dark mass*

There are other possibilities, too. If hallucination were the cause of the phenomenon, then perhaps it was spontaneously generated in the witness's brain. Or was it caused by some outside agency – perhaps a force field emanating from the object that he had observed?

The second case we highlight occurred some 6 miles (10 kilometres) north of Cluny in eastern France, on 12 August 1972. The day before, people from all walks of life – most of them young folk – had gathered at the Protestant monastery at Taizé for celebrations organized by its founder, Friar Roger Schutz.

The events at Taizé in the early hours of 12 August 1972 were reported to the gendarmerie at Cluny, and afterwards to the French UFO organisation *Lumières dans la Nuit,* for whom an investigation was conducted by a schoolmaster named Tyrode.

According to the report, a group of about 35 young people had collected for discussions at a rustic open air theatre situated among the visitors' tents near the crest of a ridge on which the community's buildings also stood. This site faced westwards over a gently sloping valley, and a ridge known as La Cras, and successively higher ridges beyond that. The sky was overcast, and a light drizzle soon began to fall.

From the place where the earnest young debaters were grouped, a large ploughed field sloped down into the valley. F. Tantot, from Mâcon, a young man from Dijon and an Italian student were alerted at about 2 a.m. by Renata, from Sardinia, to a 'star' that she could see descending. Before the others could swing round, however, she was already telling them that it had 'landed'. In a few moments, all the people in the theatre could see an object, seemingly stationary, on the slopes of La Cras, facing them and at the same level as themselves. All present had also heard the whistling noise as the UFO approached, and they could now see that it was bounded to the left by a field of cereal – its light colour showed up the UFO as dark by contrast – and to the right by a large tree standing on the ridge. The size of the UFO was estimated as 'larger than a coach'.

All the witnesses now saw the UFO 'light up'. Seven yellow lights appeared in a row, then two orange ones outside and to the left of the object.

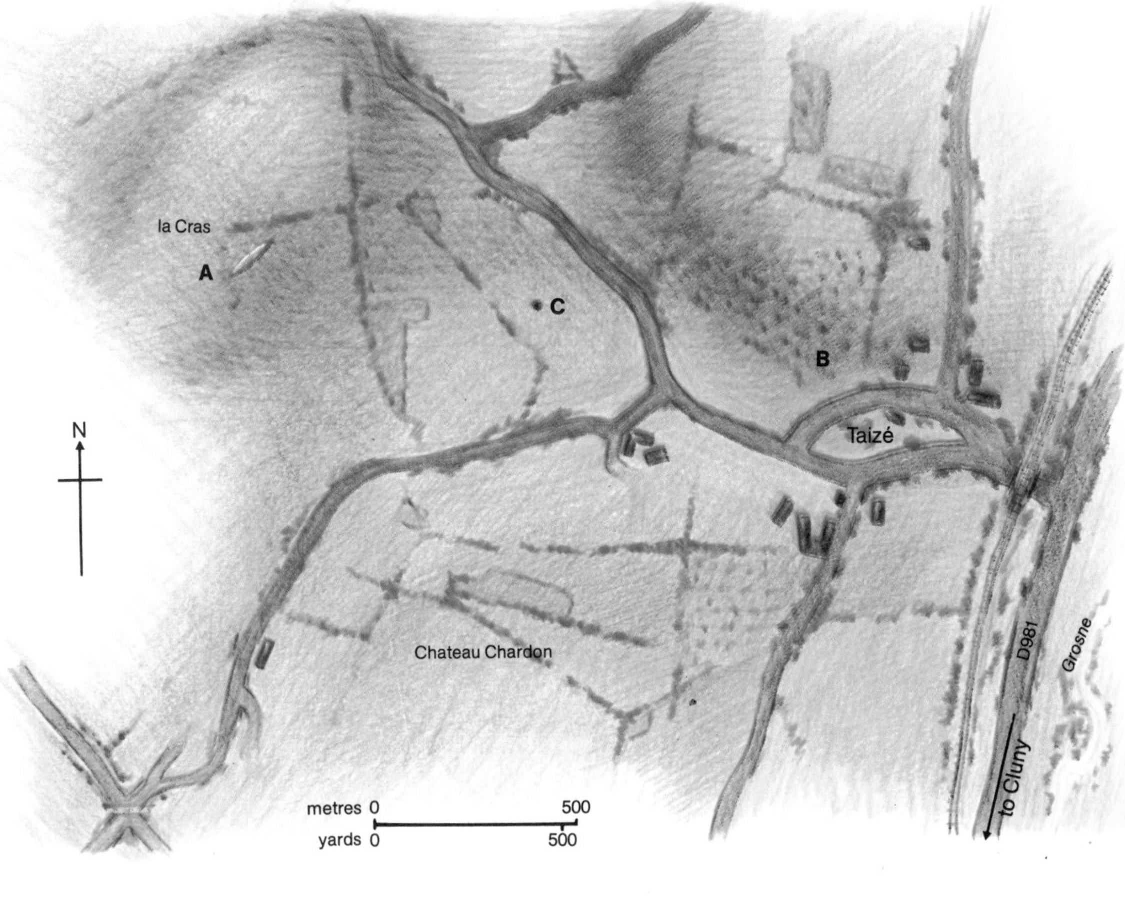

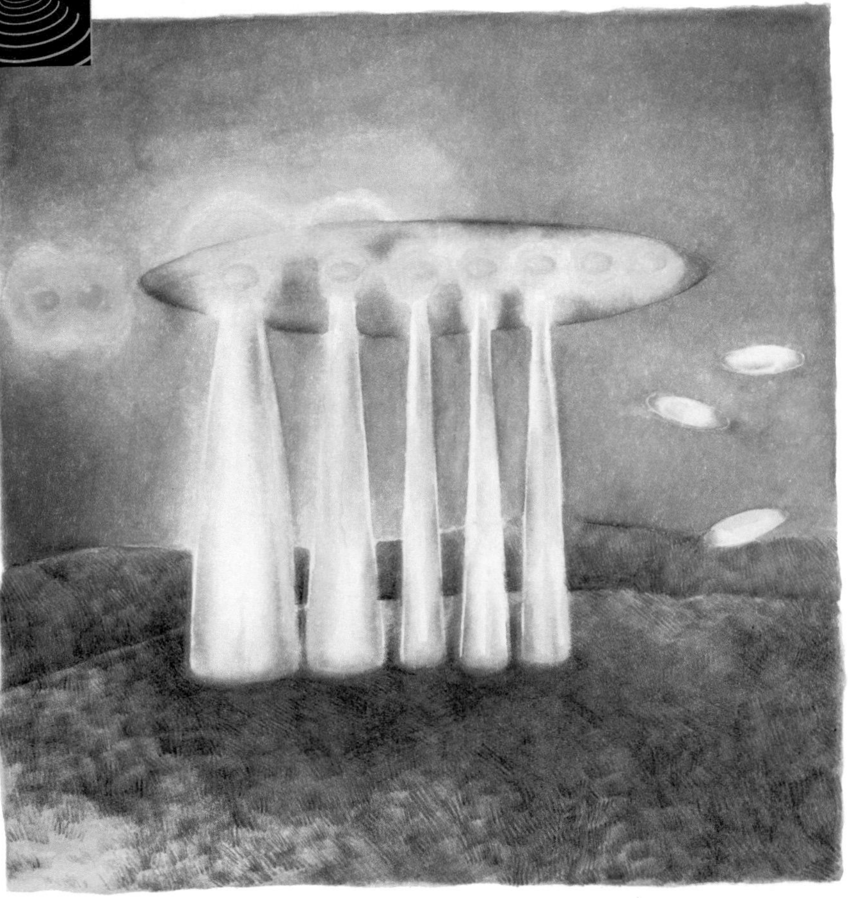

By now, the intrepid four had reached the middle of the field, and they became aware of a dark, haystack-shaped mass some 6 or 7 yards (5 or 6 metres) high, around which a point of red light moved in a haphazard trajectory. Between themselves and this mass, the witnesses thought they could see a hedge about 10 feet (3 metres) ahead – but at a point where, they knew, no hedge existed. When a torch beam was shone towards the mass, the beam suddenly turned vertically upwards about 1½ feet (50 centimetres) from the hedge and, dispersing, was soon lost in the air.

Subsequent attempts to illuminate the object, using all the torches the witnesses had with them, met with the same fate and, alarmed, the four were tempted to back off. However, when the lights on the UFO suddenly went out, only to flash back on again, and the three discs vanished into the big object, Tantot flashed his torch in that direction. As if in response, the largest beam from the UFO rose so that it shone directly at the witnesses. Dazzled, and feeling a surge of heat, they raised their hands to protect their eyes. Meanwhile, the UFO began to move away, suddenly accelerating towards Cluny. It was 4.40 a.m when the craft was finally lost from sight at Taizé.

The Taizé UFO, **above,** ***is shown emitting white pylon-like beams. In the field,*** **below,** ***a red light leaves a bright, looping trajectory around the haystack-shaped mass. The witnesses' torch beams, meanwhile, bend inexplicably up into the air.***

After that, five of the yellow lights began to emit beams that extended slowly towards the ground. What appeared to be cupolas were also observed above the two light beams at the very left of the row. When discussing the phenomenon, some witnesses said they had the impression that the beams were pylons on which the object was supported. Indeed, it was as if the beams were made of solid matter. At this point, some of the witnesses, particularly Tantot and the man from Dijon, felt tingling in their fingers and knees.

Gyrating Lights

While the 'solid' beams of light were extending to the ground, a train of red sparks was seen at the right-hand end of the object. These were soon extinguished; and where they had been, there were now seen three small discs, each with two red points of light. These began to gyrate around the main UFO, and the manoeuvres went on until the end of the sighting.

At about 3 a.m., the four original witnesses decided to have a closer look at the big object and, armed with torches, set off across the field, watched as they went by the remaining 30 witnesses in the theatre, who were later able to report that the main beams were rotating around individual vertical axes. The beam second from the left suddenly grew brighter, and showers of red particles filled the air around the four and covered the ground. A row of what looked like portholes then appeared in white light, only to disappear after approximately 20 minutes, when the large beam to the left started to flash several times.

CREATURES OF HABIT

Do we inherit knowledge from past generations? Experiments suggest we may have access to a kind of 'pooled memory' – the collective knowledge of our entire species. How do the facts support Rupert Sheldrake in his revolutionary theory of the nature of heredity?

When rabbits breed, they produce more rabbits; goldfish produce goldfish; and seeds from cabbage plants grow into cabbages. Like begets like. The general characteristics of the species are produced again and again, generation after generation; so are particular features of the race or variety, and even individual peculiarities that enable us to pick out family resemblances.

These facts are so familiar that we tend to take them for granted. But the more that is found out about the intricate processes by which embryos develop and grow, the more amazing inheritance of shape and structure becomes. Even more astonishing is the inheritance of instinct. Young spiders, for example, spin their webs without having to learn from other spiders how to do it, or what the webs are for. Among the birds, cuckoos provide a particularly striking example: the young are hatched and reared by foster parents of other species, and never see their true parents or, indeed, any other cuckoos, for the first few weeks of their lives. Towards the end of the summer, adult European cuckoos migrate to their winter habitat in southern Africa. About a month later, the young cuckoos congregate together and then they also migrate to the appropriate region of Africa, where they join the older generation. They instinctively know that they should migrate, and when to do so; they instinctively recognise other young cuckoos and congregate together; and they instinctively know in which direction to fly and their destination.

But how can these phenomena be explained? The most obvious fact is that all animals and plants develop from living cells derived from their parents. In sexual reproduction, these are the egg and sperm cells; in vegetative reproduction, detached parts of the parent organism. These cells have a complex microscopic structure, and in the nucleus of each are long thread-like chromosomes, which contain the chemical DNA (deoxyribonucleic acid).

It is well known that one of the major triumphs of modern biology has been to show that hereditary differences depend on differences in specific parts of their chromosomes (genes), and that the DNA of

Young spiders know instinctively how to weave webs, such as the one below, without having to learn the skill from other spiders. How are such instincts inherited?

different genes has a definite and characteristic structure.

DNA comes in pairs of long strands wrapped around each other in a spiral – the famous double helix. On these strands are four different kinds of chemical, usually represented by the letters A, G, T and C – adenine, guanine, thymine and cytosine. These can be arranged to spell out different chemical 'words', and the sequence of 'words' can be translated into sequences of relatively simple chemicals, amino acids, which are strung together to make up protein molecules.

The important question is whether these chemicals by themselves can explain the problem of heredity. In other words, can we account for the shape of a flower or the instincts of an insect in terms of the chemicals it contains?

The answer is that we cannot: biologists are agreed on this point. But whereas most of them assume that failure so far is due to the fact that living organisms are extremely complex and that not enough is yet known about their chemical details, some are convinced that we can never understand living organisms in terms of chemistry alone. Other, still mysterious, factors are involved in life, and play a major part in the inheritance of form and instinct.

Even orthodox biologists admit the existence of a mysterious non-chemical factor in heredity, and give it the impressive sounding name of the 'genetic programme'. It would be said, for example, that the shape of a daffodil or the instincts of a dragonfly are 'genetically programmed'. But what exactly is a genetic programme?

It is not, for a start, like a computer programme. This is put into a computer by a conscious intelligent being, the computer programmer – and materialistically minded biologists deny that living organisms have been put together by a conscious programmer or designer.

Is a genetic programme the same thing as the chemical structure of the DNA? This cannot be the explanation either, because all cells of the body contain identical copies of DNA, and yet they develop differently. Consider your arms and your legs. The DNA in them is the same, but they have different forms. So something else must have been responsible for shaping them as they developed in the embryo.

The reed warbler, above, feeds a young cuckoo in its nest. Cuckoos are hatched and reared by birds of other species and, for the first few weeks of their lives, see no other cuckoos. But, at the end of the summer, the young cuckoos, taught by no one, join up into groups to make the long flight to their winter habitat in southern Africa. They know instinctively when to congregate, how to recognise other cuckoos and how to navigate on the long journey that none of them has attempted before. How can this complex behaviour be explained?

*In*Focus

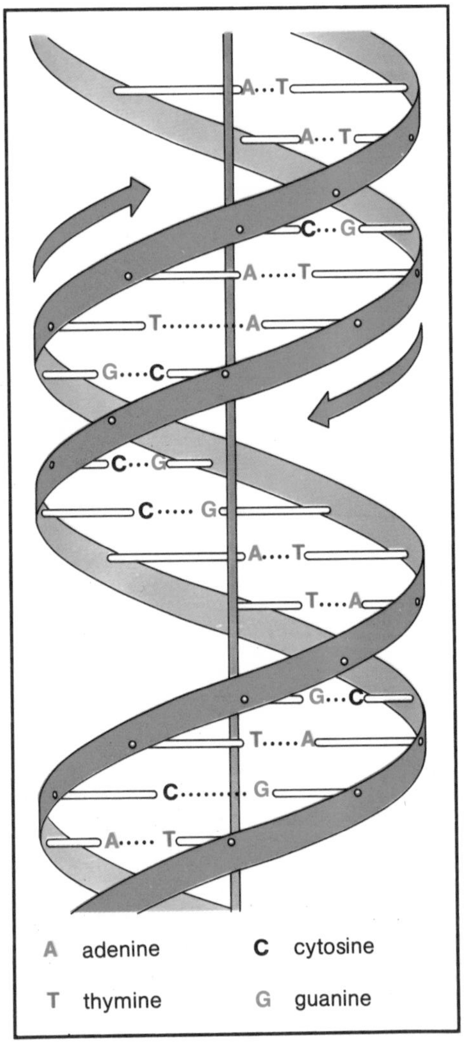

THE GENETIC BLUEPRINT

The discovery by James Watson and Francis Crick in 1953 of the beautiful double helix structure of DNA, left, is famous as one of the great breakthroughs of modern science. But the function of this substance is less well-known.

DNA – deoxyribonucleic acid – is essentially the carrier of genetic information. Found in the reproductive cells of all living things are long paired strands called chromosomes, which are the carriers of the genes. There is a fixed number of pairs of chromosomes for each species; the number for Man is 23.

Genes are made up of proteins and DNA. Scientists had believed that proteins were the genetic material, but in the early 1950s DNA – a substance that had been isolated in cells as early as 1869 – was recognised as the carrier of encoded genetic information.

It remained to break the code. The first decisive step forward came with Crick and Watson's discovery of 1953. They found that DNA consists of chains of sugar and phosphate, twisted round each other and carrying four different kinds of molecule – adenine, guanine, thymine and cytosine – which can be arranged to form various instructions. These control the selection and arrangement of amino acids, which are used to manufacture proteins. Thus DNA controls every aspect of the development of the body.

But one puzzle remains: all the cells of the body contain identical copies of DNA, and yet they develop differently. What controls this development? Orthodox science has, as yet, no answer.

The conventional explanation is that this shaping must be due to complicated chemical and physical interactions that are not yet understood. But what gives rise to the correct pattern of interactions? This is the problem that remains unsolved, and to say that it must be due to a genetic programme does not in fact provide any explanation at all: it merely creates an illusion of understanding. Similarly, to say that a spider's nervous system is genetically programmed to give the right web-spinning behaviour only restates the problem differently.

Through detailed study of embryos, a number of influential embryologists have come to the conclusion that developing limbs and organs are shaped by what they call morphogenetic fields. This term is not as daunting as it sounds, and means fields that give rise to form, or 'form-fields'. (The word 'morphogenetic' comes from the Greek *morphe* which means form, and *genesis* which means 'coming-into-being'). These fields can be thought of by analogy with magnetic fields, which have a shape even though they are invisible. (The shape of the field of a magnet can be revealed by the patterns taken up when iron filings are scattered around it.) The form-fields mould the developing cells and tissues. Thus, in the embryo, a developing arm is moulded by an 'arm-shaping' morphogenetic field and a developing leg by a 'leg-shaping' field.

The human foetus is shown* below *at various stages of development. At 28 days,* top left, *it is no more than a small blob of tissue nestled in the womb lining; at 33 days,* top right, *the limbs are just beginning to appear; at 49 days,* bottom left, *the features are recognisably human; and finally, after 340 days in the womb, the baby is fully developed,* bottom right. *Something has supervised the highly specialised development of the various parts of the baby's body: and yet, since the DNA in each of its cells is identical to that of its original single cell, this 'something' must be different from the genetic information encoded in the DNA. Its nature is, as yet, unknown.

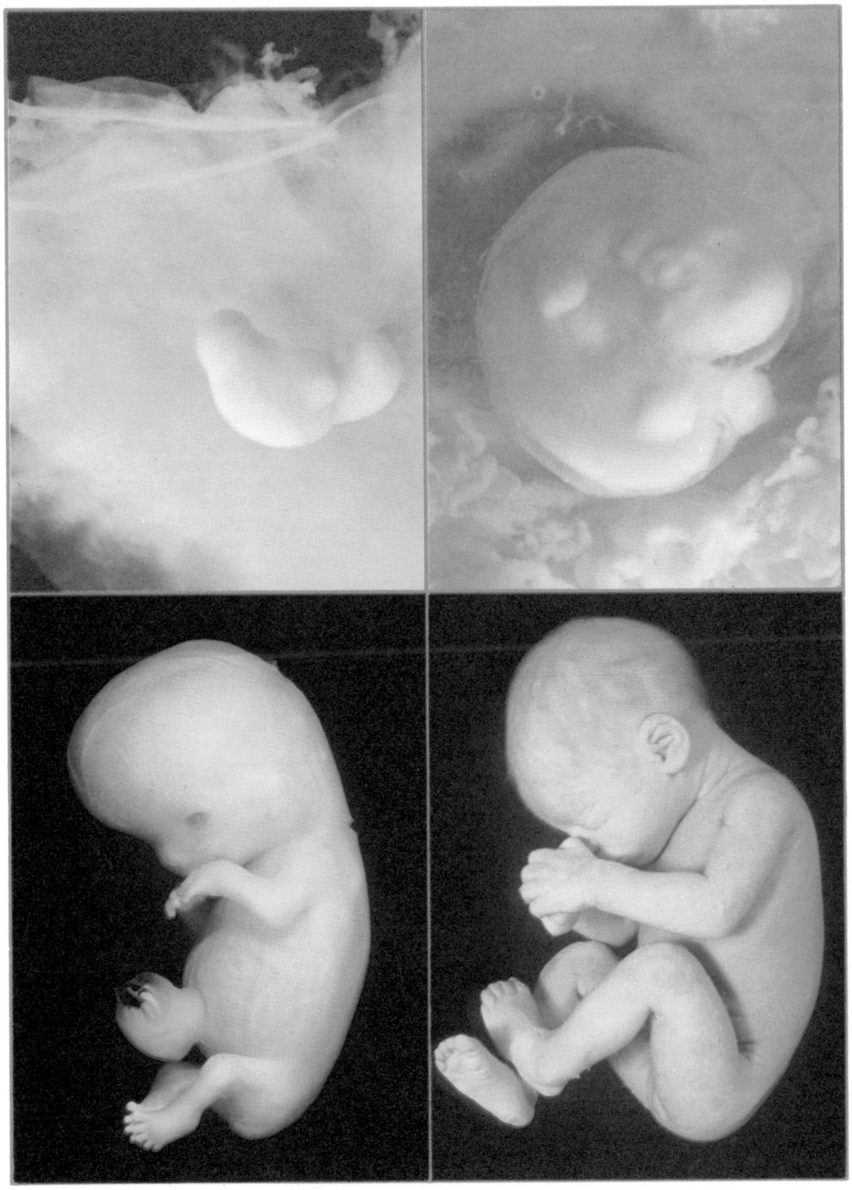

But what are these fields, and where do they come from? For over 50 years, their nature and even their very existence has remained obscure. However, they are just as real as the magnetic and gravitational fields of physics, but they are a new kind of field with very remarkable properties. Like the known fields of physics, they connect similar things together across space. In addition, they connect things together across time, so that creatures can learn from the experience of previous members of the same species even when there is no direct contact.

The idea is that the morphogenetic fields that shape a growing animal or plant are derived from the forms of previous organisms of the same species. To put it quite simply, the embryo 'tunes in' to the form of past members of the species. The process by which this happens is called *morphic resonance*. Similarly, the fields that organise the activities of an animal's nervous system are derived from past animals of the same kind; so that in their instinctive behaviour, animals draw on a sort of 'memory bank' or 'pooled memory' of their species.

LEARNING NEW TRICKS

This hypothesis, which is known as the hypothesis of formative causation, leads to a range of surprising predictions that provide ways of testing it experimentally. For instance, if a number of animals, say rats, learn a new trick that rats have never performed before, then other rats of the same kind all over the world should be able to learn the same trick more easily, even in the absence of any known kind of connection or communication. The larger the number of rats that learn it, the easier it should become for subsequent rats everywhere else.

> " THE HYPOTHESIS OF FORMATIVE CAUSATION SUGGESTS IT SHOULD BE GETTING EASIER FOR PEOPLE TO LEARN TO RIDE BICYCLES OR TYPE ... JUST BECAUSE MORE AND MORE PEOPLE HAVE ALREADY LEARNED TO DO THESE THINGS. "

Remarkably enough, there is already evidence that this phenomenon actually occurs. In 1920, the psychologist William McDougall began a series of experiments designed to find out if animals were able to inherit abilities acquired by their parents. He put white rats, one at a time, in a tank of water from which they could escape only by swimming to one of two gangways and climbing up it. One gangway was brightly lit, the other was not. If the rats left by the illuminated gangway, they received an electric shock. McDougall recorded how many trials the rats took to learn to escape by the other one.

The first generation of rats received an average of over 160 shocks each before learning to avoid the illuminated gangway. But the second generation, bred from these experienced parents, learned more quickly, and the next generation more quickly still. This improvement continued until, after 30 generations, the rats were making an average of only 20 errors each.

McDougall believed that his results provided good evidence for the inheritance of acquired characteristics. This conclusion was extremely controversial. It flew in the face of the orthodox theory of inheritance, based on Mendelian genetics, which denies that any such thing can happen. His experiments were subjected to critical scrutiny by some of the leading biologists of the time. But they were able to find little wrong with his actual procedure, and fell back on the criticism that McDougall must have been breeding from the more intelligent rats in each generation, in spite of the fact that he chose the parents at random.

McDougall replied by starting a new experiment in which he selected only the most stupid rats in each generation as parents of the next. According to conventional genetics, subsequent generations should have got slower and slower at learning. But in fact the reverse occurred, and after 22 generations the rats were learning 10 times more quickly than the first generation of stupid ancestors.

These results had such revolutionary implications that other scientists hastened to try to repeat them. Dr F.A.E. Crew in Edinburgh, and Prof. W.E. Agar and his colleagues in Melbourne, Australia, constructed tanks of similar design, using white rats of the same breed. But for reasons that no one was able to explain, from the very first generation their rats picked up what was going on much more quickly than the early generations of McDougall's rats. So striking was this effect that some of the first rats tested by Crew 'learned' to escape by the unlit gangway straight away, without making a single error.

Chromosomes are picked out clearly by a special dye in the salivary glands of the fruit-fly Drosophila, magnified above 120 times. Found in paired strands in the nuclei of sex cells, chromosomes bear the genes that are the carriers of hereditary information. When two creatures reproduce sexually, the offspring receives one set of chromosomes from each of its parents.

Agar and his group studied not only the change in the rate of learning of successive generations of rats descended from trained parents, as MacDougall had done, but also that of a parallel line of rats bred from untrained parents. In this control line, some of the rats were tested in the water tank and then discarded and replaced by others that had not been tested, who then became the parents of the next generation of control animals.

In experiments that lasted 25 years, these Australian workers observed that successive generations of rats in the trained lines tended to learn more quickly, just as McDougall had found. But so did the rats in the control line.

The fact that the same improvement occurred in rats descended both from trained and from untrained ancestors showed that it could not be due to the passing on of specifically modified genes from parents to their offspring. McDougall's conclusion was therefore refuted. With the publication of the final paper by Agar's group in 1954, the last surviving piece of evidence for the inheritance of acquired characteristics seemed to have been disposed of. Nevertheless, to this day, McDougall's remarkable results have remained unexplained in terms of orthodox science.

In relation to human beings, this hypothesis suggests that, on average, it should be getting easier and easier for people to learn to ride bicycles, or to type, or to swim, just because more and more people have already learned to do these things. Is this in fact the case? Unfortunately, precise information is hard to come by, although anecdotal evidence suggests that such improvements have in fact occurred. But even if it is so, changes in the average speed of learning are difficult to interpret because other relevant factors also change with time – for instance, machine design, teaching methods, and motivation.

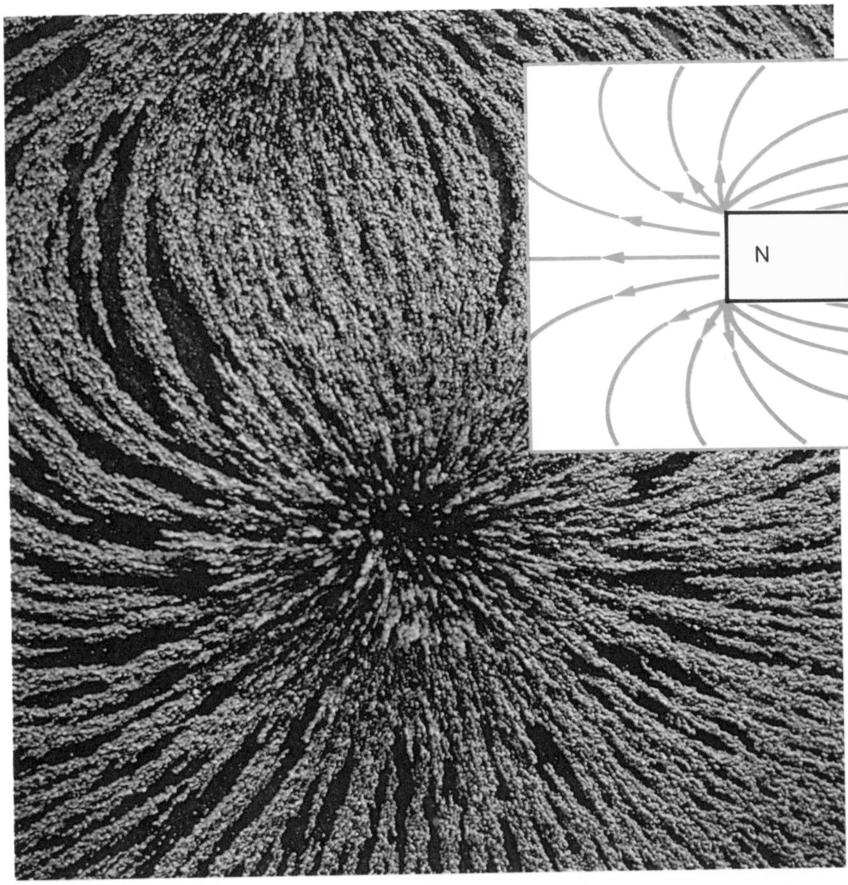

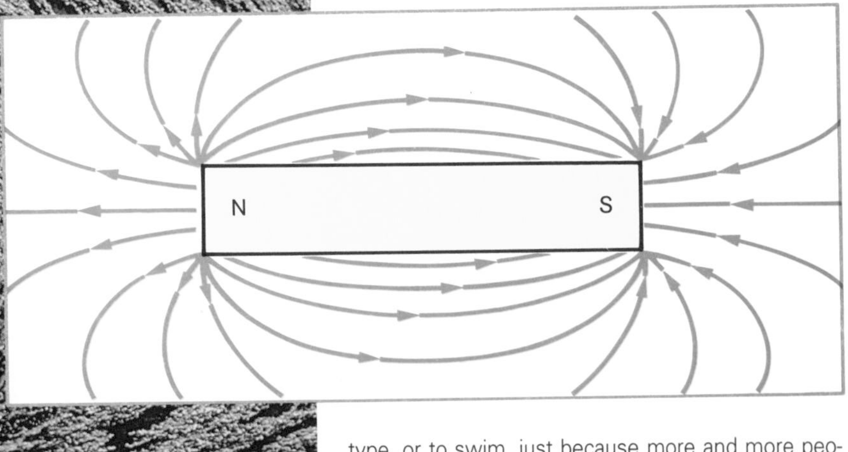

The idea of morphic resonance is perhaps easier to grasp with the help of an analogy. Imagine an intelligent and curious person who knows nothing about electricity or electromagnetic radiation. He is shown a television set for the first time. He might

*In*Focus

AS CLEAR AS CRYSTAL?

It is in the field of chemistry that the most unambiguous tests of the hypothesis of formative causation should be possible. Rupert Sheldrake's hypothesis predicts, for example, that the complex patterns in which molecules arrange themselves (like the perfect cube formed by sodium chloride, or common salt, *above* and *right*) should be influenced by the patterns taken up by previous crystals of the same substance. In other words, substances should crystallise more readily the more often they have been crystallised before.

New chemicals synthesised for the first time are usually difficult to crystallise, and do indeed form crystals more readily as time goes on. The conventional explanation is that tiny fragments of previous crystals get carried from laboratory to laboratory on the clothing of scientists, or that crystal 'seeds' travel round the world as microscopic dust particles in the atmosphere. But, as Dr Sheldrake has pointed out, it would be easy enough to eliminate these possibilities in a sealed laboratory.

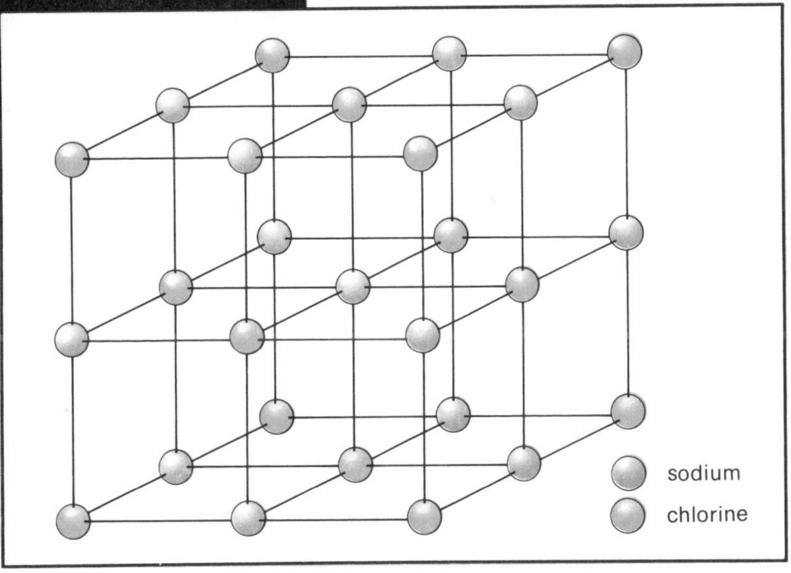

The pattern produced by a bar magnet when iron filings are scattered around it, can be seen* left. *The magnetic field that gives rise to the pattern is always there,* (see inset), *but it is usually invisible. Some leading embryologists believe that the shape of living things is formed by a morphogenetic field – a field that, although usually invisible like the magnetic field, can nevertheless mould the developing cells and tissues of an organism.

at first suppose that the set actually contained little people, whose images he saw on the screen. But when he looked inside and found only wires, condensers, transistors, and so on, he might adopt the more sophisticated theory that the screen images somehow arose from complicated interaction among the components of the set. This hypothesis would seem particularly plausible when he found that the images became distorted or disappeared completely when components were removed, and that the images were restored to normal when these components were replaced.

If the suggestion were put to him that the images also depended on invisible influences entering the set from far away, he might reject it on the grounds that this was unnecessary and obscurantist. His opinion that nothing came into the set from outside would be reinforced by the discovery that the set weighed the same switched on and switched off. While admitting that he could not explain in detail how the images were produced from complicated interactions within the set, and nothing more, he might well claim that such an explanation was possible in principle, and that it might eventually be achieved.

This point of view may resemble the conventional approach to biology. By contrast, in terms of this analogy, the hypothesis of formative causation does not involve a denial of the importance of the wires and transistors (corresponding to DNA, protein molecules, and so on). Rather, it recognises in addition the role of influences transmitted from outside the system, the 'transmitters' being past organisms of the same species. Genetic changes can affect the inheritance of form or instinct by altering the 'tuning', or by introducing distortions into the 'reception'. But genetic factors cannot by themselves fully account for the inheritance of form and instinct, any more than the particular pictures on the screen of a television set can be explained in terms of its wiring diagram alone.

Yet some of Rupert Sheldrake's tests involving human beings have produced quite startling results. On one occasion, for example, he asked a Japanese poet to provide three short rhymes, all similar in sound. One had no meaning; one was newly written; and the third was traditional. Interestingly, the English-speaking subjects (none of whom spoke Japanese) found it easier to remember the traditional rhyme. According to Sheldrake, this was as a direct result of continual repetition over many generations and the build-up of a morphogenetic field.

The hypothesis of formative causation leads to an interpretation of heredity in terms of the repetition of forms and patterns of behaviour that have occurred in the past. But it cannot in itself, of course, lead to an understanding of how these forms and patterns originated in the first place.

THE ALIEN THREAT

SOME UFOLOGISTS BELIEVE THAT THE POWERS BEHIND THE UFO PHENOMENON INTEND TO TAKE OVER MEN'S MINDS AND TURN US INTO A RACE OF ROBOT-SLAVES. WHAT EVIDENCE IS THERE FOR SUCH A CLAIM?

'Could I really be sure the people I was then talking with were representatives of the real space brotherhood who wished humankind well?' This was the dilemma facing Howard Menger, who in 1956 allegedly met a group of 'space people' who not only introduced him to space music and the space potato (with five times as much protein as the Earth-grown variety) but also revealed that he himself was Venusian, as was his second wife. The brotherhood claimed variously that they came from Venus, Mars, Jupiter and Saturn – and, as though that were not sufficiently confusing, they also announced that there were bad spacepersons as well as good. But since the bad ones always pretended to be good, how could a mere Earthling know whom to trust? Howard Menger takes up his story:

Howard Menger,* above, *was informed that he was a Venusian in an encounter with space people in 1956.

***Many people believe that UFOS presage Armageddon, as depicted in* The Great Day of his Wrath, *by John Martin,* below.**

'The man looked at me sadly. "My friend, this Earth is the battlefield of Armageddon and the battle is for men's minds and souls. Prayer, good thoughts and caution are your best insulation." I shouldn't have doubted these people for a moment, but I was quite ill at ease. I had been sheltered from the knowledge that all of the space people's work on this planet is not sweetness and light. The others I had contacted must have been on the "right side", for what I had seen convinced me they were a good people. Then the young lady spoke: "You don't know, Howard, that there is a very powerful group on this planet, which possesses tremendous knowledge of technology, psychology, and most unfortunate of all, advanced brain therapy. They are using certain key people in the governments of your world. This group is anti-God, and might be termed instruments of your mythical Satan. They are using the credulity and simple faith of many people to attain their own ends". There was both anger and frustration in her voice.'

The gathering swarms of UFOs have been taken as an indication of approaching crisis. Eric Norman, in his *Gods, Demons and UFOs,* cites the opinion of

The photograph taken by Howard Menger, **left,** *is of an alleged space woman with a shining 'gadget' on her belt. The space woman gave Menger an explicit warning that a powerful group on Earth was using advanced brain therapy techniques to further the aims of Satan.*

French theorist Jean Robin has suggested that the 'mystery planes' seen over Sweden during the 1930s, **below,** *were an early manifestation of the UFO phenomenon. He noted that it seems to stay always one step ahead of Man's technological achievement. The aim, he believes, is 'the projection of a false belief system, just beyond existing beliefs'.*

an unnamed research physicist at Stanford Research Institute, California:

'The mounting evidence leads me to believe that UFOs are extraterrestrial in origin, piloted by intelligent beings. Their appearance in recent years is probably in some way associated with the imminent second coming of Jesus Christ.'

FINAL BATTLE

Many Christians believe in the imminence of such a second coming; but traditional teachings are clear that Satan is not going to let Christ walk in and take over the Earth without putting up a fight. The belief in a 'final battle' is a key element in every scenario for 'the last days'. What is more, some say it is going to be a real war, fought by real people with real weapons. Dr Clifford Wilson, of New Zealand, has no doubt that the battle of Armageddon is scheduled for the very near future, and points out that satanic forces will need every single person who can be pressed into service. Consequently, he suggests, men and women are being brainwashed, even possessed, 'so that when the signal is given, they will be ready to give total allegiance to these beings who will then show themselves as their masters.

'Even the act of taking over humans is to be taken literally. It seems that when these beings enter the solid state which is necessary for humans to observe them, they utilise atoms from the world in which we live. They do actually take blood and other physical matter from human beings and animals alike. In this way, they are able to adapt themselves so that we limited human beings will understand them, and ultimately be programmed by them.'

The French theorist Jean Robin has taken a more subtle view. For him, UFOs are only the latest manifestation in a long tradition of strange reports; and what strikes him most forcibly about them is that they seem to be imitating – or perhaps mocking – human ideas. In 1886, he points out, Jules Verne wrote *Robur le Conquerant* which features a massive airborne 'clipper of the clouds'; a decade later, in America, there was a wave of UFO sightings in the form of airships, which at that date were purely experimental and seen only over France.

The subtitle of Robin's book is *The Great Parody*, and interestingly, every manifestation of the UFO phenomenon – the American airships of the 1880s, the Scandinavian 'mystery planes' of the 1930s, the Swedish rockets of 1946, the UFOs of today's space age – has been just one step ahead of human achievement. 'The heart of the problem,' he has insisted, 'is the projection of a false belief system, just beyond existing beliefs'.

So what is the point of this exercise? For some, it is a sign that the millennium is at hand, the advent of the brave new world brought by a new Messiah. But Jean Robin is less optimistic. According to him, we are in for 'a cursed time when there will reign beings who are almost totally dehumanised, robots or golems artificially and temporarily animated by the satanic spirit'. And, he adds, 'while it is certainly not our intention to forecast the precise form which the reign of the Antichrist will take, it is not too far-fetched to imagine him descending from a flying saucer'.

The ufonauts' purpose, it has been said, is sinister and menacing, and for that reason some say it is not a subject for teenagers and the easily terrified. It has even been recommended that parents forbid their children from becoming involved. Ivar Mackay, one-time Chairman of BUFORA, Britain's largest UFO organisation, has claimed that 'some Intelligence or Energy is ready to invade our minds'. Indeed, the process may have already started, as has been only too apparent among some researchers in recent years. But many years' intensive training may be necessary before seeking to tackle the UFO problem. Another BUFORA chairman, Roger Stanway, declared some years ago that he was now convinced that UFOs are of satanic origin. and that he was abandoning ufology. Eric Inglesby, the author of *UFOs and the Christian,* meanwhile, declared that 'Flying Saucers and Nazism are simply aspects of the same thing', and declared 'UFOs are not just dangerous – they are deadly. It is a sphere in which the Christian (and indeed everyone else) is warned to KEEP OUT'.

Welsh UFO investigator Randall Jones Pugh echoed Inglesby when, in a 1979 letter to the *BUFORA Journal,* he wrote:

'I feel we must accept, for want of a better description, the potential and probable presence of entities (as human beings) whose sole purpose is to destroy straightforward belief in Jesus Christ... I would add a note of warning to all those concerned with the investigation of the paranormal, however innocent it may be – if you wish to delve deeply into what the UFO represents, then you should indeed work with Christ, because the search for ufological knowledge can be extremely dangerous.'

Less than 18 months later, Pugh renounced the subject altogether. In a newspaper interview, he declared that:

'UFOs are dangerous and their aim is to disorientate, bemuse and eventually destroy the mind of

Many ufologists, whose thinking disagrees in other respects, agree that whatever else is going on, humanity is certainly being conned. Too many UFO sightings have a 'staged' quality, as though someone is putting on a show; too many contact encounters, with their phoney medical examinations and absurd 'messages', simply fail to ring true. One view is that the ufonauts are the liars, not the contactees. Are they perhaps lying deliberately as part of the bewildering smoke-screen which they have established to cover their real origin, purpose and motivation?

"All the indications are that before the close of the century, cataclysmic and apocalyptic events will rend the planet ... Who can doubt that certain of the UFO entities have a hand in the wrecking?"

An illustration of the 'Clipper of the Clouds' from Jules Verne's* Robur le Conquerant, *published in 1886, is reproduced* above. *A decade later, there was a wave of airship sightings over the USA at a time when such machines were to be seen only over France – an example that seems to lend support to the contention that UFOs somehow anticipate the technological advances of mankind.

In the artist's impression, right, a hideous 8-foot (2.4 metre) furry, webbed-footed creature warns UFO enthusiasts John Stuart and Barbara Turner to discontinue their UFO research. They declined to do so – with horrific results.

mankind... My first warning that I was into something very dangerous came from a friend of mine who became involved with UFOs from a scientific point of view after a sighting. After just 14 months, he came to the conclusion that UFOs were involved with the occult, and decided to burn his books. He built a bonfire in the garden, but when he threw the books on, it gave off an incredible heat. The smoke billowed up in the form of a human being, and two hands began to reach out. He was scared out of his wits, and later pleaded with me to destroy my documents, but warned me not to burn them. I took his advice, but when it came to my collection of slides, I stupidly threw them in the living room fire. Immediately there were loud cracks like explosions, and the heat was fantastic. I thought the chimney breast was going to split. It was a terrible experience, and I'm convinced the slides were satanically blessed.'

Force of the Devil

Just how dangerous it can be to play with demonic forces was well-illustrated by what is said to have happened in 1954 to John Stuart and Barbara Turner, who belonged to Flying Saucer Investigators of New Zealand. John and Barbara used to meet every night (seemingly with his wife's approval) to discuss UFO theories and all their implications. They took the demonic theory very seriously: 'There had to be some connection with Satan. But what?' As they got deeper into the subject, a change started to come over 'sweet, kind, innocent Barbara'. She, who seemingly took no interest in boys, suddenly started to interrupt their UFO-chat to say things like: 'Gee, I'm glad I'm a girl. I like to be kissed. I like to tease boys, with a partly open shirt, brief shorts, all that'. Her smile turned far more sensual, and she was even prone to whisper to John in a very suggestive manner: 'I'd like to sit here naked. Like me to?'

Images of hostile aliens feature in both **Quatermass and the Pit, below,** *and* **War of the Worlds, bottom,** *in which a UFO causes urban destruction.*

John Stuart concluded that this was 'some sort of evil possession'. However, the two UFO enthusiasts refused to abandon their studies despite many warnings, including one that seemingly originated from a hideous 8-foot (2.4-metre) creature with a furry body and webbed feet. So it came about that, one night, 13 entities came to Barbara's bedroom; and while 10 of them watched, the other three raped her for three hours, marking her all over with scratches that she showed to Stuart the following morning. This seems to have convinced her that UFO investigation was too risky, and Stuart himself was menaced by a creature that was male above the waist and female below one moment, vice versa the next – whereupon he too opted to desert ufology. There is no record of what happened to Barbara or, for that matter, to Stuart's long-suffering wife.

Such accounts seem to place the demonic theory of UFOs definitely within the lunatic fringe, but it is as well to remember that similar theories are taken seriously by some leading UFO specialists. Few researchers in Britain have contributed more to

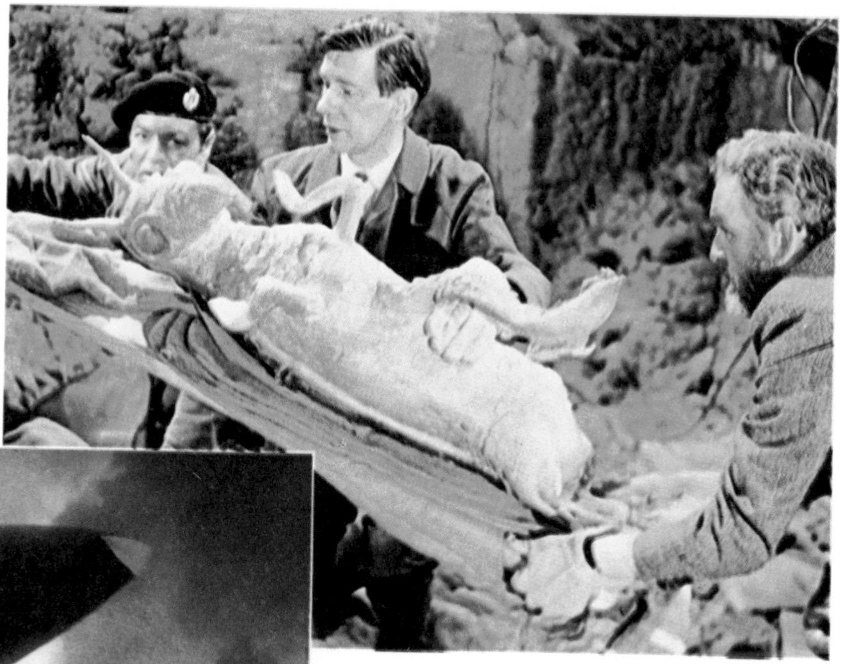

ufology than Gordon Creighton: yet he has wholeheartedly agreed with William James' observation that 'the Demonic Theory will come into its own again one day'. He has added:

'Time is running out fast. All the indications are that before the close of this century, cataclysmic and apocalyptic events will rend the planet. As the waves of senseless, irrational violence rise higher and higher on the Earth, and as the signs of moral and spiritual decay multiply, who can doubt that certain of the "UFO entities" have a hand in the wrecking, and in the stirring of the nauseating brew?'

Does the UFO evidence as it stands really support the demonists, or are they guilty of interpreting the phenomena to suit personal beliefs? We shall each of us have our own opinion on that score, but one thing is clear: in the minds of many people, Satan is alive and well and piloting a UFO.

THE GENTLE ART OF MURDER

SOME MASTERS OF THE MARTIAL ARTS ARE SAID TO POSSESS THE ABILITY TO COMMIT THE PERFECT MURDER, USING A FORBIDDEN TECHNIQUE KNOWN ONLY TO A HANDFUL OF INITIATES – THE DEATH TOUCH

George Dillman, an American karate teacher, smashes three ice blocks, each weighing 300 pounds (136 kilograms), with a single blow of his elbow, left. *Many people are familiar with such well-publicised feats by masters of oriental martial arts – but there is also said to be a secret art in which a covert 'blow', almost unnoticed by the victim and third parties alike, can kill its victim after a long delay.*

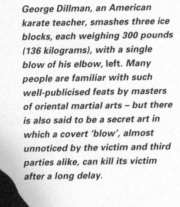

Anyone who has seen a karate expert demolish piles of bricks, boards, tiles or concrete slabs with a single blow will testify to the lethal potential of a human body when it has undergone the right kind of training and conditioning. When a man such as George Dillman, an American master of karate, shatters simultaneously 10 ice blocks each weighing 100 pounds (45 kilograms), stacked on top of each other, he leaves no doubt as to the reality of the feat: the splintered rubble that is left behind is proof enough.

But it is another matter to believe that some martial arts experts can cause internal injuries, unconsciousness and death by just the briefest pressure on certain apparently non-critical points of a victim's body; and that these effects can be deferred until hours, days or even months have passed. Yet this is exactly what has been alleged of the almost legendary art of *dim mak*, the 'delayed death touch'.

It was in search of the truth behind stories of *dim mak* and other fabled unarmed yet deadly combat systems that a Western martial arts expert,

Mourners crowd around the coffin at a Hong Kong funeral,* below. *Their grief is for the superstar* Bruce Lee, *bottom, the hero of* numerous kung fu *films. He probably died from a freak reaction to a tranquilliser, but many fans believed their hero had been killed by a delayed death touch from some unknown rival.

Dr John 'Biff' Painter is seen* below, *allegedly showing the reality of* ch'i *force, as he applies it to the auric field of his blindfolded colleague. The man sways back, even though no physical contact has been made.

John F. Gilbey, roamed from continent to continent. He finally encountered the delayed death touch technique when he reached Taiwan in 1957. There, with all the reluctance that is natural when closely guarded and dangerous knowledge is imparted to an outsider, a boxing master named Oh Hsin-yang gave him a demonstration. The human guinea pig who was chosen to be used in the experiment was his son, Ah Lin.

The blow was a light, seemingly harmless touch delivered just below the victim's navel. For the next three days, Gilbey was able to keep Ah Lin under the closest surveillance. His health was seemingly unimpaired, and his spirits were lively. The master did not come near his son until noon on the third day. Then he appeared just in time to revive him with herbal medicine and massage – for, exactly as Oh Hsin-yang had anticipated, his son had suddenly and unaccountably collapsed into a state of unconsciousness.

When Ah Lin recovered (he endured three months' convalescence to get over his experience completely), Gilbey left Taiwan convinced that he was one of the very few Westerners who had been privileged personally to witness the delayed death touch in operation.

Despite Gilbey's own expert status, the evidence remains anecdotal, as do most accounts of *dim mak*. Until 1980, no work even remotely approaching Western laboratory standards was available, and the only masters said to possess the skill refused to demonstrate it, even under the most informal conditions.

In consequence, the delayed death touch remains the supposed instrument of 'perfect murders', in which the victim dies of causes unknown, with symptoms suggesting severe, incomprehensible yet natural illness. In the East, any unexpected death of a notable person can provoke rumours of a *dim mak* assassination. The untimely death of the martial arts superstar Bruce Lee in July 1973 had precisely this effect.

INSTRUMENT OF PERFECT MURDER

Stories of the delayed death touch occur all over south-eastern Asia, but particularly in China, where the skill reputedly reached a zenith during the Tang Dynasty (AD 618-906). Although the term is applied somewhat loosely to a number of techniques, purists are careful to distinguish it from *tieh chang*, the 'iron palm' (involving toughening of the hands), and from *tu wu shou*, the 'poison hand' (involving the anointing of the hand with harmful substances). The true delayed death touch is not a ferocious movement like a karate 'chop', or one of the whiplash punches found in many styles of *kung fu:* it is more like a short-distance prod with, apparently, not enough force behind it to leave so much as a slight bruise.

Students of the 'forbidden art' must remember that a victim's vulnerability fluctuates according to the temperature and hour of the day. This is consistent with an eastern tradition that the circulation of the blood through the body varies hourly. A Western karate master, Alan Lee, has stated that the circulation passes via 36 major, 72 minor and

108 subsidiary 'blood grates', and that the expert, knowing both their location and the times when the flow of blood through each is at its maximum, can use light pressure on a strategic point to cause a fatal disruption of the flow – by, for example, a blood clot. Such knowledge takes years to acquire; but, in theory, once they are in possession of it, masters could reduce their own susceptibility to attack by regulating the pulse at crucial times.

According to Dr John 'Biff' Painter, an American master, the Chinese martial art technique of *duann mie,* a blow directed against veins or muscles, can cause the wasting and death of important organs by an interruption of the blood supply to them. At first, the victim suffers only minor discomfort, but later succumbs as the affected organ is gradually starved of its blood supply.

But some writers attribute the efficacy of the true death touch to its interference with the mysterious 'intrinsic' or 'internal' energy of the human body, *ch'i*. This energy – *ch'i* in Chinese, *ki* in Japanese – is fundamental to a number of oriental disciplines of healing and of combat that western researchers have viewed with increasing interest since about 1960. Acupuncture is a notable example. This energy is thought to pervade the human body, circulating in a 24-hour cycle along channels called meridians and feeding the body's organs. Although it is never entirely absent from each channel, the energy level is subject to a kind of tidal effect, according to the hour of the day. Oriental therapists regard illness as imbalance or blockage of *ch'i,* and seek by use of needles or by manipulations to restore the overall harmony.

The ability to control *ch'i* and to generate extra surges of it is alleged to enable exponents of the martial arts to perform feats well beyond their normal ability; and many styles of fighting feature, during their more advanced stages, exercises designed to stimulate the flow of *ch'i.*

The martial arts student may also be taught the 708 points on the meridians to which pressure can be applied to enhance or retard *ch'i,* allegedly preventing it from feeding the vital organs. The result of such an attack would again be a kind of starvation, but this time of energy rather than of blood. Unconsciousness and eventually death would ensue, without any physical clue to connect the antagonist with the damage.

Long Odds

John Painter puts the odds against an untrained attacker successfully making a lethal *dim mak* strike by pure chance at 10,000 to one. It is not enough merely to know the right points to strike, to gauge the right moment from knowledge of the timetable governing the *ch'i* circulation and to hit the target with unerring accuracy. The attacker must then, according to the theory, generate the requisite amount of internal energy. He must disrupt the victim's *ch'i* flow by transferring a certain 'voltage' of his own *ch'i* through his fingers at the moment of the strike.

Painter estimates that if the discharge of *ch'i* is 'light', the victim's end may be deferred by up to two weeks. A heavy blow might kill him in as little as 12 to 24 hours. Light-to-moderate attacks create a partial blockage, augmented each time the *ch'i* reaches the affected point on its diurnal circulation, until the meridian comes to resemble a choked water pipe. The process can be reversed only by the ministrations of someone with a superior knowledge of Chinese medicine, such as a skilled acupuncturist. However, Dr Painter regards some *dim mak* strikes as incurable: the victim should without doubt begin his funeral preparations, he has grimly advised.

> "The result of such an attack would be a kind of saturation, this time of energy rather than of blood. Unconsciousness and ... death would ensue, without any physical clue to connect the antagonist with the damage."

Many people in the East have a deeply rooted belief in the existence of the death touch. Could it therefore be possible that such a person might be killed by the mere suggestion that the touch he had just received would be fatal?

A victim's belief in the efficacy of *dim mak* certainly figured strongly in a strange story carried in English newspapers on 17 February 1976. During a brawl aboard the Royal Fleet Auxiliary Empire Gull, anchored at Marchwood, Hampshire, a Chinese cook, aged 48, stabbed to death an elderly compatriot who had hit him. His statement to the police suggested that he believed the blow had been imbued with more than physical force – that it was, in fact, a delayed death touch. He remarked: 'He died first and I will die later'. He was indeed suffering from a mysterious, undiagnosable illness that is said to have baffled three doctors. But was the illness due to his own evident conviction that the blow was to prove lethal?

There are several reliable modern accounts of martial arts experts selectively breaking one brick or tile in a stack of several, leaving those above and

Dr John Painter demonstrates the delayed death touch, above. Symptoms that followed included rising temperature, fluctuating pulse rate, profuse sweating and trembling. He claimed that severe damage would have been done if he had not taken remedial action.

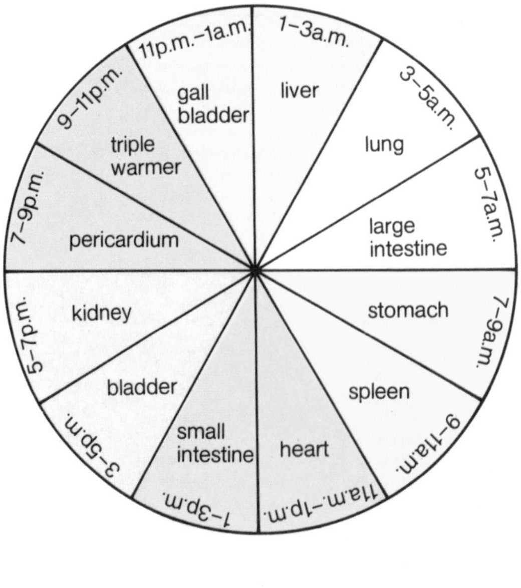

The traditional Chinese 'body clock' is shown* left. *The flow of* ch'i *is greatest in each particular organ at the hours shown. The 'triple warmer' controls the harmony of the system.

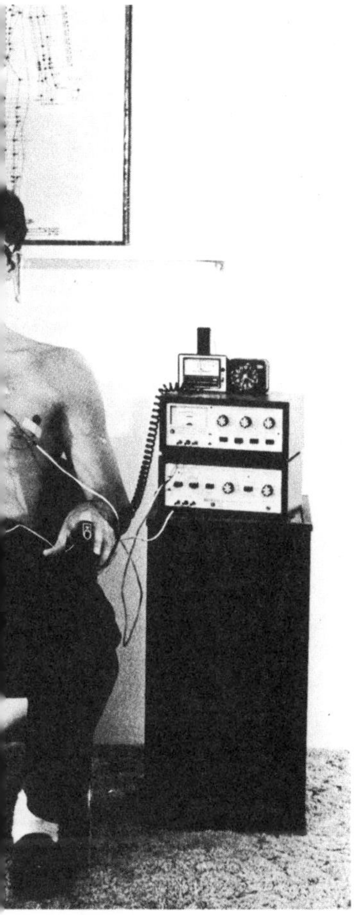

below unharmed. Such feats make it more credible that a blow could be delivered to a human body and cause internal injury without leaving any external marks – but there can be no question of bricks and tiles being influenced by suggestion.

John Painter gave a demonstration during a lecture on acupressure that goes some way towards conforming with scientific requirements. The experiment was electronically monitored and carried out before an audience that included medically qualified witnesses. The event was striking – in more ways than one.

A healthy volunteer was connected to equipment monitoring his pulse rate, temperature, blood pressure and other physiological factors. He was not informed about the exact nature of the experiment, only that it was intended to display a 'special type of acupressure'. After the initial readings had been taken, Painter applied a moderate strike to a point called *hui kui hsueh* in the chest. The subject reported no pain but said that his body felt numb and his right arm, heavy.

During the next half hour, he experienced a variety of unusual symptoms as, according to Dr Painter's thesis, the *ch'i* flow began to pass through the site of the strike. Within 10 minutes, he was suffering abdominal discomfort; and within another five minutes, his body temperature had climbed from 98.6°F (37°C) to 100°F (37.8°C). After 20 minutes, the pulse rate – which had been 62 beats per minute at the start of the test – was fluctuating wildly from less than 50 to more than 160. The subject suffered constriction of the chest muscles, profuse perspiration and trembling of the limbs. His blood pressure also soared. When Dr Painter judged that it was approaching a dangerous level, he ended the experiment by massaging the site of blockage and administering a herbal medicine. One hour later, the subject was back to normal. The onlookers accepted that, left unchecked, the *dim mak* process would have resulted in severe damage to the human guinea-pig; and Dr Painter himself believed the man would have died within two days.

Sceptics might object that the trial did not wholly exclude the possibility of the subject's expectations or the experimenter's suggestions playing a part. But the symptoms recorded seem too extreme to be accounted for solely in those terms. That a person's pulse should race because of suggestion or excitement is highly probable; that it should vary between 50 and 160 from those causes alone is far less probable. Still, one isolated experiment will not satisfy westerners that the delayed death touch truly exists. It would be preferable to study a number of *dim mak* masters demonstrating their skills in a laboratory. But such persons are rarely encountered. When identified, they habitually refuse to impart their learning to others. Painter concludes:

'Such power in the hands of the unenlightened is like a chimpanzee with a bazooka. Such power corrupts and distorts reality. It is for this reason that those who possess the full power in such arts refuse to speak of it, and why many of the wise ones regret acquisition of such knowledge and have carried their arts . . . to their graves.'

PERSPECTIVES

FEELING THE FULL FORCE

The karate expert C. W. Nicol wrote an account of his martial arts training in Japan in which he relates an almost incredible incident involving the delayed death touch. His master was the sixth-dan black belt, Hirokazu Kanazawa, *right.* One day, with a few students, he placed three bricks on the floor and broke them with a single blow. But that, he said, was nothing. He put down another pile of three bricks, determined to put his *ki* (the Japanese term for *ch'i*) into

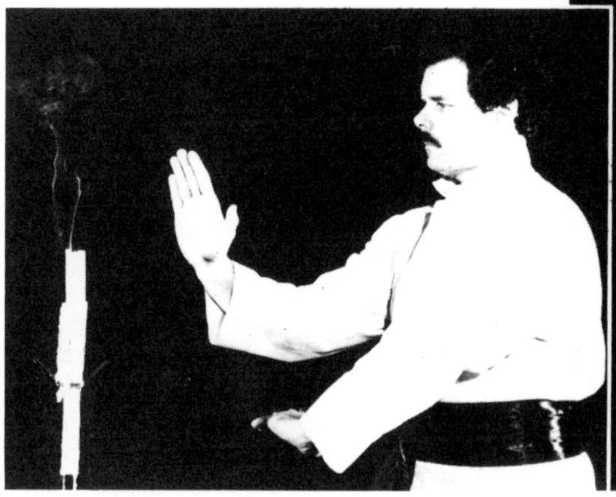

the middle brick. With a shout, he brought his fist down on the pile – and only the middle brick cracked. This was in accord with the belief that mind-force can project itself further and deeper than the actual physical presence of the fist, and can of itself alone alter the state of matter.

This is certainly the belief of Dr John Painter, who runs a martial arts institute in Arlington, Texas, USA. He believes that every human being possesses an aura consisting of *ch'i,* and that through certain forms of mental control, such as meditation, it is possible to increase the 'vibratory rate' of the aura. The 'vibrations' can be increased to a point where they are disruptive of any other living matter that comes within a certain radius of influence – up to 12 feet (3.6 metres). The power of this control of *ch'i* can also be demonstrated on a candle flame, as shown *far left.* Dr Painter explains that it took 10 minutes to extinguish this flame. He believes that beyond the delayed death touch, *dim mak,* there exists a higher art – that of killing from a distance, without the need even to touch the victim. However, there is no need to fear this skill: a condition of acquiring it is to 'clear the mind of all sensual and egotistical desires...' So, it seems, this fearful power is only possessed by those who are beyond all desire to do harm.

THE MINNESOTA ICEMAN

FROZEN IN A BLOCK OF ICE, AN 'APEMAN' IS ON DISPLAY IN THE FAIRGROUNDS OF SMALL-TOWN AMERICA. IS IT A HOLLYWOOD MODEL-MAKER'S FAKE – OR, AS EXPERT WITNESSES HAVE INSISTED, A GENUINE MYSTERY CREATURE?

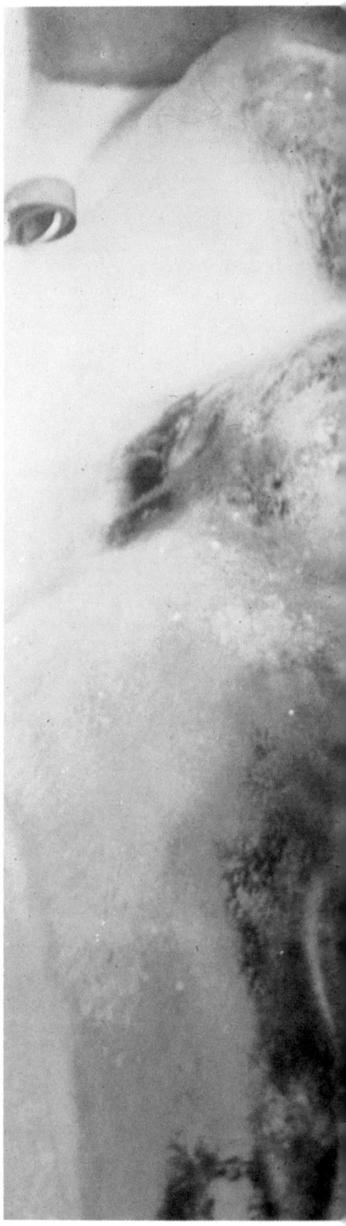

In late 1968, Dr Bernard Heuvelmans, a Belgian zoologist who had long specialised in investigating mysterious animals, stumbled on an extraordinary find. As he wrote in a letter at the time, it was something that 'will certainly crown my career as a crypto-zoologist, the discovery of a specimen of an unknown form of living hominoid. This time, it was not just a film showing a faked Abominable Snowman.' But heated controversy followed his announcement of the exceptional find a few weeks later.

The investigations that Heuvelmans had carried out into intriguing reports of the giant squid, the yeti, sea serpents and other creatures had earned him the reputation of being very much the Sherlock Holmes of zoology. He had been visiting the United States since October 1968 in order to promote a new book dealing with the sea serpent and other marine monsters, and he had intended to go on from there to central America on the trail of more creatures that were new to science. But the excitement of this new find detained him.

In early December, Heuvelmans was staying with the zoologist and writer Ivan T. Sanderson at his farm in New Jersey. They were old friends and had supported each other's researches for many years. Sanderson was well-known in the United States as an expert on the yeti and the bigfoot – enthusiasms that had made certain professional scientists wary of him.

On 9 December, Sanderson received a call from a snake dealer in Milwaukee named Terry Cullen, telling him about a curious fairground exhibit that he had recently seen. It was some kind of 'hairy man', and the showman displaying it claimed the creature was the real 'missing link' between human beings and apes.

The 'apeman', **above**, *is viewed by thousands of Americans every year. According to one account, it was found floating at sea, encased within ice.*

The creature, **left**, *is shown as reconstructed from the photographs and drawings of zoologists Ivan T. Sanderson and Bernard Heuvelmans. It resembles no known living human race.*

Sanderson and Heuvelmans stated that the creature, **right**, *was 'somewhat pug-faced, the tip of the nose turning upwards . . . the forehead is sloping . . . the mouth is slit-like...'.*

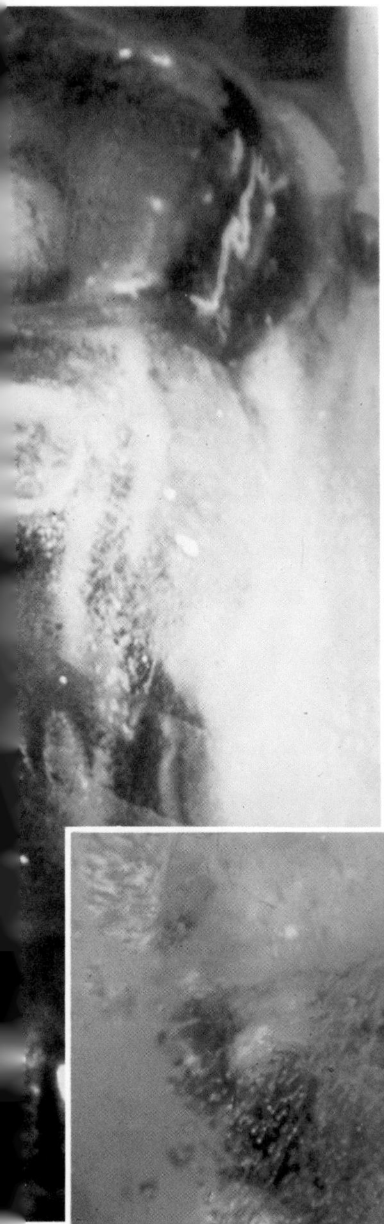

Sanderson traced the showman. His name was Frank Hansen and he lived on a farm at Rollingstone, near Winona, Minnesota. He was contacted by telephone and arrangements were made to view his exhibit for what Sanderson called 'professional reasons'. (Sanderson owned a small private zoo, and the exhibit could have been of interest to him without mention of the fact that he was also an investigator.)

> " THE SHOWMAN CLAIMED THE CREATURE WAS THE REAL MISSING LINK. "

Sanderson was the science editor of *Argosy* magazine – in which, however, science surfaces only in its more sensational forms. The magazine agreed to finance an investigative jaunt, and Heuvelmans and Sanderson drove nearly halfway across the continent, arriving at Hansen's farm on 17 December. The place was cold and bleak: it was in the depths of winter.

Parked near the farmhouse was a trailer. In this was a large freezer cabinet, and inside that, to the astonishment of the two visitors, was what appeared to be a creature unknown to science. It looked like a man covered in long brown hair.

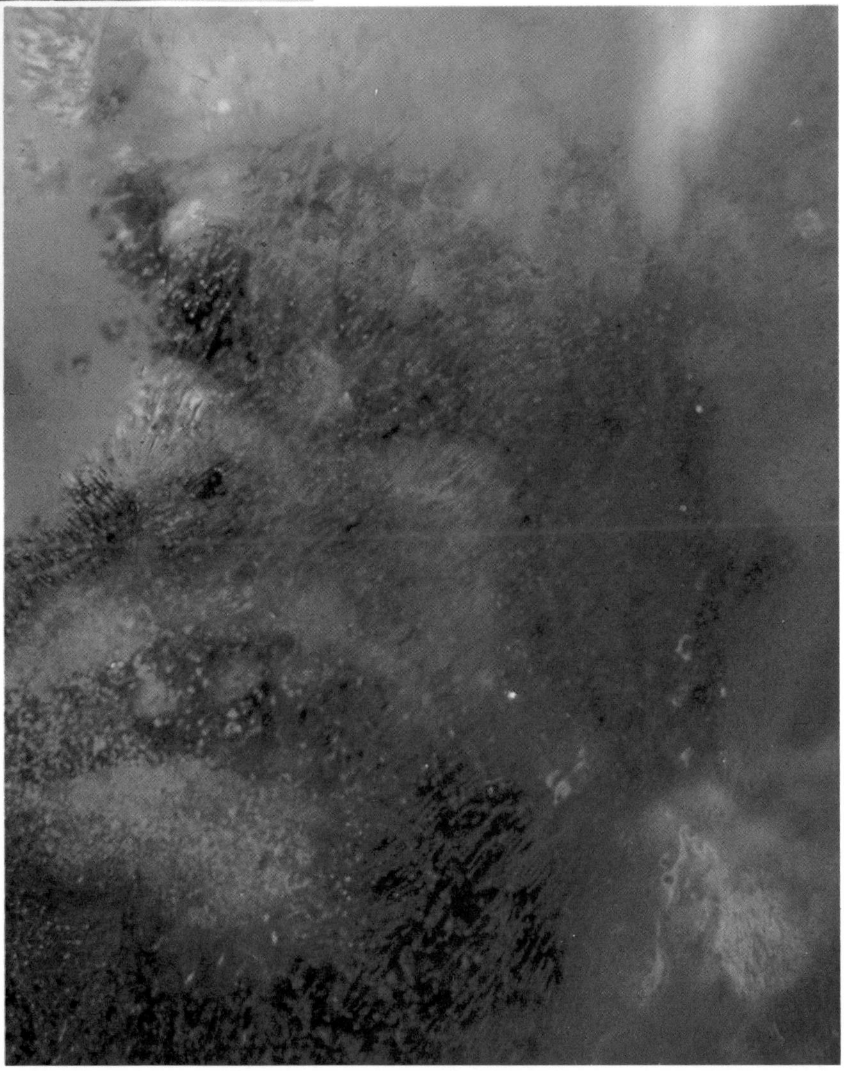

Space inside the trailer was limited. But for 11 hours each day for the next three days, Sanderson and Heuvelmans toiled to draw and photograph the creature. It was about 5 feet 10 inches (1.8 metres) tall. Sanderson had to lie on the glass top of the freezer in order to draw the 'man', one part at a time.

Using an Asahi reflex camera, Heuvelmans found that, although oblique views of the creature were easy enough, he could photograph it from above only by making four separate exposures.

The creature was hairless on the face and groin. Testicles and a narrow penis were visible, leaving no doubt about its sex at least. The creature's left arm was thrown up above its face and was obviously broken. One eye socket was empty and the eyeball of the other had been pushed out and now lay on the cheekbone. The back of the head seemed to have been shattered. This was clear, bloody evidence that the creature had been shot through the head, vainly defending itself from some sort of attack with its arm.

The blood was clearly visible to the scientists. They could detect, too, the distinctive sweet smell of decomposition. On one foot, visible through the ice, they could see the grey-tinged evidence of rotting flesh. They mentioned this to Hansen, who was disturbed by the news.

Mysterious Origins

The two experienced zoologists had no doubts as they worked that the curious object of interest in the ice block had been recently alive. But where had it come from? On this point Hansen was vague and also self-contradictory at times. Sanderson and Heuvelmans gathered that the specimen had come from the Far East, though it was never clear exactly where. At one point, Hansen said it had been found floating in an ice block in the sea off eastern Siberia. A 'dealer' in Hong Kong was also mentioned.

Hansen claimed that he was not the owner of the exhibit. It belonged, he said, to a wealthy man in California. But this mysterious mogul was never to be identified. Hansen wanted neither publicity nor an in-depth investigation of the creature, and he got Sanderson to agree not to publish anything about what he had seen. But Heuvelmans was careful not to make any such a promise. As a scientist, his first duty was to make the truth known.

Once their work was finished, Sanderson and Heuvelmans returned to New Jersey, where they separately set down their impressions. In summary, these were as follows. The creature's torso was broad and muscular. Apart from its hairy coat, the most remarkable feature was its upturned nose, which gave it a pug-like appearance. The legs were short, and the feet were broad and flat. The big toe lay alongside the small second toe, as it does in humans – there was no gap, as in other primates. The photographs, both colour and black and white, had come out very well. Now, with all this evidence to hand, what should the two researchers do next?

If the remarkable discovery were to be fully investigated, they would need to arouse the interest of the scientific community. On 4 January 1969, they drove over to Massachusetts to see an eminent anthropologist, Professor Carleton S. Coon. A man of the widest experience and learning, he was impressed by their evidence and agreed with Heuvelmans that the creature appeared to be man-like, at least from what they could tell him of the visible features. He wished them well, but did not feel that he could give them great support. He was already embroiled in public controversy because of certain racist views.

APE-MAN

On 14 January, Heuvelmans sent a note to the head of the Belgian Royal Museum. He now boldly named the specimen *Homo pongoides:* the pongids are the anthropoid apes, and Heuvelmans was thus declaring the creature to be an ape-like man. The note was received at the museum with great enthusiasm, and arrangements were made to publish it within a month. This promptness was a mark of the esteem in which Heuvelmans was held in Europe and the importance with which his colleagues there regarded his discovery.

Heuvelmans also sent English versions of his note to W.C. Osman-Hill at the Yerkes Regional Primate Center in Atlanta, Georgia, and to Dr John Napier at the Smithsonian Institution in Washington, DC, the leading scientific institution in the United States. Napier was intrigued by the news, and it was he who was the first to use the term 'iceman'. Heuvelmans hated this kind of journalistic nickname, however, which he said 'tends to ridicule the most serious problems'. But it was as the 'Minnesota iceman' that the creature was soon to become widely known.

Hansen was upset when he heard about the publication of Heuvelmans' scientific report. Since the creature was being referred to as a man and, moreover, a man who had been shot, he became alarmed at the prospect of some kind of police investigation.

Sanderson had indeed contacted the FBI in New Jersey on 18 January. But they were not interested: such a killing is murder, it seems, only when it is inflicted on *Homo sapiens*.

On 11 March 1969, the first press report appeared, in a Belgian newspaper. Within days,

Bernard Heuvelmans, above, Belgian 'crypto-zoologist' or student of mystery animals, was convinced of the authenticity of the iceman and coined the name Homo pongoides for it.

Ivan T. Sanderson is seen below testing a geological specimen. His sensationalist approach to scientific subjects damaged his reputation with many researchers.

journalists all over the world were pursuing the story. Two days later, the Smithsonian, prompted by Dr Napier, officially requested Frank Hansen's co-operation in an investigation of the creature. Although Dr Napier had known about the discovery for well over a month, he had not taken the opportunity to travel to Minnesota to see the specimen for himself. Now it was too late. Harassed by the press and scientists alike, Hansen panicked and promptly disappeared with the iceman.

The press sensation that followed was farcical. Heuvelmans had been anxious to set a high tone by having his photographs published in a reputable journal, such as *Life, Look* or *National Geographic* magazine: but he failed. The photographs finally appeared with an article by Ivan Sanderson in *Argosy* in May 1969. Sanderson had rather unfortunately nicknamed the specimen 'Bozo' after a well-known television clown. This levity influenced press treatment: no one in America could take seriously a creature named after a clown.

This sort of approach marred much of Sanderson's work at this time. Heuvelmans was even dismayed to find that his friend could hardly utter a sentence that was not a gross exaggeration. Scientists in America were only too well-aware of Ivan Sanderson's peculiarities, and many must have suspected it was all a hoax from the very start. (The bizarre aspects in Sanderson's personality were finally explained in 1973 when he died as the result of a brain tumour.)

Suspicions of a hoax seemed to be confirmed by an anonymous revelation that the iceman was a model that had been made in a Hollywood monster factory. The hair, it was alleged, had been implanted by a certain Pete Corrall, who was a professional model-maker.

After a month's 'vacation', Hansen himself reappeared and said that this was indeed the case: his exhibit was a model. Photographers and journalists now flocked to see it and to interview Hansen.

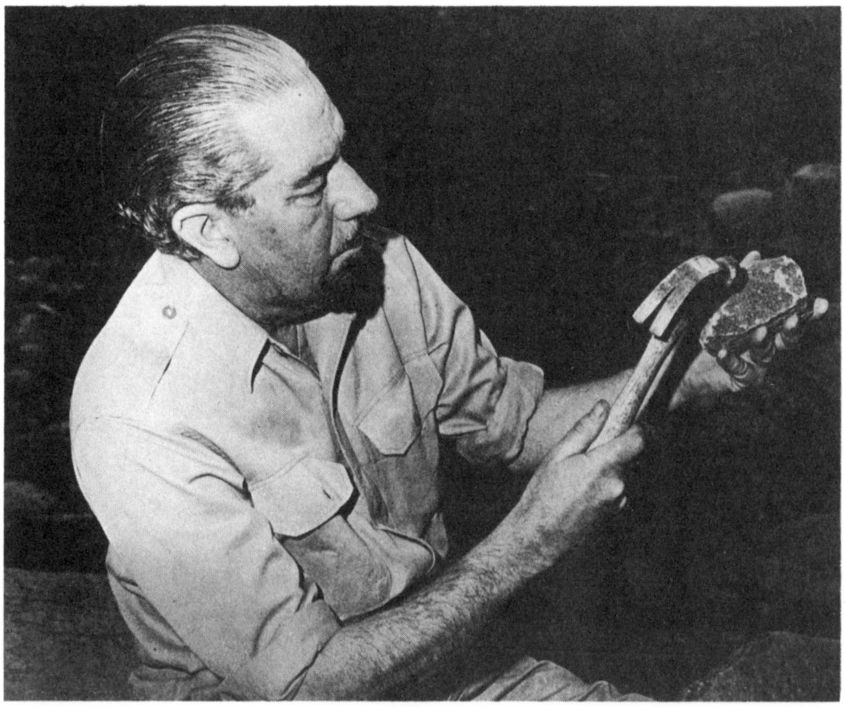

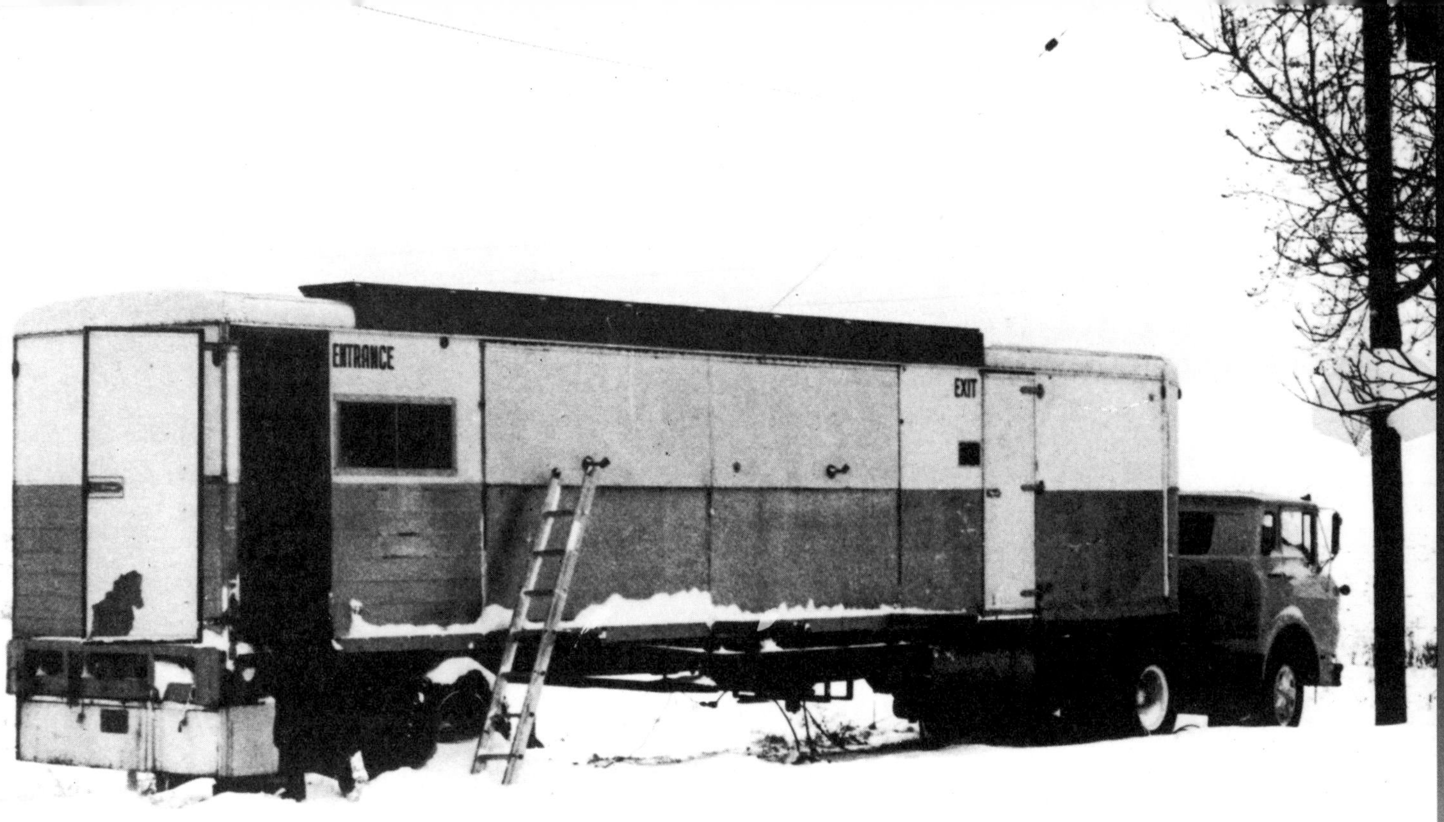

While on his 'vacation', Hansen had defrosted the corpse and made some changes in its arrangement. In the new photographs that were published, some details – such as the left hand and the large teeth in the now open mouth – were clearly visible. Nevertheless, though it looked different, it was the same creature – and Heuvelmans and Sanderson still had no doubts that, whatever they had seen, it was no model. Moreover, Heuvelmans pointed out that no observer had seen the supposed model at the time of its manufacture, and that stories about this were little more than rumours.

But as far as the media were concerned, the affair had been exploded as a hoax and it was accepted that what the two enthusiasts, anxious for a great discovery, thought was a primitive man in fact originated in the imagination of a Hollywood artist. (Sanderson himself even came round to this view eventually.)

The giant trailer, **above**, *was used to haul the iceman from fairground to fairground. Big though the vehicle was, Heuvelmans and Sanderson found themselves cramped when they were drawing and photographing the iceman.*

Frank Hansen, **below**, *told scientists that his exhibit was a model, while hinting to the public that it was genuine. He even claimed on one occasion to have shot the creature himself while hunting in the Minnesota woods.*

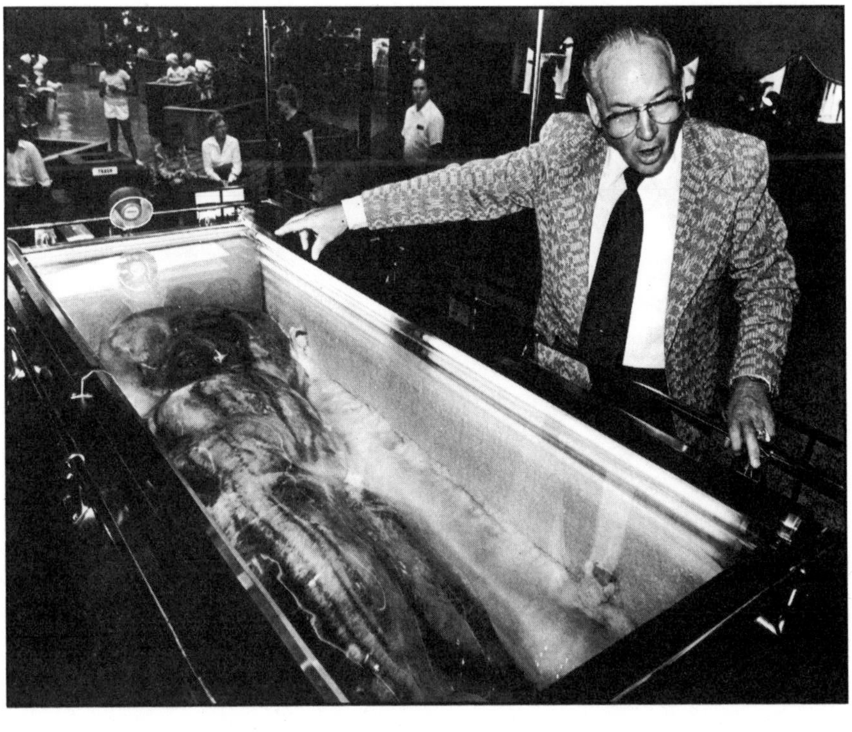

Then, in an article in another adventure magazine, Hansen claimed that he had shot the creature on a hunting trip in Minnesota some years before. 'Fact or fiction?' the headline asked. Later, a thorough investigation of this story by a Chicago newspaper showed that there could be no truth in Hansen's new tale; nor could there be any truth in a later story from a girl who claimed she had killed the creature while it was trying to rape her. The Minnesota iceman had now clearly become the property of the lunatic fringe.

What remained strange, however, was that Ivan Sanderson and Bernard Heuvelmans, two zoologists of great experience, had been taken in so easily. But Heuvelmans was certain that he had not been fooled. The creature was real, he insisted, and he believed he had a full explanation of what it was and where it came from.

> THE CREATURE'S TORSO WAS BROAD AND MUSCULAR. APART FROM ITS HAIRY COAT, THE MOST REMARKABLE FEATURE WAS ITS UPTURNED NOSE, WHICH GAVE IT A PUG-LIKE APPEARANCE. THE LEGS WERE SHORT, AND THE FEET WERE BROAD AND FLAT. THE BIG TOE LAY ALONGSIDE THE SMALL SECOND TOE, AS IT DOES IN HUMANS – THERE WAS NO GAP, AS IN OTHER PRIMATES.

COME DOWSING!

MANY PEOPLE FIND THE VERY IDEA OF DOWSING INCREDIBLE – YET WITH A LITTLE PRACTICE, YOU MAY BE ABLE TO LEARN HOW TO FIND BURIED OBJECTS OR UNDERGROUND WATER FOR YOURSELF. READ ON, AND FIND OUT HOW TO DEVELOP LATENT DOWSING SKILLS, AS WELL AS HOW TO MAKE YOUR OWN DIVINING ROD

One of the most fascinating aspects of dowsing is that it is surprisingly simple to learn. Most people should have a fair chance of immediate success when they try it. Dowsing is essentially a skill, and you can go about learning it in much the same way as you would any other practical activity. In many ways, the hardest thing about learning to dowse is reaching an understanding that it is so simple. Indeed, there is so little to it that it seems people have been forced to invent rules and complications simply for the sake of doing so.

Although dowsing may seem a highly unconventional skill, a dowser's responses conform to the same pattern as other reflex responses (such as the blink reflex that makes you shut your eyes when something approaches rapidly). But successful dowsers are often better at noticing a contrast than a uniform 'target', so that a dowser will usually find it easier to find a hairline crack in a pipe than to discover that he is standing over a huge water

Psychic Ruth Lowe is seen below, *using angle rods to dowse near the Bronze Age stone circle at Rollright in Oxfordshire. Many dowsers claim to be able to find not only minerals, underground water and buried objects, but also ley lines and areas of paranormal significance.*

*In*Focus

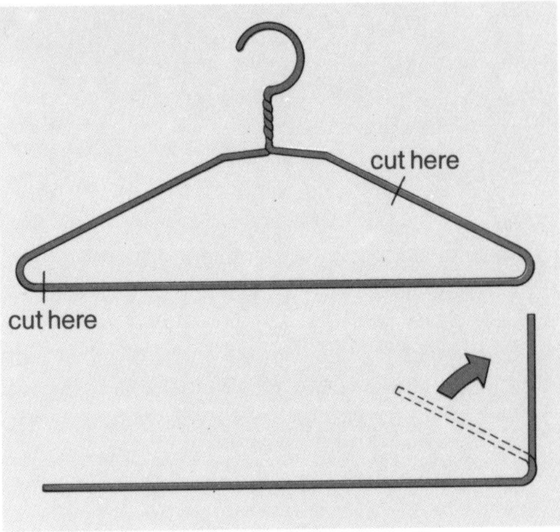

A NATURAL REACTION

Angle rods – types of divining rod that are especially easy to use – can be made from a pair of wire coat hangers, as shown *above.* In use, they are held lightly in the closed fists, so that they can freely rotate. If preferred, they can rest in sleeves made of thin tubing or dowelling through which a hole has been bored, or even a stack of two or three cotton reels. The neutral position of the rods is pointing straight ahead (1). If you tilt your fist slightly forwards, the rods will take up this position naturally. To become familiar with the behaviour of the rods, practise making them turn by small movements of your fists. This will help you to recognise spontaneous movements of the rods, apparently not caused by you. (In fact, such movement indicate involuntary reactions of your muscles, too subtle to be perceived.) Turning your hands inwards makes the rods swing together and cross (2), while twisting the fists outwards (3) makes the rods twist outwards. Twisting the fists in the same direction makes the rods swing to one side, while remaining parallel (4). Whenever such a movement occurs during a search, it has its own interpretation, which must be learned by experience.

reservoir. In most field work, dowsers are sensing with nothing more paranormal than electromagnetic and other physical forces. The element that is still unexplained, however, is exactly how the dowser can filter out minute variations in a bewildering variety of information.

The skill, in fact, lies in this very filtering of information. It is common to all forms of perception: engineers speak of 'signal-to-noise ratio', and computer-users speak of 'foreground-background operation'. But the most common term is 'the cocktail-party effect' – our ability to follow a conversation in a crowded, noisy room while disregarding all the other voices, or to ignore a clock's ticking until we are reminded of it. In other words, we select which items of information are to be meaningful – or are to be 'signal' – and which ones will be ignored as 'noise'. We understand how these selection mechanisms work in machines, since we build in the mechanisms ourselves, but we have no idea how the cocktail-party effect in human perception works. Dowsing, however, is known to be a way of actually putting it to use.

The dowser, above, is seeking water in a city garden. The rods have just swung into a crossed position, indicating the presence of water at that point – possibly in a domestic water main.

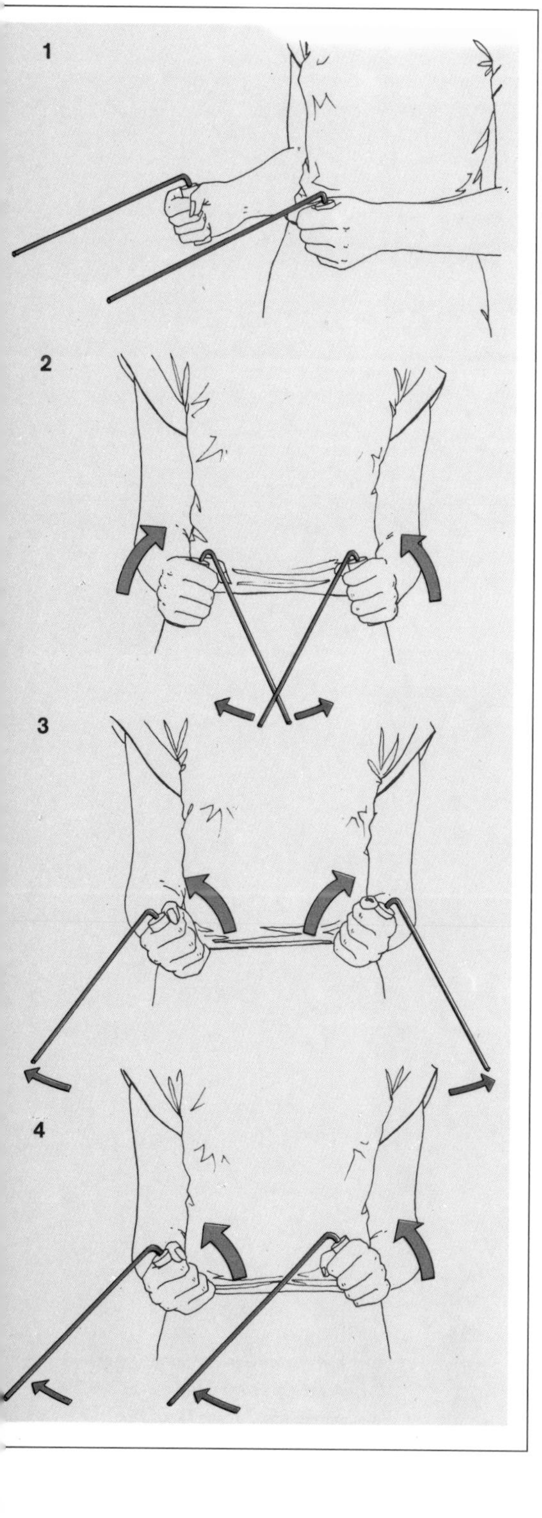

The traditional hazel twig is quite difficult to use: and in any case, is not all that common in the middle of a city, so you may find it easier to use 'angle rods' to start with. These are just two lengths of bent wire that can be cut from coat hangers.

To use them, hold one rod in each hand, the short arm of each resting in a loosely clenched fist, and left free to rotate. The long arm of each should point straight ahead: it is easier if you tilt them down a little from the horizontal, so that they are parallel to each other, pointing ahead of you. Hold them about body-width apart. You should look as if you are about to go into a gunfight holding two very thin pistols!

X Marks the Spot

Using angle rods is rather like learning to ride a bicycle. On a bicycle, you have to begin by thinking about what you are doing. But once you have got the knack of balancing on the bicycle, you no longer have to worry about it, and you can concentrate on directing the bicycle where you want to go. The same is true of the rods. In their neutral position, pointing straight ahead, they correspond to the bicycle rolling forward: with a little practice, they will stay in that position, regardless of uneven ground, wind or other disturbances. But as with the bicycle, which is useless if it will travel only in straight lines, the rods must be capable of changing their position, to indicate clearly when your body has reacted to whatever it is that you are looking for.

Given that the normal or neutral position of the rods is parallel, pointing forward, three significant types of reaction include the rods crossing over, both swinging round while remaining parallel, or only one rod moving. The last can probably be considered to be a mistake. The first response, signalling 'x marks the spot' as you move over the target object, is the most common type of reaction. The parallel movement tends to indicate a direction, such as the line of a pipe or cable. It takes a degree of practice to interpret this correctly.

For a while, just wander around, holding the rods, making sure that they can move freely but yet remain balanced. There is no need to worry about looking for anything in particular at first – just play with using the rods. This is where the knack comes in: you need to be able to recognise when the rods are moving because of something such as wind or rough ground, and when they seem to be moving of their own accord.

The strangest part is that the rods may well seem to have a life of their own. It is perhaps a good idea to remember that they do not; rather, it is your hands that move them. It might feel otherwise, but this effect is similar to that produced in a familiar childhood game: you press outwards hard against a door frame, your palms inwards; and when you stop pressing, you find your arms move upwards of their own accord. The motion is quite involuntary – as are the movements of the dowser who is controlling the divining rod. These movements, however, are imperceptible.

So far, you have simply been experimenting, without looking for anything in particular, and any results – such as the rods crossing over – have been 'noise', rather like the noise produced by an untuned radio. It is now time to be specific about what you are looking for, in order to learn what should be taken as 'signal' rather than 'noise'.

There seem to be no rules at all in dowsing about methods of targeting: almost anything that reminds you of what you are looking for will do. Some people use a sample of what it is they are looking for, holding the rod against a small bottle of water or a matching piece of cable, for example. Others use coloured discs to symbolise the object; some, a written description of the object.

All these techniques are, in the end, simply ways of reinforcing the image of what you are searching for. Indeed, without a clear image of that object, it is very difficult to ensure that the angle rods will move in a way that is clearly recognisable. So another knack that is useful in dowsing is the technique of visualisation.Try holding an imaginary orange in your hand. Even though it is not physically there, make it real in your imagination. Feel its texture. Take an imaginary knife, cut the orange open – feel the knife breaking through the tough peel, smell the tang as the juice reaches the air. Taste it! Now do the same for a sewer or a gas main, and you will appreciate that dowsing can have its unpleasant aspects, too, at times.

Practise for a while looking for pipes and cables, but not both simultaneously. Remember that the reflex response you are trying to use works best with contrasts rather than with featureless targets and that you need something physical to get to grips with. It is probably best if you look for a target in a location that is unknown to you, but in some area where you can check your results – such as a water main at a friend's house.

Dowsing in Depth

Finding something is one thing; but finding how deeply buried it is, or how big it is, is another matter. This is where dowsing becomes even more bizarre. To find depth, for example, find the position of the object – a pipe, say – and stand over it. Now start again, only this time look for the depth of the pipe. If you like, while you are walking along, imagine yourself walking downward, actually through the earth to the pipe. At some point, you should now have a completely new reaction. The distance out from the point where you started – and which you marked for reference – to where you are now is probably the distance down from your starting point since distance out equals distance down. (This is known in dowsing circles as the Bishop's Rule.) But sometimes this rule proves ineffective, and dowsers find 'distance out is half distance down' a better guide

Dowsing is perhaps best described as a state of mind. You will certainly find that your mental attitude has a critical effect – in both senses of the word – on the dowsing process. The trap is that a negative approach – 'it can't work, of course', or 'I suppose it will never work for me' – will usually interfere with or jam up the whole process. But the same is true of an over-confident approach – 'it must work for me' – involving trying too hard and concentrating fiercely, rather than just being receptive. The best advice as far as dowsing is concerned is just let it work by itself.

Here, shaman Michael Bromley is seen dowsing over a map with a pendulum.

HOWLS OF HORROR

THE IMAGE OF SOMEONE TURNING INTO A WOLF IS ONE THAT HAS HAUNTED HUMAN IMAGINATION FOR CENTURIES. IT FINDS ITS CHIEF EXPRESSION IN THE TERRIFYING LEGEND OF THE WEREWOLF. BUT COULD THERE BE MORE TO SUCH TALES THAN MERE SUPERSTITION?

The lonely figure of a wolf, above, gives its blood-curdling howl. Although stories of men taking on the forms of other beasts – such as werebears, or werehyenas – exist, werewolf tales are by far the most common in Europe, probably because the wolf was one of the most vicious and powerful animals known to Man.

Towards the middle of the 19th century, on a picturesque hill near the Vistula, a river in Poland that flows past Cracow and Warsaw, a large gathering of young people were celebrating, with music, singing and dancing, the completion of the harvest. There was food and drink in abundance, and everyone indulged freely.

Suddenly, while the merry-making was in full swing, a terrible, blood-curdling cry echoed across the valley. Abandoning their dancing, the young men and women ran in the direction from which the cry had come and discovered, to their horror, that an enormous wolf had seized one of the village's prettiest girls, recently engaged to be married, and was dragging her away. Her fiancé was nowhere to be seen.

The most courageous of the men went in pursuit of the wolf and eventually confronted it. But the furious monster, its mouth foaming with a fiendish rage, dropped its human prey on the ground and stood over it, ready to fight. Some of the villagers ran home to fetch guns and axes; but the wolf, seeing the fear of those who remained, again seized the girl and vanished into the nearby forest.

Many years elapsed; and then, at another harvest feast, on the same hill, an old man approached the revellers. They invited him to join in the celebrations, but the old man, gloomy and reserved, chose to sit down to drink in silence. A countryman of roughly the same age then joined him and, after looking at him closely for a moment or two, asked with some emotion: 'Is it you, John?'

The old man nodded, and instantly the countryman recognised the stranger as his older brother, who had disappeared many years before. The merry-makers quickly gathered round the old visitor and listened to his strange tale. He told them how, having been changed into a wolf by a sorcerer, he had carried his fiancée away from that same hill during a harvest festival and had lived with her in the nearby forest for a year, after which she died.

'From that moment on', he continued, 'savage and furious, I attacked every man, woman and child, and destroyed every animal I came across. My trail of bloodshed I cannot even now completely wipe away.' At this point he showed them his hands, which were covered with bloodstains.

'It is some four years since, having once again changed back to human shape, I have wandered from place to place. I wanted to see you all once more – to see the cottage and village where I was born and grew up to be a man. After that... well, I shall become a wolf again.'

No sooner had he uttered these words than he changed into a wolf. He rushed past the astonished onlookers and disappeared into the forest, never to be seen again.

The fairy-tale aspects of this story make it very difficult to take seriously. Could too much drink have enhanced the already colourful imagination of the peasant folk? Could detail have been built upon detail with each new telling until the story reached

PERSPECTIVES

BORN TO BE WILD

The French anthropologist, Jean-Claude Armen, has reported that on several occasions during the 1970s he saw a 'human gazelle' in the Syrian desert.

The creature, was a 10-year-old boy who galloped 'in gigantic bounds amongst a long cavalcade of white gazelles'. According to Armen, this 'gazelle boy' seemed to have adapted himself to the life of the herd, licking and sniffing at the animals in the friendliest of ways.

This seemingly well-authenticated account is just one example of many reports dating back to the Middle Ages of encounters with human children who have supposedly been reared by wild animals.

The most frequently-featured foster-parents in such accounts are wolves – animals that haunted the ancient forests of Europe and beyond, and that became a staple element of folk tales.

One of the earliest of wolf stories is that of Romulus and Remus, the legendary founders of Rome, who as babies were suckled by a she-wolf. In modern times, however, one of the most intriguing cases of children supposedly reared by wolves occurred in India in 1920. Two girls, aged two and eight, were allegedly found in a wolf-lair at Midnapore in West Bengal by an Anglican clergyman, the Reverend J.A.L. Singh.

Singh kept a diary of his efforts to humanise the two, whom he named Amala and Kamala. Civilising them proved a difficult task, for they ran on all fours, howled like wolves, and ate only raw meat. The younger child, Amala, died within a year of being found, but Kamala lived for a further nine years, learning to walk upright and to speak over 30 words.

It remains a mystery as to whether these children and their like were truly reared by wolves or whether, as it was asserted by the child psychologist Bruno Bettelheim, they were abandoned autistic children who had simply crawled into an animal's den.

its present apparently fanciful form? It is a strong possibility... and yet, like so many werewolf horror stories of its type, it is reported by many mythologists and historians, folklorists and psychologists as pure fact – James Stallybrass, for instance, in *Teutonic Mythology*, John Fiske in *Myths and Myth-makers*, and Walter E. Kelly in *Curiousities of Indo-European Tradition and Folk-lore.*

The origin of the werewolf superstition – the belief that a human being is capable of assuming an animal's form, most frequently that of a wolf – has never been satisfactorily explained.

Herodotus, the Greek historian who lived in the fifth century BC, says that the Greeks and the Scythians who settled on the shores of the Black Sea regarded the native Neurians as wizards, who were transformed into wolves for a few days of every year. He even speaks of a race of men who could change themselves at will into the shape of wolves and, when they desired, could just as easily resume their original form.

The excessively hirsute – such as Jojo,* right, *dubbed the 'dog-faced boy' – have sometimes been thought to be werewolves, but erroneously so.

***Elements of the werewolf legend passed into the story of Little Red Riding Hood, as shown in the illustration by Doré,* below.**

CRAVINGS FOR HUMAN FLESH

Centuries before the birth of Christ, the demon werewolf was looked upon as a human being possessed of an unnatural craving for human flesh who, by magical arts, had found a way to change at will into the form of a ravening wolf in order more readily to gratify this horrible appetite. Once transformed, the ancient sages believed, the werewolf possessed the very strength and cunning of the savage wolf-beast, though retaining his recognisably human voice and eyes.

The transformation of men into wolves is found in Roman literature also as a work of magic. Virgil, writing in the first century BC, is the first Latin poet to mention the superstition. Petronius, director of entertainment at Nero's court from AD 54 to 68, also tells a fine werewolf yarn in his satirical picaresque romance, the *Satyricon.*

Certain Greek and Roman traditions represent the transformation of man into wolf as a punishment for sacrificing a human victim to a god. On such occasions, said Pliny (AD 62–113), the victim was taken to the edge of a lake and, having swum to the far shore, changed into a wolf. In this condition, he roamed the countryside with fellow wolves for a period of nine years. If, during this time, he abstained from eating human flesh, he resumed his original form, which would not have been exempt from the ravages of increased age.

Another mythological instance of shape-changing as a punishment for sin is recorded by Ovid (43 BC–AD 18) in his narrative poem *Metamorphoses*. In it, he recounts legends involving miraculous transformations of shape from the Creation to the time of Julius Caesar. He tells, for instance, how Lycaon, mythical King of Arcadia, presumed to test the omniscience of Jupiter by placing before him a dish of human flesh – for which crime he was immediately transformed into a wolf, to become for evermore a source of terror to his pastoral subjects.

The methods used to effect such transformations differed widely. Sometimes the change was spontaneous and uncontrollable; sometimes, as in the transformations described in Norse and Icelandic sagas, it was achieved simply by assuming the skin of a real wolf. But, in many cases, all that was needed was the use of a charm that, while involving no actual change in the human body, caused all onlookers to imagine that they really saw a wolf. Some transformed men claimed they could regain human form only by means of certain herbs, such as poisonous aconite or hemlock, or by rubbing ointments on their bodies.

Witches and Werewolves

So genuine was belief in such tales of transformation that, in the 15th and 16th centuries, werewolves throughout Europe were regarded in the same light as witches and wizards, and anyone suspected of being a werewolf was burnt or hanged with the utmost cruelty, especially in France and Germany. As Elton B. McNeil explains in *The Psychoses*, commenting on this era of flagellantism (self-injury), tarantism (dancing mania), mass hysteria, hypochondriacal delusion, projection or hallucination, and werewolfism:

'Attitudes reflected a psychology influenced by the belief that whom the gods will destroy, they first make mad. Madness, as an expression of the will of God, became epidemic. Its cure became a religious ritual designed to use the psychotic as a target for religious persecution and as a means of reaffirming the worth of the blessed, innocent, and pure. Blessed were those who exposed persons who had sold their souls to the Devil. The classic hunt of the witches was a side product in the search for salvation.'

The hunt for werewolves was a manifestation of much the same sort of religious feeling; indeed, witch trials and werewolf trials are clearly interrelated. But it is in witch-crazed France that the most numerous instances of werewolves are to be found. In one period of little over 100 years – between 1520 and 1630 – France could record a staggering 30,000 cases of werewolfism – a fact documented in the proceedings of werewolf trials that are preserved in the public records.

In 1573 at Dôle, near Dijon in central France, a werewolf named Gilles Garnier was accused of devastating the countryside and devouring little children and, after confessing to the crimes, was burnt at the stake.

***A werewolf devours his victim,* below, *in an illustration from the former South African magazine* Die Brandwag (The Fire-Watch).**

The illustration,* bottom, *shows an 18th-century werewolf transformation. It was believed that, if the werewolf's clothes were hidden, he would be unable to resume human form.

Years later, in 1598, in a wild and desolate area near Caude, a group of French countrymen stumbled across the horribly mutilated, blood-spattered body of a 15-year-old boy. A pair of wolves, which had been devouring the corpse, ran off into a nearby thicket as the men approached. They gave chase – and almost immediately they found a half-naked man crouching in the bushes, sporting long hair and an unkempt beard and long, dirty claw-like nails, which were clotted with fresh blood and the shreds of human flesh.

The man, Jacques Rollet, was a pathetic, half-witted specimen under the curse of a cannibal appetite. He had been in the process of tearing to

In the 16th-century engraving, left, a wolf-headed Lycaon, mythical king of Arcadia, carries an axe to kill Jupiter, the supreme Roman god. Lycaon had presumed to test if Jupiter could distinguish between human and animal flesh, and was punished for his arrogance by being turned into a werewolf.

pieces the corpse of the boy when disturbed by the countrymen. Whether or not there were any wolves in the case, except those that excited imaginations may have conjured up, it is impossible to determine. But it is certain that Rollet supposed himself to be a wolf, and killed and ate several people under the influence of this delusion, a psychiatric condition known as *lycanthropy*. He was sentenced to death, but the law courts of Paris reversed the sentence and charitably shut him up in a madhouse – an institution where most suspected werewolves should probably have lived out their days rather than being executed.

DEVIL PACT

Another significant werewolf case occurred in the early 17th century. Jean Grenier was a boy of 13, partially idiotic and of strongly marked canine physiognomy – his jaws stuck forward, and his canine teeth showed under his upper lip. He believed himself to be a werewolf. One evening, meeting some young girls, he terrified them by saying that, as soon as the Sun had set, he would turn into a wolf and eat them for supper.

A few days later, one little girl, having gone out at nightfall to tend to the sheep, was attacked by some creature that in her terror she mistook for a wolf, but that afterwards proved to be none other than Jean Grenier. She beat him off with her sheep-staff, and fled home.

When brought before the law courts of Bordeaux, he confessed that, two years previously, he had met the Devil one night in the woods, had signed a pact with him and received from him a wolfskin. Since then, he had roamed about as a wolf after dark, resuming his human shape by day-light. He had killed and eaten several children whom he had found alone in the fields, and once he had entered a house while the family were out and taken a baby from its cradle.

A careful investigation by the court proved that these statements were true, certainly as far as the cannibalism was concerned. There is little doubt that the missing children were eaten by Jean Grenier, and there is no doubt that the half-witted boy was firmly convinced that he was a wolf.

In more recent times, the werewolf phenomenon has retreated somewhat into the realms of fantasy, but has done so without losing any of its grim horror. Nevertheless, tales of real werewolves do crop up from time to time. Three werewolves were said to haunt the forested Ardennes area of Belgium just before the First World War, while in Scotland at about the same time a hermit shepherd in the area of Inverness was rumoured to be a werewolf. In 1925, a whole village near Strasbourg testified that a local boy was a werewolf; and, five years later, a French werewolf scare terrorised Bourg-la-Reine, just south of Paris, in an incident related by Pierre van Paasen in his book, *Days of Our Years*.

MURDEROUS BEAST

In more recent years, werewolf scares have also occurred the world over. In 1946, for instance, a Navajo Indian reservation was frequently plagued by a murderous beast that was widely reported as a werewolf. (Navajo traditions are rich in werewolf tales). Three years later, in Rome, a police patrol was sent to investigate the strange behaviour of a man suffering from werewolf delusions: he regularly lost control at the time of a full moon and let out loud and terrifying howls.

In Singapore, in 1957, police were again called to look into what the authorities believed was a long series of werewolf attacks on the residents of a particular nurses' hostel on the main island. One nurse awoke to find ' a horrible face, with hair reaching to the bridge of the nose,' and long protruding fangs, glaring down at her. The mystery was never solved, nor was the case of the 16-year-old schoolgirl at Rosario do Sul, in southern Brazil who, in 1978, suffered terrible 'evil visions and demons', and who believed she had been taken over by the spirit of a savage wolf

In 1975, Britain's newspapers were full of the most extraordinary reports about a 17-year-old youth from the village of Eccleshall, Staffordshire. In the awful belief that he was slowly turning into a werewolf, he terminated his mental agonies by plunging a flick-knife into his heart. One of his workmates told the inquest jury that the youth had made a frantic telephone call to him just before his death. 'He told me,' said the witness, 'that his face and hand were changing colour and that he was changing into a werewolf. He would go quiet and then start growling.'

The werewolf tradition may be built on ignorance and delusion, but its influence on the mind of the weak and sick has always been powerful and most probably will remain so.

RIDDLE OF THE GREEN CHILDREN

THIRTEENTH-CENTURY MONASTIC RECORDS TELL OF THE MYSTERIOUS APPEARANCE, IN THE SMALL SUFFOLK VILLAGE OF WOOLPIT, OF TWO STRANGE GREEN-SKINNED CHILDREN. THEIR ORIGIN CAUSED CONSIDERABLE SPECULATION

The reign of Stephen, last of the Norman kings, was a dark period in the history of England. Stephen, who seized power in 1154, was a weak and foolish ruler who diminished the monarchy's immediate power by a policy of giving away titles, lands and royal rights to anyone prepared to support him, who fought a costly civil war, and who allowed the governmental machine to run down and his subjects to lose touch with the Crown. For the vast majority of ordinary people, it was a time of anxiety and strife.

Life went on, of course, in the towns, manors, villages and fields; the land was tilled and the harvests gathered, but it was hard to make a living and constant fear of war or invasion unsettled economic life to a marked degree. And, as often happens in times of great hardship, the suffering, uncomplaining thousands clung with increasing desperation to the emotional shelter offered by the Church. As Dorothy Stenton remarks in her *English Society in the Early Middle Ages*: 'Their lives . . . were hard

***The unexplained arrival of the two green children in the village of Woolpit,* below, *is commemorated in a village sign,* left.**

A paranormal event would have been greeted quite differently in medieval times from the way in which we would regard it today: it would have excited fear, awe, interest – but not surprise. And with this attitude went, unavoidably, what we would now regard as credulousness. Clearly, the veracity of any inexplicable occurrence of the medieval period must be considered in the light of such an outlook – and with extreme caution.

Monastic chroniclers of the time understood this. Among them was William of Newburgh – a monastery in Yorkshire – who, looking back to Stephen's reign in 1200, began his account of the strange green children who materialised at Woolpit, near Bury St Edmunds in Suffolk, with the following words: 'I must not there omit a marvel, a prodigy unheard of since the beginning of all time, which is known to have come to pass under King Stephen. I myself long hesitated to credit it, although it was noised abroad by many folk, and I thought it ridiculous to accept a thing which had no reason to commend it, or at most some reason of great obscurity, until I was so overwhelmed with the weight of so many and such credible witnesses that I was compelled to believe and admire that which my wit striveth vainly to reach or follow'.

Harvest Miracle

After this diffident preamble, the chronicler continues more confidently:

'There is a village in England some four or five miles [7 or 8 kilometres] from the noble monastery of the Blessed King and Martyr Edmund, near which may be seen certain trenches of immemorial antiquity which are named in the English tongue, Wolfpittes, and which give their name to the adjacent village. One harvest-tide, when the harvesters were gathering in the corn, there crept out from these two pits a boy and a girl, green at every point of their body, and clad in garments of strange hue and unknown texture. These wandered distraught about the field, until the harvesters took them and brought them to the village, where many flocked together to see this marvel'.

and brief and they accepted unquestioningly a religion that offered to the poor and hungry an eternity of satisfaction'.

If anything, this understates the case. Religion was the very crux of medieval life, and with religion went a belief that the unworldly, or noncorporeal, existed as fact. What the eye could not see was every bit as real as the visible world; that spirits were invisible to human eyes was only an indication of Man's distance – through sin – from God. To some people was given the gift of seeing spirits; and at certain times, these incorporeal beings were apt to appear, either spontaneously or through invocation. For Saint Isidore of Seville (AD 560-636), demons, for instance, were quite real. In his *Etymologia*, he describes them as creatures that:

'Unsettle the senses, stir low passions, disorder life, cause alarms in sleep bring diseases . . . control the way lots are cast, make a pretence at oracles by their tricks, arouse the passion of love . . . when evoked they appear; they take on different forms, and sometimes appear in the likeness of angels.'

The mysterious Sir Bertilak, the Green Knight of the 14th-century English poem* Sir Gawaine and the Green Knight, *is seen above as he meets his death. His green colour immediately suggests to onlookers that he is a magical creature. Similarly, the greenness of the Woolpit children served to emphasise their magical quality.

The monk,* right, *is depicted seeing the devil of conceit behind a fashionable lady. Most medieval people regarded devils and spirits as real – something that should be taken into account when evaluating medieval reports of paranormal events.

Abbot Ralph of Coggeshall, a monastic scribe working in Essex, some 30 miles (50 kilometres) south of Woolpit, was less sceptical about the green children, but also less definite about the colour of their skin, claiming only that they were 'tinged of a green colour'. He continued:

'No-one could understand their speech. When they were brought as curiosities to the house of a certain knight, Sir Richard de Calne, at Wikes, they wept bitterly. Bread and other victuals were set before them, but they would touch none of them, though they were tormented by great hunger, as the girl afterwards acknowledged. At length, when some beans just cut, with their stalks, were brought into the house, they made signs, with great avidity, that they should be given to them. When they were brought, they opened the stalks instead of the pods, thinking the beans were in the hollow of them; but not finding them there, they began to weep anew. When those who were present saw this, they opened the pods, and showed them the naked beans. They fed on these with great delight, and for a long time tasted no other food. The boy, however, was always languid and depressed, and he died within a short time. The girl enjoyed continual good health; and becoming accustomed to various kinds of food, lost completely that green colour, and gradually recovered the sanguine habit of her entire body. She was afterwards regenerated by the laver of holy baptism, and lived for many years in the service of that knight... and was rather loose and wanton in her conduct.'

The girl apparently married and settled down with a man from Kings Lynn. Here, she was often asked about the origins of herself and her companion, and how they arrived at Woolpit. The two monastic accounts differ at this point, though not substantially. Abbot Ralph records that they came from a country that was entirely green, inhabited by green people; it was said to be sunless but twilit. They had been tending their flocks one day when they came to a cave:

'On entering which they heard a delightful sound of bells; ravished by whose sweetness, they went for a long time wandering on through the cavern, until they came to its mouth. When they came out of it, they were struck senseless by the excessive light of the sun, and the unusual temperature of the air; and they thus lay for a long time. Being terrified by the noise of those who came on them, they wished to fly, but they could not find the entrance of the cavern before they were caught.'

The grossly sentimentalised creatures in an illustration from* Fairyland *by Richard Doyle,* above, *share one characteristic with their medieval counterparts: their use of the magical and slightly sinister colour green.

*In*Focus

THE BLUE MAN

Science fiction stories frequently feature accounts of aliens in the form of little green men. An actual sighting some 25 years ago, however, seems to indicate a somewhat different shade of humanoid colouring.

In January 1967, one rather bleak day, several young schoolboys were walking home together over Studham Common in Britain's Chiltern Hills when one of them thought he had spotted a strange figure – subsequently described as a small, blue man with a tall hat and a beard – lurking behind a bush in the distance.

The lad immediately pointed him out to a friend and, curious, they both determined to approach him. Gingerly venturing towards the man, they got to within about 60 feet (18 metres) of him, but he promptly vanished into thin air, in a puff of smoke, as if anxious not to be seen.

Utterly intrigued by now, because of what they had witnessed, the two boys got their pals to join in a hunt for the little blue man; and, sure enough, before too long he reappeared not far away, only to vanish again and then return – a trick he kept repeating. The boys also reported hearing odd, foreign-sounding voices at the time, and soon began feeling distinctly nervous about the whole episode.

They mentioned the occurrence to their teacher; and, questioned later by investigators who had been looking into reports of recent UFO sightings by local people, the boys wrote independent accounts of their adventure. The blue man, they all agreed, had been about three feet in height and had sported a tall hat. Mysteriously, too, he had worn a wide, dark belt with a six-inch (15-centimetre) square box at the front where a buckle might have been. The purpose of this was not, however, obvious.

To this day, the boys' experience remains unexplained, as do the humanoid's peculiar blue colouring and his persistent vanishings and reappearances. Two UFO landings had been spotted on the common not long previously; but the boys themselves had not noticed alien craft of any kind.

CASEBOOK

AN EVERGREEN STORY

An interesting postscript to the Woolpit tale is the story of the green children of Banjos, a tiny village in the Spanish province of Catalonia. The story goes that in August 1887, some peasants found two strange children crying at the mouth of a cave. The young boy and girl spoke in a tongue incomprehensible to the villagers – and, it was claimed, specialists called in from Barcelona failed to recognise it. They were clad in clothes that were made from an unknown material: but, strangest of all, their skins appeared bright green. What is more, their odd colouring appeared to be due to natural pigmentation.

The children seemed terrified at first, so the mayor of the village took them home to comfort them. He offered them food, but they refused every dish and for five whole days they starved, drinking only spring water. Then they spotted a basket of raw green beans and ended their fast. From then on, they lived solely on green beans and water; but the boy had been gravely weakened through lack of food, and died within a month. His sister, on the other hand, thrived and soon began to learn Spanish. Eventually, she could speak well enough to be able to describe the place that she and the boy had come from. It was a land of eternal twilight where the Sun never shone; and its natural boundary was a large river across which could be seen another land bathed in sunshine. Life in their twilit country had been pastoral and peaceful, until one day a great noise deafened the children, and they suddenly found themselves transported to sundrenched Banjos.

On hearing this, the intrigued villagers searched for an entrance to this hidden world, but without success. The girl, meanwhile, reconciled herself to her new life. Her skin gradually lost its green hue, and she died peacefully five years later, taking with her the secret of her origin.

The story sounds strangely familiar. In fact, its similarity to the story of the green children of Woolpit at first seems uncannily close: the only differences lie in that the Banjos children are described as having 'almond-shaped, Asiatic eyes', and that the girl dies after five years. But when we learn that the name of the mayor who looked after the children is Ricardo de Calno, credulousness is stretched beyond its limits.

A certain Sir Richard de Calne had met with the Woolpit green children, remember. Unless there is some extraordinary Fortean coincidence at work, it can probably safely be assumed that the green children of Banjos are a complete fabrication.

But how did the Banjos story ever come to be accepted as true? Until the 1950s, the Woolpit tale was little known, but in 1959 Harold T. Wilkins – who was responsible for the publication of the alleged Kidd-Palmer map showing buried treasure on Oak Island, Canada, included the story in his popular book *Mysteries Solved and Unsolved.* It was Wilkins who first suggested that these children might have come from a 'fourth dimensional world [that] existed side-by-side with ours'. He also felt that the story could 'imply that they had been teleported from some world in space . . . where men live underground'.

Wilkins's extravagant views encouraged an unscrupulous author – as yet unidentified – to update and relocate the story. An imaginary village in a remote part of Catalonia was invented – there is no such place as Banjos – making checks difficult for anyone who knew nothing of the tale's ancestry. And so the tale came to be accepted as fact, even though no one has ever produced testimony of any kind for the story – despite a claim that 'documents concerning the case exist, together with all the evidence given under oath by witnesses who saw and touched and questioned the children'.

The illustration, below, *shows the two terrified green children, found at the entrance to a cave in a Catalonian village.*

In William of Newburgh's account, on the other hand, the children are found in a cornfield, not a cave. The girl says:

'We are folk of St Martin's land; for that is the chief saint among us... One day we were feeding our father's flock in the field, when we heard a great noise, such as we hear now when all the bells of St Edmund's peal together. When, therefore, we were listening with all our ears to this marvellous sound, suddenly we were rapt in the spirit and found ourselves in your harvest field.' She adds that theirs was a Christian land with churches of its own, a land separated from a land of light by what she called a wide stream – presumably a sea.

That two alien, mysterious children turned up somewhere near Woolpit and were discovered there by the local villagers seems fairly credible. Times were hard, and it is not difficult to imagine that a family, too large and unable to provide for all, might choose to offload two of its younger members. In those impoverished times, it happened frequently. It even happens today. But it is the children's greenness and the other 'facts' of the case that make this such an extraordinary incident – and at the same time call upon a number of medieval superstitions and beliefs that cast considerable doubt upon the entire story. The reports claim that the children were green, or green-tinged. No other colour has such supernatural significance. In folklore, it has a curious dual significance: it is the colour of life and fecundity, but also a magical and slightly sinister colour, often associated with fairies. The most famous example of the association that the colour green had in medieval times is the 14th-century anonymous poem *Sir Gawaine and the Green Knight*. The weird hue of the Green Knight – who turns out, as his colour suggests, to be an ambivalent character, neither good nor evil, immediately identifies him with the world of faerie. In Brian Stone's translation from the Middle English, the description of the Green Knight runs as follows:

A greetings card of around 1870, above, shows the ancient custom of the dance of Jack-in-the-Green on May Day. His leafy green costume represented the return of life to nature in spring.

The pub sign,* left, *shows the Green Man – an enigmatic figure who characterises the forces of nature – sometimes benevolent and sometimes seemingly malicious towards Man.

'The assembled folk stared, long scanning the fellow
For all men marvelled what it might mean,
That a horseman and his horse should have such a colour
As to grow green as grass and greener yet, it seemed,
More gaudily glowing than green enamel on gold.
Those standing studied him and sidled towards him
With all the world's wonder as to what he would do.
For astonishing sights they had seen, but such a one never;
Therefore a phantom from Fairyland the folk there deemed him.'

If Woolpit's two foundlings were green, it is likely that they would have been regarded as in some way supernatural by the villagers. But what if someone who was present at their sudden appearance decided that they were, in any case, supernatural: how long would it be before their colour became part of the legend, the 'fact' evolving from the rumour? This is a contrived theory, but not a difficult one to swallow. Further evidence to support this argument is provided by the Woolpit children's predilection for green beans. Traditionally, beans are the food of the dead and of ghosts, and the souls of the dead are said to dwell in bean fields. But beans have good properties, too – scattered round the house, they are said to ward off evil spirits; and in witch country, a bean was to be kept in the mouth to be spat at the first witch one encountered. The detail of the two children eating nothing but beans merely compounds the notion that they were other-worldly. There is more than a hint here that someone has included this detail for emphasis, and that it is not intended to be taken literally.

What is most likely is that two foreign children had been abandoned by their nomadic parents, and were later found in a state of near exhaustion and starvation. Their greenness could have been some form of jaundice or even secondary anaemia. Perhaps, on the other hand, they were just green with queasiness – the simple effect, maybe, of eating far too many green beans?

BACK TO LIFE

A SMALL GIRL, DANGEROUSLY ILL, 'DIED' FOR A QUARTER-OF-AN-HOUR. ACCORDING TO HER OWN ACCOUNT, SHE WENT TO A NEW WORLD IN THE STARS, MET LONG-DEAD RELATIVES AND HAD AN INTERVIEW WITH GOD. HERE, HER FATHER TELLS HER ASTONISHING STORY

Late in the autumn of 1968, Durdana, the younger of my two daughters, then about two-and-a-half-years old, 'died' for around a quarter of an hour. She had been ill for some months, getting progressively worse. She had even begun to become paralysed, and later developed episodes of vomiting and blindness. I was an army doctor in those days, posted to a small unit high in the foothills of the Himalayas. We took Durdana to the military hospital, some miles away, for examination, but investigations proved inconclusive. A suggestion was made that the symptoms might be the after-effects of a viral encephalitis that had claimed the lives of some dozen children in the area some time before.

I was busy in the medical inspection room one morning when my orderly came running to tell me that my wife was calling me – something had happened to baby Durdana.

My living quarters were a large hut in the station compound, adjacent to the inspection room. Durdana had been very bad the night before and, fearing the worst, I hurried home. My wife was in the garden, standing beside the child's cot. A hurried examination revealed no sign of life in the little girl. 'She's gone,' I said. With a look almost of relief, for the child had been in extreme pain, my wife gently lifted the limp little form from the cot and carried her inside. I followed. Certain emergency measures are mandatory under army regulations, and one of my staff, who had followed me from the inspection room, hurried off to get the requisite equipment.

My wife carried the child to our bedroom and laid her down on my bed. After another examination, I began to carry out the prescribed emergency procedures, rather half-heartedly, knowing that they were unlikely to have any effect. While doing so, I found myself repeating, half unconsciously, under my breath: 'Come back my child, come back.'

As a last resort, my wife poured a few more drops of the *nikethamide* – a heart stimulant that we had given Durdana the night before – into the child's mouth. They trickled out of her lifeless mouth and down her cheek. We looked sadly on – and then, to our amazement, the child opened her eyes and, making a wry face, gravely informed us that the medicine was bitter. Then she closed her eyes again. Quickly, I examined her – and, as I watched her, signs of life began to reappear, albeit very faintly at first.

One day soon afterwards – when Durdana had somewhat recovered from her 'death' and my wife from her shock – mother and daughter were in the garden. 'Where did my little daughter go the other day?' asked my wife. 'Far, far away, to the stars,' came the surprising reply. Now, Durdana was an intelligent and articulate child; and whatever she said had to be taken seriously, or she would become annoyed. 'Indeed,' exclaimed my wife, 'and what did my darling see there?'

'Gardens,' said Durdana.

'And what did she see in these gardens?'

'Apples and grapes and pomegranates.'

'And what else?'

'There were streams; a white stream, a brown stream, a blue stream, and a green stream.'

'And was anyone there?'

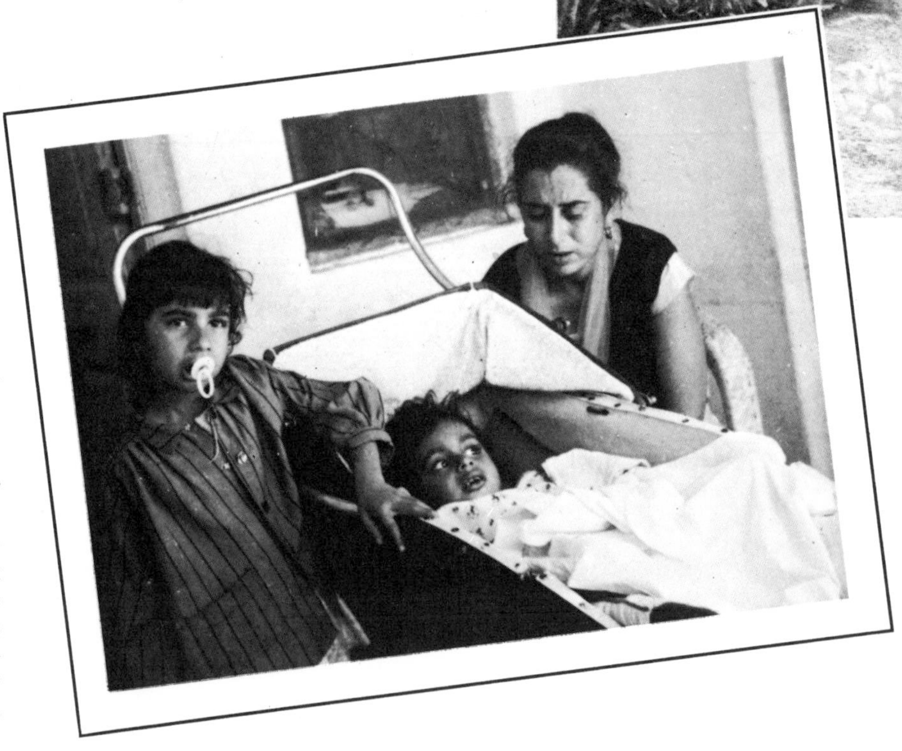

Durdana's impression – painted in 1980 – of what she saw on her visit to the 'stars' is seen* left. *She found herself in a garden with four streams – white, brown, blue and green in colour. Subtle differences showed Durdana that she could not be on Earth: there appeared to be no Sun, but everything shone with its own faint luminescence, and physical objects seemed to have no substance. Durdana painted the picture,* below, *to show what the scene would look like on Earth.

'Yes, my grandfather was there, and his mother, and another lady who looked like you.'

My wife was greatly intrigued. 'And what did they say?'

'Grandpa said he was glad to see me, and his mother took me in her lap and kissed me.'

'Then?' 'Then I heard my daddy calling me, "Come back my child, come back." I told Grandpa that Daddy was calling me and I must go back. He said we should have to ask God. So we went to God, and Grandpa told him that I wanted to go back. "Do you want to go back?" God asked me. "Yes," I said, "I must go back. My Daddy is calling me." "All right," said God, "Go." And down, down, down I came from the stars, on to Daddy's bed.'

This was more than interesting. Durdana had indeed 'come to' on my bed – an unusual place for her to find herself, for the children slept or played in

Durdana, aged two-and-a-half years, is pictured* left *with her mother and older sister, after she had 'died' for a quarter-of-an-hour as the result of a neural illness. Once she was well enough to speak, her parents asked her where she had gone during that quarter-hour. 'Far, far away, to the stars,' was Durdana's disconcerting reply.

***Questioned soon after her experience, Durdana said that she had heard her father's voice calling her home, and had asked God's permission to return to Earth. When asked to describe what God looked like, she could only say 'blue' and drew the impression,* left.**

their own beds or their mother's, never in mine. And when Durdana regained consciousness, she was in no state to know where she was. But my wife was more interested in Durdana's interview with the Almighty.

'What was God like?' she asked.

'Blue,' came the startling reply.

'But what did he look like?'

'Blue.'

Try as we might, then and later, to get the child to describe God in more detail, she could only repeat that he was 'blue'.

Soon afterwards, we took Durdana to Karachi for treatment at the neuro-surgical department of the Jinnah Post-Graduate Medical Centre. After a complex operation on her skull, Durdana gradually began to recover. I returned to duty, while my wife stayed in Karachi with the convalescent Durdana. Before they left to rejoin me, they visited several of our relatives and friends in Karachi. While visiting the house of one of my uncles, as they sat chatting over a cup of tea, Durdana started to wander about the room, holding on to pieces of furniture for support – for, extremely weak after illness, she was still unable to stand unaided. Suddenly she called out 'Mummy, Mummy!' My wife ran to her. 'Mummy,' said Durdana excitedly, pointing to an old photograph displayed on a side table, 'this is my grandpa's mother. I met her in the stars. She took me in her lap and kissed me.'

Durdana was quite right. But my grandmother had died long before Durdana was born; only two photographs of her exist, and both are in the possession of my uncle. Durdana was visiting his house for the first time in her life, and in no way could she have seen this photograph before.

We later moved to London, and Durdana's story began to attract interest from the media. The BBC featured her in a 1980 *Everyman* programme on survival of death and, before the filming began, the producer, Angela Tilby, came to visit us. She admired a number of paintings by Durdana that were hanging on the walls. Durdana had become a gifted landscape painter, and had received many awards and prizes for her work. Mrs Tilby made the interesting suggestion that Durdana should try to paint what she had seen when she was in the stars.

Durdana was later featured on the BBC programme *Pebble Mill at One*, and her paintings of the stars were shown and discussed at some length. The day after the programme had been broadcast, I received a telephone call from a certain Mrs Goldsmith, one of my patients – a very intelligent, well-read German-Jewish woman. She said she had seen Durdana on the television the day before, and expressed the wish to meet my daughter personally and to see her paintings again. It turned out that Mrs Goldsmith had been through an experience of near-death that was very similar to Durdana's. 'I nearly jumped out of my chair when I saw this picture on the television,' she said about one of the paintings. '"My God," I said, "I've been to this place..."'

Durdana stands with her father, below, and shows one of her paintings of the scenes she saw during the time she was apparently dead. One of Durdana's father's patients – a Mrs Goldsmith, above right – saw the paintings when they were featured on the BBC television programme* Pebble Mill at One *– and immediately recognised the landscapes as those she, too, had seen during a near-death experience.

Listening to her speak, I felt that she seemed a little over-excited – until I realised that what she was trying to tell us was not that she had been to similar gardens in this life, but that she had visited the actual spot that Durdana had painted. It appeared that she had seen more of the place than Durdana had: apparently, I had called Durdana away too soon! Mrs Goldsmith recognised everything that was in Durdana's picture, and also described things that were not in the picture. They sat and talked about what was round the bend in the stream that Durdana had painted, and about the location of the other streams that Durdana had described to her mother.

New Freedom

But what of Durdana's feelings during her experience? They are strikingly similar to those reported by Mrs Goldsmith, and by many other people who have gone through near-death experiences. She was very happy in the stars, and returned only out of a sense of duty, because I was calling her. She had a feeling of freedom: she felt she was everywhere at once, and could reach wherever she wanted to. There was no source of light, and hence no shadows. Everything was visible through its own luminescence. There was no sound, and there were no animals – at least, she saw none. Physical objects were ethereal images: they seemed to have no substance, no weight. She felt she knew everything and everybody.

I have presented Durdana's story as simply as possible, as it happened. But what does it imply? Where was it that Durdana spent her quarter-hour of 'death'? Durdana herself believes that her experience somehow reflects her own expectations: 'If I had been a Martian, perhaps I would have been sent to a replica of Mars. There, perhaps, God would have appeared red.' And yet Durdana's experience must be more than a dramatisation of her own imagination, for Mrs Goldsmith recognised the very same place.

Such questions remain unanswered. This is merely an account of the experience of one little girl – an experience that is strange, thought-provoking and more than a little awe-inspiring.

TELEPATHIC COMMANDS AND EVEN WORLD DOMINATION THROUGH MIND CONTROL: WHO WOULD HAVE DREAMT THAT PSYCHICAL EXPERIMENTATION IN THE USSR WAS ORIGINALLY INSPIRED BY CIRCUS STUNTS?

'Human intelligence has discovered much in nature that was hidden,' wrote Lenin, 'and it will discover much more, thus strengthening its domination over her.' Although, in the aftermath of the 1918 Bolshevik Revolution, he did his best to stamp out ancient superstitions and beliefs, before his death in 1924 the young Soviet Union had become the first country in the world to provide official support for research into nature's most baffling area – that which was later to be called parapsychology. Thus, an interest dating back at least to 1891 – when the Russian Society for Experimental Psychology was founded to study psychic phenomena – was maintained unbroken.

Half-a-century later, it was clear that Soviet scientists had learned a good deal about this 'hidden' branch of knowledge, and were ready to put their discoveries to good use. But there is a very sinister ring to some of their terminology – 'distant influence', 'mental suggestion' and 'transfer of motor impulses', for instance – indicating a desire to make people act and think according to instructions of which they are not consciously aware. Indeed, the theme of domination, as forecast by Lenin, runs through much Soviet work in parapsychology, and little imagination is needed to speculate on the uses to which such practices could be put.

Soviet interest in psychic matters was not initially inspired by Lenin, nor even by a scientist, but by a circus performer, Vladimir Durov, one of the most skilful animal trainers of all time. His animals, especially his dogs, delighted audiences with their well-rehearsed tricks. Although these were produced not by telepathy but by means of thorough training and the use of signals from an ultrasonic whistle, Durov was convinced that he could make direct mind-to-mind contact with his performers and persuade them to carry out tasks far more-complex than their routine circus stunts.

'Suppose', he said, 'we have the following task: to suggest that the dog go to a table and fetch a book lying upon

A PSYCHIC REVOLUTION

Behind the walls of the Kremlin, below, Soviet military leaders and politicians are believed to have planned the use of psychotronic weapons against the West.

Vladimir Bekhterev, above right, carried out pioneering work on animal behaviour that led him to experiment with human mind control.

it... I take his head between my hands, as if I am symbolically inculcating in him the thought that he is entirely in my power... I fix my eyes upon his... ' Durov would then visualise the exact nature of the task to be performed, adding: 'I fix into his brain what I just before fixed in my own. I mentally put before him the part of the floor leading to the table, then the leg of the table, then the tablecloth, and finally the book'. Then, on the mental command, the dog would rush off 'like an automaton', leap on to the table and seize the book in its teeth.

THOUGHT SUGGESTION

After watching Durov and his dogs perform at a circus, one of the country's leading neuropathologists, Academician Vladimir Bekhterev (1857-1927), a colleague of the world-renowned physiologist Ivan Pavlov, decided to put his claims to the test in his laboratory. After several demonstrations, which involved different dogs, Bekhterev was satisfied that animal behaviour could be influenced by 'thought suggestion', even when dog and trainer were out of sight of each other. Some of the tests, carried out in Durov's absence, involved tasks known only to Bekhterev himself, and he even achieved limited success with his own dog.

Vladimir Durov, one of the most popular stars of the Moscow circus, is seen* right, *with one of his trained wolves, and also sea-lions. His discovery of how to convey commands to dogs through mental suggestion inspired Bekhterev to experiment with telepathy in humans. Durov first took the dog's head in his hands and then visualised as vividly as possible the dog doing the task he was about to set. Next, he would issue a mental command – and the dog would instantly rush off 'like an automaton' and, amazingly, complete the task.

Inconclusive as it was, this work with Durov encouraged Bekhterev to take telepathy seriously. On becoming head of the Brain Research Institute at Leningrad University, he founded a Commission for the Study of Mental Suggestion in 1922 and set to work – not with dogs, but with humans as subjects. In one series of experiments, successful attempts were made to 'send' visual images to a subject who was told to write or draw whatever came into her mind. An extract from the sender's notes reads:

'Transmitted: triangle with a circle inside it. The subject completes the task [draws the target] at once. Transmitted: a simple pencil drawing of an engine. The percipient carries out the task precisely, and goes over the contour of the engine several times.'

Members of the commission then tried concentrating on objects instead of drawings, and found that, while subjects rarely identified the object itself, they often picked up unmistakable features of it, and even the sender's mental associations with it. A subject whose target was a block of cut glass, for instance, reported 'reflections in water – sugar loaf – snowy summit – iceberg, ice floes in the north illuminated by the sun – rays are broken up'. In another experiment, the sender stared at a framed portrait of a woman and noticed a reflection on its glass surface from a light bulb in the shape of the letter N. 'Napoleon – the letter N flashed by,' he said to his assistant. A minute later, the subject, who was out of earshot, announced: 'I see either Napoleon or Vespasian'. Altogether, the commission ran 269 experiments in transmission of objects or images, and reported that no less than 134 were wholly or partly successful.

At the 1924 Congress of Psychoneurology, delegates were given a spontaneous demonstration of telepathic control in action. On his way to the

> I BELIEVE THAT HIGH-ENERGY PARTICLES, WHICH BATHE THE EARTH FROM OUTER SPACE AT TIMES, CARRY INFORMATION FROM BRAIN TO BRAIN AT SPEEDS FASTER THAN SOUND, CAUSING REACTIONS WHICH WE DON'T YET FULLY UNDERSTAND. I URGE THAT SCIENTISTS EVERYWHERE TRY TO TRANSLATE THIS PARTICLE INTO THE LANGUAGE OF OUR SENSES.
>
> DR VIKTOR ADAMENKO, SOVIET PARAPSYCHOLOGY RESEARCHER

meeting, Professor K. I. Platonov happened to meet one of his patients, whom he asked to come along without telling her why. In full view of the audience, Platonov put the girl to sleep in a matter of seconds by mental suggestion from behind a blackboard, and then woke her by the same method. Afterwards, the girl asked him: 'Why did you invite me to the Congress? I don't understand. What happened to me? I slept, but I don't know why....' Platonov later revealed that this subject was so suggestible that he could send her to sleep even while she was dancing a waltz.

His experiment was repeated independently, and at almost the same time, by a group of researchers at the University of Kharkov, where psychologist Dr K. D. Kotkov reported that a series of about 30 experiments, held over a two-month period and designed to influence the behaviour of a girl student, were all successful. He described exactly how he did it.

Professor K.I. Platonov,* above, *prize-winning Soviet mathematician, caused a sensation at the 1924 Congress of Psychoneurology by putting a female subject to sleep merely by mentally suggesting (while hidden from her sight) that she do so. When she woke up, she had no conscious knowledge of the experiment. Platonov later stated that this girl was so suggestible that she could be mentally commanded to go to sleep even while she was dancing. The implications of this are far-reaching. Who knows how many people are similarly ill-equipped to withstand mental manipulation?

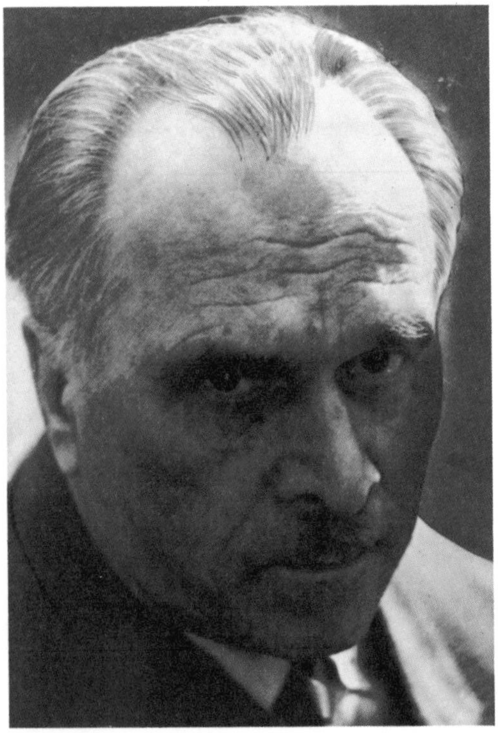

Professor Leonid Vasiliev,* left, *a former student of Bekhterev, grew up with a personal experience of telepathy and made it his life's work to study the phenomenon objectively. He proved that it is possible to send someone to sleep even at a distance of 1,000 miles (1,600 kilometres).

He would sit quietly and *mentally* murmur the words of suggestion to his subject. Then he would visualise her doing what he wished, and finally he would strongly wish her to do so. (This last stage was, he felt, the most important.) In this way, he could not only send the girl to sleep and wake her up, but even 'summon' her to the laboratory. When asked why she had turned up, the bewildered girl replied: 'I don't know. I just did. I wanted to come'. The most alarming aspect of this early example of behaviour control was that at no time was the girl aware of what was happening. 'When are the experiments about which you warned me going to start?' she kept asking – even after they had been carried out.

Remote Control

In addition to its own research, Bekhterev's Commission studied reports of spontaneous telepathy – which the Revolution had not managed to suppress totally from members of the public. One well-documented case concerned a student who had seen a bright light on his bedroom wall 'transforming itself into the clear head of a young lady'. He recognised her as his friend Nadezhda. 'After smiling at me,' he reported, 'she spoke a sentence of which I only managed to catch the last word – "decay". Then the girl's image seemed to melt into the wall and disappear.' The student wrote out an account of his experience on the same day, and six days later he learned that Nadezhda had died within minutes of his vision. Moreover, her mother testified that the girl's last words, addressed specifically to the boy, had been: 'There is neither dust nor decay'.

Impressed by the mounting evidence for telepathic phenomena, the 1924 Congress resolved that an investigation 'on strictly scientific lines' was called for. The man who was to devote his life to doing this was one of Bekhterev's students, Leonid I. Vasiliev (1891-1966). He began his career knowing that telepathy existed – because he had experienced it himself. When he was 12, he had nearly drowned after falling into a river. He begged his guardians not to tell his parents, who were 800 miles (1,300 kilometres) away; but as soon as his mother came home, she retold the whole story, right down to the detail of his new white cap being swept away by the current. She had dreamed the whole episode at the time.

Despite this personal experience, Vasiliev embarked objectively on his research into telepathy. He assumed there must be some physical explanation for it; and although he never found one, he did discover a number of practical ways in which telepathy can be made to work. In 1926, he carried out a series of experiments in a Leningrad hospital. These were designed to convey mental suggestions to a hypnotised subject, and comprised trivial actions such as raising a certain arm or leg, or scratching the nose. He was wholly or partly successful 16 times out of 19. Later, after repeating the experiment, he declared that both conscious and unconscious movements of a human body could be caused by mental suggestion alone.

Vasiliev also found that it was possible to send somebody to sleep or wake them up by a kind of mental remote control, even at distances of up to 1,000 miles (1,600 kilometres). Moreover, he found that screening the sender inside a Faraday cage (through which almost no form of electromagnetic radiation can pass) had no appreciable effect on his success rate. But Vasiliev failed in his main aim, which was to establish a physical basis for telepathy. His greatest achievement was to provide continuity between the pioneer days of the 1920s and the sudden renaissance of Soviet psi research that began after Khrushchev's historic denunciation of Stalinism in 1956.

Little is known about Vasiliev's research over the latter part of his life, although in 1940, a few months before the siege of Leningrad, he was carrying out experiments in his laboratory that showed how the muscles of an insect's intestines respond to electrical impulses emitted from contracting human muscles. Such work might not seem a vital part of the Russian war effort, yet it appears that Vasiliev was still determined to find physiological evidence for 'brain power' transference.

Master Spy?

1940 also saw none other than Joseph Stalin himself acting as psychical researcher for a short while, after showing an interest in one of the country's most popular stage performers, telepathist Wolf Messing. According to Messing's story, as published in the Soviet press (and never officially denied), Stalin put the telepathist's power of mind control to the test by having him persuade a bank clerk that a blank piece of paper was a cheque for 100,000 roubles. He then walked unchallenged through the dictator's own security guards after hypnotising them into thinking that he was secret police chief, Lavrenti Beria. If his report is true, Messing, who died in the early 1970s, could have been the greatest spy of all time.

The work of Wolf Messing, the popular Soviet stage telepathist,* above right, *even attracted the attention of Joseph Stalin.

Czech parapsychologist Dr Milan Ryzl,* below, *feared Vasiliev's best research was kept secret.

However, despite Messing's undoubted popularity, and Stalin's private views on the subject, telepathy was defined in the 1956 *Great Soviet Encyclopedia* as 'an anti-social, idealist fiction about man's supernatural power to perceive phenomena which, considering the time and place, cannot be perceived'. Vasiliev's whole life had apparently been spent in vain, at least as far as public recognition was concerned. Yet, after a typically sudden policy reversal by the Soviet authorities, Vasiliev was allowed to re-enter the field of parapsychology, with the full backing of the government, in 1960. The specific task of his Laboratory of Aero-ions and Electromagnetic Waves at Leningrad University (where he had by then become head of the physiology department) was 'to study the phenomena of telepathy'. He must have felt his life had come full circle after 40 years.

Czech parapsychologist Milan Ryzl has claimed that Vasiliev was almost certainly engaged in secret work, and it seems plausible that it was the prospect of discovering the mechanism of telepathy that kept research funds flowing in. If indeed they had discovered it, the Soviet authorities would have had in their power a means of domination of which even Lenin probably never dreamed.

SIGHTINGS OF UFOS OVER LARGE CITIES ARE RARE, BUT ONE WAS SEEN AND PHOTOGRAPHED OVER THE LONDON SUBURB OF STREATHAM

CITY SIGHTING

Photographs ought to provide good evidence of a UFO sighting, but they are not always so reliable. Sometimes, for example, a UFO can appear on a picture when the photographer did not actually see one at the time. Sometimes, too, the object appears differently on the photograph from the way that the observer remembers seeing it. So evidence from genuine pictures, too, is often ambiguous.

Sightings of true UFOs over London, as over any major city, are a rarity. Many reports are made, but these often prove to be misidentifications of lights in the sky. This is hardly surprising, considering the great volume of aircraft flying over the city on the way in or out of Heathrow airport. There are also many other aircraft flying over at great height and, at night, satellites reflect the rays of a sun already well below the western horizon. Few who report sightings in fact fulfil the condition of having seen a UFO at close range – that is, near enough to be classified as a close encounter of the first kind.

One sighting towards the end of 1966, however, may have fulfilled this condition and the report was reinforced by photographs that seem to show remarkable changes in the shape of the images.

The day of the sighting was Thursday, 15 December 1966. It was one of the shortest days of the year: the Sun set at 3.53 p.m. The weather was unpleasant – misty, dull and damp, with drizzle, rain and low cloud – and maximum visibility was 2 miles (3 kilometres).

At approximately 2.30 that afternoon, Anthony Russell was standing by the open window of his flat in Lewin Road, Streatham, south-west London. Lewin Road is at the southern end of Streatham High Road and just west of Streatham Common. The window by which Russell stood faces approximately north-north-west. A keen photographer, he was testing for resolution two new 2 X converters for his Zenith 3N single lens reflex camera (focal length 135 millimetres increased to 270 millimetres by one converter). During the testing, Russell was aiming the camera at the gable of a house on the far side of Lewin Road, about 28 yards (26 metres) from the lens. The camera was loaded with 35-millimetre Gratispool colour film.

The first photograph taken by Anthony Russell is shown right. There is a hint of an efflux from the base of the object on the right. The bar seen on the gable of the house across the road supports a chimney that is off-camera.

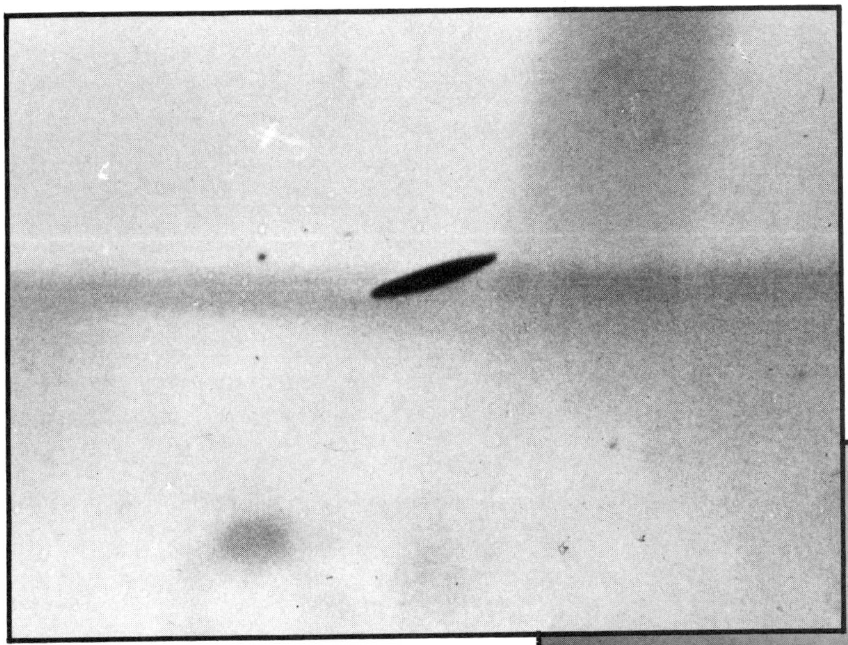

It is reasonable to assume that the eight blank frames were due to the speedy rolling-on of the film between shots in the excitement occasioned by an incident that lasted two minutes at most. The following is a reconstruction of those two minutes.

After the initial swift descent and abrupt halt of the UFO, Russell took his first two shots. He used the single converter that he had been testing, set at 1/125 second (f/5.6). He then hurried away from the window and fitted the second (Panagar) converter. With a focal length now of 540 millimetres, he set the exposure at 1/25 second (f/11). Returning to the window, he saw the object 'stand on end' and present its full circular shape to him before turning

Suddenly, Russell became aware of an object in the sky falling, stopping dead, and then drifting slowly earthwards with a pendulum-like motion. Amazed at first, but rapidly collecting his wits, he 'slapped the camera to infinity' and began snapping. He thought he got 12 photographs. The last two shots were taken as the object moved away, at first slowly and then at much greater speed.

The witness had enjoyed only limited contact with UFO literature before, in as much as his father had designed a cover for the book *Flying Saucers Have Landed* by George Adamski and Desmond Leslie. Russell did not think much of the book, however; and, after meeting Adamski, thought even less of the subject. But his scepticism received a jolt as he stood photographing the strange object.

Russell left the rest of the film in the camera so that he could take photographs at Christmas and sent it away for processing after the holiday period. In the meantime, he told a few friends what had happened. They were inclined to laugh off the incident, but he felt it was worth investigating. He did not wish for the publicity a newspaper might have brought him, but he was not sure who would be genuinely interested. Fearing he would get short shrift from established bodies such as the Royal Astronomical Society or the Royal Aeronautical Society, he looked through the telephone directory under the word 'flying' and happened on *Flying Saucer Review.* He wrote to the magazine, explaining what he expected to be found on his pictures when the film was returned, and the magazine arranged for R.H.B. Winder and Gordon Creighton to help in an investigation once the pictures were available for study.

From the start of the investigation, there was a measure of disappointment for the witness, as only three of the 12 frames came out well. A fourth – the last to be taken – revealed a dim shape that had little definition. Russell was puzzled by the object's apparent changes of shape because he did not recall seeing such changes. He remembered seeing only changes of aspect.

Russell's second photograph,* top, *shows the UFO edge-on which emphasises its disc shape. The expert who examined the photographs for fraud could not explain the strange shadow effects on this shot.

The third photograph,* above, *caught the UFO in a slanted position, perhaps in the ascent since it was taken just before the object sped away. When enlarged, the picture revealed a marked efflux to the left.

SUDDENLY, RUSSELL BECAME AWARE OF AN OBJECT IN THE SKY FALLING, STOPPING DEAD, AND THEN DRIFTING SLOWLY EARTHWARDS WITH A PENDULUM-LIKE MOTION. AMAZED AT FIRST, BUT RAPIDLY COLLECTING HIS WITS, HE 'SLAPPED THE CAMERA TO INFINITY' AND BEGAN SNAPPING.

through 90° about a vertical axis until it was edge on. The UFO then started to move to his right. During all that period, Russell shot only two successful snaps, though he could not have known this at the time. It was during the moment of movement to the right that the third good picture was captured. Then the fourth followed as the UFO accelerated away. By the time Russell reset the camera for the next shot, the object had gone.

CASEBOOK

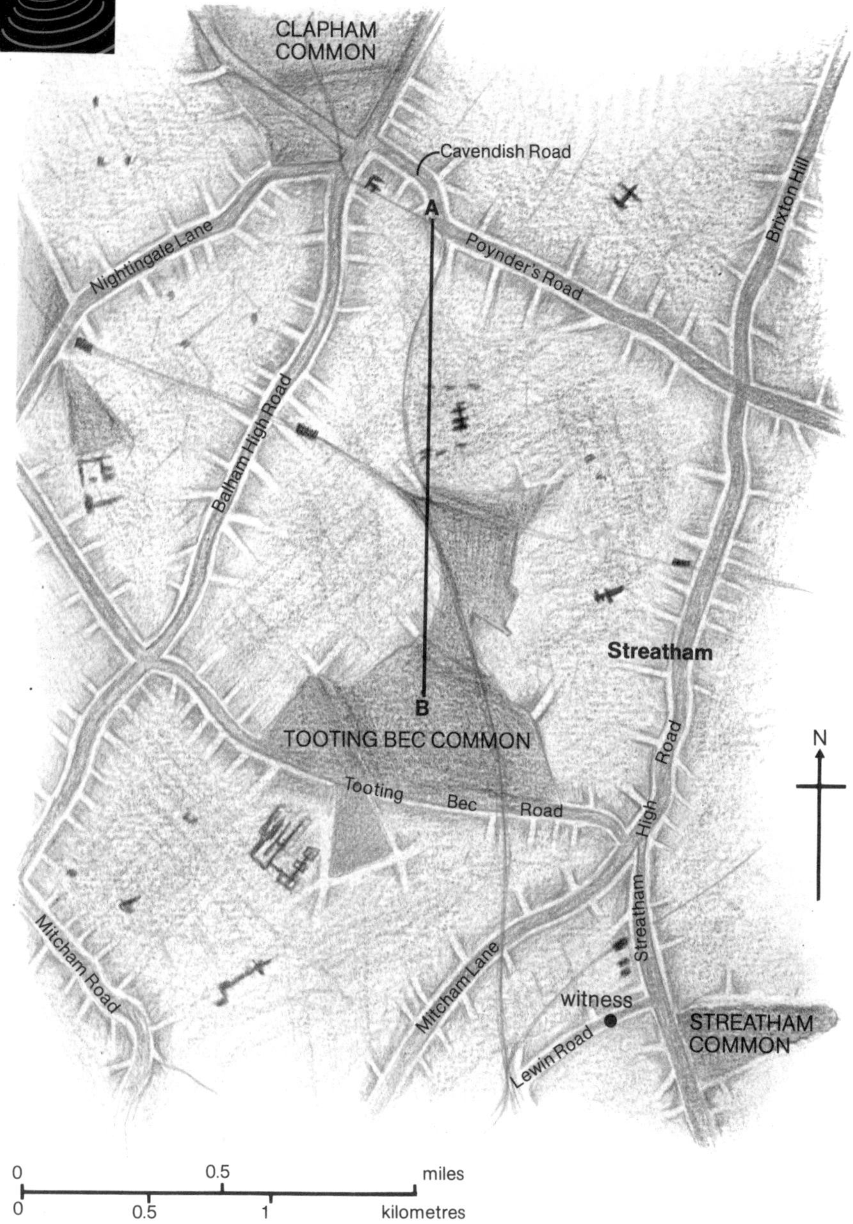

object might have been anything up to a mile (1.6 kilometres) away. In the photograph, there is a hint of an efflux streaming to the right from the base of the UFO – a feature that was more clearly seen when the image had been enlarged and viewed on a projector.

Winder pointed out that the silhouette image of the UFO on the first photograph bore a remarkable similarity to the shape drawn by Police Constable Colin Perks after his sighting of a UFO at Wilmslow, Cheshire, on 7 January 1966, at 4.10 a.m. PC Perks was checking the back door of a shop when he heard a high-pitched whine. He turned and looked over the car park behind the shops. There he saw a solid-looking object – stationary – some 35 feet (10 metres) above the grass of the meadow beyond the car park. It was about 100 yards (90 metres) from him. Perks said the UFO's upper surfaces glowed steadily with a greenish-grey colour, a glow that did not hide the definite shape of the object. He said the lines in his sketch 'represented rounded, but fairly sharp changes in the profile, matched by shading in the glow'. Nowhere could he see openings like portholes or doors. His estimate of a diameter of 30 feet (9 metres) for the base was based on a mental comparison with a 30-foot (9-metre) bus. After about five seconds, the object moved off east-south-east with no change of sound. Then it disappeared.

Russell's other photographs brought no further comparisons to mind. But in the second picture, there are strange shadow effects, particularly one that slants away in the '7 o'clock' position. Hennell could offer no explanation for this.

The third photograph seems to have been blurred either by the motion of the object – it was beginning to move away – or by camera shake. An efflux effect is also noticeable to the left of the object. This in fact was quite pronounced when the picture was enlarged.

Judging from Russell's position and the 2-mile (3-kilometre) visibility limit, the object appears to have been somewhere on a line from a point on Tooting Bec Common to Cavendish Road.

After investigation, the researchers handed the transparencies to *Flying Saucer Review's* photographic consultant, Percy Hennell. After examining them, he made plate negatives from the first three, and stated that they were 'genuine photographs of an object in the air'. He could detect no signs of the transparencies having been tampered with. Later, the transparencies were projected on to a 12-foot (3.5metre) square screen. Close inspection revealed nothing suspicious.

The investigators ascertained that the object was not luminous, and that it would have been virtually impossible for the witness to distinguish any colour, owing to the fact that it was being viewed as a dark object against a light background. Russell merely suggested it might have been maroon.

The first photograph shows the gable of the house opposite Russell's flat with a near-horizontal bar to the right that acts as a support for a chimney that is off-camera. Winder estimated that the bar would have been at an angle of elevation of 10° from the lens of the camera. Russell thought the

The map, seen top, shows the area in which Russell spotted the UFO over Streatham. The object appears to have been somewhere along line A – B.

The drawing, above, was made by PC Colin Perks after he saw a UFO in Cheshire about a year before Russell's sighting. The two reports are strikingly similar.

A contact at Heathrow airport told the investigators that the object was not observed on the radar screens, but it is possible that it missed the radar sweep by virtue of its plummeting fall between sweeps.

The Ministry of Defence (Air) was asked about weather balloons on 15 December 1966. The answer was that four were released in south and south-west England earlier than the sighting, but that they would not have migrated to the London area. The precise nature of this urban sighting remains unidentified.

THE DOOM BOOM

PROPHECIES OF DOOM ARE IN FULL SPATE – PERHAPS PROMPTED BY THE APPROACH OF THE YEAR 2000, WITH ITS SUGGESTIONS OF THE CHRISTIAN MILLENNIUM. SOME WARNINGS OF ARMAGEDDON EVEN SEEM TO COME THROUGH PARANORMAL CHANNELS

In Great Britain, there were three main detonations – one in Hammersmith, west London, one in Manchester, and one in Hull. The London blast details were as follows. 'Date and time of detonation: Wednesday 11 September, 1980, 09.16 hours; 50 per cent survival rate = 2.5-mile [4-kilometre] radius; type of detonation: 20 megatonne fission ICBM airburst at approx. height 7,800 feet [2,400 metres].'

So wrote investigator Andy Collins in one of the strangest documents in the history of paranormal research. He entitled his paper *The Past Three Years (1978-1981)*, but it was published during 1978. It concerned a psychic, given the pseudonym

The Riders of the Apocalypse ***by Vasco Taskovski,*** **below,** ***depicts the sinister horsemen of*** **The Bible's Book of Revelations** ***as machine-like beings with mechanised weapons, wreaking destruction on humanity.***

she is beaten, in a last desperate attempt, the Soviet Union decides to finish the situation completely by using a 'Doomsday' bomb. This is a large orbiting satellite, the size of Skylab. It is released from its orbit, after which it spirals slowly towards its target – a large fault-line in north-east Africa. The detonation is immense – 500 megatonnes – and it appears to be due to a cobalt-salted device. 'The idea was to destroy as much of the planet as possible. They knew that everybody would die anyway, so they thought they would speed up the process. This was detonated during December 1980 and produced horrific effects.'

This tendency to foresee doom for mankind is reflected in the growing number of alleged

Paul Grant, who was put under hypnosis, progressed to a point three years in the future and told to describe his 'memories' of the intervening period. Collins wrote up the results and gave copies to a few selected researchers so that their accuracy could subsequently be checked.

The nuclear Armageddon, of which the events in London formed a part, did not arrive on schedule – fortunately. But the few people in possession of these predictions gave careful thought to their movements on 11 September 1980. There was no sense in taking any chances!

The three-year period, as foreseen by Paul Grant, was filled with war, pestilence and all manner of fantastic events, and it was almost totally in error. On the whole, it was similar to fantasies produced in other progression experiments, and expresses the fear that has gripped mankind ever since the detonation of atomic bombs over the Japanese cities of Hiroshima and Nagasaki in 1945. The imminence of such 'end times' seems all too credible now.

Yet, in the decades since that first use of nuclear weapons, 'war has reigned merrily' (to borrow a phrase from the 16th-century French prophet Nostradamus), although nuclear bombs have never been employed widely, as could have been the case. Logically therefore, our nuclear fears should have decreased from a high point. Instead, 'Doomsday' has become big business. Best-selling writer Charles Berlitz even turned his attention away from such matters as crashed spaceships and little green men, to write a book that not only suggests a deadline of 1999 for Armageddon but offers us a choice of endings, from self-inflicted destruction – perhaps by means of Earth-splitting devices – to pole-shifts and ice ages.

Paul Grant seems to have been aware of the range of methods by which we could commit planetary suicide. Indeed, in his scenario, the Soviet Union unleashes the Third World War after a conflict with China has got out of hand. But then, realising

In 1978, a psychic published his predictions, made under hypnosis, for the years 1978 to 1981. The prophecies were dominated by a nuclear holocaust which was to be followed by the arrival of help from aliens. He foresaw the destruction of cities such as London by hydrogen bombs, like the one shown* top*, each of which could dwarf the atomic bomb that levelled Nagasaki,* above*. This was supposed to happen on 11 September 1980; but on that day, London went peacefully about its business.

communications made by paranormal means. Uri Geller and his associate Andrija Puharich, for instance, worked together to receive messages via automatic writing and telepathy. Their source was said to be 'The Nine', powerful intelligences that not only provided Geller's powers but were to use a small band gathered together by Puharich as instruments in the prevention of Armageddon. The team raced around the world in a fantastic attempt to use their psychic powers to avert war and world destruction by pole-shift. They claim that they

"THE ANTICHRIST VERY SOON ANNIHILATES THE THREE, TWENTY-SEVEN YEARS HIS WAR WILL LAST. THE UNBELIEVERS ARE DEAD, CAPTIVE, EXILED; HUMAN BODIES, BLOOD AND RED HAIL COVER THE EARTH."

NOSTRADAMUS

succeeded; and since the world is still here, who can argue with them?

It is significant that this 'intelligence' (whether external or within Geller's mind) should be so concerned about the fate of the Earth. It is not an isolated instance. Other psychic groups also believe they are being worked hard by unseen intelligences, for the greater good of the world. Even when Geller quarrelled with Puharich, the latter had no difficulty in bringing together a fresh team of disciples to carry on the work.

It is not surprising that cases of UFO contact, a common type of paranormal experience in modern times, should display similar patterns. A typical example occurred in the Dolomite mountains of Italy in July 1968. A man was sleeping in a car parked on a lonely road. Waking, he got out of the car and noticed a smell of burning. Nearby, he saw a large disc and a figure in a tight suit with a glass dome on his head. The alien 'spoke' to him telepathically and told him that he came from a distant galaxy. At this point, the frightened witness actually pricked himself to prove he was awake. The extraterrestrial told him how our planet was facing imminent destruction as a result of a pole-shift that would be followed by a tremendous cracking of the Earth's crust. After giving this warning, the alien then flew back to the safety of his far-off home.

Popular music has also responded to the fearful mood of society, and many lyrics talk of the coming end. These are not anti-nuclear cries of the sort that appeared during CND's original popularity in the 1950s, but seem much more deeply felt. Justin Hayward, for example, sang of being 'frightened for our children' and of fearing that sunshine will turn to rain 'when the final night is over'. The UK rock band Barclay James Harvest sang of a survivor of the nuclear holocaust who, after 'the last green falls', rubs his eyes and looks around, but finds that there is nothing left, anywhere. One trend in such apocalyptic themes has been to bring in the UFO as saviour. Extraterrestrial saviours are seen as Earth's last hope; and in one of his lyrics, the Scottish singer and songwriter Al Stewart even begs the 'silvery ships' to reach down from the stars.

One can also find signs of forebodings of war in the movements of human population. The British Census of 1981, for example, showed an exodus from traditional residential areas in cities. The migrants had dispersed, so that there were very few areas of dramatic expansion. But one area to which people did move *en masse* was mid-Wales, even though amenities there were few. A map, published at around the same time, shows probable targets for nuclear destruction in the event of war. It points to only a few parts of the country as emerging relatively unscathed. One is mid-Wales.

The anti-nuclear movement,* below, *experienced a rebirth in countries around the world during the early 1980s. Alongside this activism, however, a more fatalistic preoccupation with the prospect of Armageddon manifested itself in doom-laden songs and stories.

In the Dolomite mountains of northern Italy in July 1968, a space being dressed in classic fashion emerged from a UFO, as shown in the artist's impression,* left. *His telepathic message to the frightened witness referred to one of the standard range of planetary disasters – a pole-shift. The alien proved to be no more successful at prophecy than his terrestrial counterparts, however.

CASEBOOK

REFUGEES FROM ANOTHER WORLD

The notion of apocalypse seems to underlie the story of the Janos people, reported by the ufologist Frank Johnson. An English family believe that, in June 1978, they were taken on board a UFO and taught about the distant planet, Janos. For unknown reasons, ancient inhabitants of Europe migrated to Janos thousands of years ago. But this beautiful planet was to be destroyed by the disintegration of one of its twin moons, Saton. The event was long foreseen, and a fleet of spaceships began evacuation of the planet. But Saton broke up sooner than expected because of damage caused by Janos spaceships. Much of the population of Janos was trapped in underground shelters as the surface was bombarded by rock fragments. Meteoric impact also caused nuclear power stations on the planet to explode, and radioactivity brought a lingering death to the trapped people. Survivors in the orbiting space fleet, however, set out for their old home, the Earth. They are now waiting somewhere in the solar system, hoping to be allowed refuge somewhere on this planet in exchange for the benefits of their technological knowledge and wisdom. Frank Johnson even suggested that the interior of South America, Australia or Canada might be set aside for them.

The Janos saga combines several familiar elements of the literature of UFO encounters and apocalypse – the idyllic life of the sky people, and disaster brought on by technological arrogance – but now salvation is sought by aliens, not offered.

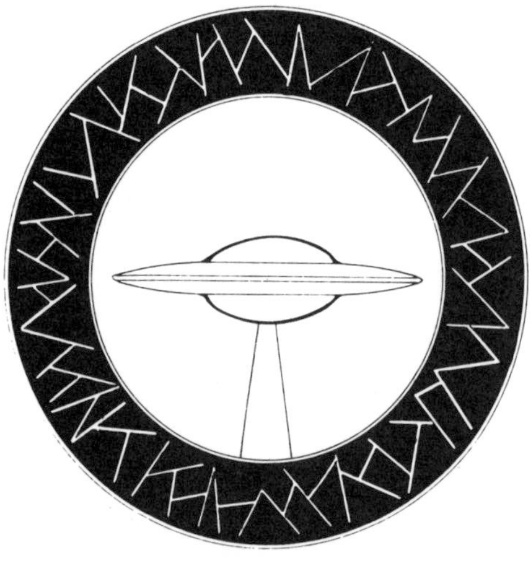

The badge,* left, *supposedly worn on a spacewoman's belt, shows her spacecraft.

Could it be that, on a deep level, many people are aware of this, choosing where to live to maximise their chances of survival?

At any time of special concern and fear for the future, many people turn to new or old prophets. The most famous of past seers was undoubtedly Nostradamus. His book *Centuries* (1555) contains over 900 enigmatic verses, but these are widely considered so vague that they can often be applied to many different historical events. Some devotees, however, claim that such inventions as aeroplanes and submarines are foretold in them, while those prophecies that seemingly are yet to be fulfilled paint a picture of global destruction.

A psychic, using the pseudonym 'Paul Grant', once predicted that key people, including himself, would be protected from the coming global disaster in huge underground complexes. But the only bunkers that have been made public in Britain,* below left, *are cramped quarters intended to house civil servants – seen as an elect who will survive Armageddon, as the anti-nuclear demonstrator,* left, *protests.

More modern prophets have made similar claims. Edgar Cayce, for instance, who worked in the early decades of this century, spoke of planetary upheavals in the last quarter of the 20th century, causing whole cities to sink. Jeane Dixon, America's most famous seer, also claimed to have had a vision in which a child, born in the Middle East during February 1962, would become of great importance to the future of the world. She further talked of war in the late 1980s and early 1990s, and of catastrophic destruction. But it is hard to know to what extent such people are influenced by the prophecies of Nostradamus and others, or whether they are somehow tapping into a source of knowledge about the near future on which they superimpose slightly different personal interpretations.

Interestingly, some of the claims of Gaynor Sunderland, a Welsh contactee, coincided with those of Jeane Dixon. She, too, had a vision of a child born in the Middle East, who will prove to be of world importance but claimed never to have heard of Jeane Dixon.

An element common to many of the claimed precognitions that have been reported throughout the world is the rescuing of an elite group. Paul Grant also featured it in his 'memory':

'The British government had realised that certain people involved with certain aspects of UFO research had information pertaining seemingly to the future, and would be of great use to them ... at which point it was decided to start to get these people together.'

Paul 'saw' a massive underground complex to which these people were taken. He even learned the names of the government officials who ran it. He, of course, was among the important people who went there.

A belief also exists that major disasters, such as air crashes or fires, cast a hazy shadow before them. After the tragedy at Aberfan, South Wales, in 1966, for instance, when a wet slag tip subsided on to a school packed with children, studies showed that there had been premonitions of this event. Some came in the form of dreams and psychic visions, and were either straightforward images of the disaster, or consisted of relevant images mixed in with other material. Others appeared in children's drawings. Unfortunately, however, no one acted on these messages, and disaster claimed many lives.

If the human mind is indeed capable of picking up faint signals from future events, and subconsciously adapting behaviour accordingly, what might it do when faced with a stimulus as powerful as an approaching nuclear catastrophe? It seems reasonable to suggest that Armageddon would trigger numerous 'psychic alarm bells'.

The rock band Barclay James Harvest, **below**, *are seen staging a suitably apocalyptic display to match the mood of a song concerned with nuclear doom. The question remains as to whether the streak of foreboding that runs through popular books and song lyrics is a product of the collective imagination – or of collective premonition?*

" IN THE YEAR 1999, AND SEVEN MONTHS, FROM THE SKY WILL COME THE GREAT KING OF TERROR. HE WILL BRING BACK TO LIFE THE GREAT KING OF THE MONGOLS, BEFORE MARS REIGNS HAPPILY. "

NOSTRADAMUS

VOICES FROM THE DEAD

THE VOICE OF THE CHINESE PHILOSOPHER CONFUCIUS IS SAID TO HAVE BEEN HEARD OVER 2,000 YEARS AFTER HIS DEATH, SPEAKING IN OLD CHINESE. WAS THIS MORE THAN MERE VENTRILOQUISM? WHAT EVIDENCE IS THERE FOR 'DIRECT VOICE' PHENOMENA?

Margery Crandon, a Boston medium of the 1920s, was exposed as a fraud by Harry Houdini, below left, *who demonstrated her tricks as part of his stage act. The medium's 'spirit guide' (her dead brother Walter) allegedly left his thumbprint,* below, *after a seance but this was later proved to be that of a previous sitter,* below right. *The whorls and ridges (as numbered) can be seen to match exactly.*

Jack Webber, right, *often produced ectoplasm. He was also said to produce ectoplasmic 'voice boxes' so the dead could speak through them.*

John Campbell Sloan could have made a small fortune had he exploited his direct voice mediumship commercially. For, in his presence, the dead were said to speak in their own voices and to hold long conversations with their living relatives and friends. But Sloan, a kindly, ill-educated Scotsman, chose to be a non-professional medium. For 50 years, he gave seances for which he never charged a penny, working instead as a tailor, a Post Office employee, a packer, garagehand and also a newsagent.

Many of the astonishing direct voice seances that Sloan gave were recorded in a best-selling book written by Spiritualist author J. Arthur Findlay, *On the Edge of the Etheric*. In this, Findlay gives an account of the very first seance he attended with Sloan, on 20 September 1918. It took place, as is often the case with direct voice phenomena, in a darkened room.

'Suddenly a voice spoke in front of me. I felt scared. A man sitting next to me said, "Someone wants to speak to you, friend," so I said, "Yes, who are you?" "Your father, Robert Downie Findlay," the voice replied, and then went on to refer to something that only he and I and one other ever knew on earth, and that other, like my father, was some years dead. I was therefore the only living person with any knowledge of what the voice was referring to,' Findlay wrote. He continued:

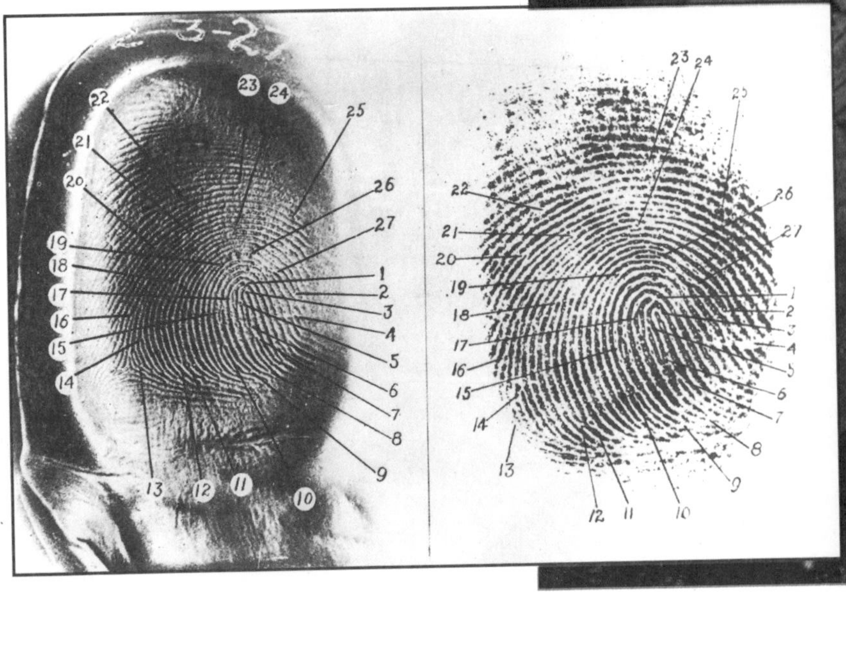

'That was extraordinary enough, but my surprise was heightened when, after my father had finished, another voice gave the name David Kidston, the name of the other person who on earth knew about the subject, and he continued the conversation which my father had begun.'

How do sceptics explain such occurrences? Perhaps the medium was a ventriloquist and had chanced upon the information thought to be known to no one else, they say. But Findlay dismisses such explanations with this answer:

'No spy system, however thorough, no impersonation by the medium or by any accomplices could be responsible for this, and, moreover, I was an entire stranger to everyone present. I did not give my name when I entered the room, I knew no one in that room and no one knew me or anything about me.'

Sloan himself was sometimes able to produce two or three spirit voices simultaneously. On occasions, he went into trance at the start of a seance; on others, he remained conscious and held conversations with the spirit communicators.

Another gifted direct voice medium was Etta Wriedt of Detroit, Michigan, USA. She never went into a trance, nor separated herself from the other sitters by using a cabinet, as many mediums do. Instead, she would remain with the sitters and join in conversations they had with the spirits. If, however, a foreign language 'came through', she would get out her knitting. She could speak only English.

George Valiantine*, above, was a *'trumpet medium', and accomplished fraud.

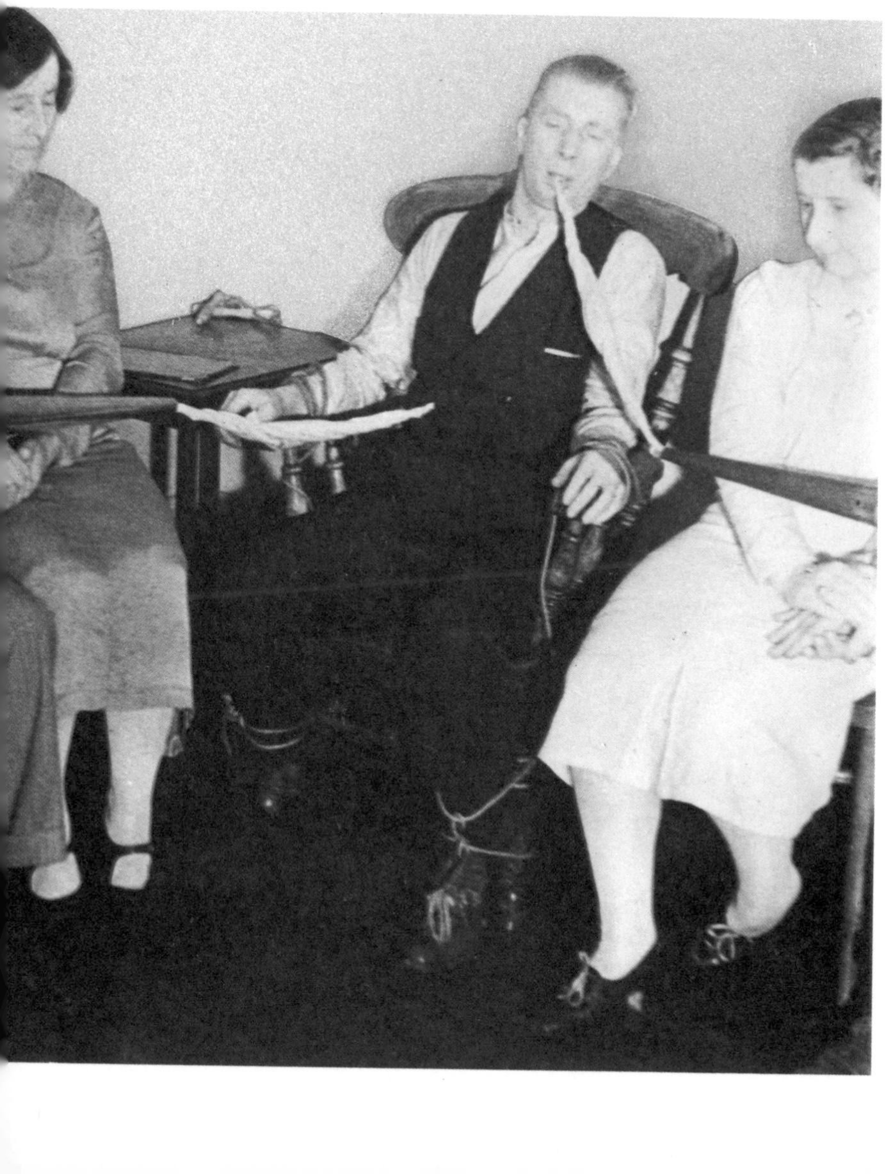

A British vice-admiral, W. Usborne Moore, also had the opportunity of sitting with Mrs Wriedt when she visited England in the 1920s and testified: 'Frequently two, sometimes three, voices spoke at the same moment in different parts of the circle. It was somewhat confusing.' Of an American seance with the same medium, Moore said: 'I have heard three voices talking at once, one in each ear and one through the trumpet; sometimes two in the trumpet'. These conversations were so realistic, he maintained, that he sometimes forgot that he was talking with 'those whom we ignorantly speak of as "the dead"'.

Another testimony to Etta Wriedt' s direct voice mediumship came from the Dowager Duchess of Warwick, who had been one of King Edward VII's mistresses. She first invited the medium to her home because it had been plagued with strange phenomena. On her arrival at Warwick Castle, Mrs Wriedt was shown to her room, while some of her belongings, including a seance trumpet, were left in the hall outside her door. Lady Warwick, while waiting for her guest to appear, ventured to pick up the trumpet and placed it against her ear. Immediately, she heard the characteristic voice of King Edward, deceased, speaking to her, and she found she was able to carry on a conversation with him, partly in German, oddly enough.

Thereafter, the king became a regular and persistent communicator at direct voice seances held at the castle – to such an extent that other communicators could sometimes hardly get a word in edgeways. Finally, in view of her former lover's apparent possessiveness from beyond the grave, Lady Warwick decided to terminate the seances that had been organised with Mrs Wriedt.

Psychically speaking, New York medium, George Valiantine was a late developer. He did not discover his mediumistic powers until he was 43, but soon made something of an impact, particularly with direct voice seances. In 1924, English author, Dennis Bradley, brought Valiantine to England, where he gave seances almost every day for five weeks. The invited guests included 50 prominent people, and around 100 different spirit voices were said to have communicated. Caradoc Evans, the novelist, for instance, spoke to his father in idiomatic Welsh, while other spirits spoke in Russian, German and Spanish.

CONFUCIUS, HE SAY

Probably the most impressive communication of all, however, came at a seance in New York in the late 1920s. Strange and unintelligible voices had been heard previously, and so Dr Neville Whymant, an authority on Chinese history, philosophy and ancient literature, agreed to attend. Dr Whymant did not remain a sceptic for long. First he heard the sound of a flute played in a characteristically Chinese way, then a quiet, almost inaudible voice said *'K'ung-fu-Tzu'*, which is the Chinese version of the name Confucius, the 6th-century Chinese philosopher and teacher. Few people, except the Chinese, can pronounce it properly. Even so, Dr Whymant did not at first believe it was the famous

Etta Wriedt, left, *was one of the most powerful direct voice mediums of all time. Often two or more voices spoke together. On a visit to England, she was invited to Warwick Castle where the Dowager Duchess,* below, *was experiencing strange phenomena. While showing her to her room, the Duchess picked up Mrs Wriedt's seance trumpet and was astonished to hear her ex-lover King Edward VII, speaking to her partly in German. He later became so persistent that the Duchess gave up attending Mrs Wriedt's seances.*

philosopher who was communicating. After all, perhaps it was just someone else speaking his name. But when Dr Whymant began to refer to a passage from Confucius that he believed had been transcribed wrongly, and quoted the first line:

'At once, the words were taken out of my mouth, and the whole passage was recited in Chinese, exactly as it is recorded in the standard works of reference. After a pause of about 15 seconds, the passage was again repeated, this time with certain alterations which gave it new meaning. "Thus read," said the voice, "does not its meaning become plain?" '

Subsequently, after having the opportunity to speak to the voice again, Dr Whymant declared that there were only six Chinese scholars in the world capable of displaying such knowledge of the language and of Confucius, none of whom was in the United States at the time. Dr Whymant also testified to hearing a Sicilian chant at one of Valiantine's seances, and he conversed in Italian with another communicator.

The man who brought Valiantine to England, Dennis Bradley, claimed that Valiantine had apparently passed on his direct voice powers to him; and another regular sitter, an Italian, the Marquis Centurione Scotto, also developed direct voice mediumship.

One of the great British mediums to demonstrate direct voice phenomena was a Welsh miner, Jack Webber, whose powers gradually developed at weekly seances run by his in-laws. He refused to use a cabinet because he knew it would be regarded with suspicion. Instead, he would be tied to a chair, and a red light was turned on at intervals throughout the seance so that sitters could confirm he was still bound. He also allowed infra-red photographs to be taken at some of his seances, to record a number of physical phenomena including levitation, partial materialisation, and the demonstration of direct voice through trumpets.

His powers were recorded by famous healer Harry Edwards in his book *The Mediumship of Jack Webber,* which tells of events recorded over the 14-month period leading up to December 1939, when Webber suddenly died. In that time, more than 4,000 people witnessed Webber's mediumship.

Edwards heard the spirits of men, women and children communicating through Webber's seance trumpets: some spoke in foreign tongues, their messages frequently containing intimate personal information. He also testified on one occasion to hearing two spirit voices singing simultaneously through a single trumpet.

The photographs taken at Webber's seances seem to throw some light on the apparent mechanism of direct voice mediumship. Ectoplasmic shapes appear to connect the medium with the levitated trumpet; and in some of the pictures, small round shapes, about the size of a human heart, are seen to be attached to the small end. These are said to be 'voice boxes' through which the dead are able to speak.

TESTING TIMES

In the United States, one of the most famous physical mediums, 'Margery' (whose real name was Mina) Crandon, allowed some ingenious devices to be used during the investigation of her direct voice mediumship. 'Margery' was married to Dr L. R. G. Crandon, who was for 16 years professor of surgery at Harvard Medical School. Their seances began in 1923, and a variety of physical phenomena soon developed .

One piece of apparatus used to test her powers was developed by Dr Mark Richardson, a Boston resident, and consisted of a U-shaped tube containing water, with floats placed on the surface. 'Margery' had to blow into this through a flexible tube, causing one column of water to rise. She then had to keep her tongue and lips over the mouthpiece throughout the seance to prevent the water returning to its original level. (Witnesses could verify this even in the dark because the floats were luminous.) She did as she was asked, the water level remained as it should, and yet it was found that her regular 'spirit' communicator – her dead brother, Walter Stinson – spoke as loudly as ever.

An even more ingenious piece of equipment was invented by B. K. Thorogood: this was a box comprising seven layers of different materials and containing a large and sensitive microphone. This was closed, padlocked and placed in the seance room in order to record spirit voices. Two wires ran from it to a loudspeaker in another room. People in the adjoining room were able to hear Walter's voice coming out of the loudspeaker, while those in the seance room could hear nothing spoken into the microphone.

Not all these mediums were above suspicion, however. George Valiantine was accused of fraud

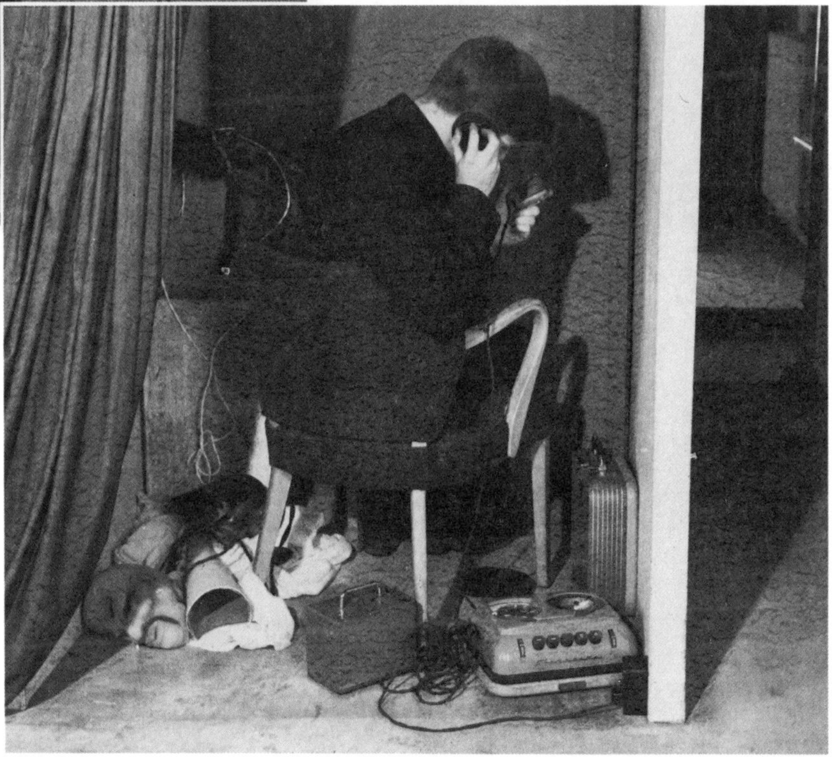

on a number of occasions, and when both he and Mrs Crandon allowed themselves to be investigated by the *Scientific American* – a publication offering $2,500 for a demonstration of objective psychic phenomena – they failed to convince the magazine's committee.

But it was not their direct voice mediumship as such that was to be challenged. Valiantine had produced a series of wax impressions that were said to be the actual thumbprints of famous dead people. He was eventually exposed by Dennis Bradley – the man who had championed him in two previous books – and the damning evidence was published in a third book, *And After,* in which Bradley said the prints 'were produced by Valiantine's big toes, fingers and elbows'.

IDENTICAL PRINTS

'Margery' also ran into trouble with a thumbprint, which was said to have been produced when her dead brother Walter's materialised hand left an impression in wax. In the early 1930s, the Boston Society for Psychical Research showed that the thumbprint was identical to that of Mrs Crandon's dentist, who had been a sitter at her early seances.

Sceptics believe that if these mediums did produce some of their phenomena fraudulently, then it is more than likely that it was all phoney – though how they produced some of their most startling direct voice effects, it is difficult to imagine.

One man who did find a way, and performed successfully for many years, was William Roy – one of the most brilliant and ruthless frauds in Spiritualism's history. His real name was William George Holroyd Plowright, and he was a small-time crook before he devised a fraudulent mediumistic routine to make money out of gullible people. He even claimed to have made a total of £50,000 from his 'direct voice' seances.

The technique was simple. He used a confederate whose job it was to search people's coats, wallets and handbags after they were safely settled in the seance room. The assistant then conveyed any information thus gleaned to the medium via a sophisticated communication system that came into operation when William Roy placed metal plates on the soles of his shoes on to tacks in the floor that were apparently holding down the carpet. The 'medium' then used a small receiver in his ear. The same device could be clipped to the end of a trumpet so that the confederate could produce one 'spirit voice' while Roy produced another, simultaneously, using a telescopic rod in order to levitate the trumpet.

Roy was exposed as a fraud in 1955 and sold his confession to the *Sunday Pictorial* (now the *Sunday Mirror*) in 1960. Despite being a self-confessed fraud, Roy (who had left the country) returned to Britain in the late 1960s and began giving seances once more, this time using the name Bill Silver. His sitters were numerous, and even included some of The Beatles.

It subsequently transpired that many people who were now attending 'Bill Silver's' seances actually knew he was William Roy, the self-confessed cheat. Yet they now believed that the powers he was demonstrating were genuine. When challenged by a Sunday newspaper, however, he claimed that his earlier published confession was nothing other than 'a pack of lies', published only for the money it would bring him.

William Roy, top, was a self-confessed fake who claimed to have made £50,000 from his direct voice seances. His confession in 1960 included an exposé of his tricks, such as the use of a confederate in the next room, as shown above. Even so, he later claimed that the confession had been a pack of lies and again set himself up as a medium, this time under the name 'Bill Silver'.

A HOLLOW THEORY?

IT HAS LONG BEEN HELD THAT THE EARTH IS HOLLOW – BUT IT WAS NOT UNTIL 1968 THAT ANY SORT OF PROOF WAS FORTHCOMING. IN THAT YEAR, PHOTOGRAPHS TAKEN BY SATELLITE SEEMED TO SHOW AN ENORMOUS HOLE AT THE NORTH POLE. OR DID THEY?

In early 1970, the Environmental Science Service Administration (ESSA) of the US Department of Commerce released to the press photographs of the North Pole that had been taken by the ESSA-7 satellite on 23 November 1968. One of the photographs showed the North Pole wreathed in its customary cloud cover; the other, showing the same area without cloud cover, revealed an enormous black hole where the Pole should have been.

Little did the Environmental Science Service Administration know that their routine weather reconnaissance photographs would lead to one of the most sensational and highly publicised controversies in UFO history.

In the June 1970 issue of *Flying Saucers* magazine, editor and ufologist Ray Palmer reproduced the ESSA-7 satellite photographs with an accompanying article, claiming that the enormous hole shown on the photograph was real.

The mysterious ice cave at Signy Island, Antarctica, above, is believed by some to be an entrance to the Underworld.

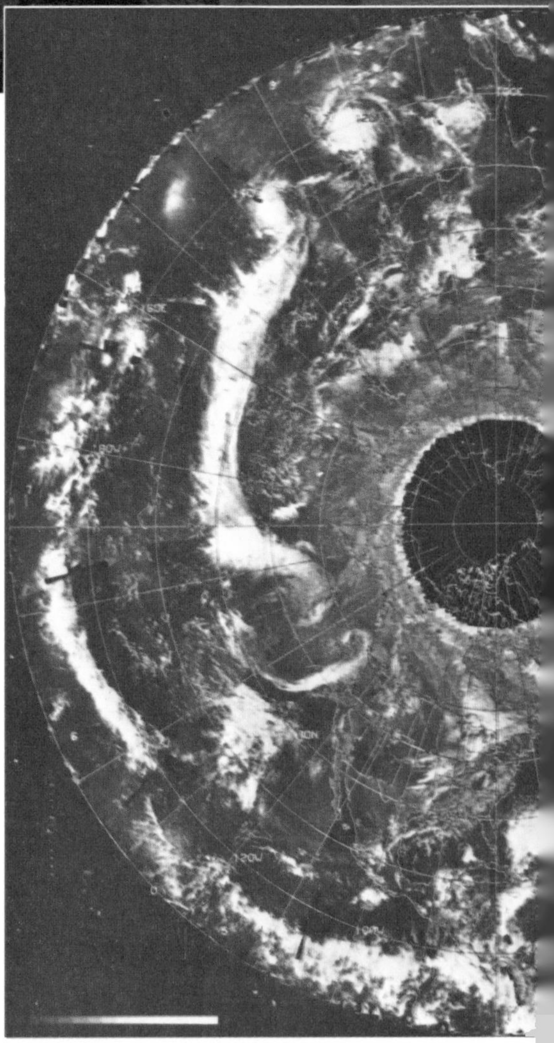

The controversial photograph of the North Pole taken in 1968 by the ESSA-7 satellite, right, shows a strange black hole where the Pole should be. For certain UFO enthusiasts, this provided proof that the Earth is hollow.

Rear-Admiral Richard E. Byrd, above, led expeditions that provided inspiration for believers in the hollow Earth theory.

According to Greek legend, Orpheus, **below right,** ***mourned for Eurydice, who was kept prisoner in the Underworld.***

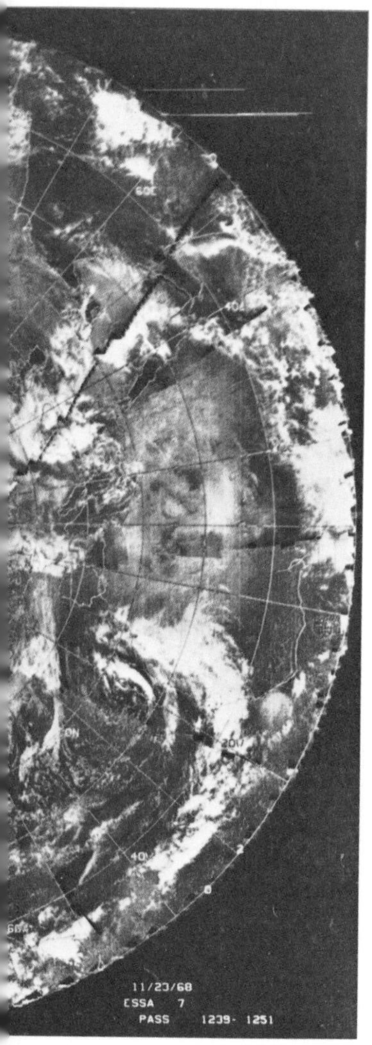

It had long been the belief of Ray Palmer and a great many other ufologists that the Earth is hollow, and that UFOs emerge from and return to a civilisation of superior beings hidden deep in the Earth's unexplored interior. Now, with an actual photograph of an enormous black hole at the North Pole, Palmer was able to assert that a subterranean super-race could well exist, and might be reached through holes at the North and South Poles.

According to Palmer, the ESSA-7 satellite photograph was proof that an enormous hole existed at least at the North Pole, and in subsequent issues of *Flying Saucers* he strengthened his case by resurrecting another long-standing 'hollow Earth' controversy, involving the expeditions of Rear-Admiral Richard E. Byrd to the North and South Poles.

BEYOND THE POLE

Rear-Admiral Byrd (1888-1957) of the US Navy was a distinguished pioneer aviator and polar explorer who made the first flight over the North Pole on 9 May 1926 and then led numerous exploratory expeditions to the Antarctic, including the first flight over the South Pole on 29 November 1929. From 1946 to 1947, he was in charge of a programme known as Operation High Jump, which allegedly sighted 1.5 million square miles (3.9 million square kilometres) of Antarctic territory, 25 per cent of it seen for the first time. It was the flight of one of the exploratory party that caused a minor sensation. On 11 February 1947, a snow-free area of rock covering 100 square miles (260 square kilometres) and dotted with lakes was discovered in the Bunger Hills, near the Shackleton Ice Shelf. A navy press release described it as a 'Shangri-La' and reported, erroneously, that vegetation had been seen there.

Byrd's most famous polar expeditions were first drawn into the hollow Earth controversy when a great many articles and books – notably *Worlds Beyond the Poles* by Amadeo Giannini and *The Hollow Earth* by Dr Raymond Bernard – claimed that Byrd had actually flown, not across the North and South Poles, but down into the great hollows that led into the Earth's interior. Ray Palmer, quoting extensively from Giannini's book (as did Dr Bernard), introduced this theory in the December 1959 issue of *Flying Saucers,* and thereafter ran a voluminous correspondence on the subject.

According to Giannini, Bernard and Palmer, Rear-Admiral Byrd announced in February 1947, prior to a supposed flight of 1,700 miles (2,750 kilometres) beyond the North Pole: 'I'd like to see that land beyond the pole. That area beyond the Pole is the centre of the Great Unknown.' Giannini, Bernard and Palmer also claimed that, during Byrd's supposed flight over the North Pole in February 1947, the Admiral reported by radio that he saw below him not ice and snow, but land areas consisting of mountains, forests, green vegetation, lakes and rivers and, in the undergrowth, a strange animal that resembled a mammoth.

As it happens, records show it is unlikely that Byrd ever made a flight over the North Pole in February 1947, when he was very much preoccupied with his Operation High Jump in Antarctica.

What is more, according to Giannini, Bernard and Palmer, in January 1956, after leading his last expedition to the Antarctic, Rear-Admiral Byrd claimed that his expedition had penetrated 2,300 miles (3,700 kilometres) beyond the South Pole. They further claimed, that before his death in 1957, Rear-Admiral Byrd had called the land beyond the Pole 'that enchanted continent in the sky, land of everlasting mystery'. That land, according to other hollow Earth theorists, was actually the legendary Rainbow City, home of a fabulous lost civilisation.

For exponents of the hollow earth theory, these comments merely confirmed what they had suspected all along: that the Earth is shaped 'strangely' at both Poles, something like a doughnut, with a depression that either goes down an enormous distance into the bowels of the Earth or forms a giant hole running right through the Earth's core, from one Pole to the other. Since, geographically speaking, it would be impossible to fly 1,700 miles (2,750 kilometres) beyond the North Pole or 2,300 miles (3,700 kilometres) beyond the South Pole without seeing water, it stands to reason – at least according to hollow Earth logic – that Rear-Admiral Byrd must have flown down into the enormous convex

depressions at the Poles, and thence into the Great Unknown of the Earth's interior. Had he flown further, it has been claimed, he would have arrived eventually at a secret UFO base belonging to the hidden super-race – inhabitants of the legendary Rainbow City that Byrd had possibly seen reflected in the Antarctic sky.

So when, in June 1970, Ray Palmer was able to publish satellite photographs that actually showed what seemed to be an enormous black hole at the North Pole, hollow Earth theorists all over the world were confirmed in their beliefs – and the controversy started. But is the Earth really hollow? And do such holes at the Poles exist?

The possibility that the Earth might be hollow, that it may be entered through holes at the North and South Poles, and that secret civilisations still flourish inside it, is one that has fired the imagination since time immemorial. The Babylonian hero, Gilgamesh, in search of immortality, is said to have visited an ancestor, Utnapishtim, in the bowels of the Earth; the Greek hero, Orpheus, tried to rescue his dead wife Eurydice from an underground hell; the Pharaohs of Egypt were rumoured to be in touch with the underworld, which they could reach via secret tunnels concealed in the pyramids; the Incas, in flight from the rapacious Spaniards, reportedly carried much of their treasure into the 'inner Earth'; and Buddhists long believed (and still do) that millions live in Agharta, a veritable underground paradise.

Illustrious Believers

Perhaps, surprisingly, the scientific world was not immune to the hollow Earth theory. Leonhard Euler, an 18th-century mathematical genius, deduced that the Earth was hollow, that it contained a central Sun and was inhabited. Dr Edmund Halley (1656-1742), discoverer of Halley's comet and Astronomer Royal for England in the 18th century, also thought that the Earth was hollow and that it even contained inside it three planets.

In the early 1820s, John Cleves Symmes, an American, failed to obtain United States government backing for an expedition to prove his theories that the Earth was hollow, but his ideas were published in 1826 in a book, *The Symmes Theory of Concentric Spheres, Demonstrating that the Earth is Hollow, Habitable Within and Widely Open About the Poles.* He hoped thereby to persuade the world that the interior of the Earth could be reached through large holes at the North and South Poles, and that inside the Earth would be found 'a warm and rich land, stocked with thrifty vegetables and animals, if not men'. Among those who jumped on to the Symmes's bandwagon were Cyrus Read Teed, who founded a hollow Earth religion; William Reed, who wrote the controversial book, *Phantom of the Poles;* and Symmes's son, who added to his father's theory the even more fanciful notion that the inhabitants of the inner Earth were the Ten Lost Tribes of Israel.

None of these theories was supported by anything other than wishful thinking, but they sat comfortably side by side with various works of fiction on the subject, the most notable of which were Edgar Allan Poe's *Narrative of Arthur Gordon Pym,* in which the hero and his companion have a chilling confrontation with emissaries from the interior, and Jules Verne's *Journey to the Centre of the Earth,* in which an adventurous professor, his nephew and a guide enter the inner Earth through an extinct volcano in Iceland, and there encounter new skies, seas and giant, prehistoric reptiles roaming wild in the forests.

Nonetheless, the idea of a hollow Earth became so widespread that Edgar Rice Burroughs felt obliged to write *Tarzan at the Earth's Core,* in which the famous child of the jungle goes to Pellucidar, a world lying on the inner surface of the Earth and lit by a central sun. H. P. Lovecraft's *The Shadow out of Time* brought the theme into the modern age by introducing an ancient, subterranean race that had dominated the Earth 150 million years ago and had since, in the safety of the inner Earth, invented airships and atomic-powered vehicles, as well as mastering time-travel and ESP.

There can be little doubt that Lovecraft's famous novel influenced the lengthy article entitled *I Remember Lemuria* by Richard S. Shaver, first published in the March 1945 issue of *Amazing Stories* magazine and claimed, by the author, to be fact rather than mere fiction. In his article, Shaver stated that the interior of the Earth is laced with a network of gigantic caves, and that these are filled with a race of malformed, subhuman creatures known as *deros* or *abandonderos* (so-called because they

PERSPECTIVES

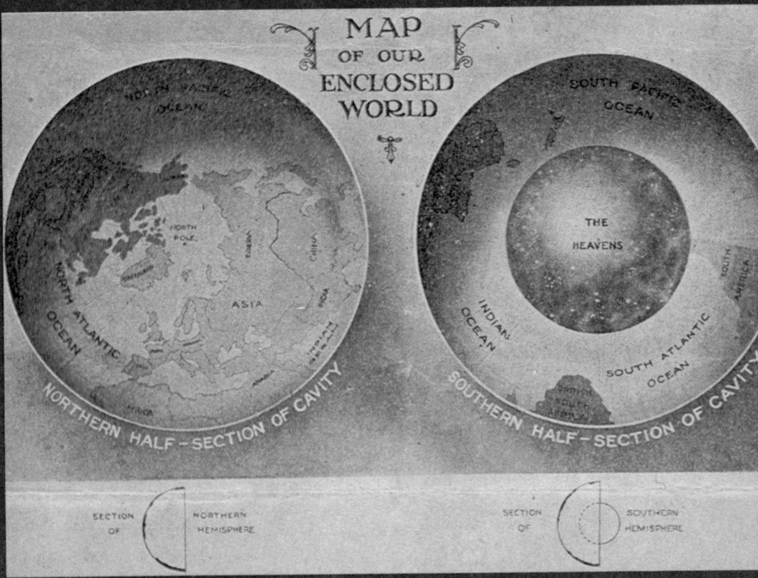

THE EARTH TURNED INSIDE OUT

If *Journey to the Centre of the Earth* remains the most popular of hollow Earth novels, perhaps that with the most baleful influence was Edward Bulwer-Lytton's *The Coming Race,* in which the hero descends into a deep mine and finds himself in a subterranean world inhabited by highly advanced, vindictive beings who have harnessed 'Vril

The leaflet, above, entitled* The Earth – with a New Map of our Enclosed World *is by the Dowager Lady Blout, and was published in 1921. Her view of the Earth's 'real' structure was similar to that of certain Nazis; the Earth is concave and 'the heavens' are inside the cavity of the southern hemisphere.

fluid', a kind of energy that can be conducted over vast distances and used for good or evil.

Vril fluid in some ways resembles the power of Kundalini, the spinal fire of Tantric tradition. The inhabitants of this subterranean world, Vril-ya, descended into the Earth during the Flood, but are planning to return to the Earth's surface in order to conquer an intellectually decadent mankind.

Bulwer-Lytton's novel proved the inspiration of various occult groups, including the 'Luminous Lodge' or Vril Society, which was established in the early days of Nazi Germany. Members of the Vril Society confused Bulwer-Lytton's fiction with their own murky visions of an Aryan master race inhabiting the lost world of Thule which, according to legend, disappeared 'somewhere in the far north'. They were determined that, when this master race returned to the Earth's surface, they would be their equals and not slaves.

Loosely connected with these beliefs was the persistent theory that the Earth possessed concave curvature, so that mankind lived inside the globe, with a small sun and tiny starry heaven at its centre. So insistent on this theory were certain members of the Nazi Party that, in April 1942, Dr Heinz Fisher and a group of leading scientists were sent to the Baltic island of Rügen with a mass of radar equipment to obtain reflections of radar beams from the far side of the Earth. They returned in defeat.

abandoned the surface Earth 12,000 years ago). The *deros* had once been slaves of a Lemurian master race from outer space, but now occupied themselves in persecuting humans of the surface world and were responsible for some of our most momentous calamities.

ADVANCED CIVILISATIONS

Shaver's insistence that a Lemurian underworld actually existed – and that he had been taken down into it by the *deros* – was given enormous publicity in the United States, leading to a resurgence of interest in the possibility of a hollow Earth and hidden, highly advanced civilisations. So it was perhaps not an accident that the UFO age was ushered in two years later, on 21 June 1947, with the reported sighting of five disc-shaped, unidentified aircraft over the Canadian border by Harold Dahl and, three days later, by Kenneth Arnold's famous sighting of 'flying saucers' over the Cascade Mountains in the north-west USA.

After these two sightings, UFO mania swept the United States and eventually the world. Two of the most popular theories were that the UFOs were either extraterrestrial spacecraft from some distant galaxy or the craft of a species of highly advanced beings inhabiting the interior of the Earth. According to the latter theory, the flying saucers both left and re-entered this world via enormous holes at the North and South Poles.

John Cleves Symmes,* top, *was a 19th-century American hollow Earth theorist who believed the inner world to be a warm and rich land, stocked with vegetables and animals, if not men.

***The illustration,* above, *is of the central sea, featured in Jules Verne's* Journey to the Centre of the Earth.**

Betty and Barney Hill,* right, *alleged they were UFO abductees whose captors explained that there were many UFO bases in or under the Earth – and even below the sea.

***A statue of the Babylonian hero Gilgamesh, who travelled deep into the Earth in search of immortality, is shown* far left.**

"... HE SAW BELOW HIM NOT ICE AND SNOW, BUT LAND AREAS CONSISTING OF MOUNTAINS, FORESTS, GREEN VEGETATION, LAKES AND RIVERS AND, IN THE UNDERGROWTH, A STRANGE ANIMAL THAT RESEMBLED A MAMMOTH. THAT LAND, ACCORDING TO OTHER HOLLOW EARTH THEORISTS, WAS ACTUALLY ... HOME OF A FABULOUS LOST CIVILISATION."

Such theories led to a resurrection of belief in the 'lost' civilisations of Atlantis, Lemuria and Thule. However, it was also widely believed that another likely source of UFOs was to be found in the Antarctic. This theory was encouraged by the publication of John G. Fuller's remarkably persuasive factual book, *The Interrupted Journey,* in which the author tells the story of Betty and Barney Hill, an American couple who, during psychiatric treatment for an inexplicable period of amnesia, recalled under hypnosis that they had been temporarily abducted by extraterrestrials, examined inside a flying saucer,

and informed that the extra-terrestrials had secret bases located all over the Earth, some of them under the sea, and at least one in the Antarctic.

This sensational case, coupled with Aimé Michel's widely read *Flying Saucers and the Straight-line Mystery* – from which many people deduced that the saucers generally flew in north-southerly directions – strengthened the growing belief in the Arctic and Antarctic as likely locations for the secret bases of the flying saucers. We still, however, await conclusive proof.

The theory of a hollow Earth certainly offers archaic charm; but, as several scientists have suggested, if it were so, then the Arctic Ocean would surely drain to the centre.

CURSE OF THE HEXHAM HEADS

The discovery of two carved stone heads in the back garden of a house in Hexham, Northumberland, seemed unremarkable enough at first. But when the heads triggered the appearance of a wolf-man, the nightmare began

One afternoon in February 1972, 11-year-old Colin Robson was weeding the garden of his family's council house in Rede Avenue, Hexham, a market town some 20 miles (32 kilometres) west along the Tyne valley from Newcastle-upon-Tyne. To his surprise, he suddenly uncovered what appeared to be a lump of stone about the size of a tennis ball, with a strange conical protrusion on one side. Clearing the earth from the object, he found that it was roughly carved with human features, and that the conical protrusion was actually meant to be a neck.

Excited by the find, he called to his younger brother Leslie, who was watching from an upstairs

It was in the back garden of a council house in the small town of Hexham in northern England, **below left,** *that two small boys unearthed a pair of crudely carved stone heads, apparently carrying some ancient curse. A distinguished archaeologist suggested that they were around 1,800 years old, and designed to play a part in Celtic head rituals – but Desmond Craigie,* **left,** *claimed that he had made them himself.*

window. The boys continued to dig, and soon Leslie uncovered a second head.

The stones, which soon became known as the Hexham heads, appeared to be of two distinct types. The first had a skull-like face, seemed to be masculine to everyone who saw it, and was dubbed the 'boy'. It was of a greenish-grey colour, and glistened with crystals of quartz. It was very heavy – heavier than cement or concrete – with hair that appeared to be in stripes running from the front to the back of the head. The other head – the 'girl' – resembled a witch, with wildly bulging eyes and hair that was combed backwards off the forehead in what was almost a bun. There were also traces of a yellow or red pigment in her hair.

After the heads had been unearthed, the boys took them inside the house. It was then that the strange happenings began. The heads would turn round spontaneously, and objects were broken for no apparent reason. It was when the mattress on the bed of one of the Robson daughters was showered with glass that both girls moved out of their room. Meanwhile, at the spot at which the heads had been found, a strange flower bloomed at Christmas and an eerie light glowed.

It could be argued that the events in the Robson household had nothing to do with the appearance of the heads – that they were, instead, poltergeist phenomena triggered by the adolescent children of the Robson family. But the Robsons' next door neighbour, Mrs Ellen Dodd, underwent a truly unnerving experience that could clearly not be explained away so easily. As she recounted:

'I had gone into the children's bedroom to sleep with one of them, who was ill. My ten-year-old son, Brian, kept telling me he felt something touching him. I told him not to be so silly. Then I saw this shape. It came towards me and I definitely felt it touch me on the legs. Then, on all fours, it moved out of the room.'

Ellen Dodd later described the creature that had touched her as 'half human, half sheep-like'. Mrs Robson also recalled that she had heard a sound like a crash as well as screams from next-door on the night in question. Her neighbour told her that the creature that made them was like a werewolf. And when Mrs Dodd went downstairs, she found, that her front door was open. Whatever caused the phenomenon, Ellen Dodd was terrified, and as a result was rehoused by the local council. Eventually, the heads were removed from the Robsons' house, the abode itself was exorcised, and all became quiet in Rede Avenue.

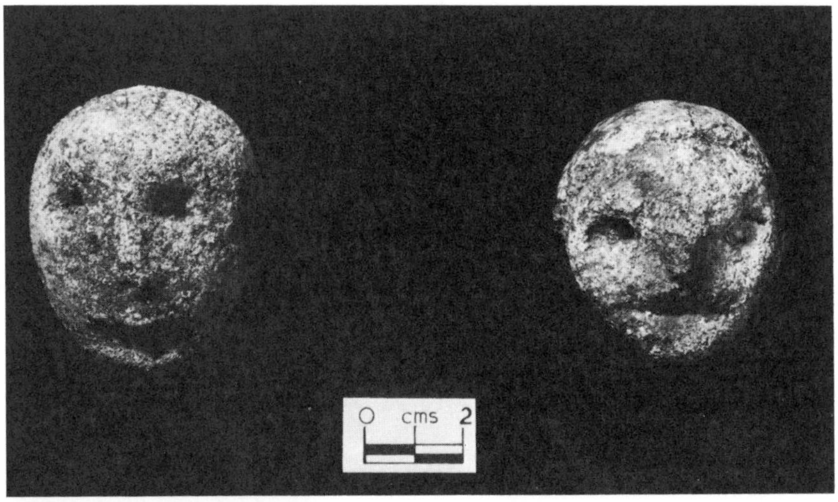

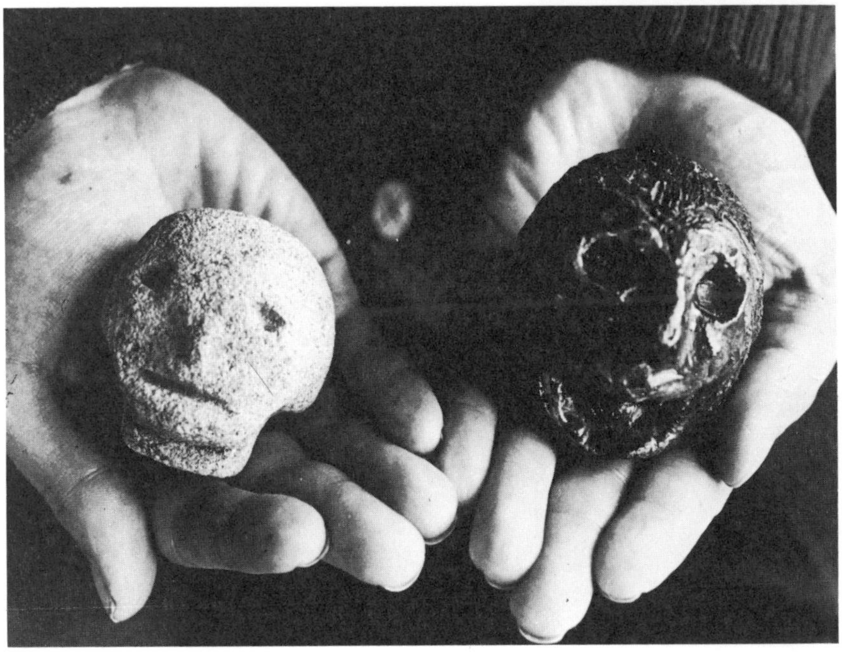

The Hexham heads, **top,** *are presumed to be those of a male,* **left,** *and a female. A comparison with heads that are known to be modern,* **above,** *reveals striking similarities. The head on the left was made by Desmond Craigie, in an attempt to prove that he made the original heads; the one on the right, curiously enough, was made by one of the boys who unearthed the Hexham heads shortly before their discovery.*

CELTIC RITUALS

Meanwhile, however, a distinguished Celtic scholar, Dr Anne Ross, had become interested in the stones. In an article for *Folklore, Myths and Legends of Britain,* Dr Ross had claimed that the heads were around 1,800 years old and had been designed to play a part in Celtic head rituals. When the heads were banished from the Robsons' house, Dr Ross took charge of them. She recalls what happened next:

'I didn't connect it with the heads then. We always keep the hall light on and the doors kept open because our small son is a bit frightened of the dark, so there's always a certain amount of light coming into our room, and I woke up and felt extremely frightened. In fact, panic-stricken and terribly, terribly cold. There was a sort of dreadful atmosphere of icy coldness all around me. Something made me look towards the door, and as I looked, I saw this thing going out of it.

'It was about six feet [2 metres] high, slightly stooping, and it was black against the white door. It was half-animal and half-man. The upper part, I

The figure of the wolf-man, **left,** *which appears in legends throughout the world, is similar in appearance to a creature said to appear in the presence of the Hexham heads.*

> " I DIDN'T CONNECT IT WITH THE HEADS THEN ...THE UPPER PART, I WOULD HAVE SAID, WAS WOLF AND THE LOWER PART WAS HUMAN. IT WAS COVERED WITH A KIND OF BLACK, VERY DARK FUR ... I FELT COMPELLED TO RUN AFTER IT. "

would have said, was wolf and the lower part was human. It was covered with a kind of black, very dark fur. It went out and I just saw it clearly and then it disappeared and something made me run after it – a thing I wouldn't normally have done, but I felt compelled to run after it. I got out of bed and I ran, and I could hear it going down the stairs. Then it disappeared toward the back of the house. When I got to the bottom of the stairs, I was terrified.'

That, however, was not the end of the story. A few days later, Dr Ross and her husband arrived home from London one evening to find their teenage daughter in a state of shock. Dr Ross described her daughter's experience as follows:

'She had opened the front door and a black thing, which she described as near a werewolf as anything, jumped over the bannister and landed with a kind of plop. It padded with heavy animal feet, and it rushed toward the back of the house and she felt compelled to follow it. It disappeared in the music room, right at the end of the corridor, and when she got there it had gone. Suddenly, she was terrified. The day the heads were removed from the house everybody, including my husband, said it was as if a cloud had lifted; and since then there hasn't been, really, a trace of it [the paranormal activity].'

Before the heads were removed, however, there were a number of other manifestations of the unwelcome 'lodger'. During those frightening months, Dr Ross insisted, the creature appeared to be very real. It was not something shadowy, or only glimpsed out of the corner of the eye. It was noisy, and everyone who came to the house commented on a definite presence of evil. While he never observed it directly, Dr Ross' archaeologist husband was fully aware of his unwelcome 'guest's' presence, although he is not usually sensitive to psychic phenomena. The phenomena ceased after the heads had been removed and the house was exorcised – but not before Dr Ross had disposed of her entire collection of Celtic heads.

The complex but ordered shape of copper sulphate crystals,* below, *reflects the regularity of its subatomic structure. Dr Don Robins,* below right, *an inorganic chemist and one of the many people to experience the disquieting effect of the Hexham heads, put forward the theory that crystal structures can store information in the form of electrical energy. The Hexham heads contain a high proportion of quartz – a crystalline substance; and Robins explains their apparent ability to induce paranormal effects by suggesting that these are derived from the place in which the heads were made.

Home-Made Toys?

The story took on a new twist in 1972 when Desmond Craigie – then a truck driver – announced that the 'Celtic' heads were actually a mere 16 years old. They had not been fashioned as votive offerings by a head-hunting Celt – for, Craigie claimed, he himself had made them as toys for his daughter, Nancy. He explained that he had lived in the house in Rede Avenue that was now the Robsons' home for around 30 years; indeed, his father had remained a tenant there until the previous year. One day, his daughter had asked him what he did for a living. At that time, Craigie worked with artificial cast stone, making objects such as concrete pillars. In order to explain to his daughter what he did at work, he made three heads especially for her in his lunch break, and took them home for her to play with.

'Nancy played with them as dolls,' he said. 'She would use the silver paper from chocolate biscuits as eyes. One got broken and I threw it in the bin. The others just got kicked around and must have landed up where the lads found them.'

Embarrassed by the publicity that his own handiwork had attracted, Desmond Craigie said he was concerned merely to set the record straight. Speaking of the heads, he said: 'To say that they were old would be conning people'. But Dr Ross was not entirely convinced. 'Mr Craigie's claim is an interesting story... Unless Mr Craigie was familiar with genuine Celtic stone heads, it would be

" THE DAY THE HEADS WERE REMOVED FROM THE HOUSE, EVERYBODY – INCLUDING MY HUSBAND – SAID IT WAS AS IF A CLOUD HAD LIFTED; AND SINCE THEN THERE HASN'T BEEN A TRACE OF THE PARANORMAL ACTIVITY. "

In Focus

HEADS OF THE HOUSEHOLD

Hundreds of stone heads have been found in the north of England, Scotland and mainland Europe. Most of these primitively carved objects can be positively identified as dating from the pre-Roman Celtic period – but some of them are of more mysterious origin.

The Celts of the kingdom of Brigantia, in north-east England, were among those who revered the human head both as a charm against evil and as a fertility symbol, and would set the severed heads of vanquished enemies over the doors of houses and barns. Historians believe that it is an echo of this gruesome cult that lies at the heart of later Celtish veneration of stone heads, such as those shown *left*.

West Yorkshire is particularly rich in such heads. Many are mounted in the walls of buildings, by doorways, on gables, or close to wells, where they seem to be serving their original purpose of warding off evil. But the curious thing is that many of these stone relics of the Celts' grisly cult are no more than a century old. Consciously or unconsciously, Yorkshire men and women have been perpetuating a tradition that is probably more than 2,000 years old.

extraordinary for him to make them like this. They are not crude by any means.' Scientific analysis has, surprisingly, been unable to determine the age of the heads.

Stored Energies

If the heads are indeed Celtic, it is easy to imagine that they may be the carriers of some ancient curse. But if they are not, why is it that they appear to provoke paranormal phenomena? The evidence that they do so is strengthened by the testimony of inorganic chemist Don Robins, who has explored the idea that mineral artifacts can store visual images of the people who made them. He also suggested that places and objects can store information that causes specific phenomena to occur – an idea similar to Tom Lethbridge's notion that events can be 'tape-recorded' into the surrounding in which they take place. He has stated, too, that certain minerals have a natural capacity to store information in the form of electrical energy encoded in the lattice structure of their crystals. Summing up this theory, Dr Robins stated:

'The structure of a mineral can be seen as a fluctuating energy network with infinite possibilities of storage and transformation of electronic information. These new dimensions in physical structure may well point the way, eventually, to an understanding of kinetic imagery encoded in stone.'

Robins was interested, too, in reports of sounds that had allegedly accompanied the phenomena and been induced by the presence of the heads, and drew a tentative parallel with a creature from Norse mythology, called the *wulver,* powerful and dangerous, but well-disposed towards mankind unless provoked. There are several reports of sightings of this creature in the Shetlands this century.

Dr Robins' interest in the heads prompted him to agree to take charge of them. As he put them in his car in order to take them home, however, and turned on the ignition, all the dashboard electrics suddenly went dead. He turned to look at the heads, telling them firmly to 'Stop it!' – and the car started!. No one could have been more surprised than he was.

Back home, Dr Robins, in his turn, began to find the presence of the heads disquieting. Curiously, they seemed, in some way, constantly to be watching him. 'There was no doubt that any influence that the heads possessed came from the girl [head]. I felt most uncomfortable sitting there with them looking at me, and eventually we turned them round. As we did so, I had the distinct impression that the girl's eyes slid round watching me.'

Perhaps disappointingly, however, Dr Robins did not witness any paranormal events that might have been caused by the heads. There were, however, some perturbing moments. One day, leaving the house, he muttered to the heads: 'Let's see something when I get back!' Moments later, he re-entered the house to collect a book he had forgotten. Outside, it was fresh and blustery – but in his study the atmosphere seemed 'almost electric with a stifling, breathless quality'. Attributing the effect to the 'girl' head, he left hurriedly. He found nothing amiss on his return home.

The present whereabouts of the Hexham heads is not known. There also remains the mystery of their age and why they should have produced such startling phenomena.

ROADS OF FEAR

CLOSE ENCOUNTERS WITH ALIEN ENTITIES ON LONELY ROADS ARE COMPARATIVELY FREQUENT OCCURRENCES AND KNOWN TO HAPPEN AS FAR APART AS FRANCE AND TASMANIA. STRANGELY, SOME SUCH EXPERIENCES EVEN OCCUR REPEATEDLY

One of the more curious aspects of the UFO phenomenon is the way in which certain individuals are sometimes singled out for more than one visitation. Our first story concerns one such 'repeater', who experienced UFO sightings and related phenomena for nearly 20 years, culminating in a terrifying encounter on a lonely road in southern France.

The second story is a close encounter of the second kind – with a difference. In addition to the interference with electrical equipment that has come to be regarded as normal in UFO sightings, there were more unusual side-effects: after the sighting, for instance, the witness noticed that the front of her car, which had been dirty, was as clean as if it had just been washed, and her hair, which had recently been treated with a permanent wave, went completely straight!

It was 10.45 p.m. on 29 August 1975 and R.Cyrus – a former policeman turned businessman, aged 48 – was driving along route D10 from Longages to a point south of Noé where the road joins Route Nationale 125. It is a country district, deep in the Haute-Garonne region of south-western France. The sky was clear, the weather was mild, and a light south-east wind was blowing. Under a bright moon, he had travelled about three-quarters of the way along the road when he observed, in a field to the right, an aluminium-coloured machine. When, a second or two later, he was almost level with this object, the underpart became illuminated with a phosphorescent glow, and it floated in the air, at bonnet height, towards the front of the car.

Cyrus rammed on the brakes just as the object tilted back to present its underside to the driver. At that moment, the luminosity increased enormously and, blinded by the fierce light, Cyrus threw up his arms to protect his head and eyes. His car swerved

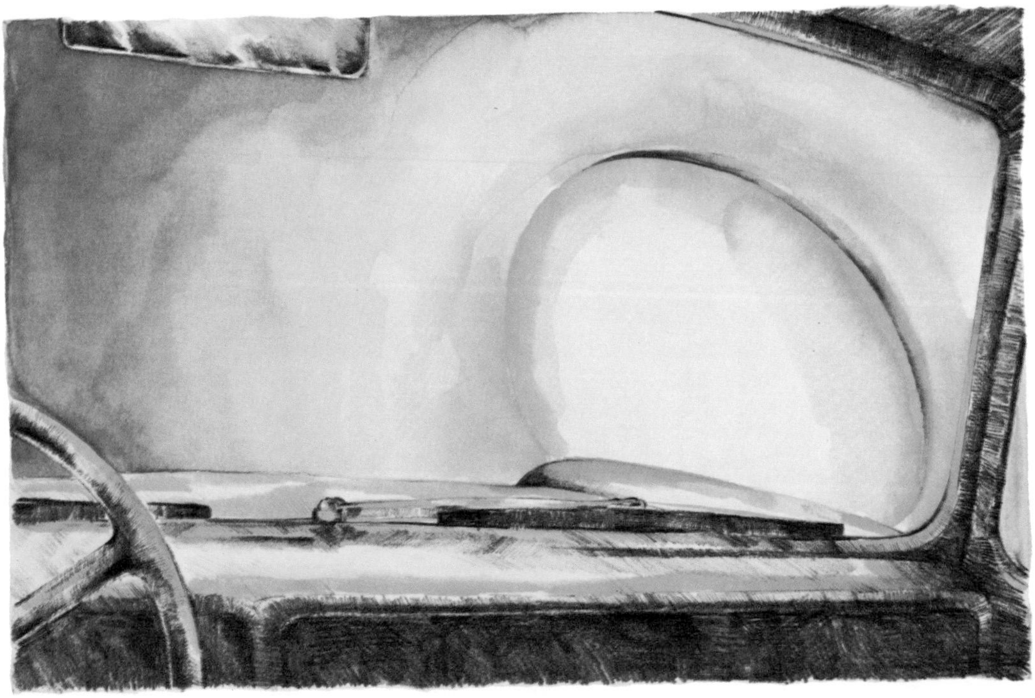

A blinding white light shone towards the car, as shown **left** *in the artist's impression, and finally forced the witness into a ditch.*

As depicted in the illustration, above, a beam of light, reddish in tinge, illuminated Cyrus car, but not the surrounding area.

off the road and ended up in a shallow ditch. Even as that happened, the UFO shot straight up and hovered, as a bright point of light in the sky, directly above the car. All this took place in the space of five seconds or so, and there was no sound whatsoever from the UFO.

For a moment, Cyrus sat motionless, getting out of his car only when a passing motorist stopped nearby and came over to open the door for him. 'I thought your car was exploding,' the motorist said.

The former gendarme, shocked and unsteady, touched himself 'to see if he was still alive'. Then he muttered: 'Good heavens – is this it?'

Meanwhile, the light of the UFO, high above, was fluctuating in intensity, and had taken on a reddish tinge. Cyrus stood where he was, watching the phenomenon for some 15 minutes. A compact beam shone down from the object, illuminating the car but not the surrounding area.

By now, a number of people had arrived on the scene, and the consensus of opinion was that Cyrus should report the matter immediately to the gendarmerie. But he declared: 'You all know me; I'll go to the gendarmerie tomorrow. Now I'm off home!' It was a statement that subsequently puzzled him. His wife later said that, when he arrived home, he was utterly distraught.

When questioned, Cyrus said he could not recall having been 'paralysed' by the UFO's presence, but he did remember that his throat was all 'jammed up', and he was unable to utter a sound until the motorist opened the car door. There were other physiological effects, too. After the encounter, the witness experienced bouts of sleepiness, even when driving; whenever he stopped doing anything, he found himself falling asleep. His eyesight, too, was briefly affected: when awakening on the two mornings following his experience, he had black spots before the eyes, but these gradually faded.

Surprisingly, there were no signs of burns or scratches, nor changes of colour on the car after the event. And there was another unusual feature about the sighting: the engine did not stall during the event, and the lights continued to work normally throughout.

Attempts were made by investigators to locate landing marks, but nothing was found. Aerial photographs also failed to reveal anything.

It was unfortunate that the motorist who approached Cyrus after the sighting presumably declined to make a statement, and refused to allow his name to be mentioned. There were, however, two other independent but vague reports of lights in the sky, and of one in a field some distance from the road.

During the course of their investigation for the French UFO organisation *Lumières dans la Nuit* (Lights in the Night), the researchers, a certain M.Cattiau and his colleagues, greatly assisted by the good-natured collaboration of Cyrus, unearthed the remarkable fact that he appeared to be one of the group of witnesses known as 'repeaters': it transpired that he had been through at least three earlier UFO experiences.

In 1957, he had been at a vineyard at Quillan in Aude, south-west France, during the grape harvest, when he saw, at about 8.30 one evening, two orange-coloured, cigar-shaped objects some 200 yards (180 metres) away. They were hovering over rows of vines while a cart passed below, its driver apparently oblivious to what was happening. Cyrus had called other vineyard workers from their dinner. When they saw the intruders, they ran towards them, whereupon the objects departed silently.

Again, one midnight in the autumn of 1974, Cyrus had been driving with his wife from Noé to the town of Muret when they saw a strange object to their left. It seemed to be composed of flashes of light, but these were suddenly succeeded by a huge orange sphere that illuminated the countryside, and kept pace with their car for about 5 miles (8 kilometres). When they arrived at the village of Ox, they were able to compare its size with that of the church: the sphere appeared enormous. Then, as they passed, a nearby transformer appeared to explode. It was confirmed next day that the circuit-breaker had tripped during the night for some unknown reason.

Twice in 1975, a few weeks before the encounter of 29 August, Cyrus also stated that he heard guttural voices speaking in an unidentifiable

CASEBOOK

language on his car radio each time he had the radio switched off. While this is not strictly within the UFO realm, some investigations have been forced to wonder whether or not Cyrus is a deep-trance subject, or perhaps possesses a degree of clairvoyance – in which case, something could well have been 'beamed in' on him, setting him up for the big encounter of 29 August.

Tasmanian Encounter

A year previously, a Tasmanian woman, who wishes to remain anonymous, experienced a not dissimilar phenomenon. Late on the afternoon of 22 September 1974, she arrived at the junction of the Diddleum and Tayene Plains roads, around 30 miles (50 kilometres) north-east of Launceston. It was raining, and the mountains were shrouded in mist as she parked her car around 200 yards (180 metres) from the junction and waited for the arrival of the relative she was due to pick up. Because there was a steep bank to the left of the road, she parked her car on the other side to ensure that any of the heavy log trucks that frequently used the narrow road would see the vehicle clearly.

Over the car radio, she heard that the time was 5.20 p.m. Then, suddenly, the radio developed a high-pitched whine and the whole landscape lit up, bright light flooding the inside of the car. She leaned over to switch off the radio and, looking up through the windscreen, saw a glowing orange and silver object moving between two trees and coming downhill towards her. It was the size of a large car, moving slowly 50-60 feet (15-18 metres) above the ground, and dropping steadily towards the road.

The UFO,* below, *was seen by a woman on a Tasmanian road in 1974. It was silver-grey, and featured several wide bands beneath a dome that emitted an intense orange-yellow light.

Not surprisingly, the woman panicked. She started the car and hurriedly began to reverse up the road, away from the UFO. But the object went on approaching until it was at the level of the fence at the side of the road. It then hovered over the middle of the road about 30-35 yards (25-30 metres) from the woman's car. It appeared to be domed on top, although it was difficult to make out its exact shape because of the intense orange-yellow light that it emitted. Beneath the dome, the UFO was silver-grey in colour. There was also a wide band on which the witness said there could have been portholes, and six to eight horizontal bands below it, decreasing in diameter. At the bottom of the object was a small revolving disc, and below this what appeared to be a box or tube, which protruded from the base a short way.

After reversing about 100 yards (90 metres), the woman accidentally backed the car over the edge of the road, and the wheel stuck fast. The UFO now stopped in front of the witness. It then dipped to the right and moved away to the south-west over a valley beside the road. It next rose vertically upwards, fairly quickly, until lost from vision. The entire sighting had lasted 3 to 4 minutes.

The witness jumped out of her car and ran all the way to her house, about a mile (1.6 kilometres) away. All the while, she had the feeling that she was being watched, and kept looking up to see if the UFO was following her: she did not, however, see anything. When she arrived home, her husband and son went to inspect the car. They could see nothing unusual.

The next day, however, when the car was towed home, it was noticed that the front of the car was exceptionally clean, although the rest of it was as dirty as it had been before the encounter. Previously, there had been cat footprints all over the bonnet, but it seemed to have been given a good polish. It appeared impossible that the rain of the previous day could have cleaned the front of the car while leaving the back dirty.

State of Shock

For some days after her terrifying experience, the witness was ill with nervous tension and seemed in a state of shock. Her hair, which had been newly treated with a permanent wave, turned straight after her encounter. Furthermore, the car radio, which had been in perfect working order before the sighting, afterwards suffered from distortion. This, of course, is a common phenomenon in close encounters with UFOs.

The witness initially reported the sighting to the Royal Australian Air Force (RAAF), who could not supply her with any explanation, but they ruled out such things as weather balloons, aircraft, and meteorological phenomena. The case was also investigated by the northern representative of the Tasmanian UFO Investigation Centre, and subsequently reported to *Flying Saucer Review*. As yet, however, we do not know whether this particular individual's experience will be repeated.

Picture Acknowledgements

The Publishers would like to thank the following for supplying pictures;

Klaus Aarsleff
Murray Aikman
Lorna Ainger
Aldus Books
Ardea Photographics
Associated Press
Richard Baker
John Beckett
Stephen Benson
Graham Bingham
Anne Bolsover
Bord Failte
Janet & Colin Bord
Bridgeman Art Library
Paul Brierley
British Library Board
British Museum
Brooke Bond Oxo Ltd.
Paul Bryant
Richard Burgess
Cambridge Evening News
Robert Candy
CBS Records
Center for UFO Studies
J. L. Charmet
John Cleare
Bruce Coleman
W. E. Cox
George E. Crouter
John Cutten
Daily Telegraph Colour Library
Dali Institute, St. Petersburg, Florida c DEMART PRO ARTE BV/DACS 1992
Philip Daly
Peter Day
Demetrius
Department of the Environment
Paul Deveraux
Tim Dinsdale
Tony Dodd
J. Dowding
Droemer-Knaur Verlag
H. Edgar
Colin Edwards & Partners
Sam Elder
Robert Estall
Mary Evans Picture Library
Fate Magazine
John Featherstone
Vivien Fifield
Findhorn Foundation
Joel Finler
Flicks
A. L. Flowerdew
Flying Saucer Review
Fortean Picture Library
Foto Mönsted
French Government Tourist Office
Leif Geiges
General Motors
Glaister & Rentoul
GLC
John Glover
Henry Gris
Ground Saucer Watch Inc.
Sonia Halliday
Robert Harding Associates
Norma Harvey
Mrs. Nancy Heinl
W. N. Henry
Michal Heron
Hertford Museum
Bernard Heuvelmans
Professor F. Hodson
Michael Holford
Holiday Inns
Mike Holland Studio
Hulton Picture Company
Robert Hunt Picture Library
Anwar Hussein
Hutchison Library
Institute of Advanced Study, Princeton
Japanese National Tourist Organisation
Alix Jeffry
Juliette John
Frank Johnson
Stephen Kerry
Keystone
Dr. A. G. Khan
Kitt Peak National Observatory
Kobal Collection
Dieter Kuhn
Frank W. Lane/Roy C. Jennings
Lauros/Giraudon
Linden Artists
London Express
London Features International
London Scientific Fotos
Long Island University
Longman
Stephen MacMillan
William Macquitty
City of Manchester Art Galleries
Mansell Collection
Janos Marffy
MARS
Martin Aircraft Co.
Iain McCaig
Paul McElhoney
Medical Illustrations Support Service
Duane Michals
R. B. Minton
Moderne Verlag
Graham Morris
Marion Morrison
Tony Morrison
Musee de l'Homme
NASA
National Archaeological Museum, Athens
National Archives
National Film Archive
National Gallery
National Gallery of Art, Washington
National Portrait Gallery
Natural Science Photos
Vautier de Nauxe
New Scientist
Peter Newark's Historical Pictures
Newcastle Chronicle & Journal
News Ltd.
Novosti
S. Ostrander
Photo AFP
Photographers Library
Photri
Pictorial Parade Inc.
Pictorial Press
Picturepoint
Guy Lyon Playfair
Popperfoto
Press Agency (Yorkshire) Ltd.
Harry Price Library
Psychic News
The Psycho-Physical Research Foundation
Henry Puharich
Punch
Radio Times
Rank Xerox
Religious News Service Photo
Retna
Rex Features
Edward Rice
Royal Greenwich Observatory
Tony Roberts/Young Artists
Roger-Viollet
Ann Ronan Picture Library
Routledge & Kegan Paul
Frank Ryan News Service
Science Photo Library
Paul Screeton
Sheridan Photo Library
Paul Sieveking
Dr. Stanley Singer
Harry Smith Collection
Smithsonian Institute
Brian Snellgrove
Paul Snelgrove
R. Solecki
South West News
Space Frontiers
Neville Spearman Ltd./Jacques Vainstain
Spectrum Colour Library
Spooner Pictures
Sri Sathya Sai Baba Trust
Roy Stemman
Greg Stringer
Ed Stuart
Studio Briggs
Homer Sykes
Syndication International
Tao Ch'i Chuan Kung Fu
Tate Gallery
Michael Taylor
Simon Thomas
Tony Stone Worldwide
Topham Picture Source
D. Towersey
Transworld Feature Syndicate
U.S.A.F.
UKAEA
UPI, New York
Van Duren Publishers
John Walsh
Peter Warrington
Washington Post
John Webb
Werner Forman Archive
Steve Westcott
Professor C. Wickramasinghe
Wurttenbergisches Landesmuseum, Stuttgart
Yorkshire Evening Press
Zanka Woodward Picture Library
Zefa